W9-BXP-124

INSIDER TRAVEL SECRETS

You're NOT Supposed to Know!

Tom Parsons

Best Fares USA, Inc.
www.bestfares.com

Copyright © 1996, 1997 by Best Fares USA, Inc.

All rights reserved. No part of this book may be reproduced or transmitted in any form or by any means, electronic or mechanical, including photocopying, recording, or by any information storage or retrieval system, without the prior written permission of the publisher.

Library of Congress Catalog Card Number: 96-83477

ISBN 0-9650960-0-9

Book and cover design by Lisa Leonard-Koger.
Illustrations by Al Rod.
Map illustrations by Mike Ellis.

The information published in *Insider Travel Secrets* is derived from industry sources which are considered reliable at the time of publication. Promotions and fares are subject to change and withdrawal without notice; therefore, it is the responsibility of the consumer to verify reliability on an individual basis based on specific consumer needs. *Insider Travel Secrets* assumes no responsibility, and extends no guarantees, for discount promotions, fares, or changes in travel industry programs listed in this publication.

For the latest insider travel deals and
subscription information about
Best Fares Discount Travel Magazine
visit our web site at www.bestfares.com
or call 800-880-1234.

INSIDER TRAVEL SECRETS is dedicated

to my parents, John and Margie Harman, for teaching me the true value of a buck;

to my children, Stephanie, Michael and Bryan, for giving me a good reason to spend everything I've saved;

to the Wright Amendment for opening the Dallas/Fort Worth skies to creative ticketing and helping to show me how to bring low prices to America

and to Southwest Airlines, the number one low-cost carrier in the U.S., for proving that you can give passengers a fair deal and still make a profit.

ABOUT THE AUTHOR

Tom Parsons has spent almost 15 years learning how to save you money on every aspect of travel. He has looked behind the scenes, analyzed airline pricing and promotions and taken apart the systems that govern travel piece by piece.

Parsons grew up in South America where wheeling and dealing is woven into the culture. He earned his degree in Criminal Justice (specializing in white collar crime) and was a military investigator in Vietnam. He worked for a major international corporation as a specialist in tearing systems apart to uncover embezzlement and other corporate theft. His ability to be innovative and create new and unique ways of looking at things helped form an extremely effective investigative division known as the "Can Do Unit."

Parsons became a frequent flyer. His company handed him a corporate credit card and left him on his own. He was a greenhorn with no experience in the travel industry. It was the early 1980s, not long after the airline industry was deregulated. Before deregulation, all fare comparisons were apples-to-apples. Then a new world of discounts, price wars, frequent flyer programs and special promotions opened up, as airlines aggressively offered fares so varied that no one seemed able to keep up with them.

After putting his best efforts into getting the lowest possible fare, Parsons learned that a co-worker purchased a ticket on the same flight three days later for $100 less. He was frustrated, challenged and vowed that it would never happen again.

He discovered that there were literally tens of thousands of possible fares on any given day several hundred on one route alone all subject to change at a moment's notice. He studied airline guides, airline computer systems, fare rules, trends and promotions. He realized that, even though his travel agency was trying to find him low fares, they worked under handicaps: a commission-based system that provided no direct financial benefit for locating low fares, a computer reservation system geared toward major air carriers' interests rather than those of consumers, and an ever-changing array of discount offers that didn't appear in any computer reservation system.

His corporation went through some belt-tightening and offered a double bonus to anyone who could reduce travel costs. "Can do," he replied and proceeded to cut corporate-wide travel expenses by $800,000 in 14 months. He got the bonus and an award as "The Man Least Likely To Give Up A Buck." His two-page travel tip newsletter, distributed within the company, was in demand by friends and associates of management and soon generated a mailing list of 300 people. In 1983 it grew into *The DFW Report*, a regional newsletter. Parsons anticipated a subscription base of 800-1,000, but subscriptions kept coming in as people in other parts of the country wanted to know about travel, Parsons' style. In 1987 *BEST FARES Discount Travel Magazine*–The National Edition made its debut. It now serves over 45,000 subscribers. Tom Parsons collects airfare discounts like kids collect baseball cards and the magazine is his means of sharing 250-300 deals every month some of them as hot as a Babe Ruth Signature Card.

"The Guru of Cheap Airfares" is a sought-after guest on national and local radio and television. What started as occasional appearances on local stations has grown into an average of 80-100 talk shows each month giving millions of people across the United States a free clinic on how to reduce travel costs. Many stations report that Parsons is their most requested return guest.

His knowledge of hidden discounts and travel industry secrets is regularly featured on shows including *Good Morning America*, *The Today Show*, *CBS This Morning*, *CNBC*, *CNN* and *Nightline*; in newspapers such as *The Wall Street Journal*, *The New York Times* and *USA Today*; in magazines including *U.S. News And World Report*, *Fortune* and *Money*. He has testified by invitation before the United States Congress on consumer airline issues.

Parsons' understanding of travel industry strategies is well documented. He consults with executives of most major airlines and has a working relationship with them. Airlines, travel agents and consumers all must focus primarily on their own needs and wants. Parsons tries to understand all sides. He believes that business deserves a profit but he is also strongly pro-consumer. He does not mind taking a stand and being vocal when he sees something wrong with the industry. At the same time, he is quick to praise when they do something right. He is the true watchdog of the travel industry, usually first to inform the national media of changes that affect consumers.

For years, Parsons has been asked when he was going to write a book that would include all the tips he passes out each day and all the information that can't fit into a 64-page monthly magazine format. After 13 years of research and two years of writing, *Insider Travel Secrets* is here.

INTRODUCTION

Have you ever called every airline for prices, checked with travel agents and done all your homework only to find out that the person sitting next to you on the plane paid much less than you did? Have you noticed that when you check in at hotels the desk clerks circle the rate you're paying rather than confirming it out loud? It's standard policy to avoid alerting you to the fact that the person next to you may be paying $89 for a room that's costing you $129. Have you ever booked a cruise and been content with a free cabin upgrade until you talked to a friend that sailed on the same ship to the same ports of call a week or two later and was given a two-for-one deal? Have you ever paid high dollar for a rental car while the next person at the counter rented a better car for half of what you paid? It's as if there are two worlds of travel–one in which consumers pay what they're told to pay, and one in which rates are discounted as much as 70%.

In the summer of 1995, I took a Delta flight from Los Angeles to Dallas/Fort Worth and sat next to a seasoned traveler who flies Delta six or seven times a week. He thought he knew all the tricks. He used promotional deals. He charged his travel on American Express. He did everything he knew to maximize his bonuses. I told him that, for an additional $25, he could take his spouse or one of his children with him on any Delta flight, including roundtrips to Hawaii or Europe–and he could do it without cashing in 25,000 or 40,000 frequent flyer miles. There were three clues available on the flight and I challenged him to find them.

Forty-five minutes passed and he was no closer to the answer. We were on a 767 with a two-minute video presentation preceding the movie. The video had mentioned the free ticket offer. The in-flight magazine–the same issue he had probably paged through on an earlier flight–mentioned it. The pop-up display card on his dinner tray promoted the deal. AT&T was offering a free companion ticket to people who signed up for their new 500-number service (a number that can reach you anywhere in the U.S.). After $25 worth of calls–calls paid for by the people placing them–you received a buy-one-get-one-free certificate good for a Delta roundtrip anywhere in the world. My frequent flyer friend took the AT&T service, and he subscribed to my magazine. I also gave him my new 500 number knowing that, when he called me, his call would help me reach my own $25/free ticket goal.

On the same flight, I asked the flight attendants if they were ever asked for free tickets. Most of them said yes. None of them knew about the AT&T promotion even though they were the ones who loaded the video, distributed the magazines and served the meals.

Don't fault them for being unobservant. If you closed your eyes right now and tried to describe details of some of the things you see every day, you would have a hard time. In this information age we're constantly subjected to input. We have to screen some of it out just to survive. What we don't want to ignore is information that saves us money. The AT&T deal was so good that even if you never planned to use the 500 service, the $25 investment was a great bargain. Who wouldn't spend $25 for a roundtrip ticket to Europe or Hawaii?

My monthly magazine is full of the newest promotions and hidden deals. That's what makes it important to travelers. This book supplements the magazine and provides the foundation you need to locate and use the deals that are best for you. The book has two major missions–**to reduce your travel costs and to show you how to get as many free perks as possible**. A lot of travel books and travel experts paint pretty pictures about the advantages and details of certain locations. This book will show you how to **go where you want to go and get you there for less**. Read the guide books. Check out the writer who's been to Maui and wants to tell you about the beaches and restaurants. **Read this book to save money.**

We'll give you a triple play of lower fares, free upgrades and perks you never thought you could get. If we can't save you on a particular airfare because the fare is already low, we can show you how to get free perks and upgrades. Whether you want to fly first class at coach prices or fly a college student home for half the usual cost, we'll show you how. We'll tell you who to call and what to ask. Whether you fly 200,000 miles a year or once every blue moon, you'll benefit from this book and learn to use the loopholes the travel industry has created.

We picked an ace detective to help you become a super sleuth of travel savings. Be sure to check out the maximizers (highlighted by magnifying glasses) that begin each chapter. They're my favorite all-around ways to save. Begin with Airlines then follow the footsteps through Car Rentals, Hotels and Cruises. "More Dollars And Sense" and "Travel Guide" hit on hundreds of unique ways to save and simplify travel. The final section–"Know Who To Call"–is your own private directory of all the numbers a savvy traveler needs.

As you read this book, remember the basics. There are deals and there are **better** deals. Don't settle for ten percent off when you can save five or six times more. Be flexible and be patient. You may not need to change a thing in your travel pattern except the prices you're paying. You may find that making a minor change can cut your fare in half or save you even more. Knowledge is power and this book will give you the knowledge you need to get lower fares no matter how you prefer to travel. You'll learn that airlines are your worst places to shop and that good travel agents are your most important allies.

Sit back and get comfortable as we show you that finding bargains is neither as complicated nor as time consuming as you think. Bargain hunting can be fun. You don't have to dedicate your life to it; you simply have to be willing to take the time to learn the methods that will consistently bring you the thrill of beating the system. Any game is fun once you're an expert at playing it. This game pays off in cash.

TABLE OF CONTENTS

AIRLINES

DON'T LET THE AIRLINES TAKE YOU FOR A RIDE 1
GETTING THE BEST BANG FOR YOUR BUCK 5
   Free & Reduced Ticket Coupons .6
   Reading A Coupon's Fine Print. .9
   Niche Airlines 10
   Fare Wars At Your Command 15
   Companion Fares 17
   Weekend Discounts 18
   Choosing & Using Consolidators. 18
   Off-Season Savings 19
CREATIVE TICKETING 20
   Alternate Cities 20
   Back-To-Back Tickets 26
   Hidden City Discounts Up To 80% 28
   Split City Discounts Up to 70%. 31
   Code Share Airport Money Savers 31
   Last Flight In/First Flight Out .32
   Backhauling Benefits 32
   How To Use Standby Travel 33
   Throw-Away Tickets 33
   Open Jaw Tickets 33
   Circle Tickets and Free Stopovers 34
PACKAGE TRIPS & TOURS 35
   Tour Savings Strategies 36
   Evaluating Tour Companies 38
   Steps To Successful Tours 42
OTHER WAYS TO SAVE 45
   Senior Airfare Discounts & Coupon Books 45
   International Senior Discounts .49
   Children's Travel 50
   Children Flying Solo 50
   Student & Youth Fares. 52
   Bereavement & Compassion Fares 53
   Military Fares 54
   Family Fares 54
   Free & Low-Cost Upgrades 54
   U.S. Regional Passes 55
   Ticket Rebates 56
   Coupon Brokers 57
   Buying From The Classifieds 57
   Courier Travel 58

International Travel Passes 59
Around-The-World Fares 63
Other International Savings 64

BUSINESS TRAVELER EXTRAS 67
On-Time Arrivals 68
Membership Programs 71
International Business Travel 72

PRE-FLIGHT INTELLIGENCE REPORT .73
Airline Reality Check 73
Contracts Of Carriage De-Coded. 75
Passenger Allies. 78
Airline Tickets De-Mystified 79
Saving With Re-Issued Tickets 80
Lost & Stolen Tickets. 82
Pre-Paid Tickets 84
Ticketless Travel 84
Getting Bumped 85
Delayed & Cancelled Flights 87

ON BOARD BASICS 89
Seat Assignments. 89
Airline Smoking Policies 90
Upgrades/Seating/Boarding Passes 91
Airline Meals 93
Special Meals 94
Healthy Flying 96
Making Flying Safer 97
Flying With Children 98
Fear Of Flying 100
In-Flight Medical Assistance 100
Passengers With Disabilities 100
Safe Flights For Pets 101
In-Flight Added Costs 103
Airport Clubs 104
Airport Policies & Prices 107
Airline Terms 108

FREQUENT FLYER TWISTS & TURNS 110
Earning The Most Miles 112
Purchasing Incentive Miles 113
Expiring Miles 114
Redeeming Miles 115
Airline Credit Cards 116
Travel & Entertainment Cards 117
Bank Cards 118
Domestic Airline Programs 121
International Airline Programs 131

HOTELS

INN-SIDER TRADING 141
CLUES TO THE BEST BARGAINS .143
  50%-Off Hotel Directories 143
  Direct Discounts 144
  City Discount Cards 144
  20-70%-Off Hotel Consolidators 144
OTHER WAYS TO SAVE 146
STANDARD DISCOUNTS FOR THE ASKING 150
  More Savings Tips 155
OTHER LODGING OPTIONS 157
'INN'-SIDER INFO 162
  Hotel Jargon 162
  Hidden Hotel Costs 164
  Hotel Amenities 166
  Mega-Chains & Independents 167
  Hotel Safety 168
HOTEL HIGHLIGHTS 170
  Booking Hotels Internationally 183

CAR RENTALS

ARE YOUR CAR RENTAL DOLLARS GOING UP IN FUMES? 187
CLUES TO THE BEST BARGAINS .189
THE RUNDOWN ON THE COMPANIES 192
OTHER WAYS TO SAVE 194
  Corporate Savings 194
  Senior Rates. 195
  Weekend & Holiday Deals 196
  One-Way Rentals 197
  Limiting Rental & Fuel Costs 198
PLAY THEIR GAME & WIN 202
  License & Record Checks 202
  Financial & Age Requirements 203
  Waivers & Insurance 204
  Options & Add-Ons 206
  Headaches To Avoid 208
  Safety Tips 210
INTERNATIONAL 'COUNTER' INTELLIGENCE 211

CRUISES

DON'T LET YOUR CRUISE DOLLARS MELT AWAY 221
Cruise Discounters 223
Getting The Best Bargains 224
AN OCEAN OF SAVINGS POSSIBILITIES 225
Promotions & Creative Discounts 226
Booking For One 227
Air Travel Options 229
WHY CRUISE NOW? 230
New & Upcoming Ships 231
All-Inclusive Pricing. 233
CRUISE CONTROL 236
Cruise Insurance 239
Shore Excursions 240
Safety & Health Issues 241
Other Seaworthy Tips 242
CRUISE LINE PROFILES 244
Shipshape Information 250
Off The Beaten Wave 255
Cruise Line Itineraries 259

MORE DOLLARS & CENTS

COUPON CORNER 263
U.S. Discounts & Deals 266
International Offers 272
Student & Youth Savings 274
Senior Savings 275
SAVE BY HOW YOU PAY 276
The Truth About Credit Cards 276
Other Savings With Plastic 280
Using ATM Cards 281
Emergency Cash Options 282
Travelers Checks & Cash 283
International Savings 284
Travel and Taxes 286
TIPS ON TIPS 288
TRAVEL INSURANCE 292
CALLING FROM THE ROAD 295
RAIL TRAVEL 301
International Rail Travel 303

TRAVEL GUIDE

A CONSUMERS' GUIDE TO TRAVEL AGENTS 311
TRAVELERS' CAUTIONS 317
   Travel Scams 317
   Problem & Complaint Resolution 323
   Safe Travel 327
LUGGAGE LOGIC 330
   Airline Baggage Policies 330
   Cruise, Rail & Bus Policies 332
   Buying New Luggage 333
   Packing Tips 334
HEALTHY TRAVEL 336
TRAVEL BY LAND 340
SPECIAL TRAVEL CATEGORIES 346
   Traveling Solo 346
   Senior Travel 348
   Children & Travel 350
   Traveling With Animals 356
   International Travel 358

KNOW WHO TO CALL

Airport Paging 367
Airlines 369
Car Rentals 374
Ground Transport/Rail Travel 375
Hotels/Motels 375
Cruise Lines 378
Outdoor & Adventure Contacts 379
Attractions & Theme Parks 380
Mobility Impaired Travel 382
Ski Resorts 383
Dining & Theater 383
State Tourism Offices 383
International Tourism Offices 390
ATMS/Wires/Credit Cards 391
Lost/Stolen Travelers Checks 392
Regional Passport Offices 392
Shipping & Air Freight 392
Travel Insurance 392
Weather 392

Don't Let The Airlines Take You For A Ride

Let's face facts. The major airlines' primary job is to try to squeeze every possible dollar out of every passenger. Last year they reported over $2 billion in profit. They cut back on service, meals, seat comfort, travel agent commissions and even took the lettuce off dinner plates to keep profits soaring. I'm not here to ruffle their wings, but I want to make your bank account healthier. After you read this book, you'll be able to get deals like these:

Triple whammies that let you use three separate discounts on one ticket price.

Rock bottom airfares that don't require Saturday stays.

Special promotions offering free tickets and big discounts on multiple tickets.

Niche and regional airlines that can cut your travel costs by up to 75%.

Creative ticketing methods that are some airlines' best kept secrets.

Discounts on almost any ticket costing $150 or more.

The airlines would love it if you agreed to pay $600 for every coach ticket you bought. They've hiked fares over 35 times since June of 1992 (five times in the first six months of 1996). Why? They don't listen to what consumers want, but they do pay attention to competition. If there's a niche carrier in a given market, the fares stay low to select destinations. That's why travelers who live in cities where there are no low cost airlines end up paying more. Should I, with Dallas/Fort Worth as my home airport, pay two or three times more for a ticket than someone in Austin or Oklahoma City? Of course not–but that's exactly what the airlines try to engineer.

The airline industry and consumers have had to adapt to many major changes in the years since deregulation. Oldtimers such as Pan Am (returning this year as a niche carrier), Peoples Express, Eastern and Braniff have disappeared from the skies. Wall Street observers predicted three of four years ago that we'd end up with only three major airlines. My answer to that is "hogwash." Their crystal balls must have been functioning under foggy conditions.

We've seen America West, Continental and TWA successfully emerge from bankruptcy. Niche airlines like Western Pacific, Valujet, Southwest and Southwest wannabees are building their own airfields of dreams. They offer sensible ticket prices based on the actual distance flown. Southwest is the only one of the top ten carriers that has shown a profit every year of its existence. That proves that airlines can base their fares on distance flown and still make money. They survive, profit and open the door for air travelers to make their own airfields of dreams, built around low fares.

We probably won't see new coast to coast airlines, but there are 24 new airlines awaiting approval right now from the Department of Transportation. We're going to see more and more competitive upstarts making names for themselves in specific markets. They and their predecessors are going to keep airfares down, make creative ticketing more widespread and help us save as much as 75% on every ticket we buy, compared to what the major airlines would love to charge.

This chapter will give you an arsenal of arrows to shoot through the hot air balloons of airline pricing. Read it carefully and you will know how to use every angle, every trick and every advantage you need to cut travel costs dramatically. You will know ticketing options the airlines frown on and perfectly legitimate ticketing options they say violate their rules. Since I've been publishing **BEST FARES** *Discount Travel Magazine*, the airlines have come up with many new rules, and I've come up with many new strategies to use these rules to the consumers' advantage. I believe **you** should be able to make the decisions on how you spend your dollars.

Relax, fasten your seat belts and hold on to your hats as we begin a trip to bargains you never dreamed you could have. We will cover areas not usually seen by the average traveler and change the way you travel forever. You have entered "my world of travel"–a world of secrets **they** don't want you to know–secrets that we are going to unlock together, page by page.

RECENT AIRLINE CHANGES THAT AFFECT ALL TRAVELERS

THE FOUR BIGGEST EVENTS

The #1 Consumer Windfall: the continued strength of upstart airlines. Western Pacific had the biggest recent impact. Their presence in Colorado Springs, their attention-grabbing aircraft graphics and their effect on prices out of Denver International earn them applause. ValuJet's profits tripled, new mini-hubs were added, they continued their Northeast expansion and ordered 50 new jets. Southwest slashed fares in Florida, revamped its frequent flyer program and earned its fourth consecutive Triple Crown–the Department of Transportation (DOT) award for best on-time performance and baggage handling and fewest customer complaints. No other major airline has ever received this honor.

The #1 Industry Windfall: heightened airport security requiring domestic passengers to show photo ID. Tens of thousands of people with non-refundable tickets, who used to sell them for half-price or equal dollar, were stopped in their tracks. The ID check coincidentally uncovered people trying to fly on tickets issued in other passengers' names. The airlines have the right to yank these tickets and force passengers to pay full fare. Even if security levels relax, you can bet airlines will do their best to keep this security procedure in place.

The #1 Mixed Blessing: The government, with the negotiating skills of the Hatfields and McCoys, skidded into a budget stalemate that suspended the airline excise tax. Most airlines responded by lowering most ticket prices by ten percent–an amount equal to the excise tax. This consumer windfall could ultimately cost the government billions of dollars. Somewhere down the line, someone will have to pay the piper.

The #1 Sham: It happened in early 1995 when we received our settlement for price-fixing allegations. The discount certificates gave us up to a paltry ten percent off–a discount you can beat any day of the week. The attorneys sold out consumers in exchange for $14 million in fees. They got the big bucks. The airlines got a great advertising tool. We got scraps of paper best used as bookmarks.

Delta cut travel agency commissions on domestic airfares over $500. Most other carriers followed. It became harder to find agents willing and able to spend the time needed to find low fares. Agencies said Delta's action would force many of them out of business. One year later the number of agencies increased one percent, sales were up six percent but domestic commissions were three percent lower. They now have to work harder to make the same revenue.

Five of the six airlines that capped domestic ticket commissions saw their total 1995 traffic go up. Delta, the airline that incurred the most agency wrath, saw its traffic go down. Agencies would like to think they were responsible, but the decrease was mostly attributable to Delta's restructured route network. Delta had hoped to save $80 million due to commission caps. In reality, they saved $157 million, making Delta very happy.

Airlines raised leisure airfares five times in 1995 and kicked off 1996 by raising them four times in four months. If car insurance rates went up that often, we'd be up in arms.

Midwest Express and American Transair lengthened the time a reservation will be held from 24 to 72 hours. Finally, you actually have time to make plans before confirming a reservation.

Weekend travelers in select hub cities got a break from American, United, TWA, Northwest, Delta and USAir. Fares for many destinations were cut. American, for example, slashed prices up to 80% from Dallas and Chicago with CableSavers and NetSavers. Weekend load levels went up and fares for last minute, weekend travel went down. It's part of a trend of select market advertising with some deals promoted on cable television, some promoted via the Internet and all deals re-capped in *BEST FARES Discount Travel Magazine*.

United got creative with 50 different non-stop flights from Chicago and Denver for Thanksgiving 1995 for only $50 roundtrip. They also became the first airline to fly the new Boeing 777.

Five of the major airlines eliminated eight-coupon senior coupon books, traditionally the most cost effective option for travelers 62 and older. TWA kept their eight-coupon deal and added companion coupons, allowing passengers of any age (flying with a senior coupon travel user) to enjoy their own discounts.

Airlines cut corners, raised fees and cut the number of cities served. Meal quality, meal frequency and comfort all took a dive. Fees for many services went up. You had to pay a higher fee for children flying solo and some airlines even began charging the fee for non-stop flights.

American, America West, Delta and other airlines introduced doggie bags with fancy names like "Bistro Meals" and "Sky Deli." You picked up your meal as you boarded the plane. They used to load the meals early, until they found that the meals weren't that satisfying. People de-planing pick up another meal on the way out.

TWA successfully exited from bankruptcy leaving the airline a potent force in domestic and international travel.

Continental Lite's fight to survive ended as the airline was unable to successfully copy the Southwest style. Mark Air and Grand Air disappeared from the skies with Mark Air's demise temporarily raising prices in and out of Denver International, their home base.

United and Southwest promoted ticketless travel, perhaps encouraged by the great success ValuJet and Morris Air had with all-ticketless travel. Airlines save a fortune, and passengers are protected from lost ticket nightmares.

Virgin Atlantic added new, non-stop San Francisco to London service, effectively lowering the cost of traveling to Europe from any west coast city. They also initiated Washington, DC to London service in June of 1996.

TWA made comfort more affordable by eliminating high dollar, first class fares to Europe and offering Business One, 57-inch seating and Premium Class service with more affordable fares. America West added first class to all its jets. The single first-class seat they used to have on some flights is now a curious artifact of the past.

GETTING THE BEST BANG FOR YOUR BUCK

S PECIAL PROMOTIONS

Special limited promotions and coupons are the buried treasure of airline discounts. They're like hundred dollar bills you can pick up and use, if you know where to find them. Getting your hands on the right coupon can even give you a free flight, or you can save hundreds of dollars on a single roundtrip. Some coupons even allow you to discount up to seven passengers traveling together, and some will permit you to fly First Class, even on the cheapest excursion fares. You can even use them on most fare war prices.

Every major U.S. airline and many international airlines issued hidden discount, dollar-off coupons in 1995. It is estimated that between 750 million and one billion discount certificates were issued in 1995. Did you get your "fare share?"

The deals pop up in traditional and unexpected places. They can appear in your junk mail or as inserts in your credit card statement. They can be offered on displays at your supermarket, at the drug store, a furniture store or on the hangtag of a pair of boxer shorts. You can get $100 off of a flight for choosing a specific car rental company and $4,000 worth of discount coupons for buying a $40 book.

A popular discount coupon form is the free companion ticket offer. Sometimes you get them for specific purchases. Other times they're inserted with credit card bills. Most people don't look through all the inserts stuffed in with their bills, but if you buy airline tickets, you might be overlooking the equivalent of five hundred-dollar bills hiding behind that 473rd long distance carrier enticement.

Some airlines accept some coupons sponsored by competitors. The main exemptions are frequent flyer award tickets or upgrades (although some discount coupons issued to frequent flyers are transferable). If you'd like to use a coupon on a non-issuing airline, check with their reservation desk and ask if they will honor it.

Some coupon deals are so good it can be worth buying a product just to get the coupon. Would you develop a roll of film to get a $100-off airline coupon? Most people would, even if they had to borrow the camera. Would you buy five pair of boxer shorts to get a free, roundtrip ticket to London? You would, even if you had to give the boxer shorts as gifts. Would you buy $20 worth of golf balls so that two people could fly roundtrip to Hawaii or Alaska for a total price of $600? Of course. You don't have to dedicate your life to this treasure hunt because we have. This chapter is the basic guide, and *BEST FARES Discount Travel Magazine* is the monthly map that puts these deals at your fingertips. Literally hundreds of discount coupons are available at any point in time.

Last Year's Hot Promotions

We don't want to make you feel bad about what you missed, but we do want you to know what kind of bargains you can use if you keep on top of discount deals. Here is just a small sample of hidden travel promotions and certificates that appeared in *BEST FARES Discount Travel Magazine* last year:

Free Tickets

A free roundtrip ticket on Delta with no Saturday stay restriction just for purchasing furniture from Thomasville.

A free roundtrip ticket to any of 53 cities in Europe, the Middle East, the Far East or Africa from Austrian Airlines for charging two tickets on American Express.

A free ticket on Northwest for spending $25 per month for 12 months with your long distance carrier.

A free domestic roundtrip for purchasing a transatlantic ticket on British Air.

A free companion ticket to London on Virgin Atlantic for buying five pairs of boxer shorts.

A free roundtrip companion ticket on United for obtaining their Mileage Plus Visa.

A free roundtrip companion ticket on Air France for spending $10 on computer disks.

Buy-one-get-one free on Northwest for switching your long distance service.

A free domestic roundtrip on Southwest, America West, United or Alaska Airlines for buying one roundtrip at as little as $78.

A free companion ticket for TWA frequent flyers for switching to a new long distance carrier and using their service for three months.

A free companion ticket on Delta, American or America West for buying a box of golf balls.

A **buy-one-get-one-free on Delta** for spending $25 on AT&T's long distance service.

A **buy-one-get-one-free on American** for upgrading your credit card.

A **buy-one-get-one-free to Mexico** for enrolling in Aeromexico's Frequent Flyer program.

A **buy-one-get-one-free on American** for signing up for their Citibank card.

A **buy-one-get-one-free on over 11 international airlines** for charging your tickets on American Express.

A **buy-one-get-one-free on Delta worldwide** when you purchase $30 in computer software.

A **buy-one-get-one-free on TWA** for using your MasterCard.

Reduced Companion Tickets

A **$149 companion ticket on Northwest** for clipping a coupon from specific issues of ten national magazines.

A **$129 companion ticket on Northwest** for charging your tickets on Diners Club.

A **$99 roundtrip on Northwest** for kids ages two to 17 for visiting Target.

A **$50 Delta roundtrip** for kids ages two to 11 between any U.S. cities Delta services. Just ask for the coupon.

Half-price American Airlines companion tickets for seniors who clip a coupon and charge the tickets on American Express.

Four United $50-coupons, plus one half off of the companion fare for referring a friend to Bank of America or opening your own account.

Northwest companion tickets–$99–and up to $100 off single roundtrips for partic-ipating in the Visa Rewards program.

Half-price companion fares to Palm Beach on USAir by requesting a discount coupon from the Palm Beach Visitors Bureau.

Fifty percent off of a companion ticket good to all U. S. cities United services for opening a checking account.

Dollars-Off Coupons

Up To $100 off each of 40 TWA tickets by using the Dine-A-Mate coupon book, available for under $50.

Up to $920 off American flights with four coupons from another discount directory, selling for under $50.

Up to $75 off Continental after just one stay at Howard Johnson, with room rates starting at $25.

$100 off TWA for booking a car from Alamo.

$80 off Northwest for joining Holiday Inn's no-fee Priority Club.

$400 in savings on USAir ($200 per traveler) for renting an Alamo car in Florida.

Fly two kids, ages two to 11, roundtrip on Delta for $99 each within the 48 states when you buy $50 in toys.

Up to $400 off Continental roundtrips when you purchase a 1996 edition of an *Entertainment Publications* discount book.

Up to $100 off America West for paying with American Express.

Up to $250 off of a Delta flight by using a coupon enclosed in select American Express mailings.

Up to $100 off Continental for processing one roll of film at any of 2,300 nationwide drug stores.

Up to $100 off USAir for processing one roll of film at participating Target stores.

Up to 70% off Northwest roundtrips for purchasing $50 in groceries.

Twenty percent off of any published Delta fare costing $198 or more to any city in North America.

$100 off of USAir roundtrips for renting an Alamo car in California.

Up to $400 off American for placing a $50 order with a mail order company.

A $50-off coupon on Southwest. Just ask your credit card company.

$75 off Continental roundtrips for filling up at Exxon stations in nine states.

Up to $200 off USAir roundtrips for enrolling in the AT&T "True Rewards" program.

Up to $95 off American with a "Windows '95" purchase.

$75 off Continental roundtrips for opening a Payless Cashways charge account or charging $75 to an existing account.

Up to $150 off Continental for buying two tickets to a hit Broadway show.

Up to $100 off Continental for buying the right jar of Taster's Choice coffee.

Up to $200 off American roundtrips to Barbados for charging your tickets on Visa and requesting a special promotion code.

Up to $500 off of two Delta tickets anywhere they fly, any fare class–including sale fares–for charging tickets to American Express.

Up to $100 off TWA for charging tickets to Mastercard.

A $25-off Southwest coupon for renting a car from Alamo in their spotlight city of the month.

Up to $75 off Continental for contributing $25 to participating PBS stations.

Special Zone Fare Deals

Discount roundtrips on Continental (starting at $178) for spending $25 at any of seven east coast shopping malls.

Northwest roundtrips for as little as $198 for shopping at any of 11 northeast Malls.

Roundtrip on TWA for as little as $98, coupon included with Visa and MasterCard statements.

America West roundtrips at deep discounts for purchasing groceries at select Pack & Save, ABCO and Safeway food stores.

Up to 70% off Continental for purchasing $25 in merchandise.

Up to 75% off TWA for spending $80 on groceries.

$100 off a Northwest roundtrip for purchasing $100 in groceries.

Turn a $7 certificate into hundreds of dollars in savings on Northwest for using a joint promotion sponsored by Northwest and California's Coast Federal Banks.

Other Neat Promotions

Coast to coast on Continental for $378 with no Saturday stay.

Children, ages two to 11, fly TWA for $99 roundtrip when traveling with an adult using any published airfare.

Fly two people to the 1996 Olympics from over 23 U.S. cities for $199 roundtrip.

Children, ages two to 11, fly Delta for $50 roundtrip within the continental U.S. or Hawaii, the Caribbean and Canada when traveling with an adult and joining

---

Average level of cabin humidity in passenger jets: 25%.

Delta's "Fantastic Flyer" program.

Weekend roundtrips on Delta from Cincinnati to any of 69 cities for as little as $78 roundtrip.

Up to 80% off last-minute roundtrips on American when flying out of Dallas/Fort Worth, Chicago, Miami, Nashville, Los Angeles and New York.

A free Sony Watchman color TV for flying roundtrip on any Finnair transatlantic flight.

Roundtrip air on Delta plus a five-attraction Disney World Passport for as little as $179.

Fly TWA roundtrip to Europe for $249, plus 15,000 frequent flyer miles.

Up to 46% off USAir for students who acquire a particular no-fee credit card.

First class to Hawaii for $995 roundtrip.

Seniors fly Southwest coast-to-coast for as little as $99 using special sale fares.

Two-for-one to Europe on select airlines for American Express Platinum level cardholders.

Roundtrip to Puerto Rico from the northeast for $99 when you stay at a participating Hyatt Resort.

Two free days of golf at any of 17 courses for flying Myrtle Beach Express.

A First Class roundtrip to Europe for seniors plus four months of almost unlimited domestic travel on Continental for $1899, far less than the cost of just the ticket to Europe.

Double and Triple Whammies

My favorite way to get discounts is to pile them up. Double whammies–getting two discounts on one ticket–are terrific. Triple whammies almost make buying airline tickets fun. Examples:

Wait for a fare war (discount #1), find an alternate city routing that offers a significantly lower price (discount #2) and use one of the free companion tickets or dollars-off coupons you've been collecting (triple whammy!).

Creative ticketing, double and triple whammies are cost-cutting, kissing cousins. Use back-to-back ticketing, an open jaw itinerary and buy your tickets with coupons. Read *Creative Ticketing* to find out how to do the first two parts of this triple whammy.

Reading A Coupon's Fine Print

The biggest trick to learning a coupon's rules and restrictions is getting a look at the coupon when and if you have to request it by mail. This is common when the coupon is offered in return for a specific purchase.

Unless you know the policies, you have no way of knowing if the coupon will be beneficial for a specific trip. All advertising concerning the free coupon offer should include the major terms and limitations. If it does not, ask some questions before you buy the necessary product or find out the promotion code for the coupon. With this as a reference, you can call the specific airline and usually get full details, including travel and blackout dates and other important restrictions of use. Make sure you can use the discount when and how you plan to use it.

Check to see if a handling fee is specified. A $10 handling fee plus a $15 expediting fee that gets you a coupon with a value to you of $25 is not a good deal. If the offer is for a free companion ticket, however, grab it.

Are the discounts graduated? Many coupons offer a discount range of $25-100, depending on the cost of the flight.

What airports and dates are blacked out? You can usually work around the blackout dates, but an airport blackout can be a problem.

What are the advance purchase and minimum stay requirements? Most discount coupons require a minimum stay of one Saturday night. Some of the most valuable coupons can be the ones that don't have a minimum stay requirement. Two-for-one offers without this restriction can be extremely valuable to business travelers.

How many passengers can use the coupon? The most valuable coupons allow travel for up to seven people (on the same itinerary), each getting the discount.

Remember that even though you're not allowed to sell or buy airline discount coupons (except as part of an authorized program such as the *Entertainment* coupon books), you can give them away. If a coupon falls into your hands or is easy to acquire, you're completely free to give it to anyone who can use it. The one possible exception? Discount certificates issued in your name. They may not allow you to transfer the offer to another party, but some do. Read the fine print.

⊘ NICHE AIRLINES

✐ **One of the most important keys to getting the lowest fares** is knowing where all the players fly, especially niche and low-cost airlines. They have allowed us to create a whole new airfare system, even from cities that may not have niche airlines.

Niche airlines offer significant savings with their point-to-point pricing policies, fare structures and the competition they create. Southwest was the trend setter and pioneered the concepts most niche carriers are now trying to emulate.

Niche airlines have made ticket prices plummet in every market where they have a presence. The major airlines tried to ignore them at first, but now they usually match their prices. Fares go down, sometimes as much as 75%. This has happened in cases where there's just one niche airline serving a market. When Southwest Airlines originally entered the Baltimore market, airfares plummeted and traffic increased dramatically. Now Baltimore has the reputation of being a low-cost airport.

Niche airlines offer great one-way prices because they don't penalize you for not purchasing a roundtrip. This is a very big plus for business travelers who prefer not to stay over a Saturday night, or leisure travelers seeking a cheap one-way ticket. You can even get a good last-minute fare because their walk-up rates are far lower than the fares the majors charge when you don't meet their advance purchase requirements. Niche airlines also tend to allocate a higher percentage of seats to their lowest prices than do their major carrier competitors.

Some niche carriers base their fares on advance purchase and peak and off-peak times, varying by airline. Others use inventory-controlled pricing, meaning that a certain number of seats are sold at the lowest price, then the price goes up. Inventory-controlled fares are not usually affected by advance purchase requirements, but your chance of getting the lowest fare is better the earlier you book.

Niche carriers tend to be dynamic, adding new routes frequently. Our magazine monitors these changes monthly. Here's a listing of niche carriers, regional carriers and their markets. (*An asterisk (*) in front of an airline name designates a niche carrier that flies charter aircraft*).

NICHE AND REGIONAL AIRLINES			
AIRLINE	**GATEWAY**	**CITIES SERVED**	**FARE STRUCTURE**
AIR 21 800-359-2472	Fresno, CA	Colorado Springs, Fresno, Grand Junction, Las Vegas, Los Angeles, Palm Springs, Salt Lake City and San Francisco	One ticket price per itinerary
AIR SOUTH 800-247-7688	Columbia, SC	Atlanta, Columbia, Jacksonville, Miami, Myrtle Beach, Raleigh/Durham, Tallahassee and Tampa	Peak and off-peak; 7- and 21-day advance plus walk-up fares
AIRTRAN AIRWAYS 800-247-8726	Orlando	Akron-Canton, Albany, Allentown, Birmingham, Buffalo, Cincinnati, Dallas-Fort Worth, Dayton, Greenville-Spartanburg, Hartford, Kansas City, Knoxville, Nashville, Newburgh, Norfolk, Omaha, Orlando, Providence, Rochester and San Antonio	Inventory controlled; no advance purchase variations
AMERICA WEST 800-235-9292	Columbus (Ohio), Las Vegas and Phoenix	Albuquerque, Anchorage, Atlanta, Austin, Baltimore, Boston, Burbank, Chicago Midway & O'Hare, Columbus, Dallas-Fort Worth, Denver, Detroit, El Paso, Houston International, Kansas City, Las Vegas, Long Beach, Los Angeles, Los Cabos, Mazatlan, Mexico City, Milwaukee, Minneapolis, New York Kennedy & La Guardia, Newark, Oakland, Orange County, Orlando, Phoenix, Portland, Puerto Vallarta, Reno, Sacramento, Saint Louis, Salt Lake City, San Antonio, San Diego, San Francisco, San Jose, Seattle, Tampa, Tucson, Vancouver and Washington National; Miami starting 11/15/96	7-, 14- and 21-day advance; some companion fares

NICHE AND REGIONAL AIRLINES

AIRLINE	GATEWAY	CITIES SERVED	FARE STRUCTURE
AMERICAN TRANS AIR 800-225-2995	Boston, Chicago Midway, Indianapolis, Milwaukee, Los Angeles and San Francisco	Boston, Chicago, Fort Lauderdale, Fort Myers, Grand Cayman, Honolulu, Las Vegas, Los Angeles, Maui, Miami, Milwaukee, Montego Bay, Orlando, Phoenix, St. Petersburg, St. Thomas, Salt Lake City, San Francisco, San Juan and West Palm Beach	Peak and off-peak; no advance purchase variations
CAPE AIR 800-352-0714	Hyannis, Massachusetts	Boston, Hyannis, Fort Myers, Key West, Naples, FL and New Bedford	Inventory-controlled and frequent flyer coupon books
CARNIVAL 800-824-7386	Islip (Long Island) and Fort Lauderdale	Fort Lauderdale, Islip, Los Angeles, Miami, Nassau, New York, Orlando, Port Au Prince, San Juan, Tampa and West Palm Beach	Inventory-controlled
EASTWIND 800-699-3592	Trenton	Boston, Greensboro and Trenton	Inventory-controlled
FRONTIER 800-243-6297	Denver	Albuquerque, Bismarck, Chicago Midway, Denver, El Paso, Las Vegas, Los Angeles, Minneapolis/St. Paul, Omaha, Phoenix, Salt Lake City and San Francisco	7-, 14- and 21-day advance
JET TRAIN 800-359-4968	Pittsburgh	Newark, Orlando and Pittsburgh	7- and 21-day advance
KIWI INTERNATIONAL 800-538-5494	Atlanta and Newark	Atlanta, Chicago Midway, Bermuda, Las Vegas, Newark, Orlando, San Juan (Puerto Rico), Tampa and West Palm Beach. Code shares to Columbia, SC, Jacksonville, Myrtle Beach, Raleigh/Durham and Tallahassee	1-, 3-, 7- and 14-day advance
LAKER AIRWAYS 954-359-7609	Fort Lauderdale	London and Orlando	Inventory-controlled
LONE STAR 800-877-3932	Fort Worth	Aspen, Dallas/Fort Worth and Eldorado, Jonesboro, Harrison and Hot Springs, Arkansas	7-, 14- and 21-day advance

Number of surviving airlines from among the 48 launched since 1991: 14.

NICHE AND REGIONAL AIRLINES

AIRLINE	GATEWAY	CITIES SERVED	FARE STRUCTURE
MIDWAY 800-446-4392	Raleigh/Durham	Allentown, Boston, Cancun, Charleston, Fort Lauderdale, Fort Myers, Hartford, Hilton Head, Jacksonville, Las Vegas, Long Island, Myrtle Beach, Newark, Newburgh, New York La Guardia, Norfolk, Orlando, Philadelphia, Providence, Raleigh/Durham, San Juan, Tampa, Washington National, West Palm Beach and Wilmington	7-, 14- and 21-day advance
MIDWEST EXPRESS 800-452-2022	Milwaukee and Omaha	Anderson (Indiana), Appleton, Atlanta, Boston, Cincinnati, Cleveland, Columbus, Dallas/Fort Worth, Dayton, Denver, Des Moines, Detroit, Flint, Fort Lauderdale, Fort Myers, Grand Rapids, Green Bay, Indianapolis, Kalamazoo, Kokomo, Lansing, Las Vegas, Los Angeles, Louisville, Madison, Muskegon, New York La Guardia, Newark, Omaha, Philadelphia, Phoenix, Rochester, Saginaw, San Francisco, Tampa, Toronto, Traverse City, Washington (DC) and Wausau	7- and 21-day advance; all seats are business class at coach prices
NATIONS AIR 800-248-9538		Discontinued scheduled service; in the process of converting to charter service; call for update	
PAN AM (Summer 1996 start-up)	Miami	Chicago, Los Angeles, Miami, New York and San Francisco	Not known at press time
RENO AIR 800-736-6243	Reno and San Jose	Albuquerque, Chicago O'Hare, Colorado Springs, Las Vegas, Laughlin, Los Angeles, Orange County, Palm Springs, Portland, San Diego, San Jose, Seattle, Tucson, Vancouver and (seasonally) Anchorage and Fairbanks	7- and 14-day advance

Average number of hours each day a Southwest aircraft spends in the air: 11.

NICHE AND REGIONAL AIRLINES

AIRLINE	GATEWAY	CITIES SERVED	FARE STRUCTURE
SOUTHWEST AIRLINES 800-435-9792	Burbank, Dallas, Houston Hobby, Nashville, Oakland, Phoenix, St. Louis and Salt Lake City	Albuquerque, Amarillo, Austin, Baltimore, Birmingham, AL, Boise, Burbank, Chicago, Cleveland, Corpus Christi, Columbus, Dallas, Detroit, El Paso, Harlingen, Houston Hobby & Intercontinental, Indianapolis, Kansas City, Las Vegas, Little Rock, Los Angeles, Louisville, KY, Lubbock, Midland-Odessa, Nashville, New Orleans, Oakland, Oklahoma City, Omaha, Ontario, Orange County, Orlando, Phoenix, Portland, Reno, Sacramento, St. Louis, Salt Lake City, San Antonio, San Diego, San Francisco, San Jose, Seattle, Spokane, Tucson, Tulsa, Tampa and Fort Lauderdale	7- and 14-day advance fares with peak and off-peak pricing
SPIRIT 800-772-7117	Detroit	Atlantic City, Boston, Detroit, Fort Lauderdale, Fort Myers, Orlando, Philadelphia, Tampa and West Palm Beach	Inventory-controlled
*STERLING ONE 800-759-7283	Long Beach	Chicago O'Hare and Long Beach	Inventory-controlled
SUNJET 800-478-6538	Clearwater and Dallas	Clearwater, Dallas/Fort Worth, Fort Lauderdale, Long Beach, Newark and Orlando	Inventory-controlled
TOWER AIR 800-348-6937	New York JFK	Amsterdam, Bombay, Los Angeles, Miami, New York, Paris, San Francisco, San Juan and Tel Aviv	Peak and off-peak; low-cost upgrades
TRI STAR AIRLINES 800-218-8777	Eugene	Eugene, Los Angeles and Reno	Inventory-controlled
VALUJET 800-825-8538 (Currently In Reorganization)	Atlanta & Washington Dulles	Atlanta, Boston, Charlotte, Chicago Midway, Columbus, Dallas-Fort Worth, Detroit, Fort Lauderdale, Fort Myers, Hartford, Indianapolis, Jackson, Jacksonville, Kansas City, **(Continued next page)**	7- and 21-day advance

Amount of wages paid by the U.S. tourism industry in 1993: $102.9 billion.

NICHE AND REGIONAL AIRLINES

AIRLINE	GATEWAY	CITIES SERVED	FARE STRUCTURE
VALUJET **(Continued)** 800-825-8538	Atlanta & Washington Dulles	Louisville, Memphis, Miami, Nashville, Newport News, New Orleans, Orlando, Philadelphia, Raleigh-Durham, Savannah, Tampa, Washington Dulles and West Palm Beach	7- and 21-day advance
VANGUARD 800-826-4827	Kansas City	Chicago Midway, Dallas/Fort Worth, Denver, Des Moines, Kansas City, Los Angeles Minneapolis/St. Paul, Salt Lake City, San Francisco and Wichita	Peak and off-peak fares
WESTERN PACIFIC 800-930-3030	Colorado Springs	Atlanta, Chicago Midway, Colorado Springs, Dallas/Fort Worth, Houston Intercontinental, Indianapolis, Kansas City, Las Vegas, Los Angeles, Nashville, Newark, Oklahoma City, Phoenix, San Antonio, San Diego, San Francisco, San Jose, Seattle, Tulsa, Washington Dulles and Wichita	7- and 21-day advance; peak and off-peak fares; 3-day advance companion tickets with controlled availability
WORLD AIRWAYS 800-967-5350	New York JFK	New York JFK and Tel Aviv	3-, 7- and 14-day advance; peak and off-peak fares

⌕F ARE WARS

If you plan far enough in advance, you can almost always take advantage of fare wars. During 1995, we saw a new domestic fare war begin approximately two to three weeks after each fare war ended. If you can plan at least 60 days in advance, you have a very good shot at being able to get fare war prices.

Don't be fooled by the airline ads that say they'll honor the new fare if ticket prices go down. What they fail to mention is that you have to **give them $50 or more in processing fees** (sometimes waived if you accept the difference in airline vouchers).

If you use a buy-one-get-one-free coupon or a $100-off travel certificate on a fare that subsequently goes down, you cancel any savings you could have received if you had waited and used your discount on a fare war price.

International fare wars recur approximately four to five weeks after the old fare wars expire. There are more fare wars to Europe than to any other international destination. Planning trips to Europe at least 90-120 days in advance, especially to London, Paris or Frankfurt, should ensure a fare war reduction in the base fare of 20%-40%. Using a wholesaler such as World Travel, 800-576-2242, you

---

Number of international arrivals in the United States in 1993: 45.5 million.

could save another five to 30 percent. By combining both discount opportunities (the fare and the wholesaler), you get a double discount. You'll know when fare wars occur if you check the front page of your daily newspaper's business section, the evening television news or network morning television news programs.

Fares wars pop up so regularly because yield management people send out the word that sales need a boost. They're usually initiated at the beginning of the week. One airline usually starts the fare war by lowering prices on select flights. Highly competitive routes are most likely to be the prime focus. Within hours other airlines in competitive markets fall in line. They might match the fares the leader initiated, or they might undercut them.

Airlines update fares in their computers three times a day, Monday through Friday, usually at 12:30 p.m., 5 p.m. and 8 p.m. EST. On weekends they update at 5 p.m. Saturday and 3 p.m. Sunday. When a major airline starts a fare war they try to take advantage of the 8 p.m. weekday or 3 p.m. Sunday update so the competition is prevented from matching fares until the next update time–12:30 p.m. the next day. This gives the originator a 24-hour price and advertising advantage.

It can pay to wait a day or two after a fare war starts to allow the airlines time to scramble, meet prices, open up seats and try to come up with advantages that scoop the airline that initiated the price cuts. The downside of waiting is that you can lose available seats. Buy 24 hours of time by reserving a fare war seat immediately so it's there as a backup. Then you can let the dust settle to see if lower fares or fares with less blackout dates are released.

During the first day of a fare war, travel agents get confusing information on their computer systems. New prices may not be entered yet, they may be entered with the system not showing any of the rules and policies and they may not allow the agents to ticket.

Fare wars increase the number of ticket prices available on a single flight. One recent fare war offered over 250 different fares for a New York/Los Angeles roundtrip, ranging from $290-2,334.

Don't assume that a fare war price is the lowest available price. A niche carrier may have driven the ticket price even lower on a specific daily flight. An airline not even in the fare war fray may offer a ticket price below the publicized discount rates. For example–Hawaiian Air recently offered roundtrips to Honolulu at $80 less than other carriers' fare war prices.

Ask your travel agency if they will void your ticket at no cost if the fare goes down before they submit their weekly Airline Reporting Commission (ARC) report and reissue the ticket (with payment of a change fee) at the lower fare.

Mini-fare wars get less media play but can save you a lot of money. They occur when two carriers enter into competition in a specific market. Early 1996 mini-fare wars took place in Florida cities as Southwest slashed fares to make a splashy entry into the markets. They took place in 1995 when ValuJet expanded flights out of Atlanta. Market wars on domestic and international fares also start when an airline adds a new city to their system. The best way to tune in to these discounts is to keep up with the activity of niche carriers and the majors (who are less changeable, but still prone to duke it out in a desirable market).

1995 brought a few fare war surprises that may be repeated in '96. Fare wars designed to increase sales for Thanksgiving travel offered some tickets requiring just a one-day advance. Others required no Saturday stay. America West slashed some fares in November by as much as 75%, taking them to their lowest level in three years. American's MX/HURRY fares cut international ticket prices in October. September fare wars dropped blackout dates for both Thanksgiving and Christmas travel.

Anatomy Of A Fare War

In mid-October of 1995 Northwest kicked off a fare war, discounting some routes by 50%, major hub routes by 30%-40%. TWA entered the battle, offering 50% discounts across the board and reducing the 21-day advance requirement to seven days. When one airline sees the signs of another airline's impending fare war, follow-the-leader is always played with a hefty side dish of one-up-man-ship. The first airline gets the lion's share of media attention–the others try to grab their own glory with new twists and turns.

Timing and persistence are important when shopping for airfares. To illustrate this point, we checked daily on one airline's lowest price for a Dallas/Fort Worth-Boston roundtrip coach ticket. The $257 price on the 18th is $406 lower than the highest quote and $386 lower than the initial quote given two weeks earlier. Calling just a day later than the 18th produced a price $40 higher than the lowest rate. How do you know when the magic date will occur? Neither a whiz-bang computer nor a 900 psychic line can tell you. Collect your coupons. Start shopping early. Call often. Outside of the seven-, 14- and 21-day advance influences, it's a wide open game. Here's how prices fluctuated in one month's time:

DAY	PRICE	DAY	PRICE
1	$643	17	$322
2	$643	18	$257
3	$643	19	$297
4	$643	20	$297
5	$643	21	$663
6	$643	22	$663
7	$643	23	$643
8	$643	24	$643
9	$643	25	$643
10	$643	26	$643
11	$643	27	$643
12	$643	28	$663
13	$362	29	$663
14	$322	30	$663
15	$322	31	$663
16	$322		

OMPANION FARES

Two-for-one can be the best deal of all, but there are some things you need to know before taking your piggy bank to the travel agency.

Companion fares, in some cases, are based on a higher priced ticket than you will be able to buy when flying alone. The savings enter in when you divide the cost of the paid ticket by two and get what is usually the lowest possible per-ticket price.

Companion fares require that both people travel together on all segments of the flight. Sometimes they are limited to travel on specific days of the week. They almost always have blackout dates.

Not all airlines offer companion tickets consistently. They tend to pop up in certain markets when load factors are down. Make sure your travel agent checks down to the bottom of the computer screen where companion fares, family fares and other deals may hide. Then do your math and compare all your options.

Be sure to check companion ticket availability to alternate cities. They may not be available for your exact destination, but a nearby airport may work.

WEEKEND DISCOUNTS

Several airlines are coming up with new ways to fill their planes on weekends. Fortunately, these ideas benefit consumers.

American Airlines offers three weekend discount options.

* **Cablesavers**, available out of Dallas/Ft. Worth, for example, are released each Wednesday for travel the following weekend. The airline checks their load levels and picks out the destinations with the lowest percentage of booked seats. You fly roundtrip at discounts of 75% or more.

* **Netsavers**, available for both Dallas/Fort Worth and Chicago, offers low rates via personal computer. Check American Airlines computer WEB site for details.

* **Break AAway fares** represent savings of up to 85%. They're available out of six locations: Dallas/Fort Worth, Chicago, Miami, Nashville, Los Angeles, and New York. Recently prices varied from $79-269 roundtrip, depending on the destination. A Memphis-Dallas/Ft. Worth roundtrip, for example, was $99; Dallas/Ft. Worth-Newark was $199.

Niche carriers, and therefore their competitors, customarily discount off-peak travel. Off-peak is likely to be after 7 p.m. weekdays and all day Saturday and Sunday.

You'll almost always pay more when you fly weekends to international destinations because you're flying during the time of highest demand.

CONSOLIDATORS

Consolidators offer discount tickets released to them in bulk by the airlines. Domestic consolidators usually advertise without mentioning airline names. Domestic tickets sold by consolidators are perfectly legitimate. Almost every airline in the world that offers international travel also has wholesalers or consolidators that sell these unpublished, discounted airfares to the general public. International tickets technically are forbidden by a 1958 law stating they cannot be sold below their published price, but the DOT and the Department of Justice has not enforced the law in almost 40 years. International consolidator tickets purchased from reputable vendors are usually safe consumer purchases. In fact, some consolidators are actual partners with the airlines whose discount seats they sell.

* **Consolidator prices are rarely exactly as advertised**–but good consolidators will get very close. If there is a big discrepancy, ask why. Always compare a consolidator rate to the airline's quote, making sure you're comparing prices for the same ticket.

* **They don't require advance purchase**, except for the time needed to get the ticket to you if you're purchasing by phone.

* **International tickets sometimes waive** minimum/maximum stay requirements other discount tickets may carry. Many fare war prices permit a maximum of 30-45 days to complete travel. Many consolidator tickets allow 90-365 days to complete travel. You can also get discounts of up to 50% off the lowest published fares.

- **The price paid for those advantages may include** non-endorsable status, meaning you won't be placed on an alternate carrier in case of extremely delayed or cancelled flights. On some consolidator tickets, you forego frequent flyer points, advance seat assignments and special meal options. Any refunds are required to be made by the consolidator.

- **Always deal with reputable consolidators** and always pay by credit card.

- **Double check your tickets** by calling the airline direct 24 hours after you've purchased your consolidator ticket. If the airline does not show your reservation, call the consolidator immediately.

International carriers are taking advantage of the domestic airline commission cap for travel agents and doing all they can to strengthen their relationship with agents. They're hoping more agents will concentrate on international tickets where commissions are not capped. British Airways now guarantees the best price (even compared to consolidators) for tickets bought through travel agents at least 90 days in advance. Their "All Seasons APEX Fare" takes $100 off 21-day advance purchases.

Even though we recommend World Travel, 800-576-2242, whose data base offers over 40 consolidators and discounters worldwide, you should also check local Sunday travel sections from gateway cities. If you're flying to Europe, check the *New York Times* and the *Boston Globe*. If you're flying to South America check the *Miami Herald*. If you're flying to the South Pacific or the Orient, check the *Los Angeles Times* and the *San Francisco Chronicle*. Most major city libraries will carry these out-of-town papers so you can review them for free. If you can't find them there, try a book store or newspaper stand that carries out-of-town papers.

OFF-SEASON SAVINGS

International fares, in most cases, are determined by the date of the outbound leg of your flight. Save hundreds of dollars simply by booking your departure a few days earlier or later when you travel near seasonal breaks. Always ask your travel agent if your travel dates are in or near high, low or shoulder season. The seasons vary by destination. For instance, you can save about $250 on travel to London from Chicago if your flight originates from November 1 through December 14, 1996, or December 25, 1996, to March 31, 1997.

During the Christmas season, you can save $100-200 on domestic roundtrips for departures December 24 or December 25, depending on the day Christmas falls. You may also be able to save on international tickets for flights leaving Christmas day.

Acknowledging high, shoulder and low rate seasons can help you save. If you are the adventuresome type with flexible time demands, you can plan your itinerary based on where the deals are or wait to make a desired trip until rates are at their lowest. In early 1996 you could fly roundtrip to London from Los Angeles, San Francisco, Chicago or Dallas for as little as $299.

Remember that consolidator fares can be up to 50% less than published fares in all seasons of travel. Consolidator fare contracts and new prices are usually released two times per year: in September and October for travel between November 1 and March 31, in late January and February for travel from April through October.

CREATIVE TICKETING

HIDE THIS BOOK

Now we're getting into areas where the airlines post their "RESTRICTED ENTRY" signs. We've all watched late-night movies and seen Dracula flinch at the sight of a cross. That's the same effect you could get if airline personnel see you carrying this book. Keep it hidden at the airport. What's going to be extra green to you will be like a red flag to airline gate agents. Airlines would like to intimidate you into believing that creative ticketing is a black and white situation. As you'll see, it's really a big gray area–the same shade as all the tax code loopholes that most of us try to find.

As you read this section, you'll find that we have either legitimately countered any airline's claim that creative ticketing is wrong or given you ways to use creative ticketing while staying within the boundaries of each airline's rules. They won't be happy, but you'll be walking around with a much healthier checking account.

Many travel agents have problems with creative ticketing because the airlines try to intimidate them. Airlines have tried to fill them with fear of reprisal if they take one step outside of what the airlines want them to do. The airlines' contracts with travel agents mandate that they cannot offer creative ticketing methods to their customers, even if it saves them hundreds of dollars. You must remember that the travel agency cannot afford to lose their contract to write tickets. Give your agents an out by telling them what you want. Then, when and if the airlines come back at them, they can legitimately say that they were not promoting creative ticketing.

ALTERNATE CITIES

Eight members of a family want to attend their family reunion in New York City, but tickets from their home in Denver to La Guardia or JFK are $538 per person. The total cost for this family would be $4,304. Instead, the family uses two alternate cities. They fly out of Colorado Springs and into Newark, for a per ticket price of

---

A General Disclaimer

❝ Many of these creative ticketing methods, namely **back-to-back and hidden city** ticketing, make the airlines' wings ruffle. BEST FARES Discount Travel Magazine has received many letters from airlines stating that back-to-back ticketing and hidden city fares violate their rules. I believe that each ticket is its own separate contract and as long as you abide by the rules of each contract, you've met your responsibility. The airlines try to claim that they have the right to guess at what you're doing when using multiple tickets. My opinion is that they only have province over each individual ticket. The Department of Justice and the Department of Transportation have stated that the use of the creative ticketing options are legal. However, they also have stated the airlines have the right to deny boarding or charge you more money for the ticket. ❞

1949 Pan Am round trip fare from New York to Hawaii on the double-decker Clipper: $288 plus tax.

> 66 *For the past 15 years I have been talking about hidden cities on radio and TV and using creative ticketing methods properly on the majority of my flights across the country. Other people have also used them for years. I have always felt that if the airlines really believe that creative ticketing in any way, shape or form legally violates any rules, more passengers would be challenged. To this date, no one has been sued, fined or come up in front of a court of law relating to creative ticketing issues. Whether or not you choose to use these methods is entirely up to you! Just make sure you do it correctly.* 99

$218. They save $320 per ticket, or $2,560 total. The additional driving time is less than two hours total. With savings of $2,560, forget renting a car, they could hire a limo–and deserve it.

Sometimes a reasonable change in departure or arrival airports (or both) will save you hundreds of dollars. This can be due to a price war in a certain market, an upstart niche-carrier that's causing prices to plummet or other market factors. You can also get to popular destinations at peak times–such as New Orleans' Mardi Gras–by being one of the first to think of using alternate cities. Can't get tickets to Memphis for Elvis' birthday? Buy a ticket to Little Rock where you'll be a two-hour drive away. Use ground transportation to get to and from these alternate cities or, in some cases, add a commuter flight that will still give you a less expensive bottom line.

Any city serviced by Southwest, ValuJet, Western Pacific and, for long haul service, America West, offers great alternate-city savings. Niche airlines, low-cost airlines and introductory fares are what make alternate city savings possible.

Compare the savings against any possible inconvenience, then decide. Is $50 savings worth an 80-mile drive? Probably not. But what about a $350 savings and an 80-mile drive?

An added plus to alternate city travel is the likelihood that you'll fly into a less congested airport with fewer delays and car rental ease you thought disappeared a decade ago. Just be sure to make an advance reservation to account for the more limited availability.

Use alternate cities for travel to Europe by checking fares from major U.S. gateway cities. If you live in Philadelphia, for example, check the fares out of New York City.

- **If you're going anywhere near London**, consider using the low fares almost always available to that city–coupled with rail travel or Visit Europe Air Passes–to reach your ultimate destination.

- **Flights to Scandinavia** are usually more expensive than flights to other European destinations. Flying into Germany puts you 100 miles from Denmark with easy access by rail and ferry.

- **Iceland Air** flies into Luxembourg which is next to Belgium, France and Germany. Its fares are almost always bargains, and the airline will even assist you in discount train travel to Paris or Zurich.

The best way to find an alternate city is to take out a U.S. or world map. Check major airports near your origination and destination cities, then refer to the follow-

---

Cost of a 1953 roundtrip from Cincinnati to Phoenix on a TWA "Quickie Vacation:" $85.05.

ing chart. For example, you live in Dallas and want to fly to Cincinnati. The airfare to that city is not on sale and costs $450 roundtrip. When you look at a map you will see that Dayton and Columbus (Ohio), Louisville and Indianapolis are all approximately two hours or less driving time from Cincinnati. The airfares to any of these cities could save you up to 80%, compared to the airfare to Cincinnati.

Be sure to ask your travel agent to check these surrounding cities. Also, be sure to combine the low alternate city fares with any airline's dollars-off discount coupons for maximum savings.

Here's a chart showing commonly used domestic alternate cities with their air mile distance from the primary airport in parentheses.

ALTERNATE CITIES (AIR MILE DISTANCES IN PARENTHESES)

PRIMARY AIRPORT	ALTERNATE CITIES
AKRON, OH	Cleveland (40); Pittsburgh (70); Columbus (99)
ALBANY, NY	Hartford (80); New York City (140)
ATLANTA, GA	Chattanooga (106); Birmingham (134)
ATLANTIC CITY, NJ	Philadelphia (55); Newark (93)
AUSTIN, TX	San Antonio (70); Houston (143); Dallas/Fort Worth (183)
BALTIMORE, MD	Washington International (30); Washington Dulles (43); Philadelphia (90); Richmond (120)
BANGOR, ME	Boston (201); Montreal (244)
BATON ROUGE, LA	New Orleans (65)
BOSTON, MA	Providence (49); Hartford (91)
BOISE, ID	Salt Lake City(291)
BUFFALO, NY	Rochester (55); Toronto (68); Cleveland (192)
BURBANK, CA	Los Angeles (18); Ontario (44)
BURLINGTON, VT	Montreal (75); Hartford (177); Boston (181)
CHARLESTON, SC	Columbia (95); Charlotte (168); Atlanta (259)
CHARLESTON, WV	Columbus (131); Cincinnati (173); Louisville (226)
CHARLOTTE, NC	Greensboro (82); Raleigh (130); Atlanta (227)
CHATTANOOGA, TN	Knoxville (87); Atlanta (106); Nashville (113)
CHICAGO, IL	Milwaukee (75)
CINCINNATI, OH	Dayton (64); Louisville (83); Indianapolis (98); Columbus (116);
CLEVELAND, OH	Toledo (102); Columbus (112); Pittsburgh (144)
COLORADO SPRINGS, CO	Denver (67)
COLUMBUS, OH	Dayton (72); Cleveland (112); Cincinnati (116)

The oldest state capital in the United States: Santa Fe, New Mexico.

ALTERNATE CITIES (AIR MILE DISTANCES IN PARENTHESES)

PRIMARY AIRPORT	ALTERNATE CITIES
CORPUS CHRISTI, TX	San Antonio (135); Houston Hobby (187);
DALLAS, TX	Oklahoma City (175); Austin (183)
DAYTON, OH	Cincinnati (64); Columbus (72); Indianapolis (110)
DAYTONA BEACH, FL	Orlando (54); Jacksonville (97)
DENVER, CO	Colorado Springs (67)
DES MOINES, IA	Omaha (117); Kansas City (165)
DETROIT, MI	Toledo (49); Lansing (74); Grand Rapids (120)
EUGENE, OR	Portland (106)
EVANSVILLE, IN	Louisville (98); St. Louis (161)
FORT LAUDERDALE, FL	Miami (21); West Palm Beach (42)
FLINT, MI	Lansing (45); Detroit (56)
FORT MYERS, FL	Tampa (104); Fort Lauderdale (112)
FRESNO, CA	Oakland (152); Sacramento (167)
GRAND RAPIDS, MI	Lansing (48); Detroit (120); Chicago (134)
GREEN BAY, WI	Milwaukee (107); Chicago (181)
GREENSBORO, NC	Raleigh (67); Charlotte (82)
HARLINGEN, TX	Corpus Christi (107)
HARRISBURG, PA	Baltimore (70); Philadelphia (83); Washington Dulles (94); Washington National (94)
HARTFORD, CT	Boston (91); New York City (105)
HILTON HEAD, SC	Savannah (31); Jacksonville (133)
HOUSTON, TX	Austin (143); San Antonio (191)
HUNTSVILLE, AL	Birmingham (74); Atlanta (151)
INDIANAPOLIS, IN	Cincinnati (98); Dayton (110); Louisville (111)
JACKSONVILLE, FL	Savannah (117); Orlando (143)
KALAMAZOO, MI	Lansing (62); Detroit (113); Chicago (116)
KANSAS CITY, MO	Omaha (152)
KEY WEST, FL	Miami (126)
KNOXVILLE, TN	Nashville (152); Atlanta (152)
LANSING, MI	Grand Rapids (48); Detroit (74)
LEXINGTON, KY	Louisville (63); Cincinnati (70)

Cost of Hong Kong's new Chep Lap Kok airport: $20 billion; cost of Denver's new airport: $5 billion.

ALTERNATE CITIES (AIR MILE DISTANCES IN PARENTHESES)

PRIMARY AIRPORT	ALTERNATE CITIES
LINCOLN, NE	Omaha (55); Kansas City (152)
LITTLE ROCK, AR	Memphis (130)
LOS ANGELES, CA	Burbank (18); Orange County (36); Ontario (47)
LOUISVILLE, KY	Cincinnati (83); Indianapolis (111)
MADISON, WI	Milwaukee (74); Chicago (119)
MANCHESTER, MA	Boston (26)
MCALLEN, TX	Harlingen (37); Corpus Christi (119); San Antonio (232)
MEDFORD, OR	Portland (222)
MEMPHIS, TN	Little Rock (130); Nashville (200)
MIAMI, FL	Fort Lauderdale (21); West Palm Beach (62)
MILWAUKEE. WI	Chicago (75)
MOBILE, AL	Pensacola (64); Birmingham (216)
MONTREAL, CANADA	Burlington (75); Boston (254)
NAPLES, FL	Fort Myers (26); Fort Lauderdale (101); Tampa (134)
NASHVILLE, TN	Memphis (200); Atlanta (214)
NEW ORLEANS, LA	Baton Rouge (65); Pensacola (186)
NEW YORK, NY	Newark (14); Philadelphia (93); Hartford (115)
NEWARK, NJ	New York (14); Philadelphia (81); Hartford (115)
NORFOLK, VA	Newport News (23); Richmond (75); Washington, DC (142); Raleigh (160)
OAKLAND, CA	San Francisco (11); San Jose (30); Sacramento (75)
OKLAHOMA CITY, OK	Tulsa (111); Wichita (156); Dallas (175)
OMAHA, NE	Des Moines (117); Kansas City (152)
ONTARIO, CA	Orange County (30); Burbank (44); Los Angeles (47)
ORANGE COUNTY, CA	Ontario (30); Los Angeles (36); San Diego (76)
ORLANDO, FL	Tampa (80); Jacksonville (143)
PALM SPRINGS, CA	Ontario (65); San Diego (85); Los Angeles (110)
PENSACOLA, FL	New Orleans (186)
PHILADELPHIA, PA	Newark (81); Baltimore (90)
PHOENIX, AZ	Tucson (110)
PITTSBURGH, PA	Cleveland (105); Columbus (144)

Comparative cost of flying 500 miles within the U.S. and within Europe: U.S./$296; Europe/$516.

ALTERNATE CITIES (AIR MILE DISTANCES IN PARENTHESES)	
PRIMARY AIRPORT	ALTERNATE CITIES
PORTLAND, ME	Boston (95)
PORTLAND, OR	Seattle (129)
PROVIDENCE, RI	Boston (49); Hartford (66); New York (146)
RALEIGH, NC	Greensboro (67); Charlotte (130)
RENO, NV	Sacramento (112); Oakland (180)
RICHMOND, VA	Newport News (52); Washington, DC (97)
ROANOKE, VA	Greensboro (85); Raleigh (120); Washington, DC (192)
ROCHESTER, NY	Buffalo (55); Syracuse (79); Toronto (106)
SACRAMENTO, CA	Oakland (75); San Francisco (86); Reno (112)
SAGINAW, MI	Lansing (58); Detroit (98)
ST. LOUIS, MO	Indianapolis (229)
SAN ANTONIO, TX	Austin (70); Houston (191)
SAN DIEGO, CA	Orange County (76); Los Angeles (109)
SAN FRANCISCO, CA	Oakland (11); San Jose (30)
SAN JOSE, CA	San Francisco (30); Oakland (30)
SARASOTA, FL	Tampa (40); Orlando (109)
SEATTLE, WA	Vancouver (127); Portland (129)
SHREVEPORT, LA	Little Rock (182); Dallas/Fort Worth (190)
SOUTH BEND, IN	Chicago (75); Indianapolis (137); Detroit (157)
SPOKANE, WA	Seattle (224)
SYRACUSE, NY	Rochester (79); Buffalo (134)
TAMPA, FL	Orlando (80)
TOLEDO, OH	Detroit (49); Cleveland (102); Columbus (121)
TUCSON, AZ	Phoenix (110)
TULSA, OK	Oklahoma City (111)
VANCOUVER, CANADA	Seattle (127)
WASHINGTON, DC	Baltimore (30); Richmond (94)
WEST PALM BEACH, FL	Fort Lauderdale (42); Miami (62); Orlando (142)
WICHITA, KS	Oklahoma City (156)
WORCHESTER, MA	Providence (44); Boston (45); Hartford (47)

Cost of increased security at 83 U.S. airports from August 1 through October 31, 1995: $13.8 million.

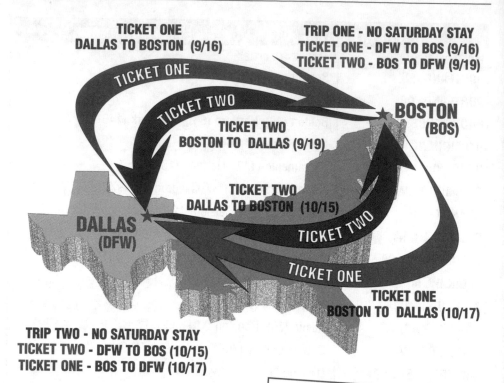

TICKET ONE
DALLAS TO BOSTON (9/16)

TRIP ONE - NO SATURDAY STAY
TICKET ONE - DFW TO BOS (9/16)
TICKET TWO - BOS TO DFW (9/19)

TICKET ONE

TICKET TWO

TICKET TWO
BOSTON TO DALLAS (9/19)

BOSTON
(BOS)

TICKET TWO
DALLAS TO BOSTON (10/15)

TICKET TWO

DALLAS
(DFW)

TICKET ONE

TICKET ONE
BOSTON TO DALLAS (10/17)

TRIP TWO - NO SATURDAY STAY
TICKET TWO - DFW TO BOS (10/15)
TICKET ONE - BOS TO DFW (10/17)

BACK-TO-BACKS

Airline pricing is geared to shaft business travelers. For example, a business traveler flies from Dallas to Boston every other week, spending two days each time. He never stays over a Saturday night but he hates paying three or four times more for each ticket than he'd pay with a Saturday stay. He learns about back-to-back ticketing and is able to fly on the lowest possible excursion rate. He buys two tickets: one set originating in his actual departure city and the second set originating in his actual destination city. It looks like he has Saturday stays because he flies to Boston on the first segment of one ticket and back on the first segment of the other. On his second trip he uses the second portion of each ticket. He buys his tickets from two different airlines to avoid even the smallest risk.

> **❝***Always know the rules of the tickets you're buying if you fly on seven-, 14- or 21-day advance purchase fares. For more flexibility, you may want to use a higher-priced excursion fare that gives you up to a 365 day window for your second trip on each ticket.* **❞**

Back-to-backs are sometimes called "nested" or "cross" tickets. You can use them when you're flying to and from the same destination at least two times within the fares' maximum stay period, usually 30 days on excursion tickets. Back-to-backs are useful when you don't have a Saturday stay and would otherwise be forced to buy an expensive ticket. Sometimes, particularly during fare wars, savings are so significant that you can save money by buying two back-to-backs when you only plan on making one roundtrip.

If you're going to use the same airline for both sets of tickets, buy one from your travel agent and one from the airline so the ticket numbers won't be sequential. Or buy them both from your travel agent, but buy the second set one day later after making sure they're on a 24-hour hold. Better yet, use two airlines–one for each set of tickets–whenever possible. If you buy one ticket from Airline A and one ticket from Airline B, neither one has the right to claim you can't use them as you see fit because you're staying completely within each airline's rules.

The return dates on both tickets can be changed by payment of a nominal change fee, giving you even more flexibility. Make sure that your original return reservation is in the computer so you can call from the road and change it. If, for example, you're not sure of your return date but you know it will be within the next 30 days, extend your return to the last possible return date your ticket allows.

Always be sure to use your ticket coupons in order, and don't hand both sets of tickets to the gate agent to "figure it out." Either action could be a sure way to alert the gate agent to the fact that you're using back-to-backs.

Variation #2: Keep your Saturday night stay in your home city and make the back-to-back process less complicated by buying a one-way ticket for the first leg of your first trip–perhaps using a niche airline, an alternate city or a hidden city to keep the price low. Then use the first part of your roundtrip ticket to fly home, saving the return ticket for your next trip back to the same location. You can make date changes for the "return" flight, usually for $50, within a reasonable length of time. What you've done is slid through a perfectly valid loophole because nothing in airline rules and tariffs state that your weekend stay cannot be in your home town.

Variation #3: Gain even more low-cost flexibility by using back-to-back ticketing with open jaw ticketing. It works when you plan to travel to two separate cities. Your first trip, for example, would be Detroit to New York. Your second trip would be Detroit to Chicago. Using open jaw ticketing (fully explained on page 33), you can purchase back-to-backs with open jaw routing. You can do this with any routing that meets the primary rule of open jaw ticketing–your return flight must be more than half the distance of your originating flight. If you're traveling, for example, on a 1,381 mile flight, your open jaw return flight must be 691 miles or more.

Variation #4: Back-to-backs with a hidden city. If you want to use back-to-back ticketing but don't plan to make two trips to the same location, adding hidden city ticketing lowers your cost and makes your savings more significant. Buy a lower-priced roundtrip using a hidden city (see the next page for details), and either buy a one-way return ticket on a niche or other low-cost carrier or buy a cheaper second round trip originating in your actual destination city.

Variation #5: Double option back-to-backs. Sometimes you fly to New York. Sometimes you fly to Washington, DC. Your schedule is rarely set in advance. Buy back-to-backs routed with a flight that connects in Washington before going on to New York. If you need to go to Washington, you have a non-stop. If you need to go to New York, you make the connection. Either way, you're covered. If you want to return on a different date, pay the change fee and instruct the airline to put you on a non-stop flight.

Year that American Airlines began service as American Airways: 1930.

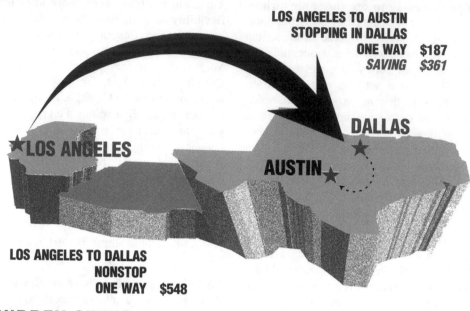

**LOS ANGELES TO AUSTIN
STOPPING IN DALLAS
ONE WAY** $187
SAVING *$361*

DALLAS

★LOS ANGELES

AUSTIN ★

**LOS ANGELES TO DALLAS
NONSTOP
ONE WAY** $548

HIDDEN CITIES

Airlines often lower fares from destinations that connect through their hub cities. They do it to counter competition from other carriers at the originating airport. You can take advantage of these fares for one-way travel. Book your ticket to the hidden city, but get off the plane when it makes its stop at the hub airport. Remember to take carry-on luggage only, and make your exit as unobtrusive as possible.

Hidden cities can lower your fare by as much as 80%–sometimes even more. Anytime you are flying to a major airline's hub city and you're flying only one-way, are not planning a Saturday stay or have no advance notice, you're likely to save by using a hidden city.

Most airlines no longer base their prices on the distance flown. They've hidden the cities that provide the best ticket values, and it's up to us to find them. Say you want to fly from Los Angeles to Dallas. You're quoted a fare. What you're

not told is that a longer flight from Los Angeles to Austin with a change of planes in Dallas costs $361 less. The airlines expect you to pay more even though you're not flying as far. In this case, Dallas is the hidden city.

> **"**It's not as if you have to find Atlantis. Hidden cities is a term I coined years ago to recognize that the cheapest distance between point A and point B is often a ticket to Point C. Now the phrase "hidden city" is being used by most of the travel and transportation writers worldwide.**"**

Hidden cities came from deregulation. The Civil Aeronautics Board (CAB) set tariffs prior to deregulation and allowed what were called "Point Beyond" fares— the predecessor of hidden cities. The CAB highly recommended Point Beyond fares because they believed it was unfair for people on the same plane to be able to fly farther for less than was paid by the passengers who de-planed at the stopover city. Travel agents could legitimately issue a ticket from Point A to Point B, but charge the lower fare for Point A to Point C. They simply circled the fare on the flight coupon to let the airline know they were using a Point Beyond fare calculation. The airlines even offered advice on how to get the best Point Beyond fares. After deregulation, the airlines were allowed to set their own prices, and they decided Point Beyond fares were not in their best interest.

Hidden cities are not for everyone. The intent of this section is to show you how to book a cheaper one-way flight with little or no advance purchase. It also eliminates the need to stay over a Saturday night.

Always book a hidden city ticket that's routed to fly on the first segment. The hidden city segment is the one you plan **not** to use. If you try to fly on the second segment without having checked in for your first flight, you're likely to find that your entire ticket was cancelled as a "no show." A hidden city should have two separate segments for each roundtrip. For example, purchase a roundtrip from Dallas/Ft. Worth to Toronto, planning to deplane in Chicago, the connecting city. If roundtrips to Toronto are $190 and roundtrips to Chicago are $480, you'll save $290. If your return ticket is on the same ticket, the airline will cancel both the Toronto to Chicago and Chicago to Dallas/Ft. Worth return flights since you never checked in for your outbound Chicago to Toronto flight. That's fine if all you wanted was an inexpensive one-way ticket to Chicago. It's a small disaster if you actually had planned to use a return flight.

There are two ways to use hidden cities intelligently:

- **One-way travel.** This is the simplest and most common form of hidden city usage. Roundtrips run the risk of having the return segments cancelled if an airline computer scan shows that you missed one segment of your outbound trip. Never use hidden cities for roundtrip travel except...

- **Roundtrip travel with an open jaw return.** Say you want to go from Denver to New York City. You have a 21-day advance and plan on staying over Saturday, but the roundtrip fare is still $544. You could buy a roundtrip ticket with an open jaw return, departing from Denver but returning to Colorado Springs. Make sure the return flight makes a stop in Denver and de-plane there. Remember that you must carry your luggage on your return trip, or it will end up in Colorado Springs. Because you paid 50% of the excursion fare on each part of your open jaw ticket, and because the Colorado Springs fare is cheaper, you saved about $100. Anytime you use an open jaw in this manner, be sure your return flight is scheduled to stop in your actual destination.

Never call and cancel any leg of a flight you don't plan to use. It's technically fraud because it comes under the definition of altering a ticket. Even if you never plan to get on that segment, let the reservation stand.

Many travel agencies will not book hidden cities because, on the off chance that the airline detects it, they may try to charge the agency the difference in the ticket cost. You can purchase your tickets directly from the airlines, making sure never to mention the term "hidden city," or you can purchase tickets from your travel agent.

The longest air route flown in 1931: KLM's Amsterdam to Batavia (now Djakarta) on four-passenger planes.

AIRLINE HUBS	
AIRLINE	**HUBS**
ALASKA	Anchorage and Seattle
AMERICAN	Chicago, Dallas/Fort Worth, Miami and San Juan
AMERICA WEST	Columbus, OH; Las Vegas and Phoenix
CONTINENTAL	Cleveland, Houston and Newark
DELTA	Atlanta, Cincinnati, Dallas/Fort Worth, Orlando and Salt Lake City
NORTHWEST	Detroit, Memphis and Minneapolis
SOUTHWEST	Houston Hobby, Dallas Love, Phoenix, Salt Lake City, Nashville and St. Louis
TWA	New York JFK and St. Louis
UNITED	Chicago, Denver, San Francisco and Washington Dulles
USAIR	Baltimore, Charlotte, Philadelphia, Pittsburgh and Washington National
WESTERN PACIFIC	Colorado Springs
VALUJET	Atlanta and Washington Dulles

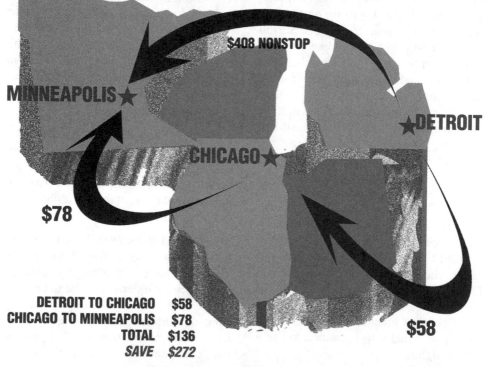

SPLIT CITY EXAMPLE

$408 NONSTOP

MINNEAPOLIS ★

★DETROIT

CHICAGO ★

$78

$58

DETROIT TO CHICAGO	$58
CHICAGO TO MINNEAPOLIS	$78
TOTAL	$136
SAVE	*$272*

Airport from which Amelia Earhart departed in 1937 for her ill-fated, around-the-world flight: Oakland.

SPLIT CITIES

You can save up to 70% and avoid the financial trauma of one airline's route monopoly by splitting your ticketing in half and buying two tickets: one to the intermediate city and one to your final destination. In many cases you can do this on the same airline. In others you may have to use two airlines. In both cases your extra effort could pay off with hundreds of dollars in savings per passenger.

For example, a student likes to fly home from Detroit to Minneapolis as often as possible. It's hard to plan in advance and last minute fares are prohibitive. Split cities allow the student to fly one major carrier to Chicago and a second carrier on to Minneapolis. The two separate roundtrips together cost less than a 21-day advance Detroit/Minneapolis fare and up to 70% less than a last-minute roundtrip.

Niche carriers increase your split-ticketing options. If you book one leg on a niche carrier, you frequently put yourself close enough to your destination to get a cheap second-leg ticket on a major carrier. Niche carriers' walk-up fares are higher than their advance fares, but the ratio is much lower than it is for major carriers. On niche airlines that use inventory-controlled pricing, you may even be able to get their lowest fare, particularly for off-peak travel.

Head back to the niche airline chart to see which connecting cities offer the best opportunities for split-city ticketing.

Sometimes you can make your entire trip on major carriers by using two airlines, one for each segment. To get your savings, you need at least one segment at a low-cost fare. Then you can fly the same airline at a tremendously reduced fare. You can do this if one of two factors is in play:

- **Competition** is keeping fares low on a particular route either through the presence of a niche carrier or competition for dominance of a particular route.

- **Fare war prices**, not in effect for the roundtrip you want, are in effect for one segment of your flight.

There are two cities in the United States that permit low-cost air travel without a weekend stay: Reno and Las Vegas. You only have to stay in these resort areas a minimum of two days–any days. The rule holds true on all tickets, even the lowest priced 21-day excursion fare. If you want to fly from New York to Los Angeles, for example, departing and returning during the week, route your travel through Reno or Las Vegas, buying one New York/Las Vegas roundtrip and one Las Vegas/Los Angeles roundtrip. You can save 75%-80% off of regular mid-week fares plus, if you like, enjoy a vacation in the resort city, taking advantage of low hotel and meal costs.

Use split cities for international savings. If you're going to Europe, check east coast gateways like New York, Boston and Washington. Or check the fare to London and also the fare from London to your next destination. If you're going to South America, check Miami. If you're going to the South Pacific or the Orient, check fares from Los Angeles, Seattle and San Francisco. Those are the cities likely to have the best promotional fares. Check consolidator prices from gateway cities, too. This can help you lower your fare even more.

CODE SHARE AIRPORTS

Nearby airports can have code-share arrangements that also can mean additional savings and convenience. For instance, with certain types of airfares, Baltimore/Washington/Dulles are considered code-share airports. This means you can fly or stand by for flights at any of the three airports with the same ticket. Naturally you would book your flight from your point of origin to the airport that offers the best fare. Then, if needed, use your code-share option to fly to the airport of your choice. Other examples include San Francisco/Oakland/San Jose, New York La Guardia/JFK/Newark and Miami/Ft. Lauderdale.

LAST FLIGHT IN/ FIRST FLIGHT OUT

It may be impossible to fly to a city for a same day, early morning meeting. Your schedule may prevent you from departing the day before. Consider taking the last flight of the day to a hub which gives you an early morning connection the next day to your destination city.

Let's say you live in Dallas and need to be in New York City for a 10 a.m. meeting Tuesday. You won't be able to leave Dallas before 7 a.m., which is already 8 a.m. in New York City. That means you can't fly early Tuesday and still be on time for your meeting. The last flight out of Dallas to New York City Monday night departs at 7:40 p.m. Depending on your work schedule—and the Dallas traffic—you may not be able to make that flight. Even if you could, you don't want to check into a New York City hotel at 1 a.m. If you book the last Delta flight to Atlanta on Monday, departing at 10 or 11 p.m., and layover in a hotel near the airport, you can get a good night's rest and take Delta's first flight out in the morning, in plenty of time to make your meeting. Atlanta is in the same time zone as New York City, and because it's a Delta hub, has frequent flights beginning early enough to get you to Manhattan with time to spare. This utilizes the airlines "Last Flight In, First Flight Out" rule. You don't have to pay the airline extra for the layover

in Atlanta or pay an extra airfare since this is considered a connecting flight.

You can also use last flight in/first flight out to your advantage when low priced fares to your destination are sold out. Say you want to fly from Orlando to New York City, but the cheapest fare available is $700. Checking a flight that connects in Atlanta, you find availability on the last flight of the day, as it arrives in Atlanta too late to make a connection to New York. The next morning you take the 6 a.m. Atlanta-New York flight with available seats since it leaves too early for other flights to feed passengers to it. You've just flown for $200–saving $500 off the lowest quoted fare.

> **"**As an added bonus, I have found that hotel rates near hub airports are usually much more reasonable than rates in major metropolitan destinations. For instance, in the example above, I could get my hotel room in Atlanta for $69. That's cheap compared to New York City hotel rates.**"**

BACKHAULING

Some flights are more direct than others, but those flights that get you to the same destination via a more circuitous route can offer lower fares to fill empty seats. You will usually need a good travel agent to locate these deals. They're called backhauls because you fly **away** from your destination for part of your trip. For example, a Dallas-Los Angeles fare can sometimes be lowered by routing it through St. Louis.

STANDBY BENEFITS

You may be able to fly standby if you're holding a ticket for a future date and want to fly between the same city pairs (or their code-share airports) prior to your ticketed times.

Airlines have different rules on when passengers can stand by for ticketed reservations. Some, such as Alaska Airlines, insist that your ticket be for travel on the same day you're attempting standby. Others (such as American and TWA) allow standby based on tickets for any future date.

Standby travel is usually not confirmed until ten minutes before departure.

There are other types of standby travel most often attainable on (but not limited to) international routes and for passengers 25 and under. Ask about these options when you call for ticket quotes.

Some domestic coupon travel such as youth and senior coupon booklets permit a standby option with no advance purchase.

Virgin, Air Canada and IcelandAir frequently discount international tickets purchased one day or less before travel, but only on select flights with a decent percentage of empty seats.

THROW-AWAY TICKETS

Throw-away tickets are the easiest form of creative ticketing. They're used when you wish to fly one-way and can't get a fare you can live with using a niche carrier, alternate or hidden cities. You simply buy a roundtrip ticket, use the outbound segment or segments and throw away the return ticket. You save money because sale-priced roundtrip excursion tickets (requiring a Saturday night stay) are usually substantially cheaper than a major airline's one-way ticket.

Never throw away the first portion of a ticket and attempt to use the return segments. When you don't fly on the outbound segments, your reservation cancels and the airlines can charge you for a full fare, one-way ticket.

OPEN JAWS

While not exactly a creative ticketing method by itself, open jaws are assets in several forms of creative ticketing. If you draw a simple diagram of open jaw routing, it looks exactly like its name. Open jaw ticketing is used when you want to fly in to one city and out of another. The fare is calculated by taking half of the round trip fare to each destination and combining them. You can use open jaws on almost any fare basis.

There are geographical limits to open jaw ticketing. Domestically, you can get an open jaw roundtrip when the mileage on your return flight is one-half or more the distance of your originating flight. For example, flying out of New York to Salt Lake City and returning to New York from Los Angeles can be done on an open jaw ticket. Returning from Chicago would not be allowed.

There are two types of open jaw tickets.

• **The originating and ending cities are the same,** but the open jaw cities are different. You would, for example, fly from Houston to Newark and return from Boston to Houston.

• **The destination city is the same** but you are originating in one city and returning to another. For example, you fly from Milwaukee to Boston and return from Boston to Detroit.

Remember that all open jaw tickets require that both your flights are on the same airline. A Saturday stay is usually required.

Open jaws can provide particularly good options for international travel. You'll probably pay more than you'd pay for the cheapest ticket in and out of the same city, but you'll gain flexibility and avoid backtracking if you plan to cover several cities or countries.

CIRCLE TRIPS

Circle trips allow you to visit two cities at half of the lowest roundtrip excursion fare. Circle trips offer destination choices you can't get on open jaws, due to geographical restrictions. You must make your entire trip on the same airline and your trip must include a Saturday night stay. You can't make three or more stops without giving up the benefits circle trips offer.

Each airline has its own rules on circle trips. In general, the first leg must be the farthest point from your originating city and the first leg destination must be where you take your Saturday night stay. Delta, however, allows the Saturday stay requirement to be met on any portion of the trip. United allows you to choose the Saturday-stay city in select markets. Always ask for the individual airline's policy.

A sample circle trip itinerary would be New York City to Denver, Denver to Dallas/Fort Worth and Dallas/Fort Worth to New York City.

FREE STOPOVERS

Airline rules state that on travel within the 48 states you can have up to four hours between connecting flights. Anything over four hours bases your fare on one-way prices. The four-hour rule gives you an ideal window in which to visit families, conduct short business meetings or take a quick city tour for free.

Say, for example, you're a business traveler flying from Los Angeles to New York, but you have clients you'd like to see in Dallas/Fort Worth or Memphis. If you simply ask for a connecting flight, the reservationist will usually book you on a connection with less than one hour between flights. If you route your travel through a hub city, you're likely to have your choice of several connecting flights–all within the four-hour rule. You can see your client in Memphis without adding a penny to your Los Angeles/New York trip.

Get two free stopovers by using the four-hour rule on your outbound and your return flights. Continuing with the previous example, stop in Dallas/Fort Worth on your way back. You've just seen three clients for the price of one. Ask your travel agent to review the rules and pull up proper connection cities on the computer. All approved cities should show up.

The last flight in/first flight out section showed you another way to get a free stopover. In that case, you get an overnight stay. This is enough time to see the sights, particularly in cities with great nightlife such as New York and Chicago.

The connecting-time rule on international flights tends to be 12 hours, but be sure and check each airline for its individual policy. Some international airlines will give you up 24-hour stopovers without charging you more.

PACKAGE TOURS

DO THEY WORK FOR YOU?

Positives & Negatives

Tours are like the fabled little girl with the curl in the middle of her forehead. When they're good, they're very, very good, and when they're bad, they're horrid enough to give the pleasures of travel a bad name.

The package tour simplifies arrangements with one-stop shopping and can save you money. There is, however, no more fertile field for the seeds of disaster. If you choose the wrong company, your one stop could turn out to be either a series of bad dreams or a complete nightmare in which your money is gone with absolutely nothing to show for it.

We're going to show you how to avoid disaster and how to get the truly good deals and well-planned packages. The three irrevocable rules of booking a tour:

- **Deal only with reputable, well-recommended tour companies**. The cost of your entire vacation is at stake. Almost anyone can print a glossy brochure or open a well-appointed office.

- **Always pay by credit or charge card.** Even if you have to pay a little more to use your card, the protection it affords is better than many insurance add-ons and, in most cases, a faster way to get your money back when a tour company defaults in any way.

- **Always compare package prices** against booking each tour component separately, using discount options. Tours advertise savings of ten to 50 percent, but compare tour prices against two-for-ones, coupon deals, half-price hotels and other discount options, including the limited offers detailed in monthly issues of *BEST FARES Discount Travel Magazine*. Tour companies often compare their prices against rates travelers rarely have to pay, such as non-discounted airfares and full rack rates at hotels.

Type of aircraft that accounts for 25% of the commercial jets now in service: Boeing 737.

Sample Savings

This chart shows sample savings on tour packages based on winter 1995-1996 prices. All the savings are real, yet we could have also done a chart showing tour prices versus savings on deals you get by creative booking techniques explained in this book. Which way do you save the most? If you're not inclined to put time into booking your trip, tours offer convenience and some savings. If you are willing to invest some time, booking each component using special offers should save you even more.

SAMPLE SAVINGS ON PACKAGES VS. NON-DISCOUNTED TRAVEL				
ROUTING	VENDOR	COST	EXCURSION FARE AIR ONLY	PACKAGE INCLUSIONS
Los Angeles to Maui	Delta Dream	$479	$660	Air and 5 nights hotel
Los Angeles to London	United Vacations	$664	$788	Air and 5 nights hotel including breakfast
Los Angeles to Acapulco	Aeromexico Vacations	$449	$515	Air and 4 nights hotel
Tampa to Las Vegas	GoGo Tours	$279	$388 hotel	Air and 3 nights
Washington, DC to London	British Airways Holidays	$669	$579	Air and 6 nights hotel including breakfast
Phoenix to Los Cabos Vacations	Alaska Airlines	$298	$347	Air and 2 nights hotel
Dallas to Cancun	MLT Vacations	$261	$293	Air and 4 nights hotel (last minute sale price)
Houston to Banff, Canada	Continental Grand Destinations	$429	$609	Air and 3 nights hotel

Savings Strategies

Traveling on weekdays might give you more for less. A four-night Sunday to Thursday trip may cost the same or less as a three-night Thursday to Sunday package with identical inclusions.

Off-season travel offers substantial savings. Changing your travel dates by as little as a day or two can take you into off-peak rates and hundreds of dollars in savings.

Independent tour companies using charter air want to fill their planes even if it means selling a small number of air-only tickets. If you're traveling to a city popular with tourists, check the tour company ads in the Sunday paper for possible one-way and roundtrip bargains.

People traveling to conventions can sometimes beat the prices offered by convention sponsors by using vacation packages. This works best in popular vacation cities with clusters of nearby hotels. You may not get the same hotel as your group, but staying nearby could save you more money.

Airlines also use fly/drive or land/air packages to create artificial airfare discounts that in many cases prevent the competition from matching a published fare. Often, the airfare with hotel and car is cheaper than just the airfare. Hawaii is a great example. This is also true of many international destinations.

> **66**Hot bargains can be found in the large tour company ads in the travel section of your local Sunday newspaper. You'll find the most extensive international listings in papers from major gateway cities, such as Los Angeles and New York. The best deals focus on season-openers and last-minute "fire" sales. It's possible to pick up bargains like $99 Dallas-Las Vegas roundtrip flights or $149 three-night packages, including air and hotel.**99**

Charter Airlines

Charter airlines were the real pioneers of ticketless travel. You booked and paid for your flight, went to the airport and picked up the best seat assignment you could get. That's still the way they operate.

Charters offer the truest standby bargains. They count on filling all or most of their seats on every flight. As departure dates get closer, they bring down the price to attract more passengers. The best place to find these deals is in ads in the Sunday newspaper travel section. Try to find an agency that is open on Sunday so you have first crack at the available seats. Often they're listed at the bottom of each ad.

The king of charter destinations is Las Vegas. Charters go where vacationers want to go so you'll also see a concentration of charters to Orlando, Mexico, parts of the eastern Caribbean and, surprisingly, Minneapolis. No, it's not because the Mall of America is there. Two of the biggest charter companies have their home bases in Minneapolis.

Some of the most established charter companies are MLT, Funjet, Adventure Tours, TransGlobal and Go-Go Tours. Some of the best charter companies are directly affiliated with major airlines. In the United States, MLT and Northwest are the best example. Internationally, Air France, Lufthansa and KLM all have charter partners.

The Department of Transportation requires that all charter airlines maintain escrow accounts and financial performance bonds. They must also file with the DOT. Currently about 100 charter companies are on file. If you have any doubts about a charter's track record and solvency, ask for proof that they are meeting the provisions the law dictates and check with a reputable travel agency regarding the charter's track record.

Charter flights usually are scheduled based on three-, four- and seven-day roundtrips. A small percentage have 14-day configurations. You are usually limited to the scheduled departure and return dates, unless the charter agrees to sell you one-way tickets. If they do allow one-ways, the number sold will be restricted.

Charter flights fly under regulations that differ from those of scheduled air. Most charter flights are public charters, with ticketing done by travel agents, tour operators or (rarely) by passengers dealing directly with the airline. Affinity charters are planes leased by a particular group or organization.

- **Companies can cancel charters up to ten days before departure,** but that rarely happens. They're also allowed to make changes in their schedules, which is rarely done, except on an anticipated, seasonal basis.

- **They are allowed to delay flights for up to 48 hours** with no compensation mandated. Many charters do not have inter-line agreements, so they won't be able to put you on an alternate carrier.

- **Most charter tickets have no refund value.** If you're not able to take the flight, you lose the entire purchase price unless you've purchased cancellation insurance and fulfilled the terms for compensated cancellations. Always ask if insurance is available. If you're buying a last-minute, $98 roundtrip, there's no reason to buy insurance. If you're investing $2,000 in a package tour, it's probably a desirable thing.

> *“World Airways was considered to be the oldest charter airline in the U.S. The Virginia-based carrier began flying in 1948. It became a scheduled airline, went back to charter only from 1979-1986 (because of deregulation) and is now back in the scheduled air business.”*

EVALUATING TOUR COMPANIES

Name Recognition

Name recognition tells you very little about tour operators. Certified Vacations, for example, is a company you've probably never heard of, yet they package most American Express, American Automobile Association and Delta Airlines tours.

- **Some 80% of tour business is done by 20% of all tour companies.** The best tour companies can be useful adjuncts to your travel planning. The worst give the travel industry a bad name.

- **Defaults and bankruptcies** are statistically unlikely, but practically horrendous if yours is one of the vacations lost to an unscrupulous operator. If it looks too good to be true, it probably is.

- **Federal law requires all tour companies** to hold funds in escrow. If you have doubts, ask for specifics on escrow provisions. Best option: book tour companies where checks are made payable directly to an escrow account.

- **Use agencies** that hold a membership in one or more trade organizations, establish their own escrow accounts and/or have direct affiliations with an airline. Tour operator membership organizations include:

The American Society of Travel Agents, 703-739-2782

The U.S. Tour Operators Association, 212-750-7371

The National Tour Association, 800-682-8886

> *“Members of the United States Tour Operators Association (USTOA) have a unique consumer protection plan, initiated in the fall of 1993. Each active member of the organization must put up $1 million in security for consumer protection. It can be a bond, letter of credit, or certificate of deposit.”*

SELECT TOUR COMPANIES

COMPANY	FOCUS	PHONE	DIRECT BOOK	AFFILIATIONS
ATS Tours	South Pacific	800-423-2880	No	USTOA, ASTA
Apple Vacations West	Mexico, Caribbean, Las Vegas & Hawaii	800-727-3400	No	ASTA
Apple Vacations East	Mexico, Caribbean, Las Vegas & Hawaii	800-365-2775	No	ASTA
Central Holidays	Europe & North America	800-935-5000	Yes	USTOA, ASTA
CIE Tours	Escorted Europe	800-243-8687	Yes	USTOA, ASTA
Colette Tours	U.S. & International	800-717-9191	Yes	USTOA, ASTA
DER Tours	Europe & Asia	800-782-2424	Yes	USTOA, ASTA
Europlus/ Rail Europe	European Train Travel & Packages	800-438-7245	Yes	USTOA, ASTA
Funway Holidays Funjet	Nevada, Florida, California, Mexico, the Caribbean & Europe	800-558-3050	No	USTOA, ASTA
Globus & Cosmos Tourama	U.S. & International; Largest escorted tour operator	800-221-0090	No	USTOA, ASTA
MLT Vacations	Caribbean, Mexico, Las Vegas & other U.S. cities	800-328-0025	No	ASTA
Pleasant Holidays	Hawaii & Mexico	800-242-9244	Yes	USTOA, ASTA
Special Expeditions	Small group International Adventure Travel	800-762-0003	Yes	USTOA, ASTA
Tauck Tours	Worldwide Escorted Tours	800-468-2825	Yes	USTA, ASTA
TBI Tours	Japan, China, Southeast Asia & Indochina	800-223-0266	Yes	USTOA, ASTA
Trafalgar Tours	Europe & Mid-East	800-854-0103	No	USTOA, ASTA
TransGlobal Vacations	U.S., Mexico & Caribbean	800-338-2160	No	ASTA, USTOA, CLIA

The Smart Travelers Planning Kit is offered by the U.S. Tour Operators Association. The free brochure is clearly useful to infrequent travelers, yet has a range of information likely to contain several new tips for the experienced. Write to USTOA, 211 E. 51st St., Suite 12B, New York, NY 10022 or call 212-750-7371 to order by voice mail.

Where to book Parrot Head packages to destinations mentioned in Jimmy Buffett's song: Paradise Tours/Miami.

Independent Tour Companies

Independent tour companies come in a multitude of configurations. Some specialize in escorted tours. Some use only charter air. Others use multiple airlines, including scheduled air flights. Some have specific departure dates, others offer greater flexibility.

Some cities such as Atlanta, Dallas, New York and Minneapolis have a large number of charter choices. Others offer less.

Your best source for regional information: your Sunday travel section or a trusted travel agent. Many of the largest independent tour operators only book through travel agents.

Airline Tour Divisions

Many airlines have their own tour divisions. Tour packages aren't available to all destinations they serve and are usually limited to vacation-oriented cities.

* **You must call the vacation division directly** because the airline's general reservationist cannot access package options.

* **You can call all airline tour divisions directly except** for MLT, which books Northwest and KLM tours, as well as charter packages. MLT must be booked through travel agents. It is the one agency that spans both categories.

* **Most vacation divisions are open standard weekday business hours** and limited hours on weekends.

Protecting Yourself

Travel agencies may begin concentrating more and more on package tours since the major airlines capped commissions on air-only tickets. This will perhaps lead to increased expertise in tour packages. No travel agent can be an authority on all the thousands of options available. What they can and must do is assist you in determining the reliability of every tour company whose packages they sell.

Always pay for tours with a major credit card. It's your primary defense against loss of money in case of default or service violating your tour contract. Check the rules of the lending institution that issued your credit or charge card to see the time parameter on contesting a charge for a purchase not delivered as promised.

Choose to use the card that affords you the most protection. Some tour operators won't accept all major charge cards. Some charge a three to five percent surcharge for specific cards, most commonly Discover or American Express. Don't give in to the temptation to write a check. Even if you must pay a small surcharge, don't surrender the protection that paying by credit card affords.

Trip cancellation insurance is available from the larger tour operators, cruise lines and private insurance companies. Provisions may include coverage for illness, injury, emergency medical evacuation, lost and damaged baggage, cancellation and defaults. Refund value in case of traveler cancellation decreases incrementally the closer you get to departure. Cancellation is only covered for very specific medical reasons. Make sure the insurance fund is administered by an entity with financial separation from the tour or cruise operator. Otherwise, if the operator goes under, you've just increased your loss.

* **Policies** are sold by travel agents and private companies. Sources include Travelers, 800-243-3174; Mutual of Omaha's Travel Assure, 800-228-9792; Health Care Abroad/Global, 800-237-6615; TravelMed, 800-937-1387 and Worldwide Assistance, 800-821-2828.

MAJOR AIRLINE TOUR DIVISIONS			
AIRLINE	TOUR DIVISION	PHONE	CUSTOMER PROTECTED BY
AEROMEXICO	Aeromexico Vacations	800-245-8585	ASTA, USTOA
ALASKA AIRLINES	Alaska Vacations	800-468-2248	Alaska Airlines
AIR CANADA	Canadian Holidays	800-776-3000	Air Canada
AIR FRANCE	Jet Vacations	800-538-0999	ASTA
AMERICA WEST	America West Vacations	800-356-6611	America West Airlines
AMERICAN AIRLINES	Fly Away Vacations	800-321-2121	American Airlines, ASTA
BRITISH AIR	British Air Holidays	800-876-2200	British Airways
CATHAY PACIFIC	Cathay Pacific Tours	800-762-8181	Cathay Pacific Airlines
CONTINENTAL AIRLINES	Grand Destinations	800-634-5555	Continental Airlines, ASTA
DELTA AIRLINES	Delta Dream Vacations	800-872-7786	Delta Airlines, USTOA
EL AL	El Al Tours	800-352-5786	El Al Airlines
ICELAND AIR	European Vacations	800-223-5500	ASTA
MEXICANA AIRLINES	Mex Sea Sun	800-531-9321	ASTA
MIDWAY AIRLINES	Midway Vacations	800-996-4392	ASTA, USTOA
NORTHWEST AIRLINES	KLM/Northwest World Vacations	Must Go Through Travel Agent	ASTA
QANTAS	Qantas Vacations	800-641-8772	Qantas Airlines
RENO AIR	Quick Escapes	800-736-6247	Reno Airlines
SINGAPORE AIRLINES	Asian Affair Holidays	800-742-3133	Singapore Air
SOUTHWEST AIRLINES	Fun Pack Vacations	800-423-5683	USTOA, ASTA
SWISSAIR	SwissPak	800-688-7947	ASTA
TWA	Getaway Vacations	800-438-2929	TWA
UNITED AIRLINES	United Vacations	800-328-6877	United Airlines, USTOA, ASTA
USAIR	USAir Vacations	800-455-0123	USTOA, ASTA
VIRGIN ATLANTIC	Virgin Vacations	800-364-6466	USTOA

> **❝**Tour cancellations by travelers can exact high penalties, sometimes the entire cost of the trip. You're used to being able to cancel a regular airfare ticket and still retain the ticket's value. This is often not the case with tour packages. Be sure you know the cancellation policy in detail before making any payment.**❞**

KNOW THE FINE PRINT
Steps To A Successful Tour

Be sure to read the most important part of any tour brochure: the terms and conditions. This small print explains the terms of the contract you are entering into with the tour company. It should clearly explain:

- **payment provisions**

- **deposit and payment protection**

- **cancellation and refund policies**

- **insurance options**

- **departure rules and provisions changes**

- **baggage allowances and protection**

- **rules on reconfirming flights**

- **Visa and passport information**

- **a written guarantee covering their obligations and what they will do if they are not met**

A deposit will hold your tour and leave the majority of your funds at your disposal until the final payment deadline.

- **The stiffest cancellation penalties** don't go into effect until final payment is made.

- **Be sure you know** how and when the final payment must be made. The tour operator and agent have no legal responsibility to remind you of the deadline.

- **If you miss your payment deadline,** your deposit and your reservation most likely will be lost.

After you've read the fine print, get any variances in writing. Make sure your tour is not subject to a minimum number of participants. If it is, be sure you want to accept that risk.

Advertised prices always reflect the cheapest possible price and limited availability. Any variation will probably raise the rate considerably.

- **Prices are almost always based** on two people traveling and reflect the cost for one person only.

- **Weekend travel rates** can be higher.

- **Holiday travel** almost always carries a per-person surcharge.

- **Trips to foreign destinations** (including Mexican resorts) are advertised minus taxes and fees.

- **Price changes after you've booked** are

unlikely; however, they can occur when local currency versus the U.S. dollar fluctuates dramatically. Make sure your rates are fixed.

Changes options are limited. Flexibility may be the price you pay for tour savings and planning. Some packages give you travel date and length options. Others are built around schedules that dictate exact dates of departure and return. Any change to your original reservation may be prohibited or incur the payment of change fees. Know what risks are involved and the options available to you as a consumer.

Charter air is used by many tour companies. Since you give up protections inherent in scheduled air travel, a missed flight may be major trouble.

- **Tour companies are under no legal obligation to compensate you** for any problems resulting from a flight you fail to make even if it means your holiday is over before it begins.

- **If you miss the flight home** you may be forced to pay enormous one-way fares on scheduled air. The tour company may try to help you out, but they are under no obligation to provide alternate transportation.

- **Choose well-established tour companies** with enough flights and volume to possibly have an alternate seat within a reasonable time frame.

Scheduled flights on major airlines will offer more options, but you are still dependent on the airline's desire to maintain your good will. If you need to return home later or earlier, you could be faced with a higher airfare plus a $50 change fee.

All-inclusive tours can ease budget planning, but be sure you know exactly what is included. Travelers who enjoy exploring on their own usually do best to decline an all-inclusive option. "Free" meals are of no use unless you plan to be at your hotel or resort for all mealtimes.

Escorted tours provide a more structured travel experience and more direct companionship. Know the credentials of your tour leader, the size of the tour and the types of people who comprise the group. Three key phrases indicate how much time will be spent on specific attractions:

- **"View"** may indicate a passing glance.

- **"Visit"** can mean ten minutes or several hours.

- **"Orientation"** means you'll be given basic information and sent off to explore on your own.

Hotel ratings may be skewed by the tour operator to make a budget property look more appealing. Check the hotels in an independent ratings guide to get a true picture. Remember that amenities matter only if they matter to you. If you just want a comfortable base, choose the economy package.

Reserved seating, standard on tours using scheduled air (but be sure to check), is rare on tours using charters. Check in early for best seating options.

Ask for contact information so you know who to call if you have questions or problems. Some large companies have on-site representatives to address problems as they occur. At a minimum, get an 800 number plus the hours it is staffed. Many times this information is provided with your final tour documents.

Take advantage of helpful information available from your tour provider. They can tell you about weather conditions, the best beaches, local customs, special shopping values, dining options and clothing suggestions.

Airline with a complimentary hair style consultant on select flights: Virgin Atlantic.

Ask for special coupon books often available as part of the most popular tour packages such as Disneyland/Orlando and Las Vegas. Check for special deals on meals, attractions and car rentals.

Carry the necessary documents for international travel. Customs procedures do not relax just because you travel with a tour group.

Tour Terminology

Scheduled air: seats on an airline operating published, scheduled flights available to the general public.

Charter air: an entire flight booked by a tour operator and re-sold on a seat-by-seat basis as part of a tour package.

Best available: a commitment to provide a specified standard of hotel accommodation with the possibility of upgrade on arrival.

Run of the house: any available room.

Ground operator: a company responsible for airport-to-hotel transportation, sightseeing and other options.

Transfers: ground transportation either from the airport to the hotel or from the hotel to an attraction.

Land Package: excludes air or other transport to the destination. It can also include hotel, car rental and attraction tickets.

FIT: Foreign Independent Tour is usually unescorted, sometimes with guide options for some segments.

Stopover: an approved trip interruption, usually for 12 hours or more. The passenger de-planes at a connecting city and rejoins the tour at another scheduled departure time.

Recently,

BEST FARES Discount Travel Magazine showed savvy travelers how to get up to $100 off a Continental or USAir roundtrip when you develop a roll of film.

Call 800-880-1234 to subscribe.
See page 395 for your discount subscription offer.

Cost of a 23-day, private jet world tour, hotels included: $33,900.

OTHER WAYS TO SAVE

The airlines offer a lot of special status discounts, but before you hand over your credit card, always check to see if there are better deals out there.

SENIOR DISCOUNTS

The traditional ten percent senior discount, available on most single airline tickets, should only be used when it's the best possible discount opportunity, although some airlines extend the ten-percent discount to companions of any age. You can often save more by using senior coupon books, promotional discount coupons and special offers.

Senior coupon books come in four-, six- and eight-coupon formats; the eight-coupon books provide the best per-seg-

ment cost. Reservations generally require a 14-day advance. Many airlines permit standby travel–even on the day of purchase.

- **Each coupon book is valid for one year** from the date of purchase and allows one-way travel to or from your destination. Some destinations require two coupons per direction.

- **There are limited numbers of seats** set aside for coupon holders. The percentages and exact policies are never clearly stated. Your best bet is to allow as much advance booking time as possible.

- **Seniors using coupons must be at least 62,** except on Southwest (age 65). Southwest's advantage is they allow you to purchase one coupon at a time.

Airline with one plane painted in Aboriginal artwork: Qantas.

- **Companion coupon books** are offered by Continental and TWA for passengers traveling with the senior. USAir offers seniors a companion deal for grandchildren traveling with a senior coupon user.

- **When deciding which senior coupon book to buy**, take into consideration the cities serviced by each airline.

- **Don't use your senior coupons when** you can beat the price with a separate ticket. Be particularly careful on short trips, and always check fare war prices to see if they beat your per-coupon cost.

- **Coupon books can be purchased** from the airlines or from travel agents.

- **Always carry proof of age** when you travel on senior coupons.

- **Seniors may only need to be 60** for international flights, including Canada, Mexico and some Caribbean destinations.

The chart on pages 47 and 48 detail senior coupon deals. The chart on page 49 shows international senior discounts.

Senior Freedom Passports

Continental Airlines has a fantastic deal for travelers ages 62 and above who plan to do a lot of concentrated traveling or would like to do more if it was affordable. You pay one price for an array of travel benefits, and companion passports (at the same price) are available for people traveling with the primary passport holder–regardless of age.

Freedom Passports come in four- and 12-month versions. You are basically entitled to a one-way trip per week during the term of your passport. Domestic travel can be made from noon Monday to noon Thursday and anytime Saturday. Travel to Europe is permitted all day Monday through Thursday and anytime Saturday. Blackout dates do apply, and a Sunday stay is required between trips. You can visit the same U.S. city up to three times per passport term. There is no limit for your home city.

Add-on coach and First Class roundtrip options are available on Domestic Freedom Passports. For example, add the Caribbean for $250 (First Class, $400); Hawaii for $400 (First Class $550) and Europe for $500 (First Class $1,000).

The Global Passports allow domestic travel plus one roundtrip each to Hawaii, Alaska and Central America and two roundtrips each to Europe, Mexico and the Caribbean.

Choose your passport based on your travel needs:

4-month Domestic Coach Passport.....$999

12-month Domestic Coach Passport...$1,999

12-month Domestic First Class Passport...$3,499

12-month Coach Global Passport...$4,499

12-month First Class Global Passport...$6,999

The bargain value of Freedom Passports depends on the amount of travel you do. For example, if you take six roundtrips on a four-Month Domestic Coach Passport, you pay an average of $166 per trip. If you take 20 domestic roundtrips on a 12-month Domestic First Class Passport, you pay an average of $175 per roundtrip–an unheard of price for First Class travel.

Get a free brochure detailing your passport options, including an application form by calling 800-576-2242.

SENIOR COUPON BOOKS			
AIRLINE	PRICE PER BOOK (COST PER COUPON)	TERMS	DESTINATIONS
AMERICA WEST Senior Saver Pack 800-235-9292	4 coupons: $495 ($123.75) 8 coupons: $920 ($115)	14-day advance; travel from noon Monday to noon Thursday and all day Saturday; some holiday blackouts; stand-by allowed; you do earn miles	All U.S. cities
AMERICAN Senior TrAAvler 800-237-7981	4 coupons: $596 ($149)	14-day advance; travel any day; stand-by allowed; you do earn miles	Continental U.S., Mexico, U.S. Virgin Islands. Hawaii requires 2 coupons each way
CONTINENTAL Freedom Trips 800-248-8996	4 coupons: $579 ($144.75) 8 coupons: $999 ($124.88)	14-day advance; travel any day; stand-by allowed; some holiday blackouts; you do earn miles	All U.S. cities; Alaska, Hawaii, Mexico and the Caribbean require 2 coupons each way
	4 month senior pass: $999 Companion pass: $999	Unlimited travel for a 4-month period within 12 months of purchase date; travel noon Monday through noon Thursday and anytime Saturday; Sunday stay required	48 U.S. states; Montreal and St. Thomas; add-on rates available for Hawaii and Alaska
DELTA Young At Heart 800-221-1212	4 coupons: $596 ($149)	14-day advance; stand-by travel permitted, including on the day of purchase; you do earn miles	All U.S., mainland cities plus Hawaii, Alaska and San Juan; 2 coupons needed for Hawaii, Alaska and St. Thomas
KIWI Senior Discount Pack 800-538-5494	6 coupons: $678 ($112)	Reservations must be made 7 days or less before departure; travel any day; no blackout dates or change fees	All U.S. cities

Member of the board of directors of Amtran, American Trans Air's parent company: ex-vice president Dan Quayle.

SENIOR COUPON BOOKS

AIRLINE	PRICE PER BOOK & PER COUPON	TERMS	DESTINATIONS
NORTHWEST UltraFare Coupons 800-225-2525	4 coupons: $540 ($135)	14-day advance; valid any day; stand-by allowed; you do earn miles	All U.S. cities; Alaska, Hawaii and the Caribbean require 2 coupons each way
SOUTHWEST Senior Fares 800-435-9792	No minimum purchase; $29 to $129	No advance purchase required, but you must reserve in advance; valid any day on flight, but seats are limited; tickets are fully refundable	All cities
TWA Senior Travel Pak 800-221-2000	4 coupons: $498 ($124.50) 8 coupons: $938 ($117.25) 4 companion coupons (any age): $598 ($149.50); 8 companion coupons (any age): $1029 ($128.60)	14-day advance; travel any day except Sunday, noon to 7 p.m. and holiday blackouts; Hawaii and San Juan travel has additional black-outs and restrictions; stand-by allowed; you do earn miles	All U.S. mainland cities plus San Juan; Hawaii requires 2 coupons each way; coupon books include a 20% discount coupon for travel to Europe
UNITED Silver TravelPac 800-633-6563	4 coupons: $541 ($135.25)	Travel any day. Reservations must be made 14 days in advance; stand-by allowed; you do earn miles	All U.S. cities, Canada and San Juan; Hawaii and Alaska require 2 coupons each way (except Seattle/Fairbanks and Seattle/ Anchorage)
USAIR Golden Opportunities 800-428-4322	4 coupon book: $542 ($135.50) Up to two children 2-11 can use the same coupon book when traveling with a senior	14-day advance; travel any day; stand-by allowed; some holiday blackouts; you do earn miles	Continental U.S., San Juan, St. Thomas, Mexico and Canada

The two biggest expenses for U.S.-based airlines: labor and jet fuel.

INTERNATIONAL SENIOR DISCOUNTS

AIRLINE	MINIMUM AGE	SAVINGS
AEROLITORAL 800-237-6639	62	Half-price flights inter-Mexico and to and from Texas and Arizona cities
AIR CANADA 800-776-3000	60 & 62	Seniors 60 and above get 10% off Air Canada; 62 and above get 10% off code share flights; the Freedom Flyer program for passengers 60 and above discounts multi-itinerary tickets.
AIR FRANCE 800-237-2747	62	10% off most fares, including the Concorde
AIR INTER 800-237-2747	60	40%-60% off full fare tickets on inter-France flights
ALITALIA 800-223-5730	62	10%-15% off, depending on destination; some discounts require membership in United's Silver Wings travel club
BRITISH AIRWAYS 800-247-9297	60	10% off 7 and 14-day advance Apex fares for seniors and companions; 21-day advance fares aren't discounted but cancellation and change penalties are waived; Privileged Traveler Tours by British Airways offers discounts on tours.
EL AL 800-950-5000	60 & 55	15% off Apex fares for seniors 60 and above and spouses 55 and above
FINNAIR 800-950-5000	62	50% off New York/Helsinki flights for seniors and companions
IBERIA 800-772-4642	60	10% off published fares for seniors and companions
KLM 800-777-5553	62	10% off published fares for seniors and companions
LUFTHANSA 800-645-3880	60	10% off published fares for seniors and companions
MEXICANA 800-531-7921	62	10% off for seniors and companions, except during summer and holiday blackouts
SABENA 800-950-1000	62	10% off most tickets and discounts on specific destination tickets
SCANDINAVIAN (SAS) 800-221-2350	62	10% off for seniors and companions
SWISSAIR 800-221-4750	62	10% off for seniors and companions on airfares and packages
TAP/AIR PORTUGAL 800-221-7370	62	10% off for seniors and companions

The average cost of a gallon of jet fuel in 1995: 60¢.

CHILDREN AND TRAVEL

Once children reach their second birthday, an adult-fare ticket is required on almost all domestic flights. USAir does discount a few flights for children ages two to 11 flying with an adult and for ages 12-22 with student ID's. Southwest offers "baby" fares and modest discounts for children ages two to 11 accompanied by an adult. Children ages two to 11 almost always receive discounts on international flights.

Children under two (lap children) flying with adults do not require tickets for domestic travel, but they will not have an assigned seat, nor is there an increase in baggage allowance.

International travel for lap children costs ten percent of the adult ticket. A separate seat is not guaranteed.

If you're one of the few travelers willing to pay for a ticket for your child under two, you will increase safety and comfort factors, but you should also have an approved safety seat–to avoid negating the safety benefits of a separate seat.

Proof of age can be requested. If your children look older than they are or if they're near the age limit for a particular form of travel, take along birth certificate copies.

International travel (including travel to Canada) requires the proper documents for all children, including infants. Check on up-to-date requirements with the U.S. Tourism Office or the embassy of the country you plan to visit.

Solo parents and children traveling to Mexico, Brazil, Australia and other countries must have a letter of consent from the absent parent. This is designed to guard against kidnapping. Even a married parent may be asked to provide proof that the absent parent is aware of and approves the trip.

Minor children traveling with anyone other than the custodial parent require written permission for medical treatment. A simple sentence authorizing medical care via permission of the accompanying adult will suffice. Have the statement notarized for extra assurance.

Kids Flying Solo

Children flying alone are subject to each airline's age minimums. Also, consider your child's individual level of maturity.

The majority of airlines demand that the child traveling alone be at least five years old and fly non-stop only.

Children can make supervised connections for an additional fee. The age minimum varies. (See the chart on next page.) An airline attendant will accompany the child to the connecting flight.

Children 12 and older are allowed to travel alone on all flights, including connecting flights.

When children travel alone you must complete a form at the airport, providing the name, address and phone number of the adults taking the child to the first flight, and the adults picking the child up on arrival.

The escort fee for a child traveling alone is usually not paid in advance. If you are unable to pay it at the airport, the airline is

---

Cost of fuel consumed by a Boeing 747 in an average hour of flight: $2,000.

likely to deny your child boarding, even if you were not advised of the fee when you reserved your ticket. Charter and niche airlines each have their own policy on children flying alone. In all cases, you must make arrangements when making your reservation. Be sure to ask for specific "unaccompanied minor" policies and fees.

Make sure children flying alone have safe journeys. An estimated 20,000 unaccompanied minors fly on domestic airlines each day. Their flights are overwhelmingly trouble-free, but you want to do all you can to make sure your child's flight is safe.

- **Make sure the person meeting the flight** has accurate flight information and will call the airline for flight updates.

- **Don't put your children on the last flight of the day**, especially if they are making a connection. That flight could be cancelled, leaving your child in a strange city overnight.

- **Send some money with your child** to cover incidental expenses.

AIRLINE POLICIES ON CHILDREN FLYING ALONE			
	AGE MINIMUM		
AIRLINE	**NONSTOP OR DIRECT**	**CONNECTING FLIGHTS**	**ESCORT FEE EACH WAY/PER CHILD**
ALASKA 800-426-0333	5	5	No fee for non-stops; $30 on connecting flights
AMERICAN 800-433-7300	5	8	No fee for non-stops; $30 on connecting flights; no solo children allowed on the last flight of the day to Chicago
AMERICA WEST 800-833-8602	5	7	No fee for non-stops; $30 on connecting flights
CONTINENTAL 800-248-8996	5	8	No fee for non-stops; $30 on connecting flights
DELTA 800-323-2323	5	8	No fee for non-stops; $20 on connecting flights
NORTHWEST 800-225-2525	5	5	$30 for non-stops and connecting flights
SOUTHWEST 800-435-9792	5	12	Escorts are not available because Southwest technically has no connecting flights
TWA 800-221-2000	5	8	No fee for non-stops; $30 on connecting flights
UNITED 800-241-6522	5	8	$20 for direct, non-stop and connecting flights
USAIR 800-428-4322	5	8	No fee for flights that don't involve changes of plane; $30 on connecting flights

Name of the first woman in space: Valentina Tereshkova of the former USSR; she orbited the earth in 1963.

STUDENT & YOUTH FARES

Student and youth fares come from three sources: consolidators, student membership programs (sometimes co-sponsored by an airline) and directly from the airlines.

The Student Identity Card, available to students ages 12-25, costs $15 per year. Council Travel, the agency segment of the non-profit Council on International Educational Exchange, issues a free catalogue available by calling 800-226-8624. It explains the many discount possibilities accessible simply by owning the card.

USAir and AT&T offer discount coupons to full-time college students who acquire the AT&T Universal card. You get discounts on three roundtrip tickets for use within a six-month period and discounts on other domestic and international flights. Call 800-438-8627 to apply.

Continental and American Express offer the Student Privileges program. Full-time or graduate students who have an American Express card can receive discount certificates for travel on Continental Airlines with varying terms and restrictions. Roundtrips can be as low as $158. To join, call American Express at 800-582-5823. New programs are usually announced every September.

Airline student and children's fares come and go. USAir, for example, has offered one-ways under $30 for flights of less than 750 miles. You have to call each airline and ask for the current offerings. When available, they will carry unusual restrictions and requirements so be sure you're made aware of all of them. Current offerings (all subject to change) include:

- **America West:** ten-percent discount to students 17-25 years of age on flights from the U.S. to Mexico; the discount applies to all published fares. You must show proof of age and a student ID card.

- **Carnival:** 25% discount for children two to 17 years of age per ticketing code KW.

- **Delta:** The Fantastic Flyer Program offers various promotions to new members. Membership is open to children ages two to 12. Past promotions have included certificates for a $50 roundtrip for children flying with a parent and a 20% off discount coupon that can be used for up to four family members traveling on the same itinerary and flights. These specials seem to be offered every four to five months. If you have more than one child, consider staggered memberships to take advantage of as many specials as possible. Call 800-392-5437.

- **Southwest:** Infant fares for children under two range from $29-99, one-way. Even though these children could fly free, the infant fares guarantee a seat and provide improved safety.

- **TWA:** The Student Getaway program offers ten percent off most published domestic and international airfares. The program is open to full time students ages 16-26. A one-year discount card is $15; two years, $25. There are no blackout dates. Call 800-221-2000.

- **TWA:** The Student Travel Pak, available to students ages 14-24 provides five coupons. The first four permit one-way travel among the 48 contiguous states and San Juan. The fifth is valid for a 20% discount on travel to Europe. The current cost is $548, an average $137 purchase per one-way trip. A 14-day advance purchase is required, but students are allowed to attempt standby travel. Call 800-221-2000.

BEREAVEMENT & COMPASSION FARES

Bereavement fares can provide 35%-50% off last-minute flights in the case of the death of an immediate family member. You must provide verifiable documentation, including the name of the deceased, their relationship to you and the name and phone number of the funeral director.

Compassion fares are offered by some airlines. They provide discounts for situations such as accidents or life-threatening illness. They are generally not granted for the passenger's own illness. Documentation required includes the name of the ill or injured person, their relationship to you and the name and phone number of the attending physician or hospital.

Compassion and bereavement fares are one of the rare ticketing situations in which travelers do best by calling the airlines direct. This is particularly true with airlines that have policies that are, to some degree, up to their customer service department's discretion. Call your travel agent to see if there are better options such as niche carriers and creative ticketing. If major airline bereavement and compassion rates seem to be your best bet, call the airlines.

> *As options to bereavement and compassion fares, seniors can still utilize senior coupon books which permit standby travel. Youths ages 16-24 can use TWA Youth Packs. Alternate cities may also save you a bundle over bereavement and compassion fares.*

This chart compares bereavement and compassionate fares against no advance, roundtrip fares between Washington, D.C. and San Francisco. Remember that you can often beat bereavement and compassion rates by using creative ticketing options and/or niche carriers.

BEREAVEMENT AND COMPASSION FARES

AIRLINE	LOWEST NO ADVANCE ROUNDTRIP	ROUNDTRIP BEREAVEMENT FARE	ROUNDTRIP COMPASSION FARE
AMERICA WEST	$1388	$639	None
AMERICAN	$1378	$808	$808
CONTINENTAL	$1378	$679	$679
DELTA	$1378	$689	None
NORTHWEST	$1378	$722	$722
TWA	$1378	$686	$805
UNITED	$1394	$814	$814
USAIR	$1378	$689	$689

MILITARY FARES

The prime advantages of military fares are flexibility and possible savings on last-minute flights or one-way travel. They're available to active duty military and, in some cases, to military dependents. Tickets generally cost $25-50 less than seven-day advance fares, but they cost much more than 21-day advance fares. Remember to also check niche carriers, split-city options and special promotional coupon offers for last-minute flight savings.

Military fare tickets cannot be mailed, require military ID at the time of ticketing and at check-in and are only available within the U.S.

FAMILY FARES

When the whole family is flying together, particularly on international flights, including Mexico, Canada and the Caribbean, you may have some money-saving clout. Companion tickets and family fares are two options. The best family discounts are usually graduated, with each family member getting a larger amount off the ticket price. Families flying to Tel Aviv may be able to take advantage of specials consistently offered. The first child pays full fare; the second gets 25% off. The third gets 50% off. Additional children get 75% off. Never be afraid to ask if a family discount is available; they're surely worth it when you find them.

When traveling outside the U.S. with children ages two to 11, be sure to check children's fares. They're often discounted 25%-50% as compared to adult fares, including fare-war tickets. America West, for example, offered a special introductory offer from Phoenix to Puerta Vallarta and Los Cabos for $120 roundtrip for adults and $80 roundtrip for kids ages two to 11. What a great family deal!

❝Children flying on Delta during the summer can take advantage of "Dusty's Dens," toy-stocked playrooms at eight major airports. Don't forget Delta's Fantastic Flyer program and its discounts for children. Add in Delta's $1 charge for headphones for children in-flight (versus $3 or $4 for adults), and you have three 'kid-friendly' Delta features. ❞

FREE AND LOW-COST UPGRADES

There's nothing democratic about the free upgrade process. Checking in early won't earn you a single advantage. Gate agents determine who will be upgraded based on space available, your frequent flyer status and the fare you paid.

❝A compassionate gate agent will sometimes upgrade a passenger traveling on an emergency basis or under unusual conditions. One of BEST FARES Discount Travel Magazine's readers was upgraded on her return flight as a 'thank you' for assistance she provided with a critically ill passenger on her outbound flight. On a recent Delta flight, a blind passenger was upgraded for free. This is what helps make a good airline. ❞

Can you charm your way into Business or First Class? It doesn't happen regularly, but passengers with winning personalities have been upgraded for handing a bunch of flowers to the gate agent, claiming to be on a honeymoon or mentioning a real or imagined injury that would make sitting in coach an uncomfortable prospect.

Use frequent flyer miles to upgrade according to the policies of your membership plan. Most carriers charge 10,000 miles minimum, so reserve them for long haul and international flights.

Elite status frequent flyers are often upgraded on a space-available basis. Some programs allow you to request the upgrade in advance. Others will only take requests at the gate.

> *"Seniors ages 62 and over, be sure to check the senior section for information on Continental's Freedom Passport–an array of bargain benefits including great First Class deals."*

You can get a low-cost upgrade if you are a frequent flyer using a full coach fare. The upgrade will be much less than the cost of purchasing a First Class ticket. Upgrade costs are usually based on flight lengths. Airlines offering this "near First Class" pricing include Alaska, America West, Canadian, Continental, KLM, Northwest, TWA, USAir and Virgin Atlantic.

Other ways to upgrade for less:

- **Continental** has, unfortunately, discontinued their $20 standby upgrade program, but they will upgrade frequent flyers for a fee based on the distance traveled: $50 each way for flights under 500 miles, $100 for flights from 500-1200 miles and $150 for flights from 1201-2300 miles.

- **The best upgrade deal** Continental now offers is their "Executive Pack," available to new One Pass members. For $49.95 you get four free, one-segment, one-class standby upgrades; a certificate good for a $99 companion ticket; two free passes to the Continental Presidents Club; 5,000 immediate bonus miles; 2,500 bonus miles after your first flight and free GTE airphone air time. Call 713-952-1630 to enroll. Allow about four weeks for delivery.

- **Reno Air** offers standby upgrades at $20-40, depending on the distance traveled.

- **American often runs promotions** with their frequent flyer partners. In the recent past, American AAdvantage members received a free one-class upgrade for a qualifying stay at Wyndham, Sheraton, Loews or Fairmont hotels.

- **TWA's** Trans World One Class offers First Class for Business Class fares on transcontinental and transatlantic flights.

- **USAir** offers Business Select premium service into select cities. Frequent travelers fly First Class at unrestricted coach fare prices.

U.S. REGIONAL PASSES

U.S. airlines offer a unique array of passes, all offering price advantages over one-at-a-time ticketing. One disadvantage: most coupon books are non-refundable. Losing one is like losing cash.

Aloha Airlines AlohaPass, 800-367-5250, offers the Island Hopper with five days of unlimited travel during off-peak hours for $199.

The America West Value Pack, 800-

235-9292, provides four one-way coupons for $299. Travel is valid between Phoenix and Albuquerque, Burbank, El Paso, Long Beach, Las Vegas, Los Angeles, Ontario, San Diego or Tucson; and between Las Vegas and Oakland, Phoenix, San Diego or Reno. Standby travel is allowed. Upgrade to First Class for $25-50 per flight. The non-transferable coupons are valid for one year, and some blackout dates apply. You also get a 1,500-mile FlightFund bonus coupon. They frequently throw in a hotel bonus such as a free weekend night stay in Albuquerque, El Paso, Long Beach, Los Angeles, Ontario or San Diego.

Carnival Airlines First Fare Pass, 800-437-2110, is for the cost-conscious First Class passenger. It provides eight flights between Los Angeles and Fort Lauderdale or Miami. The cost is $2,999. It is non-refundable, but there are no other restrictions. Changes are without charge, and no blackout dates apply. Carnival's Coach Pass includes ten one-way coupons for travel between New York City, Fort Lauderdale and Miami for $1,139.

Delta Connection-Comair Weekend Traveler, 800-532-4777, provides four coupons for $299, valid for travel weekends, Mondays until noon and during some holiday periods. Their base cities are Orlando and Cincinnati. Flights under 500 miles require one coupon. Flights over 500 miles, and all flights connecting through Cincinnati, require two coupons. Travel is valid to U.S. destinations and the Bahamas. Comair will send you a free booklet detailing the Weekend Traveler deal.

Hawaiian Airlines AirPass, 800-367-5320, has four passes good for unlimited flights during the period of validity. A five-day pass is $179, a seven-day pass (with the eighth day free) is $199, a ten-day pass is $239 and a 14-day pass (with the 15th day free) is $279. Seniors and children receive a $10 discount. Purchase requires proof of inbound travel from the U.S. and a confirmed return reservation. The Commuter Airpass allows unlimited travel for one month for $799. Commuter passes are only good from the first through the 31st of each month. They can't, for example, run from the 15th to the 15th. You also get two transferrable First Class upgrades for travel to the West Coast, access to airport lounges and 10,000 bonus miles.

Kiwi's Commuter Coupon Books, 800-538-5494, come in three varieties, each providing ten segments of travel on designated routes. The first, valid between Atlanta and Tampa, Orlando and West Palm Beach, costs $771. The second, valid between Newark and Chicago or Atlanta, or between Chicago and Atlanta or Newark, costs $1,101. The third, valid for travel between Newark or Chicago to Orlando, Tampa, and/or West Palm Beach, costs $1,281. Coupons are valid for one year with a three-month extension available for $25. Standby travel is allowed. The coupons are non-refundable.

TICKET REBATES

Some agencies offer rebates on airline tickets, usually five percent or less. There will be a minimum ticket amount. The full amount of the ticket is charged to your credit card. The rebate check is either issued with your ticket or you're asked to mail your boarding pass in after you've flown. The check is then mailed. Agencies that use the second method know a high percentage of people will not take the time to mail in their rebate request.

A five percent rebate on a standard airline ticket is not a good deal. Use rebaters primarily for reservations you've made with the airlines, either for airfare only or for vacation packages. By giving the agency the ticket designator or reservation number, your reservation can be pulled up and ticketed, and you can get the rebate.

The biggest error travelers make when first attempting to receive a rebate is giving their credit card number to the airline, then calling an agency and requesting the rebate. You only get it when you allow the agency to do the ticketing.

COUPON BROKERS

There are three main ways in which discount coupons and flight certificates change hands.

Frequent flyers have been selling their award tickets ever since the program began. Some very frequent flyers could not possibly use all their miles and selling their benefits seems logical. The airlines prohibit it, and all litigation has backed them up. Airlines want to avoid offending their best customers, but they want to protect their bottom line even more. They've become more aggressive every year in trying to stop the selling of flight coupons.

Discount coupons from special promotions can legally be given away, but they can't be sold. If your neighbor has a $100-off coupon that she doesn't plan to use, she can give it to you but, according to airline rules, no money can change hands.

Coupon brokers make a business out of wheeling and dealing in coupons. If you're going to use them, you'd better use caution. You're violating the airlines' rules to attempt to gain a financial advantage you can as easily acquire through legitimate means. Airlines have bounties on broker tickets. They pay their gate agents to discover them. If you're challenged and lose, your ticket is confiscated and you end up paying full fare. If you're flying domestically and the ticket is in someone

else's name, 90% of the time you'll be discovered through routine checking of photo ID's. Internationally, even with the ticket in your own name, you run a high risk of discovery. Be legitimate. You'll save as much or more, and you won't have to deal with all the fear and stress.

> **❝**I don't just walk away from these deals–I run from them. You may think courier travel and coupon brokers offer easy savings, but why go through so much hassle when consolidators, niche carriers and special promotions offer stress-free savings?**❞**

CLASSIFIED ADS

Even though there are some ads that offer tickets the holders just can't use, there are many more ads that attempt to sell stolen tickets and illegal tickets. Some of these scammers are in and out of a market in one or two weeks. They get all the money they can, then they disappear. The buyers don't discover that they're trying to fly on illegal tickets until they get to the airport.

It's definitely a "Buyer Beware" situation. We think it's a mistake to buy tickets from individuals through classified ads. If you must do it, at least limit your risk and pay by credit card. And never buy a ticket with someone else's name on it. In these days of increased security and the need for a photo ID, you probably will end up the loser.

Many legitimate agencies, particularly those dealing in consolidator tickets, run classified ads or small display ads in travel and business newspaper sections.

COURIER TRAVEL

Free courier travel is almost a thing of the past, and discounted courier travel is increasingly harder to find. There were only about 20,000 passengers flying as couriers in 1995, not even close to one percent of the 548 million overall passengers who traveled in the U.S. in 1995.

Courier travel used to be a great way to fly. Before the days of Airborne Express and other overnight delivery services, bearer bonds, documents and other timely materials had to be carried over the ocean by couriers. Companies bought wholesale tickets that they sold at discounts to those who agreed to serve in that capacity. Most of the companies that still use couriers now send their own employees.

There are great disadvantages to courier travel, over and above the difficulty in getting a courier flight. Many companies require that you pay a membership fee and a deposit (usually non-refundable if you decide not to take the flights that are offered). It's next to impossible to travel with a companion unless they pay for a high-dollar, last minute ticket. Most, if not all, of your luggage allowance may be consumed by the material you're being asked to transport. Worst of all, you're stuck on someone else's schedule. When you arrive at your destination, your return ticket is confiscated by a representative of the company. You are not allowed to fly back on any date other than that which is ticketed. If you have a family emergency and want to go home early, tough luck. If you're having a great time and want to stay longer, tough luck.

Even with the odds against it, courier travel continues to stimulate the imagination of some travelers. If you're one, here are some additional things to know:

- **You're likely to be charged** as much as one-half to one-third the unrestricted coach fare. Some last minute courier flights may go for as little as $100, but they are the exceptions. The closer it is to the departure date, the less you will have to pay.

- **You have to be in a major gateway city** (or be able to get to one cheaply). Most North American courier flights depart from Chicago, Dallas, Detroit, Los Angeles, Miami, Montreal, New York, Newark, San Francisco, Toronto and Vancouver.

- **The most frequent destinations for** courier flights departing from North America are major cities in Europe, Asia, South America, Australia, New Zealand, Mexico, Jamaica, Puerto Rico and Guatemala City.

Courier opportunities are advertised in the telephone yellow pages under Air Courier Services, in travel sections and in classified newspaper advertising.

Get a free audio cassette on international courier flights from The International Association of Air Travel Couriers (IAATC), 407-582-8320, but be aware, they have a vested interest in putting the best possible light on courier travel. Write to IAATC Air Courier Cassette, 8 South J Street, P.O. Box 1349, Lake Worth, FL 33460.

Good books for the courier curious:

The Insiders Guide To Air Courier Bargains by Kelly Monaghan. For information, send $17.45 to Upper Access Publishing, Box 457, Hinesburg, VT 05461 or call 800-356-9315.

The Courier Air Travel Handbook by Mark Field. Send $10.70 to Thunderbird Press, 6893 Sullivan Road, Grawn, MI 49367. Call 800-345-0096.

International charter flights usually fly certain days of the week. A good way to check their reliability is to ask how many flights they flew the previous year and how many were cancelled. The figure should be one to two percent, maximum. If the company doesn't have at least a year's worth of track record, don't use them.

> *Check our Package Tour Section for creative ways to save on international travel by using charter flights.*

INTERNATIONAL TRAVEL PASSES

Most international carriers offer passes that allow multiple stops, unlimited flights or discounted flights within a certain country. They can save you 25%-70% as compared to individual tickets. Flights within Europe, for example, can cost almost double a ticket for the equivalent distance traveled in the U.S. They do carry various restrictions, so have your travel agent read and explain them to you before you decide to buy. The most common restrictions:

- **Passes usually must be purchased in the U.S.** in conjunction with an international flight.

- **Passes usually allow just one stopover per city** unless you use that city for a connecting flight.

- **You cannot transfer to another carrier** if your scheduled flight is cancelled or delayed.

- **Some passes are seasonal:** either costing more or unavailable during peak travel times.

Examples of international passes:

Argentina

Aerolinas Argentinas, 800-333-0276, offers a four-segment pass for $450, valid for 30 days. Additional segments (to a maximum of eight) are $120 each. You cannot backtrack. The pass must be purchased directly from the airline.

Australia & New Zealand

Both these countries can be covered with Down Under Discount Deals available from nine airlines including Ansett, 800-366-1300, and Qantas, 800-227-4500. Pass prices are based on units traveled, with units determined by the distance per flight. Average savings are 50%-60% off single flight pricing. Air New Zealand, 800-262-1234, offers the Downunder Air Pass good for 60 days with flights ranging from $89-219, depending on distance.

Bolivia

Lloyd Aero Boliviano, 800-327-7407, offers the Visit Bolivia Pass for $150 if you fly to Bolivia on LAB, $175 if you take another carrier. It allows flights to six Bolivian cities within a 28-day period.

Brazil

Varig, 800-468-2744, offers a $490 (low season), $540 (high season) pass to any five cities in Brazil during a 21-day period. Additional segments (to a maximum of nine) are $100 each. No backtracking is allowed. The pass is valid for one year.

Caribbean

Liat, 809-774-2313, offers a $199 Caribbean Explorers Fare good for three flights within a 21-day period to your choice of three islands. The Super Caribbean Explorer Pass is good for visits to any island they fly to within a 30-day period for $367. The first pass does not allow changes once reservations are made. The second pass allows changes for a $35 fee.

Bahamasair, 800-222-4262, offers the AirPass, good for three flights within 21 days. There is a minimum three-day stay on each destination. The price is $250, departing from Nassau; $320, departing from Miami. Destinations include the Abacos, Andros, the Acklins, Cat Island, Eleuthera, the Exumas, Long Island, Grand Bahama, Mayaguana, Inagua, Crooked Island and San Salvador.

Chile

LAN Chile, 800-735-5526, offers the Visit Chile Fare, permitting 21 days of travel to nine cities for $550.

Columbia

Avianca, 800-284-2622, offers the Discover Columbia Pass, ten flights within 30 days for $224. The Discover Columbia Five Pass allows five stopovers in 14 days for $112.

Europe

Air France, with Air Inter, Sabena and Czechoslovak Airlines, offers Euroflyer passes. Travel must originate in Paris, Brussels or Prague and is valid to over 100 cities in Europe. The minimum cost is $360 for three coupons ($120 each); nine coupons are allowed. The minimum stay is seven days–maximum stay, two months–and is available to U.S. passengers with roundtrip international tickets on any carrier, 800-237-2747.

British Airways offers various pass plans for Western and Eastern Europe, most in conjunction with Deutsche BA and TAT European Airlines. Purchase a minimum of three sectors and a maximum of 12. There is a minimum stay of seven days between first and last sector and a maximum stay of three months.

Zone 1: Per segment, $82 on UK domestic and French domestic routes and between the UK and Belgium, Ireland, Luxembourg, Netherlands and Paris or between Gibraltar and Tangier.

Zone 2: Per segment, $107 for BA German domestic routes; between UK points and Denmark, France, Germany, Portugal, Spain and Switzerland, excluding Paris; between Germany and Italy; between Gibraltar and Morocco, excluding Tangier and between Greece and Italy.

Zone 3: Per segment, $133 between UK points and Austria, Bulgaria, the Czech Republic, Finland, Gibraltar, Greece, Hungary, Italy, Norway, Poland, Romania and Sweden; between France and Scandinavia; between France and Greece; between Germany and Norway, between Spain and Sweden; between London Heathrow and Tangier and between Germany, the Czech Republic and Switzerland DI sectors.

Zone 4: Per segment, $166 between UK points and Azerbaijan, Cyprus, Israel, Madeira, Russia, Tunisia, and Turkey; between Denmark and Spain; between Germany and Latvia, Lithuania DI sector and Russia; between Greece and Norway; between Italy and Sweden and between the UK and Morocco, excluding Tangier, 800-247-9297.

KLM, 800-374-7747, with Air UK,

Investment amount required by Kiwi from each new pilot: $50,000; from other employees: $5,000.

Transavia, Tyrolean Airways, Maersk Air and Eurowings, offers passes for passengers who fly KLM or Northwest Airlines from the U.S. to Amsterdam, Frankfurt, London or Paris. They are valid for travel among European cities, select North African cities and the Canary Islands. Travel between Amsterdam and St. Petersburg or Moscow is excluded. There is no minimum stay, and the maximum stay is the same as the transatlantic ticket. A minimum purchase of $390 is required for three coupons in peak season (June 1, 1996 through August 31, 1996 and December 15-23, 1996). Additional coupons, four and five, are $110 each; coupons six and above are $100 each. Off-peak, a $300-330 total is required for three coupons; additional coupons four and five are $80-90 each; coupons six and above are $70-80 each. A maximum of 12 coupons may be purchased. Coupons are non-refundable once purchased. Additional coupons may be purchased in Europe.

Lufthansa, 800-645-3880, with Finnair, United and Lauda Air is valid within Europe. Minimum $420 for three coupons during peak season; additional coupons are $125 each. A maximum of nine coupons may be purchased; $175 per coupon for flights on Finnair between Helsinki and Athens, Barcelona, Lisbon, Istanbul, Madrid, Milan, Nice and Rome. Per coupon, $200 on Lufthansa for travel to or from Turkey and the cities of the former Soviet Republic. No minimum stay is required. Maximum stay is the same as a transatlantic ticket.

Swissair, 800-221-4750, with Cross Air, Tyrolean Airways and Austrian Airlines; valid for travel from Switzerland or Austria to anywhere in Europe, except Lugano and Sion. Minimum cost: $390 for three coupons; additional coupons are $130 and a maximum of eight coupons

may be purchased; no minimum stay requirement; two months maximum. Only one coupon will be required on routes within domestic Switzerland. They do not offer direct service.

> **"**Several U.S. based carriers also offer European travel passes, great deals for people who plan to see several countries. TWA's InterEurope from Paris, for example, offers your choice of three to nine coupons at $99 each. Delta's Discover Europe offers four coupons at $125 each or four to nine coupons at $109 each.**"**

France

Air France, 800-237-2747, offers the La France Pass, good for seven days of unlimited travel within France–a 30-day period for $339. Air Inter, a subsidiary of Air France, offers a four-segment pass for $275, five-segments for $318 and six for $349. The passes are good for one year.

Fiji Islands

Fiji Air, 800-677-4277, offers the Discover Fiji Pass allowing four segments of travel to your choice of 15 destinations within 30 days for $199, additional segments are $50. Pass must be purchased in Fiji.

Finland

Finnair, 800-950-5000, offers the Holiday Ticket with ten segments valid for 30 days to your choice of 22 destinations in Finland. The cost is $400.

India

Indian Air Lines, 212-751-6200, offers the Discover India Pass–21 days of unlimited travel among 64 cities for $500. India Wonderfare offers seven days of unlimited travel within four regions for $200.

Indonesia

Garuda Indonesian, 800-342-7832, offers the Visit Indonesia Air Pass, ranging from $350-600, depending on the length of the pass and the amount of flights permitted. Passes last 20, 30 or 60 days. A three-city pass, for example, is $300 if you arrive in Indonesia via Indonesian Airlines and $350 if you use another carrier. A five-city pass is $500 and $550 if you fly in on another carrier.

Italy

Alitalia, 800-223-5730, offers the Visit Italy Pass good for three flights to your choice of 28 Italian cities for $299. Each additional flight is $100.

Malaysia

Malaysia Airlines, 800-552-9264, offers the Discover Malaysia pass allowing five flights within 21 days for $199.

New Guinea

Air Niugini, 714-752-5440, offers a four-flight pass for $299, with additional flights $50 each. The pass must be purchased in the U.S. in conjunction with a prepaid land package, and you must use Air Niugini to fly to and from New Guinea.

New Zealand

Air New Zealand, 800-262-1234, offers a three-segment pass for $313 and a four-segment pass for $417. Passes are valid for the duration of your international ticket.

Peru

Aeroperu, 800-777-7717, offers two Peruvian city coupons for $130, three cities for $189, four cities for $239 and five cities for $289. You can't repeat cities, excepting Lima. Passes must be purchased in the U.S.

Scandinavia

SAS, 800-221-2350, offers a 90-day pass of three-, four- and six-coupon passes ranging from $230-490. Passes are completely changeable and refundable. You can also opt for Visit Scandinavia tickets (no minimum purchase requirement) at $80 each for the first two flights and descending prices for subsequent flights. They must be purchased in the U.S., and your transAtlantic flight must be on SAS.

Solomon Islands

Solomon Airlines, 800-677-4277, offers the Discover Solomon Pass providing four flights within 30 days for $236. Additional flights to any of the 24 islands they serve are $50.

South Africa

South African Airways, 800-722-9675, offers African Explorer passes that allow four to eight flights within a 30-day period. The cost depends on the distance flown and ranges from $69-300. Costs reflect a 25%-60% discount over regular fares.

South America

Aeroperu, 800-777-7717, offers a six-segment South American pass for $1,299 (low season) and $1,499 (high season). The pass is valid for 60 days and may be used in a maximum of three countries.

South Pacific

Air Pacific, 800-677-4277, offers the Pacific Air Pass valid for 60 days. The cost depends on the sectors chosen, ranging from $150-300.

Polynesian Airlines, 800-677-4277, offers the Polypass. Costing $999, the Polypass is good for 30 days travel to America Samoa, Western Samoa, Pago Pago, Fiji, the Cook Islands and one city each in New Zealand and Australia. Add a stop in Tahiti and extend the pass seven days for $100 more.

Thailand

Thai Air, 800-426-5204, offers the National Heritage Pass good for four flights within 60 days at a cost of $259. Additional flights are $70 each.

Venezuela

Avensa Airlines, 800-428-3672, offers the Avensa Airpass good for 45 days of unlimited travel among 27 cities in Venezuela at a cost of $70 per segment. You must purchase a minimum of four segments.

AROUND-THE-WORLD FARES

Around-the-world fares save money on international trips with extensive itineraries. You book your ticket on the host airline and are also permitted to fly its affiliates during a specific time frame, usually six to 12 months. They offer an incredible value, especially for Business and First Class travel, as your entire trip can cost about the same as one roundtrip.

Around-the-world fares start at about $2,500 for coach, $3,600 for Business Class and $5,000 for First Class. Here is a sample itinerary: Chicago to Toronto and on to New York, London, Amsterdam, Frankfurt, Copenhagen, Stockholm, Ath-ens, Delhi, Bangkok, Hong Kong, Manila, Taipei, Seoul, Osaka, Tokyo, Guam, Honolulu, Seattle and back to Chicago.

Domestic airlines that offer around-the-world fares and their partner airlines include:

- **Air Canada** with Air Jamaica, Air Liberte, Australian Airways, Czechoslovakian Airlines, LOT Polish Airlines, Royal Jordanian, Sabena, Swissair and VIASA

- **American** with Alaskan, Lufthansa, Malev Hungarian and Qantas

- **Canadian** with Cathay Pacific, KLM, Philippine Airlines, Singapore Airlines, Swissair and Thai Airways

- **Continental** with Air India, Alitalia, Cathay Pacific, JAL, KLM, Malaysia Airlines, Singapore Airlines and Thai Airways

- **Delta** with JAL, Lufthansa, Qantas and Singapore

- **Northwest** with Cathay Pacific, Air India, Gulf Air, KLM, Malaysia, Pakistan International, Qantas, Sabena, South African Airlines and Thai Airways

- **TWA** with Cathay Pacific, China Airways, JAL, Korean Air, Malaysian, Qantas and Singapore

- **United** with Air France, Air New Zealand, British Airways, KLM, Lufthansa, SAS, Swissair, Thai Airways and Varig Brazilian Airlines

- **USAir** with British Air

If around-the-world fares interest you, take the time to gather route maps from the major airlines and plot a tentative itinerary. Most travel agents really can't provide the intensive time needed to plan an around-the-world-trip. Airlines offer special agents skilled in the complexities of around-the-world routing. World Travel offers a five percent instant cash rebate if you book your itinerary and then allow them to process your tickets. If your ticket is $5,000, for example, you get a $250 rebate–not a bad return for one phone call. Call 800-576-2242 for details.

OTHER WAYS TO SAVE INTERNATIONALLY

Some of the greatest current airfare bargains focus on international travel. With these bargains come some complex changes–to the consumer's advantage.

A discount-conscious travel agent can help you through the terms and conditions to help you save. Factors that will affect your international fare include:

- **The days of the week on which you travel.** You usually have to meet the day of the week requirement on departure and return to get the applicable fare.

- **The season of travel.** International airline seasons are not the same as the four seasons of the year. Sometimes changing your departure by as little as one day will substantially lower your price. Here are some examples of usual international off-seasons:

  Europe: November through March

  Asia: January and February

  Australia/New Zealand:
  April through August

  The Caribbean:
  May through December 15

South America: April through November

- **Length of stay.** A stay of 30 days or less will generally cost less than longer stays. Changing a return date may also change your fare and subject you to payment of the fare difference plus a change fee.

- **The ages of the travelers.** Children under two, generally, will pay ten percent of the ticket price. Children ages two to 11 generally pay 50%-75% of the adult fare. You may also find family fares that offer graduated discounts for multiple children. Inter-Europe flights may offer discount standby tickets for people ages 12-24. These tickets are usually confirmed 72 hours before flight time.

- **Restrictions.** Plan to spend a little extra time on the phone when booking an international ticket. Lower priced tickets generally offer less flexibility and require higher fees for any changes. Some APEX fares are even issued on a non-refundable basis. Before you purchase an international ticket ask the agent to go through the major rules with you. After you purchase it, ask to have the rules printed out and enclosed with your ticket.

China's 1995 revenue from tourism: $8 billion; number of visitors: 45 million.

You can sometimes bend the rules when you want to return earlier than your ticketed date. Let's say the change fee is $100. If you show up at the airport and request a seat on an earlier flight with plenty of available space, there is a possibility you will get on the plane without having to pay the fee. This is at the gate agent's discretion, so having a good reason for your early return is essential.

Free stopovers, also known as maximum permitted mileage, can sometimes be added to an international ticket at no extra cost. Sometimes you can even fly on another airline. For example, a New York to Norway ticket can be issued with a stopover in London at no additional cost. In some cases, you can make multiple stops. You also accrue more frequent flyer miles. There are rules and limits to maximum permitted miles, so it's best to book them through a travel agent who is well-versed in international routes.

Don't forget package prices offered by all the major airlines, many international carriers and private tour companies.

Flights between European cities can be outrageous. They can also be bargains that get you between two points for less than the cost of a train ticket.

- **Some European cities,** including Paris, London and Amsterdam are full of agencies that sell discount tickets. A good way to check prices before you travel is to head for your local library and check the classified ad sections of international papers. If you see fares that appeal to you, jot down the phone numbers and purchase your tickets in advance by credit card.

- **Europe is now evolving** into a deregulation era similar to what the U.S. did 18 years ago. New upstart airlines and fare wars within Europe are expected.

PASSPORT & VISA SERVICES

Last-minute Visas and Passports are available from special services that expedite issuance. These services are not inexpensive and can cost as much as several hundred dollars for one-day passport service. Visa services are useful for their proximity to embassies and their daily contact with them. Passport expeditors should be reserved for emergency situations only.

Some embassies do not charge for issuing visas, but policies vary by country. Some Middle Eastern countries or former Soviet satellites may charge hundreds of dollars for the privilege of visiting. The current range runs from 42¢ to over $400.

The chart on the following page lists services that secure visas and expedite passports. You can also effectively expedite your passport using local companies who deal with the nearest regional passport office.

Number of passport applications backlogged during the 1995 U.S. government shutdown: over 200,000.

VISA / PASSPORT SERVICES

MEMBERS	VISAS AVERAGE FEE	PASSPORTS (FEE ONLY)	
		48 HOURS OR LESS	3 DAYS OR MORE
ALL POINTS VISA Bethesda, MD 301-652-9055	$35.00	$95.00	$50.00
ATLAS VISA Arlington, VA 703-418-0800	$28.00		$50.00
CAPITOL VISA Silver Spring, MD 301-942-8576	$35.00	$10.00 to $100.00 Additional Charge for Rush Service	$45.00
CIBT Washington, DC 202-244-9500	$39.00	$78.00	$48.00
DMS VISA INTERNATIONAL Washington, DC 202-745-3815	$40.00	$75.00-same day $65.00-48 hours	$55.00
EXPRESS VISA Washington, DC 202-337-2442	$35.00	$125.00-same day $75.00-48 hours	$45.00
TRAVEL DOCUMENT SERVICE Washington, DC 202-638-3800	$40.00	$60.00	$40.00
TRAVISA Washington, DC 202-463-6166	$38.00	$129.00	$69.00
VISA ADVISORS Washington, DC 202-797-7976	$65.00	$125.00	$50.00
VISA SERVICES Washington, DC 202-287-0300	$45.00	$130.00	$70.00

Only U.S. airline that placed in the passengers' top 20 in a recent survey: Midwest Express.

SPECIAL NOTES FOR BUSINESS TRAVELERS

Your flexibility determines the range of savings possibilities open to you. Non-stop flying is always convenient. Flying home right after finishing the Friday business day is desirable. If cost, however, is a major factor, most of us will change travel dates, times and flights to save money. The changes can be easy to accommodate, and your savings may be significant.

- **Would you switch airlines if it cut your price in half?**

- **Would you change planes if it saved you $400?**

- **Would you put off your Friday return flight until late evening if it saved you $250 and increased your chances of a free upgrade?**

Many surveys indicate travelers care more about frequent flyer programs than value.

- **Placing price anywhere but number one on the priority scale** is a triumph of Madison Avenue over greater reality. You can have it all if you know how to play the game–from discounts that are just as available for Business Class as for coach (and they can be even more dramatic) to earning "free flights" that give you more flexibility than any frequent flyer award. If you must have miles, you can get them without sacrificing price.

- **You can often get miles while you're getting the best price** and when you can't, you're saving more than enough money to make up for the fraction of a "free" ticket that's dangling at the end of the frequent flyer carrot. When you limit yourself to one airline just to rack up miles, you've made it easy for your

---

Of the past 17, number of years in which the major U.S. airlines admit to having earned a profit: eight.

travel agent to earn commissions and easy for the airlines to charge their asking rates. The travel agent simply has to check one airline, then issue the ticket with no incentive to even look for a better price. The airline happily takes your money.

> **❝**It takes, on average, the purchase of 12 tickets to earn enough miles for a free ticket. If you pay $200 more per ticket, your 'free' ticket really costs you $2,400.**❞**

* **Use a travel expert** or become one. The time you spend educating yourself to options and possibilities will pay off handsomely in annual savings.

* **Even small companies** benefit from assigning one person to oversee travel reservations.

* **If your client is paying for your travel**, retain control over choices whenever you can. Often you can take the money they've budgeted for your travel, save money and acquire upgrades by doing the booking yourself.

ON-TIME ARRIVALS

Travel agents and airline reservation staff will find a number from one to ten next to each flight on their computer screen, designating each flight's on-time performance. A number one indicates the flight was on time ten percent of the time, and so on, to ten, for 100%. You obviously want the flight with the highest rating.

Don't get taken in by any airline's advertising claims regarding overall on-time statistics. There are two reasons why the information is misleading:

* **The statistics average the records for all flights.** Some flights—perhaps the one you're considering—may be notoriously late.

* **Airlines increase scheduled flight times** trying to obscure reality. In some cases, the same routing, on the same aircraft, flying at the same time, shows as much as 30 more minutes of flight time now compared to 1985.

Choose flights that take off and land outside of peak travel times. For most airports the busiest times are 9-11 a.m. and 4-8 p.m. on weekdays. Airports with a preponderance of leisure travel (such as Las Vegas and Fort Lauderdale) will have different peak periods.

> **❝**On-time statistics are fine to determine whether the flight you're considering is likely to arrive on time, but you also should question why a particular flight has a poor record. If it is due to frequent mechanical breakdowns, I want to know about it. I also want to know if an airline historically has a bad record on flights connecting through certain hubs. Minneapolis/St. Paul, for example, would seem to be your last choice for a winter connection, but their winter performance has been better than that of Atlanta or Dallas/Fort Worth. Another point to consider is even if your entire trip is in good weather territory, your flight might originate in a bad weather location. Always ask your travel agent to check out your flight's city of origin.**❞**

The **Department of Transportation records a monthly record** of specific flights with an 80% or worse on-time performance. Here's a look at the flights that earned that dubious distinction in December 1995:

This chart shows the 50 worst flights for on-time performance, their routing, their scheduled departure times, the percentage of times the flight was late and the average delay in arrival time.

> 66*Don't judge Delta too harshly. Of all the airlines I've flown, Delta is the most consistent in holding flights for the arrival of connecting passengers. They do it for the sake of customer satisfaction, even though it means their on-time statistics won't look as good.*99

50 WORST FLIGHTS FOR ON-TIME PERFORMANCE

CARRIER /FLIGHT #	ROUTING DEPARTURE	SCHEDULED	PERCENTAGE OF FLIGHTS MINUTES LATE	AVERAGE ARRIVING LATE
TWA #350	Seattle to St. Louis	12:02 p.m.	100.00	69
Delta #197	Atlanta to Seattle	7:00 p.m.	98.77	55
Delta #284	Salt Lake City to Atlanta	2:55 p.m.	99.77	46
Delta #961	Atlanta to Miami	5:43 p.m.	98.77	44
Delta #1181	Dallas/Fort Worth to Seattle	8:38 p.m.	95.67	53
Delta #1354	Salt Lake City to Seattle	9:50 p.m.	95.67	48
USAir #904	Chicago O'Hare to Pittsburgh	6:35 p.m.	95.00	71
Delta #284	Atlanta to West Palm Beach	9:10 p.m.	93.55	60
Delta #1854	Minneapolis to Salt Lake City	6:20 p.m.	93.55	51
Delta #677	Detroit to Atlanta	4:25 p.m.	93.55	43
Delta #1854	Atlanta to Minneapolis	5:00 p.m.	93.55	51
Delta #936	Cincinnati to Newburg	3:10 p.m.	93.55	33
Delta #2059	Cincinnati to Newburg	7:00 p.m.	93.33	43
USAir #411	San Francisco to Kansas City	2:30 p.m.	92.31	56
Delta #574	Atlanta to New York La Guardia	6:30 p.m.	92.00	71
Delta #505	Minneapolis to Atlanta	4:30 p.m.	90.32	76
USAir #411	Los Angeles to San Francisco	12:30 p.m.	90.32	74
Delta #751	Salt Lake City to Portland, Oregon	9:52 p.m.	90.32	60
Delta #187	Seattle to Portland, Oregon	10:05 p.m.	90.32	49
Delta #1055	Boston to Atlanta	1:35 p.m.	90.32	48
American #900	Dallas/Fort Worth to Los Angeles	10:55 a.m.	90.32	47

Average amount it costs a small travel agency in overhead to issue a domestic airline ticket: $22.70.

50 WORST FLIGHTS FOR ON-TIME PERFORMANCE

CARRIER /FLIGHT #	ROUTING DEPARTURE	SCHEDULED OF FLIGHTS	PERCENTAGE MINUTES LATE	AVERAGE ARRIVING LATE
Delta #568	Fort Myers to Atlanta	2:35 p.m.	90.32	41
USAir #1517	Pittsburgh to Chicago O'Hare	5:30 p.m.	90.00	58
Delta #303	Hartford to Cincinnati	5:15 p.m.	90.00	52
Delta #1132	Atlanta to Pittsburgh	5:20 p.m.	90.00	42
United #2025	San Francisco to Los Angeles	11:43 a.m.	88.89	56
TWA #561	Indianapolis to St. Louis	3:40 p.m.	88.24	72
Delta #1810	Los Angeles to San Francisco	7:35 p.m.	87.10	55
Delta #187	San Juan to Atlanta	3:25 p.m.	87.10	51
Delta #1187	Salt Lake City to Anchorage	9:35 p.m.	87.10	45
Southwest #410	Los Angeles to Phoenix	12:00 p.m.	87.10	44
Delta #507	Louisville to Atlanta	6:10 p.m.	87.10	42
Delta #1529	Atlanta to Portland, Oregon	5:20 p.m.	87.10	39
Delta #1480	Atlanta to Miami	11:09 p.m.	87.10	37
Delta #382	Louisville to Cincinnati	11:30 a.m.	87.10	36
Delta #1275	Salt Lake City to San Diego	10:00 p.m.	87.10	35
Delta #1249	Minneapolis to Atlanta	11:15 a.m.	87.10	33
Delta #240	Los Angeles to Atlanta	12:25 p.m.	87.10	33
Delta #1082	Salt Lake City to Missoula	9:30 p.m.	87.10	32
Delta #1882	Salt Lake City to Bozeman	9:32 p.m.	87.10	31
Delta #889	Atlanta to Phoenix	8:45 a.m.	87.10	28
Delta #2095	Cincinnati to Harrisburg	3:10 p.m.	87.10	25
Delta #549	Newark to Atlanta	5:40 p.m.	86.67	61
Delta #817	Hartford to Atlanta	5:40 p.m.	86.67	48
Delta #1085	Philadelphia to Atlanta	6:10 p.m.	86.67	42
Delta #2120	Cincinnati to Rochester	7:00 p.m.	86.67	40
United #2035	San Francisco to Los Angeles	2:30 p.m.	85.71	55
USAir #57	Charlotte to San Francisco	12:35 p.m.	85.00	38
Delta #1155	Charlotte to Atlanta	3:15 p.m.	84.00	31
Delta #751	Boston to Salt Lake City	5:50 p.n.	83.87	53

Percentage of seats filled on U.S. major carriers in January 1995: 61%; in August 1995: 74%.

Delta had 39 of the 50 flights with the worst on-time performance. USAir had five flights, TWA and United each had two and American and Southwest each had one.

Thirty-five of the late flights departed after 3 p.m., illustrating how on-time performance gets worse as the day goes on and late departures begin to stack up.

Most business travelers rarely even consider flying out of smaller airports to save money and avoid congestion–Burbank instead of LAX, Chicago Midway instead of O'Hare and Oakland instead of San Francisco.

MEMBERSHIP PROGRAMS

Join frequent flyer programs. Join as many as you can. No membership fee is involved. Consider other frequent traveler programs and study the potential benefits before agreeing to programs requiring annual fees. Concentrate on the two or three that benefit you the most. Use tie-in programs to accumulate points and miles, but be careful not to develop a blind loyalty that keeps you from saving many times the dollar value of your award units.

Qualify for elite level frequent flyer status to earn priority wait listing and baggage handling, preferred seating, special menu selections, liberal upgrade provisions and less limited blackout days for free travel. The requirement can be as little as 25,000 base miles per year.

Join airline clubs. Some meetings can be comfortably conducted at airports by using member-only facilities. This works best when the people you're meeting have easy access to the airport. Consider sending a car to pick them up and return them to their home or office. You'll still be dollars ahead by saving your own transporta-

tion and hotel costs. Airport clubs are also the most relaxing environment for waiting out flight delays.

Join a long distance carrier program that awards points or miles on your preferred airlines.

❝Since corporations can't earn miles or access the special discounts that individuals can receive on long distance service, I have all my long distance calls routed through my home with a home office 800 number. For example, because I spend more than $25 a month, I qualify for a 25% across-the-board discount on all AT&T calls–better than the corporate rate. I can still earn air miles on every single call I make. If I spend $600 a month, I get double miles. That's almost enough for three roundtrip tickets annually. If I wasn't doing that, I'd be throwing away three free roundtrips every year.❞

LAPTOP LOGIC

Request a visual security check rather than placing your laptop or diskettes on the conveyor belt. Keep diskettes stored safely in your laptop carrying case.

Make sure your battery is fully charged and carry a spare for contingencies.

Telephone modems, as small as credit cards, cost $100-150 and give you access to bank account balances, on-line services and bulletin boards with a wealth of city-specific information.

Don't use laptops until your flight has reached cruising altitude to avoid interfering with pilots' instrument readings. Carry pen and paper to avoid losing great ideas while laptop use isn't allowed.

If you need a hard copy but don't have a printer, fax a copy to yourself at your hotel. Most hotels charge only for outgoing faxes.

Is your laptop insured under your homeowner or renter's policy? If not, Safeware, 800-800-1492, offers $2,000 in coverage for $49 per year.

INTERNATIONAL TRAVEL

Flying Business or First Class allows extra time to recover from your flight. Often the cost difference is recouped by time saved in arriving alert and ready to conduct business. You don't have to pay airlines' premium prices for Business and First Class if you follow the advice in this chapter.

International airport-to-city train transport excels in many cities. For example, Cointrin Airport has departures every ten minutes to Geneva for $3.

Stays of two weeks or more might qualify you to lease a car. Several European companies lease cars at rates substantially lower than rentals. See our *Car Rental* section for details.

Carry appropriate adapters for modems and electrical appliances.

Don't doom international deals by ignorance of country-specific protocol. The British can be sensitive to jokes about the royal family. White is the color of mourning in Japan. Shaking hands, particularly offering the left hand, is ill-received in several countries. *Culturgrams* are available from the David M. Kennedy Center for International Studies, 800-528-6279. Each four-page briefing is written by someone who has lived in the country they cover for at least three years. Individual *Culturgrams* are $4.99, and they're updated yearly.

SPECIAL TIPS

Be sure to pack enough items to ensure your good appearance in case of stained or damaged clothing. Pack your own lost luggage insurance by always wearing a business suit on your outbound flight and carrying a change of undergarments and a clean short or blouse in your briefcase. Take a second pair of shoes even on short trips. Being late for a meeting because you're trying to get your only pair of shoes repaired is an avoidable headache.

Take along an extension cord and an extra-long phone cord to provide more mobility in your hotel room office.

If your company has discontinued cash advances for travel, you're part of a nationwide trend. Make sure you can use your corporate card for cash advances to avoid dipping into your own funds.

Use per diems wisely. Taking a hotel shuttle or mass transit into the city can free funds for an exceptional dinner or a relaxing room service meal.

Cut the cost of business entertaining by using two-for-one dining coupons, but use them discretely unless your client is more likely to be impressed than offended by your thriftiness. Take clients to breakfast to avoid hefty lunch and dinner tabs and get a productive start on the day.

When boarding rows are called, get in the back of the line that precedes your section. You'll be first in line when your section is called.

Take weather conditions at connecting airports into account. Try to travel through cities subject to minimal weather-related and high-volume delays.

Exercise meal options. Unless you're flying in business or first, a specialty meal guarantees you better and fresher food.

PRE-FLIGHT INTELLIGENCE REPORT

Now that you have the basics of cost-conscious travel, it's time to know that you have rights and choices as a passenger. Some of these matters will help you financially. Some will enhance your knowledge when dealing with airline personnel. Others pertain to comfort and amenities that can help put the fun back into air travel.

AIRLINE REALITY CHECK

As with all things in life, what "they say" and what "they mean" is not always the same. Sometimes what they *don't* say is more important. This fact is even more meaningful when dealing with the airlines. The sentences in bold state the positions the airlines' prefer you to believe. My "Reality Checks" follow.

Airlines just raise fares to remain competitive.

Reality Check:

They raise fares in cities where they have no competition and where there are no niche airlines. They lower fares because they're forced to, usually because a niche carrier has come in and cut into their expected market share.

Frequent flyer programs that cancel unredeemed miles after three years are doing it for the sake of good bookkeeping.

Reality Check:

Cancelling miles at the end of the year is well-timed to take advantage of the hol-

---

Number of airline service complaints filed with the Department of Transportation in 1995: 6,026; in 1994: 6,945.

iday season rush when you're likely to be distracted. Airlines like to send miles to NeverNever Land. They don't have to use up as many premium seats for upgrades, they create more brand loyalty as you scramble to get enough miles for redemption, they try to get you to redeem early so you don't grab the premium seats and, most of all, they help their own bottom line.

Calling the airlines direct will give you the best service and the best price.

Reality Check:

Don't ever believe this. It's the last place to go shopping. Good travel agents are your best allies, but make sure they use niche airlines and all the deals that don't appear on any computer reservation system. The one time you do want to call the airlines direct is when you need a fee waived or a special request granted. Travel agents usually can't do it. If you have to argue with someone, argue with the airline.

Flight delays are inevitable and statistics show that they aren't that big of a problem.

Reality Check:

Believe it or not, 20% of all flights are late. The frequency of late arrivals is up by 20%. You get stuck on the runway for lengthy periods of time because airlines schedule flights to please business travelers and try to have too many flights leaving during the same brief time periods. They don't leave room for inevitable mechanical and weather delays. We also have an inadequate air traffic control system. On-time departure is figured by when a plane leaves the gate, not when it actually takes off. They want to get you away from the gate so their figures look better than they really are.

Overbooking is a necessity, and few passengers are involuntarily bumped.

Reality Check:

Almost one million passengers were bumped in 1995. The DOT keeps two statistics on bumping—voluntary and involuntary. Once you agree to relinquish your seat voluntarily, you're not included in the statistics the airlines like to advertise.

Your rights are the same on every segment of a flight booked on a major carrier.

Reality Check:

If you're scheduled to change planes to a code-share partner or a commuter flight, 61 passengers or less, you're under a different set of rules.

All the information any airline passenger needs to know is printed on the ticket jacket.

Reality Check:

Some of the most important information never makes it to any airline's ticket jacket. It's in their *Contracts of Carriage*. (More on this subject later.) If you use electronic ticketing, you don't even get the usual ticket jacket information until you've arrived at the airport. Most people usually like to review contracts before they buy. Knowing your rights and being able to talk to airline personnel as an educated traveler helps you win many more battles.

If you call as soon as a fare war begins you can get the bargain rate on any applicable flight.

Reality Check:

A previous fare war may have already sold out the seats set aside for the sale. Try to be flexible on your departure time. Put the best seat possible on hold, then wait for the dust to settle to see who might be matching or beating the fare tomorrow. If you can't get a seat, try another airline or call back the next day to see if additional fare war seats have opened up. Better yet, have a travel agent check availability on all major carriers. If one airline is sold out, you have the option of using another.

All airline rules and policies are essentially the same.

Reality Check:

Many rules vary from airline to airline and on different flights flown by the same airline. On one flight you can check a bicycle for free. On another, you pay a $50 fee. Some airlines will give you a seat assignment a year in advance. Others will only do it at the check-in counter.

Ticket prices to airports near one another will be similar.

Reality Check:

The *Alternate Cities* section debunks this myth. In many cases, changing cities will be more convenient or only slightly less convenient, and you'll save major dollars. If you're going to Manhattan, Newark fares may be lower than JFK's, plus you're closer to your destination.

CONTRACTS OF CARRIAGE

When you buy any airline ticket you are automatically agreeing to the terms of a contract you have probably never seen. It goes by the name *Contracts of Carriage*. Contracts of Carriage for domestic travel vary by airline and even within subsidiaries of the *same* airline such as United/United Express or American/ American Eagle.

> **❝** *It's important to differentiate between rules made by individual airlines and laws. Most airlines don't want you to use certain forms of creative ticketing. Buried in their hard-to-access Contract of Carriage are warnings against them, implying that people who use these forms of ticketing are somehow breaking the law. Remember, creative ticketing is legal, it only violates some airlines' rules.* **❞**

A summary of each airline's *Contract of Carriage* appears on most ticket jackets, stating some, but not all, of their policies. You may have to search for the summary. For some, it is in a place not easily noticed inside the jacket.

- **If you use ticketless travel,** this summary may not be given to you unless it is included with a mailed itinerary.

- **If your tickets are delivered in a travel agent's ticket folder**, rather than the airline's, you should have a summary stapled at the front of your ticket.

- **Contract terms for international travel** are only available in the form of published *Tariff Rules*, available at airports and city ticket offices.

Each airline must make their full *Contract of Carriage* available to you on request at airport and city ticket offices. They must also mail you a copy if you request one in writing. In our experience, getting one is not very different from searching for a needle in a haystack. Many airline employees have no idea what you're talking about. If they do, they will either print a copy for you or refer you to an address, insisting that you have to request a copy in writing.

We went to the airport to request copies of the elusive *Contract of Carriage* from ten airlines. Because 548,000,000 people pass through airline gates each day, it would seem logical that gate agents would know what a *Contracts of Carriage* is. Out of ten airlines, a few offered summaries. Most gave responses including:

"I don't know what you're talking about."

"The contract isn't readily available."

"I honestly do not know how to get a copy of the contract."

"You have to request it in writing from our legal department."

"The contract will take about two hours to duplicate."

Calling the airlines produced the same frustration, except with Southwest. Their agent immediately knew what we were requesting and said it could be picked up at any of their airport counters.

What It Says/What It Means

Here's a look at one airline's current *Contracts of Carriage***.** We'll call them Airline X. Its *Contracts of Carriage* covers fare changes, *force majeure*, overbooking, delayed or cancelled flights, baggage, check-in requirements, acceptance of passengers, acceptance of children, refunds, ticket validity, claims and authority to change the contract. We'll hit the high spots and show you some loopholes the airlines write in so they are there in case they need them. Some of these loopholes can work to *your* advantage.

What It Says:

"All printed versions of the *Contracts of Carriage*...are obsolete. Print as requested. Do not print advance copies."

What It Means:

• **The rules can change so fast** that "printed" (mass produced) publications are no longer created. Instead, they are printed one copy at a time on request via the printer attached to the airline's computer system.

> ❝Insist on receiving a hard copy of any verbally indicated changes to **Contract of Carriage** policies. Do not accept any policies not in printed form.❞

What It Says:

"Airline X may, in the event of a *force majeure* event, without notice, cancel, terminate, divert, postpone or delay any flight...without liability except to issue an involuntary refund. The involuntary refund will be made in the original form of payment in accordance with involuntary refund rules for any unused portion of the ticket." **Force majeure** is partially defined as "...any shortage of labor, fuel or facilities of Airline X or others, or any fact not reasonably foreseen, anticipated or predicted by Airline X."

What It Means:

• **Beware of documents with obscure terms!** How many times does *force majeure* turn up in your daily conversation? It's beginning to sound more and more like a document executed in lawyerese. *Force majeure* usually refers to major events such as blizzards, wars and riots. If you run into the season's big snow storm, the airline will try to help, but per their contract, they don't have to do any more but offer what they call "involuntary compensation."

> *During the blizzard of January 1996, hundreds of thousands of passengers were stranded in airports trying to depart or return to parts of the Northeastern U.S. Under the force majeure clause, passengers were entitled to a full refund to their original form of payment for flights that had been cancelled. Instead, many airlines tried to compensate passengers with vouchers for future travel. If this ever happens to you, be sure to check the airline's **Contract of Carriage** for full details of what you are really entitled to.*

What It Says:

"If a flight is oversold...you will be entitled to payment...unless..."

What It Means:

- You get nothing if they get you where you're going within an hour of your originally scheduled arrival, if you checked in late (according to a time limit you may never have been advised of), if a flight is cancelled or delayed or if a smaller aircraft has been substituted.

What It Says:

"Airline X is responsible for transportation only on flight segments operated by Airline X."

What It Means:

- If Airline X wants to place you on another airline (because of overbooking, weather, etc.), they will use their interline agreement (contracts with other airlines) to reassign you. You are now under the other airline's *Contracts of Carriage*. If that occurs, don't forget to "double dip." Mail your tickets and boarding passes to the **original** airline, you get the frequent flyer miles on your original and your reassigned flight.

> *When an airline wants to place you on another carrier, ask whom their primary interline agreements are with. You may be able to choose an airline you prefer, one on which you earn frequent flyer miles or have upgrade coupons.*

What It Says:

"Unless you have checked-in, received your boarding pass and are at the boarding point ready to board the aircraft at least ten minutes before scheduled departure, your reservation is subject to cancellation. Such cancellation will apply to all segments in your itinerary, including those on other carriers."

What It Means:

- Does this mean that you can show up, breathless, at the gate check-in counter ten minutes before your flight or should you have completed the check-in process? Custom dictates that just showing up is OK, but should the airlines decide to get picky, their verbiage technically allows them to enforce it.

> *Northwest Airlines enforced a 20-minute rule during Christmas and New Years of 1994. Always ask your travel agent to send you a printed copy of the check-in requirement's and other pertinent information. Then if the airlines change check-in times, you have the original requirement in writing. Remember, the check-in counter is not the ticket counter, it is the counter at the gate of departure.*

What It Says:

"A ticket is invalid if...Airline X determines that the ticket has been purchased or used in a manner designed to circumvent applicable fare rules."

What It Means:

- This section goes on to specifically forbid back-to-back ticketing, throwaway ticketing and hidden city ticketing. Perhaps most amazing is the rule against throwaway ticketing which allows you to buy a cheaper, roundtrip ticket for one-way travel, throwing away the unused portion. To try to steer you to high-priced, one-way tickets, the airlines made a rule that says you can't fly half the distance on a purchased ticket, even though you've paid for it entirely. It's like buying a ticket for a double feature, trying to leave after the first movie and being told you can't. Some airlines aren't content to set prices. They also want to unfairly limit how you use your tickets once you've purchased them.

Rule 240

If a flight is oversold or your reserved seat is not guaranteed, you may exercise your right of passage under Rule 240. In some cases this is an unofficial rule which you won't usually find in the *Contract of Carriage*. It states that under specific circumstances the airline will get you to your destination via another carrier. You usu-ally will have to ask to be placed on a competitor's flight.

The rule is most frequently exercised in circumstances where overbooking occurs. You will also be given the option of "denied boarding compensation" plus guaranteed passage on a later flight on your original airline.

Passenger Allies

The Department of Transportation (DOT) is one of four agencies that accept complaints about airline performance and passenger service and otherwise attempt to keep the airline industry in line. The DOT receives an average of 1,000 complaints from air passengers each month. Most people don't take the time to complain or may not know where to go with their complaints.

- The DOT releases monthly statistics on airline performance and consumer complaints. The agency also helps deal with serious problems relating to baggage, flight delays and overbooking. You can record a complaint via voice mail by calling 202-366-2220. To speak with a staff member, call 202-366-5957. Address letters of complaint to Aviation Consumer Protection Division, DOT, C-75, Washington, DC 20590.

- The Federal Aviation Administration, 800-322-7873, deals with safety issues, airport security and carry-on baggage issues.

Worldwide passenger traffic (excepting to and from the United Kingdom) handled by U.S.-based airlines: 80%.

• The **Aviation Consumer Action Project**, 202-638-4000, is Ralph Nader's organization. They publish useful material and are also willing to advise passengers on their rights by phone. You're likely to get a voice mail recording. Leave a message and a representative will get back to you.

• The **International Airline Passengers Association**, 214-404-9980, publishes a bimonthly newsletter on airline safety and other travel issues.

AIRLINE TICKETS DE-MYSTIFIED

Translating Tickets

If you think airline tickets are printed in code you're right, but the code is easy to break.

The place of issue is printed just above the main green bar.

The record locator (PNR in airline lingo) is in the large, beige gap at the top of the main green bar. The first six letters and digits identify your reservation and should be used whenever you call regarding your ticket.

The type of rate is identified by a one-letter code at the second break in the main green bar. It shows if your ticket price came from the airlines, a travel agent or a negotiated corporate rate.

The class of service is designated at the center of the main green bar. "P" or "F" indicates First Class and "C" or "J" indicates Business Class. "Y" or any other letter indicates coach.

The ticket status is marked on the green bar directly below the word "STATUS." It should read "OK." Anything else indicates that your flight is not confirmed, even though a ticket has been issued.

The codes for the computer and travel agent who issued your ticket are printed to the left of the third green bar on the boarding pass.

Your form of payment is indicated on the second line under the main green bar. If you used a credit card, the type of card and your number (minus the expiration date) will be printed.

Routing and fare information are encoded on the third line under the main green bar, preceded by the two-letter airline code. It shows basic restrictions (by code) and the fare-per-segment.

The date of travel is most easily read on the fourth green bar on the boarding pass segment.

The ticket number is printed at the lower bottom of the ticket against a white background. It validates the ticket and helps protect the airlines against fraud. Each ticket issuer must account for every ticket in each numbered sequence, even voided tickets.

The fare is printed in the lower left corner. "USD" indicates the base fare. "US" indicates the federal tax. "XF" indicates the passenger facility charge, up to a total of $12 roundtrip. The total amount (printed on its own green bar) should be the exact amount you paid for your ticket.

Ticketing Rules & Procedures

Always ask the ticketing time limit when making a reservation.

• **Reservations for most domestic flights** are only held 24 hours. A few airlines are experimenting with lengthening the limit to 72 hours. At press time, Midwest Express and America TransAir were the only airlines offering this desirable service on all reservations.

- **Reservations for international flights** have ticketing time limits that vary considerably.

- **A guaranteed reservation does not guarantee a price.** As long as you observe the ticketing time limit, you'll get your ticket at the quoted price 95% of the time. Once in a while airlines raise rates in a manner that affects current reservations. **That's why reservation people usually tell you that the price is not guaranteed until you purchase the ticket.**

> **❝***It is amazing that when simple requests are made and not followed through, the airlines always blame travel agents. In many cases the errors are made in transmission from computer reservation systems. Always double check your records, including seat assignments.***❞**

Always note the reservation number when you confirm your tickets. If any special provisions or promises have been made, or if you have special needs (such as wheelchair assistance, special meals, pets on board, etc.), be sure the agent notes the information in your record. Even after this is done, you should still contact the airline at least 48 hours in advance to be sure the proper information is in your record.

When you receive your tickets, check them immediately. Make sure the destination, dates and times are correct. Make sure the dollar amount printed on the ticket is the same as the amount you were quoted. Check the status box to make sure it's been marked "OK." This is your assurance that your reservation is confirmed rather than placed on standby or a waiting

list. Make sure it is to the right city and state. Portland, Oregon is only 2,500 miles away from Portland, Maine.

Always reconfirm your reservation, even when you are holding a confirmed ticket. International travel may require it and reconfirming domestic travel assures that you're aware of any change in schedule. Often departure times are changed by ten, 20 or more minutes. The airline will try to notify you or your travel agent, but if they fail to reach you, you could miss a critical factor in your travel plans. This is particularly vital for people who only allow themselves time for quick, last-minute check-ins. Refer to Rule 240 in the event of unacceptable schedule changes.

> **❝***You may think your job is done once you get a low-price ticket. Dedicated bargain hunters, however, keep searching, even after they've purchased. Call on Tuesdays and Thursdays and check out the fares. If they're substantially lower (worth paying the $50 change fee) and you meet all the new ticketing requirements, it's time to downgrade your ticket to up your savings. The savings game continues until the day you take off.***❞**

Reissues And Downgrades

Many fares, including most excursion fares, are not refundable, but they can be exchanged.

You will want to have your ticket reissued if the fare has gone down or if you change. When an airfare goes down and you want to receive a refund for the difference, it's called a "downgrade" or "rollover."

A downgraded ticket is a good thing. It doesn't mean you have to fly in Third Class. It means that you are exchanging an existing ticket for one with a lower fare. An upstart airline, a fare war or a show of one-upmanship among airlines can lower a fare to the point where paying a change fee becomes a good deal.

All requirements for the lower price ticket must be met, including advance purchase, minimum-stay requirements and availability of seats at the lower price.

Some travel agencies have computer systems that spotlight tickets available for reissuing at lower prices and will call to give you that option. The airlines will never call and tell you about a lower fare.

If you're holding tickets and a fare war hits, call and ask if you qualify for the lower rate.

You can have tickets reissued by your travel agent, at the airline's city ticket office or at the airport. Some airlines require that certain changes be made only at the airlines ticket office or at the airport.

DOMESTIC TICKET POLICES	
AIRLINE	**DOMESTIC REISSUE/DOWNGRADE POLICIES**
ALASKA	No fee if you accept a voucher; $35 fee for refund in your original form of payment
AMERICA WEST	$50 fee whether you accept a voucher or a refund in your original form of payment
AMERICAN	No fee if you accept a voucher; $50 fee for a refund in your original form of payment; itineraries cannot be changed
CONTINENTAL	$50 fee whether you accept a voucher or a refund in your original form of payment
DELTA	No fee if you accept a voucher, unless you change your itinerary; $50 fee for a refund in your original form of payment; a non-refundable ticket can be exchanged only at the airline's reservation center
NORTHWEST	No fee if you accept a voucher; $50 fee for a refund in your original form of payment; no part of the itinerary on excursion tickets can be changed
SOUTHWEST	All tickets are non-refundable, but can be exchanged with no change fee; downgrade refunds are paid in airline vouchers
TWA	$50 fee whether you accept a voucher or a refund in your original form of payment
UNITED	$50 fee whether you accept a voucher or a refund in your original form of payment; no part of the itinerary on excursion tickets can be changed
USAIR	No fee if you accept a voucher, unless you change the itinerary; $50 fee for a refund in your original form of purchase

Approximate combined profit of all U.S.-based scheduled airlines in 1995: $2 billion.

Generally you have one year to have a ticket reissued, but some airlines allow two years and all allow you to apply for an extension. Some airlines allow you to travel up to two years after the original ticket date, but you have to make a reservation within a specified period of time.

You can extend the life of almost any ticket by having it reissued.

You cannot always change the name on a ticket without paying an additional fee, and on most tickets, the airline tickets cannot be changed or refunded.

> **66** *Some airlines will waive the processing fee if you agree to accept your refund in vouchers, the airline's play money, to be used for future flights. If you insist on a refund in your original payment form, some airlines will allow you to downgrade and pay you the cash difference, minus a processing fee. If you fly a particular airline frequently, a small voucher may be acceptable, but remember that it locks you into a specific airline. If you get a cash refund, you maintain your flexibility.* **99**

Lost & Stolen Tickets

Airline tickets are like currency. Protect them as diligently as you protect your cash. Make a photocopy of each ticket and store it safely so you have the information you need in case you need to report a loss. You'll have the ticket number and proof that you purchased the ticket because your credit card number is printed on the ticket's face.

The procedure for reporting lost and stolen tickets is the same except stolen ticket replacement or credit is hastened when you supply a police report or case number to authenticate your claim. The airline will attempt to stop anyone from flying on your stolen ticket.

Report the loss directly to the airline. You can sometimes go through a travel agent, but the process takes longer.

If your ticket is used while your refund is still pending, the airline may refuse to process the refund. They will certainly investigate your claim.

How will you get a replacement ticket? The answer is influenced by several variables, including airline policy, the type of ticket and the conditions under which it disappeared.

If you're asked to purchase a replacement ticket at full coach fare, try to negotiate to have the advance purchase requirement waived.

It's usually easier to get a quick refund on a lost or stolen international ticket. It's much more difficult to attempt to fly on the lost or stolen ticket because of passport requirements.

Partially used tickets fall under separate policies. Check with the airlines for specifics.

> **66** *One of the great benefits of ticketless travel is not having to deal with lost or stolen tickets. Passengers run no risk of losing what's stored in airline computers.* **99**

LOST AND STOLEN TICKET POLICIES

AIRLINE	LOST/STOLEN TICKET POLICIES
AIR FRANCE 800-237-2747	$70 processing fee; ticket number not necessary; must purchase new ticket at current fare; refund less $70 fee if the original ticket is determined to be unused
AMERICA WEST 800-235-9292	$60 processing fee; ticket number required; must purchase new ticket at current fare; if ticket is determined unused, the refund is processed within 120 days; fee waived only if original ticket found and returned to America West within 120 days
AMERICAN 800-433-7300	$60 processing fee; ticket number required for non-refundable tickets; must purchase new ticket at original fare; refund processed within 90 days
BRITISH AIRWAYS 800-247-9297	$70 processing fee; ticket number required; will issue new ticket at no additional charge
CONTINENTAL 800-525-0280	$60 processing fee; ticket number not required; must purchase new ticket at original fare; if ticket is determined unused, fee waived and refund processed within 120 days
DELTA 800-221-1212	$60 processing fee; ticket number required; must purchase new ticket at current fare; if ticket is determined unused within 30 days, fee waived and refund processed
LUFTHANSA 800-645-3880	$50 processing fee; ticket number not required; must purchase new ticket at current fare; refund, less $50 fee, is processed within six weeks
NORTHWEST 800-225-2525	$60 non-refundable processing fee, even if the original ticket is never used; ticket number required; new ticket issued at no additional charge; if ticket is determined unused, the fee is waived
SOUTHWEST 800-435-9792	Lost and stolen tickets are not refundable; the airline advises electronic ticketing protection
TWA 800-221-2000	$60 non-refundable processing fee; ticket number required; new ticket issued at no additional charge
UNITED 800-241-6522	$60 non-refundable processing fee; ticket number required; must purchase new ticket at current fare if your ticket was purchased from an agency not using United Airlines' computer system; 60-90 days to process refund; tickets issued by United or an agency using United's computer system are replaced at no additional charge, but the processing fee still applies
USAIR 800-428-4322	$60 processing fee; ticket number required; must purchase new ticket at original price; if ticket is determined unused within 90 days, the refund is processed; fee is waived if you find the original ticket and return it to USAir within 90 days

The rank of the United States as a world tourist destination in 1994: second.

Prepaid Tickets

Prepaid tickets allow you to pre-purchase an airline ticket and have it waiting at the airport of your choice. There is a $35 fee above the ticket price. You can arrange prepaid tickets through the airlines or through a travel agency, allowing a minimum of one hour for the transaction to be completed. An international pre-paid ticket could take considerably longer. Be sure to always check. You can use any form of payment. You must provide your name, address and phone number, plus the same information on the traveler. Positive identification will be required of the person picking up the ticket. If they are not carrying identification, the airline will allow you to select a code word, used to access the ticket.

Prepaid tickets are notorious for problems because of the speed in which the transactions are conducted and the need to guard against fraud. Always ask for the prepaid ticket number and the confirmation number (record locator number), and always call the airline to confirm that the reservation has gone through to its system. Make sure that the price charged to your credit card is accurate.

Avoid prepaid fees when you have at least an overnight before the passenger must travel. Purchase the ticket as usual and send it via overnight delivery with a guaranteed early morning arrival. Many overnight delivery companies have offices at or very near major airports. If you specify that the overnight letter be kept at that office for pickup, an 8 a.m. arrival is usually guaranteed. The cost of overnight shipment should be about $10 less if you are able use a corporate account with a negotiated, lower rate.

> **"**Prepaid ticket fees can be eliminated by utilizing ticketless travel options.**"**

Ticketless Travel

Here's what travel industry crystal ball gazers predict for the near future: Travelers will insert cards into their home computers to book airline flights, hotels and car rentals. At the airport the same card, inserted into an airline computer, will assign seats and award frequent flyer miles. Will this prediction happen? It will probably come true in some modified form. What technology can't provide is know-how and pathways to the latest bargains.

Electronic ticketing is the wave of the future, like it or not. It's estimated that airlines could save as much as $1 billion per year if all ticketing was done electronically.

Adding up the good and bad of ticketless travel may make it look as if the negatives outweigh the positives, but what is positive about e-ticketing is very positive.

* **There is no hassle and no added cost** for ticket delivery *and* there is no danger of a lost ticket.

* **Travelers don't get the abbreviated version of the Contract of Carriage** (currently printed on ticket jackets) until they're at the airport. Even then, they usually have to ask for it.

* **Business travelers don't always get ticket receipts** to attach to expense accounts, and if they're linked to their travel agent by e-mail, run a certain risk in transmitting credit card numbers.

* **You don't get an itinerary** unless you request one, so you must be particularly careful to note flight times and confirmation information precisely.

1995 on-time arrival record of the ten largest U.S. carriers: 78.6%; in 1994: 81.5%.

The Power Of Gate Agents

Never underestimate the importance of the gate agents. They have the authority to bend or even break certain rules to your advantage. In almost every case, arrogance or anger on the part of the passenger is met with an iron-clad adherence to policy. Asking for their intercession is your best course. Calmly and firmly explain why you feel you are entitled to certain benefits and ask for their help rather than demanding it.

Gate agents operate under policies that could be summarized in one sentence: "Give customers what they want to keep them happy, but don't give away any more than you have to." Some of the goodies they can select from:

- **free upgrades**, usually reserved for elite-level frequent flyers and special circumstances

- **compensation for overbooking**, based on how many seats they need to empty and how many volunteers are willing to be bumped

- **preferred seating**, a change of seat assignment or even blocking the middle seat in a row of three

- **waiving service and processing fees** on a case-by-case basis

- **providing free drink, headset and other vouchers** in the name of good customer relations

GETTING BUMPED

Two ways to look at bumping: If you have flexibility, you may want to be voluntarily bumped just to receive the compensation offered. If you're on a tight schedule, involuntary bumping is the last thing you want to occur. By law, airlines must first ask for volunteers on all overbooked flights.

You lose any claim to compensation if you:

- **fail to meet the airline's minimum check-in requirement.** Deadlines vary, with ten minutes most common on domestic flights and 30 minutes for international flights. Some airlines require you to simply be at the airport ticket counter while others demand that you be in the boarding area. If you're picking up your tickets at the airline, a ten-minute deadline may be increased to 30 minutes. If the airline's rules are not printed on your ticket jacket, call

❝How One Paid Ticket Created Two Free Roundtrips: A business traveler bought a coach ticket for roundtrip Dallas to Rapid City. It was July, and because of the extreme heat, the airline had to fly under full capacity to meet weight requirements. She could not volunteer for bumping on the outbound trip because she had to be there as scheduled. On the return trip, her schedule was less demanding. The flight departing from Rapid City was overbooked. She was given a free roundtrip ticket in exchange for volunteering to wait for the next flight, four hours later. When she reached Denver she received another free ticket, hotel accommodations and a $25 meal check because her connecting flight was overbooked and she agreed to wait for a morning flight. Her "profit:" two roundtrip tickets, a meal voucher and an overnight stay in one of her favorite cities.❞

the airline and have a reservation person document the information you're given on your record. We've found that many reservation people don't know the correct answer. If there's an error, you want a record that it was on the part of the airline. Minimum check-in times can change and, if you switch from one carrier to another, you may be under a different time limit.

- **are rescheduled to a smaller plane.** Airlines aren't required to pay any compensation if they substitute a smaller aircraft.

- **are flying on a plane that holds 60 passengers** or less.

- **fly on an alternate flight** that gets you to your destination within one hour of your scheduled arrival.

When You Want To Be Bumped

1. Arrive at the gate early. Minimum check-in times won't give you the leverage you want.

2. Be first in line when your gate becomes operational for check-in. Ask the agent if the flight is oversold.

3. Negotiate for a free roundtrip ticket or travel voucher, but keep in mind that not all airlines offer them. Go for the best possible deal while keeping in mind it's like a bidding process. Try to judge what the traffic will bear.

4. In most cases Alaska, Continental, Delta, Reno, TWA and USAir offer free flight certificates. America West, American, Northwest and United offer dollar-off vouchers.

5. Ask when your new seat can be guaranteed. Make sure the time lag is acceptable and your new seat is not just on standby status. If your new flight turns out to be overbooked, you're likely to be com-

pensated again, as long as your new seat was guaranteed.

6. If the airline won't guarantee a seat on their next flight, ask to be protected under Rule 240, (See details on page 78) allowing you to fly on another carrier. Check a flight schedule that shows what flights are being offered by competitors.

7. The ante increases when too few people volunteer to be bumped. Some airlines may then offer free tickets plus cash awards, usually $100-200, but sometimes as much as $400. When this happens, try to be the first to offer your seat because the number of people willing to do so increases with the amount of compensation offered.

> **❝**We've seen an airline offer two roundtrip tickets to the person who was first to volunteer their seat. We have also been on flights that held 148 passengers but over 180 tickets were sold. Flights on major business routes tend to have a high no show factor, so they're usually the ones that are the most overbooked. **❞**

8. If the time between your bumped flight and your next flight is more than two hours, ask the agent for a free call home (or a free phone debit card) and a meal ticket for an airport restaurant.

9. If you've already boarded and hear an announcement asking for passengers volunteering to be bumped, there's going to be a stampede to the front of the plane. They've already asked for volunteers at the gate. Now they have to do all they can to avoid involuntary bumping. If they're offering $50, stay in your seat. If the ante goes up to $250, or even $400, make your move.

10. If your new flight is overbooked, go back to #1 and start the process again.

Involuntary Bumping

Involuntary bumping has minimum compensation requirements, per policies determined by the Department of Transportation. Every passenger who is involuntarily bumped must be given a copy of these policies.

If the delay causes you to reach your destination between one and two hours after scheduled arrival, or between one and four hours on international flights, the minimum compensation required by law is the face value of the current segment of your ticket (not the fare to your final destination) or $200, whichever is less. If the delay is more than two hours, domestically, or more than four hours, internationally, the compensation must be at least double the one-way fare or $400, whichever is greater. Most commuter flights carry a $100 minimum compensation.

Some airlines will offer a roundtrip ticket, sometimes with blackout dates, requirements for last-minute reservations or even standby only. Ask specifically what limits your ticket carries, and don't hesitate to ask for less limited terms.

Other airlines try to satisfy you with "funny money"–vouchers for future travel.

Ask if you are receiving less compensation than passengers who were voluntarily bumped. No law forces the airline to match the amount, but asking for more can have a worthwhile result.

Bumping on international flights may be subject to policies that are more or less favorable to passengers. Always ask for the policies when booking your tickets.

Flights originating in the European community, for example, come under compensation rules determined by the length of the flight and the length of the delay. Any involuntarily bumped passenger should also receive meals, hotel (if the delay is overnight) and compensation for a fax or telephone call.

Delayed And Canceled Flights

Delayed and cancelled flights don't routinely entitle you to compensation by law, particularly when the reasons are considered to be outside the airline's control. Airlines don't guarantee their schedules. The help you get is up to each airline's policy and the degree of their eagerness to maintain your goodwill. If your flight is cancelled and you are not be able to take your trip, you may be (under specific circumstances) entitled to a full cash refund.

> **"**Concerned that you're not being told the truth about a delay? If the claim is a weather-related delay, check to see if other airlines are affected. Call the airline's 800 number and see what story is being given out by phone.**"**

If the delay or cancellation is due to a factor not affecting other airlines, ask that your ticket be endorsed for use on an alternate carrier. Ask specifically for coverage under Rule 240 which declares, under specific circumstances, they will get you to your destination via a higher class of service or another carrier. You have to ask to be put on a competitor's flight. Few airlines will offer it. They prefer that you wait for their own next scheduled flight. Be sure they give you a confirmed reservation with the alternate airline.

If your original airline endorses your ticket under Rule 240 and the new airline refuses to honor it, have that gate agent call the original airline's gate agent. Some discount tickets require an additional notation called a "Flight Interruption Manifest" (FIM). If it's not there, the new airline may refuse to honor the ticket.

If you're able to wait out the delay, ask for help with meals and lodging. Generally you'll get more help if the problem has come from mechanical delays or other factors the airline has some control over. It's less likely that you'll receive monetary compensation when, for example, a blizzard forces the cancellation of hundreds of flights.

If the airline declines to arrange a reduced rate room, ask the hotel directly for a "distressed passenger" discount.

Most airlines will not offer accommodations if the bump is on the outbound (beginning) leg of your flight. If your plane is making a connection and your flight is cancelled, you should demand a room, meal vouchers, phone call and transportation to and from the hotel, as necessary.

> **"**Don't accept a hotel that you are not comfortable with. In many cases, by declining the one-star dump offered, you may receive as an alternate, a four-star hotel gem.**"**

Delayed flight compensation policies are another airline secret. Discount vouchers tend to go to the people who complain the loudest, and sometimes just to those who take the time to write letters of complaint. Meals, overnight accommodations and even phone cards are at the disposal of airline airport personnel to use according to the guidelines we don't get to see.

If a delay means you may miss your connecting flight, make the gate agent or flight attendant aware of your situation. If enough passengers are involved, the connecting flight may be held. If not, alternative arrangements can be worked out while you're still in flight.

On close connections get the gate assignment of your connecting flight while you're still in the air, check the airport map in the in-flight magazine and map out your route. As soon as you de-plane, tell the customer service agent which flight you're trying for. They can either help with transportation by cart or call the departure gate and let them know you're on your way.

If a major weather problem is forecasted and you can change to any earlier departure to avoid it, ask the airline to confirm space on the flight with no change fee. It's to their advantage, as well as your own, to get you out before the bad weather hits.

ON BOARD BASICS

SEAT ASSIGNMENTS

You can make seat selections in advance during a range of time varying by airline. Always ask for your boarding pass to be included with your ticket. If you purchase your tickets before the seat selection opens, make sure to call back on the first day seat assignments can be acquired.

All advance seat assignments can be cancelled if you don't check in at least ten minutes before your flight. Usually airlines will wait until ten minutes before flight time, but you may find adherence to a 30-minute policy on heavily-booked flights. You'll maintain your reservation, but you might end up with a less desirable seat assignment. Also note that if all passengers are checked in and on the plane, the airline may depart early.

Unclaimed seats are released ten to 15 minutes before flight time. If your current seat assignment is unfavorable, ask to be put on a waiting list in case a better seat opens up.

> **"***If you do not yet have a seat assignment and you call the airline reservations line at least 24 hours in advance and are told that they cannot reserve seats because the seats are under "airport control," it's a good sign that your flight is oversold. Get there early!***"**

If you can't enjoy the comforts of Business or First Class, opt for the best selection you can get in coach.

- **Exit row and bulkhead seats** (the first row in coach) provide the most legroom. Bulkhead seats have trays that fold out of a panel between seats rather than from the seat in front and no floor storage space. All carry-ons must go in the overhead bins. Exit row seats also guarantee you won't be next to small children or infants. They aren't allowed in exit rows.

> ❝The best seat on the plane, in terms of leg room, is not in First Class but in many cases, in coach, in the emergency exit row. ❞

Some airlines don't release premium seating, such as bulkhead and exit row seats, until the day of the flight. Exit row seats can only be assigned to people 15 and over who are physically able to assist other passengers in emergency situations.

- **Seats in front of exit rows** often have less reclining capability.

- **TWA, Alaska, Kiwi and Midwest Express** offer some of the most comfortable coach seats in the skies. Midwest Express has all two-across seating with extra leg room and comfort comparable to Business Class on other airlines. TWA reconfigured seats on many of its jets in 1993 to provide increased coach leg room.

- **Wide-bodies** with two-five-two seating allow extra comfort in coach, providing that your seats are located in the outer, two-across sections rather than the five-seat across the middle area. Look for DC-10's, MD-11's and L1011's.

Never change seats without notifying the flight attendant. You'll usually have no problem getting permission to move within the same class of service but, particularly on direct flights, a passenger boarding at the intermediate city may be assigned to the seat you want to occupy.

The chart on the following two pages shows who gets preferred seating and upgrades, when you can reserve your seat and when you can be issued a boarding pass. If you can't get your boarding pass when you purchase your ticket, make a note on your calendar so you can call on the first day boarding passes will be issued. If you have an excellent travel agency, they may issue your pass at the appropriate time.

Airline Smoking Policies

Smoking is banned on all U.S. domestic flights, and both major Canadian airlines are completely smoke-free.

The United Nations has passed a nonbinding resolution calling for a ban on smoking on all international flights starting in July, 1996.

Smoking is never allowed while an aircraft is on the ground or in takeoff or landing status.

Smoking in aircraft rest rooms sets off a very loud alarm. It was banned when a fire started by a badly extinguished cigarette killed 116 passengers.

U.S. airlines flying internationally have policies that vary by airline. They can also vary on segments flown by a code-sharing carrier. When two planes fly the same route in the same day, one is often designated smoking and one non-smoking. The best rule for people who really want to smoke in-flight and for those who really want to avoid smoke; ask about the policy before you purchase your ticket.

Number of new aircraft delivered to the nine largest commercial U.S.-based airlines in 1995: 93.

UPGRADES/SEATING/BOARDING PASSES

DOMESTIC AIRLINES	PREFERRED SEATING	WHEN YOU CAN RESERVE YOUR SEAT	WHEN YOU CAN ACQUIRE YOUR BOARDING PASS
ALASKA 800-426-0333	MVP & MVP Gold members	When ticket is purchased	When ticket is purchased
AMERICAN 800-433-7300	Full fare, air pass and AAdvantage members	331 days in advance	30 days in advance
AMERICA WEST 800-235-9292	Full fare tickets	When ticket is purchased	When ticket is purchased
CONTINENTAL 800-525-0280	OnePass members	340 days in advance	35 days in advance
DELTA 800-221-1212	Full fare tickets	120 days in advance	30 days in advance
MIDWAY 800-446-4392	No preferred seating	When ticket is purchased	Check-in only
MIDWEST EXPRESS 800-452-2022	Full Y fares	When ticket is purchased	When ticket is purchased
NORTHWEST 800-225-2525	Full fare tickets and preferred WorldPerk members	90 days in advance	35 days in advance
RENO 800-736-6247	None stated	When ticket is purchased	Check-in only
SOUTHWEST 800-435-9792	No assigned seats	No assigned seats	Check-in only
TOWER AIR 800-221-2500	Full fare, premium and business class tickets	60 days in advance	Check-in only
TWA 800-221-2000	Frequent flyers	Requests accepted 11 months in advance but no seat assignments until 30-45 days in advance	45 days in advance
UNITED 800-241-6522	Premier frequent flyers	331 days in advance	30 days in advance
USAIR 800-428-4322	Gold Plus members	130 days in advance	30 days in advance
VALUJET 800-825-8538	Full fare tickets	21 days in advance	1 hour prior to flight

First name of both the pilot and the co-pilot on the first Concorde flight: Pierre.

UPGRADES/SEATING/BOARDING PASSES			
INTERNATIONAL AIRLINES	PREFERRED SEATING	WHEN YOU CAN RESERVE YOUR SEAT	WHEN YOU CAN ACQUIRE YOUR BOARDING PASS
AEROMEXICO 800-237-6639	Aero Miles members	30 days in advance	Check-in only
AIR CANADA 800-776-3000	Full fare M & Y class and elite or prestige level frequent flyers	364 days in advance	30 days in advance
AIR FRANCE 800-237-2747	Full fare, red service tickets and Frequency Plus 2000 members	11 months in advance	Check-in only
ALITALIA 800-223-5730	None stated	332 days in advance	Check-in only
BRITISH AIRWAYS 800-247-9297	Full fare and Executive Club members	364 days in advance for full fare tickets; promotional fare seat assignments at check in only	Check-in only
CANADIAN 800-426-7000	Canadian Gold Plus & Club members	3 days in advance	Check-in only
CATHAY-PACIFIC 800-233-2742	Full fare and Marco Polo Club members	165 days in advance	Check-in only
EL AL 800-223-6700	Business & first class and frequent flyers	30-60 days in advance	Check-in only
LUFTHANSA 800-645-3880	Full fare and Mile & More members	364 days in advance	Check-in only
MEXICANA 800-531-7921	None stated	90 days in advance	Check-in only
QANTAS 800-227-4500	Frequent flyer members	When ticket is purchased	Check-in only
SABENA 800-955-2000	None stated	90 days in advance	Check-in only
VIRGIN ATLANTIC 800-862-8621	Virgin and Delta frequent flyers	60 days in advance	Check-in only

Longest regularly scheduled flight in the world: South African Airways New York to Johannesburg: 14:25 minutes.

AIRLINE MEALS

The big news is fewer airline meals are being served, and airlines are spending less for each meal on domestic flights. You can fly coast-to-coast on some connecting flights, and the sum total of nourishment provided will be two bags of peanuts and a couple of plastic cups of soda.

Midwest Express serves the best food overall on domestic airlines. Their one-class service provides for meals ranging from $10.32 and $10.65 per passenger depending on the meal cycle, double that of most competitors.

WHEN AIRLINES SERVE MEALS	
AIRLINE	POLICY
AMERICAN	No meals on flights under two hours or on longer flights that occur outside of "traditional meal hours," roughly defined as 7 a.m. to 9 a.m., 11 a.m. to 1 p.m. and 5 p.m. to 7 p.m.
AMERICA WEST	No meals on flights under two hours or outside traditional meal-times unless competition demands
CONTINENTAL	No breakfast on flights under 90 minutes; no lunch or dinner on flights under two hours; no hot food on flights under 3.5 hours, meal service is generally only during traditional mealtimes
DELTA	No meals on flights under two hours; on longer flights breakfast is served if you spend 50% or more of the time between 7 a.m. and 8 p.m. in the air; lunch if you spend 70% of the time between noon and 1 p.m.; dinner if you spend 80% of the time between 6:30 p.m. and 7:30 p.m.
MIDWEST EXPRESS	Full meals during traditional meal times when flights are longer than two hours; snacks and drinks all other times
NORTHWEST	No meals on flights shorter than 105 minutes and meals are only served on longer flights during traditional mealtimes
SOUTHWEST	Peanuts and trail mix on all flights
TWA	No meals on flights shorter than 740 miles; cold snacks during the day and hot snacks in the evening on flights between 741 and 1,156 miles; longer flights have a higher percentage of hot meals but may still serve cold snacks only
USAIR	No meals on flights of 89 minutes or less; light snacks and beverages on flights of 90-120 minutes; meals on mealtime flights 150 minutes or longer
UNITED	No meals in coach on flights shorter than 500 miles; meals are served on longer flights according to the time of day and what the competition is doing
VALUJET	Muffins and beverages on morning flights; peanuts and beverages on other flights
WESTERN PACIFIC	Peanuts and pretzels on all flights

First international in-flight meal: ham sandwich eaten by Charles Lindbergh during his flight across the Atlantic.

> **"***First and Business Class passengers often get food service even when meals are not served in coach. They may also get full meals while the back of the plane has to settle for snacks.***"**

Ten major airlines spent almost one-and-a-half billion dollars in 1995 on passenger food. Midwest Express spent an average of $10.41 per meal in 1995, giving them easy claim to the number one position. Mike Allen, the wizard of Back Information Services in Toronto, provided us with a food expense breakdown for other airlines based on revenue passenger miles flown. The 1995 figures are based on the first three quarters of the year:

Airlines	1989	1995
Alaska	$8.65	$4.12
America West	$2.71	$2.39
American	$5.77	$4.92
Continental	$4.38	$2.90
Delta	$5.36	$3.47
Northwest	$4.50	$2.99
Southwest	$ .42	$ .24
TWA	$4.60	$3.55
United	$4.51	$4.12
USAir	$5.82	$3.53

If you want to make sure you get your choice of the two standard menus offered on a flight, ask the flight attendant to take your request when you board the plane.

Special Meals

Special meals can be ordered on most airlines and most flights with six to 24 hours advance notice. They are usually better and fresher than the standard coach fare. If a special meal is important to you, it's best to re-confirm, particularly if you ordered it far in advance of your flight. Not all meal choices are available on all flights.

> **"***Kid meals are some of my favorites and are often superior to the adult meals the airlines offer.***"**

Several airlines, including America West, Delta and American, hand out bagged lunches at the gate in lieu of some meal service. They jazz up the concept, if not the contents, with names like American Airlines "Bistro Service."

Northwest serves many meals a la carte, literally. Passengers choose what they want and how much from a selection of food that may include bagels, fruit, yogurt and other easy-to-serve items.

The easiest route to the best meal in the air is to book a flight that is the first domestic leg of an international flight. Meal service is markedly better.

If you're on a special medical diet, keep in mind that schedule changes can result in your requested meal not being available. Carry back-up food if necessary.

Infant and baby meals are generally only guaranteed on international flights.

Vegetarian meals can always be ordered and often include sub-varieties, including egg-free and ethnically oriented menus.

Pounds of lettuce used in one day's meals for Delta passengers departing from Atlanta: 2,712.

SPECIAL MEAL AVAILABILITY

AIRLINE	CHILDREN'S MEALS	SPECIALTY MEALS
AMERICAN	Children's (peanut butter & jelly/ hamburger/hot dog/ fried chicken), Junior Food, Infant (strained fruit/meat with vegetables/ rice cereal with fruit)	All American Breakfast, Seafood, Fresh Fruit Bowl, Great American Hamburger, Heart Healthy, Diabetic, Non-Lactose, Low Calorie, Low Sodium, Low Cholesterol, Gluten Free, Bland & Soft, Low Carbohydrate, Kosher
AMERICA WEST	Children's (chicken nuggets/ peanut butter & jelly, cereal, pastry & fruit or french toast & sausage), Infant	Fruit Plate, Low Calorie, Low Sodium, Low Cholesterol, Diabetic, Kosher
CONTINENTAL	Children's (chicken fingers/ hamburger/hot dog, cereal & banana/ snack w/grapes, carrot sticks & celery), Infant	Fruit Plate, Seafood, Diabetic, Kosher, Low Calorie, Low Cholesterol, Low Fat, Low Sodium/No Added Salt, Passover/Good Friday Meals
DELTA	Children's (chicken nuggets/ hot dog/pizza /peanut butter & jelly, cereal), Toddler, Infant	Fruit Plate, Cold or Hot Seafood, Bland, Diabetic, Gluten Free, Low Calorie, Low Cholesterol/Low Fat, Low Sodium/No Salt, Kosher
NORTHWEST	Children's (hot dog/hamburger/ peanut butter & jelly), Infant, (strained meat/ vegetable/fruit), Orphan Meal (easily digestible/ usually for newly adopted children flying to the U.S.)	Hot or Cold Seafood, Fruit Plate, Bland, Diabetic, Low Calorie, Low Sodium, Low Cholesterol/Low Fat, Low Carbohydrate, Gluten Free, Sulfite Free, Soft Diet, Kosher
TWA	Children's (chicken nuggets/ hot dog/cheeseburger, cereal & banana)	Seafood, Fruit Plate, Low Calorie, Low Cholesterol/Low Fat, Low Sodium, Low Carbohydrate/Low Sugar, Diabetic, Kosher
UNITED	Children's (McDonald's Happy Meals®/hot dog/ peanut butter & jelly, breakfast w/cereal & fruit), Infant (strained meat/vegetables/ fruit/graham crackers	Fresh Fruit Plate, Seafood, Bland, Chef's Salad, Diabetic, Gluten Free, High Fiber, Kosher, Low Calorie, Low Cholesterol, Low Fat, Low Sodium, Low Protein, Non Diary
USAIR	Children's (chicken & tater tots/ hot dogs & macaroni and cheese/peanut butter & jelly/ pancakes or french toast)	Cold Seafood, Fruit Plate, Bland, Low Calorie, Diabetic, Gluten Free, High Fiber, Kosher, High Protein, Low Cholesterol, Low Fat, Low Protein, Low Sodium

The only difference between a Moslem airline meal and a Kosher airline meal: a rabbi blesses the Kosher meal.

HEALTH ISSUES EN ROUTE

Pressure build-up occurs in the ears during take-off and landing. Ease it by swallowing often and pinching your nostrils shut, then **gently** blowing against them. Chewing gum may also help.

Economy Class Syndrome is a medically recognized complaint caused by cramped leg room and dehydration–symptoms inhibiting blood flow. Ask your doctor about taking one aspirin to thin your blood. Limit smoking before boarding and try to move and stretch as much as possible during the flight.

Dehydration is countered by increasing your consumption of liquids before the flight. Drink at least eight ounces of water or juice per hour of flight time. Limit alcohol and caffeine consumption; both are diuretics. A small plastic atomizer of water will release a mist to replenish your skin.

Closed cabins and crowded situations increase the number of germs in the air. Breathing through your nose rather than your mouth helps purify the air you take into your lungs.

Airline pillows and blankets are guaranteed germ carriers. Airlines may only change them every 24 hours, not after every flight. If you need a pillow, consider carrying a small inflatable version. Try to keep warm with a coat or jacket rather than covering yourself with a blanket that may be a challenge to the best immune systems.

Slip off your shoes and elevate your feet. Put a small pillow behind the small of your back. Buy a special inflatable pillow that cradles your neck and head.

If you experience severe cramps, gas-like pains or swelling in the waist area, you might ask the flight attendant to check the cabin pressure. It sometimes requires an in-flight adjustment.

Tension and muscle tightness resulting from sitting too long in one position will ease if you rotate your head, roll your shoulders in a modified shrugging motion and shake out your hands. Relax your legs by pointing and flexing your feet and spreading your toes.

Jet Lag

Jet lag is your body's reaction to the disruption of its 24-hour cycle coupled with the demands placed on your body by lengthy flights. It's more common on eastbound flights. Every frequent international flyer has a cure to recommend, including wearing battery-operated visors, said to send the proper, balancing light into the retina. Jet lag is like hangovers and common colds. There are no cures, but there are some things you can do to ease the symptoms:

- **Set your watch** to your destination's time as soon as you take your seat.

- **Adapt** your flight behavior to the time of day you're scheduled to arrive. Try to relax and rest as much as you can so you wake up to a morning arrival. Try to stay awake if you will be arriving at night.

- **Deep breathing** can replace some of the oxygen deprivation that occurs from lowered cabin pressure.

Countries that spray arriving passengers with pesticide: Argentina, Grenada, India, Kiribati, Madagascar.

- **Melatonin, a hormone,** is reputed to lesson the symptoms of jet lag. The British Medical Journal, claims *Lancet* improves symptoms by 50%. However, the Federal Aviation Administration does not recommend it for pilots' use, and the Air Force strictly prohibits it. Synthetic melatonin is available in health food stores. It is not recommended for pregnant women, nursing mothers, children, couples trying to conceive and people with auto-immune diseases.

- **The U.S. Department of Energy** will send you a free copy of their *Anti-Jet Lag Diet*. Send a stamped self-addressed envelope to Arizona Chemical, 9700 S. Cass Ave., Argonne, IL 60439, 708-759-8901. Be forewarned: following this diet requires the willingness to adopt a relatively strict eating regimen for four to five days prior to each flight.

- **Aromatherapy to ease jet lag?** Air New Zealand, British Air and Delta think so. First and Business class passengers are given kits with plant-based, fragrant oils to be inhaled, dabbed on pulse points or used in the bath or shower. Make your own kit by asking for help from a shop selling aromatherapy products. They can help you select the oils said to produce the effects you desire.

PERSONAL SAFETY IN THE AIR

You've heard it before, but it merits repeating: You're far safer on the plane than you are on your drive to the airport. On average more people in the U.S. are killed each day in car accidents than are killed each year in plane crashes. A statistical passenger would have to fly once a day for 26,000 years before encountering the odds of a fatal air crash.

On January 1, 1997, commuter airlines will be held to the same safety standards as major airlines. Until then, the commuter airlines that feed passengers to the major airlines come under two categories: those carrying 30 or less passengers and those carrying 31 or more passengers. The smaller planes are still allowed looser safety standards. If you can't avoid a commuter flight, at least avoid the smallest planes. The reservation person can tell you the type of aircraft and the number of passengers it carries, but you must always ask for that information.

> **❝**Don't believe that low-cost airlines have a worse safety record then major carriers. Southwest Airlines, in its 25-year history, has never lost a passenger. None of the top five airlines can make that statement.**❞**

Aircraft with fewest lavatories per number of seats: Boeing 757.

International air travel safety is sometimes on a par with that in the U.S., but some countries are notorious for risky flying and poorly managed air traffic control systems. The FAA has begun publishing a list of countries considered to be lax in airline safety standards. Ask your travel agent to check out your destinations.

For safe flying:

- **Use electronic equipment in-flight** only according to stated airline rules. Don't use laptops and CD players at all during takeoffs and landings.

- **Never carry weapons on board.** They're forbidden by all public carriers. Swiss Army Knives may be an occasional exception.

- **When told to put on your oxygen mask,** do so without delay. Apoxia, caused by a lack of oxygen, not only affects your thinking, it also affects eyesight in just a few seconds. If you're traveling with young children, put your mask on first, then help your children.

- **Wear natural fiber clothing** and avoid highly flammable synthetics. The worst thing you can wear on a plane is panty hose. If there is a fire they will quickly melt against your skin.

- **Avoid the temptation to overload overhead bins** or place heavy objects inside.

- **Keep your seatbelt fastened at all times.** It may be a minor annoyance, but it can save you from injury in case of unanticipated turbulence or a sudden drop in altitude.

- **Don't carry sharp objects** in pockets or wear jewelry with sharp edges.

- **Carry a small, high beam flashlight** to provide light for situations that may extinguish the emergency back-up lights.

- **Pay attention to safety instructions** and review the information card in the pouch in front of your seat. Even frequent flyers can get confused.

- **Count the rows to the nearest exit** so you can get there by touch. Locate alternate exits.

- **Keep alcohol intake to a level** that does not appreciably compromise alertness and reaction time.

- **Urinate frequently.** A full bladder increases the odds of internal injury in case of a serious crash.

- **Survivaid escape hoods** cost about $35 and give you 30 extra minutes of added safety from fire and smoke. If you can't find them in stores, call the manufacturers at 817-923-0300. An alternative: Cover your mouth and nose with wet cloths.

> **❝**Eighty-five percent of the cabins in commercial U.S. aircraft do not meet the suggested fire resistance standards set in 1990. The reason? It costs an average of $1 million per plane to bring them up to par.**❞**

Traveling With Kids

The safest flight position for babies without assigned seats is within the arms of an adult, but outside of the adult's seat belt. Enclosing your baby within your seat belt actually increases the risk of injury. If there is an empty seat next to you or if you've purchased a seat for your baby, ask for a small loop belt that attaches to the front of regular seat belts.

Don't place a small children in a seat alone during takeoff and landing unless you're using an approved safety seat.

Best seating options for families vary by opinion. The bulkhead seat (the first row of coach) provides additional leg room. Be aware that the arm dividing the seats does not lift up because it contains the fold-out meal tray. The rear of the plane, with its increased engine noise, seems to lull some infants to sleep. One point of agreement: children want window seats. When traveling in pairs, select window and aisle seats only, leaving the middle seat free. On all but the most crowded flights they'll remain unclaimed and give you extra room. Be sure to get advance seat assignments to assure that your family will not be split up on crowded flights.

Airlines do not usually provide diapers (except on some international flights), changing tables (except on larger, newer aircraft), milk, refrigerators, microwaves or plentiful supplies of fresh water. Pack accordingly. Be sure to check for child or infant meals prior to your flight. International flights may offer cardboard bassinets and a few more baby-care items.

Airport play areas and privacy rooms for nursing mothers are available at New York's La Guardia and other clever airports. Usually you have to ask since they're not identified with signs. They can be invaluable in the case of delayed flights. Delta's "Dusty's Dens" provide child-friendly waiting areas in several major airports.

Collapsible strollers are supposed to be checked baggage, but if you "forget," you can use it all the way to the boarding gate and the flight attendant will find a place for it. If you do check the stroller it won't count against your baggage limit.

Always do a "gate check" and request the flight attendant to put a special tag on the stroller. When the ground crew empties the baggage you will be able to pick up your stroller at the gate and not at the baggage claim area. Be very clear when you request a "gate check." Take the flight attendant's name so you will be able to refer to it if any problems arise.

Takeoffs and landings are easier for infants if they are sucking bottles, breasts or pacifiers. Older children should chew gum or hold their nostrils shut while blowing against them very gently.

Kid meals are available on most airlines, but there is no guarantee that your children will like them. (See the chart on page 95 for a sample of choices.) Carry enough food with you to keep everyone satisfied throughout the flight.

Get your pillows and blankets as soon as you board. Supplies can run out. Busy flight attendants may not offer promotional items such as pilot's wings and entertainment kits unless you ask.

Dirty diapers should not be handed to flight attendants because they also handle food and beverages. If you must do it, place the diaper in the coated airsick bag first.

Deal with crying and fussiness by keeping children interested, comfortable (no dress-up clothes), unafraid and fed. If the worst occurs and you think every passenger is glaring at you, do your best and don't add to the problem by becoming overly anxious and angry. That just increases the problem.

Enroll your children in the frequent flyer programs. Even if the miles don't add up to a free ticket or an upgrade, they'll feel important and enjoy carrying their cards.

Ratio of frequent flyer airport waiting time spent reading versus making phone calls: 8 to 1.

Fear Of Flying

Small fear levels can be managed by sitting in the front of plane or over the wing (where the ride is the smoothest), talking to your seat mate and not focusing on your fears.

If you want every statistic on your side, sit in the back of the plane, the same place where the famous black box (which is actually bright orange) rides. Your ride will be a bit less smooth, but you will be in the area least likely to be destroyed in an accident. The second best option is over the wing where the aircraft structure is most stable.

"Thairapy," by aviation psychologist Glen Arnold, 714-967-0772, offers a $30 audio-cassette kit summarizing the teachings of his seminars. Three of his tips:

* **Plan a relaxing day** before your flight.

* **Fight claustrophobic feelings** by thinking of the cabin as protective, rather than confining.

* **Remember that turbulence** is a natural quality of air that airplanes are designed to accommodate.

Major problems that prohibit flying require either psychological treatment or enrollment in one of the special programs that deal successfully with aerophobia.

* **The Pegasus Fear of Flying Association** provides an effective one-day program. Call 800-332-7668.

* **USAir's Fearful Flyer Program** is offered in 11 cities and takes place over a five-week period. The cost is $325. Write to Box 100, Glenshaw, PA 15116 or call 412-366-8112 for details.

* **Flight To Freedom** is a two-day weekend seminar regularly conducted in Dallas, New York City, Chicago and Orange County, California, by a former American Airlines pilot. The cost is $350. Write to 2407 Crockett Court, Grapevine, TX 76051 or call 817-424-5108. Program information also is available through America Online at F2FREEDOM or the internet: http://www.jstrelax@aol.com.

In-Flight Medical Assistance

Babies are born and people die on air flights, but neither happens very often. The Federal Aviation Administration has minimal standards for medical emergencies in the air. They include:

* **first aid instructions** plus an annual refresher course for all flight attendants.

* **a first aid kit** containing bandages, antiseptic and standard "small emergency" equipment.

* **a medical emergency kit** containing a stethoscope, syringes, needles and basic drugs that may only be used if an authorized medical person is aboard the flight as a passenger or flight attendant.

* **contact by radio** with either airline staff physicians or a private firm offering 24-hour medical back-up.

OTHER IN-FLIGHT ISSUES

Travelers With Disabilities

Most disabilities can and must be accommodated by U.S. law. The Americans With Disabilities Act of 1990 and the Air Carrier Access Act of 1986 mandates full rights for all people with disabilities in airports and on all U.S.-based airlines. All carriers must accommodate you and give assistance as needed.

Plan ahead and make use of services including by-request airline assistance in getting on/off the airplane, moving to and from rest rooms and retrieving baggage. Advise the carrier of the extent of your disability with regard to mobility, hearing, sight, etc.

"Access Travel: A Guide To Accessibility Of Airport Terminals," is available at no cost from the Consumers Information Center, Pueblo, CO 81009, 719-948- 3334.

You do not have to give notice of your disability unless you use a respirator hook-up, stretcher, on-board wheelchair or special battery packing for your wheelchair. Airlines can insist on attendants only for passengers who have severe mental illnesses, are on stretchers or are quadriplegic and unable to respond to safety instructions.

Pet Concerns

Small dogs and cats, rabbits, ferrets, birds, guinea pigs and other small, warm-blooded animals are allowed to accompany you in the passenger cabins of most major airlines. Each airline has its own specific rules and policies regarding the size of the animal and how many are allowed on each flight. Always check 24 hours in advance to be sure your pet will be allowed on the plane.

If you are shipping your pet in the baggage compartment, airlines permit only one pet per kennel. Airlines also have restrictions on when they will carry pets during weather extremes.

Snakes, pot-bellied pigs and other more exotic pets are not allowed in aircraft cabins, but may be transported in the cargo area. Individuals cannot transport poisonous snakes.

Most pets dislike air travel which can be stressful for them. Make sure your reasons for taking your pet outweigh the risks and disadvantages.

Never try to fly with an animal who is:

- **overly excitable or subject to motion sickness.** As a rule, animals who are good car travelers will tolerate air travel.

- **in heat, pregnant, under eight weeks old or elderly** (age varies according to breed).

- **pug-nose dogs and cats** should never travel as cargo; even passenger cabin air can inhibit their breathing due to the structure of their faces.

There are four basic modes of air travel available for pets. Terminology and rules differ from carrier to carrier.

- **Carry-on travel** is restricted to pets who fit comfortably in a 16" x 21"x 8" high carrier and are traveling with a human.

Some airlines allow small animals to travel in soft-sided pouches available from pet supply stores.

Rates average $50 per direction.

Reservations are mandatory, so be sure to make arrangements as far in advance as possible.

First animal transported on an international flight: Nico the bull in 1924 on KLM from Rotterdam to Paris.

- **Checked baggage** allows your pet to travel in conjunction with your ticket in an approved carrier in the cargo hold.

The average rate is $50 roundtrip.

After you reserve your ticket, advise the agent you are bringing an animal and call the baggage department to make separate arrangements.

Don't confirm your reservation until your animal's reservation is accepted. You want to check the conditions in cargo as well as the availability of space.

- **Priority shipment is best** for unaccompanied animals. You specify the precise flight.

Rates vary according to the animal's size and weight.

Be sure to have your animal picked up within the specified time frame or the airline may send the animal to a boarding facility and bill you for the fee.

Know exactly when and where your pet may be claimed.

- **Regular cargo** allows you to specify the day of shipment, but not the flight. This option should be used rarely, if ever. Your pet may be treated like freight and spend hours in a warehouse or on the pavement in bad weather.

Foreign travel usually allows the same four options listed above. You must check individual airline rules as well as the entry rules of your destination. Many countries require quarantine periods. Remember that different cultures view animals in different ways. Dogs frequent the cafes of Belgium and France, but even assistance animals are still uncommon in Japan.

Don't be too trusting. Airlines carry animals only as a secondary service.

- **Have the gate attendant call and confirm** your pet has been loaded before you board the plane.

- **Make sure the pilot is aware that animals are on board.** One quick sentence from you may save your animal's life in case of a lengthy ground delay.

Lengthy flights only mandate that your animal be fed every 24 hours and watered every 12 hours. This includes transfers, layovers and ground delays. If you can avoid them, do so. If not, remember that your intervention may be the only thing that makes the trip bearable for your pet. Tape a strong plastic bag full of your pet's usual food to the kennel if the airline will be feeding your animal.

In-flight water is best provided by filling the carrier's plastic water container three-fourths full and freezing it before you leave home. The ice should melt slowly throughout the flight. You may want to gradually switch your pet to a national brand of bottled water and maintain usage throughout your trip. This avoids digestive problems from a sudden switch in water supply.

Tranquilizers are not desirable unless your vet believes your animal must have them. Travel-induced excitement is only a problem for animals who harm themselves when excited.

Pets flying cargo should not wear collars and tags that can get hooked on metal grates. Identification will be attached to the carrier when you check in. Never put a lock on carriers. Locks delay access if your pet needs emergency attention.

Select a non-stop flight whenever possible. Avoid peak travel periods. If you must use a connecting flight, be sure the size of each plane accommodates your pet carrier. Avoid the last connecting flight. You may arrive at your destination and because you had a short connection, your bags and animals may not arrive until the following day.

Purchase an approved kennel from a discount pet store or, better yet, borrow one from a friend. Airlines sell them but you will pay a premium price. Be sure the kennel is large enough for your pet to stand up comfortably. Place a blanket and a favorite toy in the kennel and let your pet explore it before you go.

Get the required health certificate from your vet. This must be dated no more than ten days prior to your originating flight. It includes documentation of current immunizations (including rabies) and certifies that your animal is fit to travel. These papers will be affixed to the kennel by the airline. Make a copy to carry with you.

Exercise your pets before the flight so they are more relaxed and prone to sleep. Don't feed them for five to six hours prior to take-off and limit water two hours before the flight.

In-Flight Added Costs

Frequent flyers find the convenience of in-flight phones worth the high per-minute charge. The newest innovation is the ability to receive incoming calls while you're on a flight. You pay a $2.50 per flight activation fee and $2.50 per minute. Two companies service the telephone needs of most airlines: GTE and Claircom. GTE was the first to offer incoming options. You can get full information and an application for an Air Phone Calling card by calling 800-247-6636.

Receive in-flight faxes on select United and Delta long haul flights. This is also an option of GTE Air Phone.

ADDED COSTS		
AIRLINE	**HEADSET COST DOMESTIC COACH**	**ALCOHOLIC DRINKS DOMESTIC COACH**
AMERICAN	$4	Beer & Wine $3 Cocktails & Cordials $4
AMERICA WEST	$4	Domestic Beer & Wine $3 Imported Beer & Cocktails $4
CONTINENTAL	$4	Domestic Beer & Wine $3 Cocktails $4
DELTA	$3, $1 for kids	Beer & Wine $3 Cocktails $4
NORTHWEST	$5	Beer & Wine $3 Cocktails & Imported Beer $4
TWA	$4	Beer & Wine $2 Cocktails $3
UNITED	$4	Beer & Wine $3 Cocktails $4
USAIR	$4	Beer & Wine $3 Cocktails $4

Brewed weight of the Starbucks coffee United Airlines will serve in 1996: equal to that of 27 Boeing 737-500s.

Ask your travel agent or the airport gate supervisor for free coupons for drinks or headset use. Don't be shy. Be charming. You're almost guaranteed to get them at the gate if you're qualified for an upgrade and there's not enough room to accommodate you.

Headsets are free with Business and First Class domestic tickets and on all international flights.

Beer, wine and mixed drinks are always free in First and Business Class on both domestic and international flights. They're also free in coach on all international flights, except Continental's flights to and from Mexico, where the charge is the same as for domestic coach drinks. Free international drinks are only available during flight portions that occur over international waters.

AIRPORTS

Airport Clubs

Not all Airport Membership Clubs are created equal. All the major domestic carriers (except Southwest) and most large international carriers have membership only clubs. There are about 150 of them in the U.S. and internationally. Membership usually requires an initial membership fee plus annual dues. Spousal membership is at a reduced rate. Some charge for beverages and conference room use; some do not. They can be havens from airport crowds and discomfort but they can also get overcrowded during busy travel times.

Many airport clubs offer short-term memberships. United, Delta and American, for example, sell one-day passes for $25 or $30. The one-day fee includes your immediate family or two, unrelated guests. Continental sells a 30-day membership for $30. Diners Club and American Express also sponsor more than 50 clubs worldwide, with free admission to all cardholders but guests of cardholders may be charged a fee.

Advantages of any airport club membership include:

- Special check-in services.

- Secure storage should you choose to leave your luggage behind while you move about the airport.

- Business amenities including fax, copiers, computers and meeting rooms.

Join the club that has the best services at your home airport. The next consideration: airports you fly to most frequently or connecting city airports.

Ask about policies regarding the requirement of a same-day ticket to access the airport club. Most clubs have it in their rules but only enforce it at crowded airports during peak travel times. Delta is reportedly the most stringent enforcer of this policy.

Airline Club Fees And Policies

Here's a chart to help you sort out which airline club may best suit your needs. Please note that American Express Platinum cardholders are entitled to complimentary visits to Northwest WorldClubs and Continental Presidents Club each time they fly that airline.

AIRLINE CLUB FEES AND POLICIES			
AIRLINE	FEES	BEVERAGE CHARGES	CONFERENCE ROOMS
AMERICAN Admirals Club 800-237-7971	Initiation fee $100 Annual fee $175/spouse $75 Lifetime $2600/spouse $1500 Senior lifetime $875/spouse $425	Non-alcoholic - .75¢ Beer & wine - $3 Liquor - $4	$35 per hour; may be higher in New York & Chicago
ALASKA Board Room 800-654-5669	Initiation fee $100 Annual fee $150/spouse $70	Complimentary with a three-drink maximum (two for guests)	Free up to two hours
AMERICA WEST VIP Lounge 602-693-2994	Initiation fee $50 Annual fee $150/spouse $75 Lifetime $1300/spouse $625	Complimentary	Free up to two hours; then $20 per hour
CONTINENTAL Presidents Club 800-322-2640	Initiation fee $50, or 30-day introduction $30 Annual fee$150/spouse $75 3 years $375/spouse $150 Lifetime $1775/spouse $675 Senior lifetime $875/spouse $400	Non-alcoholic - Free Beer & wine - $3.50 Mixed drinks - $4.50 (Free in Houston)	Free
DELTA Crown Room 800-323-2323	Initiation fee $100 Annual fee $200/spouse $100 (or redeem 30,000 miles/ spouse 10,000 miles) 3 years $500/spouse $250	Complimentary	Free
NORTHWEST WorldClubs 800-225-2525	Initiation fee $50 (waived for Lifetime or World Perk Gold/Preferred members) Annual fee $175/spouse $75 3 years $450/spouse $200 Lifetime $2800/spouse $1500 Senior lifetime $1000/spouse $650	Complimentary	$35 per hour

The average business traveler's per diem expense for food and lodging in New York: $338; in Las Vegas: $156.

AIRLINE CLUB FEES AND POLICIES

AIRLINE	FEES	BEVERAGE CHARGES	CONFERENCE ROOMS
TWA Ambassadors Club 800-527-1468	Initiation fee $25 Annual fee $150/spouse $75 3 years $300/spouse $150 Lifetime $1500/spouse $500	Non-alcoholic - Free Beer & Wine - $2 Imported Beer - $2.25 Mixed drinks - $4	$25 per hour
UNITED Red Carpet Club 602-881-0500	Premier members: No initiation fee Annual fee $150/spouse $75 3 years $400/spouse $200 Lifetime $2500/spouse $1500 Non-Premier members: $100 initiation fee Annual fee $175/spouse $75 3 years $475/spouse $200 Lifetime $2500/spouse $1500	Varies By Location Non-alcoholic - $1 avg. Mixed drinks - $4 avg. Wine - $3 avg. Bottle beer - $3 avg. Draft beer - $2.50 avg. Champagne - $3.50 avg.	$35 per hour except Denver, which is $50 per hour
USAIR USAir Club 910-661-8083	Initiation fee $50 Annual fee $150/spouse $50 3 years $375/spouse $150 Lifetime $2000/spouse $1000 Senior lifetime $850/spouse $100	Non-alcoholic - Free Bottle beer - $3 Draft beer - $2 Mixed drinks - $4 Wine/Champagne - $3	$25 per hour

VIP Lounges

A dozen or so VIP airline clubs exist for preferred passengers. The only admission cost is the price of your first class ticket. New York's JFK Airport is the mecca for those who require the ultimate in service. The best VIP lounges offer extraordinary amenities that may include candlelight dinners, caviar and premium champagne. They offer specially trained agents to tend to almost any need or wish.

Some VIP lounges offer little more than standard airport clubs, particularly those that share facilities with other airlines.

Airport Alert Levels

Airport security is the main line of defense against terrorism activities against U.S. aircraft. Alert levels are numbered one through four, with four being the most intense.

Historically our airports operated on Level One security. The only noticeable security measure were the metal detectors leading into gate areas.

Level Two security has now become the norm. Its main features include an increase in security personnel, more random searches of luggage and more requests for passenger identification.

Level Three and Four procedures are put into effect as deemed necessary. They include all Level Two provisions plus undercover security forces, bans on curbside parking and check-ins, closing of parking lots within 300 feet of terminals and extensive inspection of checked luggage.

Smoking In Airports

Airport smoking policies are changing rapidly with more and more U.S. airports banning smoking entirely. Almost one-third are already smoke-free. Those that still allow smoking limit it to fewer areas. More than half of all airports have no direct control over smoking policies as they are mandated by city, state or county law.

Most violations of airport smoking policies are handled by verbal warnings, though there have been cases of fines ranging from $10-125, levied when the warnings weren't heeded.

Airports that don't allow smoking in their terminals usually do not restrict smoking outside though some (such as Boston and Miami) ask that you only smoke when standing away from terminal exits and entrances.

How Much Is That Hot Dog In The Airport?

Airport food has traditionally been on a par with most airline food–plus you had to pay inflated prices. The airport is still not the place to head for a gourmet meal but better options and trends are coming. Look for gourmet coffees, healthy snacks, ethnic specialties and fresh fruit and vegetable plates. The following chart show average prices for our old stand-bys:

AIRPORT PRICES							
AIRPORT	HOT DOG	SODA	COFFEE	BEER	FROZEN YOGURT	PIZZA	MIXED DRINKS
ALBUQUERQUE	$2.75	$1.58	$1.15	$3.90	$2.06	$2.75	$4.25
CHICAGO	$3.24	$1.85	$1.31	$3.01	$2.09	$4.06	$4.50
DALLAS/FT. WORTH	$2.95	$1.88	$1.15	$2.50	$2.40	$3.50	$4.50
HONOLULU	N/A	$1.55	$1.20	$3.50	$1.82	$3.00	$4.75
KANSAS CITY	$2.59	$1.29	$ .89	$3.25	$2.53	$2.99	$4.85
MIAMI	$2.79	$1.49	$1.09	$3.25	$1.49	$3.50	$4.25
NEW YORK LA GUARDIA	$1.89	$1.59	$1.09	$3.75	$1.90	$2.69	$4.75
SALT LAKE CITY	$2.50	$1.50	$1.25	$2.50	$2.00	$3.50	$4.50
SAN FRANCISCO	$1.79	$1.10	$ .89	$2.95	$1.99	$3.29	$3.95
WASHINGTON NATIONAL	$2.75	$1.25	$1.15	$2.75	$2.70	$1.89	$4.07

Commercial airports in North America that are smoke-free: 33%; percentage restricting smoking: 93%.

AIRLINE TERMS

Here's a quick reference to terms you'll hear most often when arranging air travel.

Apex: Advanced Purchase Excursion Fare. One of the lowest-priced but most restricted ticket types.

ATB: Automated ticket and boarding pass, usually coded with a magnetic strip.

Back To Back: Overlapping, roundtrip tickets used to fulfill Saturday stay requirements and lower costs.

Blackouts: Holiday, major event and seasonal dates when specific discount fares are not available.

Bucket Shops: A name originating in Britain to describe shops selling consolidator and wholesale airline tickets.

Bulkhead: The first row of seats in any commercial aircraft coach cabin.

Bumping: The voluntary or involuntary removal of confirmed passengers from overbooked flights.

Cancellation Penalty: The dollar amount or percentage of your ticket price you lose if you request a refund.

Charters: Public charters fly regularly between specified cities, usually at rates lower than scheduled air. Private charters are usually used in conjunction with vacation packages.

City Codes: Three-letter designations used by airlines and air traffic control to identify specific airports. You should always check the city code the baggage handler or gate agent puts on your luggage to make sure it is being coded to the correct airport.

City Pairs: The originating and destination cities of a flight.

City Ticket Office: An off-airport location that issues tickets for a specific airline.

Coach: The least expensive airfare (as opposed to Full Fare Coach).

Code Sharing: Two or more airlines flying a route under one airline's name. One of the carriers may offer a lower service level or flights via commuter carriers. The Department of Transportation (DOT) mandates that passengers be informed when they are flying on code share flights.

Commuter Aircraft: Defined by the DOT as 62 passengers or less. Commuters may be affiliated with major airlines but operate under separate rules and regulations.

Companion Fares: Pricing based on two people traveling together on an entire itinerary.

Concorde: SST (Supersonic Transport) operated by Air France.

Connecting Flight: Requires one or more changes of plane.

Consolidator: A company that purchases bulk tickets from the airlines and sells them at a discount.

Contract Of Carriage: The terms of the contract you enter into with an airline each time you purchase a ticket.

Cross-Border Ticketing: International tickets written to take advantage of lower fares or more favorable currency rates.

CRS: Computer reservation systems, interactively linked.

Department Of Transportation: Known as the DOT, this federal agency is in charge of monitoring airline compliance with rules and policies.

Deregulation: The 1978 law that phased out the Civil Aeronautics Board and some government regulation of routes and fares.

Direct Flight: Makes one or more stops and may even require a change of planes on code share flights.

Double Booking: Two reservations for the same person on the same route and date. If the airlines detect it, they'll cancel, without notification, the last reservation entered.

Excursion Fares: Roundtrip fares with minimum and maximum stay requirements and advance purchase requirements.

Gateway City: An airline's point of entry to a particular country.

Group Rate: A nominal discount usually offered to groups of ten or more people traveling together.

Hidden Cities: Flying (usually one-way) to a second city but deplaning in the stopover city to take advantage of a lower fare.

Hub & Spoke: A hub is a central connection airport for an airline. Passengers are further routed to (spoked) to their final destination.

Interline Connection: A change of planes and airlines.

Narrow Body: An aircraft with one center aisle.

Niche Carriers: Upstarts who creatively route and price scheduled flights usually based on point-to-point fares.

Non-Stop Flight: Goes directly to the ticketed destination without a stop.

Open Jaw: Ticketing that allows travel to and a return from two separate cities with the fare based on 50% of each roundtrip.

Open Ticket: Good for transportation between specific points with no specific reservation needed.

PFC: Passenger facility charge, usually $3 per airport, added to the cost of all airline tickets.

Red-Eye Flights: Once a great discount source, late night flights now rarely come with reduced prices except for America West's night flights.

Revenue Passenger Miles: Airline seats sold times distance flown. Commonly used in compiling airline statistics.

Segment: A portion of an airline itinerary.

Split-Ticketing: Two low-priced tickets purchased to reach a high-price destination dominated by one non-stop carrier.

Standby: Waitlisted travel with no confirmed reservation. It normally requires pre-purchasing a ticket.

Ticketless Travel: Electronic ticketing that does not require paper tickets.

Waitlist: A holding-pattern for ticketed passengers without confirmed reservations. Tickets are confirmed as space becomes available.

Waiver: The airline's agreement to waive specific rules, conditions or fees attached to your ticket, itinerary or changes you wish to make.

Yield Management: Computerized tracking and adjustment of fares based on anticipated demand and closely monitored activity of competitors.

FREQUENT FLYER TWISTS AND TURNS

American Airlines gave birth to one of our favorite little monsters in 1982. Their frequent flyer program was designed to create airline loyalty. Frequent flyer miles are always at the top of the list when surveys ask business travelers why they choose certain airlines. The ingenious-ness of American's innovation is apparent in one simple statistic: reportedly only about 15% of all airline miles are ever redeemed. Use the frequent flyer programs to your advantage–but don't remain loyal at the expense of your own bottom line.

> ❝What can be upsetting with frequent flyer miles is that for years, the airlines have hung that carrot out for free dream trips. We save our miles, we shop with our credit cards, we do everything we can to be loyal travelers and earn our carrot. When it's our turn to redeem air miles, we find out that that our dream trip to Hawaii is not available for eight or 12 months, or not at all. Try finding a seat to Europe during summer '96. I don't think so. Why does this happen? If American Airlines, for example, allotted only a half of their frequent flyer tickets for free trips to Hawaii, they would have to fill two 250-passenger DC10's each day to meet frequent flyer demands.❞

Percentage of passengers on U.S. airlines who change planes to get to their destination: 33%.

FREQUENT FLYER FACTS

A frequent flyer mile is literally worth 2¢. Some quick math will let you know if it's worth spending more on tickets just to get extra miles. If an airline gives you 1,000 miles for a flight but charges $50 more than competitors, you've just spent $50 to get $20 worth of value. If a car rental gives you 500 miles but the rate is $20 more than a competitor, you've spent $20 to get $10 in value.

Join as many frequent flyer clubs as possible but try to concentrate your miles on one or two airlines. There are no membership fees and you never know which card will give you the best advantage in a particular situation. Carry them like a deck of plastic cards always available for bargain-acquiring tricks. You'll also end up on desirable mailing lists that make you aware of special discounts, sometimes only available to frequent flyer members.

Decide where to concentrate your mileage by examining what each program offers. If you fill out a membership form read it carefully. If you sign up by phone, ask that the program's specifics be nailed to you. Some programs offer more liberal upgrade policies. Some are best for international awards. Hotel and car rental affiliations are important because they add approximately 25% to the average traveler's annual mileage total. If your entire family flies, utilize programs that allow you to transfer miles among family members.

Remember that frequent flyer programs can change.

- **Don't rely on long term plans** for spending or earning your miles. There are some constants, but affiliations change to some degree with each airline. Sometimes the changes are month-to-month. The miles you'll need to get what you want may change too.

- **We recently saw the number of miles needed** for a basic award jump 25% from 20,000-25,000 miles. You can also end up paying more than expected to circumvent blackout dates and capacity controls.

- **Not all locations of partner companies participate in frequent flyer programs.** Never assume that you'll be earning miles for a car rental or hotel stay until you've been specific-

❝With the code share program between USAir and British Airways, you have more reasons than ever to join British Airways' frequent flyer program, especially if you are traveling with the family. To date, British Airways has the only frequent flyer program that permits air miles to be accrued for an entire family (up to four) under one frequent flyer account. For example, a family of four flying from Los Angeles to London on American Airlines earns 10,000 miles per family member. After the trip's completion, none of the four passengers have anywhere near enough miles for a free roundtrip ticket. On British Airways' family plan, 40,000 miles have accumulated–enough for two free roundtrip tickets within the U.S. on USAir. When you travel domestically, give USAir your British Airways frequent flyer number, especially when traveling with family members. By doing this you will have access to total mileage for all family members.**❞**

Percentage of frequent flyers who say they would not trade perks and points for lower fares: 76%.

ally guaranteed that the location you plan to use will award the miles.

- **Many awards from car rental agencies and hotels** are contingent on paying specific rates. Always ask for the lowest applicable rate.

Always scan the inserts that come with your frequent flyer statements. You're likely to find some good discount deals plus periodic listings of travel routings that offer double or triple miles.

Inter-Continental Hotels has the most liberal policy for awarding airline miles. In most cases you'll get the same number of miles per night that other hotels award per stay.

> **66** *Corporations with a substantial amount of business travel aren't likely to keep miles earned by employees flying on business. It's been tried by various corporations and, in most cases, met with severe employee resistance and abuse.* **99**

There are so many frequent flyer miles on the debit side of the airlines' ledgers that they are coming up with merchandise, trips-for-bid and other enticements meant to try to lower the massive total. Delta offered a trip to the 1996 Olympics, requiring a minimum bid of 400,000 miles. United auctioned a four-day trip to France with a minimum bid of 200,000 miles. Continental auctioned a ten-day Far East cruise for two—minimum bid, 100,000 miles. Some airlines also now permit miles to be used in buying membership to their airport clubs.

Inside Flyer, published monthly by Randy Peterson, lists bonus programs and new

partnerships and explores one airline's program in depth in each issue. Call 800-333-5937 for subscription information.

The Inside Flyer group also offers some excellent programs for frequent flyers such as Award Guard, Award Extender and Privilege Flyer. Call 800-487-8893 for information.

Earning Miles

Go for the best accumulation of miles possible while always factoring in price. Remember that you do not usually earn miles when using consolidators, wholesalers, barter or bucket shop tickets.

Not all code share flights earn frequent flyer miles. Be sure to check. Many international airlines, for example, only issue air miles if you pay full fare Business or First Class. You may want to switch to an international carrier that offers miles on discounted tickets. Your decision should be based on the price of the ticket **and** the miles offered.

> **66** *Some airlines will, in effect, permit you to buy miles. If you receive 10,000 miles for buying a $60 upgrade–that's a good deal. If you have to pay $300 for 8,000 miles–that's a bad deal. Many travelers have received their frequent flyer miles just by asking gate agents to review their records and then requesting that their frequent flyer miles to be credited. Remember, nothing ventured nothing gained.* **99**

- **The higher your level of membership** the more benefits you get, particularly those that are discretionary. Benefits include priority upgrades, waitlisting and baggage handling; special contact numbers; access to coach seats reserved for elite levels; limited blackout dates; and bonuses you earn only after reaching a certain level. Learn what level of travel is required for elite membership and, if you're going to play the game, go for the gold.

- **Elite status** is an accomplishment attained by less than ten percent of all travelers. Most airlines will not count miles earned by means other than flights when determining elite status and they won't count miles earned on flights on their partner airlines.

Here are the miles you need to reach the first level of elite status:

5,000 miles: TWA (White Card)

15,000 miles: Alaska Airlines

20,000 miles: America West, Continental and TWA (Gold Card)

25,000 miles: American, Delta, Northwest and United

30,000 miles: USAir

More and more companies are trying to get your business or keep you a satisfied employee by giving miles through a variety of programs:

1,000 miles for a king size mattress purchased from Dial-A-Mattress.

One mile for every mile you move when using some Allied Van Line locations.

5,000 miles to some Merrill Lynch brokers for each five clients they sign up for financial planning.

5,000 miles periodically offered by Visa as a "referral fee" for recruiting new cardholders.

The two mega-mile award sources are airline affinity credit and charge cards, and long distance carriers. They both give you miles for expenses you routinely incur. Read all about them beginning on page 116.

Purchasing Incentive Miles

Airlines have had a big problem with frequent flyer members selling miles but now they've decided it's OK to purchase miles, as long as you buy them from the airlines. They're available to corporations only for use as customer and employee incentives.

If your company is interested in buying miles, which airline's miles should you buy? The rules are virtually the same for all six airlines that have incentive miles purchase programs. The cost per mile (2¢) doesn't vary. The minimum purchase requirement is either $1,000 or $1,200. The standard service charge per purchase is $60-75. Miles must be deposited in an individual's frequent flyer account within one year of the date of purchase. The miles then are subject to the same expiration policies as miles earned through other means.

There are two areas to focus on when making a decision:

- **Which airline's miles** will provide the best incentive to your market or your employees? Which airline offers the widest array of service from their home airport? Which airline do they prefer to fly?

- **What's the highest number of miles** you want to be able to award to one person each year? Continental's Miles of Thanks is the only program with no limit. All other programs have a cap of 20,000-50,000 miles per recipient per year. If, for example, you plan to give 20,000 miles to your employee of the month, you'd be unable to reward the same employee more than once a year with four of the six incentive programs.

The only airline that has a frequent flyer program for pets: Carnival.

INCENTIVE MILES PURCHASE PROGRAMS

AIRLINE PROGRAM	MINIMUM PURCHASE	SERVICE FEE	MAXIMUM ANNUAL AWARD TO ONE PERSON
AMERICAN *AAdvantage Incentive Miles* 800-771-5000	$1,200/60,000 miles	$75	35,000 miles
CONTINENTAL *Miles Of Thanks* 800-340-9318	$1,000/50,000 miles	$60	No limit
DELTA *SkyRewards* 404-715-9426	$1,200/60,000 miles	$75	25,000 miles
NORTHWEST *Miles Above* 800-469-6453	$1,000/50,000 miles	$75	20,000 miles
UNITED *Mileage Plus Reward Miles* 800-742-5825	$1,200/60,000 miles	$75	20,000 miles
USAIR *VIP Miles* 800-883-1019	$1,000/50,000 miles	$75	50,000 miles

Expiring Miles

Frequent flyer programs have different policies on expiring miles.

- **American, Northwest and United** delete all three-year-old miles on January first of each year.

- **Alaska** deletes three-year-old miles accrued before January, 1996. New miles do not expire.

- **America West, Continental, Delta and Midwest Express** have no expiration date providing you have flown the airline in the past three years.

- **Southwest, TWA and USAir** have no expiration date and no flight activity requirements.

Don't let the airlines take your miles. If they're about to expire or if you have too few miles to be of personal value to you, donate them to charity. Most airline-sponsored programs use the miles to provide free transportation to sick children or adults.

- **Continental's OnePass program** gives donated miles to the Americares Foundation, the Brass Ring Society, the Multiple Sclerosis Society and Careforce. You must donate by mail. Address your request to OnePass Service Center "Give the Extra Miles" P. O. Box 4365, Houston, TX 77210.

- **American AAdvantage's Miles For Kids, 800-882-8880** allows frequent flyer miles to be assigned to various charities.

- **Delta's Sky Mile's SkyWish 800-323-2323,** requires donations in blocks of 5,000. Choose from among three designated charities: CARE, the Make A

Wish Foundation or United Way of America. Delta will add 1,000 miles for every 5,000 miles you donate.

- **Northwest WorldPerks Air-Cares, 800-447-3757**, converts donations of miles to Fly-Write coupons. A different charity is chosen quarterly.

- **United's Mileage Plus Charity Miles program, 800-399-2400** accepts miles for several national and international charitable organizations as well as the charity of your choice.

- **TWA's Frequent Flyer miles never expire,** but the airline does distribute donated miles to charities through its "Operation Lift-Off." Call 800-325-4815.

Redeeming Miles

Keep track of your mileage totals. There are no statistics on error rates but logic will tell you that the odds of mistakes being made are astronomical when billions of miles are swarming around in data bases.

Save all your boarding passes and the receipt portion of your ticket until you receive your frequent flyer statement and are sure all your miles have been credited. If they haven't been, send photocopies (never originals) to the frequent flyer program.

Redeem your miles in the manner most likely to get you what you want for the lowest possible expenditure.

- **Plan three-15 months in advance.** Even then, you may not get tickets for choice destinations. Keep checking back with the airline for your original dates. Some airlines do open up additional frequent flyer seats on flights with good overall availability.

- **Have alternate dates in mind whenever possible.** The best availability is usually for Tuesdays and Wednesdays. The best months are October and May.

- **Consider alternate cities.** This is particularly workable when you're trying to get tickets to Europe during heavy travel times.

> **"**Alaska Airlines releases all unsold seats for frequent flyer award travel 48 hours before departure. **"**

- **Ask about mileage saver or mileage stretcher tickets** that fly off-peak times and seasons for a lower mileage cost.

- **Ask to be waitlisted** for flights without frequent flyer seats available or call at one minute after midnight when newly available seats appear on computer screens.

- **If you can't get coach award tickets**, check on Business Class. They'll cost more miles but they're likely to be more readily available than coach tickets.

- **Check with partner airlines**. They may have award seats available after the base airline has run out of inventory, especially where code-share flights are included.

- **If you're a few thousand miles short** of what you need to earn an award, ask the program if you can buy enough miles to make up the difference.

- **You'll pay a fee for many redemption services.** Expedited service, when available, always carries a charge. You're likely to have to pay from $20-50 for expedited service, repositing miles or changing international awards.

Award travel tickets do not give you the same rights as purchased tickets. You're not apt, for example, to be able to invoke Rule 240 in the case of cancellations or delays. Don't hesitate to ask for an exception to any frequent flyer ticket limitations as you remind the airline that your accumulated miles prove that you should be treated as a valued customer.

CREDIT & CHARGE CARDS WORTH CONSIDERING

Airline Credit Cards

Airline Credit Cards are joint offerings of a specific airline and a financial institution. They allow you to earn extra miles on all purchases charged to the card – generally one mile for every dollar spent. Annual fees and interest rates vary. Airlines that offer credit cards include:

- **Alaska** Sea First Bank Card from Visa and MasterCard, 800-552-7302.

- **America West** Flight Fund Card from Visa and MasterCard, 800-508-2933.

- **American** Citibank AAdvantage Standard and Gold MasterCard or Visa, 800-359-4444.

- **Continental** One-Pass MasterCard and Standard and Gold Visa, 800-850-3144.

- **Delta** Sky Miles American Express/ Optima Card, 800-759-6453.

- **Midwest Express** Elan Standard and Gold MasterCard, 800-388-4044.

- **Northwest** WorldPerks Standard, Gold or Classic Visa, 800-360-2900.

- **TWA** EAB Visa or MasterCard, 800-322-8921.

- **United** MileagePlus First Visa and MasterCard, 800-752-8888.

- **USAir** Classic and Gold Visa, 800-294-0849.

> ❝The major airlines sponsor Visa and MasterCards that give you a mile per dollar charged in addition to your frequent flyer miles. Some also provide collision insurance for rental cards. Airline sponsored cards are tempting, but have limitations. You can only earn miles on the sponsoring airlines and its partners plus you are subject to any expiration policy the airline puts in place.❞

Travel & Entertainment Cards

Travel and Entertainment cards offer the same benefits as airline credit cards with added flexibility.

> *"The major travelers' charge cards offer advantages that are literally unbeatable. American Express and Diners Club unquestionably offer the greatest overall advantages to travelers."*

American Express Platinum Card
800-297-6453

- **The $300 annual fee** seems high but the benefits far outweigh the initial cost.

- **When traveling on Northwest or Continental Airlines,** cardholders are allowed free entry into Northwest's "WorldClub" and Continental's "Presidents Club" airport lounges. The combined annual memberships are normally $425.

- **Members receive complimentary enrollment** in the premier service programs of Avis, Hertz and National. The annual enrollments are normally $125.

- **The Platinum Card** has historically provided special Business and First Class buy-one-get-one-free and free upgrade offers when traveling to certain international destinations. Participating airlines have included Aeromexico, Alitalia, Air New Zealand, Iberia, Sabena, Scandinavian, Lufthansa and Varig.

- **Other promotional discounts** on travel are provided regularly.

- **Current American Express cardholders** can call the number on the back of their credit card to request an application for a Platinum Card.

American Express
Membership Rewards
800-297-3276

- **One membership mile $1 charged.** One membership mile equals one airline mile.

- **Participating frequent flyer programs** include Aeromexico, Austrian Airlines, Delta, Continental, El Al, Mexicana, Sabena, Southwest, Swissair and USAir.

- **Participating frequent guest programs** include Marriott, Sheraton, Hilton, Westin and Renaissance.

- **A one-time threshold of $5,000** must be charged and paid in full to convert membership miles.

- **Membership miles can also be used for special** hotel and cruise awards or other benefits.

- **Eligible cards** include the Personal Card, Gold Card, Rewards Plus Gold Card, Platinum Card, certain Corporate Cards, certain Optima Cards and up to two additional cards per basic consumer account. Membership miles are awarded cumulatively.

- **Annual fee of $25; waived the first year.** Annual corporate fee of $50.

Diners Club
Club Rewards
800-234-6377

- **Two points for every dollar charged.** Two points equal one airline mile with a 1,000-point minimum required for conversion/redemption.

- **Participating frequent flyer programs** include Air Canada, Air France, Alaska Airlines, American, America

West, Austrian/SwissAir, British Airways, Continental, Delta, Hawaiian, LatinPass, Mexicana Airlines, Midwest Express, Northwest, Sabena, South African Airways, Southwest, Thai Airways, TWA, United and USAir.

- **Participating frequent-guest hotel programs** include Best Western, Hilton, Holiday Inn, Hyatt, Sheraton, Marriott, Ramada and Westin.

- **No minimum charge requirement** and no expiration date on points. There is no limit to the number of points you can earn.

- **Annual fees** may be waived as part of corporate agreements or may average $40 for corporate members; $80 for individual members.

Best Bank Cards

Some bank cards offer points, miles and travel discounts that can improve on plans offered by airline frequent flyer programs. Free tickets, in some cases, are awarded at amounts as low as 16,000 points. You also usually get your choice of airlines and are not always limited by blackout dates or inventory controls.

> *"Bank card offerings have to be examined closely. If you get great initial rates and benefits, make sure to stay on top of changes that make using the card less attractive. Some cards offer great enrollment bonuses but the price you pay to use the card is unfavorable. In that case, take the bonus then run back to the cards that give you consistently good deals."*

Star Bank
Visa or MasterCard StarMiles
800-999-0619

- **Enrollment bonus only for current** Star Bank cardholders who switch to StarMiles; bonus points based on your total charges for the past six months.

- **One point per $1 spent** up to a maximum of 5,000 points per month. Points expire four years from purchase date.

- **Award tickets begin at 25,000 points** to any destination within the 50 states.

- **Award tickets require a 14-day advance** and Saturday stay. No blackout dates apply. Maximum ticket value is $500.

- **Annual membership fee $25.**

American Savings Bank
Visa Gold Check Card
714-252-4881

- **A debit card requiring a minimum of $300 to activate.** Bank locations throughout California.

- **1,000 point enrollment bonus.**

- **One point per $1 spent.** Monthly balances over $2,500 earn one extra point for every $10 above the minimum.

- **Twenty-five thousand points earns $500 toward any U.S. airline** flight within the 50 states. If the airfare exceeds $500, the card member pays the difference.

- **No blackout dates.** Tickets are purchased based on published airfares and require a 21-day advance.

Number of passengers who went through O'Hare Airport in 1994: 66.5 million.

Amalgamated Bank of Chicago
MasterCard Cardmiles
800-365-6464

- **One Cardmile $1 spent.**

- **Discount certificates** automatically mailed for every 5,000 miles accrued. Certificates are valid on the airline of your choice.

- **Five thousand miles equal $25 off.** Ten thousand miles equal $50 off. Fifteen thousand miles equal $75 off. Twenty thousand miles equal $100 off. Twenty-five thousand miles equal an additional $100 certificate, making the maximum accumulated discount $350. Additional miles repeat the cycle.

- **Certificates can be redeemed** individually or combined to $350 maximum.

First of America Bank
Visa FirstAir Classic Card
800-835-9373

- **Five thousand bonus points** the first time card is used.

- **One point per dollar charged.**

- **Award ticket at 25,000 points,** good for travel within the continental U.S. on any domestic airline.

- **Fourteen-day advance Saturday stay** required but no blackout dates apply.

- **Annual fee Classic/$35; Gold/$49.**

Bank One
TravelPlus Visa Card
800-945-2023

- **One-thousand-point enrollment bonus.**

- **One point $1 charged.**

- **Award ticket at 16,000 points** good for travel within one of three zones on any domestic airline, with a $350 price

limit. Twenty-four thousand points earn a ticket for travel within the continental US with a $500 price limit. Thirty thousand points earn a ticket to Mexico, the Caribbean or Canada with a $700 price limit. Forty thousand points earn a ticket to Alaska or Hawaii with an $850 price limit. Fifty thousand points earn a ticket to Europe with a $1,000 price limit. Seventy-five thousand points earn a ticket to Asia with a $1,775 price limit. Eighty-five thousand points earn a ticket to Australia with a $2,000 price limit. Members may opt to pay the amount over the price limit.

- **Fourteen-day advance and Saturday stay** required. No blackout dates and no seat restrictions.

- **Points expire after five years.**

- **Annual fee Classic/$25; Gold/$55.**

Old Kent Bank Cardmiles
800-949-3733

- **One thousand cardmiles enrollment bonus.**

- **A $100 travel certificate** is automatically issued when 5,000 miles are accrued.

- **Certificates can be used on any airfare,** domestic or international. They are valid for two years from date of issue and are transferable.

- **Up to three certificates can be combined** to receive up to $300 off any fare.

- **Four certificates can be combined** to receive a free ticket on specific U. S. airlines for travel within the continental U. S. or a $350 discount off many international airfares. A 14-day advance and Saturday stay are required.

- **Maximum point accumulation per monthly cycle** is 10,000; 60,000 per year.

- **The annual fee varies** by the plan and rate you choose and is waived the first year.

MBNA America Bank
Visa Travelmax
800-858-0905

- **One thousand bonus points the first time card is used.**

- **Cardholders using a revolving balance** earn one point per dollar charged. Balances paid in full monthly earn one point per $3 charged.

- **Twelve thousand points earn a ticket on any airline** for travel to locations within Eastern and Central time zones, or within Pacific and Mountain time zones. Twenty thousand points earn a ticket on any airline flying within the contiguous 48 states.

- **Award tickets require a 21-day advance and Saturday stay**. No blackout dates apply.

- **The $25 annual fee is waived the first year.**

Stop & Shop MasterCard
SupeRewards
800-997-9116

- **One point per dollar charged.** Double points for purchases at Stop & Shop.

- **Awards include** $100 off select Delta Dream vacation packages for 1,000 points; $200 off for 2,000 points. Ninety-nine dollars off Northwest coach fares for 5,000 points; a free coach companion ticket for 15,000 points; a coach ticket within the 48 states for 30,000 points. Royal

Caribbean Cruise Line two-category upgrade on select cruises for 500 points; free cruises for two children or third & fourth passengers/same cabin on select cruises for 7,500 points; a free companion ticket on select three to four night cruises for 2,500 points.

- **No annual fee.**

Chase Bank
Flight Rewards
800-984-6767

- **One point per $1 charged.**

- **Twenty-five thousand points earn a $500 voucher** on the airline of your choice. There are no blackout dates.

- **Twenty-five-dollar annual membership fee.**

- **Interest** is calculated in two segments –a lower rate for cardholders in good standing with a balance of up to $1500; a higher rate if your balance is over $1500.

Wells Fargo
MasterCard BusinessCard
800-359-3557

- **Business owners earn one air mile for every dollar** they or their employees charge, up to 180,000 miles annually.

- **Miles are good toward travel on most commercial airlines** to all 50 states, Canada, Mexico and the Caribbean.

- **Redemption is flexible.** Tickets may be issued to the business owner or to employees.

- **Membership includes MasterAssist which may provide up to $300 per day** in cash advances, a credit line of up to $50,000, $250,000 in travel insurance, free American Express travelers checks and Hertz Car Rental discounts.

MasterCard/AT&T Universal's Travel U 800-438-8627

- **Available to full-time students** only and geared to first-time credit card users.

- **A MasterCard, AT&T Calling Card and cash card program** all in one. SafePurchase is included to afford protection from damage or theft of items purchased by the card for up to four years.

- **Enrollment bonus of three USAir coupons** for existing and new student cardholders good for discounts on three roundtrips within a six-month period. At the end of that period, additional certificates are issued.

- **No annual fee.**

- **Apply by computer** at http:\\www.att.com/ucs/.

American Express Student Privileges 800-582-5823

- **Available to full-time or graduate** student cardholders.

- **An MCI Calling Card,** good for 30 minutes of free long distance calls each month of the program is issued with the Student Privileges card.

- **Enrollment bonus of five discount** certificates valid for travel within the 48 states and to international destinations serviced by Continental Airlines

- **Enrollment is free**.

DOMESTIC AIRLINES FREQUENT FLYER PROGRAMS

Alaska Airlines Mileage Plan

Customer Service Center
P.O. Box 24948
Seattle, WA 98124-0948
Reservations: 800-426-0333
Service Center: 800-654-5669

Award Requirements: 20,000/coach; 30,00 First Class, if all travel is on Alaska Airlines.

Minimum Award Miles: 500 minimum miles on Alaska, Northwest and Horizon; actual miles on other partner airlines. Alaska First Class gives a 50% bonus, including upgraded travel. British Airways, Northwest, Qantas and TWA First Class and Concorde flights earn a 50% bonus; Business Class, 25%.

Policies: Account may be canceled if no mileage is credited during the first nine months of membership or if an account is inactive for more than three years. Miles earned after January 1, 1996 are not subject to expiration. Miles earned before that date expire on January 1, three years after accumulation. Award certificates and tickets are valid for one year.

Award Redemption: Reservations can be made before award certificates are received, except on TWA flights. Complete the award request form on your statement and return it to the service center. Allow three weeks from date of receipt for delivery. Tickets are issued at any Alaska Airlines or Horizon Air ticket counter, except TWA awards, which are ticketed by TWA. Expedited award delivery (three-award limit) is $60, payable by major credit card. Instant award autho-

---

rization is $75, and tickets will be express mailed the same day if your request was received by 1 p.m. (PST); the following business day if received after 1 p.m. Overnight service is not available for TWA awards.

Airline Affiliations–Miles & Redemption: Alaska Airlines Commuter, British Airways, Horizon, Northwest, Qantas, SAS and TWA.

Car Rental Affiliations: Alamo, Budget and Hertz. Earn 500 miles per rental from participating locations. Rentals do not have to be in conjunction with a flight.

Hotel Affiliations: Coast Hotels-Canada, Hilton, Holiday Inn, Hyatt, Kimpton, Preferred, Princess Tours Hotels, Red Lion, West Coast, Westin and Westmark. 500 miles per stay at participating hotels. Most partners do not require a flight in conjunction with your stay.

Credit Card Affiliations: Alaska Airlines Seafirst VISA and MasterCard, 800-352-7302, gives 1,000 mile sign-up bonus plus one mile per $1 charged. Diners Club converts Club Reward points to Mileage Plan miles: two points equal one mile.

Phone Service Affiliations: AT&T and ALASCOM give one mile per $1 spent. Sprint gives five miles per $1 spent on residential long distance.

Other Affiliations: The Flower Club gives 300 miles on minimum orders of $29.95 and an additional 100 miles for every $10 over $34.99. Alaska Airlines Vacations or Horizon Air Holidays leisure packages give 500 bonus miles. Three miles per $1 spent at participating DineAir restaurants.

America West FlightFund

FlightFund Service Center
P. O. Box 20050
Phoenix, AZ 85036-0050
Reservations: 800-235-9292
Service Center: 800-247-5691

Enrollment Bonus: 2,500 miles.

Minimum Award Miles: 20,000/domestic coach; 60,000/European coach; 30,000/Hawaiian coach; 20,000/domestic upgrade.

Minimum miles: 750 for America West; 500 for America West Express, Aeromexico and Continental. Fifty percent bonus for America West First Class or full-fare coach and Aeromexico Class Premier. Air New Zealand Business Class earns a 25% bonus; First Class, 50%.

Policies: Account may be cancelled if no mileage is earned during the first 12 months after enrollment or with no activity for 24 months. Miles do not expire as long as you fly once within a three-year period. Award ticket valid for one year from issue date.

Award Redemption: Receive four award certificates for every 20,000 miles accrued. Request tickets by mail or exchange certificates at ticket locations. If additional certificates are required for an award ticket and your account has available mileage, up to four individual 5,000-mile certificates may be requested by calling the service center. There is a $35 fee for this service, payable by credit card. Allow two to three weeks. Partner award certificates should be sent to the service center with a completed request form. Allow six weeks for mail delivery. Expedited deliveries are $35, payable by credit card or get tickets in two days at the airport ticket counter.

Airline Affiliations–Miles & Redemption: Aeromexico, Air New Zealand, America West Express and Continental.

Airline Affiliations–Redemption Only: Air France and Northwest.

Car Rental Affiliations: Earn 1,000 miles at participating Avis and Dollar locations; 1,500 miles at Thrifty with special rates in conjunction with a flight.

Hotel Affiliations: Earn 500 miles per stay at participating Hilton/Conrad International, Radisson and Westin. Earn two and a half miles per $1 spent at participating Holiday Inns and Crowne Plazas. Some hotel partners require a conjunction flight within 24 hours of your stay.

Credit Card Affiliations: America West FlightFund Visa, 800-508-2933, gives a sign-up bonus of 2,500 miles plus one mile per $1 charged. Diners Club converts Club Rewards points to FlightFund miles –two points equal one mile.

Phone Service Affiliation: 2,000-mile sign-up bonus plus five miles per $1 spent on Sprint residential long distance.

Other Affiliations: Chairmen's Club members receive a 3,000-mile sign-up bonus. America West Vacation packages earn 500 bonus miles. Phoenix Club membership earns 2,500 sign-up miles. The Flower Club gives 300 miles on minimum orders of $29.95 plus 100 miles for each $10 spent over $29.99.

American Airlines AAdvantage

MD 5400, P.O. Box 619688
DFW Airport, TX 75261-9688
Domestic Reservations: 800-433-7300
International Reservations: 800-624-6262
Service Center: 800-882-8880
Fax: 817-963-7882

Award Requirements: 25,000/domestic coach; 60,000/European coach; 35,000/Hawaiian coach; 20,000/domestic upgrade.

Minimum Miles: American and all domestic partners (except Hawaiian Airlines) give 500 minimum miles. Fifty percent bonus for First Class; 25% for Business Class. Canadian and Hawaiian Airlines inter-island flights of one to 250 miles earn 250 minimum miles; flights of 251-500 miles earn 500 minimum miles. Flights within Canada at discounted economy fares earn 50% of mileage flown. Hawaiian Airlines mainland flights earn 50% of miles flown on discounted fares; 100% of Y or V fares. Flights on international partners earn actual miles.

Policies: Three-year-old miles expire on January 1 of each year. Award tickets are valid one year from issue date.

Award Redemption: Request certificates by phone, mail or fax. Allow 21 days. Airline certificates can be exchanged for tickets at any ticketing location. Same-day expedited service (for airline tickets only) is $75, payable by credit card. Order at least two hours before the ticketing location closes. Overnight delivery of tickets and car and hotel certificates is $50, payable by credit card. Allow two business days for delivery when calling after 2 p.m. (CST) weekdays or anytime weekends and holidays. Quick Claim service for airline, car and hotel certificates is $50, payable by credit card. Call the service center by 2 p.m. (CST) weekdays. You should receive your award by 5 p.m. the following day. Four-business-day expedited service on airline, car and hotel certificates costs $40, payable by check. Send claim form and check payable to AA Expedite Service via overnight delivery to American Airlines Expedited Award Service, 4200 Amon Carter Blvd., Fort Worth, TX 76155-2604.

Airline Affiliations–Miles & Redemption: American Eagle, Canadian, Cathay Pacific, Hawaiian, JAL, Midway, Qantas, Reno Air, Singapore and South African Airways.

Airline Affiliations–Redemption Only: British Airways and British Midland.

Car Rental Affiliations: Alamo, Avis, Hertz and National rentals at participating locations earn 500 miles per qualifying rental in conjunction with any American Airlines or partner flight in the U.S., Canada and Puerto Rico. Rentals at participating international Alamo and Avis locations require no flight in conjunction with rental.

Hotel Affiliations: Earn 500 miles per night at Inter-Continental Hotels; 250 per stay at Fiesta Inns; 750 per stay at Sheraton Tower or Suites; 1,000 per stay at Sandals; and 500 per stay at Courtyard, Hyatt, Fairfield, Fairmont (Platinum/Gold members only), Fiesta Americana, Forte, Forum, Hilton/Conrad International, Holiday Inn, Crowne Plaza, ITT Sheraton standard rooms, Le Meridien, Loews, Marriott, Plaza, Red Lion, Vista, Westin and Wyndham. Earn 1,750 bonus miles on Courtyard and 1,000 bonus miles on Fairfield Inn after your 12th stay.

Credit Card Affiliations: Citibank AAdvantage Card, 800-359-4444, gives one mile per $1 charged with a 60,000 mile limit (waived for AAdvantage Platinum & Gold members). Diners Club converts Club Reward points to AAdvantage Miles–two points equal one mile.

Phone Service Affiliations: 500 mile sign-up bonus plus five miles per $1 spent on MCI residential long distance. One mile per $1 spent in select areas on SNET MobileCom.

Other Affiliations: AAdvantage Dining members earn three miles for every $1 spent, excluding gratuity. FTD Direct gives 300 miles for a minimum order of $29.95 plus 100 miles for every additional $10 spent. The American Traveler Catalog awards miles based on purchase amounts. AA Money Market Fund-Mileage gives one mile per $10 invested. Computer City gives one mile per $1 spent. Fly AAway Vacations gives 500 bonus miles with each vacation package. One mile for every dollar spent with ServiceMaster. Miles for mortgage interest payments at participating financial institutions and one mile per $1 spent on real estate purchased from specific brokers. (Participants vary by location.) Numerous additional affiliations. American AAdvantage offers the most options on earning additional miles.

Continental OnePass

P. O. Box 4365
Houston, TX 77210-4365
Domestic Reservations: 800-525-0280
International Reservations: 800-231-0856
Service Center: 713-952-1630
INFOPASS: 713-785-8999
Award Travel: 800-344-1411
Partner Awards: 800-344-3333

Enrollment Bonus: 2,500 miles with first flight.

Award Requirements: 25,000/domestic coach; 50,000/European coach; 45,000/Hawaiian coach; 20,000/domestic upgrade.

Minimum Miles: Continental and its partners give 500 minimum miles. Fifty percent bonus for First Class; 25% for Business and Business First. Air Canada discount fares earn 50% of actual miles within Canada.

Policies: Account may be cancelled if no mileage is deposited for 18 consecutive months, but you will receive a certificate for the highest award for which you are eligible. Miles do not expire as long as you have flown within the past three years. Award certificates are valid for one year from the issue date, except MileageSaver awards, which are valid for six months. There is a $35 fee for award redeposits, international changes, airport ticketing and expedited service. Stopover awards incur no fee.

Award Redemption: Request awards by calling the appropriate award desk. Allow two weeks. Expedited two-day delivery is $35/U.S., $40/Canada & Hawaii, $50/other locations–all payable by credit card when ordered by phone or by check payable to Continental OnePass when ordered by mail.

Airline Affiliations–Miles & Redemption: Aer Lingus, Aerolinas Argentina, Air Canada, Alitalia, America West, BWIA, GP Express, Iberia, Frontier, Lan Chile, Malaysia, Qantas and SAS.

Airline Affiliations–Miles Only: SkyWest Airlines.

Car Rental Affiliations: Avis, Europcar, Hertz, National, Nippon, Thrifty and Tilden. Hertz gives 500 miles; other agencies give 750 miles at participating locations in conjunction with and within 24 hours of a Continental or partner flight. Thrifty gives 500 miles with no flight conjunction requirements.

Hotel Affiliations: Aston Deluxe, Fiesta Inns, Marriott, Radisson and Sheraton give 500 miles per stay. Camino Real Hotels, Fiesta Americana, Melia and Sol Hotels give 1,000 miles per stay, all subject to eligible rates. Some hotel partners require a flight in conjunction with the stay.

Credit Card Affiliations: Continental OnePass Marine Midland Standard and Gold Visa and MasterCard, 800-850-3144, give one mile per $1 charged. Diners Club

converts Club Reward points to OnePass miles–two points equal one mile. American Express converts Membership Miles into OnePass miles on an equal basis.

Phone Service Affiliations: five miles per $1 spent on Capital TeleTravel long-distance plus 2,500 sign-up bonus. Five miles per dollar spent on MCI residential long-distance service plus 500 mile sign-up bonus.

Other Affiliations: A $29.99 Flower Club order earns 300 miles plus 100 miles for each additional $10 spent.

Delta SkyMiles

Hartsfield Atlanta International Airport, Dept. 745
P. O. Box 20532
Atlanta, GA 30320-2532
Domestic Reservations: 800-221-1212
International Reservations: 800-241-4141
Service Center: 800-323-2323
Automated Service: 800-325-3999

Award Requirements: 25,000/domestic coach; 50,000/European coach; 30,000/Hawaiian coach; 10,000/domestic upgrade.

Minimum Miles: 500 per qualifying Delta or Delta Connection flight. Actual flight mileage for airline partner flights except Singapore Airlines which does not credit coach miles. Class of service bonuses with Delta and most partner airlines (except Aeromexico, Austrian and Finnair): 50% for First Class; 25% for Business Class. Some international airline partners only give miles on certain fares and offer reduced class of service bonuses.

Policies: Account may be cancelled with no activity within 12 months of enrollment. Miles do not expire providing you have flown within the past three years. Certificates must be ticketed for travel

---

Color of the "black box" which records vital flight information on all commercial flights: orange.

within one year from issue date. Award tickets are good for one year.

Award Redemption: Mail completed award request from your statement and allow two to three weeks. Tickets can be issued at ticket offices or airport ticket counters. Expedited delivery for flight certificates can be redeemed at ticket counters and city ticket offices for $60. There is no fee for expedited upgrades. Express mail expedited service is $35 per account transaction for general members; $20 for Medallion/Royal Medallion members–each payable by credit card. Awards are processed within 48 hours of receipt.

Airline Affiliations–Miles & Redemption: Air New Zealand, Aeromexico, ANA, Austrian Air Lines, Finnair, Sabena, Singapore, Swissair and Varig.

Car Rental Affiliations: Alamo, Avis and Hertz give 500 miles per rental with a flight in conjunction with the rental.

Hotel Affiliations: two and a half miles per stay at Holiday Inn; 65 miles per stay at Holiday Inn Express; 500 miles per night at Inter-Continental; 250 miles per stay at Forte Hotels. Five hundred miles per stay at Courtyard, Crowne Plaza, Fairfield Inn, Hilton/ Conrad International, Hyatt, Le Meridien, Marriott, Preferred, Radisson, Sheraton and Swissotel. Seventeen-hundred-and-fifty-mile bonus option after 12th Courtyard stay; 1,000 miles after 12th Fairfield Inn stay. Conjunction flights not required.

Credit Card Affiliations: Delta SkyMiles American Express, 800-759-6453, gives one mile per $1 spent. American Express Membership Miles convert to SkyMiles on an equal basis. Diners Club converts Club Reward points to SkyMiles–two points equal one mile.

Phone Service Affiliations: five miles per $1 spent on AT&T long distance on $25 minimum monthly billing; five miles for each AT&T True Rewards point.

Other Affiliations: Special credits on Renaissance Cruise Lines promotional bookings. Three hundred miles for a $29.99 Flower Club order plus 100 miles for each additional $10.

Midwest Express Frequent Flyer

P. O. Box 37136
Milwaukee, WI 53237-0136
Reservations: 800-452-2022
Service Center: 800-452-2022
Fax: 414-747-0192

Minimum Miles: 500 on Midwest Express and Skyway Airlines. Other airline partners give actual miles.

Policies: Miles do not expire providing you have flown within the past three years. Certificates are valid for one year from issue date.

Award Redemption: Mail or fax award request form from statement to the service center. Qualifying miles from Midwest Express and Northwest can be combined for awards on Midwest or Northwest flights for $50. Allow two to three weeks for Midwest Express awards, six weeks for partner awards and four weeks for combined mileage awards. Tickets are issued at airport ticket counters or city ticket offices. Expedited service is $35, payable by credit card or check, with delivery within three business days. Award requests are processed immediately on receipt.

Airline Affiliations–Miles & Redemption: Air New Zealand, Northwest, Skyway Airlines, Swissair and Virgin Atlantic.

Car Rental Affiliations: Alamo, Avis, Hertz and National give 500 miles at participating locations. Rentals must be within 24 hours of a Midwest Express or Skyway Airlines flight.

Hotel Affiliations: The American Club, Grand Geneva Resort, Heidel House, Loews, The Pfister, and Wyndham. Earn 500 miles per stay at participating partner locations. Stays do not have to be in conjunction with flights.

Credit Card Affiliations: one mile for each $1 charged on the Midwest Express Elan MasterCard, 800-388-4044, plus a sign-up bonus of 1,000-2,500 miles, depending on the type of card you select. Double miles when you purchase Midwest Express and Skyway Airline tickets using your Midwest Express Elan card. Diners Club converts Club Reward points to miles–two points equal one mile.

Phone Service Affiliations: five miles per $1 spent on MCI residential long distance plus a 500-mile enrollment bonus.

Other Affiliations: Holidays with Style tour bookings earn 500 miles. Midwest Parcel Express usage earns 50 miles. Three hundred miles given for minimum $29.99 order from Midwest Express Flower Club. Varying points awarded for Amtrak travel.

Northwest WorldPerks

P. O. Box 11001
St. Paul, MN 55111-0001
Reservations: 800-225-2525
Service Center/Award Reservations:
800-447-3757
Fax: 612-727-4245
Automated Service: 800-327-2881

Award Requirements: 25,000/domestic coach; 35,000/European coach; 40,000/Hawaiian coach; 20,000/domestic upgrade.

Minimum Miles: Northwest/NW Airlink gives 500 minimum miles. A 50% bonus for First Class; 25% for Business Class. KLM, flights between Europe and Africa, the Indian subcontinent, and South and Central America may be limited to 3,000 miles. Aloha operated/Northwest designated flights give 250 minimum miles. KLM flights between Europe and Africa, the Indian subcontinent and South and Central America give a 100% bonus for World Business Class. Alaska Airlines gives actual miles.

Policies: Accounts with no activity for three consecutive years may be cancelled with miles forfeited. Miles earned after Jan. 31, 1995 expire on January 1 of the third year after accrual. Certificates are good for one year from date of issue.

Award Redemption: Tickets are issued at city ticket offices or by the service center. International flights must be ticketed at the service center. Tickets are delivered via U.S. mail to the member's address. Expedited service (two-day minimum) requires a $50 fee payable by check, money order or credit card. Three-day service is $35 via Federal Express and same day service, $60.

Airline Affiliations–Miles & Redemption: Air New Zealand, Air UK, Alaska Airlines, Aloha, America West, Asiana, Horizon, KLM, Midwest Express, Northwest Airlink, Pacific Island Aviation and USAir.

Car Rental Affiliations: Alamo, Avis, Europcar, Hertz and National give 500 miles per rental from participating locations. Rental must be in conjunction with Northwest, KLM, or partner airline flights and be booked within 24 hours of arrival.

Hotel Affiliations: Two and a half miles per $1 spent at Crowne Plaza; 65 miles per stay at Holiday Inn Express; 500 miles per stay at Hilton, Holiday Inn, Hyatt, Marriott, New Otani, Peabody, Radisson,

Sheraton, Shangri-La, Trans-States and Westin. All hotel partners except Holiday Inn and Radisson require a flight in conjunction with your stay.

Credit Card Affiliations: Northwest WorldPerks Visa, 800-360-2900, gives a 1,000-mile sign-up bonus plus one mile per $1 charged. Diners Club converts Club Reward points to WorldPerks miles –two points equal one mile.

Phone Service Affiliations: five miles per $1 charged on MCI residential long distance and MCI F&F pagers.

Other Affiliations: 500-2,500 miles for World Vacations packages. Two miles per $1 spent with Dining for Miles. Three hundred miles for Flower Club orders of $29.99 plus 100 miles for each additional $10 spent.

Southwest Rapid Rewards

P. O. Box 36657
Dallas, TX 75235-1657
Reservations: 800-435-9792
Service Center: 800-445-5764

Award Requirement: 16 credits equal one free roundtrip.

Minimum Miles: The program is operated on a credit system: one credit per segment flown.

Policies: Credits expire one year from the date of your first flight. Award tickets are valid for one year from issue date.

Award Redemption: An actual ticket is automatically issued when 16 credits have been earned. You can reserve a specific roundtrip or use your award ticket for any available seat by presenting it at the ticket counter. Southwest does not limit seats available for award travel. Expedited mail service is $12 with a maximum 14-day processing time and one to two business

days for express mail.

Car Rental Affiliations: Eligible rentals from Alamo, Budget and Hertz earn one credit.

Credit Card Affiliations: Diners Club converts 2,000 Club Reward points to one Rapid Rewards credit. American Express Membership Miles converts 1,250 miles to one Rapid Rewards credit.

Phone Service Affiliations: one credit for every $150 spent on MCI residential long distance.

TWA Frequent Flight Bonus

P.O. Box 800
Fairview Village, PA 19409
Domestic Reservations: 800-221-2000
International Reservations: 800-892-4141
Service Center: 800-325-4815
Fax: 610-631-5280

Enrollment Bonus: 3,000 miles after your first flight.

Award Requirements: 20,000/domestic coach; 35,000/European coach; 40,000/ Hawaiian coach; 20,000/domestic upgrade.

Minimum Miles: 750 on TWA and TWExpress. Partners give actual miles. First Class bonus of 50%; 25% for Business Class.

Policies: No expiration. Award certificates must be redeemed within 12 months of issue date unless specifically exempted. Award tickets are valid for one year from issue date.

Award Redemption: Mail or fax the completed request form to the service center for TWA and partner awards. If the request is for the exact member or a family member with the same surname, it can be made by phone. Allow four weeks for processing. Certificates will be sent to the address on your account. If requested travel dates are not available you can exchange your certificate for a ticket at any TWA ticket office at the time of travel. Expedited service is $50, payable by credit card. Tickets for travel within seven days can be delivered next day if your request is called in before 2 p.m. (CST). Requests made after 2 p.m. or for travel within eight to 21 days will get two-day delivery. Airport pick-up is available for U.S. members only for $100, payable by credit card. Allow two to three days for processing on airport pickups.

Airline Affiliations–Miles & Redemption: Aerolinas Argentina, Air India, Alaska Airlines, Horizon Air, Ladeco Chilean Airlines, Philippine Airlines and TWExpress.

Car Rental Affiliations: Alamo, Avis and Thrifty give 500 miles per rental at participating locations. Some partners require a flight in conjunction with your rental. Thrifty gives 750 miles with a flight requirement. Rentals must be within 24 hours of a TWA or TWE flight and have specific rate requirements.

Hotel Affiliations: 500 miles per night at Inter-Continental Hotels. Five hundred miles per stay at Adam's Mark, Forte, Marriott and Radisson Hotels. Flights in conjunction with your stay are not required by most properties but there may be rate requirements.

Credit Card Affiliations: TWA EAB Visa or MasterCard, 800-322-8921, gives one mile per $1 charged. Diners Club converts Club Reward points to Frequent Flight Bonus miles–two points equal one mile. The TWA Getaway card (an airline charge card good for air travel only) earns one mile for each $1 charged.

Phone Service Affiliations: 2,000-mile enrollment bonus with Sprint, plus five

miles per $1 spent on residential long distance. Members who reside outside the U.S. get a 1,000 mile sign-up bonus for the TWA/Sprint FONCARD plus five miles for every $1 spent. 1,000 mile enrollment bonus for LDDS WorldCom.

Other Affiliations: A minimum $29.99 purchase from The Flower Club earns 500 miles plus 100 miles for each additional $10 spent. The TWA Business Club gives 5,000 miles with a one-year membership, 10,000 miles with a three-year membership and 15,000 miles with a lifetime membership. TWA Getaway Vacations gives 5,000 miles for each international vacation when your transatlantic flight is on TWA and 2,000 miles for other vacations when you fly TWA.

United Mileage Plus

P.O. Box 28870
Tucson, AZ 85726-8870
Domestic Reservations: 800-241-6522
International Reservations: 800-538-2929
Service Center: 605-399-2400

Award Requirements: 25,000/domestic coach; 50,000/European coach; 35,000/Hawaiian coach; 20,000/domestic upgrade.

Minimum Miles: 500 on United and most partners. A 50% bonus for First Class; 25% for Business Class. Two hundred and fifty on Aloha and National Airlines of Chile flights within Chile; actual miles on flights outside of Chile.

Policies: Miles are automatically converted into AwardCheques, which are valid for three years. All three-year-old miles expire on January 1 of each year. Award tickets must be used within one year of the date issued. Upgrades can be requested when reservations are made in full coach or with any fare if you are a Premier member. Upgrades are confirmed 24-100 hours prior to departure, depending on your membership status.

Award Redemption: Certificates can be ordered by mail or at United ticket airport and city ticket locations. Awards can be express-mailed in two days or automatically transferred to a ticket counter in 24 hours for a $50 fee, payable by credit card.

Airline Affiliations: Air Canada, Air France, ALM Antillean Airlines, Aloha, Ansett, British Midland, Cayman, Gulfstream, Lufthansa, National Airlines of Chile, SAS, Sunaire, Thai, TransBrasil, Transportes Aeromar and United Express.

Car Rental Affiliations: Earn 500 miles at participating Alamo, Avis, Budget, Dollar, Hertz and National locations. Some agencies require rental within 24 hours of qualifying flights.

Hotel Affiliations: 500 miles per night at Inter-Continental hotels. Five hundred miles per eligible stay at Deneure, Forum, Groupo Sol, Hilton/Conrad International, Holiday Inn, Hyatt, Libertel, Radisson, The Ritz-Carlton, Shangri La, Sheraton, Vista and Westin. Hotel stays do not have to be in conjunction with a flight.

Credit Card Affiliations: United Mileage Plus Visa, 800-752-8888, gives one mile per $1 charged plus a variable enrollment bonus. There's a 10,000 mile maximum in a billing period and a 50,000 mile maximum per year (both waived for premium level members). Diners Club converts Club Reward points to miles–two points equal one mile.

Phone Service Affiliations: five miles per $1 spent on AT&T long distance or monthly bills over $25. One AT&T True Rewards point converts to five Mileage Plus miles.

Other Affiliations: 800-FLOWERS gives 300 miles with a minimum $29.99 order. Special promotions award miles

from Crystal, Norwegian, Renaissance and Royal Cruise Lines. Elite level frequent flyers earn ten miles per $1 spent at participating restaurants.

USAir Frequent Traveler

P.O. Box 5
Winston-Salem, NC 27102-0005
Reservations: 800/428-4322
Service Center: 800-872-4738

Enrollment Bonus: 2,000 miles.

Award Requirements: 25,000/domestic coach; 40,000/European coach.

Minimum Miles: 500 on USAir, USAir Express and USAir Shuttle. Partner airlines give actual miles. Fifty percent bonus for First Class and 25% for Business Class.

Policies: Miles do not expire. Award certificates and tickets must be redeemed within one year of the date issued.

Award Redemption: Mail completed award request on statement or request the form by mail. Award requests are not accepted by telephone. Allow four weeks from receipt of request for processing. Reservations must be made within 30 days. Tickets are issued at city or airport ticket offices or through tickets by mail. Hotel and car rental certificates must be exchanged at check-in. Cruise awards must be redeemed by calling 800-455-0123. Expedited service is $40 for domestic members and $50 for international members, payable by credit card. Allow four business days for delivery.

Airline Affiliations: Air France, Alitalia, ANA, British Airways, LatinPass, Northwest, Qantas, Sabena, Swissair, USAir Express and USAir Shuttle.

Car Rental Affiliations: Alamo, Avis, Hertz, National and Tilden give 500 miles per rental at participating locations.

Rentals must be made within 24 hours of a qualifying USAir flight.

Hotel Affiliations: Earn 500 miles per stay at participating Courtyard, Fairfield Inn, Hilton/Conrad International, Hyatt, Marriott, Omni, Radisson, Renaissance and Westin hotels. May earn 1,750 bonus miles after your 12th Courtyard stay and 1,000 miles after your 12th Fairfield Inn stay. Some partners require stays within 24 hours of a paid, qualifying flight and have specific rate requirements.

Credit Card Affiliations: USAir/Nationsbank Visa, 800-294-0849, gives one mile per $1 charged. American Express converts their miles to USAir miles on an equal basis. Diners Club converts Club Reward miles to Frequent Traveler miles–two points equal one mile.

Phone Service Affiliations: five miles per $1 spent on AT&T residential long distance on monthly bills $25 and over; ten miles per $1 on monthly bills over $75. One AT&T True Rewards Point equals five Frequent Traveler miles.

Other Affiliations: The Flower Club gives 300 miles for a minimum $29.99 purchase.

INTERNATIONAL AIRLINE FREQUENT FLYER PROGRAMS

Aer Lingus TAB

122 East 42nd Street
New York, NY 10068-0016
Reservations: 800-223-6537
Service Center: 212-557-1090

Minimum Miles: Varies by destination. Business Class fares earn a 100% bonus.

Car Rental Affiliations: Avis, Europcar and Hertz, only in conjunction with an Aer Lingus flight.

Hotel Affiliations: The Jury Hotel Group, with some rates not allowing miles.

Aeromexico Club Premier

P.O. Box 922016
Houston, TX 77292-2016
Reservations: 800-237-6639
Service Center: 800-247-3737
Fax: 713-939-7242

Minimum Kilometers: 1,000 on most Aeromexico and partner airline flights; 25% bonus for First Class within Mexico; 50% for international First Class and for America West First Class of full fare coach.

Policies: one flight per year required to keep account active. Kilometers expire two years from date of accrual. Award tickets are valid for one year from the date issued.

Award Redemption: Request by phone, fax or mail. When requesting by fax or mail, include signature, account number, and PIN. Awards are sent within ten business days. Express award delivery is available in the U.S. for $25 handling plus a courier fee, payable by credit card only.

Airline Affiliations–Kilometers & Redemption: Aeroperu, Air France, America West, British Airways, Delta, Japan and Mexicana.

Airline Affiliations–Kilometers Only: Aerolitoral and Aeromar.

Car Rental Affiliations: Avis and Budget give 625 miles at participating locations in Mexico; 500 miles at participating locations outside Mexico. Avis miles can also be used in conjunction with American West flights. Rentals must be within 24 hours of an Aeromexico or selected partner flight.

Hotel Affiliations: Earn 500 miles per night at Inter-Continental Hotels. Earn 500 miles for stays outside Mexico or 1,000 kilometers for stays within Mexico at Crowne Plaza, Fiesta Americana, Fiesta Inn, Holiday Inn and Radisson. Your hotel stay must be within 24 hours of an Aeromexico or selected partner flight.

Credit Card Affiliations: American Express Membership Rewards converts their miles into Aeromexico kilometers on an equal basis. The Banca Serfin Visa credits 1.6 kilometers per $1 spent.

Phone Service Affiliations: eight kilometers per $1 spent with Globe One.

Air Canada Aeroplan

P.O. Box 15,000
St. Laurent Quebec Canada H4Y1H5
Reservations: 800-776-3000
Service Center: 800-361-8253
Fax: 514-395-2496
Automated Service: 800-361-8253

Minimum Miles: Within Canada, discount fares earn 50% of regular miles; all other flights earn 500 minimum miles. A 50% bonus for First Class; 25% for Executive First and Business Class.

Policies: Some airline partners require Canadian residency for mileage accrual. By law, all Canadian frequent flyer programs must have an end-date but the mileage expiration date has always been extended annually. Award certificates are valid for one year from the date issued, unless otherwise stated.

Award Redemption: Award certificate requests by mail or fax require three to four weeks processing. Requests may also be made by telephone. Award certificates must be redeemed at ticketing offices or authorized travel agencies within 21 days of issue date. Requests made four to 14

business days prior to departure can receive expedited service for $35 Canadian, payable by credit card. AeroRush service for Air Canada and Air Canada Connector tickets is available via airport and ticket offices in four days or less for $75 Canadian. Requests made within 36 hours of departure cannot be guaranteed.

Airline Affiliations–Miles & Redemption: Air Canada Connectors, Air Creebec, Air Schefferville, Austrian Air, Bearskin Airlines, Cathay Pacific, Continental, Finnair, First Air, Interprovincial, norOntair, Swissair, United and Vista Airlines.

Airline Affiliations–Miles Only: British Midland, Royal Jordanian, Iberia and Korean Air.

Car Rental Affiliations: Avis and Budget give 500 miles when you rent from participating locations. Rentals do not have to be in conjunction with flights. Not valid on certain discounted rates.

Hotel Affiliations: 1,000 miles per stay at Sheraton; 250 miles at Holiday Inn Express; 500 miles per stay at Crowne Plaza, Hilton/Conrad International, Holiday Inn, Hotel Des Gouverneurs, Marriott, Ocean Pointe Resort, Radisson, Regina Inn, The Charlottetown, United and Westin. Your stay does not have to be in conjunction with a flight. Not valid on certain discounted rates.

Credit Card Affiliations: one mile per $1 charged on Diners Club/en Route and CIBC Aerogold Visa (Canadian residents only). Diners Club converts Club Reward points for U.S. residents only–two points equal one Aeroplan mile.

Phone Service Affiliations: five miles per $1 spent on Unitel residential long distance.

Other Affiliations: 2,500 miles on Air Canada Vacations. One mile per $1 spent with Air Canada Collection Catalogues. One mile per dollar spent ($100 minimum) with Air Canada In-Flight Duty & Tax Free Boutique. Two hundred and fifty miles when you use Park 'N Fly.

Air France Frequence Plus

Paris Nord II-BP
60082 - 95973 Roissy
Charles-de-Gaulle Cedex, France
Reservations: 800-237-2747
Service Center: 800-237-2747
Fax/France: 33-(1)-49-38-64-00

Enrollment Bonus: 3,000 miles.

Minimum Miles: 1,000. First Class and Concorde earn 150% bonus miles; Business Class, 100% bonus miles.

Policies: Mileage expires two calendar years from date of travel.

Award Redemption: Complete award request application and return to an Air France agent or mail to the service center. Tickets are mailed to the member or can be picked up at an Air France office within three weeks. No expedited service available.

Airline Affiliations: Aero Mexico, Air Canada, Air France, Air Inter and Eurowings.

Car Rental Affiliations: Avis and Hertz give 100-400 miles depending on rental rate. Rentals must be in conjunction with Air France flights.

Hotel Affiliations: Le Meridien and Forte Grand. A free-night voucher is given after five stays at partner hotels–L'Invitation or Carte Noire–or exchanged for 4,000 miles.

Credit Card Affiliations: European residents with American Express cards can convert Membership Miles into Frequence Plus miles. Diners Club converts Club rewards points to Air France miles.

Other Affiliations: Varying miles awarded for Euro Disney ticket purchases.

All Nippon Goldpass

2050 West 190th Street, Suite 100
Torrance, CA 90504-6228
Reservations: 800-235-9262
Service Center: 800-262-4653
Fax: 310-782-3185

Enrollment Bonus: 2,500 miles.

Minimum Miles: Actual miles in Economy Class; 70% of miles in discount Economy Class. First Class provides a 50% bonus; Business Class, 25%.

Asiana Bonus Club

3530 Wilshire Boulevard, Suite 145
Los Angeles, CA 90010
Reservations: 800-227-4262
Service Center: 213-365-4516

Minimum Miles: 500. Business Class earns a 25% bonus; First Class, 50%.

Airline Affiliations–Miles & Redemption: Northwest.

Car Rental Affiliations: Hertz Korea and National/Nippon give 500 miles per qualifying rental.

Hotel Affiliations: 500 miles per stay at Alana Waikiki and participating Holiday Inns, Radissons and Westins.

Phone Service Affiliations: 500 mile enrollment bonus with MCI plus mileage credit varying by plan.

British Airways Executive Club–USA Program

P.O. Box 1757
Minneapolis, MN 55440-1757
Reservations: 800-452-1201
Service Center: 800-955-2748

Minimum Miles: Actual miles on long haul flights and all Qantas and Alaska flights. A minimum 500 miles on short haul flights and USAir, TAT and Deutsche BA flights. British Airways First Class and Concorde earn a 50% bonus; Club World and Club Europe, 25%. Qantas, Alaska/Horizon and USAir First Class earn a 50% bonus; Qantas and USAir Business Class earns a 25% bonus.

Policies: Must reside in the U.S., Bahamas, Bermuda, or Puerto Rico. Accounts inactive for five years expire. Award certificates and tickets are valid one year from date issued.

Award Redemption: Order by phone or mail. British Airway tickets require two weeks. Other words require three to four weeks. Tickets are sent to the member's address. Seven to ten-day service is available for $50, payable by credit card.

Airline Affiliations–Miles & Redemption: Aeromexico, Alaska, Qantas and USAir.

Airline Affiliations–Miles Only: Deutsche BA and TAT European Airlines.

Car Rental Affiliations: Alamo and Hertz give 500 miles per eligible rental at participating locations. Rental must occur within 24 hours of a British Airways flight.

Hotel Affiliations: 500 miles per stay at Hilton/Conrad International, Mandarin Oriental, Marriott, Radisson/Edwardian, Ritz- Carlton, The Savoy Group, Southern Sun and Taj Hotels. Not all rates are eligi-

ble. Stays do not need to be in conjunction with a flight to earn miles.

Credit Card Affiliations: one mile per $1 charged on BA/Chase Visa. Diners Club converts club Reward points to Executive Club miles.

Phone Service Affiliations: one AT&T True Rewards point converts to five miles.

Other Affiliations: 30-750 miles at Travelex Foreign Currency Exchanges (depending on amount exchanged). Three hundred miles for minimum $29.99 order with the Flower Club plus 100 miles per additional $10 spent. Two hundred miles per booking at Camelot Chauffeur Drive. Miles are also awarded for some transactions with Abercrombie & Kent International, Cunard Cruise Line and Venice Simplon-Orient Express.

Canadian Plus

P.O. Box 7737 STN MAIN
Vancouver BC Canada V6BSW9
Reservations/Service Center:
800-426-7007
Fax: 604-270-5476

Minimum Miles: Miles are tabulated as points. Two hundred minimum on Canadian and most domestic partners; 50% bonus for First Class; 25% for Business Class; a 500-minimum points on American/American Eagle and Aloha. Actual points on Air Labrador or 500 points on full fares.

Policies: National law requires an expiration date each year, which is traditionally extended. Award certificates and tickets are valid one year from date issued.

Award Redemption: Requests by mail will be responded to within three days. Tickets can be picked up at travel agencies or ticket offices. American Airlines and Canadian Holidays awards tickets must be issued directly by Canadian. Two to five-day service on tickets and award certificates is $35 Canadian, payable by credit card.

Airline Affiliations–Miles & Redemption: Air Alma, Air Atlantic, Air Labrador, Air New Zealand, Aloha, American/American Eagle, Calm Air, Canadian Regional Airlines, Island Air, Lufthansa, Mandarin Airlines, North-Wright Air, Pem-Air, Ptarmigan Airways, Qantas and Varig.

Car Rental Affiliations: 500 points at participating Europcar, National, Thrifty and Tilden locations. Rentals do not have to be in conjunction with a flight.

Hotel Affiliations: 500 points per night at Inter-Continental Hotels. Five hundred points per stay at Albatross/Gander, Cambridge Suites, Canadian Pacific, Coast Hotels, Delta Hotels, The Evaz Group, Forum Hotels, Inter-Canadian, Ramada, Shangri-La and West Coast Hotels. Stays don't have to be in conjunction with a flight.

Credit Card Affiliations: 2,500-point sign-up bonus plus one point per $1 Canadian on Royal Trust Visa. American Express (AMEX Bank of Canada) converts Membership Rewards points into Canadian Plus points on an equal basis.

Phone Service Affiliations: Long distance points varying by plan with BCTel, MT&T, MTS, NMTel and SakTel.

Other Affiliations: 250 points per one-way ticket with Brewster Transportation & Tours and for each Park & Jet, Aeropark and YVR Park usage. One point per $1 spent with AMJ Campbell/Atlas Van Lines. Three hundred points for $30 Canadian order with Flowers 24 Hours; 100 additional points per $10 spent. Varying points per membership level for Canadian Holidays packages.

Finnair Plus

228 East 45th Street
New York, NY 10017
Reservations: 800-950-5000
Service Center: 800-950-3387
Fax: 212-499-9036

Minimum Miles: Actual miles. Business Class provides a 100% bonus.

Airline Affiliations–Miles & Redemption: Lufthansa.

Car Rental Affiliations: Avis, Europcar, Hertz, National Interrent (U.S.) and Tilden Interrent (Canada) give 500 miles per rental at participating locations. Rentals must be in conjunction with flights.

Hotel Affiliations: 500 miles per night at Arctia Hotels, Hotel Inter-Continental, Hotel Savoy/Moscow, Hotel Scandic Crown/London and Scandic Hotels in Gothenburg and Malmo.

JAL Mileage Bank Americas

300 Continental Boulevard, Suite 401
El Segunda, CA 90245
Reservations: 800-525-3663
Service Center: 800-525-6453
Fax: 310-414-0149

Enrollment Bonus: 5,000 miles after your first flight.

Minimum Miles: 500. Actual miles in Full Fare Economy; 70% in Discount Economy. Fifty percent bonus for First Class; 25% for Business Class.

Policies: Mileage expires at the end of the second calender year. Award certificates are valid for three months from the date issued (travel must be completed within six months). Positive-space upgrade certificates are valid three months from date of issue, space-available upgrades one year and hotel awards six months.

Award Redemption: Order by phone, mail or fax at least three weeks prior to departure date. Tickets can be issued at any JAL ticket office. Expedited service is not available.

Airline Affiliations–Miles & Redemption: Air France and American.

Airline Affiliations–Redemption Only: Aeromexico and Aeroperu.

Hotel Affiliations: Nikko Hotels give 1000 miles. Hotel New Otani Tokyo gives 500 miles.

Korean Air Skypass

FTBS Mileage Dividend Program
Passenger Marketing Department
1813 Wilshire Boulevard
Los Angeles, CA 90057
Reservations: 213-484-5780
Service Center: 213-484-5780
Fax: 213-484-5790

Minimum Miles: 500, First Class bonus is 50%; Business Class, 25%.

Policies: Miles do not expire. Award tickets must be used within three months of issue date, and three 90-day extensions may be requested for a particular award. The first extension is free and can be validated at the ticket counter. Each subsequent deducts 5,000 miles from the member's account. Requests must be made through the service center and made two weeks in advance of the current expiration date.

Award Redemption: Tickets are issued at the local office, or by mail. If the award request is made at a Korean Air office it will take one week to process; two weeks if mailed. Car rental and hotel awards must accompany a request for a flight award and be used in conjunction. Expedited service is not available.

Car Rental Affiliations: 100 miles per

rental day for a maximum of seven consecutive days at participating Korean Rent A Car locations. Rentals do not have to be in conjunction with a flight.

Hotel Affiliations: 300 miles per night at KAL Hotels, the Omni Los Angeles, the Sheraton Anchorage and the Waikiki Resort Honolulu. Maximum of 15 consecutive nights. Stays do not have to be in conjunction with a flight.

LatinPass

1600 NW LeJeune Road
Miami, FL 33166
Service Center: 800-445-2846

Minimum Miles: 500 on international flights, actual mileage on domestic. First Class earns a 50% bonus, and Business Class earns 25%.

Airline Affiliations: Aces, APA, Avianca, Aviateca, BWIA, Copa, Faucett, Lacsa, Ladeco, Lloyd Aero Boliviano, LANChile, Mexicana, Nica, Saeta, Taca and USAir.

Car Rental Affiliations: 500 miles for an Avis rental or a Hertz rental in Latin or North America and the Caribbean.

Hotel Affiliations: 500 miles per stay at Radisson. One mile per $1 spent at Holiday Inns. Sixty-five miles per night at Holiday Inn Express.

Credit Card Affiliations: Diners Club Club Rewards and American Express Membership Miles convert to LatinPass miles.

Phone Service Affiliations: five miles per $1 spent with AT&T residential long distance.

Lufthansa Miles & More

P.O. Box 243
East Meadow, NY 11554-1096

Reservations: 800-645-3880
Service Center: 800-581-6400
Fax: 516-296-9474

Minimum Miles: Lufthansa and most European partners give 500-1,000 minimum in coach; double miles in Business Class. 200% bonus for First Class; 100% in Business Class. Canadian gives 500 miles minimum on short hauls and 1,000 on long hauls. United gives 1,000 minimum on domestic U.S. flights. Varig gives actual miles. First Class earns a 200% bonus; Business Class, 100%.

Policies: Miles expire two years from date accrued. Certificates for flights and upgrades are valid six months from date issued. Certificates issued for non-airline partners are valid for 12 months. Award tickets are valid for one year.

Award Redemption: Redeem by mail or phone. Make your requests at least 14 days in advance. If an award ticket is not issued within 21 days of your reservation, the reservation is cancelled. Tickets are mailed to the member's address. Award certificates can be exchanged for tickets at ticket offices or airport ticket counters. Phone orders are sent by mail. Expedited service is available for a fee.

Airline Affiliations–Miles & Redemption: Air Dolomiti, Business Air, Canadian Airlines, Eurowings, Finnair, Lauda Air, Luxair, ModiLuft, Thai International, Tyrolean, SAS, United/United Express and Varig.

Car Rental Affiliations: 500 miles per qualifying rental at participating Avis, Budget and Sixt locations. Rentals do not have to be in conjunction with a flight.

Hotel Affiliations: 500 miles per qualifying stay at Forum, Hilton/Conrad International, Inter-Continental, Holiday Inn, Kempinski, Luxury Collection, Marriott, Ramada International,

Renaissance, Sheraton and Vista USA. Stays do not have to be in conjunction with a flight.

Mexicana Frecuenta

3201 Cherry Ridge Drive, Suite 200
San Antonio, TX 78230
Reservations: 800-531-7921
Service Center: 800-531-7901

Enrollment Bonus: 6,400 kilometers.

Minimum Kilometers: 1,000 per flight. Y Fare International earns a 50% bonus; Mexican Republic Y fares: 25% bonus.

Affiliated Airlines–Kilometers & redemption: Aeromar, Aeromexico and Mexicana Inter.

Car Rental Affiliations: 1,000 kilometers per rental at participating Avis and Executive Car Rental locations.

Hotel Affiliations: 1,000 kilometers per stay at Camino Real, El Cid Mega Resorts, Fiesta Americana, Fiesta Inns, Hilton/Conrad, Presidente Inter-Continental, Radisson and Maeva hotels.

Credit Card Affiliations: BITAL MasterCard. American Express membership Rewards converts to Frecuenta kilometers. Diners Club converts 2,000 Club Reward points to 1,600 Frecuenta kilometers.

Qantas Frequent Flyer

360 Post Street
San Francisco, CA 94108-9727
Reservations: 800-227-4500
Service Center: 800-348-5607
FAX: 613-820-9690

Minimum Miles: Miles are accrued as points. Full coach earns one point per mile; discount fares earn 70% of actual mileage. First Class earns a 50% bonus;

Business Class, 25%.

Policies: Points are valid for five years. Award tickets are valid for one year.

Award Redemption: Redeem at local reservations offices or by mail. Allow two weeks minimum for delivery. Expedited service is available for a fee.

Airline Affiliations–Points & Redemption: Air Pacific, American, British Air, Canadian, SAS and USAir.

Car Rental Affiliations: eight points for every $1 Australian spent in Australia; 1,000 points for international rentals with participating Australia and Thrifty locations. Rentals must be in conjunction with a flight.

Hotel Affiliations: 500 points per night at Inter-Continental Hotels. Fifteen hundred points per stay at Qantas Resorts and Radissons. Five points per $1 Australian spent in Australia and 500 points a night for stays outside of Australia at Australian Resorts, Burswood Resort Hotels, Country Comfort Inns, Forum, Hilton/Conrad International, Holiday Inn, Hotel Nikko/Sydney, Ibis, Mercure, Novotel, Quality Hotels, Regent International, Rockman's Regency Hotel, Rydges Hotels, Sheraton, Sofitel and Southern Pacific. Stays must be in conjunction with Qantas flights.

Credit Card Affiliations: American Express Membership Miles convert to points on an equal basis.

Phone Service Affiliations: four points per $1 Australian spent with Telecom Australia calling cards.

Sabena Frequent Flyer Programme

P.O. Box 100
Etterbeek 4
B-1040 Brussels, Belgium

Reservations/Service Center:
800-955-2000

Minimum Miles: Miles are accrued as points–400 minimum points per flight. First Class earns a 200% bonus; Business Class, 100%.

Airline Affiliations–Miles & Redemption: Austrian and Swissair.

Car Rental Affiliations: 200-400 points from participating Avis locations.

Hotel Affiliations: 250 points per night with Hilton/Conrad International, Holiday Inn, Sabena and Vista Hotels.

Credit Card Affiliations: 3,000 point enrollment bonus for residents of Belgium and Luxembourg with the Diners Club/Sabena card plus ten points for every 1,000 BEF spent. American Express membership rewards convert to miles for European members.

Other Affiliations: ten points for every 1,000 BEF spent on Transair/Jet packages.

SAS EuroBonus

9 Polito Avenue
Lyndhurst, NJ 07071
Reservations: 800-221-2350
Service Center: 800-348-5607
Fax: 201-896-3725

Enrollment Bonus: 2,500 points.

Minimum Points: 600. EuroClass or full fare tickets earn a 100% bonus.

Policies: Membership may be cancelled with no activity in three years. Points expire on December 31, two years after accrual. Awards are valid for one year from date issued.

Award Redemption: A minimum of seven days advance booking is required. Allow three weeks for delivery. Open vouchers are issued for car rental awards.

Year in which the first regularly scheduled, non-stop transatlantic flights began: 1956.

Make reservations directly with any Radisson SAS Hotel. Make reservations through the service center for other partner hotels. Expedited service is not available.

Airline Affiliations–Points & Redemption: Air New Zealand, British Midland, Continental, Lufthansa, Qantas and Skyways.

Airline Affiliations–Points Only: Icelandair.

Car Rental Affiliations: 500 points for qualifying rentals with Avis and Hertz: in conjunction with an SAS or partner flight or a Radisson SAS Hotel stay.

Hotel Affiliations: 500 points per night at SAS International Hotels. 500 points per qualifying stay at Hilton/Conrad International, Inter-Continental, Radisson, Vista and Swissotels. Stays must be in conjunction with an SAS or a partner flight.

Credit Card Affiliations: Diners Club enrollment earns 2,500 points for residents of the U.K., Ireland, Denmark, Finland, Iceland, Norway and Sweden.

66Remember to keep a close tab on ongoing changes to your frequent flyer programs. Sign-up bonuses and other details of frequent flyer programs may change without notice and the changes aren't always likely to be in your favor. If your program has added new ways to earn miles, you want to know about it. If they've tightened their award terms, you definitely want to know about it. 99

Phone Service Affiliations: 500 points when EuroBonus membership is linked with the Tel2/Cable & Wireless Calling Card plus 500 points per $200 spent.

Virgin Freeway

747 Belden Avenue
Norwalk, CT 06850
Reservations: 800-862-8621
Service Center: 800-365-9500

Enrollment Bonus: 2,000 miles plus 25,000 bonus miles with first Upper Class roundtrip.

Minimum Miles: Actual miles for premium Economy and Mid-class fares. Double miles for Business and Upper Class. Actual miles for Economy if the members fly either one Upper Class or Premium roundtrip or three Economy roundtrips in a one-year period. Actual miles on full fare Air New Zealand and SAS; 500 minimum on British Midland; minimum 1,000 on SAS flights within Europe; 3,000 miles for your first Virgin/SEEA roundtrip to Athens; 50% bonus for SAS EuroClass to Europe or Asia; 100% bonus for Air New Zealand First Class; Business Class, 50%; Economy Class, 25%. Fifty percent bonus for Austrian Business or Grand Class.

Airline Affiliations–Miles & Redemption: Air New Zealand, Austrian, British Midland and SAS.

Airline Affiliations–Redemption Only: Delta and Midwest Express.

Car Rental Affiliation: 500-1,500 miles for qualifying rentals with Avis.

Hotel Affiliations: ten miles per pound spent at Virgin Hotels. One thousand to 6,000 miles per qualifying stay at Blakes, Doyle Hotels, Inter-Continental, Le Manoir aux Quat'Saison, Omni Hotels, Asia Pacific, Radisson/SAS and Summit International Hotels.

Other Redemption Only Affiliations: Eurostar and Radisson/SAS in London.

SOLVING THE HOTEL MYSTERY: 'INN'-SIDER TRADING

This isn't the stock market and all this information is legal! When I travel, I want premium service at top-rated hotels for about half the going rate and that's exactly what I get. I often do live radio shows from my room, so I look for hotels staffed by people willing to make the extra effort to accommodate my needs. I need two separate phone lines and as many in-room business amenities as possible. I won't even consider staying at a hotel that still collects surcharges on telephone calls. My five favorite ways to get premium rooms at discount prices:

Sunday newspaper travel sections and special promotions

50% off Hotel directories offered by membership clubs that discount
the same rooms your travel agent books at double the price.

Booking direct for rates toll free reservation line agents don't even know about.

City discount cards that save money on lodging,
plus offer discounts on dining, entertainment and shopping.

Consolidators whose high volume of business provides 20%-70% off.

Amazingly, a high percentage of travelers actually pay rack rates–the highest possible price. Others settle for the nominal discounts available through corporate rates. These discounts should only be used as last resorts. You gain control over lodging costs by knowing all the discount possibilities and, each time you book, using the one that saves you the most.

A room at The Ritz-Carlton will always cost more than one at Motel 6, but every room can cost you less once you learn the "inn"-sider secrets of the hotel industry. Did you know that...

- **You can stay at higher-amenity hotels that only seem to be out of your price range?**

- **Business travelers can save enough each night to cover the cost of three good restaurant meals?**

- **Families can get deals like a room for four near Disney World for just $39 a night, including meals for the kids.?**

- **Staying at a $40 a night budget hotel can give you $75 off your next airline ticket?**

- **A free added night at an all-inclusive luxury resort can give you an extra day in paradise without the extra $400 cost?**

The first four sections of this chapter are all about getting the best rates. They explain the secrets mentioned above, all the standard discounts and other creative ways to virtually set your own rates.

Other Lodging Options **also tells you about alternative lodging** for leisure travel and how the cost of any family vacation can be reduced by using them.

'Inn'-sider Info **tells you how to avoid the over billing** that appears on 30%-40% of all hotel bills. It also updates you on business amenities, the phone surcharge situation, hidden costs, non-smoking rooms, and other key factors that can make or break any hotel stay.

Hotel Highlights **looks at all the major hotel chains** and lets you know what they're offering in the way of corporate, senior and frequent guest programs; rate breaks; and amenities. It explains the wide range of prices available within some hotel chains and lets you know what the average rack rate is at all of them.

International Tidbits covers the how-to's of obtaining great deals in other countries for business travel, leisure travel and extended stays.

You have more control over the price of a night's stay than you realize. Check-in to this section and you can rest easy, knowing that you've paid the lowest possible price for every room you book.

CLUES TO THE BEST BARGAINS

S UNDAY TRAVEL SECTIONS

While you're planning your trip, check the Sunday travel section hotel ads in your destination city and nearby cities. For example, if you're traveling to Los Angeles, check the papers for Los Angeles, San Diego or San Francisco; if you're traveling to New York check Boston or Washington, D.C.. Though designed to fill rooms with local and area residents, these discounts can pay big dividends to the opportunistic "inn"-sider.

Access these papers at newsstands or libraries. Your best bet is to begin checking several weeks in advance and check weekly until you find the ad that fits your needs.

5 0%-OFF HOTEL DIRECTORIES

Hotel discount directories and the ability to book rooms at up to 50% off are available via memberships that usually run from 12-15 months. You're issued a listing of all participating hotels and a membership card. Most travel agents will not book rooms through hotel directories because the agent gets no commission and must call each hotel direct. You can use these programs by phoning or faxing the hotel, giving them your membership number, and checking on available space. If they have availability on the night(s) you need, the room is yours for up to 50% off. These discounts are usually available when the hotels' projected occupancy for the nights you wish to book fall below 80%. During major events you may have difficulty locating a room under this program. Programs include:

- **America at 50%**, 800-248-2783, discounts over 1,200 budget properties. $19.95 per year provides discounts on hotel, car, RV and condo rentals. Lodging discounts are in the ten to 25 percent range.

- **Carte Royale**, 800-847-7002, offers discounts at 350 first-class and deluxe hotels. Membership is $69 per year; $49.95 for two years if you pay with MasterCard.

- **Encore**, 800-638-0930, offers discounts on over 2,000 hotels plus many second night free deals. Membership is $49 per year. You also get car rental and tour package discounts.

- **Entertainment Publications** 800-445-4137, publishes national and regional editions. The national edition discounts about 1,800 hotels and costs about $45.

- **Great American Traveler**, 800-331-8867, discounts more than 1,400 economy and first-class hotel properties. Membership is $49.95 for the first year; $29.95 each subsequent year.

- **ITC-50**, 800-342-0558, covers about 3800 hotels. It has international listings with particularly good coverage of Asia and the South Pacific. Membership is $36 per year.

The most popular bar drink in U.S. hotels in 1995: margarita; in 1970; the highball.

- **Privilege Card International**, 800-236-9732, provides a directory that discounts about 1,800 hotels. It covers 50 countries including the U.S., the Caribbean, Bermuda, the United Kingdom, Canada and Mexico. Annual membership is $144.

- **Quest**, 800-638-9819, covers over 2,200 hotels for an annual membership fee that varies according to the program you select. Offerings include 25 percent off dining, coupons offering discounts on Northwest Airlines and car rental discounts.

⊙ALL DIRECT

Negotiate directly with the hotel. They're authorized to give deals the 800 lines don't even know about. The on-site staff will also know more about the property, room choices, and specific availability. Call in the early morning or late evening when long distance rates are lower. The favorable discount you'll get by calling direct is likely to be many times the cost of your long distance call. Shop the 800 numbers first to get their best deal and the phone number to the hotel.

Introductory Discounts are worth requesting for your first stay at any hotel. You can almost always get them at boutique hotels such as The Whitehall in Chicago. Hotels want to attract new allegiances, particularly if they believe you travel frequently to their city.

Never pay rack rates–the "retail" prices routinely quoted by agents on 800-number reservation lines. Unless you're trying to find the last room in town for Superbowl weekend, paying rack rate is like agreeing to the asking price on a used car. The average occupancy rate hovers at 69%, so you have room to negotiate and you should. You don't have to possess the negotiating skills of a pro-football player's agent. You just have to learn the possibilities.

⊙ITY DISCOUNT CARDS

City Discount cards are issued by tourism offices. They sometimes take the form of a small card that you show for your discount. Other times, you're given a listing of hotels offering special deals. City discount cards are a particularly good way to get discounts on distinctive hotel properties that may not be part of any hotel chain. Some deals are oriented toward seniors; some to families; some are general use. You'll also get deals on meals and attractions. Discount offers are accessed by calling city or state tourism offices. Their worth varies according to the aggressiveness and innovation of the tourism bureaus and the importance they put on attracting tourists. Business travelers are free to use these discounts.

> **"** Coupon Corner details dozens of these offers and tells you where to call to get them. Also check the "Know Who To Call" section for tourism numbers. **"**

⊙ONSOLIDATORS

Hotel Consolidators provide discounts ranging from 20%-70%. They're able to offer deep discounts to consumers because they guarantee volume business to the hotels they represent. Hotels in turn provide these substantial discounts for this guaranteed business. Part of the savings are passed on to the consumer.

- **Consolidators specialize.** Some serve limited areas; others cover most major cities. Good ones know the cities they serve inside and out. They know the market, the deals and may even be able to find you rooms during special events when availability is difficult. Others offer discounts only when projected occupancy for the date and hotel you request is under 80%.

- **Some consolidators offer two-tiered discounts** using pre-paid vouchers. The higher discount gives you a non-refundable voucher. Vouchers purchased at the lower discount may be refundable.

- **Learn the terms of the consolidator's cancellation policy.** When you book through a consolidator, you're subject to their rules. Make sure you are aware of all requirements.

Hotel Reservations Network, 800-964-6835, is a no-fee service serving London, Paris and U.S. cities including Anaheim, Los Angeles, San Francisco, San Diego, Chicago, Boston, New York, Orlando, Miami Beach, New Orleans, and Washington, DC. Specific rates vary from month to month but discounts can be up to 65%. Here's an example of savings available in December, 1995:

HOTEL RESERVATIONS NETWORK SAVINGS COMPARISONS			
HOTEL	**RACK RATE**	**HRN RATE**	**SAVINGS**
THE COPLEY PLAZA/Boston	$120–145	$85	$35–60
THE TUSCAN INN/San Francisco	$159	$109	$50
HOLIDAY INN SOMERVILLE/Boston	$125–138	$69	$56–69
HILTON & TOWERS/Washington, D.C.	$265	$99	$166
HOWARD JOHNSON/Los Angeles Airport	$58–124	$49	$11-75
ESSEX INN/Chicago	$89–115	$75	$14–40
THE HYATT ISLANDIA/San Diego	$149	$99	$50
THE SIR FRANCIS DRAKE/San Francisco	$140–180	$99	$41–81
THE CALIFORNIAN HOTEL/San Francisco	$85–105	$59	$26–46
THE PARIS HILTON/Paris	$420	$169	$251

Population of Bora Bora: 4,000. Number of hotel rooms: 409.

OTHER WAYS TO SAVE

DAY RATES

Day Rates are available at many hotels. The charge is usually about half the rack rate. Hours of availability vary but usually fall between 7 a.m. and 5 p.m. They're useful for business meetings, leisure travelers who prefer night driving and international travelers dealing with excessive layovers. You can sometimes get corporate and senior discounts on day rates. And yes– you are allowed to sleep on the bed.

PLAN AHEAD

Advance Reservation Rates require booking seven to 30 days in advance. Chains including Marriott, Days Inn and Sheraton often discount 21-day advance reservations as much as 50%. Advance purchase rates are often available at premium business hotels. The Boston Marriott, for example, has a $189 corporate rate that you can beat with a 21-day advance rate of $139.

- **Some advance rates require pre-payment** for your first night's stay.

- **Advance purchase rates** are often non-refundable and unchangeable.

OFF SEASON SAVINGS

It's always off-season somewhere and if you travel regularly you're likely to run into seasonal rate breaks. You'll never know about these rates unless you ask. Business travelers locked into the corporate rate mentality sometimes end up paying more, not less, because habit blinds them to variables like this that can lower rates. The Knickerbockers in Chicago, for example, discounts all rooms in January, February, July and August. If you make a business trip to Chicago each month and pay the same corporate rate each time, you'll miss four months of savings. Here are some places and times when hotel prices should go down:

- **Arizona**–summer, when temperatures routinely rise above 100. You can get ultra-luxury hotels at up to 75% off.

- **Florida**–Easter to mid-December. Daytime temperatures are 80-90 degrees. September and October may be rainy enough to stop tourists, but business travelers will still save.

- **Florida Panhandle**–after Labor Day through early March. Winter highs are in the 60s and 70s.

Number of doors in San Jose's 160-room Winchester House: 2,000.

- **Orlando**–January 7th through February 15th.

- **Southeast Coast**–Labor Day to Memorial Day.

- **New York City**–mid-May to mid-September.

- **Chicago**–January through March.

- **New Orleans**–Memorial Day through Labor Day.

- **Palm Springs**–June to September. Rooms get as cheap as $29 per night.

- **Las Vegas**–After Thanksgiving through December 20th, also weekdays Sunday-Thursday, most anytime when there is no convention in town. Rates during major conventions can soar. Call Las Vegas Convention Bureau to check on convention activity.

- **San Francisco**–November through March.

- **Hawaii**–September and October.

- **Northeast Coast**–Columbus Day to Memorial Day, but be aware that many resort-area hotels close for the winter.

- **Pacific Northwest**–November to April. You can even get Storm Watchers Discounts at coastal hotels.

- **The Caribbean**–Mid-April through October. Room rates are often cut in half, yet there's very little variation in climate. The discounts reflect the lowered demand when North Americans are enjoying their own versions of summer. (Hurricane season generally runs from August to October.)

- **Europe:**

  Rome–July through August.

  Paris–November through March.

  London–November through March

with cheapest rates in January and February, and July and August.

  Athens–November through March.

- **Brazil**–April through November.

- **Jamaica**–May through mid-December, except Thanksgiving.

- **Canada Rockies**–October through April.

- **Mexico**–May through October. Luxury resorts go for as little as $50 per night.

- **Australia & New Zealand**–Fall and winter.

Peak travel periods also contain bargains as hotels compete for tourist bookings. Discounts may also be available at the beginning and end of peak seasons. Skiers, for example, can save 25%-30% in early December, in April and May and all Sundays through Thursdays.

HOLIDAY DISCOUNTS

Holiday rates at resort hotels are as high as demand warrants but business-oriented locations are almost steals. They're open and fully staffed, yet business guests have disappeared. To avoid a five-to-one staff-to-guest ratio, they may offer whatever discount is required to raise the holiday population.

SPECIAL PROMOTIONS

Hotel chains constantly court your business with ever-changing promotions. Stay with them and they may send you a dozen roses, bake you chocolate chip cookies, give you a free cellular phone or hand you a coupon to cut the cost of your next airfare. They'll lower their rates, give you an extra discount for paying with a certain credit card or even give you a second night's lodging free. It's all designed to avoid the hotel manager's recurring nightmare: empty rooms. These limited, promotional offers are advertised in hundreds of daily and monthly publications, tucked in with your credit card statement and added to the reservation systems used by travel agents. *BEST FARES Discount Travel Magazine* details the best of each month's offerings. A recent sampling of some of these offers:

- **A free compact car for the length of your stay** at any participating Outrigger Hotel in Hawaii–the convenience of a rental car with no rental cost.

- **Up to $40 off per night on Hilton Concierge Class upgrades.** These exclusive rooms generally cost at least $60 more than standard rooms. By taking advantage of Hilton's frequent guest coupon book promotion, the upgrade at any Hilton is $20 or less. If you like the security and amenities of concierge floors but don't like the prices, this offer puts them in reach.

- **Your third weekend night free** at select Wyndham Hotels nationwide. Almost all hotels offer weekend rates but you have to ask for this free-night deal specifically.

- **$49 per night at the Tropicana/Las Vegas** when paying by American Express. You save $20 per night just by using a specific credit card.

- **Free day-long tours and free breakfast** at San Francisco's ANA Hotel... at a price below the regular room-only rate.

- **Your choice of a free upgrade or a food and beverage credit** at any Inter-Continental Hotel.

- **Stay across the street from New York's Central Park** for $119 per night. The Mayflower Hotel offers premium class lodging at a hard-to-believe Manhattan price.

- **Stay first-class at London's Gainsborough Hotel** for $109 per night. The only mystery in European hotel reservations is who has the best promotion for the time you want to travel.

- **Stay at participating Loews and Fairmont Hotels** and pay the published hotel rate with your Visa credit card and fly first class on American Airlines with a free one class upgrade.

OWN A PIECE OF THE ROCK

Stockholder Discounts are more and more available as mergers swallow up hotels and hotel chains. Check annual reports to see if you hold stock in a company with a lodging subsidiary. If you own Disney stock, for example, you'll get preferred rates plus a degree of VIP treatment at all Disney hotels. Sometimes as little as one share qualifies you for hotel discounts.

> **❝***Hotel discounts are often overlooked, even by travelers who routinely seek out discounts on airfare. If you're not planning to stay with relatives, the cost of your hotel stay for multi-day trips often will be more than your airline ticket. Why ignore discounts on another high-dollar, travel expense?* **❞**

CHARGE CARD PROMOTIONS

Charge card promotions offer special discounts and value-added features when you pay for your room with a specific credit card. It pays to know about these promotions in advance, so you should always scan your credit and charge card statements to see what travel-related offers are enclosed. Many hotel ads also mention discounts, added-values and other bonuses you can get just for paying for your room with a specific card. Check your frequent flyer statements to see if the airline is offering special inducements when you stay with a particular hotel chain.

Even if you have no advance notice of a charge or credit card discount program, you might still be able to get a discount just by asking the hotel reservationist if there is a special discount program available for using a certain card. Most offers require that the card you use to hold your reservation is the same as the card you use for final payment.

> *"Affinity credit cards are offered by Best Western, Hilton, Marriott, Ramada and other chains. You get hotel points on all your purchases. They are not as beneficial as airline affinity credit cards and there is generally no good reason to use them."*

Recently, ***BEST FARES Discount Travel Magazine*** showed savvy travelers how to take up to two children on a roundtrip flight for $99 each when you buy two moderately priced toys.

Call 800-880-1234 to subscribe.
See page 395 for your discount subscription offer.

Hotel designed as a drive-in theater, serving buttered popcorn: The Best Western Movie Manor in Monte Vista, CA.

STANDARD DISCOUNTS FOR THE ASKING

Standard hotel discounts such as corporate and senior rates are good fallback rates when the best discounts and special promotions aren't available. You can access them directly or get them through travel agents. Some require membership in certain programs (usually free or very low cost) and others are yours just for the asking. Standard discounts are generally available any time a hotel has rooms available.

FOR THE CORPORATE TRAVELER

Corporate Rate discounts of ten to 20 percent are usually yours for the showing of a business card. Major corporations negotiate preferred corporate rates (20%-40% off) in exchange for the promise of high use. Smaller companies that may not get the IBM rate, should get a usable discount for times when better deals aren't available.

Percentage of hotel rooms booked by business travelers: 59%.

- If you're making a business call on another company, ask the hotel about that corporation's discount. You may find that the corporation, due to the large number of guests it sends to the hotel, has negotiated an excellent rate that will beat any rate you can receive on your own.

- Don't assume the corporate rate is lower than the standard rate. It usually is, but a small percentage of hotels actually set corporate rates higher to cover the cost of extra business amenities you may not require.

Frequent Stay and Customer Recognition Programs provide discounts, extra amenities and added values such as upgrades, free meals and other bonuses. Many chains are scaling down frequent guest programs in lieu of bonus airline miles. Surveys indicate that most guests prefer the miles. When it comes to Frequent Guest programs and extra miles, it's an either/or situation, except at Hilton and Westin where you get both. There are still benefits to joining frequent guest clubs, but never make them your reason for choosing a particular hotel.

- The average extra worth of a frequent guest stay is $10 per visit. Some fee-for-membership programs offer per-stay benefits worth more.

- Some hotels only let you accumulate credits for one year. If you don't use them, your balance goes to zero. Others have no expiration date, but if you don't stay at a member hotel at least once in a given year, your account is deactivated.

Airline Affiliate Programs usually provide an added value in the form of 500-1,000 free miles per stay. They are usually offered in lieu of hotel points.

- Some chains, including Hilton, allow you to "Double Dip" (receive hotel points and airline points for the same stay). Intercontinental Hotels usually offer bonus miles for each night's stay (if you stay a required number of nights) rather than one bonus per stay. Marriott provides a 5,000-mile bonus for any five-day stay. Be sure to ask for these programs.

- Some programs require a flight on a particular airline in conjunction with your stay to qualify for bonus miles.

- At 500 bonus miles per stay, you have to stay 50 nights to earn a free airline ticket. Saving just $10 per night by not being locked-in to miles gives you $500 to buy your ticket and it won't have the restrictions frequent flyer tickets carry.

- Bonus miles are incredibly popular even though they defy financial logic. Perhaps it's because business travelers usually get to keep bonus miles and saving corporate money on the room rate provides no direct benefit to them.

SPECIAL TIPS FOR BUSINESS TRAVELERS

Check corporate rates but be aware that unless you work for a major company that's negotiated its own deal, you're getting a rate available to anyone carrying a business card. Half-price hotels and other discount programs will save you more.

Be loyal–to a point. If a particular chain makes you feel most welcome, you've found a valuable asset, but monitor competitors to make sure your preference is based on current information.

Avoid high city center rates on trips where a central location is not crucial. Choose hotels located near where you'll be doing the bulk of your business. A nearby location often means being able to do without a rental car, learning to navigate in a strange city and factoring in time for extensive commutes.

Develop strategies to avoid hotel phone fees. Check our *Calling From The Road* section for tips and strategies.

If you tend to use room service regularly, stay away from hotels that charge service fees or have minimums.

When staying at high-amenity hotels, take advantage of all the free services, including hotel shuttle and concierge floor food and beverages. Avoid the mini-bars in your room. Food and drink from a mini-bar is costly. Their best use is free refrigeration for items you buy outside the hotel and carry in.

Hotel business class rooms should offer modem ports, in-room fax with personal fax numbers, no phone surcharges, basic business supplies and 24-hour access to printers and copy facilities. They're worth the added cost for late-night work or on weekends when hotel business centers are closed. When you book a business class room, be sure of what you're getting. That designation can mean anything from a few small added amenities to a full-scale office-on-the-road. If you use the 50%-off hotel directories, you may want to consider purchasing two or three different brand books to increase your choice of hotels. Also, remember to use consolidator companies, such as Hotel Reservation Network, 800-964-6835.

If you can live without a guaranteed upgrade, take a small gamble. Book at a lower rate then request a free upgrade when you arrive or use your frequent stay card for upgrades.

Lower your cost on quick trips by using day rates.

Always audit your bill when you check out. Surveys have shown an almost 40% error rate in hotel bills. Front desk staffs are quick to correct errors–but you must point them out. You can make this easier by making sure all optional charge totals end with the same digit. For example, add tip amounts to make totals end in the number "5." If your bar tab is $17.12 make the tip $2.73. If your room service tab is $19.70 add a tip of $3.05. You can scan your bill quickly and locate any unauthorized charges.

Free breakfasts are a valuable offering at many hotels.

Look for free gym use with many frequent stay programs.

WEEKEND RATES

Weekend rates are lowered in an attempt to fill space in business-oriented hotels when the work week is over.

• **Some hotels discount rooms on a per night basis**; others require a two-night minimum stay to qualify for weekend rates.

• **Many throw in extras** like free breakfast, champagne or dinner.

• **A chain may offer several different weekend deals**, applicable by location. One chain's properties within one major city may offer six or seven different weekend rate deals. If you don't like the first one quoted, and if you are willing to book at another location in the same city, ask the reservation agent to check for an even better deal. Some weekend rates are extended to Monday if you stay over a Saturday night, but not if you check in on Sunday.

Cost of a 1933 room at The Drake Hotel/Chicago: $3; breakfast: 45¢.

FAMILY DISCOUNTS

Family discounts come in several forms including second rooms at 50% off and added values.

- **There is usually no charge at U.S. hotels** for children 18 and under (17 at some chains and 19 at Holiday Inns) staying in the same room as their parents. The age maximum in Europe may be 12 or 14.

- **Several U.S. chains offer free meals** to children under 12 who dine with their parents.

- **Some hotels**, such as Hyatt, offer travelers one room with the option to book an adjoining room at 50% off. Consider hotel chains such as Embassy Suites which offer two living areas, one for adults and one for kids.

AFFILIATE & GROUP DISCOUNTS

Organizational Discounts are offered to members of AAA (American Automobile Association) and other automobile clubs. They tend to be ten percent but, in some cases, can range up to 50% when special promotions are offered.

Group Discounts are available when you book a specific number of rooms, sometimes as few as five. Some discounts require the same payment form on all reservations. When requesting a group discount, first negotiate the lowest price for one room, then ask for an additional discount for your multiple booking.

Government Discounts are available to government employees and retired or active members of the military.

SENIOR DISCOUNTS

Senior discounts are widely available. Senior rates are always subject to availability, with maximum discounts being obtained by booking in advance.

- **Even when there is no official senior discount policy,** most hoteliers will accord you a discount, of ten percent or more.

- **Minimum ages vary** by chain. Always carry an AARP (American Association of Retired Persons) membership card, which is available to people 50 and above. AARP has official arrangements with about 25 chains but almost all hotels honor AARP's cards.

- **Other senior memberships that accord hotel discounts** include the Catholic Golden Age Club, Mature Outlook, the National Alliance of Senior Citizens and United's "Silver Wings."

- **Many hotels allow you to book second rooms at the senior discount rate,** as long as one room is occupied by a senior.

- **You may also get discounts on hotel dining**, particularly at Omni, Hilton, Doubletree, Marriott, Holiday Inn and Radisson.

- **Some senior discounts require** membership in the hotel's senior program.

Best mansion converted to U.S. hotel: The Mansion on Turtle Creek in Dallas.

STANDARD RATE COMPARISONS

How do rack rates, corporate rates, senior discounts and weekend rates compare?
You have to pick one and you want to pick the most favorable. There is no hard and fast
rule except to get the applicable options, then select the one that's best for you. Also,
check with consolidators as they will often have rates that beat any standard discount.

STANDARD RATE COMPARISONS				
HOTEL	RACK RATE	WEEKEND RATE	CORPORATE RATE	SENIOR May Require Advance
MARRIOTT/Charlotte	$135	$59	$109	$69
INTER-CONTINENTAL/Chicago	$149–179	$129	$139	$129
CONCOURSE HOTEL/Columbus	$98–111	$70	$101	$79
THE FAIRMONT/Dallas	$139–209	$79	$125–188	$119–179
SHERATON/Hartford	$129–153	$85	$119	$97–115
RADISSON INN/Los Angeles	$65–85	$49–69	$59–69	$49
HILTON/Los Angeles Airport	$99–209	$79	$89–109	$75–149
CROWNE PLAZA/Los Angeles	$109–139	$89	$99–109	$88–101
FAIRMONT/New Orleans	$125–195	$79	$105–169	$99–129
WALDORF ASTORIA/New York	$284–875	$219	$284–314	$259 up
HILTON/St. Louis	$129–149	$75	$111 up	$97–115
ADAMS MARK/St. Louis	$149–179	$99	$129–179	$109
RAMADA/Downtown Seattle	$72–150	$89	$79	$59–119
SHERATON/Atlanta Airport	$113–153	$85	$98	$85–115
HOLIDAY INN/Atlanta Peachtree	$52–169	$89	$74–92	$42–133
SHERATON/Baltimore Inner Harbor	$145–185	$85	$145	$107–139
INTER-CONTINENTAL/Chicago	$139–239	$99	$139 up	$122–214
QUALITY INN/Downtown Chicago	$69-119	$39–49	$59	$62–109
OMNI-NETHERLAND/Cincinnati	$135–225	$99	$135	$79–119
BEST WESTERN/Denver	$95–125	$69	$90–115	$85–112
MARRIOTT/Fort Lauderdale	$89–219	$89	$104–179	$45 up
SHERATON/Hartford	$109–134	$89	$109	$77–102
WYNDHAM/Houston	$159–250	$119	$119	$129 up
RADISSON/San Diego	$79–155	$69	$79	$79 up

Hotel where you can stay in the Barbara Mandrell or the Burt Reynolds suite: The Crowne Plaza, Lake Buena Vista.

TIPS FOR SAVING

NEGOTIATE

Negotiate your own rate anytime you choose to book directly with hotels. The process is easy and the alternative (accepting rack rate) is akin to tossing $20 bills out an open car window.

> **❝***Challenge the reservation agent to find you the lowest possible rate in the quickest possible time. Since they're trained to offer the highest rate first, you have to ask for the lowest rate–then ask again.***❞**

- **Pick a rate range that fits your budget.** Generally, you are better off with a lower-priced room in a luxury hotel

than a top-of-the-line room in a moderate hotel. You get the amenities and the service level no matter what class of room you're in. Conversely, if all you need is a comfortable place to sleep, stay away from hotels with rates that must cover the costs of spas, health clubs and multi-amenities.

- **Make your needs clear.** If you must have specific business amenities in your room or access to 24-hour room service, state that at the beginning of your call. If a view or the extra benefits of the concierge floor are important to you, make that clear. If you are eligible for any standard discounts, tell the reservation agent upfront.

- **Ask about rate breaks,** promotional rates and frequent guest rates. Some deals are available only to members of

---

Average rate for a hotel room in the United States in 1994: $63.63.

frequent guest clubs but many memberships are yours for the asking. If you've never stayed at the hotel, ask for an introductory rate.

- **If you're booking multiple nights**, check on day-to-day rate variances. If the cheapest room available is $79 for the first night, $139 for the second night and $89 for the third, ask if you can get the $79 rate for each night of your stay. If the initial response is negative, point out that your multiple-night stay should merit special savings.

- **Ask if a lower rate is available for limited maid service.** Some hotels offer a discount if you agree to forego daily changes of bed and bath linens. The bed will get made and some towels will be replaced but the room won't be turned around as if it's being prepared for a new guest. The hotel saves on maid-time and laundry cost. You should save on the rate.

- **If you're booking a room due to a family emergency,** ask for a compassion rate. There are no hard and fast policies, but most hotels will respond to your request for a discount in the case of an ill or deceased family member or other special needs situations.

- **Ask if the hotel is undergoing any substantial renovation.** Fifteen percent of all hotels are, at any given point in time. You want to book a room away from the sounds of construction and you want a discount.

- **Before you agree to the lowest of the "lowest" prices** you've been offered, try to get an upgrade, free breakfast or another added value.

- **When you get a rate you like**, note the rate code so you can cite it if the price you're given when you check in or out

differs from your quote. Always keep the confirmation number and the name of the booking agent.

- **When you book a last minute room**, do it by phone, even if you're already in town. If you try to get a rate break while standing at the front desk, you're negotiating from a weakened position.

SHOP AROUND

Hotels offer a variety of choices in rates, services and amenities, particularly in large metropolitan centers.

For instance, in New York, average rates can range from the Super 8 Suburban $50 to the Marriott Financial Center $235. Chicago rates range from Travelodge Des Plaines at $47 to Hotel Nikko Downtown at $235. Atlanta's rates range from Holiday Inn Downtown at $49 to the Hotel Nikko Buckhead at $215. San Francisco's rates range from the Astoria Fisherman's Wharf at $52 to the Grand Hyatt Downtown at $145. Dallas rates range from Red Roof Highway at $29 to the Crescent near downtown at $245.

❝You can find the amenities at the rate you want if you shop around. Remember you're going to be a smart consumer and use a half-price hotel directory, a promotional offer or consolidator so you can get your best hotel option for even less.❞

OTHER LODGING OPTIONS

If you're looking for variety, a break from hotel rates or a new outlook on an old vacation, consider an optional lodging choice.

BED & BREAKFASTS

Bed & Breakfasts offer rooms in home-like settings with meals often built around regional cuisine. They're best for travelers seeking interaction and a more direct slice-of-life experience.

* **The rules of your stay** are determined by the family that owns the B&B. You sacrifice some of the privacy and anonymity of hotel stays, but the pay-off is in charm, ambiance and person-alized service.

* **Check listings** at the library, at book shops and in newspaper travel sections. Don't rely on any guidebook over a year old.

* **There are about 200 B&B reserva-tion services in the U.S. alone.** Many reservation services come and go. If you use one, ask how long they have been in business.

* **The Thrifty Family Bed and Breakfast Club**, 800-599-3730, pro-vides lodging worldwide at about $10 per night for a family of four. You may sleep on the floor in sleeping bags or you may have a private room. An an-nual $50 membership gives you the information you need to arrange stays directly with host families.

Questions to ask before booking a Bed & Breakfast:

* Is there a private bath?

* Is there a phone and/or television in the room?
* Are there pets in the house?
* Is smoking permitted?
* Do guests have kitchen privileges?
* Are children permitted and welcomed?
* What time are meals served?
* Are there locks on the guest room doors?
* What forms of payment are acceptable?
* What are the cancellation policies?

ELDERHOSTEL

ElderHostel, 617-426-7788, offers won-derful seniors deals combining lodging, meals and activities. A total charge of $325 for a week's lodging, meals and pro-grams isn't uncommon. These programs are very diverse and can be based on active pursuits (such as hiking) or cerebral activities (such as bridge). Deals in the U.S. and Canada are the real finds. European prices are usually close to the price of standard package tours.

UNIVERSITIES AND COLLEGES

University and College rooms usually go for $15-30 per day. They are most available in summer when dorms are empty but some are offered year-round. Some institutions offer rather deluxe lodg-ing in homes and apartments.

* **Get a listing of 700 U.S. and interna-tional schools** which offer dormitory room accommodations. Send $12.95 for *U.S. and Worldwide Travel Accommodations Guide*, Campus Travel Service, Box 5483, Fullerton, CA 92636. It also lists YMCA's,

YWCA's, bed and breakfasts, farms, cottages and home exchange programs.

- **A free listing of 60 British universities** offering private rooms and family lodging can be acquired by writing to the General Secretary, British University Accommodations, Box 91, University Park, Nottingham NG72RD England, or call 011-44-115-950-45-71.

> **❝**Most university and college libraries have these guides. You can look through them and copy the pages that interest you.**❞**

YMCA'S AND YWCA'S

YMCA's and YWCA's are available in the U.S. and in Europe. Get domestic YMCA information by calling 312-977-0031 or by writing to 101 N. Wacker Dr., Chicago, IL 60606. For YWCA's: 212-614-2700 or 726 Broadway, New York, NY 10003. Call 212-308-2899 for international locations and rates.

YOUTH HOSTELS

Youth Hostels aren't just for young people. They're most plentiful in Europe, but you'll find them in the United States as well as other countries. Some are basic. Others have pools, coffee bars, bike rentals, scuba lessons and other amenities.

- **Hostelling International**, 733 15th St. NW, Suite 840, Washington, DC 20005, will send you a free directory if you're a member. If you're not, the cost is $8. You can also call 202-783-4943. Membership cost is $10 for people 17 and under; $15 for people 55 and older; $25 for people 18-54 and $35 for fam-

ilies. They also have guides for Europe, the Mediterranean, Asia and Australia for $13.95 each.

- **You can reserve a bed up to six months in advance** at over 300 international locations by calling Hostelling International's Booking Network, 800-444-6111, open 9 a.m. to 6 p.m. Eastern Standard Time. The average per-night cost is $10-30. There is a $5 reservation fee. They can also help you locate rooms at $25-60 per night.

Before you make a final selection, check to make sure a particular hostel meets your needs.

- Are men and women housed in separate dorms?
- Are family rooms or private rooms available?
- Are there set times when you must be up and about and when you must be back in your room?
- Are there kitchen facilities and/or communal meals?
- Should you bring your own towel and soap or bedding?
- Is a membership card required?
- Is there a limit on the length of stay?

RETREATS

Crave quiet? Ashrams, monasteries and retreats offer inexpensive lodging options. Some require you to get up early and contribute a bit of work. Others accept you on a guest-only basis.

- *U.S. and Worldwide Guide to Retreat Center Guest Houses* is available for $17.95 postpaid from CTS Publications, Box 8355, Newport Beach, CA 92660. Call 714-720-3729.

- **Tourism Offices in specific countries** (Spain and Italy chief among them) have free listings of monasteries and abbeys that take guests.

- **The Trappist Monastery in Hong Kong**, 852-2987-6292, will let you stay for $15 a night and give you three meals. The only catch? Lights out at 10 p.m.

RENTALS AND SUBLETS

Rentals and sublets can be arranged for stays as short as one week. Savings can be remarkable. A London flat, for example, can be acquired for about $900 per week versus over $2,000 for a comparable hotel suite. Prime vacation area rentals often are booked six months to a year in advance.

- **Rentals are easiest to find** in beach and ski areas and tourist-attractive cities such as San Francisco, London and Paris. They range from studio apartments to full mansions.

- **Go through a broker** or make arrangements on your own. If you are unfamiliar with short-term rentals and sublets, using a broker affords you some protection.

- **Check for urban rentals** in the *International Herald Tribune*, the Sunday *New York Times*, and other big city newspapers.

- **The Barclay International Group**, 800-845-6636, has listings in the U.S., Europe and Australia. They also offer *The Savvy Consumers' Guide To Short-Term Apartment Rentals*. Mail a stamped, self-addressed, business-size envelope to 150 E. 52nd St., New York, NY 10022.

DUDE RANCHES AND FARM STAYS

Dude Ranches and Farm Stays offer hands-on experiences and good vacation values for families.

- **Farm Stay information** can be acquired from state tourism bureaus, 4H headquarters and agriculture-extension offices.

- **Pennsylvania Dutch Farm Stays**– 800-723-8824, ext. 2335

- **Italian Farm Stays**–Write to Corso Vittorio Emanuelle 1010, 00189 Rome, Italy or call 011-39-6-685-2342.

- **Farm Stays in Switzerland** can cost as little as $10-20 per night. Call the Swiss National Tourist Office, 212-757-5944.

- **An extensive directory of dude ranches** (inexpensive to J. R. Ewing-style) is available for $5 postpaid from The Dude Ranchers Association, P.O. Box C471, LaPorte, CO 80535. Call 970-223-8440.

- **American Wilderness Experience, Inc.,** has catalogs and brochures on Old West Dude Ranch Vacations or Back Country Adventures. Write to P.O. Box 1486, Boulder, CO 80306 or call 800-444-3833 in the U.S. and Canada.

HOME EXCHANGE

Home Exchanges list and reference-check people willing to exchange stays in their homes for stays in another location.

- **You may need** about a year's advance to accomplish an effective exchange.

Hotel owned by author Crescent Dragonwagon: The Dairy Hollow House, Eureka Springs, Arkansas.

- **You'll want** full information (including photographs or videos) on what you're getting. Check the contract thoroughly and check your homeowner's insurance to make sure you're completely covered.

- **You should** correspond with the people with whom you'll be trading. Don't rely solely on the agency's information and reference checks.

Three listing sources:

- **Intervac USA**, 800-756-4663

- **The Invented City**, 800-788-2489

- **Trading Homes International**, 800-877-8723

HOME STAYS

Home Stays are all-inclusive programs that place you with a couple or family. They're typically two weeks in length and your hosts will be English-speaking. You generally get a private room and bath.

- **American International Home Stays**, 800-876-2048, covers Eastern Europe, Russia and China.

- **Servas**, 212-267-0252, covers the United States and 80 other countries.

- **Friendship Force**, 404-522-9490, covers Europe.

Recently, ***BEST FARES Discount Travel Magazine*** showed savvy travelers how to take up to $100 off four Continental Airlines roundtrips when you buy five frozen entrees.

Call 800-880-1234 to subscribe.
See page 395 for your discount subscription offer.

Hotel owned by Frank Sinatra with a tunnel from his cabin to the lounge: Cal-Neva Resort, Lake Tahoe.

RENTALS AND SUBLETS		
SOURCE	ANNUAL FEE	COVERAGE
AT HOME ABROAD 212-421-9165	$25	Europe, Caribbean, Mexico
B & V ASSOCIATES 800-755-8266	None	Europe
BUTTERFIELD & ROBINSON 800-678-1147	None	France and Italy
CARIBBEAN DESTINATIONS 800-888-0897	None	Caribbean
CREATIVE LEISURE 800-426-6367	None	Hawaii, Mexico, Caribbean, U.K.
EUROPALET 800-462-4486	None	Europe
HIDEAWAYS INTERNATIONAL 800-843-4433	$99	U.S., Europe, Mexico, Caribbean
INTERVAC 800-756-4663	$78	Worldwide
IN THE ENGLISH MANOR 800-422-0799	None	London apartments; manors and castles in the U.K.
PARIS CONNECTION 954-475-0615	None	Paris
DHR WORLWIDE 800-633-3284	None	Worldwide
VILLAS INTERNATIONAL 800-221-2260	None	Europe, Mexico, Caribbean
WORLD-WIDE HOME RENTALS 800-299-9886	$18	Worldwide; semi-annual catalogue

Hotel with decor featuring 100 self portraits of the same woman: The Cliffside Inn in Newport, Rhode Island.

'INN'-SIDER INFO

DECIPHERING LODGING LINGO

Understanding hotel jargon will help you read the map that takes you through the hotel rate labyrinth. Is an American Plan room in a Boutique hotel better than the European Plan at an Extended Stay rate? If you're a walk-in, are you likely to be walked? Here are some commonly used terms:

Advance Deposit–a partial payment to secure your room, often required if you don't reserve with a major credit card.

Confirmed Reservation–acknowledgment that a room is being held for you until a specific time, usually 4 or 6 p.m.

* **Hotels overbook** just as airlines do and there are no laws protecting you if you arrive and find there's no room at the inn. You must rely upon your diplomatic insistence and the hotel's desire to maintain a decent level of customer satisfaction.

Guaranteed Reservation–a double-sided coin that doesn't necessarily flip to the advantage of the consumer. You give your credit card number and, if you don't cancel by the deadline, you're billed for one night's lodging whether you use the room or not.

Deadlines vary by property. 4 p.m. or 6 p.m. were once the standards, but some hotels now require that you cancel by noon or 24-72 hours in advance. A few even set the limit at seven days. Always know the time zone in the city you are visiting to be sure you don't violate the deadlines.

* **Always write down your cancellation number** and the name of the person you spoke with when you cancel a guaranteed reservation. It's good protection if an unwarranted charge appears on your credit card statement.

* **Some hotels bill your credit card** when they guarantee your reservation. If you'd rather not pay until you've been served, register your protest by selecting another hotel.

First hotel in China to bear the name of an international hotel chain: The Great Wall Sheraton Hotel Beijing.

- **Early-departure fees** are being test-marketed by Hyatt and a few other hotels. If you don't stay the entire length of your reservation, you may be billed $25-50.

Walk-in–a guest arriving without a reservation.

Walked–what happens to you when you arrive at a hotel that guaranteed your reservation but didn't save you a room. You want a comparable room in a nearby hotel at no charge, taxi fare to the hotel, a complimentary long distance call to advise your family/office where you'll be and a discount coupon or upgrade guarantee for a future stay. If you're expecting calls, make sure the switchboard is notified and will transfer your calls or refer callers to your new number.

Sold-Out–a changeable state in the land of hotel reservations. Hotels can be sold out one minute and have rooms available the next. People double- and triple-book hotels, plus hotels set aside rooms for eventualities that may not occur. If your heart is set on a particular hotel, check back to see if availability has opened up. Hotels that are literally sold out may be able to accommodate you at a discount in the living-area section of suites that have been booked as single rooms.

All-Inclusive–room, meals, amenities and activities (such as water sports) are included. Not all-inclusives are created equal so get the details on what is included. Can you order premium brand drinks? Are meals ordered from a full menu or buffet-style? At resort properties, will all water sports be included or do some require additional fees? All-inclusives do not include taxes–a hefty last minute shock if you don't take them into account.

Modified American Plan–includes three meals a day with some menu restrictions.

Full American Plan–includes three meals a day chosen from the full menu.

European Plan–meals are not included.

Continental Plan–includes a light breakfast that can range from tea and toast to a rather hearty cereal, fruit and bagel buffet.

Double Occupancy Rate–a misleading way of quoting half the real cost of a room or hotel package. If an ad does not prominently state that the rate is per person, double it to get your real cost even if you're traveling solo.

Single Supplement–the additional charge for a single person occupying a double room.

Extended Stay–five nights or more. You deserve a per-night reduction. Suite hotels may have an additional rate break at 30 days.

Soft Opening Rates–provide discounts on new hotels or hotels near the end of major refurbishment. Most areas are open but there's still some construction clamor or one or two amenities out of commission.

Connecting Rooms–have doors that allow room-to-room access without going into public corridors. When the door is closed, each room is self-contained. Connecting rooms are usually booked as single rooms by unrelated guests. If you're booking two rooms and you want them to connect, make your desire clear when you book your reservation to avoid getting rooms across the hall or even further separated.

Double Room–can mean two single beds, one double bed or two double beds. Some hotels have king-size beds in double rooms. In Europe, it usually means two single beds. If it seems confusing, you get the picture. The bottom line: if bed types and numbers are important, specify your exact needs when you make your reservation.

Club or Concierge Floor–extra amenities at a higher room rate. Free food, business services, special access lounges and the security of a members-only floor.

- **Club floors in most hotels** are a big step above standard floors. In a few hotels they offer little more than weak drinks, microwaved canapes and a higher price.

- **Club floor upgrades can sometimes be yours for the asking** if you're a frequent guest. When a hotel nears capacity and standard rooms are booked, you can often get a club floor room at the standard rate.

Junior Suite (Parlour Suite)–a room with a partition separating bed and sitting areas–not what you want if you're looking for privacy.

Suite Hotels–may offer junior suites or suites with separate living and sleeping rooms plus a full-size (apartment-style) kitchen. Some suite hotels, particularly those specializing in long-term stays, have many floor plans, including units with fireplaces.

Oceanfront Rooms–face the water but there could be a grove of palm trees and a four-lane highway between you and the view.

Oceanview Rooms–could provide a splendid view of the ocean or a speck of blue visible only to an extremely agile contortionist.

Mountainview Rooms–mountains or mole hills–make sure the mountains are not blocked by a McDonalds or other modern day facades.

Gardenview Rooms–usually the least scenic option.

Boutique Hotels–small, intimate and usually expensive. The standard of service tends to be exemplary.

Full Service Hotels–should and usually do have 24-hour room service, fine restaurants, business centers and full amenities. A few hotels may take extreme liberties with advertising claims and offer only a bellman and a cafe that closes at 8 o'clock.

Tourist Class Hotels–a term borrowed from Europe, where it means simple, comfortable rooms and the likelihood of a shared bath. In the U.S., it means a standardized, economy facility with very small bars of soap.

Late Charges–can be added to your bill even after you check out. These can include last minute room service, mini-bar purchases or telephone and fax charges. They can also include mistakes. Because you won't know about them until the bill reaches you, jot down any legitimate last-minute charges so you can easily compare them to the final bill when it arrives.

SERVICES & AMENITIES
Hidden Costs

Hidden costs can create shockwaves in your wallet at check-out time if you don't ask the right questions before you make your reservation. Quoted rates do not include taxes, surcharges, phone fees, parking, fax charges and, in some cases, room service minimums and service fees above and beyond any gratuity. The only way to control these hidden costs is to inquire about the hotel policy on each individual service that you require. If you need a shirt laundered at the Crowne Plaza/Manhattan you'll pay $8.05. The cost of a clean shirt at Atlanta's Sheraton Inn is just $2.50. A pot of coffee delivered to your room at the Orlando Hilton is $3 but it can cost you $12-15 at hotels with room service minimums. You pay the base charge whether you order a cup of coffee or a three course meal. Taxes are one uncontrollable variable but be sure to take them into account when budgeting for hotel stays. Check our *Calling From The Road* section for ways to avoid phone surcharges. Here are some examples of variances in taxes and surcharges (set by states and municipalities) and room service fees (set by each hotel).

HOTEL AMENITY COMPARISONS				
LOCATION	QUOTED RATE	TAX RATE	RATE INC. TAX & SRCHG	ROOM SERVICE POLICY
CHICAGO	$180	12%	$201.60	10% mandatory service charge not including gratuity
DALLAS	$104	13%	$117.52	15% mandatory service charge not including gratuity
DENVER	$104	9.8%	$114.20	$1.50 service charge not including gratuity
HONOLULU	$145	10.17%	$169.75	15% mandatory service charge includes gratuity
LOS ANGELES	$139	8.5%	$150.82	$2.00 service charge not including gratuity
MIAMI	$149	12.5%	$167.53	$1.50 service charge not including gratuity
MINNEAPOLIS	$99	12%	$109.88	15% mandatory service charge not including gratuity
NEW ORLEANS	$139	11%	$154.29	15% minimum; $1.50 delivery fee plus 16% mandatory service charge includes gratuity
NEW YORK	$185	13.25% + $2	$211.52	$1.50 delivery charge not including gratuity
NEWARK	$129	12%	$144.48	20% mandatory service charge includes gratuity
ST. LOUIS	$119	13.25%	$134.77	No fee or minimum
SAN FRANCISCO	$130	10%	$143.00	15% mandatory service charge not including gratuity
SEATTLE	$119	115	$132.19	15% mandatory service charge not including gratuity
WASHINGTON, D.C.	$135	13% + $1.50	$154.05	$15 minimum; no fee; not including gratuity

Number of business trips by U.S. residents in 1994 that included children: 43.4 million; in 1990: 26.6 million.

Business Amenities

Keeping business amenities up-to-date has been a big job for hoteliers this past decade. Technology has created a demand for data ports, two incoming phone lines, in-room faxes, computers, laser and laptop printers.

Hotel business centers have equipment availability and variety you won't find in any individual room. Some even have on-site secretaries. Business center usage is usually billed by the hour. Some premium class rooms include the services in their base room rates.

Travelers who want to work in the privacy of their rooms have options ranging from simple dataport availability to recreated offices. Rooms equipped with business basics go for $15-20 above standard rates. Highly equipped rooms will cost $35-50 above standard rates.

Desirable but hard-to-find is the true two-phone-number hotel room–much more useful than the commonly offered two-line phone. Hotels are slowly installing two lines per room to accommodate today's business traveler. For example, Embassy Suites is currently converting all their suites to provide two lines for their guests. Always check with the hotel prior to booking.

Express Options

Express check-in and check-out options are on the rise. The lodging industry is following the lead of car rental companies in seeking market share via promises of saving you time. Here are some ideas now being tested and implemented:

Check-in:

- **Hand-held computers** operated by roving employees who check you in before you reach the front desk.

- **Pre-issued check-in folios** waiting for you when you reserve with a pre-approved credit card.

- **ATM-like check-in machines** that issue your key in return for the answers to a few key prompts. Hilton has pulled their machines based on the belief that guests want to interact with humans when they arrive at the hotel.

- **Toll-free number check-in.** You call for your room assignment and complete all necessary check-in procedures by phone. When you arrive at the hotel, your key is waiting.

- **Streamlined front desk procedures** (pioneered by Hilton) that cut check-in time from the average three-minutes-plus to about 30 seconds.

Check-out:

- **Bills are slipped under your door** the night before your scheduled departure.

- **Bills are accessible via in-room television**. You see updates as soon as they're entered. A few luxury hotels even have in-room printers so you can print out your own bill copy before you leave your room.

- **Breakfast check-out** being tested by Hilton, Hyatt and Marriott. Your hotel bill is presented with your food tab. Review it, sign it and be on your way.

- **Check-out by machine or computer kiosk.** Guests are more willing to deal with a computer at check-out time. The main problem comes if you find an error on your bill and end up at the back of the line you're trying to avoid.

The Concierge

The concierge is a person designated by the hotel to assist guests in any way they may need or desire. Services include

---

making arrangements for dinner, travel, car rental, tickets for sporting events or other entertainment, reservations, babysitting, a nurse, notary and secretarial services, and of course flowers. If you enjoy the services a concierge provides, tip accordingly and let the management know. What has long been an expected source of assistance for travelers is disappearing in the quest for lower overhead.

Smoking and Non-Smoking Rooms

If you smoke, or if you don't, the hotel industry is interested in giving you what you want. Almost 90% of U.S. hotels offer non-smoking rooms, setting aside, on average, almost 40% of their inventory for exclusive use by non-smokers.

- **It costs hotels about $600** to complete all procedures necessary to change one room from smoking to non-smoking status.

- **During peak periods,** hotels are tempted to remove ashtrays from rooms and call them non-smoking. Your nose will know. If you run into this ploy and still want the room, demand a discount.

- **The ultimate non-smoker's room** is also an allergy-sufferer's dream. "Green Rooms" have special air and water filters, hypo-allergenic toiletries and chemical-free carpeting.

- **Hotels with a high percentage of international guests** have more relaxed anti-smoking rules in public areas and a lower percentage of rooms set aside for non-smokers.

- **If you plan to conduct business meetings in your room,** take your colleague's smoking preferences into account. A clash in smoking/non-smoking preferences can make meetings disastrous.

- **Hotels are subject to municipal anti-smoking** regulations. Boulder, Colorado and some California cities ban smoking in all public buildings and in outdoor areas.

- **The penalty for smoking** in a non-smoking room? Nothing more than a dirty look from the maid and, possibly, mild censure from the front desk.

Hotel Ratings

Hotels are rated with various euphemisms, systems of stars and even (at Days Inns) suns. Your best guide to where a particular hotel is positioned, in the economy-to-luxury spectrum, is the cost of the rooms.

- **Travel agents can access ratings** from the *Official Hotel Guide* (OHG).

- **Guides that offer more subjective ratings** are useful only if they clearly state the basis for the ratings and are based on current information. In some cases, ratings will change dramatically in the time it takes to print the book. Popular guides are published by AAA and Mobil.

- **Hotels in some countries are rated by their governments**. These ratings tend to be very pragmatic and are based on cut and dried statistics like room size and percentage of rooms with private baths.

Mega-Chains

Some hotel chains have radically different components. A Crowne Plaza and a Holiday Inn Express are both owned by Holiday Inn, but they are very different. Stay at one of the 2,900 properties managed by Choice Hotels and you can pay as little as $35 for a room at Sleep Inn; or $115 for a room at a Clarion Hotel. Most chains operate under the directives of the

---

Percentage of U.S. hotels offering smoke-free rooms: 85%.

corporate office with member hotels abiding by corporate-wide standards and policies. Franchise hotels (Best Western and Hampton Inns, for example) have more individual control, thus more variance. Best Westerns, in particular, tend to adopt the personalities of their owners. Don't count on uniform policies. Ask about those that matter most before you make your reservation.

Independent Operators

Don't overlook traditional hotels. There are still unique, American hotels that have identities of their own and have avoided major chain affiliations. Others have capitulated to a degree, but retain their names and sense of style. All offer a full range of amenities and competitive prices for their class of hotel. They're great ways to break up the tedium of business travel.

SAFETY TIPS

No matter how long the flight and how tired you might be, never leave your luggage unattended.

The safest rooms are on preferred guest floors with restricted access. A no-cost option is to request a room near the elevators to minimize walking through empty halls.

If the desk clerk announces your room number at a volume that can be heard by anyone including you, ask that it be changed. Safety-conscious front desks let you know your room number without sharing it with the entire lobby.

Women can maintain their privacy by registering under their last name and first initial.

Valuables belong in the hotel safe or, better yet, at home. All states have innkeepers' laws stating that hotels are not liable for anything of value left in your room. The ceiling for losses on items kept in hotel safety deposit boxes is usually around $300.

If you must stash cash and valuables in your room, don't put them all in the same place. With luck, a burglar will find one stash place, and go away. The only dan-

ger–forgetting where you've put everything and leaving things behind when you check out.

Always leave the TV on when not in your room. This can deceive would-be thieves into thinking the room is occupied.

Don't fall for crime-prevention gimmicks such as travelers locks for dresser drawers. They're like arrows pointing out the good stuff.

Number of hotel keys lost or not turned in per year: 30 per room.

Inspect the safety features of your room as soon as you check in. Check patio doors, connecting doors and all door locks. Read the safety notice posted on the door.

Always engage all door locks when you are inside your room. Hotels should change locks between guests but many don't. A chain lock won't keep a determined person out, but it will slow him down and let him know the room is occupied.

Choose hotels with electronic card key locks. The code is changed with every guest.

Keep the "Do Not Disturb" sign on your door even when you're not in the room.

Confirm identities before opening your door. If you haven't requested hotel staff, call the desk even if the person at the door is in a recognizable uniform.

Don't invite strangers to your room. Their seemingly innocent presence in the hotel guarantees nothing–not even that they're guests.

Unattended pool areas and workout rooms should be used with caution.

Small hotels and inns may have windows and balconies easily reached from outside. Be sure they are adequately secured.

Memorize the direct number to hotel security in case you need to reach them in an urgent situation.

Never lay your room key down on a restaurant table or in any public area of the hotel.

Use the main hotel entrance during low traffic periods, even if it means a longer route to your room.

Sleep with your room key and travel flashlight on the nightstand so you can find them immediately in case of fire. Add any items you'd want to take with you if you had to evacuate quickly.

Don't fall asleep wearing headphones. Those soothing sounds can mute unusual noises and alarms. Falling asleep with the television on will also block out what could be important warning sounds.

If you're issued two keys, don't leave one in your room.

Lost or stolen keys should be re-coded or re-keyed immediately. Do this even if your travel partner still has a copy of the original key.

Call security if you see anything suspicious. They're trained in discretion. If you're being overly cautious, no harm will be done.

Plan a fire exit route as soon as you check in. Be aware that many stairways in international hotels are not fire-protected and may not provide safe escape routes.

If you smell smoke and your room door feels hot, don't open it. Turn the air conditioner or heater off and put a wet towel under the door. Call for help. If the phone system is working, let the desk know you need assistance or call 911 and give them your room number.

HotelDocs, 800-468-3537, will send a physician and necessary medication to your hotel room in 30 U.S. cities. The fee is $150. Compare that against using walk-in clinics, which usually charge about $50 per visit. Use the specialized service when a hotel call is worth the added cost.

Price of an egg, bacon, hash browns and toast breakfast at the Holiday Inn, Las Vegas: $1.29.

HOTEL HIGHLIGHTS

HOTEL CHAIN PROFILES

Hotels within a chain can vary by location. With that in mind, here's a look at what some of the most prominent chains are doing to attract your lodging dollar. Rate breaks listed include ongoing offers plus special, limited promotions–many of which tend to recur each year.

> **GX:** Guarantee Time–The time your reservation is released if you have not checked in. (PP: indicates deposits or prepaids are required on all reservations).
>
> **Kid:** Maximum age for children staying free in parent's room.
>
> **V:** Designates a high degree of variance in policy.

ADAMS MARK (800-444-2326), 13 locations ($110-165), plus a West Central Florida Golf Resort and a Daytona Beach Resort. The independently owned hotels do participate in chain-wide business and senior discounts, which vary by property. **GX**: 4 p.m.; **Kid**: 17 & under.

AMERISUITES (800-833-1516), 19 locations ($69-89), featuring two phones and a dataport in each suite, complimentary continental breakfast and free local transportation.

- **Americlub** frequent stay program gives the thirteenth stay free, added amenities and car rental discounts. **GX**: 6 p.m.; **Kid**: 17 & under.

ASTON RESORTS & SUITES (800-922-7866), 30 locations ($100 & up), all in Hawaii.

Only U.S. hotel with underwater rooms: Jules' Undersea Lodge in Key Largo, $195 per night.

- **Sun Club for seniors** 55 and older provides 20%-30% discounts plus free or discounted car rentals. Membership is free, but some locations require you to enroll in advance of your first discounted stay. Deposit or pre-payment is required. **GX**: PP; **Kid**: 17 & under.

BEST WESTERN INTERNATIONAL (800-528-1234), 3,400 franchise locations ($44-90), that share the same name and reservation number. Best Western reviews each member hotel annually, hoping to exact some uniformity in standards while still encouraging individual owners to put their imprint on their hotels. It has a large international presence with over 1,000 European locations, and 360 in Asia and the South Pacific. North American locations either have on-premise food service or are within 500 feet of a restaurant. Many programs are chain-wide, but be sure to check specific inclusions. **GX**: 6 p.m.; **Kid**: V.

- **The Gold Crown International Club** is a frequent guest program based on points redeemable for travel benefits. Six hundred points, for example, earn a free day's car rental; 8,000 earn a roundtrip airline ticket within the continental U.S.

- **Best Western Seniority** offers guests 50 and above 15% off and frequent-stay points redeemable for awards and gifts. **Mature Benefits** offers guests 55 and above ten percent off. Ask which program is in effect at the inn where you plan to visit.

- **Young Travelers Club** operates like a frequent stay program. Children 16 and under get their own points, redeemable for games, collector cards, CDs and other age-appropriate gifts.

- **Rate breaks** include special rates for two people sharing a room, added-value benefits that vary by location, Best Rates and Breakaway Weekend Escape packages.

- **The Guestcheque program** offers vouchers for North and South America and the Caribbean. **Euro-Guestcheques** cover over 900 hotels in seven price categories.

- **Trucker discounts** are available.

- **Scam-O-Grams,** produced by the corporate office, fax fraud alerts to participating hotels.

BUDGET HOST INNS (800-283-4678), 180 locations ($25-60), is a network of individually owned economy inns in 36 states and Canada. Most offer senior and commercial discounts, available even without advance reservations. Calls to the toll-free reservations number are switched to the inn you select–a helpful innovation enabling you to ask location-specific questions without paying for a long distance call. Many locations have special parking for 18-wheelers. **GX**: V; **Kid**: V.

BUDGETEL INNS (800-428-3438), 108 locations ($39-49). Individually owned, limited-amenity hotels based in Milwaukee and concentrated in the Midwest. Their business plan rooms include fax machines, printers and modem jacks–features that some hotels at double the price offer only in premium room categories. **GX**: 6 p.m.; **Kid**: 18 & under.

- **The Roadrunner Club** gives a free night after 12 stays.

- **Seniors 55 and above** and AARP members get ten percent off.

CANADIAN PACIFIC (800-441-1414), 25 locations ($110 & up), is the largest owner-operated hotel company in Canada. Properties tend to be historic, chateau-style buildsings. Most were refurbished in 1988 and include modern amenities such as pools and full health clubs. Many guest rooms have data ports, portable phones and printers available on request. **GX**: V; **Kid**; 18 & under.

- **Canadian Pacific Club** for frequent guests is a no-cost enrollment program. You get express service, late check-out, health club usage, 15% discount at on-site shops, free luggage storage and an exclusive toll-free number. Rooms are set aside specifically for club members.

- **Reservations Plus** is a premium frequent guest program for business travelers.

- **Entree Gold** premium floors have their own concierge, boardroom, private lounge and private check-in and check-out.

- **Senior discounts** range from ten percent to 30% for ages 65 and older.

- **AAA** members sometimes get as much as 50% off.

CHOICE HOTELS, 2,900 properties in 38 countries including Clarion, Comfort, Econo Lodge, Quality, Rodeway and Sleep Inns. Choice was the leader in reserving rooms for non-smokers and now dedicates half its inventory to them. Econo Lodge and Rodeway Inns have revamped Senior Rooms, which include brighter lighting, large-button telephones and remote controls, large print brochures, grab bars in baths and lever handles on doors and faucets. They also offer a free book, *Tips For Travelers Over 50*, yours on request when you check in.

- **Clarion** (800-252-7466), 106 locations ($85-125), is Choice's upscale segment with a focus on business travelers. Food courts offer multiple-choice, quick-dining options.

Room service in hotel suites includes cooked-to-order breakfasts. **GX**: 6 p.m.; **Kid**: None.

- **Comfort Inns and Suites** (800-228-5150), 1,352 locations ($45-79), the nation's fastest growing chain. Rates include continental breakfast and a morning paper. Comfort Suites have partitioned living areas. **GX**: V; **Kid**: None.

- **Econo Lodge** (800-553-2666), 643 locations ($38-49), sets aside ten percent of its rooms for guests 50 and above and offers them 30%-discounts on advance reservations. **GX**: V; **Kid**: 18 & under.

- **Quality Inns** (800-228-5151), 555 locations ($65-85), have converted 20% of their inventory to Executive Rooms with speaker phones, data ports, over-size desks, fax modems and other business amenities. Quality Suite rates include continental breakfast and evening cocktails. **GX**: V; **Kid**: 18 & under.

- **Rodeway Inns** (800-228-2000), 151 locations ($40-60), is the least expensive segment of the Choice group and typically has 60 rooms or less. **GX**: V; **Kid**: 18 & under.

- **Sleep Inns** (800-753-3746), 65 locations ($35-45), are all new budget hotels with 70 in operation and almost 100 under construction. Locations feature data ports, electronic door locks and free coffee and doughnuts in the morning. **GX**: V; **Kid**: 18 & under.

- **Ages 50 and above** get 30% off with advance reservations; ten percent without. Their senior guest benefits have resulted in a 464% jump in senior business in eight years.

- **Rate breaks** include Visa promotions

with ten percent off room rates and "LoRates" for discounts at Florida locations during off-peak travel times.

CLUBHOUSE INNS (800-258-2466), 15 locations ($60-95), offer rooms and suites in nine states. All locations have free breakfast buffets, evening cocktails, local calls and long distance access. **GX**: 6 p.m.; **Kid**: 16 & under.

- **The Best Guest** frequent stay program offers the thirteenth stay free.

- **Rate breaks** include "Kickback Weekend" rates (November to March) including a free weekend night stay after two consecutive weekend nights. "Big Splash Weekends" (April to October) offer special discount rates for two consecutive nights from Thursday to Sunday.

COUNTRY INNS & SUITES (800-456-4000), 61 locations ($55-80), the sister company to Radisson Hotels. Located primarily in resort, scenic and suburban locations in the U.S. and Canada, plus one property in Mauritius. Twelve of the 59 locations are in Minnesota and much of the country-like ambiance reflects Midwest style. Complimentary continental breakfast, cookies and fruit available throughout the day. **GX**: 6 p.m.; **Kid**: 18 & under.

- **Seniors 55 and above**, AARP and Mature Outlook Association (MOA) members get ten percent discounts.

- **Special care programs** include "Did You Forget?" which offers a dozen personal care items by request. A call from the front desk within 15 minutes of check-in, ensures everything in the room is as it should be.

- **Kids Stuff** provides a fun package to all children at check-in. The basic

package is often enhanced by special treats added by each hotel manager.

COURTYARD BY MARRIOTT (800-321-2211), 215 locations ($66-96), focusing on mid-size cities and suburban and near-highway locations in major cities. **GX**: 6 p.m.; **Kid**: 18 & under.

- **The Courtyard Club**, $10 annual membership, offers frequent guests express check-in and check-out, free fax service, one free night after twelve paid and $20 in Courtyard Cash when joining or renewing.

- **AARP members** get 15% off. Non-member seniors can request specific discounts.

CROWN STERLING SUITES (800-433-4600), 19 locations ($90-99), specializing in extended stays. Hotels are concentrated in California, the southern U.S. and Minnesota. **GX:** V; **Kid**: 12 & under.

- **Seniors 60 and above** get $10 discounts on rooms, free breakfast and cocktails.

DAYS INN (800-325-2525), 1,500 locations ($39-89), specializing in leisure travelers and targeting most promotions to families and seniors. **GX**: V; **Kid**: V.

- **September Days Club** for guests 49 and above, offers discounts of 15% to 50% plus car rental and attraction discounts. Grandchildren eat free at many locations. The annual fee is $12 with deductions for multiple year membership.

- **The Inn-Credible Club Card** provides ten percent off standard rates for frequent guests, a special reservation number, car rental discounts and other added values.

Hotel with thatched palazzi built to house the crew making the film "Hurricane": Hotel Sofitel, Marara, Bora.

DOUBLETREE (800-222-8733), 114 locations ($79-125), in 31 states and the District of Columbia plus several Doubletree Clubs with lower prices and more limited services. **GX**: 4 p.m.; **Kid**: 18 & under.

- **Senior discounts** range from ten percent to 30 percent for guests 60 and above and for AARP members.

- **Kids** under 12 eat free.

- **Rate breaks** include "Dream Deals" with two-for-the-price-of-one rooms and free breakfast. "DoubleTreat Weekends" added values include a 6 p.m. Sunday check-out time.

EMBASSY SUITES (800-362-2779), 100 locations ($99-129), featuring free, full breakfasts plus a two-hour manager's reception each evening. **GX**: V; **Kid**: 13 & under.

- **Diplomat Club** for frequent guests offering discounts and added-value benefits.

- **Seniors 55 and above** get a minimum ten percent discount plus free breakfast and cocktails.

EXEL INNS (800-356-8013), 26 locations ($28-38), primarily in the Midwest, South Dakota and Texas. All locations provide continental breakfasts. Living Rooms (available at most locations) contain complete kitchens, extra-long beds, expanded closet space and shower massage. Deluxe King Rooms (available at all locations) include king beds, recliners, in-room coffee makers and shower massage. **GX**: V; **Kid**: 17 & under.

- **The Insiders Card** for frequent guests provides a free thirteenth stay. There is no membership fee, no application to fill out and no expiration limit on benefits. You simply request the punch card at your first visit.

- **Seniors** receive a ten percent discount.

FAIRFIELD INN BY MARRIOTT (800-228-2800), 175 locations ($45-75), Marriott's economy option. All locations offer complimentary continental breakfast. **GX**: 6 p.m.; **Kid**: 17 & under.

- **INNsiders Club** offers a special reservation number, express check-in, a free night after twelve paid and free daily papers.

- **Seniors 62 and above** get ten percent discounts; AARP members get 15%.

FAIRMONT HOTELS (800-522-3437), six locations ($139-179), in the grand hotel tradition. All offer express check-in and check-out, 24-hour room service and deluxe amenities. **GX**: V; **Kid**: V.

- **The President's Club** for frequent guests has a point-system rewards program. Points are redeemable for American Airlines miles, upgrades, express service and car rentals. Suite upgrades are available at nominal charge.

- **Rate breaks** include honeymoon/anniversary promotions, golf packages and "Sale Savers," which bring some rates as low as $69 per night.

FORTE (800-543-4300), 250 locations ($179-209), including classic Le Meridien and Forte hotels such as the Hyde Park (London) and The Watergate (Washington, DC). Locations include the U.S., Europe and the Middle East. **GX**: V; **Kid**: V.

- **Rate breaks** include "Summer and Winter Passport" programs with 30% off at more than 250 hotels and the "Forte 30" program with 30% off rack rates at 200 hotels in 23 countries when bookings are confirmed with credit card at least 30 days in advance.

U.S. hotel with 15 air–conditioned, concrete wigwams: Wigwam Village in Holbrook, Arizona, $35 per night.

FOUR SEASONS AND REGENT HOTELS AND RESORTS (800-332-3442), 26 locations ($160-190). They sold 25% of their shares to Saudi Arabia's Crown Prince Al Waleed Bin Talal Bin Abdulaziz Al Saud in 1994. (Shall we count it unlikely that any location will soon bear his name?) They're using the capital to maintain their stronghold in the luxury hotel market. Amenities include complimentary shoeshine service, twice-daily maid service, monogrammed terry cloth robes, poolside iced-towels and spritzers, and overnight sandal and golf shoe repair. **GX**: 6 p.m.; **Kid**: 18 & under.

HAMPTON INNS (800-426-7866), 300 locations ($49-69), concentrated in the eastern U.S.

- **Lifestyle 50** offers seniors benefits including up to four guests per room at the single rate. **GX**: 6 p.m.; **Kid**: 17 & under.

HAWTHORN SUITES (800-527-1133), 17 locations ($79-109), primarily in the southern U.S. Rate breaks include "Hot 'N Suite" packages, which offer tickets to area attractions. **GX**: V; **Kid**: 18 & under.

HILTON (800-445-8667), 240 locations ($90-162), a major player in the city center market with extensive business amenities. Four Hilton Garden Inns mark the chain's entry into the budget/suburban market. Six all-suite hotels are also in operation and there are 12 Conrad International Hotels. **GX**: 6 p.m.; **Kid**: 18 & under.

- **"SmartDesk" rooms** ($25-$35 above regular business rates) include a full-size desk, Intel-486 computer with all major business programs pre-loaded, fax/modem, laser printer and copier (with a parallel cable for laptop printing). Most hotels have dual line phones and over 150 hotels have dropped phone access fees.

- **HHonor program** for frequent guests awards points plus 500 bonus miles if you fly in on an affinity airline and show your ticket at the front desk. Members also receive priority reservations and express check-in and check-out. You can also purchase advance upgrade certificates. A book of five is $100; $75 for Gold VIP members. Using them can save about $40 per night on upgrades to concierge level rooms. Membership in HHonors is free and enrollment is available via the Internet.

- **Senior HHonors** offers 20%-25% discounts on rooms, 20% off many restaurant meals and discounts on Hertz cars. Dues are $50 per year or $265 for a lifetime membership.

- **Express service options include** Zip-In, Check-In and Check-Out, which Hilton claims has reduced the average transaction time to 30 seconds.

- **Rate breaks** include "Bounceback Weekends" with rates starting at $79 (including continental breakfast), and "Summer World of Savings" at International hotels offering 30% off room rates plus Hertz upgrades.

- **Free cellular calls to Hilton's toll-free reservations number** are offered in Seattle, the test market for what may become a nationwide benefit.

HOLIDAY INN (800-465-4329), 2,005 worldwide locations ($55-175), divided into ten categories; from Holiday Inn Express budget hotels to high-end Crowne Plazas. Holiday Inn was the first chain to offer full booking capabilities via the Internet. **GX**: 6 p.m.; **Kid**: 19 & under.

The world's largest hotel: The MGM Grand/Las Vegas with 5,005 guest rooms.

- **Priority Club** for frequent guests of all segments of the chain (except Holiday Inn Express) awards a point per dollar spent, excepting promotional room rates. Benefits vary by location but may include room upgrades and extended check-out. There is a $10 annual fee.

- **Holiday Inn Express** has over 300 locations worldwide. They offer a free breakfast bar at all locations.

- **Holiday Inn Garden Courts** are in small European towns and cities.

- **Crowne Plaza** hotels are designed for business travelers. They all offer meeting facilities, health clubs and fine restaurants. Executive Floors are available at most locations.

- **Crowne Plaza Preferred** provides points and benefits for frequent guests. There is a membership fee of $10. Points are redeemable for travel packages and upgrades as well as merchandise from their Crowne Plaza catalogue.

- **The Alumni Club** for guests 60 and older offers 20% off standard rates, complimentary continental breakfast, a ten percent meal discount (even if you're not a guest) and two for one birthday dinners. The $10 annual membership fee is waived the first year.

- **Kids under 12** eat free from a special children's menu at over 1,100 hotels. The offer is limited to four children per family.

- **Rate breaks** include the "Best Breaks" weekend package and "Great Rates," which gives up to 50% off rack rates; "Family Great Rates" offering discounts up to 50% off plus free kid

meals; and "Weekender Plus" with bed and breakfast rates in Europe, the Middle East and Africa.

HOMEWOOD SUITES (800-225-5466), 29 locations ($69-99), designed for business travelers, offers extended stay rates for stays of six nights or more. They plan to double their locations by the end of 1997. Suite accommodations are built around hospitality centers that include a convenience store, exercise center, laundry, meeting space and business center. All guests receive complimentary breakfast and evening hors d'oeuvres Monday through Thursday nights. **GX**: 6 p.m.; **Kid**: V.

HOTEL SOFITEL (800-221-4542), 50 locations ($129-189), in Europe and the U.S. **GX**: V; **Kid**: V.

- **The Exclusive Card**, at $68 for the leisure traveler and $125 for the business traveler, affords ten percent off weeknight rates; plus car rental and meal discounts; 50% off weekend rates; free welcome gifts; express check-in and other added values.

- **A voucher program** covers bed and breakfast at 40 city-center hotels in 11 countries. One child under 12 stays free with an adult.

- **Rate breaks** include "Summer Sale" prices with 57% off plus 50% off the reduced rate for second-night stays at some hotels.

HOWARD JOHNSON (800-446-4656), 600 locations ($27-84), including Howard Johnson Plazas, Park Square Inns, Lodges and HoJo Inns. Seniors account for about one-half of all Howard Johnson reservations. **GX**: 6 p.m.; **Kid**: 17 & under.

- **The Business Traveler Club** guarantees corporate rates and offers awards including airfare discounts, auto club membership and cellular phones. Your first stay currently gives you free membership plus a Continental Airlines discount certificate worth up to $75.

- **The Golden Years Travel Club** gives 15%-50% discounts to members 60 and above, 20% discounts to AARP members or 15% to anyone 60 and above. Club members are also offered discounts on car rentals, airfares and insurance. Lifetime membership is $29.95 for couples or singles.

- **Rate breaks** include the four aptly named seasonal promotions: "Fall Sale," "Winter Sale," "Spring Sale" and "Summer Sale." Special promotions offering excursion airfare discounts are often available in conjunction with Continental Airlines.

HYATT HOTELS & RESORTS (800-233-1234), 181 locations ($125-145), with separately managed domestic and international divisions. **GX**: 6 p.m.; **Kid**: 18 & under.

- **BusinessPlan** rooms have in-room fax, printers and copiers and express breakfast. There is 24-hour access to copiers and printers located on the same floor. The cost is $15 above regular room rates.

- **Gold Passport** for frequent guests gives five points per dollar spent with bonus points for Delta, Northwest and USAir passengers, and for guests renting cars from Alamo or Avis.

- **Seniors** 62 and above get 25% off rack rates at most hotels and meal discounts at many locations.

- **Express check-in** is available with an advance check-in option via a special toll-free number. In-Room video check-out is also available at many Hyatts.

- **Hyatt Vacations** packages hotels with airfare and car rentals.

- **Camp Hyatt** for kids offers newsletters, supervised activities for ages three to 12 and special room rates.

INTER-CONTINENTAL HOTELS & RESORTS (800-327-0200), 182 worldwide locations ($109-169). **GX**: V; **Kid**: 14 & under.

- **Global Business Options** allow preferred business rates, plus your choice of an upgrade, a $15-25 food and beverage credit or double bonus miles.

- **Six Continents Club** for frequent guests requires a $100 enrollment fee and $25 per-year membership renewal, waived for Executive card holders each year they qualify. Members receive priority service, free upgrades, double occupancy at single rates, VIP greeting and in-room gifts, luggage tags and other added values.

- **Airline bonus miles** are awarded for stays at U.S. hotels at a rate of 500 **per day** rather than the standard 500 per stay.

- **Rate breaks** include "Leisure Options" that give your choice of a food and beverage credit, suite upgrade, free parking, second room at half-off or double miles. "Winter Spectacular" rates offer as much as 60% off in Europe, Africa and the Middle East.

KEMPINSKI (800-426-3135), 20 locations ($200-250), all overseas except for locations in San Francisco and Dallas. The Kempinski Group is represented in Beijing, Bangkok, Bombay, Brussels, Berlin, Budapest, Buenos Aires, Dresden, Frankfurt, Hamburg, Hong Kong, Istanbul, Jakarta, Leipzig, Montreal, Moscow, Munich, Santiago, Spain and

---

Only palace on American soil: Hawaii's Iolani Palace, which had electricity installed before Buckingham Palace.

Warsaw. **GX**: 48-hour; **Kid**: 16 & under.

KNIGHTS INNS (800-843-5644), 188 franchised budget locations ($38-48), in 19 states. The Royalty Club for frequent guests provides discounts and added values. **GX**: V; **Kid**; 17 & under.

LA QUINTA INNS (800-531-5900), 225 locations ($45-85), is San Antonio-based with external architecture reflecting its southwest origins. It recently completed a $55 million facelift of over 200 locations and launched a $73 million program to create Gold Medal Rooms with multiple improvements including 25-inch televisions with smart cards and dataports on all telephones. **GX**: 6 p.m.; **Kid**: 18 & under.

- **Returns Club** for frequent guests provides credits per nights paid. Benefits include the twelfth night free, express service options and a special room rate below the standard corporate rate. You can enroll after three stays. Stay more than 50 nights in one year and qualify for additional Gold status awards.

- **The Keenta Club** offers extra booking incentives for corporate travel planners. Earn gift certificates and merchandise credits for booking rooms for corporate use.

- **Seniors 65 and above** and AARP members get ten to 15 percent off.

LOEWS (800-223-0888), 14 locations ($115-145), offering frequent guests a free weekend stay after 15 nights, discount rates, upgrades and other awards. **GX**: V; **Kid**: V.

- **Business-class** rooms include computer work stations, printers and data ports.

- **Rate breaks** include "Summer Sale" rates and American Express promotions with a second room at half-price.

MARRIOTT HOTELS, RESORTS & SUITES (800-228-9290), 252 locations ($89-179), striving for the business traveler market by providing extensive business amenities. **GX**: 6 p.m.; **Kid**: 18 & under.

- **Frequent guests get a choice** of Honored Guest Awards, with bonus points for frequent stays, or Marriott Miles, giving bonus miles on nine airlines. They also offer special awards to users of specific credit cards and AT&T True Rewards.

- **Senior discounts** vary. AARP members generally get ten percent off while some locations offer as much as 50% off with 21-day advance reservations. A ten percent discount on gift shop items is also offered.

- **Rate breaks** include "Two for Breakfast" weekend promotions, which provide up to 40% off, and may include dinner discounts, late Sunday check-out and car rental upgrade.

MOTEL 6 (800-466-8356), 770 locations ($25-40), a franchise operation of budget roadside hotels, often offering the lowest priced hotel option (with the possible exception of Vic & Vickie's Bide-A-Wee Inn and other mom and pop motels). Seniors 55 and above get ten percent discounts. **GX**: 6 p.m.; **Kid**: 17 & under.

MOUNT CHARLOTTE-THISTLE (800-847-4358), 110 locations ($165-225), the second-largest group of hotels in the U.K. Almost 20% of their properties, including The Royal Westminster/ Victoria and The Arden/Stratford-Upon Avon contain award-winning restaurants. The group is in the midst of an $82.5 million renovation project. **GX**: 6 p.m.; **Kid**: None.

- **Rate breaks** include the $96 in '96 program guaranteeing a $96 per-person, per-night rate throughout the year on four night minimum stays. It includes all room taxes and service charges, full English or Scottish breakfast, rental of a four-door Rover (except in London) and a National Trust attraction voucher.

OMNI HOTELS (800-843-6664), 35 locations ($105-145), has eclectic properties with uniform excellence in service. There are 33 U.S. locations, plus hotels in Cancun and Huatulco, Mexico. **GX**: V; **Kid**: V.

- **Select Guest Program** for frequent guests offers discounts and added values including free juice and coffee delivered to your room per your request.

- **Seniors** who are AARP members get discounts up to 50% with some advance reservations.

- **Rate breaks** include "Supersavers" and "Emotional Rescue" rates, both giving up to 50% off.

OUTRIGGER HOTELS (800-462-6262), 30 Hawaiian locations ($90-120), offering budget off-beach high-rises to deluxe beachfront resorts. **GX**: PP ; **Kid**: 17 & under.

- **Seniors 50 and above** get 20% off; AARP members get 25% off.

- **Rate breaks** include free or drastically reduced car rentals at select properties and "Getaway Packages" with rooms starting at $45 per person, per night including breakfast, first night free and free rental car.

RADISSON/SAS (800-333-3333), 305 locations ($87-165), in 39 countries, including high-end Radisson Plazas, bud-

get Radisson Inns, Suite hotels and resort properties. Radisson/SAS is a sister company to Carlson Wagonlit Travel–one of the two largest travel agencies in the world. **GX**: 6 p.m.; **Kid**: 17 & under.

- **Radisson Business Class** (available in over 200 hotels in 23 countries) provides full breakfast, data port, free phone calls, movies, fax service, computer hookup and coffee. Rooms average $20 above standard rates.

- **Worldwide Hospitality Program** confirms the lowest volume rate available to corporate clients.

- **Senior discounts** are generally ten to 30 percent on rooms, food and beverages for guests 50 and older. You're guaranteed the best available room at check-in.

- **Rate breaks for leisure travelers** include "Shades of Summer" from May to September (30%-50% off plus free breakfast); "Great Fall Rates" from September to December; "Shades of Winter;" and "Bed and Breakfast Breakaways" (at 290 participating hotels) including complimentary international breakfast options.

RAMADA (800-272-6232), 700 locations ($34-111). Its franchise system allows wide variances from location to location. Ramada Plaza Hotels are high-end/full-service. Ramada Inns are on or near major highways and have a moderate level of amenities. Ramada Limiteds are budget properties with complimentary light breakfasts. **GX**: 4 p.m.; **Kid**: 17 & under.

- **The Ramada Business Card** frequent guest program works on a point system with bonuses for Alamo car rentals. Points are redeemable for travel and merchandise. Members also get preferred rates, express service and upgrades, when available.

- **Best Years Club** offers 25% off rack rates and award points for guests 60 and older. There is a $15 lifetime membership fee.

- **Kids** 12 and under eat free at participating locations.

- **Rate breaks** include "Super Saver Weekend" rates offering up to 50% off regular rates. The "Bed & Breakfast Weekend" promotion offers 50% off plus breakfast for two.

- **Seasonal information and hotel package deals** are available via the Ramada Hotline, 800-228-2828.

RED LION HOTELS & INNS (800-547-8010), 56 locations ($70-100), located primarily on the West Coast, offer upscale amenities at surprisingly moderate prices. **GX**: 6 p.m.; **Kid**: 17 & under.

- **Frequent Guest Dividends** offers discounts on future stays that can be used cumulatively or 500 bonus air miles per stay.

- **Prime Rate Discount** gives AARP members 20% off and ten percent off some meals.

- **Rate breaks** include weekend promotions with your choice of a second night free or a second room at half-price.

Red Roof Inns (800-843-7663), 210 locations ($30-57), primarily in the Eastern U.S. **GX**: 6 p.m.; **Kid**: 18 & under.

- **The Senior RediCard** offers ten percent off room rates, $15 in discount coupons and other added values. Lifetime membership is $10, $12 for couples.

RENAISSANCE HOTELS (800-228-9898), 96 locations ($115-140), including the upscale Stouffer Hotels plus Renaissance Hotels, once the high end of Ramada's corporate portfolio. **GX**: 4 p.m.; **Kid**: 18 & under.

- **Club Express** for frequent guests gives points for every dollar spent–even restaurant meals when you are not a hotel guest. Members get express check-in, free in-room lodging for spouses and quarterly newsletters.

- **60-plus rates** provide standard discounts up to 25%. Special discounts go up to 50% at some properties.

- **Rate breaks** include "Breakation" summer rates starting at $69.

- **Vacation packages** built around special interests such as golf and diving are available.

RESIDENCE INNS BY MARRIOTT (800-331-3131), 195 locations ($75-105), offering many floor plans. They also offer complimentary suites for the use of families on extended visits. All guests receive complimentary breakfast. Weekly barbecues are hosted by on-site managers. **GX**: 6 p.m.; **Kid**: 18 & under.

- **Seniors 62 and above** and AARP members get 15%-40% discounts.

> **❝**Hotels investing heavily in room business technology might take note that The Ritz-Carlton business guests listed fresh fruit as their most desired business amenity–followed by mineral water and chocolate chip cookies.**❞**

THE RITZ-CARLTON HOTELS (800-241-3333), 38 locations ($150-190), upscale and almost exclusively located in city centers. Many have special summer rates and American Express Card discounts. **GX**: V; **Kid**: None.

SHERATON HOTELS, RESORTS AND ALL-SUITES (800-325-3535), 416 locations ($58-164), including the CIGA group, purchased in 1994. Fifty hotels are designated The Luxury Collection. The Four Points Hotels comprise their mid-range option. **GX**: 4 p.m.; **Kid**: 17 & under.

- **Club International** for frequent guests spans all Sheraton types and locations. There are two levels: Basic and Gold. Basic membership is free. You are automatically upgraded to Gold after four stays (membership is $25 per year) and earn points at an accelerated rate plus automatic upgrades when available and guaranteed 4 p.m. check-out.

- **Seniors 60 and above** and AARP members get 25% off, and grandchildren stay free in the same room.

- **Business rooms** in Club Level contain computers, laser printers and fax machines. You can pull up your bill via smart-card TV and print it yourself before you check out.

- **Rate breaks** include "Suresaver" discounts of five to 40 percent off and "Endless Weekend" rates including breakfast and late check-out. Book 14 days in advance for the maximum discount. "Freedom of Europe" promotions offer up to 30% off with no minimum stay requirement. Special rates and two-for-one for Sheraton Club International members.

- **"FastBreak Breakfast,"** at all North American Sheratons, delivers breakfast to your room in five minutes or the meal is free.

SHONEY INNS (800-222-2222), 79 locations ($40-65), in 19 states, primarily in the Southeast and Midwest. Some offer complimentary breakfast. **GX**: 6 p.m.; **Kid**: 18 & under.

- **The ShoBusiness Club** provides rate breaks and added values for frequent guests and business travelers.

- **Merit Club for ages 50 and above** provides single rates for up to four occupants. Membership is free.

SIGNATURE INNS (800-822-5252), 23 locations ($58-70), in Iowa, Illinois, Indiana, Ohio, Kentucky and Tennessee. Continental breakfast is complimentary. **GX**: 6 p.m.; **Kid**: 17 & under.

- **Signature rooms** have 12-foot work centers including modem port. Guest office use is free to registered guests.

- **Signature Club** for frequent guests offers discounts and added values.

- **AARP and AAA members** get discounts, varying by location.

- **Rate breaks** include "Weekend Saver Rates" (seasonal at some locations; year-round at others).

SUPER 8 (800-800-8000), 1,201 locations ($32-50), a franchised chain that holds few surprises. Most locations offer free coffee, cable television, local phone calls and fax usage. **GX**: V; **Kid**: 12 & under.

- **VIP Club** for frequent guests provides ten percent discounts, express check-in and check-out and added values.

- **Senior discounts** vary but the majority of locations give at least ten percent off to guests 50 and above.

Home of the world's first skyscraper: Sana, Yemen where a 20-story palace was built over 2,000 years ago.

SWISSOTEL (800-637-9477), 14 locations ($134-189), including four in the U.S. (Atlanta, Boston, Chicago and New York) and ten international (Switzerland, Germany, the Netherlands, Turkey, Egypt, Thailand, China and Korea). Swissotel is owned by Swissair. **GX**: 6 p.m.; **Kid**: V.

- **"Swissoffices"** are hotel business centers available to hotel guests at no charge for the first two hours.

TRAVELODGE (800-578-7878), 450 locations ($39-59), a low-price, full service chain under the Forte umbrella. All benefits (except senior) are grouped in their Guest Rewards program. **GX**: 6 p.m.; **Kid**: 17 & under.

- **Guest Rewards** is available in the U.S. and Canada. Earn Silver status after ten stays, Gold after 20. Also, earn free lodging, upgrades and rental car discounts and upgrades.

- **The Classic Travel Club** offers 15% off for guests 50 and above. There is no membership fee.

VAGABOND INNS (800-522-1555), 48 locations ($40-50), in the Western United States. **GX**: 4 p.m.; **Kid**: 18 & under.

- **Frequent guests** earn a tenth stay free. There's no membership fee.

- **Business Club** offers a more rapidly earned free stay benefit plus other added values.

- **Club 55** offers minimum discounts of 10%. Membership is free.

WESTIN HOTELS & RESORTS (800-228-3000), 68 locations ($120-150), upscale, with a substantial international presence. *Service Express* offers access to all hotel services by dialing one number. *Travel Light* provides toothbrush, toothpaste, razor, hair dryer and alarm clock either in your room or yours for the asking. **GX**: 6 p.m.; **Kid**: 18 & under.

- **Westin Premier** program for frequent guests offers 1,000 points per night's stay. Burgundy members also earn one point per dollar charged to their room account; Gold members earn two points. Five hundred bonus air miles per stay are rewarded even if you do not have a flight in conjunction with the stay as you get points and miles for every stay. Membership is free.

- *Guest Office* **rooms** at $20 extra per night include laser printers, copy and fax machines, direct fax lines, speaker phones with data ports and no surcharge on local, toll-free, credit card calls and incoming and outgoing faxes.

- **Senior discounts** are determined by each hotel and can range as high as 50%. United Silver Wings members get special discounts.

- **Westin Kids Club** gives free meals to children 12 and under, dining with parents. They also offer gift packs, planned activities and movies. Request a Safety Kit with night light, outlet covers and children's ID bracelets.

WYNDHAM HOTELS & RESORTS (800-996-3426), 69 locations ($90-125), in the U.S., Bermuda and the Caribbean. **GX**: V; **Kid**: V.

- **Triple upgrades** are available to American Airlines frequent flyers on flights, hotel and car rentals. Promotions may double bonus miles.

- **Seniors** get a minimum ten percent discount and as much as 50% off at Caribbean resort properties.

- **Rate breaks** include weekend and holiday rates and "Third Weekend Nights Free" available at select hotels.

INTERNATIONAL TIDBITS

You'll find that many of the same standard discounts available at U.S. hotels are also available at most international hotels. You'll also find half-off hotel programs, special promotions and package rates.

> ❝Fax your reservation request rather than call. You'll save money plus you'll have written confirmation of your rate. Most industrialized countries began using facsimile machines years before they became prevalent in the U.S., so you'll find fax access a good route around language problems, high phone rates and potential confusion of information.❞

Voucher programs are relatively prevalent but don't always provide maximum value. If you buy them at standard rate, you've just purchased rack rate, international style. You pre-purchase the vouchers before you leave the U.S. A big selling point is a locked in price, regardless of the exchange rate when you travel. A guaranteed rate will do the same thing without an advance monetary outlay.

Bargains abound if you can be happy in hotels that provide cleanliness and comfort at a basic level. Europe, for example, can provide plenty of lodging choices at $50 per night. The biggest sacrifice for North Americans? A tie between shared baths and no television.

Pensions, small home-like lodging facilities, offer full meal plans or one meal per day. They are roughly similar to bed and breakfasts but tend to be less expensive.

Country that legally limits the height of hotels to that of palm trees: Fiji.

> **"**The Three Rules of checking in: 1) Never leave your passport with the front desk. The best option is to keep it in hand while showing it to the desk clerk. 2) Get matches or hotel letterhead as soon as you arrive. It's a convenient way to direct taxi drivers or ask for directions if you don't know your way back to the hotel. 3) Always keep your valuables in a safe deposit box. Keep in mind, because of the intricacies of safe deposit boxes, if you lose the key, it may cost you $100 to replace it.**"**

U.S. based budget chains with a significant international presence include Budgetel, Choice, Courtyard by Marriott, Econo Lodge, Hojo Inns, Holiday Inn Express, La Quinta, Motel 6, Red Roof Inns, Super 8 and Travelodge.

Consider staying away from city centers. You know the rate difference between city center and suburban hotels in the U.S. The same principle holds true internationally. Go to a nearby village and you save money plus you enjoy a significant amount of local charm. Inexpensive rail passes will connect you to the city and other points of interest.

Never judge hotels by their lobbies. International hotels tend to not put a lot of their budget in initial appearances. Ask to see a room. Often, you'll be pleasantly surprised.

If you liked your last night's lodging ask the hotel manager to recommend a place in the next town you're visiting.

Tourist information offices, located at airports and in city centers, have reliable room-finding services. Ask for what you need and have the location of their recommended hotel marked on the free map they will be pleased to provide.

Remember that bargaining is expected in many countries and acceptable in most.

Youth discounts (ages 18-26) are available at about 400 Ibis Hotels in Europe.

There are markdowns on rooms still not booked at 9 p.m. Rates are on a space available basis and cannot be acquired by reservation. Tourist information offices can steer you to the closest Ibis Hotel.

When shopping for international vacation packages always check the local papers at major gateway cities. For example, when flying to Europe check the Boston, New York City and Washington, D. C. newspapers. If you are flying to Asia or the South Pacific check the Los Angeles or San Francisco papers. If you are traveling to South America, review Miami's newspaper. When visiting Mexico, look in Los Angeles, San Diego, Dallas, Houston or Miami's papers.

Climat de France, 800-332-5332, is a major budget chain with mostly country inn locations and a few high-rise city center hotels. For about $50 ($20 for seniors), you can purchase a card entitling you to discounts from ten to 30 percent. The card must be purchased in France from tourism offices.

Put on the Ritz at The Ritz on Paris' Place Vendome. A mere $620 per night gives you Persian carpets, in-room fireplaces and places you on a guest list with a legacy that includes Hemingway and Bill Blass.

Get Ritz luxury at a much lower price at the Palace Hotel in Madrid. Beautifully appointed rooms start at $125.

London's most glamorous neighborhood: Mayfair, bordered by Picadilly, Oxford Street, Regent and Park Lane.

Stay in a castle for $238 a night. The Schloss Durnstein, an hour from Vienna, is an old haunt of King Richard the Lionhearted. Its features include a large chamber with 33 chandeliers that overlooks the Danube River.

Inexpensive rooms in Japan (apart from the train-berth sized sleeping rooms hawked as an alternative to exorbitant hotel rates) can be found via the Welcome Inn Reservation Center. They offer 500 hotels, pensions and inns with maximum prices of $80 per night. Fax them at (in Tokyo) at 33211-9009.

Economy lodging in the United Kingdom is available at Granada Inns and Little Chef Lodges. They're located along major motorways and are like Motel 6 rooms with an accent.

Central London Accommodations, 44-171-602-9668, has nightly offerings at as little as $22 per night.

Staying at a spa need not be pricey–at least in Bulgaria where the four-star Sananski Hotel & Spa, 120 miles south of Sofia, starts at $80 per night.

A Monthly Publication of Insider Travel Secrets
Listing the Latest Discounts for
The Cost-Conscious Traveler

Recently, ***BEST FARES Discount Travel Magazine*** showed savvy travelers how to get a buy-one-get-one free certificate on Northwest by switching long distance carriers.

Call 800-880-1234 to subscribe.
See page 395 for your discount subscription offer.

The highest revolving restaurant: The Schilthorn in the Swiss Alps at 9,748 feet.

ARE YOUR CAR RENTAL DOLLARS GOING UP IN FUMES?

Renting a car is a pain in the exhaust pipe. There's a familiar name over the counter, but because many locations are independently owned franchises, each location might operate under different policies. The person behind the counter can bear a striking resemblance to Mickey Mouse–even if you're nowhere near Disneyland.

Each time I travel, I check a current issue of my magazine (yes, I can't remember every deal) to see if I can use any special/limited time offers, particularly those for free rentals, free upgrades or free added days. Sometimes these offers are limited to cities I'm not traveling to, or require flying on an airline I don't want to use because I'm getting a much cheaper ticket from a competitor. Then I turn to five of my favorite ways to save:

Frequent flyer discounts that keep you from paying 50% more than you have to pay.

Sunday newspaper ads that turn travel sections into road maps of savings.

Counter-hopping with a competitor's best rate in hand.

Negotiated discounts set up by automobile clubs and special interest organizations.

Fly/Drive packages offering discounted cars combined with airfare.

This section starts by showing you exactly how to use these methods to your best advantage and goes on to show you even more ways to save: corporate and senior discounts, weekend rates, fuel options, packages, deadheading and more. I'll tell you when discounts you've been relying on are actually taking money out of your pocket.

Getting the best rate isn't the only way to save. You can be taken at the car rental counter as easily as you can be taken at the used car lot. Whether buying or renting, you never want to be at the mercy of a person who's employed to get the most money possible on every deal. After you have read *Play Their Game And Win*, you'll be an expert on fine print matters including Collision Damage Waiver/Loss Damage Waiver (CDW/LDW) coverage, driver qualifications and emergency road service.

Renting internationally can be that same pain in the tailpipe with a pain relief prescription written in a language you've never seen before. *Counter Intelligence* provides the cure with savings strategies, car selection tips, insurance needs and country specific information.

When you finish this chapter you'll be more knowledgeable than the person who is trying to rent you the car. It's the best possible position to be in when negotiating any deal. If you want to throw your money away, send me a check. I promise to be far more appreciative than any car rental company. If you want to save money every time you rent a car, read on. It's easier than you think. Once you know the rules of the rental road, you're the one in the driver's seat.

CLUES TO THE BEST BARGAINS

ⓕREQUENT FLYER MEMBERSHIPS

If you don't rent a car at the frequent flyer rate you can end up paying as much as 50% more than you have to pay. All major airlines have negotiated agreements with various car rental agencies (except Enterprise, which follows a strategy of lower base rates and fewer discount options). Your actual discount will range from three to 30 percent on weekday rentals and may go up to 50% on week-long rentals, depending on the specific airline/car rental agency affiliation and the market in which you're renting. In most cases, you don't even have to fly in on the partner airline but be sure to double check. When you arrive at the counter, you'll be asked to show your frequent flyer membership card and (when necessary) your airline ticket. If you don't have the card, your rate can be bumped up to the standard rate, so be sure you have your card on hand. If you carry multiple frequent flyer cards (and you should) be sure to ask the reservation agent to check the discount for each airline or to tell you which frequent flyer card will give you the best deal.

> ❝ *Plan ahead! Taking the time to sign up with multiple frequent flyer programs will pay off. You can even sign up by phone. Even if you're partial to one or two airlines, enroll in all the major programs so you can get the lowest frequent flyer rate on every car you rent. If you rent 25 days a year and save an average of $20 each time, you've saved $500. Not a bad return for a few minutes investment. Even if you're an infrequent renter, a few minutes of research will produce significant savings.* ❞

FREQUENT FLYER RATES						
	NEW YORK CITY		CHICAGO		LOS ANGELES	
RENTAL COMPANY	DAILY RATE	FREQUENT FLYER RATE	DAILY RATE	FREQUENT FLYER RATE	DAILY RATE	FREQUENT FLYER RATE
ALAMO	N/A	N/A	$51.99	$38.99	$48.56	$38.99
AVIS	$74.99	$58.79	$60.99	$51.87	$56.99	$46.87
HERTZ	$69.99	$66.49	$58.99	$49.87	$56.99	$46.87
NATIONAL	$62.99	$44.00	$52.95	$44.85	$50.99	$35.85
THRIFTY	$43.65	$42.00	$48.95	$42.00	$46.95	$33.00

Location of most rental car wrecks: on the drive out of the airport.

> **❝** If you live in a small city, pick up a newspaper from one of the larger cities (i.e. New York or Los Angeles). The larger the circulation, the better the array of travel ads offered. Many times the advertising budget is limited to certain newspapers and your local paper won't show these short-term offers. **Your local library is also a good source for these out-of-town newspapers.** Be sure to note the promotion code of the special offer when making reservations and to reserve your car by the deadline listed. **❞**

Ⓢ UNDAY TRAVEL SECTIONS

The Sunday travel sections of major newspapers provide discount information on car rentals, fly/drive packages and other news that can lower your car rental rate. Scan them carefully. A hotel or airline ad may also contain a car rental discount offer.

Ⓒ OUNTER HOPPING

Waiting until you arrive at your destination to shop around can often bring about some of the best discounts or perks available. Reserve your best rate in advance, then hop from counter-to-counter at your destination airport, checking for a better deal. You might end up with a lower rate, a larger car, or both.

Ⓝ EGOTIATED DISCOUNTS

Negotiated discounts of ten percent or more come from membership in organizations including *BEST FARES Discount Travel Magazine,* the American Automobile Association (AAA) and other auto clubs, the American Association of Retired Persons (AARP), the Small Business Association, the American Red Cross, Sam's Warehouse Club, COSTCO, The National Association of the Self Employed and other groups. AAA discounts tend to be extremely favorable and, in many cases, offer a better rate than frequent flyer discounts. Always check AAA and frequent flyer rates. If you omit this step in comparison shopping, you may overlook the best deal.

> **❝** One thing to remember, car rental companies operate no differently than airlines, hotels, or cruise lines. If an airline takes off with empty seats–they make no money; if a hotel goes with empty rooms for the night–they make no money; if a cruise line sets sail with empty cabins–they make no money. Likewise, if a car company sits with cars in the lot all weekend long–**they make no money.** Many locations are franchises, and their bottom line is to make money any way they can with their open inventory of cars. They may even have a standard policy such as... 'take that warm body and rent the car at any rate!' **❞**

ⓕ LY/ DRIVE PACKAGES

Fly/Drive packages can provide excellent savings for both leisure and business travelers. You can book airfare and car rentals as part of one package and, potentially, get discounts on both. Your car rental discount comes from the volume business the air carrier or charter company does with the car rental agency. Savings will vary dramatically and can be particularly favorable when your trip does not include a Saturday stay. Here is an example to give you some idea of what to expect:

America West Vacations, the vacation division of America West Airlines, recently offered a Fly/Drive package to Phoenix which substantially beat their best discount on airfare only. The lowest no Saturday night stay roundtrip airfare was $640 while renting a car separately would have cost $54 per day, or $162 total for a three-day rental. The total cost would be $802. America West Vacations offered a $149 Fly/Drive package with roundtrip airfare with no Saturday stay requirement and a rental car. Since most Fly/Drive packages are based on double occupancy there was also a $35 single supplement making the total airfare and car rental cost $184. The savings amounted to $618.

You have to call each airline's vacation division directly. The airline's regular reservation staff cannot book these Fly/Drive packages. Check our *Know Who To Call* section for the vacation divisions of each major airline. Some charter companies also offer Fly/Drive packages. Check the Sunday travel section for cities served from your hometown. Fly/Drive packages are most often available in cities popular with vacationers, but smart business travelers can utilize them too.

Recently,

BEST FARES Discount Travel Magazine showed savvy travelers how to buy a $15.95 commemorative baseball and get $100 off a roundtrip airfare plus up to 65% off your hotel.

Call 800-880-1234 to subscribe.
See page 395 for your discount subscription offer.

Average cost of car and driver passage between Seattle, WA and Victoria, British Columbia: $42.

THE RUNDOWN ON THE COMPANIES

WHO ARE THE PLAYERS?

Over 2,000 rental businesses exist: regional companies, independent locations, dealerships, franchises and national chains. Eight of them dominate the market. The multi-billion dollar rental car industry can be categorized as follows:

- **National companies built around substantial airport presence**. **Avis, Budget, Hertz** and **National** each have more than 1,000 U.S. locations. **Dollar** and **Thrifty** have about half that number. **Alamo** targets the nation's largest airports with about 115 locations.

- **National companies with minimal or no airport presence.** Time spent shuttling to an off-airport facility may not be much longer than the time it takes to get to airport rental sites at the larger airports. Get precise distance information and hours of operation. Or, consider **Enterprise,** the king of off-airport agencies. With 2,300 U.S. locations, Enterprise is technically bigger than Hertz. Enterprise may deliver your car to you or may take you to their nearest office. Lower overhead means rates that are often 30%-50% cheaper than their competitors.

- **Regional companies** like **Value** and **Payless** grew up around vacation destinations, but now serve a significant number of business clients.

- **Smaller national companies** like **Rent-A-Wreck** and **Ugly Duckling** have grown out of niche markets and have become more widely known. They have cars that are in far better condition than their names imply.

- **Local rental agencies** can be cost-effective choices if you can work within their limited hours and locations.

HOW DO THEY COMPARE?

All major agencies offer the same popular features such as corporate discounts, rapid check-in and car return options, cellular phones, child safety seats and navigation systems by request and for additional fees. The difference is in the degree and sophistication of services offered. If price is your primary concern, check the chart on the following page. It shows the weekday and weekend mid-size rates in three cities. There is a $35 difference between the lowest to highest price in Houston; a $29 difference in San Francisco; and a $21 difference in Boston. Weekend prices are sometimes dependent on two-day minimum rentals. You usually save a bundle as compared to weekend rates but, as you'll note, the savings vary. One or more agencies may not even offer a discount in a particular market on a particular weekend. Three of the seven agencies we checked did not. If you don't get a much lower rate for weekend rentals, check a competitor.

DAILY MID-SIZE RENTAL RATES (Weekday/Weekend)			
AGENCY	**HOUSTON**	**SAN FRANCISCO**	**BOSTON**
ADVANTAGE 800-777-5500	$35.39/$21.99	N/A	N/A
ALAMO 800-327-9633	$47.99/$26.99	$58.99/$46.99	$61.99/$25.99
AVIS 800-331-1212	$57.79/$31.99	$64.99/$45.99	$57.99/$27.99
BUDGET 800-527-0700	$54.98/$28.98	$59.99/$41.99	$56.99/$56.99
DOLLAR 800-800-4000	$39.95/$25.95	$55.95/$45.95	$55.95/$42.99
ENTERPRISE 800-325-8007	$41.99/$26.99	$35.95/$23.99	$40.99/$40.99
HERTZ 800-654-3131	$57.99/$31.99	$64.99/$45.99	$57.99/$27.99
NATIONAL 800-328-4567	$74.99/$27.99	$59.99/$37.99	$56.99/$27.99
THRIFTY 800-367-2277	$43.88/$25.88	$39.89/$42.89	$51.90/$51.90

SPECIAL OFFERINGS

Alamo

- **Alamo Atlas**, an interactive computer system that gives directions from rental office kiosks (information booths) in 11 cities.

Avis

- **Extensive fleet of hand-control vehicles**, wheelchair-accessible mini-vans and special TTY phone reservations for hearing-impaired clients.

Budget

- **The largest renter of luxury automobiles.** Budget offers Jaguars, Lincoln Town Cars and Mustang convertibles to take the monotony out of driving.

Enterprise

- **Free** pickup or delivery offered. Enterprise will either bring your car to you or take you to the nearest agency.

Hertz

- **"NeverLost Navigation System" and "NeverLost Plus,"** include an in-car phone, if requested at time of booking, on mid-size, full-size or luxury class cars.

National

- **Lets you choose** any car within your rental category from their lot.

Thrifty

- **Fifteen passenger Vanasaurus** is featured for maximum economy for large groups or family transportation.

Length of the curvaceous Romantic Road in Bavaria: 220 miles.

OTHER WAYS TO SAVE

THE CORPORATE TRAVELER

Corporate rates are available to all business clients. You apply as a company. Dollar, Enterprise and Budget encourage even the smallest companies to apply. Larger companies rate qualifications on estimated annual car rental expenditures and usually require minimums of $12,000 -25,000. The higher end of the ten to 35 percent discount range goes to high volume corporate users. The application process takes three to four weeks. Benefits that can be negotiated are:

- **Guaranteed lowest rates** that provide a five to ten percent discount on promotional rates if they are lower than your corporate rate. This assures that you won't have to choose between lowest possible rates and corporate rate protection.

> *❝ Corporate clients who use coupons and special offers may negate some of the benefits in their corporate contracts. Read the fine print on all coupons, savings certificates and ads to make sure you don't sacrifice your benefits by using them. **Alamo** is one of the few car rental companies that allows the use of discount coupons along with negotiated discounts. ❞*

- **Reduced liability** even if the optional insurance is declined. Typically, your liability ceiling for loss or damage is set at $3,000.

- **Protection against liability** from injured parties. Large corporations can often negotiate $1 million plus in coverage.

Cost of renting an Army Hummer jeep in Beverly Hills: $300 a day.

- **Waived surcharges and fees** for under age or additional drivers and waived safe driver checks.

- **Free upgrades,** rental days and amenities, including car phones.

- **Availability guarantees** to assure your rental when cars are in high-demand.

- **Discount refueling** charges that help keep your rental expenses in check.

- **Billing options.** To aid you in setting up a corporate account, the *Know Who To Call* section of this book includes phone numbers for each of the major car rental companies.

> *" Let's face facts: hotels, airlines and car rental companies are all looking for the same thing–the full rate person at their mercy... namely a business traveler. The corporate traveler is the one who subsidizes the car rental market in many ways. Some corporate travelers opt for their favorite brand, and therefore higher rates, for reasons such as convenience options and special perks. Business travelers also pay the highest rates for midweek travel, and other established policies–such as paying for a 24-hour rental on a four-hour car usage. In many cases, the business traveler is also locked into the corporate rate program mandated by their company, and often has no choice but to pay the highest rates. "*

SENIOR RATES

Senior rates are offered under provisions that will vary from company to company. Your best route to a senior discount is membership in a senior organization such as the American Association of Retired Persons (AARP), 800-424-3410. You can join AARP at age 50 and begin enjoying senior savings. Some senior discounts require membership in AARP or a similar organization. You rarely get a senior discount on promotional rates so be sure not to settle for five to ten percent off when greater discounts are available. If you're a senior and a member of American Automobile Association (AAA), you'll almost always do better with the AAA discount. Senior discounts can vary by market, type of car rented and availability, and some require advance reservations.

Here are general guidelines for the major car rental companies:

ALAMO: five to ten percent at age 50; no membership required.

AVIS: five to ten percent at age 50; no membership required.

BUDGET: five percent at age 62; age 50 with an AARP card.

DOLLAR: varies by market; must be an AARP member.

ENTERPRISE: no senior discounts available.

HERTZ: varies by market and membership organization.

NATIONAL: usually ten percent must be an AARP member.

THRIFTY: ten percent for age 55 and older; no membership required.

WEEKEND RATES

Weekend rates can be as low as one-third of the weekday rate. In a market where peak daily rates for compact cars are $28-83, off-peak rates will range from $20-30. A rental that costs $62 per day at 11 a.m. Thursday drops to $23 one hour later. Timing is everything in the hunt for these lower rates.

* **Rates are generally in effect** from Thursday noon to Monday noon. Keeping a car over Saturday night qualifies you for the cheapest rates.

* **Some companies offer one-day rentals** at weekend rates; others require two or three day minimums. Policies can change by market, rental car company and time of year.

* **Some companies cancel your weekend rate** if you return the car late. They can legitimately raise the rate of each day on your rental contract to the premium weekday rate.

* **Ask about extra-day pricing** to avoid the shock of a much higher rate should you return the car outside of the weekend rate parameters.

* **Business travelers can save** by scheduling flights to arrive Thursday late morning or early afternoon, particularly on trips lasting a minimum of two days.

HOLIDAY DISCOUNTS

Holiday discounts work the same as weekend rates, but are harder to pin down as to when and how to qualify. We find that certain reservation agents with **Hertz** and **National** are more likely to provide exact details of holiday rental periods. Coordinating holiday schedules around holiday rental parameters can provide significant savings. A difference of one day, or even the proper number of rental days, can tremendously affect the quoted rates. To give you an idea of when holiday discounts apply:

* **Over Thanksgiving weekend,** the holiday rates typically apply from 12 noon Wednesday through 11:59 p.m. the following Monday. Wednesday pick-ups require a four-day minimum rental. Others follow the weekend rate rules.

* **Christmas 1995 and New Years' 1995,** holiday rates applied from 12 noon December 21 (Thursday), through 11:59 p.m. January 2, 1996 (Tuesday). Discounted holiday rates were available anytime during that period. Monday and Tuesday pick-ups required a four-day minimum rental, Wednesday pick-up required a three-day minimum rental, and Thursday through Sunday pick-ups followed the normal weekend rental requirements. Christmas 1996 and New Year 1997 will fall on Wednesdays, so weekend and holiday rates should combine to cover the period from December 19 (Thursday) through January 5, 1996 (Monday).

Special offers and discount coupons can be found in credit card inserts, newspapers and frequent flyer newsletters or from travel agents who are supplied by rental agency sales representatives.

Promotional books offered by rental companies, when available, contain discounts on hotels, attractions and restaurants for the area of rental. Some examples:

* **Budget's "WorldClass" Drives** program offers free guidebooks with an average of $400 in coupons available for rentals in Florida, California, Hawaii, Western Canada, the United Kingdom and Australia.

* **Hertz Savings Certificates** feature coupon discounts in Florida, California and Hawaii.

Branch of service in which Warren Avis, founder of the rental car company, was an officer: U.S. Air Force.

- **Avis'** *Florida Discount Guide* includes coupons for everything from attractions' discounts to free orange juice.

Free rental days and upgrades are available through frequent renter and corporate rate programs plus special promotions. Budget's AwardsPlus, for example, gives a free upgrade after two rentals and a free day after four rentals. Payless' Championship Club offers an upgrade after three rentals, a free weekend rental after four, and a free weekday after five rentals.

VISITOR RATES

If friends or family from abroad want a car rental in the U.S. they can often get large discounts by booking the car in their home country and requesting a visitor's promotional rate. It's designed to promote tourism and can save 30%-60% off rates given to U.S. residents. Alamo offers this discount regularly under **code ZF**.

ONE-WAY RENTAL OPTIONS

Drop-off fees and one-way rates are set high enough to discourage the removal of cars from their usual markets. Drop-off fees can be as high as several hundred dollars. One-way rental rates are higher than usual daily rates, but are almost always cheaper than paying drop-off fees.

- **Comparison shop.** Your cost will be determined in part by each company's local surplus of cars and the need for them at your destination–factors that change daily. You'll only get the information you need by calling each car company direct at their individual location. The local number of the location can be obtained by calling the main reservation number of the car company.

- **Check weekly rates** even if you only need the car for four or five days. Often, a full weekly rental rate is cheaper than the aggregate amount of four days at the daily rate.

- **Special programs negate the usual rules.** For example, the Hertz "Rent It Here/Leave It There" program lets you rent in one of eight European countries and drop your car off in another, including 200 Hertz locations in Austria, Belgium, France, Germany, Luxembourg, the Netherlands and Switzerland. The drop-off fee is only about $50.

"Deadheading" opportunities exist when a particular company has a need to move cars to a location in another city. In this case, you rent the car from one location and drop it off for the rental company at the other. You're most likely to find this situation between two nearby cities. For example, between Austin, San Antonio, Houston, and Dallas/Ft. Worth; between Chicago and Milwaukee; between Detroit, Dayton, Cincinnati, Columbus and Cleveland, or between San Francisco, San Jose, Sacramento and Los Angeles.

- **Opportunities also exist during seasonal changes**. If you need a one-way rental from the Northeast to Florida at the beginning of winter, you'll find abundant opportunities to deadhead. The rental company will charge you a fraction of its usual rate because they must have the cars moved. Heading for the right place at the right time may mean paying only surcharges and taxes.

- **Drive-away companies** transport their customers' automobiles for a fee. Finding the right connection means you can fulfill their contract and get the transportation you need for only the cost of your gas. You must be at least 21 years of age, have a good driving record and put up a fully refundable deposit of about $200. The use of these cars is limited to transportation from your city to the destination city. Once you arrive, discretionary driving is not allowed.

- **Drive-away companies usually advertise in the classified section** of newspapers or the classified phone pages under Automobile Transporters and Drive-away Services. Two of the largest companies: Auto Driveaway (U.S. and Canada) at 800-346-2277 and AAA Driveaway, 800-233-4875.

LIMIT YOUR RENTAL COSTS

Don't rent for your entire trip if you only need the car part of the time. Use free hotel shuttles to and from the airport to save one or more days in rental cost, plus parking fees. When you're ready for your car, rent from an in-hotel or nearby location or call Enterprise, the only major car rental company that will deliver your car to you or pick you up and take you to their nearest office. Enterprise's rates are usually less than most daily rates at airport or off-airport locations. Their rates will vary according to your proximity to their nearest rental office. No matter which agency you use, you'll also save by avoiding surcharges, which all on-airport rental locations add to your bill.

AIRPORT/OFF-AIRPORT RATE COMPARISONS						
	AVIS		NATIONAL		ENTERPRISE	
	ON AIRPORT	OFF AIRPORT	ON AIRPORT	OFF AIRPORT	ON AIRPORT	OFF AIRPORT
CHICAGO	$60.99	$48.99	$63.95	$44.99	$43.95	$46.99
LOS ANGELES	$58.99	$38.00	$54.99	$41.99	$54.95	$38.99
WASHINGTON, D.C.	$59.99	$52.99	$54.99	$45.99	$39.99	$43.00
DENVER	$46.99	$45.96	$46.98	$39.98	$52.95	$42.99
ATLANTA	$68.99	$56.99	$63.99	$43.99	$42.89	$32.99

Observe 24-hour cycles. Car rental companies base their rates on 24-hour periods. Even if you're a business traveler using the car for eight hours, you still pay for the full 24 hours. If you return a car late, you may be able to charm your way out of the added cost, but why risk it? You'll be charged an added hourly fee up to four hours, then you pay an added day's rental. The only company currently offering hourly rentals is Value Rent-A-Car.

Number of car deer collisions reported in Ohio in 1994: 25,636.

DON'T BE A FOOL WHEN IT COMES TO FUEL

Next time you rent a car, why not try to save some money on gas? If you forget to fill the gas tank before returning a rental car, you could end up paying a stiff refueling fee which could make you fume. Most car rental companies charge nearly three times the current local price for their gas. The simplest way to avoid this highway robbery is to make sure the needle points to full on the fuel gauge before returning the car.

You have three options when it comes to refueling:

- **The first and most important option is to re-fill the tank** before returning the car. Gas up nine to ten miles from the airport to avoid paying premium rates. Don't let the pump go until the automatic shutoff activates. Most tanks read full about a gallon before the tank's limit is reached.

- **Your second option is** to take the pre-pay option and return with the gas tank empty, If you return the car 1/2 empty, your $1.09 pre-pay option becomes $2.18 per gallon. Any gas left in the tank is your gift to the rental agency.

- **Your worst value option** would be to return the gas tank empty. If you don't pre-pay, any gas needed to fill the tank will cost you about triple the gas station prices. You'll pay as much as $3 or more per gallon if the car company has to refuel the tank. **An 18-gallon tank of gas can cost as much as $54.**

REFUELING PRICE COMPARISONS

	CHICAGO	WASHINGTON, D.C.	DALLAS	LOS ANGELES
AVERAGE PUMP PRICE	$1.35	$1.23	$1.17	$1.29
ALAMO	Refill price $2.99 Prepay option $1.34	Refill price $2.99 Prepay option $1.24	Refill price $2.99 Prepay option $1.19	Refill price $2.99 Prepay option $1.34
AVIS	Refill price $3.14 Prepay option $1.29	Refill price $3.19 Prepay option $1.30	Refill price $2.65 Prepay option $1.14	Refill price $2.95 Prepay option $1.14
BUDGET	Refill price $2.69 Prepay option $1.30	Refill price $2.65 Prepay option $1.06	Refill price $2.70 Prepay option $.99	Refill price $2.69 Prepay option $1.16
NATIONAL	Refill price $3.14 Prepay option $1.19	Refill price $3.19 Prepay option $1.09	Refill price $2.87 Prepay option $1.05	Refill price $3.01 Prepay option $1.14
HERTZ	Refill price $3.14 Prepay option $1.36	Refill price $3.19 Prepay option $1.28	Refill price $3.09 Prepay option $1.10	Refill price $3.09 Prepay option $1.19

Amount saved in one year when Avis sales representatives switched to using internal charge cards: $40,000.

OTHER CONSIDERATIONS

Finding the best car rental rate can be a task as daunting as finding the best airfare. Rates aren't just dependent on which rental company you choose. They're also determined by the day of the week, the length of the rental, the type of car, the driver's age, insurance options, airport fees, affinity memberships, special offers and last but not least, your negotiating skills.

Discount programs are so common that if you don't use one you're paying a rate that subsidizes everyone else's. Some require frequent flyer or group membership affiliations. Others, like senior discounts and special promotions, are yours for the asking. Rental agents are trained to avoid mentioning discounts so a generic request for the lowest rate won't work. **You have to be as specific as citing the code number on the promotion or coupon you want to use.**

Does any company consistently give the lowest rates? To the extent that generalization is possible, Hertz holds the highest-rate distinction with Avis and National close behind. Their rates are higher, but they also offer the broadest array of services and benefits. Budget, Alamo, Dollar and Value are in the middle cost tier. Thrifty, Payless, Enterprise and local and regional companies have the lowest base rates. Value gets the prize for lowest rates in a narrow market because they're even renting cars by the hour, starting at 99¢ for compacts. Hourly rentals are available at all their outlets, most of which are in the Sunbelt states.

Advertised rates are just the base-point. Insurance, taxes and hidden fees can double the rate you expect. Ask for cost breakdowns before signing any rental contract.

Peak rates are usually applicable on weekdays, generally considered as the period between noon Monday and noon Thursday. Resort and vacation area rates may be just the reverse, with premium rates switched to weekends. New York City, where car ownership is rare, also has high weekend rates to take advantage of New Yorkers' weekend getaway rental demand.

Unlimited mileage is once again the industry standard after an ill-fated attempt to phase in mileage caps and per-mile fees. In 1995, some of the major companies tried to place mileage caps in select markets and charge a per-mile fee over the allotted mileage amount. After immediate negative response from the traveling public, unlimited mileage was reinstated. Some companies still offer both unlimited and mileage cap rates. If you plan to drive less than 100-150 miles per day, the mileage cap rate might be more economical.

> **"**Rental prices have remained flat while the price of vehicle acquisition has doubled, so rental agencies look for ways to fill in that revenue shortfall. One way is to employ hard-sell and up-sell tactics. Know what you want before you approach the counter and don't be intimidated by the rental agent's subtle pressure tactics. When you request an advertised rate (usually based on subcompacts) they may cite safety advantages of larger cars.**"**

Use **travel agents** to get a quick comp-uter listing of available rates and discount specials. All major and some secondary companies are covered and some (but not all) discounts are listed. You may want to do additional research from the starting point they give you. Rarely will an agent research all available discounts because car rentals provide only a small percent-age of travel agency revenue. A $100 car rental may only earn a $10 commission for the agency.

RESERVING YOUR CAR

Reserve in advance for price breaks and to lock in promotional rates. Many com-panies guarantee rates on reservations as much as a year in the future. Even if you like to go from counter-to-counter looking for on-the-spot deals, you'll have a guar-anteed reservation as a fall-back. Always tell the rental agent you are arriving by air. Some agencies increase rates for local renters.

Once you've confirmed your best rate, keep checking back with the car company for a better rate and watch the papers for any new discounts offered.

Always get a confirmation number when making reservations and reconfirm the rate prior to arrival. Not only will it make it easier to refer back to your origi-nal reservation, it will be insurance to make sure you get the rate you were quoted. For whatever reason, the rate quoted over the telephone may not always be the rate you are given at the rental counter. Always double check your rate once you have booked. Call back the car rental company within 24 hours, give them your confirmation number and con-firm that the rate you were quoted origi-nally matches the rate on your record.

If there is a dispute, simply call the main reservation number on-the-spot and have them bring up your record–which includes the rate quoted. This can also work if, when you arrive at the car rental counter, they do not show a reservation.

TIME VS MONEY

When time is money you may save over-all by renting from a company with major convenience features like express check-in options, frequency of courtesy buses and use of personal profile databases that keep your basic information and prefer-ences on file. These services account for about 15% of your rental dollar. Add-on features can save even more time. Budget's valet service, for example, gives you a personal ride to the terminal for a $6.95 fee. Don't get locked-in to service options such as express check-in. You are paying premium prices for these services.

> **"**Knowing the promotion code is just as important as knowing what the discount is offering. There are thousands of negotiated deals such as corporate rates, leisure rates, organization dis-counts, club discounts, and numerous special offers–each with its own promotion code. Make sure to **always have the promotion code handy** to ensure you receive your discount.**"**

HMMM.

ACME
CAR RENTALS

PLAY THEIR GAME AND WIN

LICENSE & RECORD CHECKS

You must have a current drivers license. Seem redundant? Invalid licenses are the major reason renters are declined.

Driving record checks started in 1992 in reaction to high liability judgments. Now rental agencies from Hertz to Payless may check records to a greater or lesser extent according to accessibility of the state's records and the agency's willingness to pay $4 or more per check. Enterprise and Alamo are least likely to run record checks, and you won't be subjected to them at all when renting internationally. The larger the rental car company, the greater the likelihood your record will be checked; however, mid-range companies may hold you to more arbitrary standards when they do check. The biggest companies have been first to realize that you shouldn't turn away business based on arbitrary reporting standards.

Check your own record by calling TML Information Services, 800-388-9099, the company that does 80% of the checks for the car rental industry. They'll check your eligibility against the standards of your choice of three or four companies for a $9.95 fee ($7.95 for AAA members). In about a minute, they'll let you know if you qualify. You can also get a copy of your record from the State Department of Motor Vehicles and do your own basic comparison.

The rate of denials due to record checks was almost four percent in the first year of the program. Now it's down to one percent, due to increased applicant awareness and modification of the reasons used to deny. You're no longer automatically denied for involvement in an accident causing death or serious injury because some states list them on your record even when you are not at fault. The trend is to focus on convictions for serious offenses rather than cumulative totals of relatively minor tickets. Without this refinement, you get disqualified for three moving violations in three years, no matter if you were ticketed for going ten miles over the speed limit or clocked at 95 miles per hour in a school zone.

Reasons that may trigger rejection:

- Suspended, revoked, invalid, surrendered or expired license.

- Conviction for reckless disregard for life and property.

- Conviction for driving while intoxicated or alcohol impaired or any other alcohol or substance abuse conviction.

- Failure to report an accident or leaving the scene of an accident.

- Possession of a stolen vehicle or use of a vehicle to commit a crime.

If you are denied, you will have no immediate appeal and no recourse other than to try to rent from a company that doesn't check records. You can appeal to your state's Department of Motor Vehicles if you believe the information on your record is in error. You can also appeal to the rental company that denied you by writing to the address they will give you when the denial occurs. The best advice if in doubt is to check your drivers license record prior to showing up at the car rental agency.

FINANCIAL REQUIREMENTS

A major credit or charge card is required by all the major and most local companies. Persuasiveness and an amiable rental agency manager in a small-to-medium city will sometimes get you around the credit card requirement, but the odds are stacked against you. Drivers, age 24 years and under, are unlikely to ever have the credit card requirement waived–unless young drivers have been included in a corporate rate agreement. Debit cards and secured credit cards are fine as long as enough funds are deposited to guarantee the rental and any blocked funds deemed necessary.

Cash rentals require refundable deposits which can be as little as $100 (in smaller cities) and as much as $500 or more. Screening is likely to be more rigorous and may include employment and credit checks which could prohibit a weekend rental.

Local rentals in high-crime areas may be difficult to almost impossible and are always expensive. To help guard against people renting cars to use in the commission of crimes, drivers are screened more thoroughly, charged more money and, in some cases, flatly denied.

AGE REQUIREMENTS

Drivers 25 and over meet the age requirements of all car rental companies. There is no age maximum in the United States. If you have a valid license, you can get a car and, if you're over 62 (50 with an AARP card), you may even get a discount.

Drivers 21-24 years old may be denied rentals and almost always pay a per day add-on cost unless they rent under the corporate plan of an employer who has nego-

---

tiated lifting the young driver fees. Some companies demand proof of personal car insurance. Policies are likely to be more liberal for renters with premium credit cards, and at the higher end of the 21-24 age spectrum. An impeccable driving record, a major credit card in your own name, and your willingness to pay daily surcharge ranging from $5-25 may gain you acceptance. Agency managers have discretion in these areas.

Drivers 18-20 are forced to find the few locally based agencies willing to rent to them, usually for higher daily rates. For drivers under age 21, car rental prospects in the U.S. are limited to select local operators. Even then, the provisions for rental will be stringent.

WAIVERS & INSURANCE
What They're Trying To Sell

"Persistent" is the diplomatic word for car rental company attempts to induce you to purchase their **Collision Damage Waiver (CDW) and Loss Damage Waiver (LDW)** coverage. It's rarely mentioned when you make your reservation and it's usually in the fine print of advertised rates. It can almost double your daily rental cost at rates from $7-18 per day.

Under common law, you would only be liable for damage to a rental car caused by your own negligence. When you sign a rental contract–something you can't avoid–you waive this standard right and accept liability for damage caused by any factor. Then the rental company offers CDW/LDW coverage which, if you take it, waives their right to collect from you.

Collision coverage pays for damage to the rental car only. **Liability** covers the more significant area of personal injury. Most rental companies have changed their liability coverage to secondary cov-

erage, placing the bulk of liability on the driver's personal policy. If you don't have personal insurance, the optional LDW becomes primary except in California where you would be unprotected against any liability claim.

Six states regulate optional CDW/LDW coverage. Illinois and New York ban it completely and have caps on the renter's liability in case of theft or accident. Their rental rates are only about $3 higher on average than in states still allowing CDW/LDW. Three states have mandatory rate caps: Nevada at $10; California at $9; Indiana at $5. Texas legislation says the price must be "reasonably related" to the cost of providing coverage, leaving a loophole big enough for a mini-van.

> **❝***If you decline the optional insurance, they will tell you your credit card or personal insurance coverage is risky when it really isn't.***❞**

Primary vs. Secondary Coverage

Primary coverage is the first source of payment on any claim and frees you from even considering optional CDW. **Diners Club and MasterCard BusinessCard are the only charge cards that provide full primary coverage** and handle claims without notifying your private insurer. This is such a valuable feature that other premium cards are likely to follow.

Secondary coverage is usually limited to the deductible on your private insurance policy. If you carry a card providing secondary coverage and your private insurance precludes coverage on business rentals you might want to consider buying the additional coverage from the car rental company.

Personal and Corporate Policies

Private insurance should meet all rental needs unless you're renting for business purposes. State Farm and Nationwide initiated the trend to exclude business travel and many agencies are following suit. Check your policy and, when you renew, ask specifically if there will be any changes in business coverage. Your rental coverage will be subject to the same deductible you've chosen for your personal vehicle. Inquire about special riders to enhance your coverage in specific areas. Your policy may limit liability to the replacement cost of your personal car–a problem if you like to drive more expensive rentals. Special liability coverage is available at $200-300 per year for $1 million in coverage, and it's likely to extend to overseas rentals.

Corporate insurance is, for many companies, less expensive than rental agency CDW/LDW. An increasing number of companies are electing to insure all employees driving on company business with a rider that includes coverage for rental vehicles. Be sure you're aware of any variables that can negate coverage. They might include the type of car rented, additional drivers, retaining the car for personal use and driving record considerations.

> **66**Be sure that you know in advance what your personal or employer's insurance will cover, or not cover. Are your family members covered in the event of an accident? What about other additional drivers? Are **you** covered when driving for business and leisure purposes?**99**

Credit Card Coverage

There is a difference between credit card CDW and rental agency CDW. If you pay the car rental agency's waiver, you are released from any liability in an accident except for fine-print exclusions including items like broken or cracked windows. Credit card CDW coverage either requires you to pay for damages and reimburses you or pays for damages directly.

Know your credit card coverage terms. Cards that once included CDW may not include it now. If coverage has been decreased, your bank probably didn't send you the news by telegram. Check all cards you use for travel. You're likely to find one best card for most needs, but you may want to switch to another card for special needs like truck rental coverage. Call the issuing bank and ask for specifics such as:

- **Does the cardholder pay for damages and get reimbursed** or will damages be paid directly to the car rental agency?

- **What duration of a consecutive rental period is covered?** The basic rule is 15 days on domestic rentals, 15-30 on rentals abroad. Diners Club again excels with 29 consecutive days of protection worldwide.

- **Are other drivers covered?**

- **How does domestic and international coverage differ?**

- **Which vehicles are covered?** Check for exclusions on luxury cars, minivans, trucks and sports utility vehicles.

- **Is coverage canceled** if you drive on unpaved roads?

Some cards provide optional coverage with a $10 annual fee and a per-rental charge of about $7. It's a better deal than

---

the rental agencies offer but probably more expensive than adding a rider to your personal car insurance. **Standard rules on credit card coverage:**

• **You must present the applicable card** for each rental and pay the entire bill with that card.

• **You must decline** the optional CDW/ LDW coverage from the rental agency.

• **You must be listed as primary renter** on the rental contract.

• **Consecutive coverage varies** from 15-30 days.

• **Commonly excluded vehicles** are luxury cars (except on some overseas rentals), antique and exotic cars, limousines, trucks, custom vans, full-size sports vehicles and all off-road (jeeps and alternate terrain) vehicles.

• **Damage to the other driver's car is not included.**

• **Collisions where alcohol or drug impairment are factors** may result in denial of claim.

• **Benefits are denied** if on the date of loss or claim you are in arrears for two monthly payments.

When To Reject Rental Agency CDW/LDW

Check the REJECTED box with confidence if you're protected in any of the following ways: (You aren't obligated to tell the rental agent why you're rejecting the coverage nor to justify your alternate coverage provisions). In most cases, utilizing any of the following methods will protect you sufficiently to negate the need for CDW/LDW: (If you are unsure if your private or corporate insurance covers rental vehicles check with your insurance.)

• **Diners Club or MasterCard Business Card.** They're the gold standard in cards to use when you rent a car, providing up to $25,000 in primary coverage.

• **American Express or Gold Visa or MasterCard.**

• **Airline affinity charge card.**

• **Private insurance** that covers rental vehicles.

• **Corporate insurance** that covers employees traveling on business.

• **Willingness to play the odds** and assume the risk.

Consider Agency CDW/LDW when:

• **You don't rent via a premium credit card** or a card with secondary coverage that satisfies you.

• **You don't carry personal auto insurance** or you've chosen an extremely high deductible.

• **You're traveling on business,** your personal policy precludes coverage on business rentals and your company does not have its own insurance coverage.

• **You want the liability coverage** not included on any charge cards.

OPTIONS/ ADD-ONS
Emergency Services

Emergency service provisions should always be considered when choosing a rental company. All eight major companies tow, repair and replace according to the same standards. The smaller companies try to do the same but can be limited by proximity. A full listing of car rental companies' emergency service numbers can be found in the *Know Who To Call* section of this book under *Car Rentals*.

Make sure you request a map of the local area showing the exact location of the car rental agency. You don't want to be lost trying to return you car when you are hurrying to make your flight.

Smaller companies and independents tend to have older cars and more limited emergency road service provisions. The level of assistance available varies greatly so get very specific information before you rent. Many limit towing and replacement vehicle services to business hours and simply authorize repair after hours. The smaller the company, the more likely you will be asked to pay for approved repairs and be reimbursed when you return the car.

Automobile clubs are a boon to car renters. You get car rental discounts and have an emergency road service to call if you're in an area where the rental agency's emergency service seems to be coming by way of Guam. Be sure to check the policy on rental car emergency assistance with your automobile club.

Additional Drivers

Extra driver charges apply when more than one driver uses the rental vehicle. All major companies (except Alamo) waive the extra driver fee for spouses, employees and employers of primary drivers.

There are no extra driver charges in California. Hertz waives additional driver charges for AAA members.

Special Equipment

Give at least 24 hours notice if you want a particular model, hand controls, a car equipped with a navigation system, a child safety seat, a smoke-free car, cellular phone, ski rack or luggage rack. If getting what you requested is imperative, tell the rental agent your rental is conditional on your request being met.

Cellular phones are offered by all large and mid-range rental companies. You can get caught in fairly outrageous per-minute charges so be sure to check them before engaging in heavy cellular use.

- **Renters often risk an unreasonably high liability** for lost or stolen phones–$500-800 average. Although $2.50 per day insurance options exist, they aren't widely available.

- **Taking your own cellular** subjects you to roaming charges, but roaming rates are going down and you do eliminate the $800 risk.

- **Average cellular rental rates:** $5 per day (Alamo offers some free daily rentals and other companies include cellular phones with some luxury rentals) plus about $1.25 per call and $1.95 per minute. Calling 911 should be free. If you return your cellular to an unauthorized location, you'll be charged a drop fee–usually $100.

Navigation systems are limited to select premium cars. If you find electronic assistance helpful but prefer economy rentals, there are a few options:

- **The Road Whiz Plus** looks like a small calculator and can direct you to the nearest gas station, rest stop, hotel or tourist attraction. Its database includes 45,000 facilities in 50 states. The cost is about $60. Service Merchandise and OfficeMax sell the Road Whiz or, write to Laser Data Technology, 9375 Dielman Industrial Dr., St. Louis, MO 63132. The device gives you the location, the highway exit and a mileage estimate.

- **The AAA Trip Planner** is a CD-ROM program that retails for about $60. You can create your own maps with mileage and time projections plus access data on over 30,000 AAA-rated hotels and restaurants. The program is available via AAA, 800-222-4357.

> *"Navigation systems are becoming more readily available through the car rental companies for as little as $5 per day. Currently Avis, Hertz and National offer navigation systems on premium cars in select locations throughout the U.S."*

Since rental cars equipped with hand controls are in limited supply, mobility impaired drivers should request cars equipped with hand controls 24-72 hours in advance. To guarantee availability, book as far in advance as possible.

HEADACHES TO AVOID

Cancellation Fees

You can be charged a penalty for cancelled reservations on some one-way rentals, and on pre-paid rates to vacation destinations like Florida, California and Hawaii. The standard fee is $25. If you fail to appear without cancelling, you'll be billed the entire rental amount.

- **Never reserve a car with a cancellation fee provision** unless the deal is extraordinary enough to merit the risk.

- **If the deal was too good to pass up** and you do have to cancel, note the cancellation number, the name of the person you spoke with, their location and the time of your call.

Lost Reservations

If you arrive at the counter and they don't show your reservation, be prepared to substantiate your case.

- **Know when the reservation was made**, the confirmation number and the rate code. If you rely on someone else to make your reservations, be sure you get this information before you leave. You want to be able to make it clear to the agent that you are not scamming.

- **Call the toll-free reservation number** and have them look up your reservation. Sometimes the information doesn't make it through to the on-site computer.

- **Don't immediately accept an offer to enter a new reservation** unless they give it to you at the rate you were expecting.

If you are told no car is available or that you must pay a higher rate, ask to speak to someone with the authority to honor your reservation and insist on one of the following options:

- **Have them check their reservation system** to determine when the next car will be available. Get them to commit that car to you and request a 50% reduction in the rate to compensate you for the inconvenience.

- **If you don't need the car for several hours,** you want transportation to your hotel as well as delivery of the rental car as soon as available.

- **If you must have the car immediately,** tell the agent to arrange for a rental from another company and pay for any rate difference.

Bad Cars

Rental agencies try to give you cars in good condition. They don't want your ill will or the expense involved in emergency road service. Still, every regular renter has horror stories to tell.

- **Make sure you get a low mileage car** just by requesting one at the counter.

Major street that is closed to vehicular traffic at night: Bourbon Street, New Orleans.

The agent has that information easily accessible by computer.

- **Check safety features and basic running condition** before you leave the lot. Five extra minutes spent checking the basics could save you hours of breakdown time.

- **Check for damage to the body.** Never leave the lot without checking for damages and making sure the fuel tank is full. Note all damages on your contract before leaving the lot. If you're satisfied that it doesn't affect the driveability of the car, make sure the existing damage is noted on the rental contract so you can't be held liable.

- **If it's dark outside**, find a well-lit spot on the lot and proceed with your check.

Cancelled Contracts

Avoid the temptation to falsify any part of your rental agreement. It's usually done to try to save a few dollars but you're risking a lot more.

- **If you plan to leave the state in which you rent**, make sure to tell the reserva-

tionist. Some rentals limit the range of travel permitted. Breaking the rules leaves you vulnerable to lack of help on mechanical problems and will cancel any CDW/LDW you purchased.

- **Not listing additional drivers** invalidates your contract and leaves you completely unprotected in case of an accident.

Local Trip Planning

Always ask for directions to your hotel and any other destination you plan to visit. Most car rental companies will offer maps of the local area and many will offer computer printouts with instructions.

There are many trip planning programs on the market today for the avid computer user. Whether it be on the Internet, online services such as America Online, Prodigy and Compuserve, or on home computer programs, there are excellent programs available that will plot out your trip from door-to-door.

"Save yourself a giant headache and walk around your car before leaving the lot. Check for bumps, scrapes, nicks, and dings. Remember, one minute inspecting your car can save possible hours of frustration in resolving disputed charges. Most car rental companies require their personnel to inspect your rental car when you give them your paperwork on exiting the lot. If their representative doesn't offer to inspect your vehicle, insist on an inspection before leaving the premises."

Cost of New Orleans downtown metered parking: 25¢ per quarter hour.

SAFETY TIPS

Safe Rentals

Don't rent cars easily identified as rentals either by license plate stickers or special letter and number sequences. They make it easier for carjackers to prey on people unfamiliar with their surroundings. Avoid luxury rentals in urban markets unless you are willing to be a more attractive target to thieves.

Most car rental agents distribute safety tips when you rent your car. Some agencies have computerized kiosks, information booths or counters, that will print out specific routings. Check them out and take special note of directions out of the airport. Most rental car accidents take place between the lot and the airport exit gate.

Ask for specific directions to your destination, including your freeway entrance and exit numbers, before you leave the rental counter. Do not leave the car rental area without a clear understanding of how to get to your destination. Take advantage of the free maps most rental counters offer.

Familiarize yourself with your vehicle's safety equipment. Safety check your car before you leave the lot. Make sure the locks, horn, emergency flashers and restraint devices work and that the tire pressure is correct. Make sure you have what you need for current conditions–tire chains, abrasives to build traction, snow brush, ice-scraper, booster cables, a flashlight, etc.

Make a copy of your rental car key to use if you accidentally lock the keys in the car. Carry it in your wallet. You won't get stranded if you lock your keys inside the car.

Required stopping distance on dry pavement for a car traveling 55 mph: 310 feet; on wet pavement: 380 feet.

INTERNATIONAL 'COUNTER' INTELLIGENCE

MODUS OPERANDI FOR SAVINGS

Car rental rules change a bit when you are acquiring rentals abroad. You can rent by pre-paid voucher, pre-pay a portion of the rental amount to lock in the dollar rate or pay after you use the car, just as you do in the U.S. You can get a rental car as part of a fly/drive package. You can lease a car with all insurance and taxes included in the quoted price.

- **Rentals** normally require a 14-day advance to access the lowest rates. Save the most money (up to 50%) by booking in advance and pre-paying.

- **Rates can vary by season,** but per-day, walk-up rates are generally prohibitive regardless of the time of year.

"If you're visiting multiple European countries, consider flying into the country that offers the best combination of airfare and car rental rates. Take varying tax rates and Value Added Tax (VAT) refund eligibility into account. Remember that VATs can add up to 20% to your rental cost and, in some countries, the tax is not recoupable on car rentals. See our chart on page 284 for VAT rates around the world."

Year in which the average purchase price of a new car first exceeded $20,000: 1994.

- **Promotional rates** usually require at least a three-day minimum, but be careful. If you keep the car longer, your extra time will be charged at a rate guaranteed to make you wince. Weekly rates sometimes require a minimum one-week rental, but can be had for as little as five days if the rental period includes a weekend. Always verify that the five-day period qualifies as a weekly rental.

- **One-way rental policies** are more liberal than those in the U.S., depending on when and where you travel. There are many one-way rentals with minimal or no drop-off charges. Hertz for example, offers the "Rent-It-Here, Leave-It-There" program throughout Europe with a maximum drop-off fee currently at $50. You may even be given upgrades on one-way rentals that fit into the company's car relocation needs.

Fly/drive packages may save you even more internationally than in the U.S. Always ask your airline if they are offering any car rental deals in conjunction with the purchase of your airline ticket. Some recent examples:

- **Kemwel** has offered $99 weekly rentals in Britain, fifth and sixth days free, and premiums including a $10 long distance calling card or a motor atlas.

- **Delta and Kemwel** combined to offer a free car in Europe when two passengers flew roundtrip on Delta. A solo passenger paid a surcharge of just $50. This offer was good for all European countries served by Delta.

- **Virgin Atlantic Airways and Avis** offered considerable discounts, up to seven free rental days in the United Kingdom, if reservations were booked and paid for in the United States.

- **Auto Europe** regularly offers discounted car/air packages from the U.S. to Europe, utilizing over a dozen different airlines.

Students can get across-the-board discount privileges from the Council on International Educational Exchange, 212-661-1450.

Leasing is available in Europe as a means to provide a way for locals to avoid hefty taxes when purchasing new cars. Visitors lease them for three weeks or more and "sell" them back to the dealer. Because they now qualify as used cars, the purchaser saves considerably on taxes. Lease rates include all CDW coverage and all taxes. Leasing is most widely available in Germany, France, Belgium and the Netherlands. **The minimum age is often just 18 or 19**, a bonanza for young drivers. (For leasing options, check with Auto Europe, Kemwel or Renault.)

Car or train? When service options give you a choice, regional and local trains are cheaper than car rentals unless you have three or more people traveling together. Car rental fees, higher fuel costs (as much as $5 per gallon), parking fees and tolls all add to your rental cost. Schedule renting a car for countries and situations where personalized mobility is of prime importance.

> **"Don't use your car to sight-see within cities.** City parking is only for veterans. Roads are often narrow and traffic is swift. Some city centers ban cars completely. If you are a tourist, you will see more of the city by walking and using public transportation. Business travel by taxi is faster and avoids the considerable problems and costs of parking. **"**

Impact of hitting a solid object while in a car going 30 mph: the same as falling out of a fourth story window.

GLOBAL RENTAL SOURCES

Choose from U.S.-based rental companies and specialty tour and leasing agencies. Alamo, Kemwel, DER Tours and Auto Europe each offer to beat any comparable quotes. The numbers below are for international rentals.

- **Alamo,** 800-522-9696, has locations in 12 countries. One-third of their offices are on airport sites. They offer a high percentage of larger cars geared to American tastes, and have a 15,000-vehicle fleet.

- **Auto Europe**, 800-223-5555, is a rental and leasing giant. They are tour operators and wholesalers with access to 4,000 locations in Europe, the Middle East, Africa, the Caribbean, Latin America, the Pacific and Canada. They can sometimes get you a decent rate with only 24 hours advance. U.S.A. direct numbers connect you to Auto Europe U.S. free of charge from 17 countries. They have no cancellation or no-show fees until the time of departure. They also allow some rentals with cash deposits in lieu of credit cards, provide 24-hour road service and cars equipped for handicapped drivers.

- **Avis**, 800-331-1084, has locations in 140 countries. Their aggressive international presence is bolstered by innovations including 12 rental facilities in Eastern Europe and the Discover Europe program that cuts advance reservation requirements to 24 hours. They also offer rail and drive passes, such as the France Rail and Drive combination discount package. Cell phones, rapid check-in and return options plus 24-hour international road assistance are widely available. Their fly/drive programs are available

through the Avis-owned Preferred Holidays, 800-508-5454.

- **Budget**, 800-472-3325 has locations in 118 countries and territories, including Moscow, Croatia and Zimbabwe. Signature cars at some international locations include Jaguars, Infinitis and Mercedes. They rent Harley-Davidsons in Germany, Jeeps in Israel and Latin America and camper vans and 4-wheel drives in New Zealand. WorldClass Drive programs with easy-to-follow itineraries for individual tours are available in the United Kingdom, Australia and Western Canada at no extra charge. Cell phones are available in most major European cities.

- **DER Tours** operates in 17 countries but accepts reservations only from travel agents. Have your agent obtain a quote for you.

- **EuroDollar**, 800-800-6000, has 45,000 vehicles in 35 countries with expansion plans in Africa and Moscow. They offer 24-hour rate information and general conditions of rental by fax, 800-329-6000. You can also order your car by fax. When you've mailed your confirmation voucher, you also receive information on mileage, language and other country specifics.

- **Hertz**, 800-654-3001, services 170 countries and features 24-hour international road service and expedited service at over 590 locations in 21 countries. Computerized driving directions are available at 40 locations in your choice of Danish, Dutch, English, French, German, Italian, Norwegian, Spanish and Swedish. Le Swap lets you switch from right-hand to left-hand control cars at either end of the Channel and offers package rates for Le Shuttle speed-train crossings.

The 1995 average base car rental tax for the major 50 U.S. markets: 8.2%.

- **Holiday Autos**, 800-422-7737, services 50 countries and specializes in tours. Agents are particularly knowledgeable regarding country-specific information.

- **I.T.S.**, 800-521-0643, is a tour company serving 15 countries specializing in low rates for U.K. rentals. It represents European-based car companies.

- **Kemwel**, 800-678-0678, has a CarPass Plan that allows flexibility of travel. You purchase vouchers with U.S. dollars and choose your rental dates as you travel at savings from 20%-50%. Cars are subject to availability and unused passes are fully refundable. Kemwel also offers cost-cutting short-term leases under the European Car Vacation Plan name with leases available to drivers 18 and older, subject to specific country statutes.

- **National Interrent**, 800-227-3876, has an international presence composed of Interrent, Tilden (Canada), EuropCar and Nippon Interrent (Japan).

- **Payless**, 800-237-2804, has 22 international locations.

- **Renault EuroDrive**, 800-221-1052, specializes in leasing programs for drivers requiring cars from three weeks to six months.

- **Thrifty**, 800-367-2277, offers 159 Canadian locations and 463 locations in North, Central and South America, Australia, Europe, the Middle East, the Caribbean, Asia and the Pacific.

SPECIFYING WHAT YOU NEED

Unless you know a Tipo from a Vauxhall Cavalier, (European car models), check out the specs of the car you will be renting.

- **The least expensive rentals** are likely to be appreciably smaller than American sub-compacts.

- **Cars with automatic transmissions** are not plentiful in all locations and will generally cost more.

- **Air conditioning** very often is not a standard feature. If it's important to you, be prepared to rent at least a mid-size car and even then, verify that air conditioning is included.

- **Locking trunks** don't exist in hatchbacks, which are prevalently used in the foreign rental car market.

- **Check statistics** that will help you make reasonable comparisons: trunk space in cubic feet, size of engine, length, body type and miles per gallon. How else will you be able to tell, for example, the difference between a Fiat Panda and a VW Passat? Comparing the two, the VW gives you more than ten additional cubic feet of trunk room, an engine more than twice as powerful and four additional feet of length.

- **Always tell the rental agent how many people** need to be comfortably accommodated and what your luggage requirements will be.

Service Considerations

Airport rental agency counters, except in major gateway cities, don't have 24-hour services. You'll get to off-airport offices on a "meet reservations" basis where a driver with a handheld sign waits for you at the passenger exit.

Many in-city rental offices have restricted weekend hours and some southern European offices close for lunch. Be sure to ask, at the time of reservation, for specific details on when you can get to your rental car. When you return the car, take business hours into account to avoid being charged for the time that may elapse between your arrival and the time an employee reappears.

Emergency road service is prevalent, but not always as readily available as it is in the U.S. Get emergency contact numbers from your rental agency and ask if there are special procedures for late nights or remote areas.

As a second option, temporary membership in an international auto club is often offered to members of major U.S. auto clubs for a very low rate. Inquire about and arrange for this coverage in advance as a back-up for emergency situations.

INTERNATIONAL RENTAL REQUIREMENTS

A U.S. driver's license is usually sufficient for international driving, but an international driver's permit, printed in nine languages, can be helpful particularly in Portugal, Spain, Italy, Austria, Germany, Greece, Russia and Eastern Europe. The permit is invalid without your original license. Permits are sold at AAA offices for $10. Take two passport-size photos and your driver's license when you apply. Allow four to six weeks. You do not have to be an AAA member to secure an international license. Call 800-222-4357.

Age requirements vary but generally, rentals are available to drivers 21 and older. Some countries require that you have held a license for at least one year. If you are 20 or younger, consider leasing. If you're 70 or older, mention your age when reserving the car so you don't run into difficulty when you arrive. The United Kingdom has a maximum age of 75. Holland's maximum is 69. Ireland's is 70.

INTERNATIONAL INSURANCE

Optional Collision and Damage Waiver coverage is harder to avoid on international rentals. It's mandatory in Italy, New Zealand and other high-risk areas. The $6 to $20 per day cost could be worth assuming unless you are sure that you are already protected.

- **Make sure the agency you rent from accepts your credit card coverage.** Check your coverage to see if it extends to rentals abroad. If it does, tell the reservationist that you want a rental that doesn't require additional CDW.

- **If your private insurance covers international rentals,** carry your insurance card plus a statement from your insurer itemizing foreign coverage provisions.

- **If you decline CDW coverage,** ask what dollar amount will be blocked on your card. Up to $2,500 is not an uncommon amount. Charge other expenses on a different card to keep some liquidity of funds and avoid declined charges.

- **If you rely on personal insurance or credit card coverage,** you still must settle all damage charges directly with the rental company and file for reimbursement from the provider of your coverage. This can include filling out forms, acquiring police reports and gathering repair quotes and invoices. It's one of the strongest reasons to accept the rental company CDW.

Some companies offer "inclusive" rates which provide CDW at a presumed discount. Check the deductible. At times it is almost as high as the value of the rental car.

Amount by which Budget Rent A Car reduced its salaried work force in 1995: 20%.

			TRAFFIC	
			TRAFFIC LAWS	
		SPEED LIMITS		
COUNTRY	TRAFFIC FLOW	CITY	COUNTRY ROADS	MOTOR-WAYS
AUSTRIA	Right	50km/31mph	100km/63mph	130km/81mph
BELGIUM	Right	50km/31mph	80km/50mph	120km/75mph
BULGARIA	Right	60km/38mph	80km/50mph	120km/75mph
CYPRUS	Left	50km/31mph	80km/50mph	100km/63mph
CZECH REPUBLIC	Right	60km/38mph	90km/56mph	110km/69mph
DENMARK	Right	50km/31mph	80km/50mph	110km/69mph
FINLAND	Right	50km/31mph	100km/63mph	120km/75mph
FRANCE	Right	50km/31mph	90km/56mph	130km/81mph
GERMANY	Right	50km/31mph	100km/63mph	(1)
GREECE	Right	60km/38mph	100km/63mph	120km/75mph
HOLLAND	Right	50km/31mph	80km/50mph	100km/63mph
HUNGARY	Right	50km/31mph	80km/50mph	120km/75mph
IRELAND	Left	50km/31mph	65km/40mph	95km/59mph
ISRAEL	Right	50km/31mph	70km/44mph	90km/56mph
ITALY	Right	50km/31mph	90km/56mph	130km/81mph
LUXEMBOURG	Right	50km/31mph	90km/56mph	120km/75mph
MALTA	Left	50km/31mph	80km/50mph	–
NORWAY	Right	50km/31mph	80km/50mph	90km/56mph
POLAND	Right	60km/38mph	90km/56mph	110km/69mph
PORTUGAL	Right	50km/31mph	90km/56mph	120km/75mph
SLOVENIA	Right	60km/38mph	80km/50mph	120km/75mph
SPAIN	Right	50km/31mph	90km/56mph	120km/75mph
SWEDEN	Right	50km/31mph	90km/56mph	110km/69mph
SWITZERLAND	Right	50km/31mph	80km/50mph	110km/69mph
TURKEY	Right	50km/31mph	80km/50mph	120km/75mph
UNITED KINGDOM	Left	50km/31mph	95km/59mph	110km/69mph

Age range of U.S. drivers who have the fewest accidents: 50-64.

LAWS & CONDITIONS

SEAT BELT MAN		CHILD IN FRONT SEATS	TAXES & CONDITIONS				GAS	
			VALUE ADDED TAX	AIR-PORT SUR-CHARGE	MIN AGE	MAX AGE	EST PRICE PER GAL	
F	R							COUNTRY
Yes	Yes	12 yrs	21.44%	9%	21	–	$3.50	AUSTRIA
Yes	Yes	12 yrs	20.5%	9%	23	–	$3.80	BELGIUM
Yes	No	16 yrs	22%	–	21	–	$3.80	BULGARIA
Yes	No	8 yrs	8%	–	25	–	$3.00	CYPRUS
Yes	No	48"	23%	6%	21	–	$3.95	CZECH
Yes	No	7 yrs	25%	DKK50	21	–	$3.60	DENMARK
Yes	Yes	–	22%	–	21	–	$3.95	FINLAND
Yes	Yes	10 yrs	18.6%	–	21	–	$4.30	FRANCE
Yes	Yes	12 yrs	15%	DEM13	21	–	$4.20	GERMANY
Yes	Yes	–	18%	6%	21	–	$3.50	GREECE
Yes	Yes	12 yrs	17.5%	NLG30	21	69	$4.05	HOLLAND
Yes	Yes	12 yrs	25%	7%	21	–	$3.20	HUNGARY
Yes	No	12 yrs	12.5%	–	21	70	$3.45	IRELAND
Yes	Yes	14 yrs	0%	US$15	21	–	$2.90	ISRAEL
Yes	Yes	12 yrs	19%	10%	21	–	$4.15	ITALY
Yes	Yes	10 yrs	15%	6%	21	–	$3.10	LUX
No	No	–	0%	–	21	–	$2.65	MALTA
Yes	Yes	–	23%	–	21	–	$4.55	NORWAY
Yes	Yes	12 yrs	22%	–	21	–	$3.60	POLAND
Yes	Yes	12 yrs	16%	PTE1,50	21	–	$3.55	PORTUGAL
Yes	Yes	14 yrs	5%	–	21	–	$2.00	SLOVENIA
Yes	Yes	7 yrs	15%	ESP1500	21	–	$3.10	SPAIN
Yes	Yes	–	25%	SEK50	20	–	$3.85	SWEDEN
Yes	Yes	7 yrs	6.5%	8%	21	–	$3.25	SWITZ.
Yes	Yes	–	15%	–	21	–	$2.15	TURKEY
Yes	Yes	12 yrs	17.5%	–	21	75	$4.50	UK

Age range of U.S. drivers with peak accident statistics: 16 and 75 and over.

PAYING FOR YOUR INTERNATIONAL RENTAL

Unique financial considerations apply to rentals abroad.

- **Even if you hold pre-paid vouchers,** you must present a major charge or credit card when you pick up your car or pay a substantial cash deposit. The vouchers simply show that you have paid for all normally anticipated costs.

- **Ask whether you will be required to pay** when picking up your car or when you return it. Ask if there are additional charges for driving to other countries.

- **If you opt to pay for your rental in cash,** exchange funds first at a bank exchange rate or withdraw funds directly from a local ATM.

ORIENTATION

When you pick up your car, check out the trunk space, interior room and the interior configuration. The gas and brake pedals, for example, may be much closer together than on any vehicle you have driven previously. Check tires and all safety features, lights and windshield wipers. If you have any doubts about the car, insist on a short test drive. Many European rentals have electronic anti-theft systems. Make sure you know how to override the system to start the car.

Learn basic driving symbols. The European Community has standardized signs and signs particular to each country. A car within a circle means cars can't enter; an exclamation point within a triangle means danger; a red-rimmed triangle with an X in the center indicates an upcoming intersection. All rental agencies should provide you with written safety guides of the most commonly used signs.

Seat belts are often mandatory, sometimes in both front and back seats. Children may not be allowed to travel in front seats at all until they reach a minimum age (usually between seven and 12).

When driving on the left-hand side of the road is the custom, allow yourself time to get accustomed to the different orientation.

> *"Learn to think in kilometers. One kilometer equals .621 of a mile. The easiest way to convert kilometers to miles is to cut the kilometer figure in half and add ten percent. Another method: divide the kilometers by ten then multiply by six. Sixty kilometers per hour is roughly equivalent to 35 miles per hour. Your speedometer will do most of the work, but a basic comprehension of speed and distance will help. There is a big difference between a 50 kph and 50 mph speed limit."*

Don't be timid when driving on expressways and super-roads in other countries. Buy the optional CDW coverage and drive competently but aggressively. On the super-roads stay right unless you're going at highway speeds. Be prepared to pass and be passed and don't rely on the no-passing signs for guidance, because they are routinely ignored. Cars manufactured for use in other countries tend to have more power because of the lack of emission control standards, and drivers tend to use **all** of the power their cars provide.

Fuel is charged by the liter. One gallon equals 3.79 liters. Become familiar with local terms for grades of gas. In the United

---

The cities with the highest base car rental tax: Chicago (18%); New York (13.2%); and Las Vegas (13%).

Kingdom, for example, gasoline is called petrol or benzine; diesel is called gasoil; and essence is another name for regular gasoline.

Canada

Canada requires liability insurance on all drivers with minimum coverage of $160,000 U.S. except in Quebec where the limit is $40,000 U.S.

- **Your personal insurance** is likely to provide collision and damage coverage. Be sure to ask your insurer for a Canadian Non-Resident Inter-Provincial Motor Vehicle Liability Insurance Card. Rental companies should provide you with a copy of their own insurance card.

- **Credit card CDW coverage** usually extends to Canada but may not meet the liability requirements.

- **If you're driving your own** car, carry a copy of the vehicle registration. If you're driving someone else's, carry a signed letter of permission.

Mexico

Mexico is close to the ultimate challenge in car rentals.

- **If you rent in the U.S.,** be sure you meet the provisions for taking the car into Mexico.

- **If you rent in Mexico,** you may avoid some paperwork but you will pay premium rates.

- **If your driving is confined to** within 15 miles of the border or in Baja, California, and parts of the Mexican State of Sonora, you escape much of the red tape.

- **Your basic car insurance does not cover driving in Mexico** so you must buy insurance, whether renting or driving your own car. Border-area insurance offices have sprung up to fulfill the demand. You may choose independent agencies, rental agency insurance or AAA insurance sold at border offices.

- **If your charge card covers collision damage** in Mexico (**a big "if"**), it will automatically become your primary coverage.

- **All paperwork can be done at the border.** Driving into Mexico requires proof of citizenship and a Mexican Tourist Card for stays over 72 hours. Get no-cost tourist cards at Mexican consulates or tourism border offices.

- **The Green Angels** have patrolled 20,000 miles of Mexican roads since 1960. From 8 a.m. to 8 p.m., they repair simple breakdowns at no charge, guide lost motorists and report on safety and road conditions. Reach them toll-free within Mexico by calling 91-800-90-3-92 or, in Mexico City, 250-8221. English-speaking assistance is available.

- *Traveling to Mexico by Car* is available from Mexican tourism offices. There is no charge. The number for the New York office is 212-755-7261.

Eastern Europe

Taking rental cars to Eastern Europe is permitted by some companies from specific locations. Avis will allow certain types of cars rented in Germany and Austria to be driven within Eastern Europe with a minimum seven-day rental. Hertz permits driving in select Eastern European countries from locations in Austria, Denmark, Finland, Spain and Norway. National Car Rentals' corporate account members can drive to Eastern Europe. In all cases cars must be returned in the West. You can rent cars in Eastern Europe but be prepared to compromise on style and choice.

Ninety-nine cent accident prevention: a plastic frame that holds your takeout coffee and frees both hands for driving.

INTERNATIONAL TIDBITS

Before you leave the states, check with the departments of tourism in the countries you plan to visit for their traffic laws.

Cars may own the road in America, but you'll find yourself challenged in various countries by bikes, motorbikes, pedestrians, ox-carts and other vehicular inventions.

Italy and Eastern Europe have the highest rates of rental cars never returned or recovered. Consequently, renting a car to drive in either place is subject to increased difficulty and cost. In Naples, an estimated eight percent of cars rented are never seen again.

Ireland tends to have the lowest car rental rates in Europe coupled with some of the most beautiful terrain. It's a good choice for a driving holiday abroad.

England has roundabouts or traffic circles in urban and rural areas. Vehicles on the roundabout have priority over any vehicle attempting to merge.

China, Egypt and Nepal generally offer rental cars only by arrangements that also include the mandatory services of a driver.

Poland offers Mercedes Benz rentals at $105 per day. There is, however, a $6,000 credit card deposit.

Austria, Denmark, Finland, Sweden, Norway, Singapore and all Eastern European countries have little tolerance for drinking and driving. The consumption of even one drink and getting behind the wheel can land you in jail.

Greece is attempting to make driving easier for tourists with new road signs in Greek and Latin alphabets.

Belgium appears to have the slowest drivers in Europe, most likely due to the number of bicyclists on the roads.

Bulgaria has few gas stations and, when you do find one, you may need a voucher to purchase fuel.

Czechoslovakia gives trams the absolute right of way.

Denmark law requires that headlights be on whenever you drive.

Hungary has flashing green lights that mean the same as flashing ambers in the West.

Italy tows cars parked in green zones.

Norway measures distance in miles, but a Norwegian mile equals six American miles.

Spain has a system of coastal roads with lower speed limits than those allowed on similar roads inland.

Switzerland always gives the right of way on mountain roads to ascending traffic.

> **"**There is no question that international driving can be a challenge. In the U.S., red, green and amber lights all have different meanings. In some countries, they all seem to mean "go!" I've driven in many countries, but I'm still cautious regarding roundabouts (traffic circles)–stop on a dime and the car behind you is suddenly attached to yours. As for the Autobahn–at 55 mph you are considered a highway danger for driving too slow. You should also get used to the honking of horns–they're the international anthem of drivers around the world!**"**

DON'T LET YOUR CRUISE DOLLARS MELT AWAY!

Cruise vacations arc about to be discovered by a significant number of the 93% of North American residents who have never been on a cruise. Cruising has never been a better value as over 23 new ships are scheduled to come on line and others are repositioned to smaller ports and less demanding routes. Good deals will abound for the next few years because of the increased capacity, but you want more than a good deal–you want the **best** deal. Your cruise ship will come in at a price you can handle if you use my four best bets to maximizing savings:

Cruise discounters, discount mega-cruise agencies with the volume and the connections to get you what you want for less.

Membership clubs providing negotiated club-member-only discounts that let you take advantage of deals arranged especially for you.

Sunday newspaper travel sections advertising excellent limited-time offers–with some of the best reserved for big-city papers.

Book early. Booking six to eight weeks early can provide some of the deepest discounts.

Selecting a cruise is like planning a temporary move to a floating city. The ship and the sailing you choose are key to the success and enjoyment of your holiday. Too many people follow the safe route, go to routine destinations and pay far more than they should. We're far beyond the time when cruising was looked on as the exclusive property of the elite but the full possibilities of modern cruising are still secrets to most travelers. We'll show you how to cruise to fabulous ports for less than the per-night cost of a decent hotel.

If you're planning on booking your tenth cruise or considering booking your first, this chapter will give you dozens of ways to save and the information you need to choose a cruise that will fit you perfectly. Opt for elegance just a cashmere thread from top hat and tails or a casual cruise, where comfort is the only dress code. Sleep in the splendor of a suite or make your base of cruise operations a compact cabin that still affords you the run of a $400 million ship. Take a five-hour cruise on a floating casino or a three-month voyage around the globe. Cruise the oceans or sail the rivers of the world. Select a cruise with international flavor or go all-American on one of the two new ships being built by the Walt Disney Company.

This chapter begins with all the clues you need to cut the cost of cruising. I'll tell you how my best bets work, how to calculate the true cost of confusing offers, explain all the standard discounts, let you know how to beat the single supplement and detail more creative ways to cruise for less.

"Why Cruise Now?" puts you in the best position to take advantage of the rate breaks that won't be here forever. I'll tell you about the newest ships, including those that are still in the shipyards of Europe, being prepared for their debuts. We'll look at why cruise vacations are bargains, explain all-inclusive pricing and talk about the broadening appeal of cruises.

Cruise Control gives you an idea of how cabin choice affects price, available itineraries, and how to select a cruise and a cabin. It also addresses safety, health and insurance issues.

Cruise Line Profiles looks at the major cruise lines, their repeat passenger programs, theme cruises, innovations and identifying characteristics. After you read it, you'll be able to match your personality to the personality of the cruise line that fits you best.

Off The Beaten Wave takes you to the worlds of river cruises, unique cruise options on U.S. and international waters and cruises to nowhere. You'll read about new options for seeing the world by freighter with accommodations that rival some cruise ships and ports of call no cruise line can offer.

Turn the page to embark on a sea of savings so enticing that they're likely to make a cruise vacation the wave of *your* future.

CLUES TO THE BEST BARGAINS

Cruises provide some of the best all-inclusive values of 1996. The savvy cruiser may want to play potluck, but if you want the Caribbean, so be it. During the last week of 1995, many cruise lines offered two-for-one deals. During the entire year, about 200 cruises offered two-for-ones. During the fall of 1995 we even saw–believe it or not–deals where you paid for one passenger and the second, third and fourth were free. As more ships enter the market, more deals will appear. Begin your search by checking out four savings maximizers.

CRUISE DISCOUNTERS

Cruise discounters emphasize price. Cruise-only agencies have expansive knowledge and will take the time to help you find exactly what you want. Smaller, general purpose agencies have a lot of ground and air to cover. Even with the best intentions they simply cannot keep up with all the cruise deals and options available. Be sure the agency you call is a member of the Cruise Lines International Association (CLIA) and be sure they offer specialization and discounts. There are dozens of good cruise agencies, but you want a **great** one.

The Cruise Line, Inc., 800-777-0707, will take the time to find out your preferences, match them to an appropriate cruise and give you a healthy discount. They do volume business and are therefore able to offer group rates on individual bookings. They are also the only cruise discount agency that maintains membership in the National Tour Association (NTA). They put together impressive deals such as:

- **Carnival offered several select Caribbean and Mexican cruises,** where the first passenger payed $1070 and the second, third, fourth (and possibly fifth) passengers went **free**.

- **Two-For-One** deals were offered on many Holland America ships, including the *Maasdam*, sailing a ten-night Panama Canal itinerary.

- **A 14-night Southeast Asia & Orient** cruise on Royal Caribbean's *Sun Viking* was offered for just $2499 including airfare.

- **Dolphin Cruise Lines offered a Kids Cruise Free** when accompanied by two full fare paying adults on its theme ships.

> *Ninety-nine percent of all cruise bookings are made through cruise agencies. Unlike agencies that specialize in air travel, cruise agencies can go into business for the price of some business cards. You have to know where to go, who to trust and how to wade through all the possibilities that are out there to get to the exact discount that is best for you.*

(M) EMBERSHIP CLUBS

Some membership clubs, including the American Automobile Association (AAA), arrange special, member-only deals. Some membership clubs offer a discount on one specific sailing, usually hoping to book a large percentage of club-member passengers. Others have a monthly listing of specials, but may also discount every sailing on every ship.

(S) UNDAY NEWSPAPER

The Sunday travel section showcases some of the biggest sales cruise lines offer. Any travel section will have some special offers. Big city papers have the most. Some are limited to specific regions. Holland America, for example, recently offered an extra $140 off for people in four specific states. At the same time, they deeply discounted two months' worth of cruises nationwide. A few dollars spent on a short term subscription to a few large city papers around the country can be well worth the price if you locate cruise savings in the hundreds of dollars. You also get a basis of comparison to use when you talk to a cruise agent.

- **To use this tool most efficiently,** check the paper for a couple of Sundays to give yourself a base of knowledge before you begin to call. Also, check for bargain rates in cruise departure cities. New Orleans, for example, will offer discounts in the New Orleans, Houston and Dallas Sunday travel sections–which you won't read about in your hometown paper.

- **Don't call the agencies listed at the bottom of the ad** just because it's convenient. You want to call a specialist and you want to call someone you know something about.

(B) OOK EARLY

Some of the deepest discounts go to passengers who book six to eight months–sometimes even two years–in advance. Some lines guarantee that if the price falls below what you paid, the difference will be refunded. Be sure to check the specific policy. Early booking discounts come in two variations:

- **Capacity controlled rates** that expire as soon as a certain number of cabins are sold. Ask for Royal Caribbean Breakthrough Rates, Holland America KIS Rates, Norwegian Cruise Line Leadership Fares, Costa Andiamo Rates, Dolphin MaxSea Rates and Carnival Super Savers. Many other lines offer similar programs.

- **Fixed expiration date discounts** available until the booking deadline. Fixed-date discounts are popular with Princess and Holland America Lines' Alaska and European itineraries.

> **❝**Be flexible. If you cruise during peak times or holidays you'll pay high rates. Caribbean rates are typically lowest from Labor Day to mid-December, except for Thanksgiving sailings. Alaskan cruises are best buys from May to early June and in September. European rates are lowest in the spring and fall. Spring break economy cruises are good deals if you are in the mood for college students who have escaped the pursuit of knowledge for the pursuit of one another. **❞**

Number of light bulbs used annually on Carnival Cruise Lines: 11 million.

AN OCEAN OF SAVINGS POSSIBILITIES

Free or reduced rates for third/fourth passengers (also applying to children) are commonly offered by Carnival, Premier and Royal Caribbean, usually for three-, four-, and seven-day sailings. Airfare is additional. Royal Caribbean's Fall '95 "Breakthrough" deals recently offered first and second passenger discounts and third and fourth passenger rates of $49 per person on four-day Mexican Baja Cruises from Los Angeles to Ensenada.

Fifty to 80 percent off second passenger rates really amount to 25%-40% off per person. They are commonly used by Holland America and Orient Lines but many cruise lines use them sporadically.

- **When you're offered a price with variations** for multiple passengers, divide the total cost by the number of passengers to get your real per passenger cost. Two-for-one deals are marketing ploys based on high prices for the first passenger, but can be legitimately good deals–such as a seven-night Princess Caribbean cruise at $1048 for two passengers. Check the validity of any two-for-one deal by independently checking the usual discounted price and comparing it with your actual cost-per-person.

Free upgrades are often used by Carnival, Celebrity, Norwegian and Royal Caribbean. They give you added comfort and style with no additional expenditure. Often they're not advertised and appear and disappear without public notice. Get them by asking.

The world's smallest port: Ginostra in Stromboli, Italy with passage carved through rock.

Flat rate specials charge a fixed price–usually one rate for inside cabins and one for outside cabins–and give you the best available cabin (including suites). Run of the ship rates are similar but your specific cabin number isn't usually confirmed until two weeks before or up to the day of sailing. Flat rate specials are commonly used by Princess, Crystal and Norwegian.

Full payment advance discounts are offered by some cruise lines for payment considerably in advance of departure. Silversea Cruise's, for example, offers 15% discounts to passengers who pay in full six months before sailing. Crystal Cruises has a similar program.

Senior citizen reduced rates are commonly offered by Royal Caribbean and Norwegian Cruise Lines, but are being phased out. You're currently eligible if one person in the cabin is at least 55 years old. These discounts are almost always more beneficial than rates offered directly by senior membership clubs.

Group discounts are available for multiple bookings on the sailing. There does not have to be any formal connection among the passengers. You can negotiate for discounts and free berths. What you get is contingent on the number of people traveling. If you have 16 passengers, based on double occupancy, you may be able to get one free berth.

SPECIAL PROMOTIONS

Affinity promotions save you money when you use a cruise line and its promotion partner. The partner could be a credit or charge card company offering free upgrades, discounts and shipboard credits. Visa Gold often offers bonuses on 22 major cruise lines.

Added value promotions give free days, land package add-ons, free shore excursions or free pre- or post-cruise hotel rooms. Added value perks are commonly used by Holland America, Costa, Radisson, Renaissance and Orient Lines. Free days are commonly offered on Holland America.

If you're a frequent cruiser, watch your mail for past passenger specials. Most lines sign you up automatically the first time you sail. You may not rival the couple that recently took their 172nd cruise, but benefits still accrue and, at minimum, you get mailings that give you first use of yet-to-be advertised discounts.

CREATIVE DISCOUNTS

Repositioning Cruises combine value and variety. They're available twice a year during seasonal shifts, when cruise lines move ships from one region to another. Common repositionings are from the Caribbean to Europe or Alaska, and back again. For example, an Alaska repositioning cruise may include highlights from Eastern, Western and Southern Caribbean sailings, as well as the Panama Canal and the Mexican Riviera–all in just ten to 17 days. Repositioning cruises are generally longer than normal and offer unique ports of call. Caribbean to Europe repositionings can include stops in Portugal, Tangier and Morocco. Norwegian calls their repositioning cruises "Rare Voyages" and includes stops in San Francisco and Portland or Balboa and Cartagena. Some lines feature their repositioning cruises in their brochures. Others use less advance planning so you have to ask when they're scheduled and where they'll be going.

Book a week or two on a lengthy, around-the-world cruise for a per-day cost that may be well below a standard seven-day cruise. Arrange your own discount airfare to meet the ship at the port

---

Cost of a one-hour cruise in a swan-shaped boat at Orlando's Lake Eola: $11.

you choose to create a unique short cruise experience. You get the ambiance of a different type of ship with a different passenger profile, unusual ports of call and the freedom to make choices standard seven-day cruises don't offer.

Back-to-back specials are for people with the time and money to take two or more consecutive cruises on the same ship. You buy one week and get the second free or get a big discount on both weeks. Obviously you'll want some variation in itinerary unless repeating ports of call appeals to you.

Standby rates can be as much as 55% lower than standard rates. You pay in full at the time of booking and wait to be confirmed just prior to sailing. It's the most economical way to cruise if your plans can accommodate change. If you're not confirmed you get a full refund. Standby is available from lines including Holland America, Princess, Cunard and American Hawaii.

Ask for a discount just because you're you. If you're a newlywed, or celebrating any special event, let the cruise agent know. You could save a few hundred dollars, get a free upgrade or find flowers and candy waiting in your cabin. Upgrades are often available for the asking.

Cut port spending to purchase a better cruise. The average cruise passenger spends $385 in port. If you decide in advance to limit purchases and spend your time gathering memories, you can afford a higher-priced cruise or a significant upgrade just by re-allocating your cruise budget. On some cruises, $385 is even enough to cover the cost of an additional passenger in a shared cabin. If shopping is a big part of what makes vacations fun for you, this tip won't be your cup of tea. If you can do without it, you've expanded your cruise budget and your choices.

BOOKING FOR ONE

Singles can save on cruises even though they're typically required to pay a single supplement ranging from ten to 100 percent above the standard fare. The most popular cruises are likely to charge the highest supplements. Ask how the cruise line calculates its single supplement charges. Some are based on cruise cost only while others include air. Single supplement avoidance tactics:

- **Guaranteed Single Rates** charge single passengers a price that is slightly higher than the per person/double-occupancy rate with cabin assignment at embarkation. You get what's best available (including suites) at the time of sailing. You get the privacy of a solo cabin without paying the single supplement, as advertised in each cruise line's individual brochure.

- **Guaranteed Single Shares** charge the standard double-occupancy rate and try to place you with a cabin mate of the same gender and smoking preference. If they fail, you get a private room at no extra charge. There's also a chance you'll be stuck with an incompatible cabin mate, so choose wisely.

Cruise Line's Singles Policies

The second column indicates the availability of single cabins on some or all of the line's ships. The third column indicates the line's willingness to arrange a shared room situation. The fourth column shows how much you have to pay to book a regular cabin as compared to a single cabin (based on the double-occupancy price).

CRUISE LINE'S SINGLES POLICIES			
CRUISE LINES	SINGLE CABIN AVAILABILITY	SINGLE MATCH-UP PLANS	SINGLE SUPPLEMENT
AMERICAN HAWAIIAN	Yes	Yes	160%
CARNIVAL	Yes	Yes	150–200%
CELEBRITY	Yes	Yes	150–200%
CLIPPER	Yes	Yes	150%
CLUB MED	Yes	Yes	150%
COMMODORE	Yes	No	150%
COSTA	Yes	No	150%
CRYSTAL	No	No	150–200%
CUNARD	Yes	Yes	Varies
DELTA QUEEN	Yes	Yes	175%
DOLPHIN	No	Yes	150%
HOLLAND AMERICA	Yes	Yes	125–150%
NORWEGIAN	Yes	Yes	150%
ORIENT LINES	Yes	Yes	125–175%
PREMIER	Yes	No	175%
PRINCESS	Yes	Yes	150%
RADISSON SEVEN SEAS	No	No	125%
ROYAL CARIBBEAN	Yes	Yes	150%
SEABOURN	Yes	No	110–200%
SEAWIND	No	No	110–200%
SILVERSEA	No	No	150%
STAR CLIPPERS	Yes	Yes	150%
WINDJAMMER	No	Yes	175%
WINDSTAR	No	No	150%

Most popular costume on the Star Clipper's all-nudist Halloween cruise: body paint.

AIR TRAVEL OPTIONS

Air/Cruise packages are the norm and they protect you from any flight variables that might cause you to miss embarkation. But there are a few things you should know before you set off on your trip.

- **Cruise lines reserve blocks of seats** about a year in advance. If demand is higher than anticipated, you may be assigned less convenient flights.

- **If you want a specific flight or airline** you must request it at the time the reservation is made. There is no guarantee that you'll get what you want (and there may be a deviation charge) but your cruise agent will work with you and try to accommodate your requests.

- **When your flight is confirmed** (usually three to five weeks before departure) call the airline with your frequent flyer number. You may also request seat assignments at that time.

Be sure to explore your air travel options and pick the one that most benefits you. Reduced rate air is sometimes available. An air rate of $299 from Chicago to Miami, for example, may be reduced to $149 or $99 per person. Ask about special air add-ons that may be available from your city.

Ask what deduction you will receive if you decline airfare, so you can weigh the option of shopping for a lower fare or using frequent flyer miles.

- **Factor in the cost of airport to seaport travel.** Cruise lines include all transfers if they arrange your air travel.

- **Plan to arrive early.** You might even want to fly in the day before. A delayed flight can mean a missed ship.

- **Disembarkation takes two to three hours,** so plan your return flight accordingly. Unless your flight schedule demands that you be first in line for disembarkation, relax in your cabin to avoid the lines of early birds.

Recently,

BEST FARES Discount Travel Magazine

showed savvy travelers how to get bargain American Airlines weekend fares by checking the Internet.

Call 800-880-1234 to subscribe.
See page 395 for your discount subscription offer.

Most popular gambling destination for U.S. travelers: Nevada, followed by cruise ships.

WHY CRUISE NOW?

The years 1996 and 1997 offer unprecedented cruise values. Well over five million people cruised in 1995. The industry will have to attract eight million people annually by the turn of the century to make their new multi-billion dollar ship investments pay off. Most current cruise bookings come from repeat passengers. Only an estimated eight percent of North Americans have ever been on a cruise. Hundreds of millions of advertising dollars and creative discount temptations are going to be offered to attract new passengers.

THE BROADENING APPEAL OF CRUISES

You could say that the first cruise in history was Noah's Ark. Cruises have come a long way even since their depiction in 1950s' movies. Shuffleboard and ballroom dancing can still be found but today's cruise consumers will find ships and styles varied enough to appeal to almost anyone.

One of the most frequent misconceptions about cruises is that they appeal to the older and wealthier traveler. The theory is that most grown up baby boomers are too active for shipboard life; that people in their 30's require the kind of vacation that moves with the speed of a television remote control; that people in their 20's prefer Cyber-space and MTV and would feel confined on any cruise ship.

- **Modern ships and the itineraries they sail** probably contain more adventure, option and variety than the average land-only vacation.

- **Just about anyone alive wants to reduce stress** and the floating island of a cruise ship is one of the best ways to do it.

A physicist on a *Wheel of Fortune* theme cruise is likely to be about as happy as a sun worshipper aboard an Antarctic Adventure cruise. Personal taste is a prime consideration in choosing a cruise. Taking the time to match your personality to the ship's can mean the difference between a disappointing cruise and a perfect fit.

The cruise spectrum has grown. The fastest growing group of passengers is in the 25-40 age bracket. Whether you like to bowl and barbecue; hike and meditate; play bridge and read the classics; or eat, drink and be married, you'll feel at home on the right ship.

People who like to choose their own activities won't lack enjoyable options: swimming pools, spas and fitness centers, tennis and basketball courts, show lounges, discos, full-tilt casinos, intimate bars for conversation, card rooms, video arcades and high-tech game rooms, computer rooms, book and video libraries, cinemas, shops, restaurants and cafes, even an 18-hole miniature golf course.

People who prefer organized activities will have choices from dawn to midnight: discussion groups, investment seminars, bingo, mechanical horse racing, aerobics, skeet shooting, team sports, bridge tournaments, contests and dance lessons.

While you're having your style of fun, you're also getting closer to interesting ports of call. Each time you disembark, you might be in a different country amid a different culture. You can plunge into the experience with guided tours or explore on your own.

Don't forget the wonders of nature. You're on the ocean with no land in sight. An unobscured canopy of stars shines over gently rolling ocean waves as you remember what fresh air is really like.

NEW & UPCOMING SHIPS

The success of the first mega-ships launched in this wave of new entries in the world of cruising is based on the popularity of large, multi-option ships that offer the widest array of options in cabin choice, recreation and entertainment. The majority of today's cruise passengers definitely think bigger is better. The new additions will carry between 1,740 and 2,642 passengers. Five years ago the standard was 300-900 passengers per ship. All the new ships are coming from European shipyards with their tradition of successfully combining elegance and efficiency. Nine of the 23 new ships are coming from Italian shipbuilders.

Each ship will offer its own excitements and innovations. Each ship has a unique personality built around ultra-luxury common areas that should set the tone for a new generation of cruise delights. The traditional "floating city" has become an upscale architectural gem built to appeal to a broader array of people than ever before. The industry wants an expanded demographic base and they're building ships that help them achieve that goal–a goal they must meet to keep revenue strong.

All of the new ships will feature:

- **Technical advancements** including virtual-reality theaters and game centers and in-cabin entertainment centers. More costly cabins will even have in-room computers.

- **Grand-scale public areas**, some with retractable glass ceilings.

- **Theme restaurants** offering night-by-night options to the main dining room.

- **Spas and fitness facilities** to a degree available previously only on a handful of luxury ships.

The Pacific vs. the Atlantic: (in square miles): the Atlantic: 31,800,000; the Pacific: 63,800,000.

SHIPS COMING ON-LINE THROUGH 1998			
CRUISE LINE/SHIP	**YEAR**	**PAX**	**COUNTRY OF ORIGIN**
CARNIVAL/Inspiration	1996	2,040	Finland
CARNIVAL/Unnamed A	1998	2,040	Finland
CARNIVAL/Unnamed B	1998	2,040	Italy
CARNIVAL/Unnamed C	1998	2,600	Italy
CELEBRITY/Century	1995	1,740	Germany
CELEBRITY/Galaxy	1996	1,740	Germany
CELEBRITY/Unnamed	1997	1,740	Germany
COSTA/Victoria	1996	1,900	Germany
COSTA/Magica	1997	2,100	Germany
DISNEY/Magic	1998	2,400	Italy
DISNEY/Wonder	1998	2,400	Italy
HOLLAND AMERICA/Veendam	1996	1,266	Italy
HOLLAND AMERICA/Unnamed	1997	1,320	Italy
PRINCESS/Sun Princess	1995	1,950	Italy
PRINCESS/Dawn Princess	1997	1,950	Italy
PRINCESS/Grand Princess	1997	2,600	Italy
ROYAL CARIBBEAN			
Splendour of the Seas	1996	1,800	France
Grandeur of the Seas	1996	1,950	Finland
Enchantment of the Seas	1997	1,950	Finland
Rhapsody of the Seas	1997	2,000	France
Vision of the Seas	1998	2,000	France

Highlights Of Some Of The Newest Ships

Princess Cruises' *Sun Princess* set sail in 1995. She has multiple dining rooms, a 24-hour cafe, two pools with a waterfall, computerized golf simulating play on the world's top courses, a dance club with a clear floor built over video screens and private balconies attached to 70% of the outside staterooms.

Celebrity's *Century* debuted in 1995. The *Century* and the *Galaxy,* due in 1997, each feature two 1,515 square-foot penthouse suites serviced by private butlers. More generalized amenities include a 9,340 square-foot AquaSpa (spa, gym, beauty and fitness center combined), two-tiered restaurants and private verandas.

Number of new berths added by the cruise industry in 1995: 7,000; anticipated in 1996: 16,000.

The *Century's* focal point will be a three-deck Grand Foyer with a spiral staircase and a glass ceiling. The *Galaxy* will have a sliding glass cupola and twin atriums.

Carnival's *Destiny* wins the size prize. She entered service in 1996 in excess of 100,000 tons, making it the largest cruise ship ever built. At its highest point, she is 80 feet taller than the Statue of Liberty. She will be restricted to Caribbean itineraries as she is too wide to pass through the Panama Canal. Some 2,600 passengers will have their choice of two-tiered restaurants and three pools. Decor includes Venetian glass chandeliers and atriums centered with impressive grand staircases.

Royal Caribbean's *Legend* and *Splendour of the Seas* will both have 18 holes of miniature golf making the oceans around the ships the world's largest water hazards.

Princess Cruises' *Grand Princess*, projected to be a 104,000-gross-ton vessel, is scheduled to be in operation in 1997. She will have moving sidewalks, a cantilevered nightclub extending over the aft deck, three dining rooms, three lounges and a techno-room, which the line says will allow passengers to star in their own mini-movies.

The Costa *Victoria* will have an observation lounge patterned after an Italian piazza that spans four decks, has a waterfall on one side and a floor-to-ceiling glass wall on the other. The Euro-style spa will have an indoor pool, a Turkish bath, a sauna, a 1,312-foot long jogging track and all the usual fitness center equipment.

> 66 *Low rates may not last beyond '97 as older ships are retired to avoid costly safety improvements mandated by 1992 amendments to the Safety of Life at Sea Treaty (SOLAS). Stringent amendments start going into effect in 1997 when low-level lighting, smoke detectors and remote control fire doors must be installed. It will cost $20-40 million per ship to bring older vessels up to the coming codes. If you're a fan of the beautiful wood-paneled ships, enjoy them while you still can. If you're a fan of low rates, now's the time to get them.* 99

ALL-INCLUSIVE PRICING

Cruises typically include most if not all of the cost elements of a vacation:

- **Roundtrip airfare.** Cruise lines negotiate for special rates and assign seats to passengers based on availability of their blocked seats.

- **Transportation to and from the ship.** You'll be met by a ship's representative and transported from the airport to the ship. Arranged bus service will take you back to the airport after your cruise.

- **Accommodations** in the cabin class you select.

- **Three main meals per day** plus **three buffet meals** including lavish midnight buffets. Some ships add a fourth buffet for late-nighters at around 1:30 a.m. You also can order from 24-hour room service. Cruise ship dining is easily the equivalent of fine restaurant dining and sometimes rivals anything you've experienced on land.

Reason why alcoholic drinks should be cheaper on cruises: the availability of duty-free liquor.

SAMPLE DINNER MENU FROM THE MODERATELY PRICED NORWEGIAN CRUISE LINES

Baked Crabmeat Cake on Sweet Corn Relish

Tomato Bisque Soup with Basil

*Ravioli stuffed with Ricotta with
Sweet Pumpkin Sauce*

Jumbo Shrimp with Lobster-Basil Sauce

Fresh Garden Vegetables and Risotto Milanese

Fine International Cheeses

Chocolate-Bourbon-Pecan Pie A la Mode

Fresh Fruit Potpourri

Espresso

❝ *Most cruise lines accommodate special dietary requests made by your agent. If you forget, you should still be easily able to satisfy the terms of your diet within the wide varieties of foods offered. Late sleepers should choose late dinner seating to avoid being confronted with Baked Alaska in the light of day. The most noticeable divisions on cruises are the early risers and the late risers. The twain meet but only in passing. If you find your assigned dinner companions unsuitable, discretely ask the maitre d' to reassign you and give him a minimum $10 tip as you make your request.* ❞

Cruises typically offer some of the best vacation values:

- **All-inclusive pricing** lets you know in advance what your dollars will buy.

- **Cruises tend to stretch the vacation dollar.** Because so much is included you have fewer temptations to spend.

- **You buy a consistent level of quality.** Each cruise line varies in the quality of their cuisine but there is no worry that your accommodations might be great one night and inferior the next. You don't have to pick a local restaurant and hope for the best. Cruise cuisine is consistently innovative, varied and served with lavish style.

- **Cruise service** is focused on passenger satisfaction–as evidenced by the ratio of crew to passenger. In some cases it approaches one-to-one.

- **Shipboard activities:** pools, whirlpools, games, aerobics, yoga, skeet shooting, volleyball, contests, bridge tournaments, paddle tennis, basketball, 18-hole miniature golf courses and more. Ships also have card rooms, libraries (book and video), and deck space for sunbathing and conversation. Many ships have playrooms, teen discos, video arcades, computer rooms, jogging tracks, health spas and gyms. Some have tennis and basketball courts.

- **Entertainment**: main lounge, cabarets and nightclubs, films and theme events. The main lounge is home to Las Vegas Style Reviews or Broadway shows. There are also discos and dance band lounges.

- **Visits to exciting ports-of-call,** typically four stops on a seven-night cruise. You can take part in planned activities or explore on your own.

Extras

Expenses not included in your cruise price are optional tours in ports-of-call, ship-to-shore phone calls and faxes, casino gambling, most alcoholic beverages, personal expenses such as massage, hair care and boutique purchases, cruise insurance (see *More Dollars & Cents* section for additional information on cruise insurance) and gratuities ($56 average on a seven-day cruise). Port charges and government fees ($125 average but dependent on ports-of-call) are paid at the time your reservation is confirmed.

Super all-inclusive fares do cover certain shore excursions, gratuities and alcoholic beverages. These super fares are mostly limited to five star deluxe cruise lines such as Silversea and Seabourn.

AVERAGE COST OF CRUISE EXTRAS

Ship-to-shore phone calls: $15-20 per minute

Cocktails: $2.95-3.50

Soft drinks: $.75-1.50

Coffee and iced tea: free

Half-hour massage: $35

Manicure: $20

Laundering and pressing one shirt: $1

Cruise Insurance: Packages average $65 for ten-day trips

❝*Trip insurance for cruises is usually sold by cruise and tour operators with policies underwritten by a separate financial entity. Never buy insurance directly from the cruise line–if the cruise line folds you're out of luck. Also use caution when purchasing cruise insurance during the winter months if you buy a cruise only package. A good example would be the winter blizzard of '96 which prevented many cruise passengers from getting to their cruise ships. In this case, the missed cruise was not the cruise lines' fault and was not insured.❞*

Percentage of the Arctic Ocean open to ships year round: ten percent.

CRUISE CONTROL

THE CHOICE IS YOURS

Over 72% of our planet is covered by water and there's a cruise line ready to take you through most of it. Cruise to over 180 ports on seven continents.

Choose Your Itinerary

The Caribbean remains the most popular cruise choice.

- **The Eastern Caribbean** consists of ports including Nassau, St. Thomas, St. John, St. Maarten, San Juan and St. Croix. Cruise lines add variety by persuading lesser known islands such as Hispaniola to provide new ports of call. Many lines negotiate agreements with small islands and claim them as exclusive ports-of-call.

- **The Western Caribbean** includes Jamaica (Ocho Rios or Montego Bay), Cancun, Grand Cayman, Playa del Carmen and Cozumel.

- **The Southern or Lower Caribbean** is sailed by ships based in San Juan. Their base ports allow them to visit islands including Barbados, Antigua, Martinique, Grenada, St. Lucia, St. Kitts, St. Barts, Guadeloupe, Caracas, Curacao, Trinidad and Tobago.

Other cruise itineraries include Alaska, Hawaii, New England, Europe (including the Mediterranean, the Greek Islands, the Holy Land, the Black Sea and Scandinavia/Russia), the South Pacific (South Sea Islands, Australia and New Zealand), the Orient (China, Japan, Indonesia, Singapore, Malaysia and Hong Kong), Africa, India, Canada (Nova Scotia, the St. Lawrence River, Montreal and Quebec) and South America (coastal cruises or cruises along the Amazon River). Several ships offer around-the-world cruises.

Maximum size of passenger ship allowed to dock at The Galapagos Islands: 90 passengers.

- **Pacific** routings include Inter-Hawaiian, Honolulu to Ensenada and Los Angeles to Acapulco.

- **Far Pacific** routings include Bombay to Hong Kong, Bangkok to Sydney and Los Angeles to Papeete.

- **Panama Canal** routings include San Juan to Acapulco, Fort Lauderdale to Los Angeles.

- **Trans Atlantic crossings** include New York to Southampton, Genoa to Miami, and Capetown to Buenes Aires.

- **European and Mediterranean** routings include the Greek Islands, European port cities and Mombassa to Haifa.

- **Indian Ocean** routings include Genoa to Bombay, Singapore to Bali and Mombassa to Cape Town.

- **South American** routings include Amazon River journeys, Antarctica cruises and Buenos Aires to Santiago.

- **World Cruises** last from 90 to well over 100 nights and range in cost from about $8,500-160,000. You can purchase segments beginning at about $100 per day and join cruises in progress. The *QE2*, for example, offers four segments shorter than two weeks. One certainty: a very interesting mix of passengers.

Choose Your Range

Brochure prices range from the economical to the lavish. Even though smart shoppers never pay brochure rates, they give you some idea of the relative luxuriousness of any ship you're considering. You'll learn a lot from studying the cruise lines brochures. First observe the obvious–the photographs. Do you see children? Are the models younger or older? Is the tone festive, sedate or refined? How

are they dressed? Does the brochure use words like "ultra-deluxe," "casual elegance" or "informal?" Don't overlook the least enticing part of brochures–the small-print terms and conditions, worth reading word-for-word.

- **Budget** cruise lines include Dolphin and Commodore.

- **Moderate** cruise lines include Costa, Carnival and Norwegian.

- **Deluxe** cruise lines include Princess, Royal Caribbean, Holland America and Celebrity.

- **Ultra-Deluxe** cruise lines include Crystal, Seabourn and Silversea.

Boutique cruises overlap the ultra-deluxe category but include the smaller, all-suite ships of Silversea, Seabourn and Sea Goddess and the cruise/sail ships of Windstar and Star Clipper.

Adventure and expedition cruises are available in the moderate to deluxe range.

Choose Your Ship

When you book a cruise you're booking a total environment that will surround you for the duration of your vacation. The ship you choose will be your hotel, your entertainment, your outdoor playground, your restaurant and your meeting place. It's important that you spend the time to make a good match between your own style and the style of the ship you choose.

Most cruise lines have a distinctive ambiance that carries through to all their ships. You can get an idea of which lines would be best for you by talking to friends who are cruise veterans and have tastes akin to your own or to knowledgeable cruise agents.

Let your cruise agent know your personal tastes and preferences.

Cruise line that started with a $600 sloop purchased while "painting the town red" in Miami: Windjammer.

- **Are you excited by the huge mega-liners,** or would you feel more comfortable on a smaller, more intimate ship? If you want a truly relaxing getaway choose a smaller ship with fewer ports-of-call. Your ship is your best destination.

- **Are you looking for optimum tranquility or lots of activity?** If you thrive on planned activities, choose a line that specializes in multiple options for every waking moment.

- **Do you like to be among people in your own age group or is an age mix more your style?** Try to find the ship that best fits every member of your cruising party.

- **How important is the dining experience?** No successful cruise line serves bad food but there are variations in their level of excellence.

- **Do you plan to try your luck each night in the casino?** If you love Las Vegas, make sure the ship you book has a casino large enough to challenge you.

- **What kind of ports of call would you like to visit?** If shopping is your favorite activity head for duty free ports like St. Maarten and St. Thomas.

Choose Your Cabin

Your choice of cabin is a big factor in the cost of your cruise. There are two basic schools of thought. The first says that because you spend so little time in your cabin, selecting an inexpensive one is the wisest course. The alternate view is that comfort, size and the position of the cabin on the ship matter greatly. There are no right or wrong answers but you do want to consider the following factors before you decide.

- **Cabin type**–Inside cabins have no portholes or windows but they can offer a more economical way of cruising on most ships. Outside cabins provide a window to the world but make sure your view isn't composed of traffic on a busy deck, bright orange lifeboats or other views that are something less than splendid. If you're going to pay extra for an outside cabin, you want it to be worth the expense.

- **Location**–The higher above the water line, the more expensive the cabin. On older ships, cabins mid-ship are most stable and free of noise and vibration. They're best for people prone to seasickness. On the newer ships that won't be a consideration. Passengers in wheelchairs should select cruise lines that make special provision for passengers with disabilities.

- **Beds**–Be sure you get the configuration you want. Nothing's worse than sharing a double bed when you'd rather not–unless it's sleeping in twins beds when you'd prefer to be a little closer. Most new ships have solved the problem with twin beds that can easily be moved together to create a king-size bed.

- **Bath or shower?**–Most cabins have bathrooms with showers rather than tubs. On many ships you will have to book a suite to enjoy having both.

The chart on the next page illustrates how much your choice of cabin affects the price of your cruise. We used a moderately priced, three-day Caribbean cruise for our example but the range of variation is even more extreme on lengthier cruises and more expensive ships. Chart prices are based on double occupancy and do not include airfare. Remember that whether you choose L class at $609 ($203 per day) or an S1 suite at $1,649 ($550 per day) you'll be on the same ship, enjoying the same amenities and heading for the same ports of call.

Definition of a "stretched" cruise ship: one that's been cut in half and enlarged by a mid-ship insert.

THREE-DAY CRUISE COST VARIATIONS		
CLASS	COST	DETAILS
L	$609	Inside cabin; upper/lower berths
K	$689	Inside cabin; two lower beds
J	$709	Inside cabin; two lower beds
I	$769	Inside cabin; two lower beds
H	$809	Inside cabin; two lower beds
G	$869	Outside cabin; two lower beds
F	$909	Outside cabin; two lower beds
E	$939	Outside cabin; two lower beds
D	$979	Large outside cabin; obstructed view; two lower beds
C	$1,039	Large outside cabin; some partially obstructed views; two lower beds
B	$1,089	Large outside cabin; two lower beds
A	$1,119	Deluxe outside cabin with sitting area; two lower beds; tub and shower. Some have obstructed views.
S2	$1,399	Suite with sitting area, refrigerator and two lower beds
S1	$1,649	Deluxe suite; sitting area; refrigerator; tub and shower; two lower beds

CRUISE INSURANCE

We cover all forms of travel insurance in our *More Dollars and Cents* section. There are some cruise-specific details that merit mention:

- **Because you are investing a considerable sum** in an all-inclusive cruise, insurance is always worth purchasing. The most important component is Trip Cancellation/Interruption Protection, not automatically included in all policies. It protects you from financial risks associated with your need to cancel a cruise or to interrupt a cruise.

- **Ask to have the terms and conditions mailed** and review them carefully. Coverage pertaining to medical situations, for example, will not apply to pre-existing conditions.

- **You should be able to get good coverage** for five to six percent of the total cruise price.

- **Understand the difference between a waiver and insurance.** A waiver is **not** insurance. It is a for-fee option in which the company waives its own penalties if you cancel your cruise for any reason, usually up to 72 hours before sailing. It provides no protection against operator default and is usually full of clauses that limit the acceptable conditions under which you may cancel without penalty.

Most cruise lines offer their own policies. Also check with your cruise consultant who may offer insurance options that are less expensive and more comprehensive.

Cruise line offering nutmeg syrup and pineapple paw paw jam in their gift catalogue: Windjammer.

SHORE EXCURSIONS

Shore excursions come in three categories: pure fun, general tours and theme or attraction-oriented tours. Cruise lines have never made shore excursions part of the selling package but they can be a significant part of a well-planned cruise. You'll probably have to ask about excursion options and prices if you want to know them before the post-booking pamphlet arrives with your cruise documents. Some popular excursions sell out quickly so plan on signing up as soon as you board ship. Preview lectures are given by the cruise staff prior to arriving at each port.

The price of shore excursions on Caribbean and Mexican cruises varies. Escorted activities such as city or island tours, snorkeling, beach parties and glass bottom boat rides range from $15-50 per person.

Special shore activities have higher prices:

- **Golf**: $40-90 per person.

- **Scuba diving**: $40-55 per person.

- **Seaplane or helicopter rides**: $65 per person.

- **Submarine rides**: $48-58 per person.

- **Horseback riding**: $50 per person.

- **Sailboat rides**: $30-45 per person.

- **Extended tours** such as a seven-and-a-half-hour tour to the Tulum Mayan ruins from Play del Carmen at $55 per person.

European shore excursions tend to be all-day events, thus are higher priced. A full-day tour of Copenhagen and surroundings, for example, has an average price tag of $150 per person. A full day tour of St. Petersburg, Russia with evening entertainment costs around $135.

A full day's wine tasting tour of France's Bordeaux region is about $165.

Independent tours of ports-of-call are yours for the taking. You're free to do as you like until it's time to board the ship again. In many Caribbean ports you'll find entrepreneurial taxi drivers who give private island tours. The best ones will give their own distinctive views of island high points at about $10 less than the group tour price.

Alaskan Shore Excursions And Tours

Shore excursions on Alaskan cruises offer salmon bakes for about $21 per person; two-hour motorcoach tours for around $34; 90-minute flights over Glacier Bay for $110; fishing trips; hiking trips; helicopter tours and more. There are more shore excursion options on Alaskan cruises than on any other itineraries. Because of their popularity it's a good idea to pre-purchase these shore excursions whenever possible.

Cruise tours are land extensions of your cruise experience. You don't want to travel all the way to Alaska only to miss many of its inland wonders. Cruise tours give you an overview of Alaska that you could never get in brief port visits. You can arrange these cruise-line sponsored add-ons with your cruise agent. Also ask about tours offered by Grey Line of Seattle and Alaska.

Princess Cruise's offers a five-day/six-night cruise tour, added to the end of a seven-day Vancouver to Seward cruise. Here's some of what you'd miss if you didn't know about cruise tour options:

- **Eight Cruise Day:** Leave your ship for a motorcoach ride to the Kenai Princess Lodge, a wilderness retreat on the Kenai River and your home for the next two days.

Amount of coral destroyed when a cruise ship drops anchor in deep water: five to 25 acres.

- **Added Day One:** Explore the unique peninsula area on your own with optional activities including river rafting, flightseeing or a trip to the Kenai Fjords National Park.

- **Added Day Two:** Princess transports you to Anchorage for an overnight stay.

- **Added Day Three:** Board Ultra Dome rail cars on the Midnight Sun Express for a trip to Denali National Park and an overnight at the Denali Princess Lodge.

- **Added Day Four:** Tour the Denali National Park then re-board the Midnight Sun Express for Fairbanks.

- **Added Day Five:** Fairbanks' tours include the El Dorado Gold Mine and the Trans-Alaska Pipeline plus a cruise on the riverboat *Discovery*. Spend your second night in Fairbanks and return home (by air) the following day.

CRUISE SAFETY

Modern cruise ships are a blend of man's finest technological and artistic achievements. These mega-liners are designed to ride the most angry seas and at the same time pamper passengers with once-in-a-lifetime amenities and state-of-the-art comforts. Even if you're neither Mark Spitz nor Esther Williams, you can still cruise without fear. Technological advances also have greatly improved the safety and protection features on today's cruise ships. New rules, effective in 1997, virtually eliminate flammable materials from ships' decks and cabins. The new ships are being built with these features already in place. Modern telecommunications coupled with meteorology warn ships' captains well in advance of hazardous weather conditions and offer plenty of time to take evasive action should it be necessary.

HEALTH ISSUES

Is there a doctor on board? Always. A cruise ship infirmary is not the Mayo Clinic, but it should be able to handle minor to moderate problems and stabilize seriously ill patients.

- **Most people use shipboard medical facilities** for help with seasickness and sunburn.

- **If you have a chronic condition,** be sure to carry basic medical records with you and communicate your situation to the ship's doctor.

- **In the rare event that full hospital services are required,** you will either be evacuated by helicopter or treated in a port city. The ship's doctor should be aware of the quality of care available at all the places the ship visits.

Seasickness is an easily-managed possibility. Ships are warned well in advance of hazardous weather and can alter their courses to avoid the roughest seas. Today's vessels are built with hydraulic stabilizers that electronically maintain balance and decrease the motion that brings on seasickness. If you're OK on a small power boat, you're apt to be fine on a 70,000-ton cruise ship. Should you be susceptible to motion and not prepared in advance, the ship's doctor can offer you a full range of options.

Effective ways to avoid or eliminate seasickness:

- **Over-the-counter, non-prescription** medications including Dramamine, Marazine and Bonine.

- **The "patch,"** a prescription medication –usually Scopolamine–that time-releases through the skin. It can be worn behind the ear or in the form of a bracelet.

- **Holistic options** include bands positioned to touch an acupressure point on the wrist, and ginger, chewed to relieve nausea.

If you're really concerned about seasickness, book a cruise that travels where waters generally remain calm: most of the Caribbean, the South Pacific, Alaska's Inland Passage, the Pacific Coast of the U.S. and all river voyages.

SMOKING POLICIES

Most ships have non-smoking areas and 15 lines have major smoke-free zones. Smoking is increasingly forbidden in dining rooms. Lines with strong European roots or flavor, such as Costa, will have the most liberal smoking policies. Holland America deviated from the no-smoking trend during a "Cigar Lovers" cruise, successful enough to bear repeating.

No-Smoking Dining Rooms: American Hawaii, Carnival, Commodore, Majesty, Princess and Renaissance. Premier has a no-smoking policy during early dinner seating but maintains a smoking section in the late seating. On Norwegian Cruise Line ships with two dining rooms allocate one as smoking and one as non-smoking.

You can request smoke-free cabins on Delta Queen, Majesty, Norwegian, Oceanic and Radisson Seven Seas.

No-Smoking Show Lounges: American Hawaii, Costa, Holland America and Princess.

LEGAL ISSUES

Check our Travel Guide's International section for general passport and visa information.

Cruise Specific Tips:

- **Passport and visa requirements** specific to your cruise will be detailed in the information packet sent with your tickets.

- **If you're leaving the States,** take your passport, even to Caribbean destinations where it may not be technically required.

- **Double check visa requirements** against current State Department policies.

- **Get the required visas** for all ports-of-call–even if you don't plan to disembark. Some countries require them of every passenger before the ship is allowed to dock. Others permit the cruise line to dock under the formality of a blanket visa.

SEAWORTHY TIPS

Ask your cruise agent for packing tips that specifically address the cruise you've chosen. Generally the more expensive the cruise, the more formal and elaborate the attire. Most cruise lines offer at least one formal night with a less formal atmosphere the rest of the time. All lines prohibit shorts in dining rooms at dinner seating. The culture of the ports that will be visited also helps determine what you

---

Second most comforting scent to humans: beaches. (Bakeries are first.)

need to take. The essential item for all cruises: rubber-soled walking shoes for on-deck safety and comfort during shore excursions.

If you have a physical handicap, ask for accommodations that are specifically designed to meet your needs. Does accessibility extend to the pool, boutiques and casinos? Is there a reserved area in the main lounge for passengers in wheelchairs? Do automatic door sensors have beams low enough to register people in wheelchairs? *Cruising For The Handicapped Traveler*, from Consumer Travel Advisories, offers extensive information. Request free publication by writing to 8059 W. McNab Rd., Ft. Lauderdale, FL 33321 or call 800-882-9000.

Cruise lines that love kids show it by more than special prices and catchy phrases. According to the vernacular of each line, "child" can include infants to 17-year-olds on the brink of adulthood. Children in their late to mid-teens are usually happy with any ship's offerings but younger children need activities to keep them and their parents happy. If you plan to use on-board child care, make sure to inquire about rates, times of availability, age ranges and the ratio of children to child care provider.

Call tourism offices for information on port cities. The information you gather will enhance your enjoyment of and extend your choices at ports-of-call. Check the *Know Who to Call* section of this book for contact information. *Cruise Ports Rated*, is available for $5.95 post paid from Vacation Publications, 1502 Augusta Drive, Suite 415, Houston, TX 77057. It covers almost 200 ports in the Caribbean, Alaska, the Mediterranean, South America and the Far East from must-see places to places to avoid.

Cruise documents may not arrive until two weeks before departure. Your agent may even arrange for you to pick them up at the pier. If you are carrying them with you, have the documents and proof of citizenship handy when you check in at the pier. Don't put them in checked luggage, which arrives separately and goes directly to your cabin.

Shipboard photographers and videographers are so omnipresent that their faces may become the most familiar ones on board. Videos and photographs of embarkation, lifeboat drills and passengers posed next to ice sculptures will be hawked. Carrying your own camera saves you from the lines and protects you from making too many overpriced, impulse purchases. One keepsake photo is nice but do you really need a picture of yourself in an orange life vest?

Most merchants promoted in pre-shore excursion lectures have paid fees to the cruise line or agreed to kick back a percentage of revenue. Cruise ship passengers spent about $5 million in 1994 in St. Thomas alone. Don't wear a name tag or the paper dot cruise directors sometimes stick on your lapel. They designate you as a cruise passenger and diminish your bargaining power.

All suitcases are collected the night before the ship returns to home port so they can be cleared through customs before you leave the ship. Be sure to carry an overnight bag to accommodate items you'll need between evening and morning disembarkation.

If you are dissatisfied with any aspect of your cruise, register your complaint immediately. Cruise lines' keen dependency on repeat passengers make them very attentive to problem resolution.

First cocktail lounge built on cruise line smokestack: Royal Caribbean's Viking Crown Lounge.

CRUISE LINE PROFILES

Which ship has both the Shakespeare Library and the Oz Discotheque? Where do you go for a *Wheel of Fortune* theme cruise? Where can devoted golfers play 18 holes a day on board ship? Read on for these answers and many more.

AMERICAN HAWAII CRUISES (800-765-7000) is an appealing option for repeat visitors to Hawaii who have already seen the islands by air and land.

- **The only option** for exploring the Hawaiian Islands, cruise ship style. With one ship in dry dock in 1996, book as early as possible to get space in the remaining ship.

- **Special promotions** give two free nights on Maui, Oahu, Kauai or the Big Island with seven-day cruises.

- **Children under 18** travel free through 1996 when sharing a cabin with two full-pay passengers.

- **Theme cruises** include "Whales In The Wild" and "Wine Appreciation."

CARNIVAL CRUISE LINES (800-327-9501), an 11-ship fleet with four more on the way. The most booked cruise line in the world will also have the largest ship with the 1996 delivery of the 101,000-ton Carnival Destiny, fitted for 2,642 passengers and a staff of 1,050.

- **Itineraries:** three-, four-, and seven-day cruises to the Bahamas, the Caribbean, Baja Mexico, the Mexican Riviera and Alaska. Departures are from Miami, Cape Canaveral, San Juan, Tampa, New Orleans, Los Angeles and Vancouver.

Average depth of the Arctic Abyss: 3,240 feet; deepest depth: 18,050 feet.

- **Families and a younger-than-average group** of fun-seekers gravitate to Carnival. About 30% of their passengers are under 35. Camp Carnival (on nine ships) entertains children ages five to 17, while toddler activities are offered for children ages two to four on seven ships.

- **Kathy Lee Gifford** tells us they're "the fun ships" with offerings as diverse as the Oz Discotheque or the Shakespeare Library. The *Holiday* has 62 high-tech games in their $1 million entertainment center.

- **Exceptional value** and good programs for children. Standard cabins are among the most spacious of any line. Overall ambiance is contemporary.

- **Gamblers take note:** The *MegaCash* slot machine jackpot is linked on five ships, which means it is possible to hit five jackpots by pulling one lever.

CELEBRITY CRUISES (800-437-3111) offers luxury cruising with Berlitz five-star rated cuisine.

- **Itineraries** include embarkation from San Juan, Fort Lauderdale, Vancouver and New York with seven- , ten- and 11-day cruises to Bermuda, the Caribbean, Alaska and the Panama Canal.

- **The Celebrity *Century* and the upcoming *Galaxy*** have state-of-the-art access to the information superhighway through a partnership with Sony. Ships have interactive guest service networks, video bars, interactive kiosks, conference centers with multi-media presentation systems and language translation equipment and cabins with entertainment and information services on demand.

- **Five Star advance booking rates** offer savings of up to 46% and upgrades starting at $20 per person.

- **Celebrity's VIP program** for past passengers gives advance notice of discount offers, advance dining reservations, priority check-in and debarkation, and cocktails with the captain.

COMMODORE CRUISE LINE (800-237-5361), embarks from New Orleans, a variable that opens up interesting windows of opportunity for inexpensive flights and for drive and cruise vacations. Commodore has one ship that sails the Western Caribbean. Cruises appeal to budget-oriented travelers.

- **Random passenger age mix** except during winter when seniors take control and during spring break when college students head for sun and amnesia in Mexico.

- **Winner of The Lawrence Welk Theme-Cruise Award**: "The Polka Cruise," featuring the Polkanuts band.

COSTA CRUISES (800-462-6782) sails a modern Italian-owned fleet with largely Italian crews presenting a definite twist–perhaps most graphically illustrated during private Costa beach parties where passengers absorb the island's flavor along with the sight of off-duty waiters in red Speed-O's playing volleyball.

- **Itineraries include** the seven-day Caribbean, seven- to 12-day Europe, Mediterranean, Black Sea, Greek Islands, the Baltics and Trans-Atlantic crossings.

- **Specialists in European and Mediterranean** cruises due to their home sea advantage. Even a knowledgeable cruise director cannot match crew members' knowledge of their hometowns.

- **"Costa Club" members** have special on-board parties and get advance promotional mailings on discounts.

Location of the best scuba diving in the Caribbean: the Cayman Islands.

CRYSTAL CRUISES (800-446-6620), the largest truly five-star ships in the world, best described as floating Ritz-Carltons. Their casino is operated by Caesar's Palace. Diners can choose Italian and Japanese cuisine from a la carte restaurants in addition to the main dining room experience.

- **Itineraries include** ten-day and longer cruises to South America, Europe, Mexico, Alaska/Canada, Trans Canal/Caribbean and the Orient/South Pacific.

- **The "Crystal Society"** has an extensive rewards program for past passengers. There are about ten sailings per year designed primarily as members-only discount cruises.

CUNARD (800-528-6273), sails six classic, high-end ships ranging from the 116-passenger *Sea Goddess I* to the 1,850-passenger, 13-story *Queen Elizabeth II*. Cunard sails almost every imaginable itinerary, including their classic around the world cruises. The passenger profile is upscale traditional. Prices are more varied than you might expect, with a wide range of cabin classes.

- **The "Gentlemen Hosts"** program is refined to a high art. Many cruise lines have them but Cunard may well have the best. One *QE2* host estimates that he spends seven hours a day dancing.

- **Cunard's "Cruise Miles"** can be redeemed for upgrades and free cruises, may be earned on all ships, and are valid for seven years. Cunard's "World Club" has a private newsletter, as does the "Skald Club." Membership is determined by the specific ship(s) you've sailed.

- **Theme cruises** include "British Invasions Rock 'N' Roll," "Country Western," "Dance Across The Atlantic," Jazz (with a stop at the Newport News

Jazz Fest), "Dixieland," "Murder Mystery" and "Financial Planning."

- **Delta Queen Steamboat Company** (800-543-1949), a new cruise line, offers paddle wheel cruises along the mighty Mississippi from New Orleans to St. Paul. Many theme cruises are offered.

- **The cruise line with a drawl** is the only line with two cruises built around war themes. Take your choice of "World War II in Music and Speakers" or the "Civil War." Other themes include "Big Band," "The Old South," "Fall Foliage" and "The Kentucky Derby."

- **The *Delta Queen* is a National Historic Landmark** but the *Mississippi Queen* has air conditioning.

DOLPHIN CRUISE LINE (800-222-1003), embarks from Miami and Boston. Itineraries include three- to four-day Bahamas and seven-day Eastern and Western Caribbean.

- **Moderately sized ships** (588 to 1,452 passengers) offer a quality cruise for less.

- **Hanna-Barbera cartoon characters** for the kids and good cuisine and service for the adults.

HOLLAND AMERICA (800-426-0327), was voted best overall cruise value three years in a row by *Ocean and Cruise News*.

- **Embarks from** Fort Lauderdale, New Orleans, Tampa and Vancouver. Itineraries are world-wide, lasting 70 days and longer.

- **Ambiance is sophisticated** but it does not suffocate you with elegance. Traditional cruising style with ""No Tipping" policy.

- **"The Mariners Club"** has multi-level awards based on past cruise credits.

MAJESTY CRUISE LINE (800-532-7788), is owned by Dolphin, Majesty sails one ship–the *Royal Majesty* on three- and four-day Baja Mexico and seven-day seasonal cruises to Bermuda.

NORWEGIAN CRUISE LINE (800-327-7030), features the "Family Cruise Club" with year-round savings and a free newsletter for kids.

- **Routings include** three- and four-day Bahamas, seven-day Caribbean, Bermuda, Alaska and Panama Canal.

- **"Latitudes"** for past passengers has extra perks like sweatshirts, photo frames and free copies of the ubiquitous shipboard photographs.

- **Theme Cruises** include *Wheel of Fortune* with Vanna White, "Big Band, Blues," "SuperSport Basketball" and "Fitness & Beauty."

- **Fun and active ships** with above-average entertainment, an excellent program for children and a free a la carte restaurant.

PREMIER CRUISE LINE (800-327-7113), sails two Big Red Boats, designed primarily for families with small children. The 1,550-passenger *Atlantic* and 1,809-passenger *Oceanic* sail year round from Port Canaveral on three- and four-day cruises to Nassau and Port LaCaya.

- **Tweety Bird, Bugs Bunny, Yosemite Sam** and other Warner Brothers cartoon characters make the cruise fun.

- **Twenty-four-hour child care is provided** with planned activities from 9 a.m. to 10 p.m. for ages two through 12. They've recently spent over $1 million to upgrade their children and teen activity centers.

- **Disney World land package add-ons** are available–something likely to end in 1998 when Disney finishes building two ships of their own. For now you can meet Bugs and Mickey in one vacation, stay at an all-suite hotel and get free kid meals as part of the package price.

- **Repeat adult passengers** are always welcomed with champagne and gift luggage tags. Families get free upgrades, if available, on the day of sailing.

PRINCESS CRUISES (800-421-0522), the Love Boats, sails and has a legitimate claim to inciting a dramatic upsurge in cruising via the television show of the same name. Time has passed and one of the stars of the show went to Congress while, in an odd juxtaposition of realities, the Love Boat books Holy Land Adventures and Black Sea Tours.

- **Seven-day and longer itineraries** include the Caribbean, Panama Canal, the Orient, the Mediterranean, Canada/New England and Alaska.

- **Past passengers** are members of "The Captain's Circle" with one of the best past passenger promotion programs. They also get logo pins, logbooks, mugs and special on-board parties. The most-traveled person on each cruise gets a Tiffany bowl.

RADISSON SEVEN SEAS (800-333-3333 ext. 5), is owned by Diamond Cruises and managed by Radisson Hotels International. Ships feature unique catamaran-style construction, exotic itineraries and super all-inclusive fares.

- **Itineraries** are worldwide (including Antarctica) and start at seven days. Four new Aegean and Eastern Mediterranean cruises were added in the summer of 1995. The transAtlantic crossings can be booked in nine to 22-day segments.

Country that has an official Director of Sunshine: Barbados; duties include ensuring perfect weather.

• **Attracts the cerebral and affluent** with "Great Minds Seminars" scheduled on their 350-passenger Radisson Diamond cruises. If Ivy League universities held reunions on ships, Radisson Seven Seas would be a natural choice.

RENAISSANCE CRUISES (800-525-5350), sails a fleet of newer, Italian-crafted ships–each carrying no more than 114 passengers with a crew-to-passenger ratio of nearly one-to-one.

• **Private yacht ambiance** with teak decks and suites embellished with burnished wood and marble.

• **Itineraries carry through the luxury motif** on seven-day and longer cruises to itineraries such as Hong-Kong-Singapore-Bali coupled with seven additional nights in the three port cities.

ROYAL CARIBBEAN CRUISE LINE (800-327-6700), is one of the highest-rated lines in terms of customer satisfaction. Consistent quality in cuisine, service and entertainment and excellent programs for children.

• **Soon to sail 15 ships** carrying 714-2,500 passengers on three-, four-, seven-day and longer itineraries to the Caribbean, Mexican Baja, Bahamas, Bermuda, Alaska, Europe, Panama Canal, Far East, Africa, South Pacific and the Orient–with more to come.

• **Some of the best suites** of all ships are on the newer members of the Royal Caribbean fleet.

• **The first to offer private clubs** in port cities, beginning with the inaugural clubs in St. Thomas and San Juan.

• **The Legend of the Links** is an 18-hole (miniature) golf course that debuted on the *Legend of the Seas* and will be duplicated on the upcoming *Splendor of the Seas*. The 6,000-square-foot courses are covered by retractable glass domes. There are sand traps, water hazards and other representations of full-size golf course terrain. Each hole is designed as a miniature replica of a hole from various world-renowned golf courses.

• **"The Crown & Anchor Society"** sounds like a hangout for the British Royal Navy but in fact offers past passengers discounts on select sailings or free, pre- and post-cruise land add-ons.

• **Theme cruises** include jazz, country and western, baseball, Big Band, blues, and comedy.

ROYAL OLYMPIC (800-801-6086), is a newly merged line composed of Epirotiki and Sun Line. They continue to sail under their own banners but have a central reservation number and merged itineraries.

• **Itineraries include** sailings of seven days and longer to the Caribbean, Panama Canal, South America, the Red Sea, The Greek Isles and the Mediterranean.

• **Classic Greek seamanship**, crews and cuisine plus a cultural affinity for good times appeal to passengers who enjoy traditional cruising with an added flair.

• **Initial names for the two divisions–**"The Blue World of Sun Line" and "The White World of Epirotiki."

SEABOURN CRUISE LINE (800-929-9595), sails five-star, ultra-deluxe yacht-sized ships that are the *creme de la creme* of intimate cruise shops.

• **Itineraries span the globe.**

• **Passenger profile** is refined and elegant.

• **"The Seabourn Club"** provides a 25% discount after 20 days of sailing–typically two Seabourn cruises–and free trip cancellation, accident and medical insurance.

SILVERSEA CRUISES (800-722-6655), sails five-star, ultra-deluxe ships with all-suite accommodations and super all-inclusive pricing.

- **Offers all the entertainment** and activities the big ships offer, but on a more intimate level.

- **Itineraries** include the Mediterranean, the Baltics, the Caribbean, Canada, New England, the Panama Canal, Hawaii, Mexico, the Far East, China, India, Africa and South America.

- **Boutique ship ambiance** offers plenty of tables for two in the dining rooms and cabins with private verandas.

STAR CLIPPER (800-442-0551), offers the largest clipper ships with cruise ship amenities and nicely appointed cabins.

- **Itineraries** include the Caribbean, Mediterranean and Southeast Asia. Visits smaller, more unique ports that can't be accessed by large ships.

- **Passenger profile** is active adventurers and sailing enthusiasts.

WINDJAMMER (800-327-2601), sails masted ships through global waters with a concentration on the Caribbean and the New England coast. Many cruises involve passengers as sailors.

- **Adventurers** enjoy barefoot cruising on five-day and longer itineraries on vessels ranging from 14-200 passengers.

- **Each cruise carries 40%-50% repeat passengers.** After three cruises at full fare, you pay $99 to become a "Sudden Sailor," eligible for savings of up to 51% on standby fares confirmed 14 days before departure. After five weeks sailing, you become a Sea Dog, get additional discounts and a windbreaker.

WINDSTAR CRUISES (800-258-7245), features yacht-like, high-energy ambiance on 149-passenger, four-masted, computer controlled sailing ships with deluxe cruise ship amenities.

- **Itineraries** include the Caribbean, the Greek Isles, the Mediterranean and the South Pacific.

- **Each ship has 74 outside suites** with queen beds, VCR, CD player and mini-bar.

- **Passenger profile** is upscale, intimate and unregimented.

Late 1920s event that was a tremendous boon to the cruise industry: prohibition.

SHIP INFORMATION

This major cruise ship chart lists passenger capacity (PAX), tonnage (TONS), when each ship was built, when it was refurbished (BUILT/REF) and basic amenities.

SHIPSHAPE INFORMATION				
SHIP	PAX	TONS	BUILT/REF	AMENITIES
AMERICAN HAWAII				
Constitution	798	30,090	1951/1996	2 outdoor pools, spa
Independence	798	30,090	1951/1996	2 outdoor pools, spa
CARNIVAL CRUISE LINE				
Celebration	1,486	47,262	1987	3 outdoor pools, spa, casino
Destiny	2,642	101,000	1996	world's largest cruise ship
Ecstasy	2,040	70,367	1991	3 outdoor pools, spa, casino
Fantasy	2,044	70,367	1990	3 outdoor pools, spa, casino
Fascination	2,040	70,367	1994	3 outdoor pools, spa, casino
Holiday	1,452	46,052	1985	3 outdoor pools, spa, casino
Inspiration	2,040	70,367	1995	3 outdoor pools, spa, casino
Imagination	2,040	70,367	1995	3 outdoor pools, spa, casino
Jubilee	1,486	47,262	1986	3 outdoor pools, spa, casino
Sensation	2,040	70,367	1993	3 outdoor pools, spa, casino
Tropicale	1,022	36,674	1982/1989	3 outdoor pools, spa, casino
CELEBRITY CRUISES				
Century	1,750	70,000	1995	2 outdoor pools, spa, casino
Horizon	1,354	46,811	1990	2 outdoor pools, spa, casino
Meridian	1,106	30,440	1963/1990	2 outdoor pools, spa, casino
Zenith	1,374	47,255	1992	2 outdoor pools, spa, casino
CLUB MED CRUISES				
Club Med I	400	14,000	1990	2 outdoor pools, retractable marina, spa, casino
Club Med II	400	14,000	1992	2 outdoor pools, retractable marina, spa, casino
COMMODORE CRUISE LINE				
Enchanted Isle	729	23,395	1958/1994	outdoor pool, fitness center, casino

Cruise line that carried over two million immigrants to America between 1873 and 1920: Holland America.

SHIPSHAPE INFORMATION *continued*				
SHIP	PAX	TONS	BUILT/REF	AMENITIES
COSTA CRUISE LINE				
Costa Allegra	810	30,000	1969/1992	outdoor pool, spa, casino
Costa Classica	1,300	54,000	1991	2 outdoor pools, spa, casino
Costa Romantica	1,356	54,000	1993	2 outdoor pools, spa, casino
Costa Victoria	1,950	75,000	1996	2 outdoor pools, 1 indoor pool, spa, casino
CRYSTAL CRUISES				
Crystal Harmony	960	49,400	1990	2 outdoor pools, retractable dome spa, casino
Crystal Symphony	960	50,000	1995	2 outdoor pools, retractable dome, spa, casino
CUNARD				
Crown Dynasty	800	20,000	1993	outdoor, pool, spa, casino
Queen Elizabeth II	1,810	70,327	1969/1994	indoor and outdoor pools, spa, casino
Royal Viking Sun	758	38,000	1988/1995	2 outdoor pools, spa, casino
Sea Goddess I	116	4,250	1984/1995	outdoor pool, spa, casino
Sea Goddess II	116	4,250	1985	outdoor pool, spa, casino
Vistafjord	677	24,492	1973/1994	indoor and outdoor pools, spa, casino
DELTA QUEEN				
American Queen	436	3,707	1995	outdoor pool
Delta Queen	174	3,360	1927/1992	historical landmark ship
Mississippi Queen	414	3,364	1976/1994	outdoor pool
DOLPHIN CRUISE LINE				
Island Breeze	588	13,007	1956/1991	outdoor pool, casino
Ocean Breeze	776	21,486	1955/1992	outdoor pool, casino
Seabreeze	840	21,000	1958/1991	indoor and outdoor pools, casino
HOLLAND AMERICA LINE				
Maasdam	1,266	50,000	1993	2 outdoor pools, spa, casino, retractable dome
Nieuw Amsterdam	1,214	33,930	1983	2 outdoor pools, spa, casino

Name of Germany's version of the television series "Love Boat:" "Dreamboat."

SHIPSHAPE INFORMATION *continued*				
SHIP	PAX	TONS	BUILT/REF	AMENITIES
HOLLAND AMERICA LINE (continued)				
Noordam	1,214	33,930	1984	2 outdoor pools, spa, casino
Rotterdam	1,075	38,000	1959/1989	indoor and outdoor pools, casino
Ryndam	1,266	50,000	1994	2 outdoor pools/retractable dome, spa, casino
Statendam	1,266	50,000	1993	2 outdoor pools/retractable dome, spa, casino
Veendam	1,266	50,000	1996	2 outdoor pools, spa, casino
Westerdam	1,494	53,872	1986/1990	2 outdoor pools/retractable dome, spa, casino
MAJESTY CRUISE LINE				
Royal Majesty	1,056	32,400	1992	outdoor pool, spa, casino
NORWEGIAN CRUISE LINE				
Dreamward	1,242	41,000	1993	2 outdoor pools, spa, casino
Leeward	950	25,000	1992/1995	outdoor pool, spa, casino
Norway	2,032	76,049	1962/1993	indoor and 2 outdoor pools, spa, casino
Norwegian Crown	1,052	34,250	1988/1996	indoor and outdoor pools, spa, casino
Seaward	1,504	42,000	1988/1995	2 outdoor pools, spa, casino
Windward	1,246	41,000	1993	2 outdoor pools, spa, casino
PREMIER CRUISE LINES				
Star/Ship Atlantic	1,550	35,143	1982/1991	2 pools/retractable dome, spa, casino
Star/Ship Oceanic	1,800	38,772	1965/1993	2 pools/retractable dome, spa, casino
PRINCESS CRUISES				
Crown Princess	1,590	70,000	1990	2 outdoor pools, spa, casino
Golden Princess	830	28,000	1973/1993	2 outdoor pools, spa, casino
Island Princess	640	20,000	1971/1993	2 outdoor pools, spa, casino
Pacific Princess	640	20,000	1992	2 outdoor pools, retractable dome, spa, casino
Regal Princess	1,590	70,000	1991	2 outdoor pools, spa, casino

Top spot in the world for whale watching: Southern Ocean Whale Sanctuary, Antarctica.

SHIP	PAX	TONS	BUILT/REF	AMENITIES
SHIPSHAPE INFORMATION *continued*				
PRINCESS CRUISES (continued)				
Royal Princess	1,200	45,000	1984/1991	3 outdoor pools, spa, casino
Sky Princess	1,200	46,000	1984/1992	3 outdoor pools, spa, casino
Star Princess	1,490	63,500	1989/1994	3 outdoor pools, spa, casino
Sun Princess	1,950	77,000	1995	5 outdoor pools, spa, casino
RADISSON SEVEN SEAS				
Radisson Diamond	350	20,295	1992	outdoor pool, retractable marina, spa, casino
Hanseatic	175	9,000	1993	outdoor pool, spa, fitness center
Song of Flower	172	8,282	1986/1989	outdoor pool, casino
RENAISSANCE CRUISES				
Renaissance III and IV	100	4,000	1989	outdoor pool, casino
Renaissance V, VI, VII, VIII	114	4,000	1989	outdoor pool, casino
ROYAL CARIBBEAN				
Splendor of the Seas	1,808	70,000	1995	2 outdoor pools, retractable dome, spa, casino
Grandeur of the Seas	1,950	74,000	1996	2 outdoor pools, spa, casino
Majesty of the Seas	2,354	73,941	1992	2 outdoor pools, spa, casino
Monarch of the Seas	2,354	73,941	1991	2 outdoor pools, spa, casino
Nordic Empress	1,600	48,563	1990	2 outdoor pools, spa, casino
Song of America	1,402	37,584	1982/1991	2 outdoor pools, spa, casino
Song of Norway	1,004	23,005	1970/1995	outdoor pool, spa, casino
Sovereign of the Seas	2,276	73,192	1988	2 outdoor pools, spa, casino
Sun Viking	714	18,445	1995	outdoor pool, spa, casino
Viking Serenade	1,512	40,132	1981/1991	outdoor pool, spa, casino
ROYAL OLYMPIC				
Odysseus	400	10,000	1962/1989	outdoor pool, casino
Olympic	900	31,500	1956/1993	indoor and outdoor pools, casino
Orpheus	300			
Stella Oceanis	300	6,500	1957/1993	outdoor, spa, casino

Length of Alaska from east to west: 2,350 miles; from north to south: 1,350 miles.

SHIPSHAPE INFORMATION *continued*				
SHIP	PAX	TONS	BUILT/REF	AMENITIES
ROYAL OLYMPIC (continued)				
Stella Solaris	620	18,000	1994	2 outdoor pools, spa, casino
Triton	670	14,000	1971/1991	outdoor pools, casino
SEABOURNE CRUISE LINE				
Seabourne Pride	204	10,000	1988	outdoor pool, spa, casino
Seabourne Spirit	204	10,000	1989	outdoor pool, spa, casino
SILVERSEA CRUISES				
Silver Cloud	296	16,800	1994	outdoor pool, spa, casino
Silver Wind	296	16,800	1995	outdoor pool, spa, casino
STAR CLIPPER				
Star Clipper & Star Flyer	170	3,025	1992	2 outdoor pools
SWAN HELLENIC				
Minerva	300	6,000	1995	outdoor pool
WINDJAMMER		**LENGTH**		
Amazing Grace	94	354 ft	1955	None
Fantome	128	282 ft	1927	None
Flying Cloud	74	208 ft	1935	None
Mandalay	72	236 ft	1923	None
Polynesia	126	248 ft	1938	None
Yankee Clipper	64	197 ft	1927	None
WINDSTAR CRUISES		**TONS**		
WindStar/WindSpirit WindSong	148	5,350	1986–1988	outdoor pool, casino

---

The first official world cruise: Cunard Line's Laconia, a 350-passenger ship departing from New York in 1922.

OFF THE BEATEN WAVE

CRUISING U.S. WATERS

U.S. waters offer unique experiences for cruising, American style. Here are some examples to start you planning and dreaming.

> **"**One of my favorite forms of cruise getaways is the one-day cruise to nowhere. I'll tell you why I like them and give you some other ideas for unique cruise experiences. **"**

- **Fall cruising along the harbors of Maine** on three to six-day Windjammer excursions ranging from $378 to $1,100. Food, atmosphere and ambiance is New England style. Call the Main Windjammer Association, 800-807-9463.

- **Cruise the Hudson River** from Manhattan to Troy in weeklong autumn trips with stops including West Point, America's oldest inn and a monastery. Call River Valley Tours, 800-836-2128.

- **"Rail & Sail"** combines Amtrak to New Orleans with a seven-day Commodore Cruise to the Yucatan. Xpo America puts together various Rail & Sail pack-ages. Check with your cruise agency for current offerings.

- **Follow the Lewis and Clark Route** on two to seven-day cruises from Portland, Oregon, an authentic stern wheeler with 73 suites and staterooms. Cruises range from $279 to $3,495. Call Cruise & Tour Reservations, 800-434-1232 for a free brochure.

- **American Canadian Caribbean,** 800-556-7450, offers cruises more varied than their name implies. Ships carrying 76 to 90 passengers cruise Rhode Island to Florida, New Orleans to Chicago and other U.S. routings at prices starting at $105 per day.

The world's 11th largest lake: Africa's Lake Chad which evaporates completely during droughts.

- **A true departure from standard Alaska cruises** is offered by World Explorer, 800-854-3835. They bypass cabaret revues for on-board lectures, casual attire and increased port time. Bike and Cruise itineraries are offered on three yearly sailings. Twelve to 50-mile bike trips are scheduled in eight port cities.

- **Cruise home from Alaska** after driving the 1,000-mile Alaskan Highway. You take a nine-day Gulf of Alaska and Inside Passage cruise while your car or RV is shipped to Portland by ferry. Call Gray Line of Alaska, 800-628-3843.

- **Sail California Inland Waterways** on nine-day land and cruise packages on the 138-passenger Yorktown Clipper. Spend five nights on ship and two nights each in San Francisco and Monterrey. Prices start at $2,030 including land. Call your cruise agent for details.

INTERNATIONAL OPTIONS

International options include cruise and land packages that can be big money-savers in countries where hotels and dining are high-dollar. International cruises are also an excellent way to experience parts of the world not easily seen by the traveling public. Star Clipper, for example, 800-442-0551, adds a three-night London stay for passengers on seven and 14-day French Riviera itineraries. Other options:

- **River barging in Europe.** European Waterways, 800-922-0291, has many spring, summer and fall offerings. This unique form of travel offers centrally-heated barges that cruise the south of France and Scotland well into the winter. In addition, *Le Boat*'s facilities are fully accessible for travelers with physical handicaps.

- **Seawind Cruise Line**, 800-258-8006, sails one 728-passenger ship to the beautiful, but often forgotten Leeward Islands in the Caribbean.

- **The 4,000-mile Amazon River** can be explored aboard the 620-passenger *Stella Solaris* on 14-day departures from Florida. Fares in the $3,500 range include return airfare from Manaus to Miami. Seabourn will make two Amazon cruises in 1996 through the head of the Amazon and the Anavilhanus Jungle archipelago. The 100-passenger *Explorer* takes 18-day trips from Belem to Iquitos.

- **Cruise close to nature** with Clipper Cruises, 800-325-0010. Sail up the Intracoastal Waterway in the U.S. or explore the Arctic and the Russian Far East on these masted ships.

- **Book a stateroom on a yacht** from Preferred Yacht Holidays, 800-437-7880. Usual routes are the Caribbean and South Pacific.

- **Charter cruises through Russian waterways** are as little as $1,700, air included. They last seven to 14 days with itineraries including Moscow to St. Petersburg or the Amur River through the Russian Far East. Call UniWorld at 800-868-7892 for a free 32-page brochure.

CRUISES TO NOWHERE

Check your Sunday newspaper travel section and tourism offices in river and ocean port cities for one-day cruises that can really take you away from it all.

Cruises to nowhere are one-day adventures that sail out of many port cities in the U.S. and abroad. They spend five hours to two days on the water, then return to the original port. They often feature motifs including gambling, fishing, intense spa-

---

Number of the 1,200 islands and atolls of The Maldives that are inhabited: 200.

like pampering, or dinner and dancing. Here are some examples:

- The *Midnight Gambler* **sails from Pompano Beach, Florida**. The newly refurbished 110-foot ship has about 100 slot machines, seven blackjack tables, gourmet buffet-style dining, entertainment and dancing. Five-hour cruises depart twice daily. Call 800-807-2964.

- **Discovery Cruises**, 800-866-8687, offers overnight trips from Fort Lauderdale and Miami with a stopover in Freeport. The $158.99 price includes hotel. Day trips are also offered from Fort Lauderdale on Sunday, Monday, Wednesday and Friday, and from Miami on Monday, Tuesday, Thursday, Friday and Saturday.

- **Tropicana Cruises**, 800-965-3999, departs from Miami for six-hour cruises on an 852-passenger ship. Tickets are $24-49.

CRUISING BY FREIGHTER

Freighter Cruises are for people who like being at sea for long periods of time, are able to entertain themselves and enjoy adventure. The passenger manifest of freighters include characters like the retired professor who has spent years creating his own alphabet and language.

The Most Popular Freighter Cruises:

- **U.S. Gulf Coast to East Africa (60 -70 days).**

- **Montreal to Belgium (32 days).**

- **U.S. East Coast or West Coast to Australia (70-75 days).**

- **U.S. Gulf Coast or Montreal to the Mediterranean (35-45 days).**

- **Around the world from Los Angeles (84 days).**

Specially designed dual-purpose vessels cater to the needs of cargo and passengers alike.

- **Ivaran Lines' Americana** carries 88 passengers on a 578-foot ship with plenty of deck space, a swimming pool and jacuzzi, an indoor lounge, a library and game room, a fully-equipped gym, a sauna with masseuse, and even a small casino.

- **The three newest ships in Norway's** coastal steamer fleet each carry nearly 500 passengers with surroundings and amenities similar to cruise ships.

- **Rates on these more luxurious cargo ships** average around $160 per person, per day.

- **Discounted freighter cruises** are available for off-season travel. For example, fares to Australia, New Zealand and South America are often lowered during North America's summer.

- **Several freighter carriers offer fly/sail options** that help you book half-length or segments of voyages.

- **Most freighters accept a maximum of 12 passengers,** the point after which, per maritime law, a medic has to be aboard.

- **Because freighters are working vessels**, most lines do not allow children under 12 or adults over 80.

- **Most cargo carriers prefer you be fully insured**, and may require proof of good health.

- **Freighter itineraries stretch from 30-100 days.** Cargo is priority so ships may alter course with little notice.

One of the sources for the biggest trout in the world: Lake Titicaca (Peru).

- **Freighter cabins tend to be more roomy** than many cruise ship cabins.

- **Food is good and plentiful** but don't expect ice-carvings and midnight buffets.

- **The average cost of freighter cruises** ranges from $70-100 per day, per person. You pay by the day because you are free to book only the portion of the itinerary that interests you.

- **Single rates** are the most favorable in the entire cruise industry. There is often no single surcharge and, when it does exist, it's usually only ten to 20 percent.

- **Stopover time in port cities** may be several hours or several days.

Get specific information on **freighter cruises** by subscribing to *The Freighter Cruise Newsletter*, 180 South Lake Ave., Suite 335, Pasadena, CA 91101 or call:

Freighter World Cruises
818-449-3106

Ivaran Lines
800-451-1639

Ford's Freighter
Travel Guide
818-701-7414

TravLtips
800-872-8584

A Monthly Publication of Insider Travel Secrets
Listing the Latest Discounts for
The Cost-Conscious Traveler

Recently, ***BEST FARES Discount Travel Magazine*** showed savvy travelers how to fly Delta first class to Hawaii from over 200 U.S. cities for $578 or less.

Call 800-880-1234 to subscribe.
See page 395 for your discount subscription offer.

Number of couples who renew wedding vows on Princess Cruise Line's Love Boats on Valentine's Day: 4,000.

CRUISE LINE ITINERARIES

CRUISE LINE	CARIBBEAN	ALASKA	MEDITERRANEAN	SCANDINAVIAN	FAR EAST	AMERICAS	RIVER CRUISES	OTHER ITINERARIES
American Hawaii Cruises								Hawaii
Carnival Cruise Line	X	X				X		
Celebrity Cruises	X	X				X		Bermuda
Costa Cruises	X		X	X		X		Round The World and Transatlantic
Crystal Cruises	X	X	X	X	X	X	X	Round The World, Transatlantic and Transpacific
Cunard Line	X	X	X	X	X	X		Transatlantic
Dolphin Cruise Line	X					X		Bahamas
Holland America	X	X	X	X	X	X	X	South America and Transatlantic
Majesty Cruise Line	X							Bermuda
Norwegian Cruise Line	X	X						Bermuda
Premier Cruise Lines						X		The Bahamas
Princess Cruises	X	X	X	X	X	X	X	Amazon, Transatlantic, Transpacific, Greenland & Iceland, the Middle East, South Africa, Indian Ocean and United Kingdom
Radisson Seven Seas Cruises	X		X	X	X	X		Transatlantic and Northern Australia
Royal Caribbean Cruise Line	X	X	X	X	X	X		United Kingdom, Transatlantic, Bermuda and Hawaii
Royal Olympic Cruises	X		X		X		X	The Amazon and the Red Sea
Seabourn Cruise Line	X	X	X	X	X	X	X	Transatlantic and United Kingdom
Silversea Cruises	X		X	X	X	X	X	The Arctic, Africa, the Russian Far East and Antarctica
Star Clippers	X		X		X			Transatlantic and Indian Ocean
Windjammer Barefoot Cruises	X							
Windstar Cruises	X		X					Transatlantic

Total cruise passengers in 1990: 3,640,000; in 1995: 4,327,000.

MORE DOLLARS AND CENTS!

Pennies from heaven can bring you down-to-earth savings.

We've covered four major areas of travel expense–Air, Car Rentals, Hotels and Cruises –but I've only begun to save you money. This section is packed with ideas and strategies that cut through the hundreds of ways travel costs can add up. I want you to save money at every turn–not just at the usual travel crossroads. I'll help you spend your dollars in ways that make the most sense with these money saving tips.

Coupon Corner provides thousands of dollars in discounts for the asking. It's so valuable that you could take one entry at random and save many times the cost of this book. You'll learn how one phone call can get you hundreds of dollars in savings and how to pay less for dining, shopping, entertainment and all the activities that can make any travel budget fall apart. There are big deals, location specific savings, student and senior savings and general travel aids.

Save By How You Pay cuts to the heart of every form of travel. How much cash should you carry? Is it better to get money on the road by credit card advance or Automatic Teller Machine (ATM) withdrawal? Where do you go to get the best exchange rate internationally? Which charge and credit cards are best for travel-related purchases? Which travel taxes can you avoid entirely?

Tips on Tips simplifies one of the most confusing travel expenses with a guide to gratuities that will see you through any tipping situation. What's the correct amount to tip a cruise ship waiter or a taxi driver in London? All this and more will be answered.

Travel Insurance is one of the more misunderstood aspects of travel. Many people have called in to my radio shows with horror stories of lost vacations–even when they thought their purchase of optional insurance had protected them. I'll tell you how to get some automatic coverage, your best and worst sources for optional insurance, how to evaluate coverage and the kind of travel insurance you should never buy.

Calling From The Road unravels the tangled phone cord of calling options. When I travel, the telephone is like a lifeline. I'm apt to be on the phone when I'm on a plane, in my car or at the hotel. With the volume of calling I do, getting the job done for the least amount of money is extremely important. I'll show you how I hacked my way through the long distance jungle, the advantages offered by debit cards, how to avoid phone fraud and more of my favorite ways to save.

Rail Travel focuses on a form of travel used by millions, yet often neglected when it comes time to show people how to save. Did you know that Amtrak offers regular discount programs? Did you know that they have a frequent traveler program, patterned after the airlines? I'll give you my suggestions for saving money on Amtrak and on international rail travel.

By now I'm sure you've gotten the idea that my concept of discount travel is to get the most value from every single dollar. I love it when I can show people one trick that saves them hundreds of dollars. My listeners and readers tell me they like to continue the savings theme throughout their trips. This chapter shares what I've been telling them this past year and adds some of the new information I'll be telling them tomorrow.

COUPON CORNER

BEST FARES Discount Travel Magazine spends hundreds of hours each month keeping up with the latest, greatest offerings in discount guide and coupon books published by tourism departments throughout the world. We do it because our readers have told us that these offers consistently save them money, and give them information that makes their trips both easier to plan and more enjoyable. State and national governments spend millions of dollars annually to produce these traveler-friendly guides and coupons. Failing to use them, is like turning down an opportunity to get money **from** the government, rather than giving money **to** the government.

We've gathered some of the best discounts from several years' editions When you call to order them, keep in mind that some programs are seasonal and some are replaced by similar programs with different names. If the offer you're requesting isn't available, ask what alter- native promotions are being offered. The best news–most of these offers are free just for the asking.

Many offers must be requested via the postal system. Remember to allow adequate time for items requested to make it through the system. Two to three weeks is the usual minimum, but popular offers can take even longer.

Many programs have expiration dates and restrictions that could effect your travel plans. Review and read the fine print on each coupon to make sure it's current.

> **"**A hint for hometown savings: If you live in a city that offers discount booklets for travelers, pick one up for your own use to enjoy the same discounts designed to lure tourists to your hometown.**"**

Restaurant tax in Chicago: 8.75%; in Honolulu: four percent.

DINING, ENTERTAINMENT, SHOPPING AND SPECIAL INTERESTS

Even if you're not the type to clip coupons, you need to know about and use the big discount books with coupons that give, in some cases, up to $100 off a single travel purchase. There is really no reason to fail to use coupons that provide such major savings.

Most of these programs are issued annually and require a nominal, initial investment. Some supply a membership card with a directory of participating vendors. Many include hundreds of coupons for things like fast food and two-for-one restaurant meals. Tucked in among all these offerings are travel-related discount coupons. Having all of these books in your deck of discount cards is a good idea. Having at least one is mandatory.

Dining

Dine-A-Mate publishes a national edition and 24 regional editions with prices varying by locale, but almost always under $50. What began with restaurant discounts, now includes airline coupons and other travel-related offers. Call 800-248-3463.

Dinner On Us has a membership program covering over 9,000 restaurants in 34 states. Discounts range from 20%-50%. The $49 annual membership gives you a directory covering your home region and a number to call to acquire directories for other areas. They have a hotline to help you locate member restaurants when you're traveling. Call 800-346-3241.

The Transmedia Restaurant Discount Card gives 25% off your restaurant tab (excluding tax and tip) for a $50 annual fee. Thousands of restaurants are included You must be a Visa, MasterCard, American Express or Discover cardholder in good standing. Call 800-422-5090.

In Good Taste offers an annual-fee membership credit card that discounts restaurants, hotels, theaters and parking. The program is limited to specific regions, including metro New York City, southern California, Florida and the greater Atlanta area. The annual fee is $48 for the first year; $25 for renewal. Call 212-534-0825.

If you visit a particular city often, inquire about dining discount programs at your favorite restaurants. An example: "The Gold Plate Program" at the Westin Galleria Hotel in Dallas. You earn points on dining and can redeem them for meals and guest rooms. Write to The Westin Hotel, Galleria Dallas, 13340 Dallas Parkway, Dallas, TX 75240. Call 214-934-9494.

Frequent Flyer Programs often offer special bonus points at participating restaurants. Check with your frequent flyer clubs for the latest on dining point programs.

- **Continental and United Airlines** allow frequent flyers to earn ten miles per dollar spent at over 5,600 restaurants. Members must possess the Transmedia Card ($9.95) to collect the miles. To order the card, call 800-884-3463.

- **United Mileage Plus Dining** members receive ten miles to the dollar at over 4,000 restaurants. Call 800-555-5116.

- **The American Airlines AAdvantage** Dining program awards three points for every dollar spent. Gold and Platinum AAdvantage members are automatically enrolled. Other AAdvantage members can enroll by calling 800-267-2606.

Cost of a bowl of bird's nest soup at Hong Kong's Lai Ching Heen restaurant: $50.

- **Northwest Airlines' WorldPerks** program, 800-447-3757, earns two miles for every dollar spent with a $25 minimum purchase.

- **Alaska Airlines' DineAir program,** 800-207-8232, awards three miles for every dollar spent at participating restaurants in Washington, Oregon and California.

- **TWA's Frequent Flight Bonus program** members earn ten miles per $1 spent at over 4,600 restaurants through their alliance with Dining A La Card. It's open to all levels of frequent flyers. The first 60 days of membership are free then a $49.95 annual fee is charged. Call 800-325-4815.

Entertainment

Same-day theatre tickets at half-price or less can be yours. You'll find booths that sell these tickets in most major city centers worldwide. If you don't see them, ask the concierge at your hotel or check with the local tourism office.

New York City	TKTS
Washington, D.C.	TICKETplace
Boston	BOSTIX
Dallas	TIX
Philadelphia	TIX STOP
Chicago	HOT TIX
Minneapolis	Tickets To Go
Denver	The Ticket Bus
San Diego	Auto Tix
San Francisco	STBS

There are several local companies in every city that handle theatre and special event tickets. Two companies that are nationwide but have local offices only are Ticketmaster and Ticketron. Check local listings for Ticketmaster or Ticketron in the city you're visiting.

Entertainment Discount Coupon Books are produced annually in about 125 editions covering major metropolitan areas in the U.S. and some European cities. They cost from $25-48 each. All include discount coupons for hotels, airlines, car rentals, restaurants, attractions and special events. To order a coupon book, call 800-445-4137.

Shopping & Special Interest

Outlet Malls USA lists over 600 U.S. bargain malls that feature daily discounts ranging from 25%-90%. The guide covers 49 states and includes store names, business hours and precise directions to make getting there easier for travelers. Send $5 and a stamped, self-addressed envelope to Outlet Malls USA, P.O. Box 266, Churchville, MD 21028.

Player's Club International requires a relatively hefty $144 annual fee but if you frequent gambling areas including Las Vegas, Atlantic City, the Caribbean and riverboat casinos, savings can be considerable. Discounts for hotels, food and beverages, entertainment and shows are included. Call 800-275-6600.

The Good Sam Club is an international organization of people who enjoy travel in recreational vehicles (RVs). The introductory membership fee of $12 per family provides ten percent off campground fees, propane, trip routing, telephone-messages, emergency road service, a directory of campgrounds and other discounts. It also includes events hosted by its 2,200 local chapters. Call 800-234-3450 or write to The Good Sam Club, P.O. Box 6885, Englewood, CO 80155-6885.

Disneygram is an unofficial newsletter of Walt Disney World. It keeps up with the latest attractions, reviews rides, offers tips and throws in discount dining coupons. A subscription is $9.95 per year, but you can get a free sample issue by writing to 241 Winn St., Burlington, MA 01803.

The 1996 American Casino Guide contains over $300 in coupons including three coupons for free show tickets normally selling for $40 each. They're valid at Harrah's Atlantic City, and resorts in Reno, Las Vegas, Florida, Mississippi, Louisiana and more. The Trump Taj Mahal, for example, has a coupon for a two-for-one buffet. The 192-page paperback covers 30 states, with information on Indian and riverboat casinos and money-saving coupons on cruises, shows, bus tours, food, drinks, etc. The guide costs $12.95 plus $3.95 shipping and handling. 800-352-6657 or write to Casino Vacations, P.O. Box 703-BF, Dania, FL 33004.

The Golden Eagle Pass available to any U.S. citizen, offers one year's unlimited admission to U.S. National Parks. It can be purchased for $25 at any National Park that charges an entry fee. Seniors, age 62 and up, can buy a Golden Age Pass, valid for a lifetime, for $10.

The Swimmer's Guide lists over 3,000 year-round swimming facilities in the U.S. It includes 400 facilities with discount admission offers. The cost is $13 in bookstores or $16.95 (including shipping) when you order direct. Call 800-352-6657.

The World Ski Card from The World Ski Association costs $9.95-19.95 per year depending on when, during ski season, you purchase it. It discounts lessons, rentals, lift tickets, hotels and restaurants at over 1,000 ski areas in North America and Europe. Call 303-629-7669 or write to P.O. Box 480825, Denver, CO 80248.

The Consumer Ski Guide details 21 Colorado resorts with information on lodging, lift-tickets, ski-schools and other programs. Call 800-265-6723.

DISCOUNTS & DEALS IN THE U.S.

The Best Western Road Atlas helps you find locate the hotel chain's 3,400 properties and offers much more. Published each December and available year round, it provides maps, safety tips and points of interest. Call 800-528-1234 or pick up the guide at most Best Western Hotels.

Traveler Discount Guides are designed for travel by car or RV and focus on discounts for hotels and attractions near the highway. They are updated every three months and cover Alabama, California, the District of Columbia, Florida, Kentucky, Louisiana, Maryland, Mississippi, North Carolina, South Carolina, Tennessee, Virginia, Interstate 95 from Maine to Florida and Interstate 10 from Texas to Florida. You can sometimes pick them up for free at truck stops and other businesses along the interstates. You can also order specific guides by phone by calling 800-222-3948 and paying by Visa or MasterCard. Third class mail delivery is $2 for the first guide and $1 for each additional guide; First class mail delivery is $3 plus $1 for each additional guide. Write to Travel Discount Exit Guides, 4205 NW 6th St., Gainesville, FL 32609.

Here's a state-by-state breakdown of discount deals, guide and coupon books. Most of them are available in updated editions every year. Some special promotional offers come and go, but they tend to recur and so are always worth a phone call.

California

L.A. 'Free-Ways' And Other Ways To Save, offered by the Los Angeles Convention and Visitors Bureau, offers savings of up to $400 on area attractions. Most attraction coupons are good for up to six people. Request your copy from Coupon Book c/o Los Angeles Convention and Visitors Bureau, 633 W. Sixth St., Los Angeles, CA 90071. Savings may include discounts on admissions to Universal Studios, Six Flags, Magic Mountain and Sea World; two-for-one admissions to the Los Angeles Children's Museum, The Hollywood Wax Museum, the Guiness World of Records and Ripley's Believe It Or Not Museum; a free upgrade from Thrifty Rent-A-Car; discount room rates at the Hollywood Holiday Inn; 20% off at the popular Farmers Market and restaurant discounts.

San Diego Visitors Value Pack is offered by the San Diego Visitors Bureau. It contains discounts at many hotels, restaurants and attractions: the San Diego Zoo, Sea World, San Diego Harbor excursions, golfing, ballooning, cultural arts and more. There are also discounts of ten to 20 percent at over 40 area hotels. Call 619-236-1212 or write to 401 B Street, Suite 400, San Diego, CA 92102.

The R & R Club is a joint offering of the Palm Springs Desert Resorts and the Convention & Visitors Bureau. Free club membership entitles you to reduced rates at resorts and restaurants, and other special offers, all good from April through December. Call 800-967-3767 for a membership brochure and vacation planner.

The Catalina Island Discount Card offers ten percent off cruises, gift shops, discovery tours, Pavilion Lodge and campgrounds on Catalina Island, located off the Los Angeles coastline. The discount card is valid year round. Call 800-228-2546 or 800-538-4554.

Colorado

The Denver Travel Guide is 160 pages of tips, attractions, event listings and discount offers. Call 800-645-3446, ext. 205.

Florida

The Sarasota Vacation Guide Book and **Sand Dollar Savings Card** bring you special values and discounts at over 140 area restaurants and retail shops. The card is good for the neighboring Gulf Coast areas of Longboat Key, Lido Key, Siesta Key, Casey Key, Venice, Manasota Key, Englewood and North Port. Savings are valid during off-season periods. Call 800-522-9799.

The Kissimmee-St. Cloud Vacation Guide is 80 pages of information, event listings and discounts for travelers visiting Walt Disney World or the Kissimmee-St. Cloud area. Call 800-327-9159.

The Orlando Magicard has savings on accommodations, attractions, dining, transportation and shopping. Discounts include up to ten percent on car rentals from Alamo, Avis, Hertz and Thrifty; cruise discounts; hotel discounts and more. Call 800-645-4873.

Two Florida Keys discount books contain discounts totaling over $2,500 for dive trips, excursions, admissions, dining, hotels and shops. The Key Largo edition has over $1,500 in discounts; the Islamorada edition, $1,000. Get the Key Largo edition by calling 800-822-1088; the Islamorada edition, 800-322-5397. They're both published in January and available year round.

Palm Beach Free offers $500 in discount opportunities: scuba diving, tennis and golf, museums, art galleries, theater tickets, sail-planes, shopping and more. Also included are coupons for complimentary cocktails, two-for-one dinners and vacation packages. The coupons cover an area from Jupiter to Boca Raton. New coupon books come out every April. Call 800-554-7256.

The Miami Visitors Guide is a 100-page magazine with discounts on area attractions and restaurants and extensive tourist information. Call 800-933-8448.

The Lake County Plus Vacation Card offers Orlando-area discounts at campgrounds, golf courses and local attractions. The card, good throughout the year, also entitles you to special amenities at participating hotels and inns. Call 800-798-1071.

The Florida Values Activity Guide is a joint offering from Value Rent A Car, American Express and the Florida Division of Tourism. It lists over 500 free or low-cost activities and attractions throughout the state. Guides can be picked up at Florida **Value Rent A Car** offices, Florida welcome centers and the Florida Division of Tourism. Or you can request a copy to be mailed to you by calling 904-487-1462.

The Great Fall-Winter Getaway Promotion offers seasonal discounts to visitors in the Kissimmee-St. Cloud resort area. Savings include up to 50% off at nearly 100 hotels and attractions, including Disney World. Call 800-362-5477.

USAir Discounts Universal Studios/ Florida. USAir is the official airline of Universal Studios Florida in Orlando. The studio's ongoing promotion offers special discounts to travelers who fly into Florida on USAir. Present a valid USAir boarding pass for $4 off admission for up to six people. The boarding pass must show a date within 30 days of the date on which you purchase tickets. Members of USAir's Frequent Flyer program get $5 off each ticket. Party Gold and Party Gold Plus members get $6 off. Call 800-428-4322 for full details.

The Destin/Ft. Walton Beach Savings Card includes free long distance calls and up to 20% off at restaurants, attractions and specialty shops. It also lists special events. Call the Emerald Coast Convention and Visitors Bureau, 800-322-3319.

Georgia

The Dekalb-Atlanta Guest Card comes with coupons valid for up to $500 in discounts at hotels, attractions and restaurants in the greater Atlanta area. Call 800-999-6055 and be sure to also request the 60-page Visitors Guide when you ask for your guest card.

The Souvenir Summer Guide offers Atlanta-area discounts on attractions, hotels and packages that include tickets to Atlanta Braves baseball games. Call 800-285-2682 for a copy of the guide and call the Atlanta Convention and Visitors Bureau at 404-521-6600 for other discount offers.

The Fall Fun Coupon Book offers discounts on Georgia's Jekyll Islands from August to November. The *Sweet Spot Coupon Book* offers similar discounts for November through February. Autumn discounts start with 50% off rates on lodging options from fine hotels to campgrounds. The coupon books have over $250 in discounts for golf, historic tours, bicycling, tennis, dining, fishing, specialty shops and more. Contact the Jekyll Island Welcome Center at 800-841-6586 or 912-635-3636.

Hawaii

The Hawaii Visitor Card offers information and savings at restaurants, shops and attractions for visitors who pay with American Express. Cardholders can also get a quarterly newsletter covering the latest benefits and savings opportunities. Included is an offer to save up to 55% on long distance calls from any Hawaiian island to anywhere in the continental U.S. by using a special Sprint 800 number printed on the back of your Visitor Card. Call 800-513-6068.

The Kauai Green Coupon Book offers discount coupons and vacation planner for one of Hawaii's most beautiful islands. You get discounts on hotels, bed and breakfasts, helicopter and ground tours, ocean activities and equipment rentals, dining, shopping and more. Each annual edition comes out in December and is valid throughout the year. Call 800-245-2824.

Iowa

The Iowa Travel Guide is published each December and includes money-saving coupons, a calendar of statewide events and a state map. An average of 80 coupons offer discounts on lodging, casinos and restaurants. Call 800-345-4692.

Louisiana

The New Orleans Good Times Guide provides lodging information, a calendar of events, and information on dining and entertainment throughout the Crescent City. It also contains over $2,000 in shopping and entertainment discounts. Call 800-632-3116.

The Louisiana Tour Guide covers the entire state with tourist information and discount coupons. Call 800-753-2860.

Massachusetts

The Boston Pass and Hotel Package lists discounts on area attractions such as a free child's admission to Boston Duck Tours with the purchase of two adult tickets. The information is updated twice a year. Order your first edition and you'll automatically receive the next one. Call the Greater Boston Convention & Visitors Bureau, 800-888-5515.

Michigan

The Detroit Fun Lovers Coupon Book is offered by the Metropolitan Detroit Convention and Visitors Bureau. Motor City discounts are available at over 100 stores, restaurants, hotels and popular attractions. The books are updated annually. Call 800-338-7648.

Michigan Free details a variety of free activities and tours throughout the state: concerts, plays, museums, national parks and forests, wineries, festivals, historic cemeteries, nature centers, walking tours and more. The book costs $15.95 plus $3.50 for shipping and is available from University of Michigan Press, P. O. Box 1104, Ann Arbor, MI 48107. Call 313-764-4388. Fax 800-876-1922.

Missouri

$250 worth of savings in Branson are available in a 272-page guidebook also containing trip planning tips, maps, and detailed information on Branson's restaurants, accommodations, theaters and shows. The discounts cover hotels, restaurants, shops and attractions. The *Branson Guidebook* costs $16 plus shipping and handling. Call Fodor's Travel Publications, 800-533-6478.

Nebraska

Omaha is the title of a free visitors guide to city-wide attractions and events. It's mailed with a bonus pack of coupons discounting travel services and local purchases throughout the city. Call 800-332-1819.

Nevada

Comp City: A Guide To Free Las Vegas Vacations shows you how to get complimentary stays at Las Vegas hotels that can also include free drinks, meals, shows, and even airfares. The book tells you how to meet each casino's qualifications. In bookstores the guide costs $39.95 plus shipping. Call 800-244-2224.

The Las Vegas Advisor is a monthly newsletter that guides travelers to the best deals on hotels, casinos, restaurants and other entertainment attractions. Subscription rates are $45 annually; $50 for Canadian residents. You can get a sample issue for $5. Each subscription comes with a subscriber benefit package which contains coupons for gambling, hotels, dining, car rentals and more. Call 800-244-2224.

Bargain City: Booking And Beating The New Las Vegas is a comprehensive guide to deals and freebies–everything from where to find $2 steak dinners to free hotel rooms. The cost is $11.95. If you can't find it in your local bookstore, call Huntington Press, 800-244-2224.

The *Discover Nevada* **bonus book** covers far more than Las Vegas. This Commission of Tourism 58-page publication has 132 discount coupons as well as information on the state's lesser known attractions, Nevada trivia, scenic photo spots, and information on 397 local events, parks and climate. The coupons can save up to $1500 and include free roller coaster rides, discounts on gaming, rooms, meals, tours, rental cars and much more. Call 800-638-2328.

New Jersey

The New Jersey Travel Guide is published by the Division of Travel and Tourism at the beginning of every year. It divides the state into six regions and includes a listing of special events, transportation information, tourist information centers, and a New Jersey highway map. There are also over 120 coupons with up to $2000 in savings at various hotels, bed and breakfasts, restaurants, shops and attractions. Call 800-537-7397.

New Mexico

The New Mexico Vacation Guide is a 200-page, full-color brochure spanning the state's attractions and offering discounts on lodging, skiing, galleries and attractions. Call 800-545-2040 or write to The New Mexico Department of Tourism, Room C5105, 491 Old Santa Fe Trail, Santa Fe, NM 87503.

New York

New York City information is available by calling 800-456-8369. Information topics include country weekends, historic vacations, water vacations, family weekends, romantic weekends, New York City weekends and adventure trips. You can call between 6 a.m. and 1 a.m. Eastern time, seven days a week.

Ohio

The OhioPass Travel Planner is a full-color guide to statewide attractions with over 160 pages of listings, maps and feature stories on the Amish, theme parks, hometown museums, state parks, historic sites, zoos and other attractions. Be sure to also request the *OhioPass Coupon Book.* It offers over $3000 in discount possibilities. Call 800-282-5393.

Pennsylvania

The Pittsburgh Passport gives you admission to your choice of three attractions, plus two local transportation options. Attractions include the Andy Warhol Museum, the National Aviary, the

Carnegie Museum, Phipps Conservatory, Pepsi Plaza Ethnic Festivals, the Pittsburgh Zoo, Photo Antiquities, the Carnegie Science Center and the Frick Art & Historical Center. The Pittsburgh Passport costs $10 for individuals; $35 for four people. Call 800-359-0758 and ask for the Weekend Package, or call the Greater Pittsburgh & Visitors Bureau, 412-281-7711.

The Poconos Coupon Booklet, published by the Poconos Mountain Vacation Bureau, contains over $250 in discounts on hotels, restaurants, shops and attractions. Sample savings: 15% off rates at Adventure Sports Canoe & Raft Trips; ten percent off at Foxmoor Village Outlet Center; $4 off at the Mountain Creek Riding Stable and ten percent off at the Mountain Laurel Resort. You also get a free brochure and vacation guide. Call 800-762-6667 or 717-424-6050.

The Pennsylvania Visitors Guide, available from The Pennsylvania Office of Travel Marketing, offers over $2,500 in discounts. The 228-page book also features details of year-round, statewide events and attractions and a Pennsylvania road map. Call 800-847-4872.

The Visitors Guide To Pennsylvania Dutch Country lists attractions, events and savings available in the Lancaster Country area. The 36-page guide features savings on meals, lodging, shopping and admission to many area attractions. To acquaint yourself with the Pennsylvania Dutch Country and learn of special events and savings, call 800-723-8824, ext. 2405 or 717-299-8901.

Texas

The Texas Travel Book is a free guide and discount book done Texas-style in 272 pages. Call 800-888-8839.

The Greater Houston Passport Book is offered annually by the Greater Houston Convention and Visitors Bureau and features discounts at hotels, restaurants, shops and attractions including Six Flags and AstroWorld. Call 800-446-8786.

The Texas Travel Passport is a card that extends discounts ranging from ten to 50 percent. It's free with a one year subscription to *Texas Highways* magazine ($12.50) and provides savings on hotels, attractions, restaurants and campgrounds at over 200 Texas cities. Major attraction discounts are included: Six Flags Over Texas and Wet N' Wild in Arlington, SeaWorld in San Antonio and The Palace of Wax/Ripley's Believe It Or Not in Grand Prairie, among others. Members receive an embossed plastic card and a full sized color directory with listings of all discounts by city. Call 800-839-4997.

The Dallas/Fort Worth Big Bucks Coupon Book contains up to $1,500 in discounts and information on attractions, shopping, and other entertainment options in Dallas, Fort Worth, Irving, Arlington, Addison and Grand Prairie. Reserve your free copy by calling 800-452-9292 or pick it up at the tourist information center after you arrive. Be sure to also request the *Texas Metroplex Calendar of Events and Fun Map.*

San Antonio, Something To Remember is a free vacation kit that includes discount coupons. Call 800-843-2526 or write to The San Antonio Convention & Visitors Bureau, P.O. Box 2277, San Antonio, TX 78298.

Virginia

The Virginia Beach Guide offers $200 in discount coupons for restaurants, attractions, jet-ski, sailing and bike rentals, dive trips and more. Guides cover a year-long period, from May to May. Call 800-446-8038.

Biggest U.S. national park: Wrangell-St. Elias in Alaska at 8,331,604 acres.

Washington

Seattle Super Savers discounts winter rates at over 20 downtown hotels and provides discount coupons for dining, shopping and sightseeing. Call 800-535-7071.

INTERNATIONAL OFFERS

Prices quoted may vary slightly due to exchange rate fluctuations.

Asia

Asian Affairs Holiday is offered by Singapore Airlines. You get a $100 gift certificate with a brochure promoting all-inclusive vacation packages. Call 800-742-5742.

The Singapore Plus Card, distributed by the Singapore Tourist Promotion Board, gives discounts at over 150 shops, restaurants and attractions. Retailers participating in Singapore's "Good Retailer Scheme" (GRS) must emphasize good service and display price tags on their merchandise. The annually-issued cards are good through December. Call 212-302-4861 from the eastern U.S. or 213-852-1901 from the western U.S.

Canada

The Niagara Falls Ontario Vacation Guide is updated and available each May. It contains information on the Falls, accommodations and dining, as well as over $300 in coupons for area attractions, hotels and restaurants. Call 800-668-2746 or 800-563-2557.

The Caribbean

Caribbean Jewelry and Gemstones zeroes in on the islands' glitter with a 47-page guide, available by mail for $3. It gives you the tools you need to evaluate carat, cut, color and clarity. Write to Caribbean Jewelry and Gemstones, 1100 Sixth Avenue, Suite 30, Naples, FL 33940.

The Caribbean Classic Card offers discounts ranging from five to 50 percent at restaurants, supermarkets, car rental agencies, tour companies, nightclubs, duty-free shops and pharmacies. Over 1000 merchants participate. The card covers Barbados, Anguilla, Antigua, Aruba, the Bahamas, Curacao, Grenada, Jamaica, Puerto Rico, St. Croix, St. John, St. Thomas, St. Kitts, St.Lucia, Tortola, Virgin Gorda, Trinidad, Tobago and Miami. It's issued annually in August and costs about $10. Cardholders also have a chance to win a one-week Caribbean trip for two. Contact Caribbean Classic, Inc., 18 & 20 Webster Industrial Park, Wildey, St. Michael, Barbados, West Indies; call 809-427-5046; fax 809-435-7098.

Europe

The Amsterdam Culture and Leisure Pass costs less than $20 and gives you one year's free access to museums, 25% discounts on boat tours and tourist attractions and dining discounts. You can purchase the pass at tourist offices in Amsterdam. Call 312-819-0300 for information.

The Brussels Visitors Passport is a great deal at $5-6, depending on the exchange rate. The pass entitles you to numerous discounts at popular attractions and is also good for free 24-hour city transportation. Call 212-758-8130.

The Dublin Cultural Connection Pass will save you about 30% on admissions to museums, castles and more. The pass costs $21.50 and is available from the Irish Tourist Board, 212-418-0800.

The France Club Card has a high initial price but provides substantial discounts and is good for a year from the date of purchase. Benefits include free hotel upgrades, seasonal discounts at over 500 hotels and inns, car rental discounts, three-day admission to 65 museums in

Paris and more. The fee is $65 for one person; $100 for two. Call 800-678-5000.

The France Discovery Guide is a combined offering of the French Government Tourist Office, Air France and American Express. The guide offers guaranteed hotel rates and packages. The *AT&T France Fun Book* features over 100 discount coupons. Request either or both from Air France, 800-237-2747.

The Great British Heritage Pass allows admission to over 500 castles, manor homes, gardens and other historic properties in England, Scotland and Wales. The pass costs $35 for seven days, $50 for 15 days or $75 for one month. It's available from BritRail, 800-551-1977.

The Hamburg Card and The Multiple Day Card are valid, respectively, for one and two days free admission to 11 museums, free use of public transport and discounts of up to 30% on sightseeing tours. The card is available at Hamburg subway ticket counters. The one-day version costs $8.50 per adult; $18.50 per family. The two-day version costs $19 per adult; $32 per family. Call 212-967-3110 for more information.

The Le Club Diamant Rouge De Monaco is issued by the Monaco Government Tourist Office It costs $45, but you get some rare benefits, including real VIP treatment at participating hotels, free airport transfers via helicopter, complimentary museum admissions and more. The card is good for one year. Call 800-753-9696.

The London Arts Card, available from the London Arts Information Center, is free for the asking and is good for discounts and special offers at over 100 restaurants and art venues.

The London Countdown Card offers 50% off select restaurants and shops in London and ten percent off at thousands of shops, nightclubs and services displaying the Countdown sign. The card is valid for three months and costs approximately $12. It can be purchased at Countdown Plc., 88-92 Earls Court Road, Kensington, London W8 6EH; call 0171-938-1041.

The London Museum White Card is a three- or seven-day pass allowing admittance to a dozen museums. The three-day pass is $25; the seven-day is $40. Family passes covering two adults plus two children under 17 respectively are $50 and $86. Purchase them in London at participating museums, galleries and hotels and at major tube stations. Order in advance through Edwards & Edwards, 50 Main St., 3rd Floor, White Plains, NY 10606; call 800-223-6108.

The London Visitor Travel Card provides unlimited bus and underground travel for your choice of three, four or seven days. All cards come with discount vouchers for attractions and restaurants. Cards cannot be purchased in England. U.S.-based travelers can call the British Tourist Authority, 800-462-2748. The price varies by exchange rate.

Scandinavian Travel Cards provide country specific discounts in Copenhagen, Odense and Aalborg, Denmark; Helsinki, Finland; Reykjavik, Iceland; Oslo, Norway; and Stockholm and Gothenburg, Sweden. Features and cost vary. Call 212-949-2333 for information.

The Vienna Card discounts transportation by bus, tram and underground train and provides discounts at specified restaurants, shops, museums, attractions and concert halls. The cost is approximately $17 and the card is valid for four days. It's available at most hotels and tourist offices in Vienna.

Typical price of a modest country cottage in Ireland: $16,000 U.S.

STUDENT & YOUTH SAVINGS

The International Student Identity Card is available from the Council on International Educational Exchange. Widely varied discounts for students under age 26 include savings on international ferries and trains; rafting; snorkeling; Costa Rican jungle trips; theater tickets in London and Dublin, and free admission to 30 museums and palaces in Portugal. There are thousands of discount possibilities–more than 4,000 in Canada alone. The card is commonly accepted proof of student status in most countries around the world. An annual $18 fee, proof of full-time student status and a passport sized photograph are required. Call 800-438-2643.

The Euro 26 Card discounts over 200,000 shops and services in 24 European countries. It's available to anyone age 26 and under and can be purchased at most Youth Hostel Association locations. Countries included are Andorra, Belgium, the Czech Republic, Cyprus, England, Finland, Ireland, Italy, Liechtenstein, Luxembourg, Malta, the Netherlands, Ireland, Norway, Portugal, San Marino, Scotland, the Slovak Republic, Switzerland and Wales. The phone number for YHA's National Office in London is 01727-855215 or fax to 01727-844126.

The Go 25 Card is issued by the Federation of International Youth Travel Organization and is available to people 25 and under. It discounts over 11,000 travel-related purchases worldwide. The card can be purchased from FIYTO tour operators and travel agents or you can write to FIYTO, Bredgade 25 H, DK-1260, Copenhagen K, Denmark. The best source for information by phone is Top Deck in London at 0171-244-8641.

The National Express Discount Coachcard takes 30% off adult fares on Britain's National Express Railway and Scottish Citylink Coaches. The card is available to full-time students of any age and to travelers 16 to 25. The cost is approximately $15. The card can be purchased in the UK from Eurolines at Victoria Station.

Student Tips costs just $1 and is filled with tips on youth fares, rail passes, hotels, hostels, budget travel, work/study opportunities, customs, visas, trip planning, packing and car rentals. Call 213-463-0655 or write to "Student Tips," Council Travel, 10904 Lindbrook Drive, Los Angeles, CA 90024.

The Educational Foundation For Foreign Study arranges foreign language study combined with stays in an international host family's home. Call 800-447-4273.

The price of a burger and fries in Barcelona: $3.75; in Tokyo: $7.45.

SENIOR SAVINGS

Disney's Magic Years Club provides discounts at Walt Disney World and Disneyland plus other travel discounts. You must be 55 or above. Call 714-490-3250 or write to Box 4709, Anaheim, CA 92803-4709.

Greater Fort Lauderdale Super Senior Savers discounts hotels and attractions. Call 800-227-8669 or write to Dept. MS, 200 E. Las Olas Blvd., Suite 1500, Fort Lauderdale, FL 33301.

Philadelphia Seniors On The Go is a free booklet with discounts for Visa card holders on hotels, restaurants, attractions and events. Call 215-636-1666 or write to the Philadelphia Visitors Center, 16th and JFK Blvd, Philadelphia, PA 19102.

The Silver Card, provided by the Park City, Utah Convention and Visitors Bureau, offers summer discounts on restaurants, shops and attractions and lists summer events with special appeal to senior travelers. Call 800-453-1360 or write to 1910 Prospector Avenue, Park City, UT 84060. You can also pick up a copy of the free card at participating hotels and inns.

The Golf Card is for serious senior golfers. A single membership is $95 annually, but includes free membership in the Quest discount program, detailed in the *Hotel* section. You get two free 18-hole rounds of golf at your choice of 2,700 courses worldwide, a bimonthly magazine and resort discounts on golf packages. Call 800-453-4260 or write to The Golf Card, P.O. Box 7020, Englewood, CO 80155.

The 70+ Ski Club offers organized ski trips, a newsletter, locations offering free skiing for club members and other locations offering discounts. Lifetime mem-

bership is just $5. Call 518-399-5458 or write to Lloyd Lambert, 70+ Ski Club, 104 Eastside Dr., Ballston Lake, NY 12019.

Montgomery Ward's Years Of Extra Savings Discount Club is open to members ages 55 and above. The $2.99 per month fee provides ten percent off any merchandise, even sale items, every Tuesday–plus a five to ten percent rebate on travel booked through the company's travel service. Call 800-421-5396.

SAVE BY HOW YOU PAY

CREDIT CARDS

The Best Way To Pay

Save money by how you spend it. Using the wrong form of payment can add over ten percent to your domestic trip, up to 20% on foreign travel.

There are times when your only intelligent choice is to use a credit card.

- **Diners Club and American Express** travel cards are the best choices if you can pay the entire cost on receipt of your bill. (American Express offers extended pay options for air travel only.) They give you the best overall travel benefits at no cost other than nominal annual fees.

- **Corporate cards and Gold and Platinum** level cards offer more travel protection and promotional offers than standard cards.

- **Use your card of choice** for all major travel purchases. If you don't have a credit card get one, even if it requires a deposit of guaranteed funds. You'll need it to hold reservations, rent from most car rental agencies, and to obtain room service at many hotels. You get convenience plus:

  Free buyer protection features not available with any other form of payment. If the airline from which you purchased your ticket goes under, or the tour operator through which you booked a package tour folds, your fastest and often best protection is disputing the charge with your credit card company. Even added credit card fees may be worth the consumer protection you receive.

  Free insurance to a widely varying degree, depending on the card you use.

Average amount a bank spends to gain one new credit card customer: $100.

Cash advance options that take on increased importance when you're away from home.

- **If you're asked to fax a copy of your card** when purchasing travel over the phone, state on the fax that authorization is limited to that specific purchase. Airlines and travel agencies usually mail tickets only to your credit card billing address.

- **Cash advances internationally via debit cards** are subject to the exchange rate at the time of transaction. Credit card cash advance rates aren't set until the point at which the debit is reported to the bank–usually one to three days.

Is There One Best Credit Card?

Which card is best? The answer is different from person to person and month to month. The best card for a stay-at-home isn't likely to be the best card for a frequent traveler. Diners Club and similar cards are among the best in part because you can accumulate miles on most major airlines.

- **If you tend to carry a balance,** stay away from no-fee cards that usually charge higher interest rates.

- **A no-fee card with a low interest rate** is probably best for cardholders who pay off their monthly balance.

- **Cards that offer perks** in the form of frequent flyer miles or another award point system may require annual fees and higher interest rates.

- **Cards that offer sign-up bonuses** may also have fees and higher rates but getting one for the sign-up bonus is a great move, even if you never actually use the card. If an issuing bank wants to give you a buy one-get-one free airfare coupon, for example, it's certainly worth the application process. Make sure new benefits don't come at the expense of favorable basics and remember that initial rates usually go up after introductory offers expire.

Choosing Credit Cards

Compare benefit levels on services you'll actually use. You can eliminate half the confusion of comparisons if you eliminate features that just don't apply to your needs.

Determine how interest is charged. Some cards, for example, charge interest on cash advances from the date of the advance rather than the billing cycle's due date. Some cards compound interest. You pay on the principal plus the current interest. It can raise your real interest rate by two percentage points.

Consider cards with higher annual fees. The benefits can far surpass what you pay. The American Express Platinum Card has a $300 annual fee but you get free access to Continental or Northwest's airport clubs (a $150 value each), free enrollment in your choice of premier service programs from Avis, Hertz & National (a savings of $125), plus special international offers such as free upgrades and Business and First-Class two-for-ones.

Look at the whole picture before changing cards. It costs issuing banks almost $100 to attract a new cardholder. Their rules are not carved in stone. You can attempt to negotiate, particularly if your requested change is a return to a term or condition that existed when you first acquired your card.

Travel Benefits

Credit card travel benefits vary according to the card you carry and the issuing bank. You and your partner may have the identical card at the identical level but, if they come from different issuing banks, the benefits may differ. Benefits are determined by the issuing bank and require a direct call to define. They change often in reaction to monitored costs, market competition and special promotions.

- **Car rental collision and damage waiver coverage** has been reduced in recent years. Diners Club and some corporate cards like the VISA Business Card are the only cards that offer primary coverage. Some cards exempt trucks, campers, vans, jeeps and other vehicles from any coverage. Visa and MasterCard Gold Cards tend to continue to provide secondary coverage. Call the number on the back of your card to request full details.

- **Car rental coverage abroad** is subject to the card's provisions and the willingness of the rental agency to accept it. Some foreign rental companies decline acceptance of credit card insurance benefits and place a hold on your entire credit limit if you decline their CDW coverage. Agencies in Italy, New Zealand and Mexico tend not to accept credit coverage at all.

- **Buyers protection coverage** is on virtually every credit card either in the form of an actual program or through your ability to dispute charges for defective merchandise and services. Verify the current coverage on your card by calling the number on the back of the card. Be aware of any notable exclusions. No credit card, for example, will reimburse you for the cost of items confiscated by U. S. Customs.

- **Travel accident coverage** is standard on premium cards. Diners Club excels again, in part because they cover trips taken on free and frequent flier tickets. Check your individual card to deter-

mine the extent of your coverage.

- **Travel assistance services** are available to all cardholders but will be most helpful and plentiful with premium cards. Services may include trip planning, worldwide legal referral, message delivery, emergency transportation, medical assistance and lost luggage benefits not covered by the airline.

- **Corporate cards** entice business travelers with special billing itemization, calling card links, improved express cash terms, more liberal travel insurance coverage and special discount offers.

- **Remember** you must charge each specific trip on your card to receive its travel benefits.

Affinity Cards

Affinity cards started attracting consumers by allocating a percentage of profit to an organization such as The National Wildlife Federation. Now affinity cards in co-branded and rebate varieties are available in ever-expanding varieties. Co-branded cards are based on an alliance between a retailer and a bank with both businesses splitting the profits engendered by their union. Rebate cards give a portion of profit directly back to the consumer in the form of credits or services. There are definite consumer benefits but you won't get the most favorable interest rates and you're likely to have to pay annual fees–both interest rates and annual fees tend to increase after an introductory offer expires. You have to decide if the bells and whistles are worth the added cost.

- **Evaluate** the interest rate, the annual fee and how much you have to charge to get the benefits.

- **Be sure you'll use the advantages you earn.** These cards are the Green Stamps of the '90s. Just as millions of stamps ended up unredeemed; points, miles and coupons now go unused.

- **Look for optimum grace periods** between purchase and posting.

- **Rebate cards encourage high revolving balances** by offering special awards for minimum balances. A few cards actually add a monthly service charge if you pay your full balance.

- **Know how the sponsoring bank computes** the balance subject to interest. The adjusted balance system is best but is rarely offered by bonus cards. The average daily balance is next in preference. Avoid two-cycle average daily balance systems that compute interest based on two billing cycles.

- **If you try on one of the newer cards** and its promise doesn't meet your expectations, switch back to a basic card.

- **Get the best of both worlds** by charging regular monthly purchases on bonus cards to rack up points. Pay the bill in full each month. Use your basic, lower-interest card on large purchases where balances may be carried over.

Best Bet Credit Cards

New *multi-carrier* cards offer cumulative point systems that combine all miles and give selection options on free tickets on your choice of airline. Most award one point per dollar spent and require a 14-day advance on bonus tickets. See the *Airline's On Board Basics* section for more information.

Consolidating Credit Lines

Consolidate credit lines at about 11% interest when you make your affinity card

payments through Chase Manhattan. You're mailed a monthly preprinted check made out to your card's bank. You fill in the payment amount you've chosen. Call 800-992-4273 for details on the Chase Reward Consolidator program.

Promotional Savings

Enticement offers change as often as politicians' speeches. Of course, we think *BEST FARES Discount Travel Magazine* is the best source for each month's hottest offers. Also check your mail and credit card billing inscrts. You can frequently find deals where you can get a two-for-one airfare coupon just by signing up for a particular card. The trick–you have to know who is offering the deal and when. Bonus miles are also a common sign-up award. Typical offers from recent issues:

- **Free companion tickets** on American Airlines for CitiBank charge card applicants or current members who upgrade to Gold cards.

- **Free travel certificates** on Northwest for using selected services at Shawmut Banks in Minnesota.

- **A $25 gift cheque from American Express** for charging $100 in lift tickets.

- **United Mileage Plus** with a buy-one-get-one-free airfare offer for each new member.

Traveler's Assistance

How long does it take to get a replacement when your card is lost or stolen?

- **American Express** treats all levels of cardholders the same. U.S. replacements require one to two days. Cards lost abroad can take two to four days to be replaced but they also have offices in many countries where you can pick up a replacement almost instantly.

Dollar value of government travel contracts given to American Express Travel then cancelled: $71.6 million.

- **Diners Club** replaces cards in the U.S. within 24 hours; abroad, in one to three days.

- **Discover** replaces cards in the U.S. overnight; abroad, in two days.

- **MasterCard** replaces standard cards in the U.S. within two business days; Gold cards, the next day. Standard cards are replaced abroad according to requirements of the issuing bank–usually a minimum of two days. Gold cards are replaced the next day.

- **Visa** replaces standard cards in the U.S. in one business day and trics to replace Gold cards within 24 hours. Abroad, standard cards require three days; Gold, one business day.

Blocked Funds

Your ability to use your credit card can be hampered when car rental agencies and hotels block a certain amount of your available funds against ultimate charge contingencies. This can tie-up a good portion of needed funds when you are on a trip. If the amount is reasonable and agreeable to you, mentally deduct it from your available limit or use an alternate credit card for day-to-day expenses. Remember, to counter this problem:

- **Ask if funds will be blocked** before you confirm your reservation. If you cannot avoid the block, demand that it be removed as soon as your transaction is completed. It's a brief procedure that many vendors tend to do in batches thus depriving you of your total card limit for an unwarranted length of time.

- **Blocked funds take 48 hours or more** to be replaced with actual charges. If you decide to switch payment to a card other than the one you used when checking in, it may take even longer for the blocked amount to be removed.

OTHER WAYS TO SAVE WITH PLASTIC

Automobile Club memberships cost $22-60 annually and give you free road service, trip planning and discounts. Exxon's Travel Club, 800-833-9966, offers the best emergency service due to the number of service affiliates they can utilize. AAA, 800-222-4357, offers the most extensive discount plan on travel-related purchases including hotel and car rental discounts.

Airport Club Cards admit you to member-only lounges, business facilities and other services. The rigors of travel are eased by complimentary snacks and beverages, meeting facilities, special concierge services and quiet and useful waiting areas. Per year per airline cost is about $150. See the *Airline's On Board Basics* section for complete prices and features. Join the clubs of the one or two airlines you use the most. Depending on airport configuration you can use one airline's facilities even when flying on another.

Frequent flier membership is useful even if you don't fly often. Some perks are yours even if you never actually fly the airline.

The American Association of Retired Persons (AARP), 202-434-2277, offers an $8 annual membership (spouse included) for travelers 50 and older. AARP offers savings on hotels, car rentals and air tickets plus special cruise and tour offers.

Members of credit unions also qualify for select travel discounts. Members of government credit agencies get the best deals and membership policies often include immediate family members.

Debit cards can be practical alternatives to credit cards. They can be set up to tap into your savings if you go over the deposited amount.

ATM CARDS

The Best Way To Use Your ATM Card

Automatic Teller Machine (ATM) cards are quick and easy ways to get cash. You'll find ATM's prevalent across the United States.

> *In the spring of 1996 some ATMs began charging access fees of $2-4 in addition to the usual transaction fees. What started as a regional practice (in the South and West) is likely to go national. Machines that are not owned by the banks, and particularly machines in airports and areas frequented by travelers, are likely to add the access fee. A surcharge warning may appear on the screen prior to your transaction. Your best defense is to head for a bank-run ATM with an identifying bank logo.*

Before you leave, check your daily withdrawal limit. If you're traveling internationally it may vary from the domestic limit. Request an increase if you think you may need it. Get the number you need to call if your card is lost or stolen.

Report lost or stolen ATM cards as soon as possible. Policies vary bank by bank, but your liability is usually determined by the length of time you wait until reporting the card missing. In a 48-hour period, it can increase ten-fold.

ATM withdrawals can cost less than credit card cash advances, which usually incur interest from the date of transaction and charge fees up to three percent. ATM cash advance fees are usually two percent, with a minimum charge of $2.50 and a maximum charge of $20. You must also pay the standard transaction fee.

Shopping With Your ATM Card is a free offer from MasterCard, 800-999-5136.

International ATM Use

International ATM use is relatively easy and extremely smart. You get foreign currency at wholesale rates–the same rates banks pay when transferring in excess of $1 million. There is no cheaper way to get cash abroad. Transaction fees are technically the same in the U.S. and abroad but in rare instances you'll encounter higher fees because you're dealing with multiple banks. Minimize transaction fees by withdrawing an adequate amount of cash and keeping the bulk of it in your hotel safe.

- **Money is issued at wholesale exchange rates** that range from three to five percent lower than standard bank rates, as much as 40% lower than airport exchange counters and as much as 55% lower than some hotel currency exchanges.

- **You usually get a better deal by using an ATM** than from a local bank.

- **You pay the same per-use fee as you do in the U.S.**–usually $2-3. If you're paying more, change banks.

- **Countries with two-tiered monetary systems,** whether official or tolerated, provide the exception to the ATM rule. Use tourist exchange facilities rather than banks or ATMs.

- **If your card is part of the CIRRUS network** call 800-424-7787 for locations in 66 countries.

- **If you're part of the PLUS network,** call 800-491-1145 for locations in 75 countries.

Total number of ATM machines in 75 countries: 275,000.

Member banks may have directories but few people request them, so ask a bank officer if you're told they're not available. Consider photocopying and enlarging the pages you need to get around tiny type size.

Convert your PIN to four numbers. Some international machines won't accept a longer number and some don't have alpha-numeric keypads.

Instructions are usually multi-lingual, but basic foreign language skills can come in handy if you try to use one of three percent that are programmed in one language.

> **"**If the machine says "No Foreign Cards," heed the warning or it may consume your card!**"**

Remember that 24-hour ATMs are not the rule in suburban and outlying areas. You won't always have the same degree of accessibility you have at home.

EMERGENCY CASH OPTIONS

The best way to deal with emergency cash situations is to try to pre-plan and avoid having the need arise.

- **Know your credit card and ATM limits** before you leave. If you're going to be charging expenses outside your usual charge pattern notify the bank to avoid being questioned on individual purchases. If you're traveling internationally, have sufficient funds in your main checking account as it is the only account many overseas ATMs will access.

- **Unanticipated expenses** can make the difference between easy going and financial strain. Make sure you've allowed the means to cover them. Parking rates in some cities hit $40 per day. Hotel taxes add ten to 20 percent to the quoted rate. The $10 gin and tonic and $5 cola are not uncommon.

When unanticipated situations arise and emergency funds are your only option, you have several choices.

- **Bank transfers** are safe and cost effective, providing your bank has a branch in the city or country you're in. International transfers range from $25-45.

- **Overnight services** from Federal Express, Airborne and the post office can get a cashiers check or money order to you by 10:30 the next morning. If you have a business account, the cost can be as low as $4.50. Have the funds sent in a form that is easy to cash in the country you're in.

- **Wire money** via Western Union, 800-325-4176, at fees calculated by the dollar amount sent. If you use a credit card an additional fee is charged. American Express MoneyGrams, 800-926-9400, offers lower rates but you must make the transfer in person at an affiliated outlet. You can pay for the transfers with cash, VISA, MasterCard and Discover cards as well.

- **The U.S. Department of State**, 202-647-5225, in conjunction with Western Union will send emergency cash internationally for the Western Union charge plus a $15 consulate fee. Funds can be picked up in local currency.

TRAVELERS CHECKS

Travelers checks can cost a one percent service fee but they're free for AAA members and preferred bank customers–a status you can attain with a minimum balance.

- **Avoid losing ten to 20 percent when cashing them overseas** by buying foreign denomination checks before you leave. Buying in advance also eliminates exchange fees.

- **American Express Travelers Checks** can be exchanged at low fees or sometimes for free at American Express international offices, but the exchange rate may not be as favorable as bank rates.

- **Try to closely approximate the amount you need** to avoid the expense of converting unused checks back to U.S. dollars.

- **Buy them through your travel agent or** an international travel check service.

  Thomas Cook and Sons charges $3.50 or one percent, whichever is higher. They are listed in the classified directories under Foreign Currency Exchange.

  Ruesch International, 800-424-2923, sells seven different denominations for a two dollar per currency fee plus shipping.

- **When you use travelers checks,** make copies of the numbers on your checks and the telephone number to call if they're lost or stolen.

- **American Express and Visa** offer dual signature travelers checks that allow use with either of two approved signatures.

CARRYING CASH

Carry a reasonable amount of cash to handle tips and incidental expenses.

- **Too much cash makes you vulnerable** to theft and loss.

- **Too little cash** forces you to complicate inexpensive transactions by using payment forms that require more time and may not even be acceptable.

- **Use cash when you have reason to suspect** that your credit card number might be used for unauthorized reasons. When traveling, your credit card company may not be able to reach you to question an unusual charge activity.

- **Don't exchange currency before you leave** on an international trip. You may be tempted by momentarily favorable exchange rates, but they rarely fluctuate enough to make more than a few dollars difference.

Don't count on cashing personal checks with the airline you're flying or at your hotel. The credit card age has made that traditional courtesy subject to your persuasiveness and their interpretation of risk.

Approximate amount paid by travelers each year in local, state and federal taxes: $53 billion.

VALUE ADDED TAXES

Fewer than five percent of North Americans file refunds on Value Added Tax (VAT) purchases. Thirty million dollars are left in Europe each year.

VAT refunds are available on purchases that are taken out of the country. You cannot get them for goods and services used while in the country.

Be astute about price comparisons. Not everything is cheaper in its country of origin. If you're not going to apply for your refund or if your purchase doesn't meet minimum requirements for refunds, a 20% off price versus a 25% VAT is not a bargain.

VAT rates can vary by item as well as by country. Belgium, for example, charges 11% on electrical appliances and 25% on luxury clothing and jewelry.

General VAT Rates

This chart lists VAT rates by country plus the minimum purchase requirement for applying for a VAT refund.

GENERAL VAT RATES		
COUNTRY	RATE	MINIMUM PURCHASE IN U.S. DOLLARS
AUSTRIA	16.7%	$ 90
AUSTRALIA	20%	$ 90
BELGIUM	17%	$215
BRITAIN	7.5%	None unless required by merchant
DENMARK	20%	$ 50
FRANCE	18.6%	$250
GERMANY	5%	None unless required by merchant
ITALY	19%	$200
NETHERLANDS	17.5%	$185
SPAIN	6%	$ 95
SWITZERLAND	6.5%	$340
SWEDEN	20%	$ 13

Easy Steps To VAT Refunds

There are four ways to get VAT refunds:

- **Exit refunds.** Show your passport or ticket when purchasing items and get the appropriate paperwork from the shop. Take purchases in their original containers to the airport as carry-on luggage. Customs will inspect your purchases, stamp your form and send you to another line to get a check or charge card credit. If you choose this method add two hours to your airport check-in time.

- **Direct export.** Have purchases shipped directly to the U.S. You pay the shipping costs and items may be subject to U.S. duty.

- **Mail refunds.** Forms, instructions and deadlines are available at customs and at larger stores.

- **European Tax-Free Shopping (ETS).** 60,000 member shops usually (but not always) identified with blue and silver ETS signs have simplified VAT refunds in exchange for 20% of your refund value. They fill out the paperwork, seal your packages and issue a refund check on the spot. Checks are cashed at an ETS desk after you've passed through departure customs with payment in charge card credit, U.S. or local currency. For more information call 312-382-1101.

Get help with VAT refund procedures from services skilled in untangling the red tape. There is no up-front charge. Their fee is a percentage of the refund they expedite. The minimum refund amount handled is $190 per quarter.

Saving Taxes In Canada

Travelers to Canada can obtain refunds on National Goods and Services Tax (GST) and Provincial Sales Tax (PST), charged in most provinces.

- **GST refunds** are available on purchases taken out of Canada and on hotel rooms charges. Refunds are not applicable for tax paid on meals, car rentals and gas. Forms are available at most hotels and large stores and must be mailed in with original receipts. If you're claiming less than $500 Canadian, you can file your claim at the border. Call the Canadian Consulate, 404-577-6810 or the Visitors Rebate Program, 613-991-3346 for details.

- **PST refunds** on tax rates ranging from six to 12 percent are obtained by filing by mail directly to the provincial refund office. Hotels and stores have the forms which must be completed and in the applicable office within 30 days of purchase or use of service.

MORE WAYS TO SAVE WHEN TRAVELING ABROAD

Shop wisely. Americans are accustomed to inflated prices at airport shops but European airport shopping offers some bargains and, in some cases, VATs lower than what you'll find in city shops.

Posted foreign exchange rates are affected by small-print fees, charges and commissions. Don't try to figure out all the variables. Ask a simple question: "If I give you X dollars how much local cash will you give me in return?"

Spend ten minutes familiarizing yourself with local money. Program yourself for systems that make cost comprehension difficult for Americans. For example, a meal that costs $10 may cost 12 Australian dollars or 71 Hong Kong dollars; in Japan, 940 yen; in Britain, 6 pounds; in Greece, 2,150 drachmas; in Germany, 14 marks. A small travel computer will translate for you but you may not need one if you tune your mind to the local currency.

Off the beaten path, local currency may be the only form of money that counts. Your second best alternative–using travelers checks in the local currency.

Learn when and how to bargain. The simplest strategy: make your initial offer half the asking price and let the negotiations begin. In some cultures walking away is an expected part of the process and necessary to getting the lowest price.

How to say "tap water" in German: leitungswasser.

Guarantee hotel and car rental rates by pre-paying and locking them in at the current exchange rate.

European train systems provide efficient country-to-country travel. They're cheap and comfortable alternatives to inter-Europe air travel. Don't judge them by the limitations of our own railroad system. Check our *Rail and Road* section for specific savings.

European restaurants commonly post menus with prices in their windows. Rely on them for cost estimates rather than making snap judgments based on neighborhoods and outward appearances.

Taxis may tack on fees for bags carried in the trunk. If they fit inside the vehicle, place them there.

Develop a panhandler policy. You've learned to deal with the homegrown variety but panhandlers appear in unexpected places and forms when you travel.

A free *Foreign Currency Guide* is available from Ruesch International, 1350 Eye St. NW, Washington, DC 20005. Call 800-424-2923 or 202-408-1200.

TAXING TRAVEL

IRS Travel Deductions

Take advantage of tax deductions.

- **Get a deduction in advance** by charging travel at the end of the year on any major credit card. You can claim the full transaction even if it's still outstanding.

- **If you get stuck with non-refundable airline tickets** you can deduct all taxes, terminal and fuel surcharges and passenger facility charges. On international tickets you can also deduct immigration, customs and agriculture inspection fees.

- **Charitable trips** are deductible only if you are on duty in a substantial sense. The organization involved must have tax-exempt status.

- *IRS Publication 463* details tax rules for travelers. Contact your regional office or write to Internal Revenue Service Mail Editor, 3041 Sunrise Blvd., Rancho Cordova, CA 95742.

- *120 Money Saving Travel Tips* is a CPA-written guide to help travelers receive maximum tax deductions on travel. It covers taxable and non-taxable frequent flyer awards, deductions on conventions held outside North America, IRS travel audits, spouses traveling on business trips, deductible and non-deductible travel expenses and more. Send $6.95 and a self-addressed, stamped envelope with 75¢ postage to Travel Taxes Inc., 3262 Brook Rd, Highland Park, IL 60035; call 847-266-9500.

> **“**Get receipts on all non-credit card purchases. Amounts that seem small can be cumulatively significant. The IRS permits handwritten notes for some items and for amounts under $75.**”**

Business Travel Deductions

Keep up with frequent changes and consider using the following tips:

- **Deduct the full cost** of travel and lodging and 50% of meal costs. Don't stimulate auditor attention with expenses far outside the framework of the type of business you conduct. A renowned entertainment lawyer can justify suites and gourmet meals. A just-starting-out sales representative probably can't.

- **Travel expenses equal to the first two percent of your income** are not generally deductible. If you make $75,000 per year, for example, the first $1,500 in travel expense is not deductible.

- **Business-with-pleasure combination trips** allow reasonable deductions. The strictest requirements are on international travel. The total trip must be seven days or less and 75% of your time must be spent on business. Travel time and holidays and weekends between business days count toward the 75%.

- **Spouses get travel deductions** only if officially employed with bona fide reasons to travel.

- **Airline club dues** can be deducted if a convincing case is made that they are used primarily for business purposes.

- **The cost of airline upgrades** is deductible if you can establish that the extra room and quiet are necessary to the preparation of presentations and business material. Keep journal entries citing specific projects worked on per flight.

- **Free-lancers** must demonstrate a profit for three of the past five years to claim work related travel deductions.

- **Educational trips** are only deductible if they contribute to your current area of employment.

- **Conventions** (excluding investment, political and social) are deductible. If they're held abroad there must be a valid business reason for choosing the location. If they're based on cruise travel you can deduct a maximum of $2,000 per year if the ship is of U.S. registry and all ports of call.

Other Travel Taxes

The $3 per airport Passenger Facility Charge added to the cost of every ticket you purchase has joined the other $8 billion that's sitting in the Airport and Airway Trust Fund. The money was meant to help build and improve airports. If you're the lobbying kind, you might want to tell Congress that you'd like to see some of the improvements you've been paying for.

Never underestimate the power of taxes and fees to bring shock value to the bottom line. A cruise can be advertised at $895 even though port charges and taxes take the real cost to about $1190. The $99 hotel room ends up at $125. The $24 rental car costs about $46 when non-discretionary charges are added.

Departure taxes are charged by some countries. Keep enough local currency to pay them without taking another trip through the currency exchange labyrinth.

TIPS ON TIPS

'TO INSURE PROMPT SERVICE'

T I P S stands for "To Insure Prompt Service." Curiously enough, most tips are given after the service is performed.

Tips are never mandatory but most often are factored into pay rates by the employer and are anticipated by the employee. It's best to accept tipping for decent service as a reality of modern life.

Guidelines can be broken. They exist to provide answers for unfamiliar situations and to let you know current standards. Ultimately the level of tipping is your choice.

- **Undertipping** can express your displeasure with poor service but be sure you are sending the message to the right person. Don't hold anyone liable for what they can't control. For instance, don't undertip the waiter because of an unorganized kitchen staff.

- **Standard tipping** expresses your satisfaction and fulfills your obligation. Only extraordinary circumstances merit an additional tip amount.

- **Overtipping** should be a response to unusually proficient service and should be done with discretion.

- **Try to carry coins and currency** that allow you to tip without negotiating change.

- **Hand deliver tips** when you're uncertain they'll get to your intended recipients.

Tipping On The Move

What's expected varies by where you are. The following guidelines should see you through any domestic travel possibility. Some people theorize that tips should be higher in big cities but of course that factor is naturally accommodated by their higher prices. The percentage remains the same.

The top three 1995 tourist destinations, in order: France, Spain and The United States.

- **Airport shuttle drivers**–50¢-$1 per bag only if direct assistance is provided.

- **Skycaps**–50¢-$1 per bag, minimum. This is an upfront tip that almost always pays off. A well-tipped skycap will show greater concern for your property.

- **Taxi drivers**–15%. A little more for short hops.

- **Train porters and attendants** are tipped nominally as a service is performed. Unless the service rendered is unusual, 50¢-$1 is usually fine. Tipping for meal service follows the same standards as regular restaurant dining. Sleeping-car attendants are tipped at the end of the trip at a suggested rate of $5 per night.

- **Tipping on escorted tours** is done on the last day at a suggested rate of $2-5 per person per day for lengthy tours, and half that for shorter tours.

    A guide leading a side-tour that lasts several hours is tipped according to the number of people in the group; the larger the group, the smaller each traveler's contribution.

    Personal tour guide tipping is a matter of custom and service.

    A guide with exceptional skills, such as a safari guide, should be tipped at or above the $5 per day rate.

Cruise Tipping

Most cruise tipping is easily handled near the end of the cruise. Envelopes and suggested amounts are both provided by the cruise ship staff. You should get advance notice of standards on the cruise line you choose, either in their brochure or with your reservation packet. Some ultra-luxury lines include tipping in their prices.

Never stint on end-of-cruise tipping when service has been good. Many lines pay most of their workers relatively low wages and tips make an enormous difference.

- **Cabin stewards and waiters** generally get $3-5 per day each.

- **Busboys** are tipped at about $2 per day.

- **Other service staff**–bartenders, wine stewards, masseurs and hairdressers– are tipped as services are provided. You may opt to give special consideration to child care workers but it's not required unless you use their services outside of normal operating hours.

- **Captains and ships officers** are never tipped. The best way to acknowledge their expertise is a thank you letter, copied to the cruise line's corporate office.

Tipping At Hotels

If you tipped everyone you encountered from the time you leave your car or shuttle to the time you're in your room, you would probably have been too generous. Hotel tipping is strictly for services performed.

- **Doormen** are customarily tipped $1 but not every time you enter or leave the hotel. You don't have to tip for the professional courtesy of a door being opened for you. You should tip if the doorman provides assistance such as helping you load bags into a vehicle.

- **Front desk staff** are rarely tipped. If you're given a great upgrade, you might consider a tip but it won't be expected.

- **Bellmen** are tipped according to the amount of luggage they transport. The usual 50¢-$1 per-bag rule can apply, but fit the tip to the situation. Easy

---

U.S. hotel where Ho Chi Minh worked as a busboy: The Omni Parker House in Boston, home of Parker House Rolls.

access and a large number of bags can bring the tip down to a 50¢ per bag.

- **Housekeeping staff** is "tipping optional," but $1-2 on the pillow each morning is considerate and probably well-spent, especially if you'll be there several days.

- **Room service** tipping follows the 15% rule. Tipping in cash gives the waiter immediate use of the gratuity. Adding it to your credit card charge can delay it by days.

- **Concierges** are not tipped for general information but should be rewarded for special services. If their connections result in tickets to a sold-out play or reservations at a hot new restaurant, a $10 tip is recommended.

Tipping On The Town

- **Valet parking attendants** are always tipped when you claim your car. $1-2 is fine for most vehicles. You might want to tip more if you drive a super luxury car.

- **Coatroom attendants** don't always get to keep the contents of the tip bowl so inquire before you add revenue to the establishment. If you choose to tip, 50¢-$1 is standard depending on what you check and the tone of the establishment.

- **Bartenders** receive 15%, or $1 minimum, if the tab is under $7.

- **Musicians** are tipped at least $1 for any special request and $5-10 for something remarkable.

- **Restaurant tipping** is 15% for good service; 20% for excellent service. A good way to figure an average tip is to double the tax amount. In most U.S. cities that will come to close to 15%.

> **❝**If you are with a large party, many restaurants will automatically place a 15% gratuity on your bill. The restaurant's logic behind this–large parties tend to undertip. If this is the restaurant's policy it is usually stated on the menu.**❞**

- **Fine dining** merits a few additional standards. The maitre'd should be tipped according to the status of the restaurant. You have wide discretion. Wine stewards are tipped $2-5 per bottle or ten percent of the cost of the wine, whichever is greater.

- **Buffet dining** calls for a $1 tip per person if drinks and other services are provided.

> **❝**Many people would like to see the end of the entire practice of tipping but the reality is that many people in service professions simply do not earn a high enough hourly wage to make this possible. Some people like to comment on poor service by leaving a couple pennies. Others like to earn reputations as "big tippers" in the hope of getting preferential treatment. Use tips to make a point if you choose to, but remember that their main purpose is to allow the people who serve you to enjoy a reasonable standard of living.**❞**

Amount spent by travelers in 1995 on hotel and restaurant taxes: over $5 billion.

Tipping Internationally

Service charges are automatically added to your restaurant bill in many countries. Be sure to ask and be sure to use that specific term. **In some places a tip is considered an extra gratuity over and above the service charge** but the existence of a fixed service charge cancels your tipping obligation.

Tip in local money whenever possible. Residents of some countries appreciate tips in U.S. currency but don't do it unless you're sure it's desirable. Tipping customs vary, though few places, particularly those frequented by travelers, discourage tipping. Some Asian countries traditionally frowned on it but have begun to accept it from guests. Some Latin American countries seem to require tipping to accomplish even routine matters.

INTERNATIONAL STANDARDS FOR GRATUITIES		
LOCATION	TAXI	DINING
AUSTRALIA	15%	15%
AUSTRIA	10%	10%
BELGIUM	Included in fare	Usually included
CANADA	15%	15%
CHINA	Included in fare	Included
DENMARK	Included in fare	Usually included
FRANCE	15%	Usually included
GERMANY	Included in fare	Usually included
HONG KONG	5%	10%
ITALY	10%	15%
HOLLAND	10%	Usually included
INDIA	Included	10%
INDONESIA	10%	10%
JAPAN	Included	Included
MALAYSIA	10%	10%
NEW ZEALAND	Included in fare	Usually included
THE PHILIPPINES	10%	15%
PORTUGAL	10%	15%
SINGAPORE	Included	Included
SPAIN	10%	10%
SWEDEN	10%	Usually included
UNITED KINGDOM	15%	15%

Cost of the most expensive suite at The Plaza in Manhattan: $15,000 per night.

TRAVEL INSURANCE

CREDIT CARD PROTECTION

The travel insurance provided by credit and charge cards is yours simply for using the card to make travel purchases. If you carry several cards, check the travel-related benefits of each so you can decide which to use for specific purposes. Every credit card allows you to dispute an invalid or unfair charge. If a tour operator or airline defaults, for example, you can request a chargeback and avoid the laborious and sometimes fruitless process of trying to get your money back from the supplier.

- **Charges can be removed from your bill immediately** or it can take months. The difference is the immediate clarity of the situation, the vendor's willingness to acknowledge that your request is justified and your ability to insist on prompt action. If the vendor disputes your right to a chargeback you'll be asked to provide complete documentation.

- **Interest may not be charged** on disputed amounts but the amounts will remain on your bill until the dispute is settled.

- **Dispute deadlines** vary by card and issuing bank. At minimum, you have 60 days to notify the credit card company. You can notify by phone but always follow up with a letter. Your dispute must be acknowledged within 30 days. Resolution must be achieved within 90 days.

- **If your credit card company denies the chargeback,** appeal to the appropriate regulatory entity. Visa and MasterCard are regulated by agencies covering the bank that issues their cards. Call and ask for the name and number you need. American Express appeals go to the Federal Trade Commission, 202-326-2222. You can also contact the Better Business Bureau in the city where the vendor is based. This is one area where they have a great record of achieving settlements beneficial to consumers.

The most expensive frequent flyer credit card: United Airlines/First Chicago at prime plus 9.9%.

THREE INSURANCE OPTIONS

There are three basic sources for travel insurance. Trip insurance can cover moderate risk factors as well as things that would concern only the most worry-prone. Before you purchase additional insurance, check the automatic insurance provisions on your major credit cards, your existing general policies, and coverage included with association or automobile club memberships. You can also usually add travel-related coverage to your existing general policies at an annual cost lower than what you would pay for separate, per-trip coverage.

- **Retail insurance** is sold by travel agents and insurance companies. Trip Cancellation Insurance (TCI) averages $7 per $100 in trip cost. You can get TCI coverage for more than your actual trip cost but overbuying doesn't pay because benefits are limited to the actual loss. Emergency Medical Evacuation (EME) coverage may be included in TCI packages or you can purchase it separately for about $55 for a two-week trip. For full information:

> **Access America**
> 800-284-8300
>
> **TeleTrip/Mutual of Omaha**
> 800-228-9792
>
> **Travel Insured/The Travelers**
> 800-243-3174

- **Vendor provided insurance** is sold by cruise and tour operators with policies underwritten by a separate financial entity. If the policy's financial pool is not isolated, don't purchase coverage unless you're confident in the company's solvency. Packages average $65 for ten-day trips.

- **Waiver coverage,** in which vendors agree to waive trip cancel penalties under certain conditions, can be relied on in lieu of TCI coverage. It only guarantees reimbursement for a specified portion of your cost. The closer you get to departure date, the less coverage you have. Most waivers rescind coverage a stated number of days prior to departure.

TRIP CANCELLATION INSURANCE

Trip Cancellation Insurance (TCI) protects you against four variables.

- **Serious illness or death** of the traveler or, in some cases, a family member or business colleague. Pre-existing conditions are exempt for specified time periods and injuries that occur during active sports are usually precluded from coverage.

- **Contingencies at home** that prevent you from traveling–fire, flood, car wreck, jury duty or weather catastrophe.

- **Destination disasters** including earthquakes, quarantines, terrorist activity or general strikes.

- **Operator failure**–but be aware that most coverage is contingent on the vendor officially filing bankruptcy. Most failed companies never do. Many policies won't cover default by the entity that sold the travel directly to you but they do cover failures by the airlines, tour operators and cruise lines the company used to book your trip. That means buying from an agency gives you a tier of protection not available if you buy direct.

TCI's usually pay the non-refundable portion of what you've paid for your trip minus refunds paid directly to you by ven-

---

Number of flights cancelled during the east coast blizzard of December 1995: over 10,000.

dors. If you have to postpone your departure or leave a tour midway for covered reasons they should pay for alternate transportation.

MEDICAL INSURANCE

Emergency Medical Evacuation insurance (EME) pays for air ambulances and other emergency transportation needs, as well as medical areas not always covered by standard health insurance and health maintenance organizations. It can fill in gaps on policies that limit coverage outside the U.S. and may be particularly desirable for seniors, as Medicare covers very limited medical needs internationally. If you don't carry a credit or membership card that gives you supplemental medical coverage, EME protection can be advantageous. If you travel often be sure to check with your primary insurance carrier to see if it would be less expensive to add coverage to your existing policy. You might save money over purchasing EME coverage each time you travel.

- **Emergency medical insurance** offers TCI options but exclusions on cancellation provisions are extensive. If you want TCI and EME buy TCI-based coverage. If medical emergencies are your primary concern, choose EME policies. Some of the best sources:

> **Health Care Abroad/Global**
> 800-237-6615
>
> **TravelMed**
> 800-937-1387
>
> **Worldwide Assistance**
> 800-821-2828

Evaluating Coverage

Evaluate coverage by checking which benefits are included and where they fit on the standard scale of possibilities. Also bear in mind the features that are most important to you and make them the deciding factors in your choice of coverage. Not all policies cover all of the items listed below.

- **Cost** will range from $5.50-9 per $100 of trip cost.

- **Pre-existing condition** windows for medical coverage range from 60-90 days.

- **Medical coverage** benefits range from $3,000-10,000.

- **Emergency medical evacuation** coverage ranges from $20,000-100,000.

- **Benefits for accidents** range from $10,000-100,000.

- **Baggage protection** ranges from $500 -1500 above the carrier's limit.

- **Primary Collision and Damage Waiver** benefits for vehicle rentals should be a minimum of $25,000.

CAR RENTAL INSURANCE

Collision insurance on car rentals is covered extensively in the *Car Rental* section. We'll re-cap the highlights here.

- **Most U.S. travelers with premium credit cards** can comfortably decline the $7-18 per day Collision and Damage Waiver coverage emphatically suggested by car rental companies.

- **Your private auto insurance** may also include coverage on rental cars though the trend is to limited coverage, particularly for business travel.

- **When traveling abroad,** arrange car rentals before leaving the U.S. or deal with major companies who are more likely to accept your credit card's coverage provisions.

CALLING FROM THE ROAD

THE LONG DISTANCE JUNGLE

Ma Bell now has second cousins, kissing cousins and distant relatives. You have to shop your way through the calling card maze. Your best choice depends on where you travel, calling patterns, communications needs, savings versus convenience and multiple service discounts. Choose the card with the best rates on the options you'll use the most.

The most important rule with any calling card or long-distance service is to monitor your bills. Rates change often. The great deal that caused you to choose a particular company may disappear a few months after you sign up. Unless you're a thorough reader of every bit of fine print that comes your way, you won't know about the changes without looking at the per-minute cost of every bill.

CHOOSING A CARRIER

The Big 3 or the ever-increasing 300? AT&T, MCI and **Sprint** offer the widest array of services. Smaller companies' price structures vary widely. Some small companies charge exorbitant amounts for access to their systems, others provide rates comparable or even below the "Big 3." Discount deals are possible but cut through the hype and compare facts. Disregard special introductory rates unless you plan to change carriers often.

Domestic credit card access numbers for the Big 3:

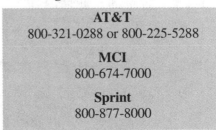

AT&T
800-321-0288 or 800-225-5288

MCI
800-674-7000

Sprint
800-877-8000

Country where phone directory listings are by first name and nickname: Iceland.

Evaluate added cost options. Special services vary from company to company and include:

- **Message delivery**–if you can't get through, leave a one-minute message at the press of a button.

- **Enhanced fax options** for multiple sends and retries.

- **500 numbers** that give your callers one number to reach you anywhere within the continental U.S.

- **800 voice mail** that allows you to retrieve messages from any touchtone phone.

- **Accounting codes** to simplify client billing.

- **Interpreter services** in as many as 140 languages.

- **Radio/telephone service** to connect you to cruise ships and seafaring vessels.

- **Travel services** that include destination-specific calling info, three-way speed calling and weather information.

"The BEST FARES Calling Card will stand up to your scrutiny with rates that will definitely save you money because we designed it for travelers. It has no start-up fee or surcharges, is good for domestic and international calls and offers free speed-dial numbers plus abbreviated dialing. You'll save 55-80¢ per three-minute call compared to major carrier rates."

PAY PHONE PARANOIA

Pay phone paranoia is a requirement of budget-wise living, unless you want to pay as much as ten times the standard rates. **Under deregulation, the only long-distance rates subject to federal restriction are AT&T's.** The theory was that operator service providers (OSP's) would lower rates through competition. As usual, when ever the government steps in, theory goes out the window. In practice many privately owned pay phones automatically connect you to their high-dollar carriers and additional fee services. A recorded announcement must precede all long-distance calls and tell you which carrier you're on. Switch to the carrier of your choice by using your access number or enter "00" and demand to be connected.

"New rate caps have been proposed, but in the meantime, don't trust the label on the pay phone."

COMPLAINTS ABOUT PRICE-GOUGING

With all the recent changes in the telecommunications field, there have been many complaints generated with regard to price gouging. Complaints should be addressed to the Federal Communications Commission (FCC), Enforcement Division, Common Carrier Bureau, 2025 M St. NW, Suite 6202, Washington, DC 20554 at 202-632-7553, or your state's consumer protection agency. You can also contact the FCC, Public Service Division by phone at 202-418-0190.

DEBIT CARDS

Debit cards are purchased for a specific dollar value and allow you the equivalent amount in phone service.

- **They are available from** vendors that range from convenience stores to travel companies.

- **Each card is good for services** equal to the purchase price. You use the card then throw it away, or if the vender allows the option, you recharge it.

- **You can pay as little as 20¢ per minute** or as much as 60¢.

- **Debit cards eliminate calling card per-call charges,** so they are particularly good for short calls, even when your calling card per-minute rate is lower.

- **Debit cards decrease phone card fraud** possibilities as theft is limited to the amount left on the card.

- **Get free bonus debit cards** during special promotions by car rental agencies and other travel-related vendors. *BEST FARES Discount Travel Magazine* keeps track of these offers and includes them in each issue.

Debit cards have been used internationally since the early '70s. Common points of sale are post offices and newsstands. Japan sells them from vending machines and local calls cost the equivalent of a dime. In France you can get debit cards at subway booths. They are routinely used by locals so ask for tips about where to buy them, how to use them and where to get the best values. Unlike U.S. debit cards, international cards cannot be used from hotel rooms.

FIGHTING HOTEL SURCHARGES

The trend is for hotels to reduce or eliminate phone access fees, usually number one in guest complaints. Resistance comes from the almost $1.8 billion in annual revenue that will be lost. Some chains allow member hotels to individually opt out of the move to eliminate fees. Beware of chains advertising the elimination of these charges when they only do so in high-dollar rooms used by five percent of the traveling public. Here's where things stood at press time:

- **Super 8, Ramada, Days Inn and Howard Johnson** are free to set their own policies. Most still use surcharges.

- **Quality Inns, Comfort Inns, Clarion and Econo Lodge** member hotels are encouraged to give free access but it's not mandated.

- **Hilton** has a no-fee policy at approximately 60% of its properties.

- **Hyatt** Business-Plus rooms eliminate the fee but other room categories are subject to 75¢ per call.

- **Marriott** has eliminated charges in about 90% of its hotels.

- **Radisson** exempts Business Class rooms and charges in others. Fees vary, but average 60¢ per call.

- **Sheraton** doesn't charge in Club Level rooms and is also phasing in the "non-fee" policy at all hotels.

- **Stouffer** has eliminated all fees.

- **Westin** charges 50¢-$1 per call; 800 numbers are free.

Don't be a captive caller. Ask about calling card access rates before you make your reservation. They can be free or cost as much as $1.25 per call. Let the reservation agent know this is a high priority item for you. Asking at check-in gives you the information but takes away your choice.

Access charges for 800 numbers have been cropping up since hotels realized customers were using MCI, Sprint and AT&T's 800 access numbers to avoid their per-call fees. You can get around the 800 number fee by entering a five-digit code before you enter your carrier's 800 access number:

AT&T
10-288-then Dial 1-Area Code and #

Sprint
10-333 gets you the Operator

MCI
10-222

Blocking specific long-distance carriers to keep you locked in to the hotel's preferred carrier is being phased out by law and most hotels have already complied. Until 1997, it remains legal if the hotel claims a cost of more than $15 per line to remove the block. If you get a persistent busy signal after you enter an access number, you may have been blocked. Call the desk and demand to be given an access route and make sure you're not charged extra for it. Hotels and pay phones, by law, must agree to your request to be allowed access to your carriers. The access rate must be the same for all three major companies, but can vary for the smaller independent carriers.

> **"**Minimize access rates by grouping calls and hitting the pound sign between each call. This should allow you multiple calls at a single-call rate.**"**

Normal discount times—nights and weekends—aren't usually discounted when you make a direct-dial call from your room. Hotels reap the savings and keep them for themselves. Always use access numbers when possible.

Calling card calls are cheaper than direct-dial even at hotels charging the highest fees. Direct-dial calls billed to your room carry up to a 40% surcharge. Rates are comparable to operator-assisted calls even though no operator intervention is required.

Complain about outrageous bills. Guests have even been charged for incomplete calls. You'll get most charges removed and, at the same time, discourage price gouging. Malfunctions and limitations in billing systems result in overcharges about 40% of the time.

Head for the pay phones to avoid per-call fees but don't get caught in an inflated rate nightmare. Rates and conditions should be posted by each phone. If they're not, ask the desk for a copy, available to you by law.

> **"**If your hotel charges for local calls and you plan to make over 30, make a deal with the front desk for a flat fee.**"**

CLEVER CLUES TO SAVINGS

Business travelers save money when calling home by making calls at pre-designated times. Check in with the office at the same time every day. They can let your callers know when their messages will be relayed. Use the same technique when calling home to avoid busy signals and wasted time.

Avoid phone felons. A small industry of industrious felons routinely try to look over your shoulder or listen in to get your calling card number. If you have to repeat your calling card number to an operator, do so in the lowest possible voice. Phone felons immediately pass your number on to a network of people who can rack up thousands of dollars in calls in an hour. The numbers are usually sold to people who make high-dollar international calls.

Cellular phones are high on thieves' wish lists. Some also like to steal the numbers, which can be picked up by scanners in slow-moving traffic. Turn your unit off when traffic slows to a crawl. Line protection features are also available.

Renting cellular phones from car rental agencies and hotels seems attractive particularly when the rental is free. Even a $5 per day charge (plus $1.75-2.50 per minute) may tempt you. Unfortunately, your liability for a lost or stolen cellular rental averages $500-800–much higher than the cost of replacing your own. You can ask about special add-on insurance but it isn't yet generally available. With roaming fees coming down, carrying your own cell phone may be your best choice.

Consider a nationwide pager. You can get a numbers-only version or an alpha-numeric pager that will relay about a paragraph of words and letters. If you choose the second option, you'll need to join a service that can transmit the text of the page. Alpha-numeric pagers can eliminate as many as half the long distance calls you usually make from the road.

Minimize use of in-flight phones. The average rate is $5 for the first minute and $2.50 for each additional minute.

Personal toll-free numbers save money on frequent calls home by sidestepping many of the fees inherent in calling from the road. The charge is about $5 per month and 20-25¢ per call. You don't have to change your current long- distance carrier to get toll-free service from a competitor. Business travelers who are calling their home office on a routine basis should consider setting up a special toll-free number for calls. If your office toll-free rate is 15¢ per minute you avoid access charges of up to 80¢ per call and rates as high as 35¢ per minute.

INTERNATIONAL CALL BACK PROGRAMS

Call Back Programs are technology's newest gift to travelers.

- **You enter an 800 number**, hang up after one ring then get an immediate call back from the switching company, providing you with a dial tone.

- **This system electronically originates your calls in the U.S.** where rates are lower and you're hooked into providers who buy bulk time at discount rates.

66Save by placing multiple calls to eliminate duplicate dial-in charges.99

- **Membership programs** may have start up fees, monthly minimums and per-call charges. You must pay for the dial-in call if you are in a country that doesn't allow access to toll-free numbers, but you will still save overall.

- **Check out details** from TeleGroup, 800-338-0225, AT&T, Sprint and MCI. They all claim 40%-80% in savings.

OTHER INTERNATIONAL SAVINGS

Public phones in other countries are used most efficiently with debit cards. You avoid the hassle of mastering and carrying foreign coins. They work for local, inter-country and long-distance calls and are available in over 170 countries. Each card can only be used in the country of issue.

Taxiphones are pay phones that calculate your cost based on call length and distance covered. Many countries have pay phones that charge by this method, even for "local" calls.

International telephone and telegraph offices are found in most major cities and offer competitive rates for infrequent callers. You give the number you wish to call to the clerk who places the call for you and shows you to a private booth. You pay on completion of your call.

Access English-speaking operators from 110 international destinations via programs available from AT&T, Sprint and MCI. You get a wallet-size plastic card with all access information. Call the following numbers to sign up for their programs:

AT&T's USADirect
800-331-1140

MCI's Call USA
800-444-3333

Sprint Express
800-877-7746

"If you travel heavily, consider a toll-free number billed to your home. Residential billings are eligible for discounts up to 25% plus you earn extra points not available on business accounts."

Most foreign directories have a page written in English with numbers for multilingual operators.

Calling U.S. directory assistance from abroad averages over $3 per call. Carry frequently called numbers with you.

In dire emergencies, friends and family can reach you via the Office of Overseas Citizens Services, 202-647-5225. This U.S. State Department service will contact the embassy in the country you're visiting and try to find you even without precise phone numbers or hotel information.

American Express cardholders with lengthy itineraries can get letters from home via a free service available through 1,700 worldwide offices. Use it to save phone costs on routine communications. Call your local AmEx office for the address for each destination you'll visit. Letters are held for up to 30 days.

RAIL TRAVEL

DOMESTIC TRAIN TRAVEL

Why Travel By Rail?

Some of the advantages of traveling the U.S. by rail are some of the same things that could be seen as disadvantages. It's a matter of perspective. Train travel buys you time to relax, transportation from city center to city center and, even in coach, seats that remain comfortable on long journeys.

Rail Cost vs. Air

Consumers are often shocked to discover that they won't always save a bundle when going by rail. The common belief is that the convenience that's sacrificed will add up to big savings. Sometimes the cost of train travel is greater than the price of an airline ticket. If you book a sleeping berth for long journeys, you'll definitely pay more. Here's a sample of how train and air fares compare.

AIR VS. TRAIN				
ITINERARY	AMTRAK COACH	AMTRAK SLEEPING BERTH	AMTRAK TRAVEL TIME	EXCURSION AIRFARE
DALLAS/CHICAGO	$352	$646	21.5 hrs.	$419
NEW YORK CITY/MIAMI	$292	$490	28 hrs.	$184
ST. LOUIS/LOS ANGELES	$492	$980	40.5 hrs.	$290
SEATTLE/NEW YORK CITY	$532	$1426	66 hrs.	$350
NEW ORLEANS/PHILADELPHIA	$370	$910	27 hrs.	$486

Britain's only disco train: The Nightclub Belle, part of the preserved Llangollen Railway in North Wales.

Fare Classifications

Coach travel is standard except for Club and Custom Class, available on some trains with more luxurious service and increased seating options. General coach seats are not reserved. Club and Custom class seats are reserved and Club service includes one meal served at your seat.

First class passengers are those with Club and sleeping car tickets. First class includes the use of private Metropolitan Lounges at stations in New York City, Chicago, Philadelphia and Washington, DC. Each lounge has comfortable seating areas, desks, phone and fax, free beverages and reading material.

Metroliner service is available in the Northeast. It designates trains with few or no intermediate stops. Metroliner service can cost as much as double other trains on the same routes and sometimes saves only 15 or 20 minutes in total travel time.

Sleeping cars will add between $60-600 per night to your ticket cost, depending on the time of year and type of accommodation. Meals are included with most tickets and choices vary by train. Here are the most common types of sleeping car accommodations.

- **A roomette** accommodates one person with an arm chair and pullout bed. The toilet and sink are in the same area. You won't be able to use them when the bed is folded down.

- **A bedroom** has either two chairs or one sofa, two folding beds and a separate bathroom.

- **A deluxe bedroom** has a sofa and two chairs, two beds, toilet and shower.

- **A family bedroom** can accommodate up to four people.

Amtrak Discounts

Standard discounts are always available on Amtrak.

- **Children ages two to 15:** 50% off when traveling with a full fare passenger. Children two and under travel for free with a full fare passenger but separate seating is not guaranteed.

- **Seniors ages 62 and above:** 15% off coach fares Monday through Thursday. The discount does not apply to sleeper cars, Auto-trains, Metroliners, Club Service or Custom Class passengers.

- **Amtrak All Aboard America** divides the nation into three regions, East, West and Central. Tickets range from $179 (off-peak/one region) to $329 (peak/all three regions) within specified travel periods. Peak season is mid-June to mid-August.

- **Amtrak Travel Packages** discount train and hotel combinations. A free "Travel Planner" is published twice a year and details special offers.

- **Amtrak and United Airlines** offer rail/air packages between 86 cities.

- **USA Rail Passes,** similar to Eurailpasses, are available only to residents of countries other than the U.S. and must be purchased in the traveler's home country. These are worth looking into for non-residents who want to see the United States from ground level.

Seasonal and promotional discounts include package trips, off-season discounts and special sales. Always ask if any special discount is being offered. One recurring promotion is "Amtrak Meets You More Than Half Way" with discounts up to 55% on tickets $75 and above. Ask about group rates if you have as few as four people traveling together. What con-

---

Length and cost of the Channel Tunnel: 23.6 miles and cost $15 billion.

stitutes a group varies by train, routing and season.

Amtrak Ticket Policies

Most tickets are fully refundable as long as no portion has been used. Passengers holding tickets for sleeping accommodations must cancel at least 48 hours in advance to avoid substantial cancellation penalties. Club Service ticket holders must cancel at least one hour in advance or be assessed a penalty equal to 50% of the fare. Lost or stolen tickets are generally not refunded.

> **"** *The fuel efficiency of three major modes of travel puts rail travel at the top of the fuel-efficiency list. According to the Worldwatch Institute, inter-city trains use one-third the fuel per passenger as commercial airlines and one-sixth the fuel used to travel the same distance in a car carrying one passenger.* **"**

INTERNATIONAL TRAIN TRAVEL

Trains Present & Future

We often see air travel as the wave of the future but other countries are counting on enhanced rail service to promote tourism, fight pollution and provide the transportation of choice for the next century. High-speed rail will soon link every major European city and help ease the loads of over 25 European airports that will reach capacity at the turn of the century, if not before. Rail traffic in India has quadrupled in the past four decades. China is investing $20 billion in rail expansion.

Saving On Trains In Europe

Most European governments are committed to mass transit. High-speed trains, excellent track maintenance and competitive rates are the result. High-tech trains attain speeds up to 170 mph, but even older trains average 90 mph. You'll save money by taking the train in Europe depending on a few key factors:

- **Number of people traveling.** A solo traveler almost always saves by taking the train. Two or more travelers should compare available car rental deals versus the cost of multiple rail fares or passes. A subcompact car is often cheaper than two rail passes but remember how small a subcompact is in European terms. Three to four people are almost always better off renting a car and can usually acquire a mid-size car for less than the cost of rail passes.

- **Itinerary.** If your trip focuses on major cities, the train gains a big edge. It takes you to the city center and saves you overnight parking costs that average $10-20 per night. If you plan to cover a lot of ground in countries with extensive toll roads (Austria, France, Greece, Italy, Portugal and Spain) you can add $5-30 per day to your cost.

- **Length of travel.** The only financially sanc rates on rental cars in Europe require a minimum of five to seven days (three in rare promotional instances). If you're spending less time, take the train.

- **Sightseeing** will be enhanced by traveling on rail. Travelers often see more of the country and parts of the country not normally seen by the average tourist.

The world's longest continuous rail line: the Trans-Siberian Railway from Moscow to Vladivostok.

Passes vs. Individual Tickets

The Eurailpass and other rail passes provide definite financial advantages if you are traveling extensively. If your inter-city travel is light, individual tickets may be your best bet. You can make your choice by calculating the number of miles you plan to cover per country and multiplying that figure by the average per-mile ticket costs. If the figure you get is markedly lower than the best rail pass option, individual tickets are for you. If you've bought a Eurailpass in the past, don't rely on what you paid then. Costs have risen between five to 18 percent in the past year. Here are average per-mile costs per country:

AVERAGE PER-MILE COSTS PER COUNTRY		
COUNTRIES	**SECOND CLASS PER MILE**	**FIRST CLASS PER MILE**
Denmark, Finland, Hungary, Poland, Portugal, Slovakia and Spain	11¢	16¢
Austria, Belgium, France, Greece, the Netherlands, Norway and Sweden	29¢	19¢
Britain, Germany, Ireland and Switzerland	45¢	30¢

An easy way to decide if a pass is more economical than individual tickets is to estimate the number of miles you plan to cover in a specific time period. If your figure is above those below, a pass is generally your best bet.

- 2,000 miles in 15 days
- 2,300 miles in 21 days
- 2,800 miles in 30 days
- 4,500 miles in 90 days

Eurailpass Specifics

The two countries in Western Europe not covered by Eurailpasses are Britain and Hungary. All other major national railways are covered.

Get the best price by buying your passes before you leave the United States. The discount pass prices are designed for visitors rather than local rail travelers. Some passes are available abroad but if they are, you will almost always pay a minimum of 20% above the advance purchase price.

Many passes can only be purchased in your home country.

Find the best Eurailpass for your needs by comparing the options available.

- **First Class** usually costs about 50% more and may be worth it for comfortable travel during busy periods. Second Class is usually available at youth and student traveler prices.

- **A full-time pass** lets you travel as often as you like during the valid period of the pass.

- **A flexible pass** lets you travel on a prescribed number of days within the period of validity. An example–five days of travel allotted within the two-month period covered by a pass.

- **A First-class Saverpass** is available for groups of three or more traveling together or two or more traveling together during October through March. One group pass is issued.

European country not included in Eurailpasses: Britain.

- **Rail/car passes** give you a specified number of rail days and a specified number of car rental days. A few passes offer rail/air options.

A Eurailpass lets you travel in all the countries included in its service range. The less expensive EuroPass is a better option for travelers planning to visit France, Germany, Italy, Spain and Switzerland only. You can visit all five or, for the cheapest option, select three countries.

A Eurailpass may also give you free or discounted travel on some suburban trains, national bus systems and ferries.

Eurail and EuroPass prices start at $255. First-class passes start at $348. Each provides five days of travel. Costs go up to $1,398 for 90 days of unlimited first class travel.

European Countries With Their Own Rail Passes

When your travel will mainly occur in one country, a country-specific rail pass may be your most economical choice. Check with your travel agent for prices or call the tourism office for the appropriate country. (Telephone numbers are listed in our *Know Who To Call* section.) When passes cover more than one country, all countries included are listed. Children under four travel free with adults except where noted. European countries offering rail passes include:

- **The United Kingdom,** (the only Western European country not participating in Eurailpasses) offers BritPass, BritGermany Pass, BritIreland Pass, and BritFrance. Various discounts are offered for children, students and seniors. Travel in Wales and Scotland is included and some passes include ferry travel.

- **The Bennelux Tourrail Pass** covers Belgium, the Netherlands and Luxembourg. Discounted Junior Passes are offered for students under 26.

- **The Greek Railpass** has a rail and fly option with Olympic Airways. Children ages four to 11 pay half price.

- **The Spain Railpass** offers rail and drive options. Children ages four to 11 pay half price.

- **The Portuguese Flexipass** has rail and drive options. Children ages four to 11 pay half price.

- **The Bulgaria Railpass** discounts fares for children ages four to 12 by 50%.

- **The Norway Railpass** offers standard and flexi-pass versions with discounted prices for low season, October through April.

- **The Scanrail Pass** covers Denmark, Norway, Sweden and Finland. Children ages four to 11 pay half fare. Rail and drive options are available.

- **The Finland Railpass** offers 50% off to children ages six to 17. Children under six travel free.

- **The Swiss Travel System** offers the Swiss Pass and Swiss Flexipass covering the Swiss Federal Railway routes plus many private railways, lake steamers, motorcoaches, cable cars and municipal buses. Children ages 16 and under are free with an accompanying adult. A discounted version, the Swiss Card, offers limited versions of the same services. Rail and drive options are available.

- **The Austrian Railpass** also covers lake ferries and steamers. Children ages seven to 15 have discounted fares; children up to six years of age travel free.

- **The European East Pass** covers Austria, the Czech Republic, Hungary, Poland and Slovakia. Children ages four to 11 pay half fare.

- **The Czech Flexipass** offers half-fare tickets for children ages four to 13.

- **The Hungarian Flexipass** offers half-fare to children ages five to 14.

- **The Polrailpass** offers half-price tickets to children under ten and discounted tickets for ages ten to 26.

- **The Central Europe Pass** covers travel in Germany, Poland, the Czech Republic and Slovakia. Children ages four to 11 pay half fare.

- **The GermanRail Pass** offers Flexi-pass options, TwinPass discounts for two or more adults traveling together, Junior Fares (ages 12 to 26) and half-price fares for children ages four to 11.

- **The Italian Railpass** offers a Flexipass option. Children ages four to 11 pay half fare.

Knowledgeable Sources For Rail Passes

Get full information on rates and options by contacting the organizations in this chart. It will be particularly helpful if your travel agent doesn't handle enough international rail business to be on top of current offerings.

RAIL PASS SOURCES		
PASSES SOLD	**SOURCE & PHONE**	**ADDRESS**
Eurail, Benelux, BritFrance, Czech Republic, European East, France, Greece, Hungary, Poland, Portugal, Russia, Scandinavia, Spain and Switzerland	Rail Europe 800-438-7245	226 Westchester Ave. White Plains, NY 10604
Eurail and most Central European passes	Forsyth Travel Library 800-367-7984	9154 W. 57th St. Mission, KS 66201
Eurail, Austria, Benelux, Britain, Germany and Italy	DER Tours/German Rail 800-421-2929	9501 W. Devon Ave. Suite 400 Rosemont, IL 60018
BritFrance, BritGermany, BritIreland, BritRail and Chunnel tickets	BritRail Travel International 212-575-2667	1500 Broadway New York, NY 10036
Benelux and Netherlands	Netherlands Board of Tourism 312-819-0300	225 Michigan Ave. Chicago, IL 60601
Austria, Czech Republic, Eastern Europe, Hungary and Poland	Orbis Polish Travel Bureau 800-223-6037	342 Madison Ave. New York, NY 10173
Eurail, Finland and Scandinavia	Scantours 800-223-7226	1535 Sixth St. Santa Monica, CA 90401

Senior Euro Discounts

Senior discounts are not automatic when you travel by rail in Europe. Some passes will provide a discount in exchange for any proof of age. Others require you to purchase an official senior ID with fees that can vary from $6-64. You also have to supply a passport-type photo so it's a good idea to carry a few extras to save the on-the-spot expense.

The Guide To European Railpasses is published annually. It lists prices for passes only available in Europe as well as prices for Eurail, country passes and rail and drive options. It can help you decide whether you're better off purchasing passes or buying tickets as you go. Write to Europe Through the Back Door, Box 2009, Edmonds, WA 98020; call 206-670-6544.

Other Available Train Passes

Please note that almost all passes must be purchased before you arrive in the host country. Students ages 12-25 get sizeable discounts when showing an International Student ID.

TRAIN PASSES	
LOCATION/PASSES AVAILABLE	**PRICE RANGE**
CANADA/CANRAIL PASS 800-561-3949	Allows 12 days unlimited travel within a 30-day period. Low season (early January through the end of May and October 1 through mid-December) prices are $270/adult; $247 for people 25 and under and 60 and over. High season is $395 and $356. Passes are invalid December 15 to January 5.
AUSTRALIA/AUSTRAILPASS KANGAROO ROAD 'N' RAIL PASS 800-423-2880	Unlimited travel ranges from $326 for 14 days economy class to $825 for 30 days in first class. Flexi-passes range from $255 for eight days of economy travel in a two-month period to 15 first class days in a two-month period for $593. Road and rail passes include bus travel and range from $491-1,148.
JAPAN/JAPAN RAILWAY (JR) PASS 800-223-0266	Passes range from $270 for an Ordinary (economy) seven-day pass to $780 for a 21-day Green (first class) pass. Children six to 11 get 50% off. Travel on all bullet trains, and some buses and ferries is included.
RUSSIA/RUSSIAN FLEXI-PASS 800-848-7245	Passes are valid for travel between all major cities. Current prices for four days of travel in a 15-day period are $289 for first class and $198 for second class.
INDIA/INDRAIL PASS 212-957-3000	Passes come in three classes: Air-conditioned First Class, Regular First Class and Second Class. Prices range from $30 for a one-day Second Class pass to $975 for a 90-day air-conditioned First Class pass.

Two classes of train travel in Japan: green (first class) and ordinary (economy).

TRAVEL GUIDE

How many times have you felt like you were lost in the travel jungle and would never find a guide who knows? This chapter begins by telling you how to find your most effective allies in discount travel. I have great respect for good travel agents. They work in a field with lightning-quick changes. Their expertise is expected to encompass an entire globe. Their work produces incredible amounts of revenue for travel vendors and, too often, they are under-appreciated and even bullied, just for trying to get their clients the best deals.

I believe that today's travelers deserve specialists. The travel world has become too big for any one person or agency to stay on top of. I'll explain how my specialist concept works, tell you how to make sure you're dealing with creative agents and show you how to help your agents get you the deepest discounts.

Travelers' Cautions deals with solving problems and getting action on your travel-related complaints. It goes on to expose the hundreds of travel scams that are costing the unwary billions of dollars each year. You'll be able to do your part to stop the dollar drain with my "scam stoppers," which plug the holes scammers are trying to poke in your pocket.

Luggage Logic details checked luggage and carry-on policies, how to deal with lost luggage, what to ask for when you're buying new luggage and details tips developed by those of us who have learned by trial and error how to pack effectively.

Health Highlights helps you to decide when medical circumstances could affect your travel plans, helps you to prepare for low stress travel and teaches you ways to help your body adapt to the demands of every trip.

Travel by Land shows you how to save money and optimize convenience when you travel by car, recreational vehicle (RV) or bus.

Special Travel Categories provides tips on five significant areas of travel:

- **Traveling Solo** can be one of the best ways to go if you recognize the positives and learn trip-enhancing singles strategies. For those who would like a travel companion, there are ideas on what to look for and where to start your search.

- **Senior Travel** reminds seniors of the power they have as travel consumers, outlines standard senior savings and looks at some unique opportunities for sensational senior trips.

- **Children & Travel** can be a perfect match if you prepare yourself **and** your children to know the basic rules of travel by air, road and rail. We'll help make it easier on the whole family while in restaurants, hotels and out and about.

- **Traveling With Animals** lets you know when you can, if you should and how to do it in ways that cause the least stress on your pet and on yourself.

- **International Travel** has nuts and bolts data on passports, visas and customs. I'll also tell you how to make language barriers disappear, the best times for European travel, where to get the great, new Hot Cards that save you money in every major international city and where to go to get enough free information to make you feel as if you've had the services of a personal travel planner.

The world becomes smaller and travel problems seem to grow larger but I've cut them back down to size. Travel can be enjoyable again—as long as you have a guide.

A CONSUMERS GUIDE TO TRAVEL AGENTS

A TRAVELER'S CHOICE

Consumers are faced with options that did not exist a week ago and prices that change in the blink of a marketing department's eye. Gone are the simple days of basic fare structures and limited choices. To get the best deals in today's market you have to know about possibilities. There are four basic sources for travel information:

Travel agencies, perhaps more than any industry, must adapt to rapid change. Many agents feel as if they're being squeezed out by changes in airline policies, commission structuring that favors volume sellers and the increased popularity of niche carriers.

Vendors (airlines, hotels, cruise lines, car rental agencies and other travel suppliers) quote prices that don't neces-

66Good travel agents are worth their weight in gold cards. When you find agents who understand you and are willing to work to get you what you want, you've found allies who will save you hundreds or thousands of dollars every year. The travel industry is neither as lucrative nor glamorous as it seems. Everyone thinks agents travel a lot. That's sometimes true for owners but not for front-line agents. They have a few perks, but they're usually too busy earning their living to use them.99

sarily reflect the best they have to offer and certainly ignore the possibility of competitors' more favorable deals. The

---

The busiest air travel day in the U.S.: the day before Thanksgiving; busiest day of the week: Friday.

vendors' main goal is to maximize profit. Yours should be to maximize savings. People who routinely bargain shop for their other purchases too often tend to accept travel price quotes as if they were etched in stone. They're not. Accepting the first price a company gives you is like paying your income tax without taking even a standard deduction.

Online computer services such as America Online, Compuserve and Prodigy, or any direct links to the Internet, such as Air Mosaic or Netscape, offer a wealth of information. Sometimes they can provide arrows to point you in money-saving directions, but their best present use is to preview prospective vacation spots, connect you to information more current than any guidebook and keep you up to date on travel sources and industry trends. The wave of the future? Perhaps, but right now, using your computer as your primary booking source will rarely save you a dime. The on-line services are great as a guide, but don't overlook your travel agent as your best source of travel information:

Insider secrets provide tools to decipher and use travel information from all sources. They are your immediate pipeline to limited offers that often result in the highest possible savings on all aspects of travel. You, as the consumer, need to be as informed as possible to supplement any source you choose. How can you keep up with the ever-changing deals and promotions? You could hire a research team, form relationships with travel suppliers, subscribe to several hundred publications, access insider computer data and devote your life to discovering and digesting each month's tricks and trends. Or, subscribe to discount travel publications such as *BEST FARES Discount Travel Magazine*, which does all of this for you.

TRAVEL SPECIALISTS

An explosion of knowledge always creates the need for specialization. Fifty years ago a general practitioner could learn all there was to know about medicine. Now you'd never consider having an oncologist do an organ transplant or a neurologist perform open heart surgery. The theory carries through to travel.

You deserve specialists with intensive knowledge of their segment of the industry. Some larger agencies have created specialty areas but that doesn't guarantee the best deal if they're still geared to selling you computer-listed or rack rates, or if it's only a segment of their business.

> **"***Travel agents are expected to be the Jacks and Jills of all travel-selling trades **plus** have photographic memories. Most of us can't even remember which gas station offered the lowest price last week. It's unrealistic to expect an agent to automatically recall that two-for-one airfare to an alternate city, the 50% off car rental deal you can get because you're arriving on Tuesday and the hotel that will give your kids two free meals a day.***"*

Specialization allows for knowledge and clout which combine to offer the biggest possible discounts to consumers.

DISCOUNT AGENCIES

Low price is the primary orientation of discount agencies. The lower the ticket price, the less commission they make on the sale. Often they require that you have a firm idea of what you want before you call. Discount agencies are usually unable to hold reservations or provide a full line of services like "full service" agencies. They are not the people to ask about hotels in New Guinea or the availability of red convertibles at Atlanta car rental agencies. They concentrate on knowing the cheapest way to *get to* New Guinea, Atlanta or anywhere else on the globe.

Weigh special services against savings. Ticket delivery is convenient but not if it costs you creativity in ticketing. It's nice to have your customer profile information kept on file so you don't have to repeat it each time you make a purchase, but is saving three minutes worth paying more? If you opt for high-service agencies, you should do so only after knowing the real price you'll pay for the "free" extras.

CHOOSING AGENTS

You need to think creatively and so does your travel agent.

- **You want agents who know about alternate cities,** hidden cities, back-to-backs and niche carriers; who keep up on basic promotions and scan industry publications to monitor changes and trends. You don't want agents who can't see beyond their computer screens. For example, the top three niche carriers, including Southwest (one of the largest carriers in the nation), can't be booked via any travel agent's reservation system.

- **You want agents who sidestep "fixed" prices in travel** in favor of the many legitimate ways to get around them–agents who **enjoy** the challenge of finding the best bargains.

- **You want agents strong enough to look out for your interest.** Bravery may seem an unlikely criteria for evaluating travel agencies, but it's vital.

Some airlines try to intimidate agencies. Stepping out of arbitrary bounds can cause an agency to lose its right to ticket on the offended airline. You want agents who understand how to bend the rules while staying completely within the bounds of legitimacy.

- **Finding the right agent** is as important as finding the right agency. The quality of agents within a company almost always varies. You want an agent able to work the system, backed by an agency that encourages them to do so.

> **❝** When you find an agency that goes out of its way to please you, return the favor by allowing them to ticket for you, even if you've reserved directly with the airlines. You won't pay any more and you will be building a business relationship that will benefit you in many ways. **❞**

- **Experience counts but creativity counts more.** Fifteen years experience means little to the consumer if the agent has never learned the knack of creative ticketing.

TELL THEM WHAT YOU WANT

Let agents tell you if they can help on a particular aspect of travel. Corporate agencies may welcome the opportunity to refer you to another source; cruise planning for example. Discount agencies may not want to book car rentals. Smart agencies know when their needs and yours are compatible.

Ask agents how they'll help you find the best deal.

Percentage of travel agency-issued airline tickets that were handwritten in 1995: an estimated four percent.

- **Will they just check the computer** for the lowest published fares? What if your best option is a niche airline, a companion ticket or a charter?

- **Do they know about** creative ticketing? Ask specifically about options you've learned about in this book–niche airlines, back-to-backs, fly/drive packages, alternate airports and so forth.

- **Will they check** promotional offers? It isn't fair to expect an agent to know about them all. About one billion travel savings coupons are issued annually.

WHAT AGENTS NEED FROM YOU

Give agents everything they need to find your best deals:

- **Tell them how flexible you're willing to be.** Express preferences but give agents the freedom to offer alternatives that will save you money.

- **Be clear** about your departure city and specific about your destination. Don't let lack of clarity have you comparing the price of a ticket to Portland, Oregon, with one to Portland, Maine.

- **Tell them the number of people traveling** and any eligibility you have for special fares such as senior or government rates.

- **Fax your travel requests.** It saves time and eliminates any confusion on your travel requirements.

EMPHASIZE PRICE

Let travel agents know you want value. If the standard rate for a flight is $900, tell the agent you want it for $300. You want the $200-a-night hotel for $60; the $189-a-week car rental for $89; the $2,000-cruise for half that price. If you don't make it just that clear you're taking money out of your own pocket.

Go for double and triple whammies. You can collect discount coupons and use them during most fare wars. Get savings-times-three by tying your purchase in with a special frequent flyer deal.

Don't be fooled by jargon about limited seating. Special offer seats **are** limited, but if at first you don't succeed, try, try again! There is more than one airline in most markets, and inventory can change in a moment's notice. With persistence, you can generally get the rate you want on the date you need.

Ask about procedures on ticket prices that go down. Some agencies have computer systems or procedures to scan ticketed itineraries during fare wars and alert clients to lower prices. You may be required to pay a change fee to the airlines, but the savings often can be many times the fee. See Airline section for specific airline "downgrade" policies.

TESTING AN AGENT

There are two easy ways to test agents on options that are invisible to those who use the computer as a crutch:

- **Pick a pair of cities serviced by a niche carrier.** Call the niche airline to get the lowest possible rate between those cities. Usually picking dates less than a week in advance or dates without a Saturday stay will show the most dramatic savings over major carriers. Then call a couple agencies and simply ask for the best rate between the two cities you've chosen. Don't mention the niche carrier. See if they offer you that option or if they merely quote the lowest available major carrier price.

- **Check the Sunday travel section for charter flights.** From Dallas/Fort

Worth to Minneapolis, for example, MLT Tours offers a roundtrip to Minneapolis at about $222 with no advance purchase required. Calling ten agencies in the market and asking for the lowest fare between the two cities resulted in MLT flights being offered only once. In our test case, using that option would have saved as much as $700 roundtrip.

Get bids on all travel needs. It's one of the best ways to determine if an agency is really going to work for you. Call several agencies and tell them what you need. Make sure to give each agent the same specifics so your rate comparisons are apples-to-apples.

Check the reputation of travel agents locally. Ask friends and colleagues for recommendations and check with the Better Business Bureau or the Consumer Affairs office in your county or state. Membership in the American Society of Travel Agencies (ASTA) is often said to be an assurance of quality. ASTA can be very helpful in resolving disputes with member agencies, but it simply has no way of knowing up-front if an agency will comply by its standards.

WHAT AGENCIES CAN'T DO

Agents don't have the power to alter or waive airline rules. Listen carefully to terms and conditions. If your agent does not tell you about refund policies, ticketing deadlines and other pertinent facts, be sure to ask–or call the airline direct. Travel agencies do not set policies for vendors. Each airline has its own restrictions and rules. Surprisingly, an airline is generally more apt to extend special favors when asked directly by a passenger than if the travel agent tries to intercede on a passenger's behalf.

Travel agents aren't mind readers. Give them your feedback, both positive and negative. If they fail to find the lowest price, let them know. Don't hold an agent accountable unless you are sure that's where the fault lies.

Some agencies extend special courtesies to favored customers. The 24-hour ticketing deadline, for example, can be stretched to the agency's weekly ticket reporting deadline. These sorts of favors are technically violations of their agreements with the airlines so should never be demanded or expected as routine.

SERVICE FEES

Most travel agency services are free, but recent commission caps and other airline changes have placed the over 35,000 U.S. agencies in the unpleasant position of deciding whether or not to charge fees.

- **The commission cap limits commission** on a single domestic ticket to $50, rather than the approximate ten percent that was customary. It's estimated that this move took over $1 million in revenue per day from travel agencies and put it in airlines' coffers. In October 1995, for example, travel agency sales were up eight percent over the same month in 1994, but domestic commissions were down five percent.

❝Never pay a travel agent a service fee. If they try to impose it, you have two options–go direct to the airline or other travel supplier, or go to another agency. Certainly the commission on a $99 ticket doesn't cover overhead, but, as in all businesses, customer service can't always be predicated on immediate profit. ❞

Premium offered in 1995 for the purchase of a Finnair business class ticket: a Sony Watchman color television.

COMMISSION OVERRIDES & VENDOR PREFERENCE

Commission overrides encourage some agencies to steer you to a particular vendor. They occur when a specific vendor has agreed to increase the commission percentage paid to an agency if a certain total dollar amount is sold. It can be very tempting for an agency to try to steer clients to that vendor. They may even imply that their preferred carrier's price is the lowest when, in fact, it's the same as (maybe even higher than) competitors. Every agency wants to maximize its profit, but, in this case, it's at your expense.

Various vendors also offer incentive programs to agencies. They are usually limited to specific time periods and may provide an increased commission percentage, a bonus point system with points redeemable for gifts or a lowered travel agent cost (book ten clients with one car rental company, for example, and get a $10-day rate the next time the agent rents).

Agents may tell you about one company's special offer and neglect to mention competitors because they've just been visited by a sales rep and a particular deal is foremost in their minds. Always ask if competitors are offering equal or better deals. Most companies play follow the leader to some extent.

PROBLEMS WITH AGENTS

Talk to the agent first and try to resolve the problem. Most agent/client problems are the result of poor communication.

If you are not satisfied, go to the owner or manager. Give them a chance to explain and correct the situation. Be clear that your repeat business is contingent on the satisfaction they provide.

If you're still not satisfied, contact the airline or vendor the agent used. They are usually very willing to try to straighten out problems that involve their companies.

If you still need help, the Better Business Bureau or a consumer affair's office will serve as your advocate. You can also contact the Consumer Affairs Office of the American Society of Travel Agents if the agency in question is a member of that organization. Write to P.O. Box 23992, Washington, DC 20026-3992.

TRAVELERS' CAUTIONS

SCAMS

Telemarketing Tricks

Telemarketing piranhas sell travelers "dream deals" that burst like bubbles. Fifteen percent of all telemarketing fraud involves travel. Here are some tell-tale tip-offs that you may be involved with a trickster:

- **You've been specially selected**–you and everyone else with a telephone and a credit card.

- **You have to decide now** or lose the offer–choose option two.

- **You can't use the offer for 60 days**–or 90 days or some other unrea-sonable time lag. This gives the scammer time to rob you of your money and get out of town.

- **You've won a "free" prize**–but you have to buy something at a huge mark-up to claim it, and the prize is never what you're led to believe.

- **You've won a free week at a resort**–but you have to buy the airfare from the telemarketer at double or triple the best bargain fare.

- **You've won a $29 flight to Hawaii**–or any other city, but you have to book accommodations and/or car rentals from the telemarketer. This is the evil twin to the ploy above.

The first U.S. airport to install a computer card access security system: Las Vegas' McCarran International.

> **"**Once there was a man who sent an incredible number of faxes to businesses claiming that he had possession of exactly 2,333 airfare discount coupons, one of which he would mail on request in return for a $4.70 processing fee. The coupon allegedly was good for a discount on the bearer's choice of three major airlines plus a completely free roundtrip. (Give me a break!) To buy some time to take the money and run, the fax said the benefits were available only during a two-week period that didn't begin for six months. When the time came, guess what? He was nowhere to be found. Remember, these con artists can send you a travel certificate that looks and feels like a million dollars, that's not worth more than the paper it's printed on. Then again, that's what a con is all about.**"**

- **We can sell you a cruise for $495, air included**–You give your credit card number and the voucher arrives the next day. The problem? It's a worthless piece of paper. The reality? You really can get cruises for $495, but not through telemarketers.

- **We can give you two tours for the price of one**–but the base price is double or triple what you really should be paying. There are many legitimate two-for-one deals and the price for the first person may well be somewhat higher than the cheapest single ticket, but the price for both travelers should always be lower than the two cheapest fares combined.

The Scam Methodology

When you're asked to pay a processing fee watch out. Scammers use them to jack-up their low price quotes to the price they've intended you to pay all along.

If you're asked to name several acceptable travel dates, beware. It makes the deal sound as if it's in such high demand that it's hard to tell where they'll find room for you. It actually means the con is buying time. If you do get any of your choices (an unlikely prospect) a long list of surcharges and extra fees will suddenly apply.

Senior travelers comprise the highest percentage of victims of travel scams. They're more likely to be found at home, have more discretionary time and income and are deemed to be more trusting. Schemers will even act like long-lost friends just to make a sale.

Some scams prey on travelers' fears of escalating prices. They try to sell you five or ten year's worth of vacations at a very appealing price. You may even get to go on the first one but you're lucky if they're still around to provide vacation number two.

Scammers want to make you feel special. They'll pretend to offer you a better price than everyone else is getting, and sometimes, will pretend to ask their supervisor for permission to grant you an imaginary favor, all part of the scripted pitch.

Scams By Mail

The same scams that attack you by phone can arrive by postcard or letter. Sometimes they invite your response via a 900 number so you can pay by the minute for the privilege of being duped. Other written material comes in envelopes emblazoned with look-alike logos designed to make you think you're hearing from a well-known sweepstakes promoter.

Scams By Computer

This is the baby monster of the fraud industry. Old scams look new when they come cruising across the Internet.

800 Number Scams

Eight hundred numbers aren't always toll-free. A postcard tells you you've won a prize and instructs you to call a toll-free number to claim it. A week or two later you receive a bill designed to look a lot like the one you get from your local phone company. It contains per-minute charges for your "free prize" call–usually $3.99 per minute. If the spiel was good enough to keep you on the line for ten minutes (and it usually is) you end up paying $40 for a "free prize" that is usually just worth a couple of dollars.

How Scams Use Reputable Companies

"Free" vacation certificates are sometimes offered in promotions sponsored by reputable stores who haven't bothered to check out the worth of the bonus they're advertising. Example: a jewelry store offers a "free airfare" honeymoon certificate to engaged couples purchasing wedding rings. They've been convinced they're giving their customers something special but they're actually exposing them to a bait & switch tactic. Maybe the airfare is contingent on purchasing an overpriced hotel package. Maybe the available dates on the airfare are so limited that high "surcharges" come into play. Don't be swayed by any offer of this type. Reputable companies do give travel discounts away with many types of purchases, but you should always recognize the name of the vendor

and confirm the details and worth of the offer before you buy.

> **❝**If you have to pay to get details it's probably a scam. If a telescammer offers to send someone to your home to pick up a check, tell them you have a relative who lives near their office who will be happy to drop off the check and pick up the travel documents. You'll usually get a very quick hang-up. You can also ask any telescammer to send you all the details in writing so you can run them by your sister, the travel agent, or your brother, the attorney. Again, a quick dial tone. **❞**

Scam Stoppers

Never check an offer from a company you don't know by calling the numbers they provide. Get the names of the vendors they're using, get the phone numbers on your own and check it out. Scammers often provide numbers answered by their own employees who tell you whatever you want to hear.

Refuse to give your credit card number over the phone unless you have placed the call to a business you know to be legitimate.

Never agree to overnight a check. You could stop payment but why go through the bother and the expense? There is usually no good reason to pay for any travel with anything other than a major credit or charge card.

Always check your credit card statements. You may think you've turned down the deal but the most unscrupulous cons will put unauthorized charges on

---

your account once you give them your credit card number. They count on the fact that a certain percentage of people never review their bills. The charge can even appear under the name of a retail store or any type of business that agrees to have their merchant accounts used for a percentage of the take.

Comparison shop. If you're quoted a tempting price, call a travel agent or call the vendors direct. Any good deal will stand up to comparison shopping.

Demand precise information. "A five-star hotel specially chosen for you" could be five-star only in its inflated ability to sound good enough to fill the pockets of the scam.

Be alert for warning signs. At the first sign of suspicion, ask for the credentials of the caller. Check with suppliers allegedly involved with the trip. Demand a bank reference. A little research on your part can save you hundreds of dollars worth of regrets.

Don't fall for the referral gambit. The satisfied customers you'll be invited to call for references might be on the payroll.

If a deal sounds too good to be true, it probably is. There are real bargains out there, but they rarely come your way by unsolicited phone calls and mailings.

Misleading Advertising

Many offers exist within the elastic bounds of legality, but stretch the truth to the breaking point. Some forms of advertising, virtually unchallenged for years, still are misleading.

- **Car rental agencies** who rarely include Collision Damage and Liability Waivers in their advertised rates, except as fine-print information. True, they are usually optional, but, when accepted, they can nearly double your quoted rate.

- **Package tours** built around tickets to the Olympics or a special sporting event without tickets included. You'll be in the right place, but no closer to the event than the hotel television set.

> **"** *In 1993, over 1,000 University of Wisconsin football fans bought Rose Bowl packages but were stuck with no tickets to the actual game.* **"**

- **Airlines advertising one-way rates,** when in fact, a roundtrip ticket purchase is almost always required.

- **Hotels that advertise** double rooms using a per person rate. A $69-room is really $138.

- **Tour operators** who advertise entire packages as cheaper than air alone, but base their comparisons on ticket prices that are hardly ever used.

Credit Card Fraud

Protect your credit card number. It's printed on ticket receipts, itineraries and hotel bills. Keep these items secure or obscure the number with a black marker. If not, you've given a crook almost everything he needs to bill your account on purchases made by phone.

Avoid using your credit card number as identification.

Never carry more cards than you really need. One ATM card and two major credit cards should suffice.

Protect your telephone credit card number against eavesdroppers and shoulder surfers at pay-phones. Once they get your number they can feed it into a network that can literally run up hundreds of dollars in calls within an hour of the theft.

Travelers on lengthy trips should arrange to have someone trustworthy check their bank and credit card statements monthly. Anyone who knows you'll be gone for awhile can manipulate your accounts, since most banks have a 90-day limit on disputing withdrawals and checks. Credit card dispute limits vary by issuing bank.

International Incidents

"Travel experts" frequent tourist spots and offer deals that are hard to resist. They ask for up-front payment and never return with the promised goods.

Variation #2: The local experts say they can get a low hotel rate available only to citizens of their country. You wait in the cafe while they purportedly book and pay for the room. They never return.

Police impersonators stop you for an imagined infraction and ask for your passport and identification. They take advantage of your confusion to remove cash and credit cards from your wallet or ask you to get in their unmarked car (which is definitely not heading for the police station).

Sneaky Scams

Scam cabs cross the line from opportunistic to blatantly deceptive. Don't be tempted even when airport lines are long.

> **❝**Ask the hotel doorman how much the cost of the cab should be. Some taxis are regulated to charge only one rate from the airport to your destination. **❞**

Time share scams hire outside agents who get up to $50 a head for getting qualified buyers to high-pressure presentations. Decline your time and your investment, until you review a written presentation.

Stolen identities are used to acquire credit cards using your name and credit history. All that is needed is your social security number. It can take months to get these false charges removed. *Coping With Identity Theft* is available from Privacy Rights Clearinghouse, Center for Public Interest Law, 5998 Alcala Park, San Diego, CA 92110, 619-298-3396.

Consumer Advocates

New federal legislation makes it easier to prosecute scams that operate across state lines.

The National Fraud Information Center, 800-876-7060 operates from 9 a.m. to 5 p.m. Eastern Time. Its sole purpose is to catalogue and aid in the prevention of scams. Be aware that cons often hit and run, so the word on the latest scams may not get to them until the con artists have scooped up the money and left town. They also offer free publications including:

Be Smart, Telemarketing Travel Fraud, and Telephone Scams and Older Consumers. You can write to them at P. O. Box 65868, Washington, DC 20035.

The Federal Trade Commission, 202-326-3128 and 326-2222, has a series of publications on travel and time share fraud. Write to 6th St. and Pennsylvania Ave NW, Washington, DC 20580.

Police Museum offering tourists a simulated LSD trip: The South African Police Museum in Pretoria.

Anti-Fraud Agencies By State

States vary in their consumer protection laws. California leads in travel industry regulation and provides a restitution fund for consumers with money coming from fees paid by all wholesale and retail travel companies doing business in that state. All states have consumer protection divisions under the auspices of the Attorney General. Notify the office in the state where the scam is based and in the state in which they're doing business.

State	Phone	State	Phone
Alabama	334-242-7334	Alaska	907-269-5100
Arizona	602-542-3702	Arkansas	501-682-2341
California	916-445-1254	Colorado	303-866-3611
Connecticut	860-566-1877	Delaware	302-577-3250
District of Columbia	202-727-7170	Florida	904-488-2221
Georgia	404-656-3790	Hawaii	808-587-3222
Idaho	208-334-2424	Illinois	312-814-3580
Indiana	317-232-6330	Iowa	515-281-5926
Kansas	913-296-3751	Kentucky	502-595-3262
Louisiana	504-342-9638	Maine	207-626-8849
Maryland	410-528-8662	Massachusetts	617-727-8400
Michigan	517-373-1140	Minnesota	612-296-2331
Mississippi	601-359-4230	Missouri	573-751-3630
Montana	406-444-4312	Nebraska	402-471-2682
Nevada	702-486-7355	New Hampshire	603-271-3641
New Jersey	201-504-6200	New Mexico	505-827-6060
New York	518-474-8583	North Carolina	919-733-7741
North Dakota	701-328-3404	Ohio	614-466-8831
Oklahoma	405-521-4274	Oregon	503-378-4320
Pennsylvania	717-787-9707	Rhode Island	401-277-2104
South Carolina	803-734-9452	South Dakota	605-773-4400
Tennessee	615-741-4737	Texas	512-463-2100
Utah	801-530-6601	Vermont	802-828-3171
Virginia	804-786-2042	Washington	360-753-6210
West Virginia	304-558-3333	Wisconsin	608-266-1852
Wyoming	307-777-7874	Puerto Rico	809-721-0940
U.S. Virgin Islands	809-774-3130		

Deadline for making a police report of theft to qualify for credit card buyer protection benefits: 36-45 hours.

> **"** *Never underestimate a scammer's ingenuity. The most recent best example: The man who setup a fake Automatic Teller Machine (ATM). Of course it couldn't service customers, but it did read their cards and provide valuable information when the magnetic strip was decoded. Second runner-up: The wily character who blocked a bank's night deposit slot with "Under Construction" barricades on Saturday afternoon and rerouted bank customers to a temporary depository. He removed the signs and picked up his loot before the bank opened Monday morning.* **"**

PROBLEMS & COMPLAINTS

Overbooked Flights

Overbooking flights is an unfortunate necessity in an industry with a high percentage of no-shows. One airline spokesman stated that his company counts on six percent of the passengers on any given flight being willing to give up their seats for compensation.

Our Airline Section tells you how to avoid being bumped and ways to make overbooking policies and the resultant bumping work to your advantage.

Lost Tickets

Lost tickets are enough of a plague to merit guarding them as carefully as you would cash.

- **Photocopy them** or write the ticket numbers down before you travel.

- **If your tickets are stolen** make a police report.

- **Report any ticket loss or theft** immediately, so the airline can try to block anyone else from using it.

- **Lost airline tickets are subject to variable policies** and factors, depending on the airline. You must fill out a lost ticket application.

- **If the airline believes** it can effective-

ly block use of the original ticket, it may issue a replacement for a fee. If not, you must buy a replacement ticket at prevailing rates.

- **Your refund may take up to six months** to process. You will be asked to pay for the lost ticket if it has been used and you can not prove theft.

Check our Airline Section and the Lost Ticket chart for airline policies.

Poor Accommodations

When your hotel room isn't up to par, you've been given a powerful negotiating tool. You have several options:

- **Demand that the problem be remedied** within a time frame that's acceptable.

- **Request a room.** With luck, the alternate room may be in a higher category.

- **Ask to be compensated** with a discount or a perk such as dinner for two or a free massage at the hotel's health club.

The first option is good for easily remedied situations like poor room preparation. Malfunctioning heat or air conditioning, defective door locks and other more major problems should first be resolved by a transfer to an acceptable room. You still want a perk in exchange for your inconvenience.

Some hotels guarantee satisfaction, or your stay is free. Most try to make you happy without surrendering all revenue from your stay.

When To Complain

You know it's time to complain when you've been:

• **Treated with excessive rudeness.**

• **Lost money.**

• **Had promises broken.**

• **Spent a considerable amount of time feeling angry** about something that's happened.

How To Complain

Isolate your complaint. What did you expect and what were you given instead? Mentioning unrelated details just confuses the situation and makes your cause less sympathetic. Stay calm and in control.

Complain when the problem occurs. Often the situation can be resolved on the spot. Airline Customer Service Representatives, for example, have authority to arrange meals and accommodations for stranded passengers, endorse tickets to other carriers, approve vouchers for bumped passengers, arrange for repair of airline-damaged luggage, and issue taxi, meal and drink vouchers as they deem reasonable.

Set a goal. Do you want reimbursement or credit against future travel? Do you want a rude person censured or an ignorant person educated? Do you think a major policy change is in order?

Find out if you have legal rights or if resolution relies on the good will of the supplier. Clear legal violations allow for adamant behavior. Negotiable situations call for charm.

Go to a person who has the power to help, but don't jump too high in the chain of command, or you risk being sent back to someone who will be less than receptive. Try to enlist the person to whom you're complaining as an ally and make them see the reasonableness of your complaint. If you don't get results, you can go on to the next level with a clear conscience–and keep going until you reach someone who acts on your complaint.

Complaining By Phone

Phone complaints can be effective, particularly with simple complaints to smaller companies. Many large companies and

> **❝**When you've looked at the situation from several perspectives and it still appears as if you've been treated like a B-movie on Oscar night, it's time to let someone know how you feel. Certain unavoidable problems can rack your nerves without really entitling you to more than empathy. If, for example, you're stuck in the Caribbean during hurricane season and the power to your hotel goes out, complaining is pointless. You've been caught in an unavoidable situation. On the other hand, if you're sitting in the dark and every attempt isn't being made to manage the situation intelligently, you have a legitimate complaint. The right kind of complaint soothes your spirits, recoups your losses and lets you get on with an enjoyable trip.**❞**

most governmental regulatory agencies insist that complaints be made in written form. Many companies that accept complaints by phone, often end up asking you to submit the details in writing. If it's worth complaining about, it's worth the time to write a letter.

Letters of Complaint

The most effective letters of complaint follow this no-lose format:

- **Letters should be typewritten,** contain your daytime phone number and be as close to one-page in length as possible.

- **Begin with the positive** to establish that you are seeing the situation in balance.

- **Describe what happened** and suggest a remedy. If additional travelers were involved, note the number of people affected by the problem.

- **Add supporting documentation** but never send originals.

- **Include any possible indication** of your worth to the company such as your frequent flier number, preferred guest number or the times per year you use the vendor.

- **Address your letter appropriately.** Decide if you want to send it to the customer service department or a company executive. It's usually worth a phone call to get the information you need to address your letter to the right person.

- **If you get a form letter** in return, re-assert your position by return mail. Set a response deadline and copy the letter and the response to an appropriate consumer organization. You may want to draft a letter then ask your attorney to send it on his or her letterhead. The fee is usually nominal.

Unresolved Complaints

Some situations demand persistence. If your initial complaint and follow-up still does not result in satisfaction, you're left with several options:

- **Accept the situation as a learning experience.** This course of action only makes sense when the damage done is small enough to make you consider that spending any more time on it would be pointless.

- **Small claims courts** can give you a favorable judgment, but you have to make sure your case falls within the court's jurisdiction and monetary guidelines. (You can't file in small claims court against a company located in another area.) Even if you should win your case, judgments can be difficult to enforce.

- **The effectiveness of the Better Business Bureau (BBB)** varies greatly, depending on whom you ask. Some people say it's a paper tiger and others predicate their consumer choices on BBB advisories. An important fact to keep in mind is that the BBB has no investigators of its own. Its power is limited to the negative ratings it can forward to future consumers calling for information. It rarely helps you acquire any monetary compensation. It is most effective on complaints directed at local businesses that rely heavily on a steady flow of new customers. They are the companies most likely to do all in their power to avoid a negative BBB report.

- **Parent organizations, governmental agencies and consumer groups** are three of the most effective second-level complaint avenues. If the company with which you have a complaint is a subsidiary of a larger corporation, the corporation is likely to have more refined complaint-resolving skills. Governmental and consumer agencies take advocacy positions for consumers. For example, a query on the letterhead of your state's attorney general will attract the attention of even the most complaint-resistant company.

- **Contact the advertiser** who led you to the vendor or the special offer. Even though they have no liability, they'll pay attention to a complaint pattern and may deny future advertising rights.

Where To Complain

Direct complaints about air carriers, hotels and car rental services should be made to the appropriate consumer affairs office of that carrier, chain or company. A complete listing can be found in the *Know Who To Call* section under each individual category. Other allies:

Problems with travel agencies: The American Society of Travel Agents, Consumer Affairs, 1101 King St., Alexandria, VA 22314. Call 703-739-2782. The problem agency must be a member.

Problems with tour companies: The United States Tour Operators Association, 211 E. 51st St. New York, NY 10022. Call 212-750-7371. The problem company must be a member.

Airline injury and service complaints: The Department of Transportation, 400 7th St. SW, Washington, DC 20590. Call 202-366-2220.

Air safety issues: Federal Aviation Administration, 800 Independence Ave. SW, Washington, DC 20591. Call 800-322-7873.

Canadian air travel: National Transportation Agency, 15 Eddy St., Hull, Quebec K1AON9. Call 819-953-9151.

Consumer rights on airlines: Ralph Nader's Aviation Consumers Action Project, Post Office Box 19029, Washington, DC 20036. Call 202-638-4000.

Lodging: American Hotel and Motel Association, 1201 New York Ave. NW, Washington, DC 20005. Call 202-289-3100.

Amtrak: Customer Relations, 60 Monarch Ave. NE, Washington, DC 20002. Call 202-906-2121.

Cruises: The Cruise Line International Association, 500 5th Ave, Suite 1407, New York, NY 10117 or The Federal Maritime Commission Office of Inquiries and Complaints, 80 N. Capital St. NW, Washington, DC 20573.

Cruise health conditions: The Center for Disease Control, 1015 N. American Way, Room 107, Miami, FL 33132.

Cruise safety: For problems during a cruise, go to the U.S. Coast Guard office in the first port city. For general complaints, write to 2100 W. 2nd St. SW, Washington, DC 20593.

Consumers Resource Handbooks are available from most county and state governments. Check the blue pages of your telephone directory. Also check the *Know Who To Call* section of this book for travel specific phone numbers and addresses.

The Consumer Federation of America, 202-387-6121, offers *How to Resolve Your Consumer Complaint*. Send a stamped, self-addressed envelope to: Consumer Complaint Brochure, P. O. Box 12099, Washington, DC 20005, free with a self-addressed envelope.

SAFE TRAVEL

While You're Away

Arrange for yard care if your trip is lengthy. Don't forget winter concerns. An unshoveled walk is as clear a sign as unmowed grass.

Program light timers and alarm systems, and have someone check regularly to make sure an electric surge or momentary blackout hasn't disrupted either system.

Notify trusted neighbors and ask one to help keep watch in your absence:

Have mail and newspapers picked up daily, or suspend delivery until you return. Don't forget the circulars that get hung on doorknobs or thrown on the porch.

Leave a complete copy of your itinerary so you can be contacted in case of emergency.

Leave numbers for a plumber, electrician and any other contact that your neighbor might need to reach in an emergency situation.

Answering machines should not have messages revealing that you're out of town. If you use an answering service, instruct operators that your out-of-town information is for their use only. Callers should simply be told you're unavailable.

Before You Go

List credit card and travelers check numbers. Make copies of tickets, travel vouchers and confirmations, and any hard-to-replace documents. Pack this material apart from the originals.

Share your excitement with discretion. Talking publicly about an upcoming trip alerts everyone, including strangers, to your absence.

Check safety data for your destination. Ask friends and colleagues for tips on safe and reasonable lodging, areas to avoid, and the relative safety of public transport. Some areas are best avoided, but if you can't resist, visit them in daylight, and go with as many people as feasible.

Identify luggage inside and out. Using a business address further protects your home in your absence. Tie an identifying marker on the handle of any look-alike piece to guard against innocents or criminals plucking your luggage from the carousel. You may also want to use your destination address on identification tags.

Consider leaving your vehicle at home to avoid the dangers of unattended airport lots. Take public transport and airport shuttles, or have a family member drop you off.

Out and About

Keep alert by resting up from travel and time-zone changes, and avoiding medications or any substance that slows down your thinking.

The country in Western Europe with the lowest automobile accident rate: Austria.

When your bags are being loaded into and unloaded from vehicles, pay close attention to ensure that all bags are accounted for.

Choose shoes and clothing in styles that won't inhibit quick escapes from risky situations.

Don't tempt muggers with expensive jewelry and watches.

Travelers checks and credit cards are safer than cash, but don't put them on display for the browsing criminal.

Carry cash in unusual places, a money belt or a neck pouch. In high crime areas, consider carrying a sacrificial wallet with a small amount of cash inside. It appeases most thieves.

The worst places to carry money are handbags and back hip pockets. If you carry a handbag that has a strap, place the strap over your head, as well as your shoulder. If you're wearing a coat or jacket, put it on over the handbag. If you must carry your wallet in a back pocket, wrap a thick rubber band around it so it can't be slipped out as easily.

Public transportation in most cities is reasonably safe if you avoid low-traffic times and high risk areas.

> *Rogue or gypsy limousine drivers will attempt to pick up riders at airports, circumventing the cabbies waiting at the curb. In many cities, this practice is illegal. If you're not sure about your drivers or their offers to transport, ask the cab stand supervisor or an airport policeman. Unlicensed gypsy cabs, and cabs without posted rates and driver ID's, should be avoided.*

Keep keys in hand when heading for your car or hotel room, to avoid delays that increase vulnerability.

Caution in subway cars and elevators comes down to instinct. Wait for the next one if your suspicions are aroused. Most subways now have transit police on board, or close by. Don't be afraid to ask an officer for assistance.

When walking in crowds, try to walk against the flow of traffic. It makes pickpockets' lives more difficult. Keep your cash/wallet/purse out of easy reach.

Have a confident attitude. Tourists are actually considerably less likely than stay-at-homes to become crime victims, unless they show obvious signs of unfamiliarity.

Try to keep your arms free. Shops will often deliver. Decline strangers' offers to help carry packages, unless you're sure you can tell the difference between kindness and larcenous intent.

Restroom stalls find you at your most vulnerable. Position belongings so they can't be grabbed from outside, or by the occupant of the next stall.

Name tags or convention badges ID should not be worn in public. A smart thief can find out where you're staying, and be in and out of your room well before you return.

There really is safety in numbers. Whenever possible, explore with a companion. Know where you're going and the best way to get there and get back.

Beware of well-dressed con artists. The better the appearance, the higher the degree of sophistication in the sham. Travelers in emergency situations have better options than asking strangers for cab fare.

Distraction theft is becoming the number one crime affecting travelers. The distractor spills a drink on you, or asks the time. The accomplice takes the opening, and your handbag or briefcase.

The latest ploy: the set-up man stands up in a crowded subway car and yells "There's a pickpocket on the train!" Instinctively, everyone grabs the place where they're carrying their money. The bold work the car, demanding valuables. The sneaky pick a key victim, follow them until their guard is relaxed, then grab for the place they know they keep their valuables.

International Concerns

Travel agents can access State Department travel updates via all major reservation systems. Compuserve and other on-line services give you direct access as part of the electronic *Official Airline Guide*.

The Office of American Citizens Service (a division of the Department of State), 202-647-5225, provides frequently updated, automated information on any unusual dangers associated with travel to specific foreign countries. Request information by fax, dialing 202-647-3000 on your fax machine phone. Recorded prompts will take it from there allowing you to request exactly what you need, and have it faxed right back to you.

Another free State Department benefit is *Your Trip Abroad*, a 30-page pamphlet that addresses safety issues. Request it from the Bureau of Consular Affairs, Room 6811, Department of State, Washington, DC 20520, or call 202-647-1488.

American Embassy and Consulate phone numbers should be noted for each country you visit. They are your local advocates in many unsafe or threatening situations.

Guard your passport. You have to carry it while in transit, checking into hotels, renting cars or cashing travelers checks. Leave it in the hotel safe the rest of the time, or carry it in a passport pouch, available for about $10. Keep a photocopy of the data page in a safe place. U.S. passports are valued highly by many thieves, often more than cash.

Be an informed border crosser. Learn exactly what you are allowed to carry. An over-the-counter medication approved in one country can be deemed contraband in another.

Understand basic cultural differences and be aware of legal penalties that can easily take a U.S. citizen by surprise. Singapore, for example, has severe punishments for littering. Clothing, quite acceptable in any American city, can provoke unpleasant encounters in the Mid-East.

Transact currency exchanges only at authorized facilities. Avoid the helpful stranger who offers unasked-for assistance or unusual exchange rates.

Learn key emergency words for countries you're visiting. There are times when you may not have time to fumble with a language guide.

> *When collecting safety data on international destinations, consider the source: tourist officials are in the business of drawing you to their countries, travel agents want to sell tickets. This is not to say that both sources can't give good information, but your most trustworthy source is the U.S. government.*

Approximate number of beer steins stolen at each Munich Oktoberfest: 250,000.

LUGGAGE LOGIC

AIRLINE POLICIES

Standardized policies with minor variations exist on most major U.S. air carriers. Niche-market airlines, commuters and charter flights have more varied provisions for carry-on or checked baggage. Check your favorite airline's specific policy whenever purchasing a ticket on a carrier new to you, or when flying to a new destination. Aloha Airlines, for example, prohibits wheeled bags as carry-ons. Reason given–they need extra room in overhead bins for life vests.

Most airlines permit three bags total, including carry-on and checked baggage. Southwest Airlines, the notable exception, allows three checked pieces plus two carry-ons.

Carry-Ons

In general, carry-ons are limited to two per passenger, though some smaller aircraft limit you to one.

- **Linear size** (height plus length plus width) must not equal more than 45 inches, and weight must be 40 pounds or less, per piece.

- **All carry-ons must fit** in the overhead bins or under the seat.

- **Garment bag dimensions** must not surpass 4" x 23" x 45" (16" x 10" x 24" when folded on Southwest).

- **Not included in carry-on limits:** Purses, camera bags and diaper bags. Some airlines technically count laptop computers and briefcases, but you are not likely to encounter problems except on airlines with a strict carry-on enforcement policy, or on crowded flights, when the passenger load is unusually heavy.

Airlines on a quick-turnaround, and most commuter airlines, may strictly enforce carry-on rules. Sizing boxes–metal-framed devices at boarding gates–are increasingly used. Average dimensions are 16" x 10" x 24" and any carry-on must fit inside. Soft-sided pieces can more easily be made to fit. Other airlines rely on visual checks by gate attendants. If you have to gate-check a bag, be consoled knowing that it is among the first bags unloaded when your flight arrives.

Most travelers support carry-on limits to eliminate obstructed aisles and increase passenger safety. Rules apply to all travelers, but are more likely to be waived for those passengers flying First or Business class, and for passengers on lightly booked flights.

Checked Luggage

Usually, checked pieces may not weigh more than 70 pounds each. Airlines measure bags in linear inches: height + width + length. The largest bag must not exceed 62 linear inches. The second checked bag has a limit of 55 linear inches and the third has a limit of 45 linear inches. Additional pieces can usually be checked at $20-35 per bag. Strollers, infant seats and two-wheeled luggage carts do not count against your maximum allowance.

Sports equipment can be carried if packed appropriately. Golf clubs and ski equipment usually are free, and count as one piece of checked baggage. Fees for transporting bicycles domestically average $45, including the cost of the carrier box. International flights often allow bicycles at no fee as part of checked baggage.

Allow a little extra check-in time.

Special-care items can be carried under specific conditions.

- **Unloaded weapons** can be packed in locked, checked baggage, but they must be declared. Ammunition is subject to quantity limits.

- **Fragile items and some musical instruments** may require special packing, and you're likely to be asked to sign a waiver releasing the airline from liability should they be damaged in flight.

International Baggage

International baggage limits roughly parallel domestic rules as long as you remain on a U.S. based carrier. There are destination-specific variances. For example:

- **On flights to the United Kingdom**, your three bags can weigh up to 70 pounds each.

- **Traveling to the Caribbean**, the total weight of your three pieces cannot exceed 140 pounds.

- **Travel on foreign based airlines** is subject to rules as varied as their home countries and the type of aircraft they fly. On some flights between two foreign cities, luggage allowance is based on weight rather than number of pieces.

If your itinerary includes multiple airlines, gear your luggage to the one with the most restrictive policies or be prepared to pay additional fees.

66Choose direct and non-stop flights when feasible, and allow adequate check in time, i.e., 45 minutes for domestic flights and 90 minutes for international flights.99

The three months during which baggage is most likely to be lost: December, January and February.

Lost Luggage

Most bags arrive without mishap: 80% of lost bags are returned within 24 hours, 90% are returned within five days. Only one percent are never recovered. Add-on insurance is available at $1-2 per $100 in coverage. Check to see if you already have coverage from your credit or charge card by calling the issuing bank. Added coverage is most valuable on overseas flights when the carrier's maximum liability doesn't adequately cover luggage contents.

If your bags are lost:

- **Liability is limited** to $1,250 per passenger on domestic flights. Efforts are being made to raise this limit to $1,850. International liability averages $645 per passenger and is based on weight.

- **File a claim** before leaving the airport. Airlines with computerized tracking can locate lost bags the fastest. Get a copy of the claim and a toll-free number. Be persistent and ask for the small emergency kit most airlines can issue to passengers with lost luggage.

- **After 24 hours**, you may request an emergency advance of $25-75. You must ask for the money and go to the airport to pick it up. Be prepared to explain why you want the higher amount. If your bags are later located, the money is yours to keep. If they are not, the advance is deducted from your final settlement.

- **After 48 hours** you're entitled to an additional $25. Again, you have to ask.

- **Be a strong negotiator.** Claims generally take three to four weeks to settle. Payment is based on depreciated value, not replacement cost. Be prepared with a list of your luggage contents and any receipts you have on hand. Items not covered include cash, negotiable documents, jewelry, furs, cameras and electronics. Airlines routinely try to deduct 20%-30% from your requested settlement.

- **Formal complaints** should be made to the customer relations division of the airline, with a copy sent to the U.S. Department of Transportation, Consumer Affairs I-25, Washington, DC 20590. Call 202-366-2220. They also publish a monthly *Air Travel Consumer Report* which ranks airlines based on consumer complaints.

CRUISE, RAIL & ROAD

Cruise luggage limits are essentially determined by the carrier that flies you to the port city and the limited storage in most cruise cabins. Cruise lines also set their own weight limit on luggage (usually 200 pounds total), but it isn't a restriction likely to be enforced unless you visibly exceed it.

Their liability for lost or damaged luggage is minimal–averaging $100 per passenger. Most lines offer a multi-use insurance option that includes lost or damaged luggage.

Amtrak baggage policies are contingent on whether or not the train has a baggage car. Without one, you're limited to two carry-ons, with no specific weight or size limit except their ability to fit in overhead compartments.

Trains with baggage cars also allow three checked pieces per passenger, with 50 pounds per piece maximum. The weight allowance can be raised to 75 pounds if you pay an additional $10 per item. You can also check three more pieces for $10 per item. Total per passenger liability is $500. Amtrak carries skis at no extra cost, and bicycles (dismantled and in boxes) for $10.

Interstate bus lines allow two pieces of checked luggage and two carry-ons. Total weight of all four pieces must not exceed 120 pounds. Maximum liability is $250 per passenger.

LUGGAGE BASICS

Buying New Luggage

Technology has produced new options to match the decline in porters and other assistance previously more readily available to travelers.

Place a bright ribbon or affix a bright, large sticker to both outsides of your luggage to make your luggage more easily identifiable.

Buy the best luggage you can afford. Increased instances of damaged luggage are caused, in part, from the use of ultra-economy pieces not designed to withstand the rigors of travel.

Hard shell luggage provides extra protection but is heavier to carry. Check the manageability by carrying the empty bag around the luggage department. If you have trouble managing it empty, it will be unacceptable when full.

Soft-sided luggage is best made of "ballistic" fabric similar to that used for bulletproof vests. Second best is fabric made of nylon or polyester yarn of at least 1,000 denier.

Plastic frames and wheels are more durable then metal. Four-wheel designs ease navigation. Look for wheels which are protected by housings or partially recessed.

Handles should be padded and riveted on rather than attached by D-rings or screws. Retractable handles are better than detachable ones, which tend to get misplaced.

Shoulder straps should be adjustable and have comfort pads.

Self-repairing zippers eliminate costly repairs.

Garment bags should open book-style and have pouches and compartments that keep items not on hangers from jumbling at the bottom of the bag.

Attachments for carrying multiple bags are useful if their design holds each bag securely.

Divided sections and waterproof pouches make packing easier.

A 'Case' Study

Remove old destination tags and make sure your luggage is well identified inside and out. Use your business address for added home security.

Decide your best luggage strategy. The most convenient is carry-on only. When using checked bags, consider using two smaller bags rather than one hard-to-carry piece. You'll also minimize wrinkles and lessen the odds of being totally inconvenienced by lost luggage. Plan to pass laptops and computer discs through security via the conveyor belt. Security arches and hand-held wands are the most hazardous to their magnetic fields.

Air recently dry-cleaned items before you pack them.

Allow for purchases made at your destination. If you always get a souvenir T-shirt, maybe you can eliminate packing pajamas and/or one shirt. If you plan to purchase Balinese batik, English tweeds or other regional specialties, deduct items they can replace from your packing list.

Make a list. It will help you eliminate what isn't needed, and remind you of things to be done before you pack, such as picking up cleaning and shopping for new items. Don't bring what you can get or use for free at any good hotel, such as an alarm clock, hair dryer, iron or basic toiletries.

What To Pack

Pack clothes that provide the right look without sacrificing comfort. Travel is not the time to try new looks, new shoes or fabrics that may not stand up to travel demands.

Consider a color scheme. Black and white have a classic style all their own and are most adaptable to dressing up or dressing down. Use accessories to change the look of basics.

Fabrics blended with a little polyester resist wrinkles best. Avoid linen, unless you plan to take along a valet. Light-weight fabrics are good for any climate, if you layer clothing. Denim's versatility makes up for its heavier weight.

Make style work for you. Clothes with usable pockets provide extra convenience. Vests come in fabrics from wool to satin and produce a finished look on their own.

Long pants are expected in many urban areas and at religious sites. Convertible shorts/pants are available in mens sizes at about $68. They have deep, cargo pockets, button-closed back pockets and khaki-type styling. A hidden zipper converts them from long pants to shorts. Call TravelSmith, 800-950-1600.

Learn the keep-cool lessons of the locals. Thin, natural fiber fabrics that cover the body loosely are actually cooler than exposing your skin to the sun.

Pack your swimsuit even in winter, so you'll be able to use hotel pool and spa facilities.

Limit jewelry to a few signature items. Don't be a glittering target for thieves. Travelers who take a lot of jewelry too often leave a piece behind when they check out of their hotel.

Take two pairs of shoes. One pair does not allow for broken heels or other footwear emergencies. Place shoes in plastic bags to avoid soiling clothes.

Packing Procedures

Set everything out, then put half back. Remember the limited reimbursement you get for lost luggage. Never carry anything you deem irreplaceable.

Place heavier items on the bottom of your suitcase. If you're packing for a long trip, start by packing what you need for the last destination, and place clothing you'll want first at the top.

Roll clothes into cylinders to eliminate creasing. Fill up empty spaces by packing socks, belts and accessories inside shoes.

Couples can place one outfit in each other's suitcase. If one suitcase is lost, at least you each have a change of clothes.

Carry-ons should include:

- **A change of clothes,** or as close to a complete change as you can get with space limitations.

If the skycap places a BET on your luggage, you're going to Bethel, Arkansas.

- **Prescriptions** in their original containers and any over-the-counter medicine you are taking or need frequently.

- **Basic toiletries** packed in a spill-proof container.

- **Address book** and contact information.

- **Keys**–but just the ones you'll need. Leave all superfluous keys at home.

- **Any essentials** or hard-to-replace items that you feel you must take.

- **Your final written inventory** of the contents of your checked luggage (an extra task that you may be glad you took the time to complete).

Packers' Tidbits

If you're traveling to a cold climate, carry your coat with you. It may seem cumbersome if you're departing from a warm weather airport but you'll be glad you have it when you land; doubly glad if your luggage is delayed or lost.

Remove or secure the hook on garment bags that will be moved on airline conveyor belts.

Lock all luggage and tie an identifying scarf or ribbon on common-appearing pieces. Retrievable luggage tags have a notice in eight languages alerting people to the itinerary inside their pouch. They're ideal for lengthy trips, and cost $4.85 for two tags. You can get them from Magellan's, 800-962-4943.

Make sure check-in agents tag your bags correctly. Know the three letter airport code for your destination. Make sure your bags are placed on the conveyor belt before you leave the check-in area.

Try to board early if you're carrying a lot of carry-on luggage. Stow carry-ons in line with your seat or in front of it, to avoid going against the traffic flow when the flight lands.

To make light work of packing, consider inflatable items:

- **The Air-Filled Car Seat,** priced at about $100, meets all safety guidelines for children 6 months to 4 years old and 20 to 40 pounds. Call Travel Safety at 800-637-7220.

- **Puffy hangers** for hotel laundry chores cost about $2 each and are widely available in travel and discount stores.

- **The Sports Pouch** keeps your keys, wallet and watch from sinking when you're on the water. Prices range from $13-25 at travel and sporting goods stores.

HEALTHY TRAVEL

SHOULD YOU GO?

Minor illnesses easily managed at home can become greater problems when traveling. Middle ear infections will almost always be aggravated by air travel and become even more painful. Stay at home if you can. Colds and sinus problems can become more uncomfortable during flights, but decongestants should provide relief.

Medical certificates are not required as a condition of air travel unless the passenger is on a stretcher, in an incubator or requires oxygen.

If you wear a pacemaker or have any metal implanted in your body, carry a physician's letter and do not go through security metal detectors.

Medical-alert tags are recognizable signals of chronic conditions and specific medical needs. They can save your life in unfamiliar surroundings. Call the Medic Alert Foundation, 800-344-3226.

Pregnancy does not have to be a barrier to any form of travel, but flying is usually the most comfortable option. Consult your obstetrician while planning your trip. If you want to fly during the last trimester of pregnancy, consult your chosen carrier and, if required, obtain written permission from your doctor. Comfort options for pregnant travelers include aisle seats and loose clothing and shoes. Don't be afraid to fasten your seat belt. Studies show that seat belts decrease risk to both mother and baby.

Don't attempt to travel if you have a serious disease transmitted by airborne bacteria. Let your conscience and your need to travel be your guide when you have a minor communicable illness. Divers should not attempt air travel within 24 hours of their last dive. Get physician's approval for travel if you have had recent surgery or suffer from heart disease, severe high blood pressure, bleeding disorders or other acute conditions.

BEFORE YOU GO

Prescription medicines should be carried in their original containers. This is particularly important when you travel internationally. It's preferable that the name on the prescription label exactly matches the name on your passport. Copy all the information on the label and keep it in a safe place in case your medicine is lost. Synchronize your dosage times when you travel to different time zones.

Out-of-state prescriptions may be difficult to obtain. Your physician may not be licensed to authorize them. Be sure to take an adequate supply of necessary medications.

Carry an extra pair of glasses or a replacement prescription.

Out-of-area medical care usually requires advance HMO or insurance approval for anything other than an immediate threat to life. Make yourself aware of the provisions of your plan and know the 24-hour authorization number.

Emergency assistance plans are travel insurance supplements that should have 24-hour contact numbers, help you locate a physician or dentist and cover emergency expenses up to $5,000 or more. Request details from Access America at 800-284-8300, or Assist-Card, 800-874-2223.

Green rooms can be booked in an increasing number of hotels. They're ideal for people with allergy or breathing problems. Many use special air and water purifiers, all natural soaps and shampoos and natural fiber carpets. All are non-smoking. The best green rooms even use cleaning supplies that are chemical-free.

ACCLIMATE YOURSELF

Extra demands are made on your body even on pleasant trips to attractive locations. Changes in climate, food and time-zones must be accommodated.

Adapt to local climates gradually. Expose yourself to close-to-the-equator sun or the thin air of high elevations slowly in order to allow your body to adjust.

Sunburn can strike in tropical destinations and on the ski slopes. Restrict your first day's exposure and wear products that block harmful rays–usually strongest between 11 a.m. and 3 p.m.

> ***Heat stroke and heat exhaustion** are aggravated by many prescription drugs including some antibiotics, anti-depressants and anti-anxiety medications. One in forty people in the U.S. takes these drugs regularly. Most aren't aware of the limitations they cause on your body's ability to cope with weather extremes.*

Increase your activity level only to a comfortable degree. Most people come home from trips exhausted because they try to fit a two-week vacation into one.

Be aware of the time in your hometown. Even though your travel activities will occur in your current time zone, your body needs some notice paid to the zone it is most used to.

DIETARY CONCERNS

Most intestinal upsets run their course with minimal treatment, usually the same over-the-counter medicine you take at home. Persistent diarrhea can cause dehydration which is almost always remedied by rapid fluid intake or rehydration powders available at all pharmacies. Be cautious of anti-diarrhea drugs unless specifically prescribed. They stop the symptoms but can also prevent your body from eliminating the cause.

Low-sanitation areas are best handled by using bottled water for drinking and brushing your teeth. Avoid ice cubes; peeled, uncooked fruits and vegetables; shellfish, and undercooked foods. Before you restrict yourself, check with your hotel. Many resort area hotels have thoroughly safe, treated water.

Treat questionable tainted water by boiling it or adding iodine or halazone tablets. Follow package recommendations and double the amount used if the water you're treating is unusually cloudy or very cold. If you're on medication, consult your physician before using any water additives.

Diet nightmares are easily avoided. You may want to splurge on regional specialties, but keep good overall eating habits. Explore the healthier aspects of each area's cuisine.

Out-of-town/Out-of-shape isn't an inevitable pairing. Walking not only gives you the best views of your travel destination, it increases your energy, strengthens your immune system and makes it easy to rationalize restaurant splurges that are usually part of any trip. Walking is also an excellent way to meet locals. Many lasting friendships have been formed between travelers and people they've met on leisurely walks around new areas.

SURVIVING THE TRAVEL JUNGLE

Accidents are a far greater risk than any travel-incurred disease. This is true if you're going to an adjacent state or to a remote destination. Exhaustion from long trips, all-day business meetings and late night festivities are one of the greatest causes of mishaps. Head off exhaustion with adequate rest. Even a 15-minute nap can rejuvenate you.

Water mishaps are best avoided by heeding all posted warnings. Be particularly careful of unknown ocean tides and currents. Check to see if other people are in the water. Some of the world's most tempting beaches are for sunbathing only, with currents too strong for most swimmers.

Stress, the biggest danger to your health at home or abroad, can result from overspending. If resources are limited, find a trip that fits and save the dream vacation for another time. Ease general stress with no-cost or low-cost options–swimming in the hotel pool, taking a sauna, relaxing in a whirlpool, exercising in the fitness center or having a massage.

Germs and bacteria are best kept in line with routine cleanliness. Washing your hands often is the easiest protection from many diseases.

Ticks can be removed by covering them with petroleum jelly or any substance that makes them remove their heads so they can breathe. Extract the pests with tweezers then disinfect the bite area. If you're in an area with a high prevalence of Lyme Disease, save the dead tick until you're sure no symptoms will appear.

Some unusual illnesses acquired while traveling don't exhibit symptoms for two to 12 months. If hard-to-diagnose rashes, fever or diarrhea develop, be sure to tell

---

your doctor where you've traveled during the past year, even if you have just traveled domestically.

INTERNATIONAL TRAVEL

Updated immunization information is available from The Center For Disease Control, 404-332-4559. They update weekly changes that the average physician cannot regularly monitor. Some immunizations are required, some are optional and a few that used to be mandatory, are now simply recommended. In extreme cases, health advisories are issued when an epidemic-level of a specific disease is present.

Polio and tetanus boosters and hepatitis immunizations are always good ideas if you're heading for tropical or developing countries. No regulatory agency demands them but, particularly if you have chronic illnesses or are of a certain age, discuss them with your doctor, then make your decision.

English-speaking doctors can be located via a free list from The International Association for Medical Assistance, 716-754-4883.

911 (the U.S. emergency phone number) translates differently in most countries that have an emergency number system. Britain uses 999; Germany, 110; Sweden, 90000; Peru, 05. Know the number for each country on your itinerary.

Foreign-made medicines should be approached with caution. Some countries sell over-the-counter products designed to look like their U.S. counterparts, but they can differ in composition and quality.

Foreign medical care varies in quality from poor to excellent. Some countries will give you free medical care via excellent public health systems. Others are to be avoided for anything other than emergency interim care. An accurate quality rating can usually be given by resident American Embassy and Consulate staff members.

After-hour pharmacies can be found in Europe by checking the placard on the door of any pharmacy. They all list the closest after-hours prescription source.

Premium level charge and credit cardholders can call 24-hour assistance lines for help in medical emergencies. The credit card company's toll-free number will work from Caribbean countries with the 809 area code but in other countries call their U.S. number collect and say "medical emergency." American Express extends this service to all cardholders. Call 800-554-2639 or, from abroad, 202-783-7474.

Travel health insurance guarantees your care in foreign countries for a cost of $3-7 per travel day. Some offer interpreter services and emergency air evacuation. They may exempt coverage for accidents involving active sports and most won't insure travelers over 70.

Country with three time zones, each a half-hour apart from the other: Australia.

TRAVEL BY LAND

TRAVEL BY CAR

Basic Driving Tips

If you're driving your own car, make sure maintenance is current.

- **Check tires** for proper inflation and remember that recommended tire pressure alters with the climate.

- **Check oil and fuel levels** and the need to add anti-freeze or snow tires.

- **Consider renting** if you have any doubt that your car can make the trip without problems.

Take frequent breaks on long drives. Every two hours or 100 miles is the recommendation of safety experts. Remember that breaks don't have to last more than a few minutes to be effective.

Rotate driving chores. Assign driving times that match the time of day when each driver feels most alert.

Headlights increase your visibility to other drivers. Turn them on whenever you use your wipers and always use them when driving during twilight and dawn.

Driving in cold climates warrants packing warm clothes and blankets, flares and food for emergency situations.

Dial *HP or 911 on your car phone to report wrecks or hazardous driving conditions.

Beware of destination-specific road hazards you may never encounter at home–mud and rock slide areas, ice, snow, or fog near large bodies of water.

Auto Clubs provide members with road maps that give up-to-date details no atlas can provide, insurance options, discounts and roadside services. Most clubs cover the primary member and his or her spouse. If you have a larger family of drivers, choose a plan that includes them all at the lowest added cost.

The longest vehicular tunnel: the 10.2 mile St. Gotthard Tunnel in The Alps.

Car Safety

According to law enforcement officials, criminals have used a number of ploys in various cities to distract motorists or get them to stop. Some of these methods may include:

1. Yelling, honking or pointing at your car as if something is wrong with your vehicle.

2. Motioning or asking you to stop and lend assistance.

3. Flashing headlights at your vehicle.

4. Bumping your vehicle from behind.

5. Obviously following you.

> **"**If any of the above trickery methods occur, do not pull over or stop; instead, drive immediately to the nearest service station or well-lighted public area and call the police (911).**"**

If another driver tries to force you off the road, don't stop even if it means damage to a rental vehicle. Use evasive action and head for a place of safety, i.e., a lighted, populated public area.

Keep doors locked and windows high enough to prevent being accosted at intersections. Keep the car in gear. If someone tries to get in, hit the horn then step on the gas.

Do not pick up hitchhikers under any circumstances. If someone claims to require assistance, send help to them, rather than taking them where they want to go.

Locking purses, wallets, luggage and valuables in the trunk or glove compartment should be a rule of thumb. Make sure your valuable items are out of sight before leaving the car rental facility.

Always park in well-lighted areas. Check inside and underneath your vehicle before entering the car. When you approach the vehicle, make sure your keys are already in your hand.

Maintain an adequate gas supply. Be particularly alert when driving a car with radically different gas mileage than the vehicle you are accustomed to driving.

Avoid driver fatigue. Time zone travel and changes in sleep patterns can create the drowsiness some studies claim to be responsible for almost 50% of highway accidents. Don't rely on caffeine. Take a 20-minute nap at a safe roadside location or get out of the car and walk around. Keep cool by lowering the air conditioner or rolling down windows. Scan the road. Don't hypnotize yourself by staring at a fixed point.

Play It Safe is a free safety brochure available from AAA. You can get it at any of their 1,000-plus locations. They'll probably be happy to give you one even if you're not a member.

If your car breaks down, evaluate your surroundings before deciding whether to go for help or wait in your vehicle. If you decide to wait, request that anyone offering assistance notify the police or highway patrol for you.

Adjust your speed. Even with increased speed limits on some roads keep in mind that miles per hour times one and a half equals the number of feet you're traveling per second. It takes one full second to react. Allow yourself a safety margin by slowing down.

People traveling alone may want to invest in a $99 inflatable man that can make you look less vulnerable. *Safe T Man* is five feet ten inches, easy to inflate and a relatively authentic looking companion, particularly for night travelers. You get your choice of skin tones and can select a clean shaven or mustached version. He comes dressed in a t-shirt and wears size large clothing. Call 800-999-3030.

Weather or Not?

Be weather-wise:

• **Tune-in radio talk shows** in the local area to get a picture of what to expect, and how bad the weather really is.

> **"**In certain circumstances, you may not even want to attempt the trip. If you are not experienced in bad weather situations or don't know the road, the safest action may be not taking the trip at all.**"**

• **If you're caught in a blizzard,** stay in your car and wait for help and keep a window cracked to prevent carbon monoxide poisoning.

• **Don't try to drive through high water.** If your car stalls in water that is moving rapidly, get out immediately and seek higher ground.

• **Don't turn on high beams in fog**. Reflections can be blinding. Use low beams and slow down.

• **When roads are icy** it takes twice as long to stop when the temperature is at the freezing point then when it is below freezing.

• **When you're driving through hot climates,** be aware of the extra strain on your vehicle's engine.

• ***Disaster Driving*** is a free pamphlet of tips available from Aetna Insurance. Call 203-273-2843.

TRAVEL BY RV

Motorhome and RV rentals give groups and families vacation options with transportation and accommodations provided at one daily rate.

It's possible to save one-half to two-thirds the cost of an airfare/car rental/hotel vacation. Average daily rental cost is $150 per day plus mileage, add-on insurance and drop-off fees when applicable.

There will either be prohibitions against travel on rough terrain or extra insurance requirements.

Be aware of the height of your rental R.V. versus tunnel, overpass and bridge heights. RV's that carry compressed gas aren't allowed to use some ferries, tunnels and long bridges.

Cruise America, 800-327-7799, is the largest renter of recreational vehicles. Discount coupons are usually available in Entertainment Passbooks. (See More Dollars and Cents.)

The Recreation Vehicle Rental Association, 703-591-7130, sells a $5 membership directory with complete information on where to rent, requirements for rental and what types of vehicles are available.

The Good Sam Club, 800-234-3450, is nearing one million members. It offers discounts at campgrounds, roadside assistance, mail forwarding and other services.

Go Camping America, 800-477-8669, would like to help you decide to buy an RV. Request a free vacation planner and/or member dealerships near you.

U.S. city where the temperature dips below 32 degrees most often: Flagstaff, Arizona's mountain elevations.

TRAVEL BY RAIL

Traveling by train is, for first-timers, something like taking on the great unknown. We live in a society where air travel is more familiar to most of us than travel by rail. Here's a collection of tips for your first trip and for all trips.

- **Book as far in advance as possible,** particularly if you're looking for discount fares.

- **Not all sleeping cars are created equal.** Before you agree to the additional expense, be sure of what you're getting.

- **Children eight and above** are allowed to travel alone on some trains and under certain restrictions. They must pay full fare.

- **Amtrak offers a free publication** detailing options and tips for travelers with disabilities and special medical needs. Request *Access Amtrak* by writing to Amtrak Public Affairs, 60 Massachusetts Ave NE, Washington, DC 20002.

- **Most trains allow three pieces of checked baggage** not exceeding 75 pounds each or 150 pounds total. Carry-ons are limited to two per coach passenger. Sleeping car passengers can carry on as much as their rooms can reasonably accommodate.

- **Take along a small pillow and light blanket** for lengthy trips when you're traveling coach. Seats recline and offer more roominess than airline coach seats. Some trains offer pillows and blankets for small fees, but supplies often run out.

- **Laptop computer users** should plan to run on batteries or bring an extension cord and a two-and-three prong adapter plug. Trains frequently enter areas that will temporarily wipe out electrical power sources.

- **Headphones are required** for radios, tape and CD players.

- **Ask for a free route guide** before you board the train. The counter staff and the conductor should all have copies. They detail the schedule and spotlight points of interest viewable from the train.

- **Trains that provide meal service** offer dining car service for dinner ($8-14); lunch ($5-7); and breakfast ($4-6). Trains without dining cars offer a limited selection of microwave cuisine.

- **Tipping** (see *More Dollars and Cents, Tips on Tips* section).

- **Smoking** is allowed in designated cars only on trips with more than four-and-a-half hours running time between stops. Smoking is also allowed in some sleeping cars.

- **On board phone service** is available on some trains including Metroliners, New England Express, San Diegans, San Joaquins and Capitols. Calls are billed directly to your credit card.

Special Amtrak Options

There are times when taking a trip by train makes getting there as exciting as being there.

- **Amtrak's California Zephyr** travels from Oakland to Chicago with a scenic route that takes you through the Sierra and Rocky Mountains, the Glenwood Canyon and the six-mile Moffat Tunnel that runs beneath the Continental Divide.

- **Amtrak's Coach Starlight** travels between Los Angeles and Seattle

---

Year in which Amtrak launched the first U.S. transcontinental passenger train: 1993–Los Angeles to Miami.

through the Blue Ridge and Appalachian Mountains.

- **Ski Amtrak** with rail travel only, rail and air packages or complete package options that include rail fare, transfers to the lodge, accommodations and lift tickets.

   From Los Angeles the Southwest Chief takes you to Lamy, NM to access Santa Fe and Taos ski areas. You're looking at an hour or two of driving once you reach Lamy, but the drive takes you through some of the most incredible scenery in the southwest. The Pioneer heads for Jackson Hole. The Empire Builder will take you to ski destinations in Montana, Idaho and Washington.

   From Chicago or San Francisco, catch the California Zephyr to access Denver and Salt Lake City area resorts.

   From Chicago and New York/ Washington DC the Broadway Limited and Capitol Limited hits budget resorts with great skiing in Pennsylvania and Maryland. The Cardinal will take you near West Virginia's Snowshoe, Winterplace and Silver Creek ski areas.

   From Washington, DC and Montreal you can access several Northeast resorts including Woodstock, Killington, Stowe Smuggler's Notch and Sugarbush.

International Train Tips

It's hard to generalize in a world of travel as varied as second class India Rail and black-tie dinners on the Orient Express. However, here are some tips that will help see you through almost any rail itinerary:

- **When traveling by pass,** you often must also make a reservation, particularly during busy travel times. Most of the time, these reservations require a nominal fee over and above the cost of the pass.

- **Many international cities have two or three train stations.** Be sure you're at the right one and that your connections allow travel time between stations, as needed.

- **Know the local spelling and pronunciation of your destination.** Both may differ greatly from the Americanized versions.

- **Make sure you're in a car** that's going all the way to your destination. Sometimes cars are detached at intermediate stations.

- **Ask if food and beverages will be available** on lengthier train trips and plan accordingly.

TRAVEL BY BUS

Greyhound and Gray Line are the two most familiar names in U.S. bus and motorcoach travel. Greyhound, 800-231- 2222, covers the map with fares usually below any other form of public transportation for short hauls. Lengthier travel may be priced higher than bargain airfares unless you take advantage of special promotions. Gray Line, 800-243-8353, offers motorcoach tours within specific cities and regions.

Ticketing Greyhound

Tickets are priced based on 21-day advance purchase and walk-up fares. You'll save a little by buying in advance and generally get the lowest price for a 21-day advance purchase. Always ask about sale fares, discounts and children's rates to get the best deal. Seniors 55 and over get 15% off walk-up fares.

Dollar amount of rail passes sold by Britrail International in 1995 to Canadian and U.S. tourists: $31 million.

Sample roundtrip fares:

New York City/Dallas fares

$178 . . . . .21-day advance

$184 . . . . .Walk-up fare

Los Angeles/Chicago fares

$198 . . . . .21-day advance

$204 . . . . .Walk-up fare

International Travel By Bus

Greyhound of Canada, 403-260-0877, offers several standard discounts.

- **Seniors 60 plus** receive ten percent off all regular and Canada Pass tickets.

- **Companion Rates** allow for 50% off the second ticket on most fares.

- **Canada Pass** offers one price for unlimited travel during time periods ranging from seven to 60 days.

Eurobus connects 19 major European cities. An unlimited two-month pass is about $325; $250 for people 26 and under. Call 800-517-7778 for precise quotes and comparisons to equivalent Eurailpass prices.

EuropaBus also connects Europe by motorcoach. Some fares work in conjunction with specific railroad systems. A good source for information is DER Tours, 800-937-1234.

Recently,

BEST FARES Discount Travel Magazine

showed savvy travelers how to get a free companion roundtrip to London for buying $55 in golf accessories.

Call 800-880-1234 to subscribe.
See page 395 for your discount subscription offer.

Country with the longest coastline: Canada at 56,452 miles.

SPECIAL TRAVEL CATEGORIES

TRAVELING SOLO

Think Positively

Solo leisure travel can provide one of the finest luxuries in life: you can do exactly as you choose. Select the destination, set the pace and answer only to your own desires. Once you've tried it, you may consider it the ultimate form of travel.

Spur-of-the-moment travel offers amazing discounts and is easiest to take advantage of if you don't have to check anyone's schedule but your own. Take the last available seat on a charter to Las Vegas. You're likely to get it for about 75% off. Pick up on a weekend special from one of the major airlines and book your destination hotel at weekend rates that don't usually carry a penalty for solo travelers.

Meeting people can be easier when you're solo. Many people even relish the anonymity solo travel provides.

Solo travelers make their own support groups. Meet amenable people on flights or at hotel clubs. You're no more likely to step into a dangerous situation on a trip than you are at home.

Build a network of friends by exchanging addresses with people you meet along the way. If you feel a little uncertain, use a business address or post office box. Soon your travels may be solo, but you'll have friends to welcome you wherever you go.

Support is just a phone call away. If you get lonely, a phone call to someone you care for will usually cure your loneliness and make you ready for new explorations.

Never get discouraged by people who can't imagine solo travel or have had bad experiences traveling alone. With careful planning, good choices and an adventuresome spirit, a wonderful trip is almost guaranteed.

Business travelers comprise the vast majority of solo travelers. They, of course, can't quite do as they choose, but even with the demands of business, small indulgences and explorations are possible. Repeat trips to cities may eventually feel almost like visits to second homes.

Strategies

Beware the double occupancy dilemma. When you check out prices and ads, you'll almost always be looking at quotes based on double occupancy. Be sure to always ask for the single rate. You don't want to arrive at your hotel to find out that the per night cost is double what you expected.

Consult our Cruise section for tips on avoiding the high cost of solo cabins.

Select destinations where you already know someone. Visit a college roommate you haven't seen for years, a favorite aunt or the neighbors who moved to Wyoming.

Ritual performed at Newfoundland's annual Screech In: drinking rum and kissing a codfish.

You may not stay with them, but they still provide a first-person source of guidance and keep you from feeling entirely alone in a new city.

Plan ahead and travel light. Those two travel basics take on even greater importance when you're traveling alone.

Consider bed & breakfasts and hostels for built-in camaraderie plus budget advantages.

Choose cities with vital centers and concentrations of activities unless your expertise and courage allow you to tackle the great urban unknown.

If you're driving, join an auto club and carry a cellular phone. Don't try to get around in a strange city after dark. Plan your arrival for a time when daylight lets you explore with greater safety.

Dine alone without apology. Some restaurants are reticent to tie up a table for one person, but most enlightened restaurants know better than to alienate you with anything other than their best service. If you want to be particularly thoughtful, avoid the busiest times and places.

Taking a book to dinner provides a margin of comfort for the timid. You can also ask to be seated at an inconspicuous table. Takeout lunches can be enjoyed in parks or wherever office workers congregate. If you're dining in Europe, don't be surprised if another solo diner is seated with you. It's a common and generally pleasant experience.

Great theater seats and tickets to sold-out events are much easier to acquire if you only need one. Build a trip around the Broadway season or a concert by a favorite group or performer.

Foreign travel? Why not? Learn as much of the language as you can or select destinations where English is a strong second language.

If You'd Like A Companion

Look for a travel companion through groups or organizations or at your religious center. You're assured of at least one common interest.

Travel partners known to you or arranged by a service should be compatible. Are you extravagant or budget conscious; neat or messy; timid or adventurous; night owl or early riser; punctual or always late?

Match-Up services are available to pair you with a person, previously unknown to you, who might make a good travel companion. **Travel Companion Exchange** is the biggest and oldest service of its kind. An eight-month membership is $159 and includes bimonthly newsletters and about 500 listings of travelers seeking companions. Call 800-392-1256 or write P.O. Box 833, Amityville, NY 11701.

Women can check with two free services for general information and travel companions. Shared Adventures can be reached at 708-852-5533 or 420 W. 75th St., Downers Grove, IL. Rainbow Adventures is at 800-804-8686 or 1308 Sherman Ave., Evanston, IL 60202.

Gallivanting specializes in active vacations for singles 25-55. Options range from international cultural excursions to white water rafting and bike trips. Call 800-933-9699.

SENIOR TRAVEL

Senior Power

Know your clout as the most powerful consumer group in America. You account for 80% of all leisure travel expenditures. You control more than half the discretionary income in the country and own 80% of the savings. You hold almost 40% of all the U.S. passports in circulation. Age discrimination tends to disappear when you travel. You get special discounts, and, particularly when traveling abroad, your age generates either additional respect or is encompassed in a spirit of general camaraderie.

Travel vendors love you because:

- **You're flexible.** You're the people who fill the mid-week period and the seasons when travel is difficult for others.

- **You purchase one-third** of all domestic travel and travel to Europe and Africa.

- **Some 90% of you have traveled before.** You have the knowledge and sophistication that makes life easier for anyone selling or providing a travel-related service.

Senior Discount Basics

We cover senior discounts thoroughly in each of our major sections–Airlines, Hotels, Car Rentals and Cruises. Here are some basic rules to follow, no matter what type of travel you're buying.

- **Always ask for senior discounts.** They aren't always advertised, and the reservation desk may not offer them. They may forget to ask, or they may be reticent about implying that you're of a certain age.

- **Check out the discount possibilities** before you make your reservation. If you wait until you're ready to make payment, it may be too late.

- **Ask age requirements.** Some discounts are applicable for people as young as 50. Others require you to be 65. Some are good for the senior only. Many will be extended to your travel companion, regardless of age.

- **Always carry proof of age** and applicable membership cards. You may not be asked to show them, but be prepared to verify your age or club membership.

- **Make sure the senior discount** is the best available discount for a particular purchase. It can frequently be bettered by discounts and special offers available to the general public.

Membership Savings

Consider a membership organization that provides the card you need to acquire senior discounts. Their affiliated travel clubs may not always offer the best value, but their cards are always worth having, particularly at the low annual rates charged for membership. If you join the American Association for Retired Persons (AARP), 800-424-3410 or 202-434-2277, for example, you'll be inundated with enticements

---

Favorite car of Marlene Dietrich: the 100 Stuttgart Cabrio C; of Errol Flynn: the Mercedes 300 S Cariolet.

by mail both from AARP and companies that utilize AARP's mailing lists. Be sure to evaluate all discount offers.

- **The National Association of Retired Credit Union People** also has a minimum age of 50. Dues are $12 per year. Call 800-937-2644.

- **The National Association of Retired Federal Employees** provides discounts and a newsletter. Write to 1533 New Hampshire Ave NW, Washington, DC 20036. Call 202-234-0832.

- **The National Council of Senior Citizens** was first formed in 1961 to help spearhead the successful lobby for Medicare coverage. Membership is $12 a year. Call 202-347-8800.

Senior Bits

Get free admission to all U.S. National Parks, monuments and recreation areas with the Golden Age Passport, available at age 62. Camping, boat launching, tours and parking are half-price. You can buy one at any National Park for $10. You can't get one by mail, but you can request information from The National Park Service, Box 37127, Washington, DC 20013. Each state also offers its own discounts. Contact state tourism offices for details.

Canadian National and Provincial Parks give you free entry if you're 62 or above just for showing your driver's license and vehicle registration. Camping is half-price on weekends.

Ask about restaurant discounts offered by your hotel. Large chains are most apt to offer them, and they can apply to your companion as well. Discounts are sometimes limited to off-peak hours.

September is special for seniors. Many locations offer discount rates or plan events designed to attract seniors and keep the vacation season going a month longer. Check the newspapers and call tourism offices in places you'd like to visit.

Educational vacations are economical and very satisfying. Sometimes you sleep in dormitories and eat college cafeteria food. Sometimes the surroundings are elegant. Examples:

- **Study in Victorian ambiance** at the Chatauqua Institute on a lake setting outside of Buffalo. The per week cost includes room and meals. Call the Program Center for Older Adults, 716-357-6200.

- **The Center For Himalayan Research and Studies** offers non-profit study opportunities that require no previous training or knowledge. They offer a range of programs from exotic cultural treks to overland trips where you stay in small hotels and guest houses. Call 800-225-4666.

- **See how Washington works** and tell it how to work better through the Close Up Foundation's package that includes hotel, meals, visiting Congress in session and even a Congressional Senior Citizen Intern Program in which you can work in the office of the congressman or congresswoman of your choice. Call 800-232-2000.

- **First class travel in Europe** is available from TraveLearn, 800-235-9114. All-inclusive two to three week tours cost about $3,000 including air and all accommodations, and amenities are superb.

- **Senior Adventures** is a network of nine colleges and universities in western states that combine education with travel. Topics range from Shakespeare to Southwestern ecology. Call 800-257-0577.

Length of time it would take to sleep one night in each of MGM Grand's guest rooms: 4,985 days.

- **University Vacations** includes students of all ages with seven to 12-day sessions at Oxford, Cambridge, Trinity College (Ireland) and the Sorbonne. Mornings are spent in study; afternoons and evenings, in exploration. Prices are bargains for the destinations offered. Call 800-792-0100.

The large variety of active senior vacations exemplifies the diversity of interests seniors have and their increasing concern with health and adventure. Here are just a few examples.

- **The National Senior Sports Association** sponsors competitive golf holidays in the U.S. and abroad. There is a $25 fee which includes a monthly newsletter, discounts on sports equipment and names and addresses of members so you can organize sports holidays on your own. Call 800-282-6772.

- **The Over The Hill Gang International** sponsors ski trips, scuba, hiking, camping, surfing... well, you get the idea. Annual membership is $37. Call 719-685-4656.

- **Bikers, motorized and pedal-powered,** have many organizations that meet to explore areas best suited for their sport. Retreads Motorcycle Club, 913-235-3893, has 30,000 members with no membership fee and a club newsletter. Roads Less Traveled Fabulous Fifties division, 800-488-8483, schedules trips in Colorado, Utah and New Mexico.

Want to make a friend in a country you'd like to visit? International Pen Pals gives reduced rates if you're 60-plus. Send a stamped, self-addressed envelope to P.O. Box 290065, Homecrest Station, Brooklyn, NY 11229. Golden Pen-Pal Association offers the same service in the United States. Send a stamped, self-addressed envelope to 1304 Hedgelawn Way, Raleigh, NC 27615.

Tourism agencies offer special packages and discounts to seniors. You save whether you're going to Branson, Missouri or Jakarta, Indonesia. You can stop by their offices after you arrive, but a phone call when you're making travel plans will yield new ideas and bargains you'll want to know about before you go. There are city, state and national offices listed in our *Know Who To Call* section. One example: The Privilege Card from the Hong Kong Tourist Association, 708-575-2828. Carrying it provides you with discounts on shopping, lodging, meals and entertainment.

CHILDREN AND TRAVEL

Saying Goodbye

Parents who travel on business learn to say goodbye a lot. There are ways to make leaving the children home easier on everyone.

- **Maps and calendar markings** help children visualize your trips.

- **Surprise them with overnight letters.** Brief notes can be supplemented

Percentage of millionaires who fly coach (according to a Warbucks marketing survey): 70%.

with small gifts–even the comics from the local paper.

- **Be in two places at once via technology.** Make audio or video tapes of bedtime stories. Keep in touch by phone, fax and computer.

- **Write a note about your day** on the back of a postcard and ask your older children to keep a short journal. Read each others notes out loud for a connecting first-night-home ritual.

Should They Go?

Your parenting style matters when making decisions about traveling with children. Should vacations be geared toward fun? Should they be learning experiences? Do you want to spend the entire vacation as a family or do you prefer some childcare options? Any answer is the right answer if it's right for you.

Leaving children at home while you take a vacation does not make you a bad parent. It's sometimes the best decision for everyone. Arrange alternate activities for your children or split your vacation into adults-only and family fun segments.

Take age levels into consideration. If you're traveling with an infant or toddler, make sure you're able to carry the child for long periods. Make sure your energy level can match that of your pre-schoolers. Account for the increased independence of teenagers. Don't expect children to necessarily like the same activities they enjoyed last year.

Minor childhood illnesses don't have to cause canceled trips if the illness is not readily contagious and is easily managed. Consider slowing down the pace for the first few days to give your child extra time to rest. Children with ear infections are prone to painful flights which often intensify their symptoms.

Taking Children On Business Trips

Working parents are taking their children on business trips 63% more often than they were four years ago. In 1994, 43.4% of business trips included children.

- **Almost 18% of hotels offer children's activities** and many of them do so throughout the week. Over 100 of the 169 Hyatt Hotels have Camp Hyatt, including childcare, activities, supervised programs and second rooms at half-price.

- **If you take your child with you frequently,** be sure he or she is enrolled in frequent flyer programs.

- **Stay away from night flights** if you are traveling with younger children. Maneuvering through airports with a sleepy child, a briefcase, garment bag and laptop is difficult.

- **Keep your child's normal schedule in mind** when traveling to different time zones.

- **Take your own nanny** if cost allows. It frees you from relying on unresearched childcare options.

Legal Issues

International travel (including travel to Canada) requires the proper documents for all children, including infants. Check on up-to-date requirements with the U.S. Tourism Office or the embassy of the country you plan to visit.

Solo parents and children traveling to Mexico, Brazil, Australia and other countries must have a letter of consent from the absent parent. This is designed to guard against kidnapping. Even a married parent may be asked to provide proof that the absent parent is aware of and approves the trip.

Number of corncobs used to build the A-maizing Corn Palace in Mitchell, South Dakota: 1,000,000.

Minor children traveling with anyone other than the custodial parent require written permission for medical treatment. A simple sentence authorizing medical care will suffice. Have the statement notarized for extra assurance.

Preparing Your Child

Allow children choices about what to pack, activities and even some budget matters. Don't try to meet every expectation. If their spending money will be limited, let them know in advance so they can plan for what is most important. If your children span a wide age range, plan activities that will appeal to each one. Disposable cameras give them something to do when the day's activities aren't particularly child-oriented.

Children taking their first flights should be prepared by conversation, books or even a trip to the airport.

* *How To Fly For Kids* covers the same ground in book form for $8.95 plus shipping and handling. It also offers games and in-flight activities. It's widely available in bookstores. If you can't find it call 800-729-6423.

* Just Planes Videos offers three videos that answer most fears and questions. They cost $11.95 each (plus shipping and handling). Call 800-752-6376 or fax 617-539-3224.

Discuss rule changes. Will bedtime remain the same? Will more snacks be permitted? What new rules are required to deal specifically with the trip?

Make the unknown known. Take the time to explain the trip to your children to alleviate fears and answer questions. Use brochures, library books and on-line travel information to excite and inform them about new destinations.

Use time to your advantage. Program free time into your travel. Underplanning can be the best friend of traveling families. Children are curious and will resist being pulled too quickly from one attraction to another. Allow extra time to get anywhere, particularly during peak travel periods.

Single parents can create a traveling family and make travel more enjoyable by joining with another compatible parent and child. The children and the adults have like-minded company, lodging costs are shared and everyone has more fun.

Taking your child's friend on a family trip can add to everyone's enjoyment but be aware of special needs and of your own liability. Be sure your guest is compatible with your child for extended periods of time. A good test is a weekend sleepover.

What To Take

A common misconception about traveling with children is that you have to carry an enormous amount of extra luggage. Be creative instead; rent or improvise when you arrive and just pack the essentials:

* Prescription medicine and copies of the prescription in case of loss or spillage plus an easy-to-read pediatric thermometer.

* Easy-care clothing that the child likes to wear and that can easily be laundered in a hotel room.

* Plastic bags of various sizes, for soiled clothes, special finds, crayons, small toys and a dozen other things you can't predict in advance.

* The stuffed toy or blanket necessary to sleep. Try to take your child's second-best comfort item or purchase a duplicate. Many travel tears are shed when "Blankie" or "Teddy" gets left somewhere along the way.

Carry infants up to five months old in

canvas slings that rest against your chest. Backpack-style carriers for older infants keep your hands free and provide them with a secure view of the world.

Surprise kits packed with treats and travel activities provide you with anti-boredom ammunition.

Personal backpacks or carry-ons allow children to take along personal treasures and favorite toys and books. As much as possible, leave this space free for what they select and what they might find interesting along the way.

Travel By Car

Approved car seats are mandatory in all states for children four and under. You can rent them for about $5 per day but often they're older, less safe models. Bring your own or look for a rental that is certified to meet the Federal Motor Vehicle Safety Standards.

When renting a car, carry a locking clip to use on free-sliding latches common on foreign and newer domestic cars. Be sure car seats can be properly secured in any vehicle you rent.

Check all seat belts and shoulder harnesses to make sure they are arranged and function in a fashion that protects every family member.

Take air bag placement into consideration when assigning children seats in rental cars.

Relieve car travel monotony to make your trips more enjoyable:

- **Head for back roads** for scenery that will awaken children's interest.

- **Leave very early in the morning** so you can cover distances by mid-afternoon and take full advantage of hotel stays.

- **Invest in inexpensive peace of mind.** Small cassette players with headphones can produce instant quiet as your four-year-old listens to a story tape and your 12-year-old tunes in to music. A child who usually reads little more than a cereal box can be fascinated by a road map or atlas.

- **Portable armrests,** available at auto supply stores, have storage compartments with lift-up lids. They create separate kid-zones when two children share a back seat.

Lodging

Use "Kids Stay Free" and "Kids Eat Free" whenever possible. Many hotel chains offer free accommodations for children under 18 sharing a room with parents. Some hotels discount a second room so families with older children can enjoy privacy at bargain rates. Holiday Inns frequently offer three free meals a day to children under 12 who are dining with their parents. Hotel Reservations Network, 800-964-6835, is a clearinghouse for special values for family hotels. Hotel chains try to stay competitive so always ask for free children's options before reserving your accommodations.

Ask for child-proof rooms to make vacation life easier. They include special safety features and equipment ranging from diaper changing areas to strollers. Safety check rooms where small children will be staying. Remember that most hotels and even grandma's house are not set up for small children. Outlet covers and routine protection you are used to at home are not likely to be present when you travel. Cribs provided by hotels may not be up to safety standards.

Consider condo rentals and suite hotels with kitchen facilities, room to spread out and separate sleeping areas.

Home of the largest ball of string (over 17,000 pounds): Darwin, Minnesota.

Supervised activities are increasingly available at hotels and resorts. They can be free or cost as much as $65 per day at ultra luxury properties. Inquire about the ratio of counselor to child, first aid training and activities provided.

Childcare options exist at most major hotels, but often they simply consist of referral numbers with minimal reference checks. If you use this service, make sure you are satisfied that your children are being left in trustworthy hands.

Caution children about added hotel expenses like in-room refrigerator items and using the hotel phone. In their eyes, every service may seem as free as the complimentary shampoo.

Hostels and college dorms are inexpensive, little-used lodging options. Some have family rooms with private baths. Some are in lighthouses or restored downtown buildings. Contact Hostelling International at 202-783-6161 for hundreds of hostel options. Get a complete list of hostels in the U.S. and Canada by sending $3, payable to Jim Williams at Sugar Hill International House, 722 St. Nicholas Ave., New York, NY 10031.

Almost 800 U.S. colleges offer dorm accommodations, mostly on a summer season basis. About 50 offer year-round availability. Call Campus Travel Service, 800-525-6633. Also investigate timeshares and house swaps. Be sure anything you select is child-friendly.

Child-Friendly Dining

Dining out with small children is simplified if you eat at restaurants that welcome them. Call ahead to see if they offer highchairs and booster seats.

Create your own room service. Milk, cereal and fresh fruit are great in-your-room alternatives to expensive restaurant breakfasts. Nested plastic bowls take up little luggage space and many hotels have nearby shopping areas where prices approach reason.

Consider a fast food meal. It may not be your idea of regional cuisine, but it can be comforting to smaller children already overloaded with change. Take the food back to your hotel and let your children enjoy their food while you order from room service. Chances are they'll think they got the better deal.

Travel Aids

All major cities offer free information on attractions for children. *New York For Kids* is available from the NYC Convention and Visitors Bureau, 2 Columbus Circle, New York, NY 10019. Similar information is available from state and national tourism organizations. Be sure to ask specifically for material pertaining to children.

Family Travel Times, published quarterly at a $40 subscription cost, is a compact source of information on traveling with children. Call 212-477-5524 or write to 45 W. 18th St., 7th Floor, New York, NY 10011.

The Family & Travel Directory includes family travel discounts and extensive information on over 500 hotels and resorts oriented toward family stays. The cost is $19.95, which also gives you access to an information hotline that connects you directly to participating properties so you can gather detailed information. Call 800-963-2645 (outside of Texas) to order.

Kid Bits

Hiking tours and outdoor-oriented vacations provide special challenges.

Let the smallest walking child set the pace. There's a lot to be seen from a kid's-eye view.

Country where it is considered improper to touch a child or adult's head: Thailand.

> **"***Train travel is a favorite of children. Sleeping berths, dining cars and observation cars are wonderful novelties. The biggest advantage may be that they can move around while en route. Amtrak offers half-price tickets for children two to 15 traveling with adults. Family Adventure Trips such as Chicago to the Grand Canyon are popular summer options with reduced train travel plus special hotel rates for overnight stays.* "**

Teach children low impact tourism by emphasizing respect for the environment and the creatures living in it.

Vacationers love sunny days but be alert to what a day outdoors can do to sensitive children's skin. Sun-blocks are almost imperative–not only on sunny days, but in high altitudes and in places where the sun's rays are strong even through cloud cover.

Don't try to see everything in one day. One of the saddest sights in any amusement park is that of impatient parents dragging children from ride to ride while wondering why they don't seem to be having any fun.

Study the maps and plot each day as carefully as if you were exploring a foreign country. Pick the attractions you most want to see and try to schedule them for less busy times.

Don't be scared away by a rainy day. Not only is the weather in both Florida and California changeable, the parks are arranged to allow for all but downpours. A little wet weather is a small price to pay for lines that may take half the time to pass through.

Dress the whole family in the same bold-colored t-shirts or caps for easier identification in crowds. Whistles worn around the neck make good alarms and calling signals.

Hands-on programs at Sea World and Busch Gardens offer children's programs from pre-school to teenage.

- **Camp Sea World**, 407-363-2380, focuses on science and conservation.

- **Busch Garden's Zoo Camp and Safari Classes**, 813-987-5555, are available on limited days.

Living history recreations and hands-on museums recognize that children like to learn by doing. Colonial Williamsburg in Virginia, Mystic Seaport in Connecticut and the six-floor Hands-On Museum in Ann Arbor are just a few places where destinations can define your trip.

International travel is more affordable and manageable than you may think.

- **Interhostel**, 800-733-9753, designed for children eight to 15, offers trips centered around university stays in places like Holland, Madrid and Slovakia.

- **A big plus of international travel** is the opportunity for your kids to interact with children from other cultures. Few things are greater eye-openers.

- **Children can introduce you to locals** and increase your ability to really get to know a destination. Take your child to a neighborhood park. You're likely to find other English-speaking parents who will be happy to share tips on top attractions for local children.

Number of students who went to Panama City Beach, Florida for Spring Break 1995: over 550,000.

Take them on a nostalgia trip and keep them interested by showing them where you went to school, the park you played at and where you went on your first date.

Don't expect them to instantly bond with cousins and other children they see infrequently. Allow them some time to get over shyness before expecting any playtime or companionship to occur.

Let them feel some sense of familiarity. A visit to McDonald's is not what you traveled 1,000 miles for, but it can help take the edge off the unfamiliarity that can distress any child.

Grandparents and grandchildren make such great travel partners that many organizations have formed to provide ideas and creative itineraries.

- **GrandTravel**, 800-247-7651, is one of the largest groups which offers specially designed grandchild/grandparent tours. The American Association of Retired Persons, 202-434-2296, offers some discounted trips.

TRAVELING WITH ANIMALS

Can You?/Should You?

Assistance animals, such as seeing-eye-dogs, are allowed to accompany you anywhere in the U.S. You don't have to receive permission, but it is a good idea to let the reservation desk know so you can be given any information available to make travel easier for both of you.

Quarantine laws are applicable anytime you travel outside the continental U.S. In most cases, the mandatory length of quarantine (as long as six months) effectively prohibits the vacationing pet. The baggage department of the airline you're flying can give you specific quarantine requirements.

Pets are not allowed on bus lines or in AMTRAK passenger cars. Some trains allow pets to travel in baggage compartments, but you are responsible for feeding, watering and exercising the animal during stops.

Travel By Car

Car trips with pets also require that you carry proof of immunization if you are crossing state lines and, in rare instances, when you cross county lines.

Documentation of the animal's most recent rabies vaccination is vital if your pet bites someone. Having it with you can save you, your animal and the person who was bitten a great deal of agony.

Road rules for pets:

- **Take short rest stops every two to three hours.**

- **Don't let dogs hang their heads out of windows** of fast-moving vehicles. Flying debris can permanently injure eyes and foreign material can lodge in their ears and nasal passages.

The most popular U.S. destination for fall travel: Florida. (Obviously it's not the leaves.)

- **Protect your animals in unfamiliar surroundings** by always keeping them leashed. Try not to leave them unattended in hotel rooms. They can be out the door the second the maid opens it.

- **Carry a recent photo** in case you and your animal are separated. An organization called Lost Paws provides you with a special ID tag and 24-hour hotline to connect lost pets with their humans. The cost is $24.95 per pet per year (less for additional animals). Call 800-676-3157.

Pet-friendly lodging is available and numerous guides exist. *Take Your Pet USA* is one of the most extensive. It's available for $13.95 postpaid from Artco Publishing, 12 Channel St., Boston, MA 02210.

Pet Protective Publications

Free pet travel tips are available for the price of a stamped, self-addressed business-size envelope.

- *Travel Tip Sheets* from the American Society for the Prevention of Cruelty to Animals (ASPCA) Education Dept., 424 E. 92nd St., New York, NY 10128. Call 212-876-7700.

- *Air Travel For Your Dog Or Cat* from the Air Transport Association of America, 1301 Pennsylvania Ave., NW, Suite 1100, Washington, DC 20004. Call 202-626-4000.

- *Pet Travel Tips* from People For The Ethical Treatment Of Animals (PETA), P.O. Box 42516. Washington, DC 20015. Call 301-770-7444

- *DogGone,* 407-569-8434, is a bimonthly magazine offering canine travel tips and information on dog-friendly destinations. A yearly subscription is $24.

Recently,

BEST FARES Discount Travel Magazine

showed savvy travelers how to get a free upgrade at Renaissance Hotels just for paying with American Express.

Call 800-880-1234 to subscribe.
See page 395 for your discount subscription offer.

Size of Arizona's Meteor Crater: 570 feet deep and 4,110 feet across.

INTERNATIONAL TRAVEL

Passports

A U.S. Passport is essential for most foreign travel and the best proof of citizenship for all travelers.

Every U.S. citizen, including infants, must carry a passport when traveling abroad.

You can travel to Mexico, Canada and the Caribbean Islands with just an original or certified copy of your birth certificate, a photo ID and a travel ticket, but you can prevent any possible problem on returning to the U.S. by carrying a passport instead.

Passport applications require proof of identity such as a driver's license or state ID (credit cards and social security cards are not acceptable) plus one of the following documents:

- **An expired passport** regardless of the date of expiration.

- **A certified birth certificate copy** or naturalization papers.

- **A baptismal certificate or** record of elementary school enrollment.

- **A U.S. citizen appearing in person** to sign a statement attesting to your identity.

Also needed when you apply:

- **Two identical passport photos** taken within the past six months. Be sure to have them taken at a place that specializes in passport photos to avoid an unacceptable pose or photos too dark or too light to be used.

- **The applicable fee:**

  $65 if you apply in person/ $55 if you apply by mail.

$40 for children under 18 applying by mail or in person.

Passports are valid for ten years. If you plan to do a lot of travel, request a passport with extra pages at no additional charge.

Apply for your passport at any U.S. Passport Agency office or any of 2,500 courthouses and 900 post offices that accept applications. Send mail applications to the National Passport Center, P.O. Box 371971, Pittsburgh, PA 15250.

Routine issuance of passports takes two to six weeks depending on the time of year (February through July is busiest) and how you apply.

U.S. Passport Agency expedited service (one week or less) is available for an additional $30 fee. You must have a ticket in hand showing that you are traveling within ten days or need your passport urgently in order to apply for visas.

Private expediting services can get you a passport in 24 hours under the same criteria listed above. You pay $100-150 for one-day service; $35-50 for seven-day service. They're listed in the classified directory under "*Passport and Visa Services.*"

Expedite your own passport if you live near one of the eight offices that issues them, but be prepared for lengthy waits in

---

Country where it is impolite to sit with feet facing the fireplace: Mongolia.

line. See *Know Who To Call* under *Pertinent Travel Numbers* for a listing of regional passport offices.

Passports: Applying for Them the Easy Way is available from Consumer Information, Dept. 356A, Pueblo, CO 81009 for a 50¢ fee.

> **"**Treat your passport as the valuable document it is. Almost 20,000 are stolen annually and another 15,000 are lost. Make two copies of the main information page. Keep one in a safe place at home and carry one with you in case you lose your passport while traveling. Never mutilate it in any way. A phone number jotted on an unused page or a torn corner is considered mutilation that can technically invalidate your passport and will definitely prohibit you from renewing by mail. **"**

Report lost passports immediately and request a temporary replacement while traveling from the American embassy or consulate. If you locate your passport after it's been reported missing, don't use it. Immigration will stop you for traveling on what they have listed as a lost or stolen document.

Visa Requirements

Visa requirements change constantly.

The Basic Visa Requirement Chart gives you the fundamentals on obtaining entry into 78 countries. It's offered by Trans-World Visa Service, which expedites visas on a per-fee basis. Send a stamped, self-addressed envelope to Trans-World Visa Service, 790 27th Ave., San Francisco, CA 94121.

- **Most Western European countries** don't require them for stays under three months.

- **Many Eastern European countries** have also dropped their requirements.

- **Most visas take two to three weeks** to acquire and you must have a passport before you apply.

The State Department fax information line, 202-647-3000, provides quick information in printed form on your choice of three countries. Request the "foreign entry requirements" option or call 202-647-5226, which gives the same data via recording.

Get for-fee expedited visa service from the same companies that expedite passports.

Customs

The basics of customs are simple and, for most people, the basics are all you will require.

- **Duty-free allowances vary** according to your country of origin and destination, existing trade policies, tax policy and in some countries, trade sanctions.

   Know Before You Go is published by the U.S. Customs Service. It offers an insight into Customs' rules and regulations. Call 202-927-6724 or write to U.S. Customs Service, "KBYG," P.O. Box 7407, Washington, DC 20044.

- **You must have been out of the country** at least 48 hours to be eligible to bring in any duty-free items.

- **You can't save unused allowances** from trip to trip, and there must be a 30-day period between exemptions.

- **You'll pay ten percent** on the first $1,000 in purchases above your $400 allowance and various rates on purchases exceeding that limit.

- **You can carry up to $10,000** in cash and negotiable instruments. Higher amounts must be reported on Customs form 4790 when entering and leaving the United States.

The Generalized System of Preference applies to 125 countries and exempts certain items from duty. *GSP & The Traveler* provides an updated list. Get it from any regional customs office or write to U.S. Customs Services, Box 7407, Washington, DC 20044.

The sensitive snout of a drug-sniffing dog can single you out for attention even if you are the picture of innocence. An incredible 97% of our currency carries trace amounts of cocaine. Don't panic, but do avoid carrying large sums of cash, particularly when visiting countries with high levels of drug activity.

The newest customs technology is INPASS, used to bypass manual inspection. Now limited to travelers who make more than three international trips per year, the goal is to extend the system to all travelers. A coded card is inserted in an ATM-like machine that prompts you to place your hand on a special plate that identifies you and checks you against a federal database. INPASS is in use at Newark, New York/JFK and Toronto airports. Call 212-206-6500 for an application.

Dutiful Tips

Purchases made in duty-free shops are exempt from tax only in the country of purchase. They're still subject to U.S. duty. Figure in the cost of paying duty when considering items to be purchased abroad.

Carry receipts on new-looking, foreign-made items that you purchased before your trip to prove they have not been purchased on your trip.

About five percent of all travelers are subject to intense scrutiny. Factors that increase the odds include:

- **Travel from known drug-source countries** or from popular shopping destinations.

- **Bulky or unusual clothing**.

- **Nervous demeanor**.

- **Obvious signs of wealth**.

Customs will confiscate certain items purchased abroad despite the assurances of shopkeepers eager to make a sale. Don't purchase lizard, snake or crocodile skin products, feathers or feather products, furs from spotted cats or marine mammals, sea-turtle products, ivory, live birds, decorative items made from wildlife or unlicensed copies of brand name products.

> **"**If you're caught trying to avoid paying duty, you could be required to pay several times more than you would have been charged had you declared your purchase. Customs agents can multiply the duty by the degree of aggravation and lack of cooperation you provide. Claims that expensive items were purchased prior to your trip can be checked via serial and registration numbers. **"**

> **❝** *U.S. Consulates and Embassies provide lists of English-speaking doctors and lawyers, special circumstance loans for travel back to the U.S., 90-day replacement passports, notary service and support for the rights of U.S. citizens in foreign jails. They can't provide loans to continue trips, cash personal checks, recommend specific lawyers and doctors or enforce American standards of justice. You are under the legal domain of each country you visit.* **❞**

International Arrests

Learn local laws and customs when you travel internationally. What is merely frowned on in the U.S. can be prosecuted under the laws of other countries. For example, Singapore is making a name for itself with laws against such society–threatening activities as chewing gum. Carrying or holding a package for a stranger could open you to drug charges in countries with laws that include the death penalty for contraband offenses.

• **If you are arrested,** notify the American Embassy and retain a lawyer immediately. Contrary to what many people assume, the embassy does not provide direct legal assistance. They guarantee that your rights as a detained U.S. citizen are protected, but those rights are defined by the laws of the country you're in.

• **The best source for an international lawyer referral:** your own attorney in the U.S. The best time to get that referral: before trouble strikes. If he or she cannot provide information on representation in countries you plan to visit, contact the International Legal Defense Council, 215-977-9982 or (for U.S. and Latin America only) the Inter-American Bar Association, 202-393-1217.

Two other potential legal pitfalls:

• **Never purchase endangered species products or antiquities.** Shop owners may assure you that you'll encounter no problems but many countries–primarily Peru, Mexico, China, Greece and other Mediterranean countries–have strict laws protecting their national treasures.

• **Exchange currency only through authorized channels.** The small amount of money you might save by dealing with a local entrepreneur is not worth risking the harsh penalties some countries impose.

Language Barriers

Crash through language barriers:

• **Learn four words or phrases a day** before you go. Two weeks gives you 56 new ways to communicate.

• **Speak distinctly and avoid slang or colloquialisms.** Don't make the common mistake of speaking louder. They hear you; it's comprehension that causes the difficulty.

• **Use commonly understood gestures** to emphasize what you're trying to say and don't try to over-communicate. Keep it simple and clear.

• **One picture can be worth a Berlitz course** if you know how to read internationally accepted symbols. "Quick-point" takes this idea a step further with the creation of easy to comprehend symbols to convey things like specific meal requests, the need for a haircut or a place to develop film. A folding card the size of a standard business envelope increases your worldwide communications skills at a $5 cost. Write to Gaia Communications, Box 239, Alexandria, VA 22313.

Accessible Travel

A comprehensive 550-page book on all aspects of travel for people with disabilities is available for $35. Order *Travelin' Talk* by calling 615-552-6670.

Unique international tour packages are offered by Flying Wheels Travel, 800-535-6790, and Accessible Journeys, 800-846-4537.

Students and Teachers

International travel can be a learning experience and a bargain:

- **If you're a full-time student of any age or you are under 25,** apply for a Student ID or Youth card to qualify for international discounts on transportation, lodging, food, movies, museums, shops and special events. The requirements: a birth certificate to prove you're under 25 or a university fee statement copy to prove you're a student, a passport type photo and an $18 fee. Contact STA, 800-777-0112. Major universities will have an STA office on campus.

- **Learn a foreign language** where it's spoken. Universities and private schools offer language programs for foreigners. Contact The American Institute for Foreign Study, 800-727-2437 or Language Studies Abroad, 800-424-5522.

- **Elementary, secondary and university educators** have their own free source of information and bargains. *Travel Options* is available from The Council on International Educational Exchange, 212-661-1414, ext. 1108.

The Three Seasons of Euro-Travel

The three seasons of European travel each offer unique advantages.

- **Peak season** (late June, July and August) offers travel when most leisure travelers are best able to go. The crowds can even be advantageous. Pick a good vantage point and get the benefit of several tour guides' interpretations within 30 minutes.

- **Shoulder season** (May, early June, September and early October) has the best mix of rates, weather and uncrowded conditions.

- **Off-season** (all remaining months) offers the best bargains. Budget hotels throughout Europe are readily available, though some hostels will be closed for the season.

Shopping Internationally

Visit the outdoor markets for bargains and a panoramic look at local culture. Whether it's a *souk* in Morocco or a *mercato* in Italy, you'll find a feast for all your senses.

Get a gem of a bargain by checking the markets where your favorite stone is king. Best bets: opals from Australia and New Zealand, diamonds from Belgium, jade from Hong Kong, pearls from Japan, sapphires from Thailand, emeralds from South Africa, agate and turquoise from Mexico, rubies from India, amber from Russia.

Check out each country's specialty items: alpaca and leather items from Argentina, chocolates from Belgium, silk from China, made-to-order suits from England, electronics from Hong Kong, batik from Bali, beaded jewelry and clothing from Nepal, sweaters and linens from Ireland. Check out public marketplaces like Ho Chi Minh City's Thanh Market where an intricately embroidered blouse is yours for about $10.

International Bits

Don't forget free attractions. London, for example, has no standard admission charge at the National Gallery, the National Portrait gallery and the Tate Gallery.

Countries where political and economic climates are in flux present special challenges. China, neither capitalist nor communist, can seem to combine the worst of both worlds. Make as many arrangements as possible from the U.S., but don't take your confirmations too seriously. Traveling in such countries requires a special sort of flexibility.

Foreign holidays and holy days can pop up in the middle of your trip. Suddenly there are crowds of people on the street or businesses are closed for the day. Take these days into consideration when making your travel plans. Be particularly aware of revered holy days in countries that take them very seriously.

Simplify taxi travel by writing out the address of your destination, or have someone familiar with the local language call it in when you request the taxi. Be prepared to translate the meter fare into local currency.

Currency adapters may take care of differences in plug styles but they don't convert electrical currents that can cause shocks, smoke and sizzled appliances. *Electric Current Abroad*, published by the U.S. State Department, lists voltage and currency fluctuations around the world. Ask for document #003-008-00203-2. The cost is $3. Order from the Superintendent of Documents, Washington, DC 20402.

One of the easiest way to be involved in an auto accident in many countries is just to walk across the street. Small cars, different driving patterns and congested streets mean you should see the sights but keep an eye on the traffic.

Not all toilets flush. You might have to push or pull, twist, step-on or squeeze a handle–or you might be surprised by an electric-eye that does the work for you. Coin-operated water closets await your need on street corners in London and Amsterdam.

Rent a cellular phone in Europe from Global Cellular Rental, 800-699-6861.

Want to save overall? Head for smaller cities rather than big international centers. You can visit them by train or rental car with a home base in a place where lodging and food are one-third to one-half cheaper. You'll also get perspectives not available to travelers who stick to the biggest tourist destinations.

Don't count on free refills. Most countries charge the same for the second cup or glass as they did for the first.

Americans are generally welcome travelers. Do your part by understanding indigenous customs, accepting warm beer, dogs in cafes and other habits common to the populace. Be observant enough to know what's appropriate.

Hot Cards started popping up all over Europe in 1995 and their popularity means they'll be around for a long time. Tourism offices provide up-to-the-minute listings of their country's cards. See our *Dollars & Cents* section for some examples.

Number of chocolate shops in Belgium: 2,100.

Soothe first-trip jitters with videos to introduce you to new destinations. Watch them for free in some large travel agencies, rent them from video shops or purchase them from retailers and tourism offices. You'll find some with exceptional production standards and creativity. The Bermuda Department of Tourism, for example, has built their 17-minute video around the Beatles *In Your Life*. Call 800-237-6832. The cost is $10.95.

Free or almost free travel information comes from many sources, including car rental agencies and airlines. Brochures geared toward attracting customers include helpful information on destinations they service. Tourism offices (listed in the *Know Who To Call* section) will always send you information on their countries. The most extensive array of information will be found on European destinations, but calling tourism offices will open doorways to almost any country in the world.

Recently, ***BEST FARES Discount Travel Magazine*** showed savvy travelers how to get a free Delta upgrade and a $99 companion fare for answering a few survey questions.

A Monthly Publication of Insider Travel Secrets Listing the Latest Discounts for The Cost-Conscious Traveler

**Call 800-880-1234 to subscribe.
See page 395 for your discount subscription offer.**

KNOW WHO TO CALL

Have you ever headed for a bank of airport pay phones, reached for the telephone directory and found an empty holder? It's hard to let your fingers do the walking when there's nowhere for them to go. It's a common annoyance you can avoid with this directory of travel contacts. There's no need to call directory assistance, hunt for a pen and get one or two numbers at a time when you really want to check multiple airlines or hotels.

On the road or at home, you'll be in control with the numbers you need to plan a trip, book it and deal with problems and complaints that might arise despite your planning.

Some of the information–such as Airport Paging numbers–are unique to this book. We included Internet contacts. We tried to give you all the numbers you need but remember that this book will be updated annually and suggestions for future editions are welcome.

This section is as accurate as hundreds of hours of checking and double-checking can make it but we know some numbers will change just in the time it takes to print this edition and get it to you. Some 800 numbers listed may not be accessible from one specific state. If you run into that glitch, make a free call to 800 directory assistance (800-555-1212) and they'll be happy to give you a number that will work from your location.

There's one number that we want to spotlight–our own. If you can't bear to be out of touch with bargains until the next edition of this book, you can subscribe to *BEST FARES Discount Travel Magazine* by calling 800-880-1234. Tell them Tom sent you.

AIRPORT PAGING

(BHM) indicates airport code

ALABAMA

Birmingham (BHM) . . . .(205) 599-0500
Mobile (MOB) . . . .(334) 633-4510
Montgomery (MGM) . . . . .CALL AIRLINE

ALASKA

Anchorage (ANC) . . . . .CALL AIRLINE
Fairbanks (FAI) . . . . .CALL AIRLINE

ARIZONA

Phoenix (PHX) . . . .(602) 273-3455
Tucson (TUS) . . . .(520) 573-8000
Flagstaff (FLG) . . . .(520) 556-1234

ARKANSAS

Little Rock (LIT) . . . .(501) 375-1509

CALIFORNIA

Burbank (BUR) . . . . .CALL AIRLINE
Long Beach (LGB) . . . .(310) 425-5555
Los Angeles (LAX) . . . . .CALL AIRLINE
Monterey (MRY) . . . .(408) 648-7002
Oakland (OAK) . . . .(510) 577-4000
Ontario (ONT) . . . .(909) 988-2700
Orange County (SNA) . . . .(714) 252-5006
Sacramento (SMF) . . . .(916) 929-5411
San Diego (SAN) . . . .(619) 231-2294
San Francisco (SFO) . . . .(415) 876-2377
San Jose (SJC) . . . .(408) 277-4759

COLORADO

Colorado Springs (COS) . . . .(719) 550-1919
Denver (DIA) . . . .(303) 342-2000

CONNECTICUT

Hartford (BDT) . . . . .CALL AIRLINE
New Haven (HVN) . . . . .CALL AIRLINE

DELAWARE

Wilmington (ILG) . . . .(302) 573-6144

DISTRICT OF COLUMBIA AREA

Baltimore/Washington (BWI) . . . .(410) 859-7111
Dulles (IAD) . . . .(703) 661-8636
National (DCA) . . . .(703) 419-3972

FLORIDA

Fort Lauderdale (FLL) . . . . .CALL AIRLINE
Fort Myers (RSW) . . . .(813) 768-4700
Jacksonville (JAX) . . . .(904) 741-3044
Gainesville (GNV) . . . .(904) 373-0249

FLORIDA (CONTINUED)

Miami (MIA) . . . .(305) 876-7000
Orlando (MCO) . . . .(407) 825-2000
St. Petersburg/Clearwater (PIE) . . . . .(813) 535-7600
Sarasota-Bradenton (SRQ) . . . .(914) 359-5225
Tampa (TPA) . . . .(800) 767-8882
West Palm Beach (PBI) . . . .(407) 471-7420

> **"**In some airports, the paging is handled directly by the airlines. You call the airline the traveler is ticketed on. We show Call Airline in these instances. Airline numbers follow this section.**"**

GEORGIA

Atlanta (ATL) . . . . .CALL AIRLINE
Macon (MCN) . . . .(912) 788-6310
Savannah (SAV) . . . .(912) 964-0514

HAWAII

Hilo, Hawaii (ITO) . . . .(808) 934-5838
Lihu, Kauai (LIH) . . . . .CALL AIRLINE
Kahului, Maui (OGG) . . . . . .Departing (808) 872-3894
. . . . .Arriving (808) 872-3893
Honolulu, Oahu (HNL) . . . . .CALL AIRLINE

IDAHO

Boise (BOI) . . . .(208) 383-3135

ILLINOIS

Chicago O'Hare (ORD) . . . .(312) 686-2200
Chicago Midway (MDW) . . . .(312) 767-0500
Moline (MLI) . . . .(309) 757-1530
Peoria (PIA) . . . .(309) 697-4741
Rockford (FRD) . . . .(815) 987-3390

INDIANA

Evansville (EVV) . . . . .CALL AIRLINE
Fort Wayne (FWA) . . . . .CALL AIRLINE
Indianapolis (IND) . . . .(317) 487-7243
South Bend (SBN) . . . .(219) 282-4590

IOWA

Des Moines (DSM) . . . .(515) 256-5050
Cedar Rapids (CID) . . . .(319) 362-8336

KANSAS

Kansas City (MCI) . . . .(816) 243-5237
Wichita (ICT) . . . . .CALL AIRLINE

Year in which AT&T purchased the nation's largest cellular telephone company: 1994.

KENTUCKY

Cincinnati (CVG) ....CALL AIRLINE
Louisville (SDF) ....(502) 367-4636
Lexington (LEX) ....(606) 255-4143

LOUISIANA

Monroe (MLU) ....(318) 329-2461
New Orleans (MSY) ....(504) 464-0831
Shreveport (SHV) ....(318) 673-5370

MAINE

Bangor (BGR) ....(207) 947-0384
Portland (PWM) ....(207) 775-5809

MASSACHUSETTS

Boston/Logan (BOS) ....CALL AIRLINE

MARYLAND AREA

Baltimore/Washington (BWI) ......(410) 859-7111
Washington Dulles (IAD) ....(703) 661-8636
Washington National (DCA) ....(703) 419-3972

MICHIGAN

Detroit (DTW) ....CALL AIRLINE
Flint (FNT) ....CALL AIRLINE
Grand Rapids (GRR) ....CALL AIRLINE
Lansing (LAN) ....(517) 321-6121

MINNESOTA

Duluth (DLH) ....(218) 727-3201
Minneapolis/St. Paul (MSP) ....CALL AIRLINE
Rochester (RST) ....CALL AIRLINE

MISSISSIPPI

Jackson (JAN) ....(601) 939-5631

MISSOURI

Kansas City (MCI) ....(816) 243-5237
Saint Louis (STL) ....CALL AIRLINE

MONTANA

Billings (BIL) ....CALL AIRLINE
Bozeman (BZN) ....(406) 388-8321
Great Falls (GTF) ....(406) 727-3404

NEW MEXICO

Albuquerque (ABQ) ....(505) 842-4379

NORTH CAROLINA

Greensboro/Piedmont (GSO) ....(910) 665-5688
Charlotte (CLT) ....(704) 359-4027
Raleigh/Durham (RDU) ....(919) 840-2123
Winston-Salem (INT) ....CALL AIRLINE

NORTH DAKOTA

Bismark (BIS) ....CALL AIRLINE
Fargo (FAR) ....(701) 241-1501
Minot (MOT) ....(701) 857-4724

NEBRASKA

Lincoln (LNK) ....(402) 475-7243
Omaha (OMA) ....(402) 422-6817

NEVADA

Las Vegas (LAS) ....(702) 261-5733
Reno (RNO) ....(702) 328-6789

NEW HAMPSHIRE

Manchester (MHT) ....(603) 624-6556

NEW JERSEY

Atlantic City (AIY) ....CALL AIRLINE
Newark (EWR) ....CALL AIRLINE

NEW YORK

Albany County (ALB) ....(518) 869-3021
Buffalo (BUF) ....CALL AIRLINE
New York Kennedy (JFK) ....CALL AIRLINE
New York La Guardia (LGA) ....CALL AIRLINE
Rochester (ROC) ....CALL AIRLINE
Syracuse (SYR) ....CALL AIRLINE

OHIO

Akron/Canton (CAK) ....(216) 499-4221
Cincinnati (CVG) ....CALL AIRLINE
Cleveland (CLE) ....(216) 265-6030
Columbus (CMH) ....CALL AIRLINE
Dayton (DAY) ....CALL AIRLINE

OKLAHOMA

Oklahoma City (OKC) ....(405) 680-3317
Tulsa (TUS) ....(918) 838-5046

OREGON

Eugene (EUG) ....(503) 341-5870
Portland (PDX) ....(503) 335-1040

PENNSYLVANIA

Harrisburg (MDT) ....CALL AIRLINE
Philadelphia (PHL) ....(215) 937-6937
Pittsburgh (PIT) ....(412) 472-3525

RHODE ISLAND

Providence (PVD) ....(401) 737-4000 ext 262

SOUTH CAROLINA

Charleston (CHS) ....(803) 767-7009
Columbia (CAE) ....(803) 822-5002

Year in which the Justice Department first sued AT&T for alleged antitrust violations: 1949.

SOUTH DAKOTA

Rapid City (RAP) . . . .(605) 393-9924
Sioux Falls (FSD) . . . .(605) 331-3733

TENNESSEE

Chattanooga (CHA) . . . .(423) 855-2200
Knoxville (TYS) . . . . .CALL AIRLINE
Memphis (MEM) . . . . .CALL AIRLINE
Nashville (BNA) . . . .(615) 275-1675

TEXAS

Austin (AUS) . . . .(512) 472-3321
Corpus Christi (CRP) . . . .(512) 289-2675
Dallas Love Field (DAL) . . . .(214) 904-5559
Dallas Ft. Worth (DFW) . . . . .CALL AIRLINE
El Paso (ELP) . . . .(915) 772-4271
Harlengen HRL) . . . .(210) 430-8600
Houston Hobby (HOU) . . . . .CALL AIRLINE
Houston Intercontinental (IAH) . . . . .(713) 230-3000
Lubbock (LBB) . . . . .CALL AIRLINE
San Antonio (SAT) . . . .(210) 821-3411

UTAH

Salt Lake City (SLC) . . . .(801) 575-2600

VERMONT

Burlington (BTV) . . . . .CALL AIRLINE
Rutland (RUT) . . . .(802) 747-7101

VIRGINIA

Norfolk (ORF) . .8:30 a.m.-5 p.m. M-F (804) 857-3351
. . . .(other times) (804) 444-3040
Richmond (RIC) . . . . .CALL AIRLINE
Dulles (IAD) . . . .(703) 419-3972

WASHINGTON

Seattle/Tacoma (SEA) . . . . .CALL AIRLINE
Spokane (GEG) . . . .(509) 455-6455

WISCONSIN

Green Bay (GRB) . . . . .CALL AIRLINE
Madison (MSN) . . . .(608) 246-3380
Milwaukee (MKE) . . . .(414) 747-5245

WYOMING

Casper (CPR) . . . . .CALL AIRLINE
Cheyenne (CYS) . . . .(307) 635-6623
Jackson Hole (JAC) . . . .(307) 733-7682

AIRLINE RESERVATIONS & INFORMATION

DOMESTIC AIRLINES

AIR NEVADA 800-634-6377
AIR SOUTH .800-247-7688
AIRTRAN AIRWAYS 800-247-8726
ALASKA AIRLINES 800-426-0333
. . .//www.metronet.com/~olesen/tree.html#AS
ALOHA AIRLINES 800-367-5250
. . .//www.alohaair.com/aloha-air
ALOHA ISLANDAIR 800-323-3345
AMERICA WEST AIRLINES 800-235-9292
. . .//www.cucruising.com/cu.amwest.html
America West Vacations 800-356-6611
AMERICAN AIRLINES & AMERICAN EAGLE
. . .//www.amrcorp.com
Reservations 800-433-7300
Fly Away Vacations 800-321-2121
AMERICAN TRANS AIR 800-225-2995
. . .//www.xmission.com/~aoi/fata.htlm
ARIZONA AIRWAYS 800-274-0662
BIG SKY AIRLINES 800-237-7788
CAPE AIR 800-352-0714
CARNIVAL .800-824-7386
. . .//www.carnivalair.com
COMAIR 800-354-9822
CONTINENTAL AIRLINES 800-525-0280
. . .//www.cucruising.com/cu/contin.html
Continental Vacations 800-634-5555
DELTA AIR LINES 800-221-1212
. . .//www.delta-air.com
Delta Dream Vacations 800-872-7786
HAWAIIAN AIR 800-367-5320
KIWI INTERNATIONAL 800-538-5494
MAHALO AIR 800-462-4256
MIDWAY AIRLINES 800-446-4392
MIDWEST EXPRESS 800-452-2022
. . .//www.cwru.edu/cleve/hopkins/midwest.htlm
NORTHWEST AIRLINES 800-225-2525
. . .//www.internet.com/~tele/nwa-info.html
RENO AIR .800-736-6243
. . .//www.sierra.net/renoair.com
Quick Escape Vacation Packages .800-736-6247
SCENIC AIRLINES 800-634-6801
SKYWEST AIRLINES 800-453-9417
SOUTHWEST AIRLINES 800-435-9792
. . .//www.iflyswa.com
Fun Pack Vacations 800-423-5683
TOWER AIR 800-221-2500
TWA (TRANS WORLD AIRLINES) 800-221-2000
. . .//www.inlink.com/~jack/twa.html
Getaway Vacations 800-438-2929

Heaviest aircraft suspended from the Smithsonian ceiling: 17,500 pounds.

UNITED AIRLINES 800-241-6522
. . ://www.ual.com
   United Vacations 800-328-6877
USAIR & USAIR SHUTTLE 800-428-4322
   USAir Vacations 800-455-0123
VALUJET 800-825-8538
. . ://www.valujet.com
VANGUARD AIRLINES 800-826-4827
. . ://www.cucruising.com/cu/vanguard.html

INTERNATIONAL AIRLINES

AER LINGUS 800-223-6537
. . ://www.hursley.ibm.com80/aer/
AERO CALIFORNIA 800-237-6225
AEROLINEAS ARGENTINAS 800-333-0276
AEROMEXICO 800-237-6639
AEROPERU .800-777-7717
AIR AFRIQUE 800-456-9192
AIR ARUBA .800-882-7822
AIR CANADA 800-776-3000
. . ://www.aircanada.ca
AIR FRANCE 800-237-2747
. . ://www.airfrance.com
AIR INDIA 212-751-6200
AIR JAMAICA 800-523-5585
AIR LANKA .800-421-9898
AIR MAURITIUS 800-537-1182
AIR NEW ZEALAND 800-262-2468
. . ://airnz.com
AIR SEYCHELLES 800-677-4277
AIR VANUATU 800-677-4277
AIR ZIMBABWE 800-228-9485
ALITALIA AIRLINES 800-223-5730
. . ://www.zenonet.com/italiatour/fly-drive.html
ALM-ANTILLEAN AIRLINES 800-327-7197
ANA-ALL (NIPPON AIRWAYS) 800-235-9262
. . ://www.ana.co.jp/
ANSETT AIRLINES OF AUSTRALIA 800-366-1300
. . ://www.ansett.com.au/
AUSTRIAN AIRLINES 800-843-0002
. . ://www.aua.co.at/aua/
AVENSA SERVIVENSA S.A 800-428-3672
AVIANCA AIRLINES 800-284-2622
AVIATECA 800-327-9832
BAHAMASAIR 800-222-4262
BALKAN AIRLINES 800-852-0944
BRITISH AIRWAYS 800-247-9297
. . ://www.british-airways.com
BRITISH MIDLAND AIRWAYS 800-788-0555
. . ://www.flybritishmidland.com
BWIA INTERNATIONAL 800-538-2942
CANADIAN AIRLINES INT'L 800-426-7000
. . ://www.CdnAir.CA
CATHAY PACIFIC AIRWAYS 800-233-2742
. . ://www.cathay-usa.com/

CAYMAN AIRWAYS 800-422-9626
CHINA AIRLINES 800-227-5118
COPA AIRLINES 800-359-2672
CZECHOSLOVAK AIRLINES 800-223-2365
EL AL ISRAEL AIRLINES 800-835-2848
EMIRATES AIRLINES 800-777-3999
. . ://www.onu.edu/~mparham/uae/emirates/emir.html
ETHIOPIAN AIRLINES 800-433-9677
EVA AIRWAYS 800-695-1188
FAUCETT AIRLINES 800-334-3356
FINNAIR 800-950-5000
. . ://www.interactive.line.com/finland/finair.home.html
GARUDA - INDONESIAN AIRWAYS 800-247-8380
GUYANA AIRWAYS 800-242-4210
GULF AIR - GOLDEN FALCON 800-553-2824
IBERIA AIRLINES OF SPAIN 800-772-4642
ICELANDAIR 800-223-5500
. . ://www.arctic.is/transport/icelandair/icelandair.html
JAPAN AIRLINES 800-525-3663
. . ://www.spin.ad.jp/jal/home e.html
KENYA AIRWAYS 800-343-2506
KLM ROYAL DUTCH AIRLINES 800-374-7747
. . ://www.ib.com.8080/business/klm.html
KOREAN AIR LINES 800-438-5000
. . ://www.koreanair.com
KUWAIT AIRWAYS 800-458-9248
LACSA - AIRLINE OF COSTA RICA 800-225-2272
LADECO CHILEAN AIRLINES 800-825-2332
LAN - CHILE AIRLINES 800-735-5526
LLOYD AERO BOLIVIANO 800-327-7407
LOT - POLISH AIRLINES 800-223-0593
. . ://www.poland.net/LOT/
LTU INTERNATIONAL AIRWAYS 800-888-0200
. . ://www.ltu.com/ltu
LUFTHANSA 800-645-3880
. . ://www.tkz.fh-rpl.de/tii/lhflug-e.html
MALAYSIA AIRLINES 800-552-9264
. . ://www.cucruising.com/cu/malaysia.html
MALEV HUNGARIAN AIRLINE 800-223-6884
MARTINAIR HOLLAND 800-366-4655
MEXICANA AIRLINES 800-531-7923
. . ://www.mexicana.com/index.html
OLYMPIC AIRWAYS 800-223-1226
PAKISTAN AIRLINES 800-221-2552
PHILIPPINE AIRLINES 800-435-9725
POLYNESIAN AIRLINES 800-272-5042
QANTAS AIRWAYS 800-227-4500
. . ://www.anzac.com/qantas/qantas.html
ROYAL AIR MAROC 800-344-6726
ROYAL JORDANIAN AIRLINES 800-223-0470
SABENA BELGIAN WORLD AIRLINES . .800-955-2000
. . ://www.sabena.com
SAS SCANDINAVIAN AIRLINES 800-221-2350
. . ://www.interaccess.com/coolsite/sas
SAUDI ARABIAN AIRLINES 800-472-8342
. . ://ee.wpi.edu/~zakharia/saudi-communications.html

Pounds of peanuts Southwest serves per day: 5,323; packages served per year: 62 million.

SINGAPORE AIRLINES 800-742-3333
SOLOMON AIRLINES 800-677-4277
SOUTH AFRICAN AIRWAYS 800-722-9675
........//saa.ca.za/saa/
SWISSAIR 800-221-4750
.../www.swissair.com
TACA INTERNATIONAL AIRLINES 800-535-8780
TAP AIR PORTUGAL 800-221-7370
THAI AIRWAYS INTERNATIONAL 800-426-5204
...//metrotel.co.uk/travlog/thaiair.html
TRANSBRASIL AIRLINES 800-872-3153
TRANS JAMAICAN AIRLINES 800-523-5585
VARIG BRAZILIAN AIRLINES 800-468-2744
VIASA VENEZUELAN AIRWAYS 800-468-4272
VIRGIN ATLANTIC AIRWAYS 800-862-8621
...//www.fly.virgin.com/atlantic

AIRLINE COMPLAINTS

DEPARTMENT OF TRANSPORTATION
AVIATION CONSUMER PROTECTION . .202-366-2220

FAA CONSUMER HOTLINE 800-322-7873

AER LINGUS 800-223-6537
Customer Service
122 E. 42nd.
NY, NY 10168
AIR CANADA 800-366-0362
Customer Relations
221 N. Lasalle Street
Chicago, IL 60601
AIR FRANCE 800-872-3224
Customer Relations
125 W. 55th Street
NY, NY 10019
ALASKA AIRLINES 800-426-0333
P.O. Box 68900
Seattle, WA 98168
ALITALIA AIRLINES 800-903-9991
Customer Service
666 5th Ave.
NY, NY 10103
AMERICA WEST 800-235-9292
Consumer Relations
4000 E. Sky Harbor Blvd.
Phoenix, AZ 85034
AMERICAN AIRLINES 817-967-2000
P.O. Box 619612
M.D. 2400
DFW Airport, TX 75261-9612
AMERICAN TRANS AIR 800-225-2995
Customer Service
P.O. Box 51609
Indianapolis, IN 46251

AUSTRIAN AIRLINES 718-670-8600
Customer Service
17-20 Whitestone Expry.
Whitestone, NY 11357
BRITISH AIRWAYS 800-422-9101
Customer Service
75-20 Astoria Blvd.
Jackson Heights, NY 11370
CANADIAN AIRLINES INT'L 403-569-4180
Calgary Administration Bldg.
Customer Relations
615-18 Street S.E.
Calgary, Alberta T2E 6J5
CARNIVAL AIRLINES 305-923-8672
Customer Relations
P.O. Box 9013
Dania, FL 33004
CATHAY PACIFIC AIRWAYS 310-640-8551
Customer Service
300 N. Continental Blvd., Ste. 500
El Segundo, CA 90245
CONTINENTAL AIRLINES 800-932-2732
3663 N. Sam Houston Pkwy. E
Ste. 500
Houston, TX 77032
DELTA AIRLINES 404-715-1450
Consumer Affairs
P.O. Box 20980
Atlanta, GA 30320-2980
EL AL ISRAEL AIRLINES 212-852-0600
Public Relations
120 W. 45th St.
NY, NY 10036
EVA AIR 310-521-6000
Customer Relations
260 W. 5th Street
San Pedro, CA 90731
FINNAIR 800-950-4768
8th Floor
228 E. 45th Street
NY, NY 10017-3303
IBERIA AIRLINES 305-267-7747
Customer Relations Dept.
6100 Blue Lagoon Dr., Ste. 200
Miami, FL 33126
ICELANDAIR .410-715-1600
Customer Relations
5950 Symphoney Woods Road
Columbia, MD 21044
KIWI INT'L AIRLINES 201-645-1133
Hemisphere Center, 6th Floor
Newark, NJ 07114-0006
KOREAN AIRLINES 310-417-5200
Complaint Dept.
6101 W. Imperial Hwy.
Los Angeles, CA 90045

Number of Boeing 747s that could be parked in Minneapolis' Mall of the Americas: 32.

LUFTHANSA GERMAN AIRLINES 800-645-3880
1640 Hempstead Turnpike
East Meadow, NY 11554
MEXICANA AIRLINES 800-353-8245
Customer Service
9841 Airport Blvd., Ste 200
Los Angeles, CA 90045
MIDWAY AIRLINES 800-564-5001
Customer Service
300 W. Morgan St., Ste. 1200
Durham, NC 2770
MIDWEST EXPRESS AIRLINES 800-452-2022
ext 3910
Consumer Affairs
P.O. Box 37414
Milwaukee, WI 53237-9977
NORTHWEST AIRLINES 612-726-2046
Dept. C5270
5101 Northwest Drive
St. Paul, MN 55111-3034
QANTAS AIRWAYS LTD. 310-726-1407
Attn: Customer Relations
841 Apollo Street, Ste. 400
El Segundo, CA 90245-4741
RENO AIR CUSTOMER SERVICE 702-686-3835
P.O. Box 30059
Reno, NV 89520
SAS SCANDINAVIAN AIRLINES 800-345-9684
1270 Avenue of the Americas
NY, NY 100
SINGAPORE AIRLINES 213-934-8833
Public Affairs
5670 Wilshire Blvd.
Los Angeles, CA 90036
SOUTHWEST AIRLINES 214-904-4223
P.O. Box 36611
Dallas, TX 75235-1611
SWISSAIR 800-221-4750
3391 Peachtree Road NE, Ste. 210
Atlanta, GA 30326
Attn: Mr. Suhr
THAI AIRWAYS INT'L 800-426-5204
Customer Relations
22 N. Sepulveda Blvd., Ste. 1950
El Segundo, CA 90245
TOWER AIR . . . . .718-553-4300 ext 289
Customer Service
JFK Int'l Airport
Hanger #17
Jamaica, NY 11430
TWA 800-221-2000
Customer Relations
1415 Olive St., Ste. 100
St. Louis, MO 63103

UNITED AIRLINES 708-952-6796
P.O. Box 66100
Chicago, IL 60666
USAIR 910-661-0061
P.O. Box 1501
Winston Salem, NC 27102-1501
VALUJET AIRLINES 800-825-8538
Customer Service
1800 Phoenix Blvd., Ste. 126
Atlanta, GA 30349-5555
VIRGIN ATLANTIC AIRWAYS 800-496-6661
Public Relations
747 Belden Ave.
Norwalk, CT 06850

FREQUENT FLYER PROGRAMS

AER LINGUS
(Travel Award Bonus) 212-557-1112
AEROMEXICO
(Club Premier/Aeromiles) 800-247-3737
AIR CANADA
(Aeroplan) 800-361-8253
AIR FRANCE
(Frequence Plus) 800-237-2747
ALASKA AIRLINES
(Mileage Plan) 800-654-5669
ALOHA AIRLINES
(AlohaPass) 800-367-5250
AMERICA WEST
(FlightFund) 800-247-5691
AMERICAN AIRLINES
(AAdvantage) 800-882-8880
ANSETT AIRLINES OF AUSTRALIA
(Frequent Flyer) 800-366-1300
BRITISH AIRWAYS
(Executive Club) 800-452-1201
CANADIAN AIRLINES
(Canadian Plus) 800-426-7007
CARNIVAL AIR LINES
(Free Flight Bonanza) 800-929-5903
CHINA AIRLINES & MANDARIN AIRLINES
(Dynasty Flyer) 800-227-5118
CONTINENTAL AIRLINES
(OnePass) 800-621-7467
DELTA AIRLINES
(Frequent Flyer) 800-323-2323
EL AL ISRAEL AIRLINES
(Matmid-Freq. Traveler) 800-223-6700
EVA AIRWAYS
(Priority One Freq. Flyer) 310-521-6070
FINNAIR
(Finnair Plus Freq. Traveler) 800-950-3387

Percentage of total British Airways budget allocated for passenger meals: six percent.

HAWAIIAN AIRLINES
(Gold Plus) 800-367-7637
IBERIA-LINEAS AEREAS DE ESPANA
(Iberia Plus) 800-772-4642
JAPAN AIRLINES
(JAL Mileage Bank) 800-525-6453
KOREAN AIR
(Mileage Dividend Program) 213-484-5780
LANCHILE
(Lanpass) 305-670-5511
LOT POLISH AIRLINES
(Frequent Flyer) 800-223-0593
LUFTHANSA GERMAN AIRLINES
(Lufthansa Miles & More) 800-581-6400
MEXICANA DE AVIACION S.A.
(Frecuenta) 800-531-7901
MIDWEST EXPRESS
(Frequent Flyer) 800-452-2022
NORTHWEST AIRLINES
(WorldPerks) 800-327-2881
QANTAS
(Australian Frequent Flyer) 800-227-4500
SABENA BELGIAN WORLD AIRLINES
(Sabena Frequent Flyer) 516-562-9281
SCANDINAVIAN AIRLINES SYSTEM
(SAS EuroBonus) 800-437-5807
SOUTHWEST AIRLINES
(Rapid Rewards) 800-445-5764
SWISSAIR
(Qualiflyer) 800-221-8125
TAP AIR PORTUGAL
(Navigator Frequent Flyer) 201-344-4490
THAI AIRWAYS INTERNATIONAL
(Royal Orchid Plus) 800-426-5204
TWA
(Frequent Flyer Bonus) 800-325-4815
UNITED AIRLINES
(Mileage Plus) 800-421-4655
USAIR
(Frequent Traveler) 800-872-4738
VIRGIN ATLANTIC AIRWAYS
(Virgin Freeway) 800-365-9500

AIRLINE CLUBS

AER LINGUS
(Gold Circle Club) 800-223-6537
AIR CANADA
(Maple Leaf Club) 312-214-7970
ALASKA AIRLINES
(Board Room) 800-654-5669
ALOHA AIRLINES
(Executive Club) 800-367-5250
AMERICA WEST
(Phoenix Club) 602-693-2994
AMERICAN AIRLINES
(Admirals Club) 800-237-7971
& 3 letter airport code
CANADIAN AIRLINES
(Empress Lounge) 800-426-7000
CONTINENTAL AIRLINES
(Presidents Club) 800-322-2640
DELTA AIRLINES
(Crown Room) 404-715-6615
HAWAIIAN AIRLINES
(Premier Club) 800-367-7637
JAPAN AIRLINES
(JAL Global Room) 800-525-3663
KLM (First & Business Class)
(Lounge Facilities) 800-374-7747
NORTHWEST AIRLINES
(WorldClubs) 800-692-3788
SWISSAIR & AUSTRIAN AIRLINES
(The Travel Club) 800-388-2878
TWA
(Ambassadors Club) 800-527-1468
UNITED AIRLINES
(Red Carpet Club) 602-881-0500
USAIR
(USAir Club) 800-828-8522

CAR RENTAL COMPANIES

ACE RENT-A-CAR	.800-243-3443
ADVANTAGE RENT-A-CAR	.800-777-5500
ALAMO RENT-A-CAR	.800-327-9633
.../www.freeways.com	
Set up corporate account	.800-732-3232
International reservations	.800-522-9696
Emergency roadside service	.800-803-4444
AUTO EUROPE	.800-223-5555
.../www.wrld.com/ae	
AVIS CAR RENTAL	.800-331 1212
Set up corporate account	.800-331-1082
International reservations	.800-331-1084
Spanish speaking	.800-874-3556
Emergency roadside service	.800-354-2847
BUDGET RENT-A-CAR	.800-527-0700
.../www.globescope.com/web.budget	
Set up corporate account	.800-527-0700
International reservations	.800-472-3325
Emergency roadside service	.800-527-0700
DOLLAR RENT-A-CAR	.800-800-4000
Set up corporate account	.800-800-0088
Hawaii reservations	.800-367-7006
EuroDollar International	.800-800-6000
Emergency roadside service	.800-235-9393
ENTERPRISE RENT-A-CAR	.800-325-8007
Emergency roadside service	.800-325-8007
HERTZ RENT-A-CAR	.800-654-3131
Set up corporate account	.800-654-4405
International reservations	.800-654-3001
Emergency roadside service	.800-654-5060
HOLIDAY AUTOS INTERNATIONAL	.800-422-7737
I.T.S. INTERNATIONAL	.800-521-0643
KEMWEL GROUP	.800-678-0678
NATIONAL INTERRENT	.800-328-4567
Set up corporate account	.800-777-6285
International reservations	.800-227-3876
Emergency roadside service	.800-367-6767
PAYLESS CAR RENTAL	.800-729-5377
Set up corporate account	.800-729-5255
International reservations	.800-237-2804
RENAULT INTERNATIONAL	.800-221-1052
RENT A WRECK	.800-535-1391
.../www.charm.net.80/~ken/	
SEARS RENT-A-CAR	.800-527-0770
THRIFTY CAR RENTAL	.800-367-2277
Set up corporate account	.800-331-3550
Emergency Roadside Service	.800-367-2277
U-SAVE AUTO RENTAL	.800-272-8728
UGLY DUCKLING RENT-A-CAR	.800-843-3825
VALUE RENT-A-CAR	.800-468-2583
.../www.neptune.com/value/value.html	
Set up corporate account	.800-327-4847

> **“**_For convenience, we have converted letters in phone listings to the complete numerical listing, i.e., 800-PAYLESS is shown as 800-729-5377._**”**

CAR RENTAL COMPLAINTS

ACE RENT-A-CAR	.800-243-3443
ADVANTAGE RENT-A-CAR	.800-777-5524
ALAMO CAR RENTAL	.800-445-5664
AUTO EUROPE	.800-223-5555
AVIS CAR RENTAL	.800-331-1212
BUDGET RENT-A-CAR	.800-621-2844
DOLLAR RENT-A-CAR	.800-800-5252
ENTERPRISE RENT-A-CAR	.314-512-5000
HERTZ	.800-654-4173
KEMWEL GROUP	.800-678-0678
NATIONAL INTERRENT	.800-468-3334
PAYLESS CAR RENTAL	.813-321-6352 EXT 137
RENT-A-WRECK	.800-535-1391
SEARS RENT-A-CAR	.800-621-2844
THRIFTY CAR RENTAL	.800-334-1705
U-SAVE AUTO RENTAL	.800-438-2300 EXT 100
UGLY DUCKLING RENT-A-CAR	.800-843-3825
VALUE RENT-A-CAR	.800-327-6459
US GOV. AUTO SAFETY HOTLINE	
(outside Washington, DC)	.800-424-9393

FREQUENT RENTER PROGRAMS

ADVANTAGE FREQUENT RENTER	.800-777-1374
ALAMO EXPRESS	.800-882-5266
AVIS PREFERRED RENTER	.800-831-8000
BUDGET AWARDSPLUS	.800-972-3414
HERTZ NUMBER ONE CLUB	.800-654-3131
NATIONAL EMERALD CLUB	.800-962-7070
PAYLESS CHAMPIONSHIP CLUB	.800-729-5255

MOTORHOME RENTALS

CRUISE AMERICA	.800-327-7778
RECREATION VEHICLE RENTAL	.800-336-0355

GROUND TRANSPORTATION

NATIONWIDE

AIRCOMM RESERVATIONS NET. 800-247-2666
CAREY LIMOUSINE 800-336-4646
CROWN LIMOUSINES 800-229-5466
DAV EL LIMOUSINES 800-922-0343
MANHATTAN INTERNATIONAL LIMO . .800-621-5466
SUN CITY EXPRESS 800-634-7774
SUPERSHUTTLE
    Baltimore only 800-809-7080
    Dallas only 800-648-7051
    Los Angeles only 800-554-3146
    Miami only 800-874-8885
    Phoenix only 800-331-3565

RAIL TRAVEL

ALASKA RAILROAD 800-544-0552
AMTRAK 800-872-7245
...//www.amtrak.com/
    Customer Service 202-906-2121
CHUNNEL TICKETS RESERVATIONS . . .800-387-6742
EURAILPASS 800-722-7151
...//www.euorail.com/
GERMANRAIL 800-782-2424
...//www.bahn.de/index e.html
MEXICAN RAIL 011-5255471097
MEXICAN TOUR 800-659-7602
RAIL EUROPE 800-848-7245
VIA RAIL CANADA 800-561-3949
...//www.viarail.ca/
WHITE PASS & YUKON ROUTE 800-343-7373

HOTEL/MOTEL RESERVATIONS

ADAM'S MARK HOTELS 800-444-2326
ADMIRAL BENBOW INNS 800-451-1986
AMERICINN 800-634-3444
AMERISUITES 800-833-1516
ANA HOTELS 800-262-4683
ASTON HOTELS & RESORTS 800-922-7866
BEST INNS OF AMERICA 800-237-8466
BEST WESTERN INN SUITES/HOTELS .800-752-2204
BEST WESTERN INTERNATIONAL 800-528-1234
...//www.travelweb.com/bw.html
BUDGETEL INNS 800-428-3438
BUDGET HOST 800-283-4678
CAMBERLEY HOTELS 800-866-7666
CANADIAN PACIFIC HOTELS/RESORTS 800-441-1414

CHALET SUSSE 800-258-1980
CLARION HOTELS 800-252-7466
CLUBHOUSE INNS OF AMERICA 800-258-2466
COLONY RESORTS - WORLDWIDE . . .800-777-1700
COMFORT INNS 800-228-5150
CONCORDE HOTELS INTERNATIONAL .800-888-4747
COUNTRY HEARTH INN 800-848-5767
COURTYARD BY MARRIOTT 800-321-2211
CROWN STERLING SUITES 800-433-4600
DAYS INNS/HOTELS/SUITES 800-329-7466
...//www.daysinn.com/daysinn.htm
DELTA INNS & RESORTS US 800-877-1133
    Canada 800-268-1133
DOUBLETREE HOTELS 800-222-8733
DOUBLETREE /GUEST QUARTERS 800-424-2900
DRURY INNS 800-325-8300
ECONO LODGES 800-553-2666
ECONOMY INNS OF AMERICA 800-826-0778
EMBASSY SUITES 800-362-2779
...//www.embassy-suites.com
EXCEL INNS 800-356-8013
FAIRFIELD INNS BY MARRIOTT 800-228-2800
FAIRMONT HOTELS 800-527-4737
FIESTA AMERICANA 800-343-7821
FIESTA INN HOTELS 800-343-7821
FLAG INTERNATIONAL HOTELS/RESORTS
   800-624-3524
FORTE HOTELS 800-225-5843
FOUR SEASONS HOTELS & RESORTS .800-332-3442
FRIENDSHIP INNS 800-453-4511
GOLDEN TULIP WORLDWIDE HOTELS .800-344-1212
HAMPTON INNS/HOMEWOOD SUITES .800-426-7866
...//www.hampton-inn.com
...//www.homewood-suites.com
HANDLERY HOTELS
    (LRI Hotel Reservations) 800-223-0888
HARLEY HOTELS 800-321-2323
HAWTHORN SUITES HOTELS 800-527-1133
HELMSLEY HOTELS 800-221-4982
HILTON HOTELS 800-445-8667
...//WWW.HILTON.COM
HOLIDAY INNS WORLDWIDE 800-465-4329
...//www.holiday-inn.com
HOMEWOOD SUITES 800-225-5466
HOSPITALITY INTERNATIONAL 800-251-1962
HOWARD JOHNSON HOTELS/INNS . . .800-446-4656
HYATT HOTELS & RESORTS 800-233-1234
...//www.travelweb.com/hyatt.html
INTER-CONTINENTAL/FORUM 800-327-0200
ITT SHERATON HOTELS/RESORTS 800-325-3535
LAQUINTA MOTOR INNS 800-531-5900
LENNOX HOUSE SUITES 800-445-3669
LEXINGTON HOTELS/SUITES/INNS . . .800-537-8483
LOEWS HOTELS 800-235-6397
LUXBURY HOTELS 800-252-7748
LUXURY COLLECTIONS 800-221-2340

The longest railroad tunnel (excluding subways): the 33.1 Selkan Tunnel in Tsugaru, Japan.

MANDARIN ORIENTAL HOTELS 800-526-6566
MANHATTAN EAST SUITE HOTELS 800-637-8483
MARRIOTT HOTELS/RESORTS/SUITES 800-228-9290
..........//www.marriott.com/
MERIDIEN HOTELS 800-543-4300
MICROTEL 800-365-6835
MIYAKO HOTELS 800-336-1136
MOTEL 6 800-466-8356
NEW OTANI HOTELS 800-421-8795
NIKKO HOTELS INTERNATIONAL 800-645-5687
OMNI HOTELS 800-843-6664
PAN PACIFIC HOTELS & RESORTS ...800-327-8585
PARK LANE INTERNATIONAL HOTELS .800-338-1338
PICCADILLY INNS 800-468-3587
PREFERRED HOTELS & RESORTS 800-323-7500
PRINCE HOTELS 800-542-8686
PRINCESS HOTEL INTERNATIONAL ...800-223-1834
QUALITY INNS 800-228-5151
RADISSON HOTELS INTERNATIONAL ..800-333-3333
..........//www2.pcy.mci.net/marketplace/radisson/
RAMADA 800-272-6232
   Inns/Hotels/Resorts & Plaza Hotels
   (destinations outside US) 800-854-7854
RED CARPET INNS 800-251-1962
RED LION HOTELS & INNS 800-232-1287
RED ROOF INNS 800-843-7663
REGENT INTERNATIONAL HOTELS 800-545-4000
REGISTRY HOTELS & RESORTS 800-247-9810
RENAISSANCE HOTELS & RESORTS ..800-228-9898
RESIDENCE INNS BY MARRIOTT 800-331-3131
RITZ-CARLTON HOTELS 800-241-3333
RODEWAY INNS 800-228-2000
SHERATON HOTELS & MOTOR INNS ..800-325-3535
SHILO INNS & RESORTS 800-222-2244
SHONEY'S INNS 800-222-2222
SIGNATURE INNS 800-822-5252
SOFITEL HOTELS - WORLDWIDE 800-763-4835
SONESTA INTERNATIONAL HOTELS ...800-766-3782
STERLING HOTELS 800-637-7200
STOUFFER HOTELS & RESORTS 800-468-3571
SUPER 8 MOTELS 800-800-8000
SUSSE CHALET 800-524-2538
SWISSOTEL 800-637-9477
TARA HOTELS 800-843-8272
MT. CHARLOTTE/THISTLE 800-847-4858
THRIFTLODGE HOTELS 800-525-9055
TRAVELERS INNS 800-633-8300
TRAVELODGE 800-578-7878
VAGABOND INNS 800-522-1555
WARWICK INTERNATIONAL 800-203-3232
WARWICK NEW YORK 800-223-4099
WESTCOAST HOTELS 800-426-0670
WESTIN HOTELS & RESORTS 800-228-3000
..........//www.westin.com
WYNDHAM HOTELS & RESORTS 800-996-3426
   (from Canada) 800-631-4200

FREQUENT LODGER PROGRAMS

ADAM'S MARK HOTELS
   (Gold Mark Club) 800-627-6275
BEST WESTERN
   (Gold Crown Club) 800-873-4653
CLUBHOUSE INNS
   (BestGuest) 800-258-2466
COURTYARD BY MARRIOTT
   (Courtyard ClubAwards) 800-321-2582
CROWNE PLAZA HOTELS & RESORTS
   (Preferred) 800-277-4567
DAYS INN
   (The Inn-Credible Card) 800-344-3636
FAIRFIELD INN BY MARRIOTT
   (INNsiders Club) 800-443-7200
FAIRMONT HOTELS
   (The President's Club) 800-553-3658
HILTON AND CONRAD HOTELS
   (Hilton HHonors) 800-446-6677
HOLIDAY INN
   (Priority Club) 800-272-9273
HOWARD JOHNSON
   (Business Traveler Club) 800-547-7829
HYATT HOTELS
   (Gold Passport) 800-544-9288
INTER-CONTINENTAL HOTELS
   (Six Continents Club) 800-462-6686
ITT SHERATON HOTELS, INNS, RESORTS & SUITES
   Sheraton Club International 800-247-2582
LA QUINTA INNS
   (Returns Club) 800-642-4258
LOEWS HOTELS
   (Loews First) 800-563-9712
MARRIOTT HOTELS, RESORTS & SUITES
   (Honored Guest Awards & Marriott Miles)
  800-367-6453
RAMADA HOTELS
   (Ramada Business Card) 800-672-6232
RED LION HOTELS & INNS
   (Frequent Guest Dividends)
  800-547-8010
STOUFFER HOTELS & RESORTS
   (Club Express) 800-824-3571
WESTIN HOTELS & RESORTS
   (Westin Premier) 800-521-2000

Number of Best Western hotels owned by Native American tribes: six.

> *66These numbers will get you to a customer relations representative, either directly or by transfer. If no number is listed, contact the hotel chain reservation number and ask for customer relations.99*

AREA RESERVATION SERVICES

> *66In this Reservation Service Section, an asterik (*) denotes HOTELS AVAILABLE AT UP TO 65% OFF regular rates. Some rates will be good, some great and some, I've found, are downright phenomenal.99*

HOTEL CHAIN COMPLAINTS

ASTON HOTELS & RESORTS	808-931-1558
BEST WESTERN INTERNATIONAL	800-528-1238
BUDGET HOST INNS	800-283-4678
BUDGETEL INNS	800-428-3438
CHALET SUSSE INTERNATIONAL	603-654-2000
CLARION HOTELS	602-953-7513
COLONY RESORTS WORLDWIDE	412-920-5700
COMFORT INNS	602-953-7513
COURTYARD BY MARRIOTT	800-831-0224
DOUBLETREE SUITES	800-528-0444
ECONO LODGES	800-637-9605
EMBASSY SUITES	800-362-2779
EXCEL INNS	608-241-5271
FAIRFIELD INNS BY MARRIOTT	800-831-0224
FORTE HOTELS	800-224-1644
FOUR SEASONS HOTELS	416-449-1750
HAMPTON INNS	800-426-7866
HILTON HOTELS	800-445-8667
HOLIDAY INN	800-621-0555
HOMEWOOD SUITES	800-225-5466
HOWARD JOHNSON HOTELS/INNS	800-544-9881
HYATT HOTELS & RESORTS	800-233-1234
INTER-CONTINENTAL/FORUM	212-852-6400
LA QUINTA MOTOR INNS	800-642-4241
MARRIOTT HOTELS	301-380-7600
MERIDIAN HOTELS	800-224-1644
MOTEL 6	800-466-8356
NIKKO HOTELS INTERNATIONAL	800-645-5687
OMNI HOTELS	603-926-8911
RADISSON HOTELS INTERNATIONAL	800-333-3333
RAMADA INNS	800-828-6644
RED LION HOTELS & INNS	360-696-0001
RED ROOF INNS	800-554-4555
RESIDENCE INNS BY MARRIOTT	800-899-7224
RITZ-CARLTON HOTELS	404-237-5500
SHERATON HOTELS & MOTOR INNS	800-328-6242
STOUFFER HOTELS & RESORTS	800-468-3571
SUPER 8 MOTELS	800-800-8000
TRAVELERS INNS	800-633-8300
TRAVELODGE	800-255-3050
VAGABOND INNS	800-522-1555
WESTIN HOTELS & RESORTS	800-228-3000

ARIZONA

Condominiums in Arizona	800-266-3680

CALIFORNIA

Anaheim*/Los Angeles*	800-964-6835
San Francisco*	800-964-6835
Santa Barbara Central Reservation Service	800-292-2222

COLORADO

Aspen Discounts	800-299-2773
Copper Mountain Discounts	800-456-8386
Durango Discount Packages	800-463-8726
Steamboat Discount Packages	800-525-2628
Vail Discount Packages	800-824-5737

CONNECTICUT

Connecticut Central Reservations	800-365-6928

DISTRICT OF COLUMBIA

Capitol Reservations	800-847-4832
Washington D.C.*	800-964-6835

FLORIDA

Central Reservations	800-950-0232
Florida: other areas Central Reservations	800-847-4835
Orlando/Disney World*	800-330-7666
Central Reservations	800-950-0232

ILLINOIS

Chicago*	800-964-6835

KANSAS

Kansas City*	800-877-4386

MARYLAND

Baltimore*	800-964-6835

Hotel chain that opened six properties in one day: Holiday Inn Worldwide on June 26, 1995.

MASSACHUSETTS

Boston* 800-964-6835

Massachusetts Central Reservations
. 800-365-6962

NEW JERSEY

Atlantic City- Accomodations Express .800-444-7666
Atlantic City Discount rates 800-833-7070
Atlantic City Toll Free Reservations 800-833-7070
New Jersey Central Reservations 800-365-6965

NEW MEXICO

Taos Bed & Breakfast 800-876-7857

NEW YORK

Accommodations Express 800-444-7666
New York City* Central Reservations . .800-964-6835
New York State Central Reservations . .800-365-6969

NEVADA

Lake Powell Resorts/Marinas 800-528-6154
Las Vegas-Accomodations Express 800-444-7666
Las Vegas Central Reservations 800-777-6555
Las Vegas-Laughlin 800-733-6644
Las Vegas/Tahoe/Reno 800-286-9195
Reno Central Reservations 800-354-4885
Tahoe North Central Reservations 800-824-6340
Tahoe South Central Reservations 800-354-4887

PENNSYLVANIA

Accomodations Express 800-444-7666

VERMONT

Special Packages 800-837-6668

WASHINGTON

Seattle 800-535-7071

MEXICO

Mexico City 800-336-5454

CRUISE LINES

ALASKA SIGHTSEEING/CRUISE WEST .800-426-7702
AMERICAN CANADIAN CARIBBEAN . . .800-556-7450
AMERICAN HAWAII CRUISES 800-765-7000
AMERIRUSS CRUISE CO. 800-279-4454
BERGEN LINE 800-323-7436
CARNIVAL CRUISE LINES 800-327-9501
          ...//mmink.com/mmink/carnival/carnival.html
CELEBRITY CRUISES 800-437-3111
CLIPPER CRUISE LINE 800-325-0010
                    ...//ecotravel.com/clipper
COMMODORE CRUISE LINE 800-237-5361
COSTA CRUISE LINES 800-462-6782
CUNARD LINE 800-528-6273
...//mmink.com/mmink/kiosks/costa/cunard/cunard.htm
DELTA QUEEN STEAMBOAT CO. 800-543-1949
DOLPHIN CRUISE LINE 800-222-1003
          ...//mmink.com/dolphincl/dolphinhome.html
DISCOVERY CRUISE LINE 800-937-4477
EUROCRUISES 800-688-3876
GALAPAGOS NETWORK 800-633-7972
HOLLAND AMERICA LINE-WESTOURS .800-426-0327
              ...//alaskan.com/promos/holland.html
IVARAN LINES 800-451-1639
MAJESTY CRUISE LINE 800-532-7788
NABILA NILE CRUISES 800-443-6453
NORWEGIAN CRUISE LINE 800-327-7030
...//www.ncl.com/ncl
OCEANIC CRUISES 800-545-5778
ODESSAMERICA CRUISE CO. 800-221-3254
ORIENT LINES 800-333-7300
PREMIER CRUISE LINE 800-327-7113
PRINCESS CRUISES 800-421-0522
PALM BEACH CRUISE LINE 800-841-7447
REGAL CRUISES 800-270-7245
RENAISSANCE CRUISES 800-525-5350
ROYAL CARIBBEAN CRUISE LINE 800-327-6700
                    ...//mmink.com/rccl.html
ROYAL OLYMPIC CRUISES 800-872-6400
RIVER CRUISES INTERNATIONAL 800-777-9480
ST. LAWRENCE CRUISE LINES 800-267-7868
SEABOURN CRUISE LINE 800-929-9595
SEAWIND CRUISE LINE 800-258-8006
STAR CLIPPERS 800-442-0551
TALL SHIP ADVENTURES 800-662-0090
TEMPTRESS CRUISES 800-336-8423
VICTORIA CRUISES 800-348-8084
WINDJAMMER BAREFOOT CRUISES . .800-327-2601
              ...//wheat.symgrp.com/symgrp/windjammer/
WINDSTAR CRUISES 800-258-7245
                    ...//www.windstarcruises.com
WORLD EXPLORER CRUISES 800-854-3835

The hotel closest to the international dateline: the Paradise International on the Tongan island of Vavau.

CRUISE LINE COMPLAINTS

AMERICAN HAWAII CRUISE LINES 312-466-6000
CARNIVAL CRUISE LINES 305-599-2600
CELEBRITY/ FANTASY CRUISES 800-242-6374
COMMODORE CRUISE LINES 800-327-5617
COSTA CRUISE LINE 305-358-7325
CRYSTAL CRUISE LINES 310-785-9300
CUNARD CRUISE LINES 800-528-6273
DOLPHIN CRUISE LINES 305-358-5122
HOLLAND AMERICA 206-270-6290
NORWEGIAN/ROYAL VIKING 800-327-7030
PALM BEACH CRUISE LINES 800-841-7447
PREMIER CRUISE LINES 407-783-5061
PRINCESS CRUISE LINES 310-553-1770
ROYAL CARIBBEAN LINES 800-327-6700
ROYAL OLYMPIC CRUISE LINES 800-445-6400
SEABOURN CRUISE LINES 415-391-7444
SOCIETY EXPEDITIONS 800-548-8669
WORLD EXPLORER 800-854-3835

NICHE CRUISES

WEDDINGS AT SEA
Cruise Line Inc. 800-777-0707
...//www.ten-io.com/clia/
FREIGHTER TRAVEL
Freighter World Cruises 818-449-3106
...//www.gus.com/travel/fwc/fwc.html

ADVENTURE / SPORTS BIKE TRIPS/TOURS

Alaskan Bicycle Adventures . . . . .800-770-7242.
American Wilderness Experience 800-444-0099
Backroads Bicycle Touring 800-462-2848
Butterfield & Robinson 800-268-8415
Chateaux Bike Tours 800-678-2453
Country Cycling Tours 212-874-5151
Easy Rider Tours 800-488-8332
Gerhard's Bicycle Odysseys 503-223-2402
Timberline Bicycle Tours 303-759-3804
Vermont Bicycle Touring 802-453-4811

CAMPING / NATIONAL PARKS

Go Camping America 800-477-8669
National Park Service 202-208-4747
Big Bend, TX .915-477-2251
Big Thicket, TX 409-839-2689
Bryce Canyon, UT 801-834-5322
Carlsbad Caverns, NM 505-785-2232
Denali, AK 907-683-2294
Everglades, FL 305-242-7700
Grand Canyon, AZ 520-638-7888
Great Smoky Mtns, TN/NC 423-436-1200
Guadalupe Mts.,TX 915-828-3251
Hot Springs, AR 501-624-3383
Mammoth Cave, KY 502-758-2251
Yosemite, CA .209-372-0200
Yellowstone, WY 307-344-7381
Zion, UT 801-772-3256

RAFTING TRIPS/TOURS

All Rivers Adventures 800-743-5628
American Adventure Exp. 800-288-0675
Arkansas River Tours 800-321-4352
Buffalo Joe River Trips 800-356-7984
Canyon Marine Whitewater 800-643-0707
Down Stream River Runners 800-234-4644
Dvorak's Kayak & Rafting 800-824-3795
Four Corners Rafting 800-332-7238
Glacier Raft Company 800-332-9995
Orion River Expeditions 800-553-7466
Performance Tours 800-328-7238
Raft Masters .800-568-7238
Royal Gorge Rafting 800-758-5161
White Water Adventure 800-366-2004

WILDERNESS TOURS

Murray's Tickets, Worldwide 800-542-4466
Outward Bound Trips 800-243-8520
Wilderness Southeast 912-897-5108
Wilderness Inquiry 612-379-3858

Cruise attended by Rod Steiger and Roger Ebert: Holland America's "Floating Film Festival."

ATTRACTIONS AND THEME PARKS

ALABAMA

Alabama Space & Rocket Center 205-837-3400

ARKANSAS

Mystic Cove .501-743-1439

ARIZONA

Old Tucson Studios 602-883-0100

CALIFORNIA

Disneyland 714-999-4000
Great America 408-988-1776
Hecker Pass (Gilroy) 408-842-2121
Knott's Berry Farm 714-220-5200
Marine World Africa USA 707-644-4000
Palm Springs Aerial Tramway 619-325-1449
Pier 39 (San Francisco) 415-981-8030
The Queen Mary (Long Beach) 800-437-2934
Raging Waters (San Jose) 408-238-9900
Raging Waters (San Dimas) 909-592-6453
San Diego Zoo 619-231-1515
Santa Cruz Seaside Co. 408-423-5590
Santa Monica Pier 310-458-8900
Sea World (San Diego) 619-222-6363
Six Flags Magic Mountain 805-255-4100
Universal Studios Hollywood 818-777-1000
Winchester Mystery House 408-247-2000

COLORADO

Pro Rodeo Hall of Fame 719-528-4761
Winter Park Resort 970-726-5514

FLORIDA

Busch Gardens 813-987-5171
Church Street Station 407-422-2434
Cypress Gardens 800-237-4826
Florida Cypress Gardens 941-324-2111
Florida Silver Springs 904-236-2121
Jungle Larry's Zoological Park 813-262-5409
NASA Kennedy Space Center/
 Spaceport USA 407-452-2121
Sea World of Florida 407-351-3600
U.S. Astronaut Hall of Fame 407-269-6100
Universal Studios Florida 407-363-8000
Disney World 407-824-4321

GEORGIA

Rock City Gardens 706-820-2531
Six Flags Over Georgia 770-948-9290

HAWAII

Atlantis Submarines 800-548-6262
Kualoa Ranch 800-231-7321
Oahu Attractions Association 800-539-6248
Paradise Cruise, Ltd. 800-334-6191
Polynesian Cultural Center 808-923-2911
Sea Life Park Hawaii 800-767-8046
USS Bowfin Submarine 808-423-1341
Waimea Valley 800-767-8046

ILLINOIS

Fishermans Dude Ranch 708-824-9821
Six Flags Great America 708-249-1776

IOWA

Adventureland Park 515-266-2121

KENTUCKY

Kentucky Kingdom Amusement Park . .502-366-2231
National Corvette Museum
 (Bowling Green) 800-538-3883
Mammoth Cave Wildlife Museum 502-773-2255

MAINE

Funtown USA Amusement Park 207-284-5139

MARYLAND

Adventure World 301-249-1500

MASSACHUSETTS

Mt. Tom Ski Resort 413-536-0516
Riverside Park 413-786-9300
Whalom Park 508-342-3707

MINNESOTA

Knott's Camp Snoopy 612-883-8600
Valleyfair 612-445-7600

MISSOURI

Branson Area Information 800-217-1260
Branson Theatre Phone #'s
 50s Variety 417-337-9829
 76 Music Hall 417-335-2484
 American Theater 417-335-8176
 Andy Williams 417-334-4500
 Anita Bryant 417-339-3939
 Baldknobbers 417-334-4528
 Branson's Magical Mansion 417-336-6037
 Branson Mall Music Theater 417-335-3500
 Box Car Willie 417-334-8696
 Branson Belle Showboat 417-336-7400
 Branson Scenic RR 417-334-6110
 Braschler's 417-334-4363
 Charley Pride 417-337-7433
 Country Tonite 417-334-2422

U.S. city with the most lightning strikes: Tampa.

Christy Lane 417-335-5111
Dixie Stampede 417-337-9400
Mickey Gilley's 417-334-3210
Glen Campbell 417-336-1220
Grand Palace/SDC 417-334-7263
Lake Queen Cruises 417-334-3015
Mutton Hollow 417-334-4947
Osmonds 417-336-6100
Ozark Jubilee 417-334-6400
Passion Play 800-882-7529
Presley's Jubilee 417-334-4874
Roy Clark 417-334-0076
Shoji Tabuchi 417-334-7469
Jim Stafford 417-335-8080
Mel Tillis 417-335-6635
Tony Orlando 417-335-8669
Thunderbird 417-336-2542
Bobby Vinton 417-334-2500
Waltzing Waters 417-334-4144
Wayne Newton 417-336-6220
Lawrence Welk 417-337-7469
Will Rogers 417-336-1333
Yakov Smirnoff 417-336-3838
Ozark Mountain Sightseeing 417-334-1850
Sevierville 800-255-6411
Tours .800-278-6877
St. Louis Zoo 314-781-0900
Silver Dollar City 417-338-2611
Six Flags Over Mid-America 314-938-5300
Worlds of Fun 816-454-4545

NEVADA

LAS VEGAS INFORMATION
Las Vegas Tourist Bureau 800-777-8342
Black Canyon River Raft Tours 702-293-3776
Boulder City/Hoover Dam Museum 702-294-1988
Bruno's Indian Museum 702-293-4865
Children's Museum 702-382-5437
Cranberry World West 702-566-7160
Debbie Reynolds Movie Museum 702-733-2243
Ethel M Chocolate Factory 702-458-8864
Grand Slam Canyon Theme Park 702-794-3912
Grayline Tours 702-384-1234
Guinness World of Records Museum . .702-792-3766
Hoover Dam 702-293-8367
Hoover Dam Museum 702-294-1988
Kidd's Marshmallow Factory 702-564-3878
Lake Mead Cruises 702-293-6180
Las Vegas Adventure Tours 702-564-5452
Liberace Museum 702-798-5595
Lied Discovery Children's Museum 702-382-5437
Menagerie Carousel at the Meadows . . .702-878-4849
Museum of Archaeology 702-397-2193
Natural History Museum 702-384-3466
Nevada Zoological-Botanical Park 702-648-5955
Nevada State Museum 702-486-5205

Planetarium 702-651-5059
Ponderosa Ranch 702-831-0691
Ron Lee's World of Clowns 702-434-3920
Wet'n Wild Water Park 702-737-7873
White Tiger Habitat 702-791-7111
GRAND CANYON SIGHTSEEING AIRLINES:
Eagle Canyon Airlines 702-736-3333
Lake Mead Air 702-293-1848
Scenic Airlines 702-638-3200
Sundance Helicopters 702-736-0606

NEW HAMPSHIRE

Canobie Lake Park 603-893-3506
Hampton Beach Casino 603-926-4541
Santa's Village Inc. 603-586-4445
Whale's Tale Water Park 603-745-8810

NEW JERSEY

Bowcraft Amusement Park 908-233-0675
Casino Pier and Water Works 908-793-6488
Fantasy Island 609-492-4000
Six Flags Great Adventure 908-928-2000
Six Flags Theme Parks 201-402-8100
Tropworld Casino & Resort 609-340-4000
Wonderland Pier 609-399-7082

NEW YORK

Darien Lake Theme Park 716-599-4641
Empire State Bldg. 212-736-3100
Fantasy Island 716-773-7591
The Great Escape 518-792-3500
Long Island Game Farm Inc. 516-878-6670
Metropolitan Museum of Art 212-535-7710
Radio City Music Hall 212-247-4777
Statue of Liberty/Ellis Island 212-269-5755
United Nations 212-963-1234

NORTH CAROLINA

Carowinds .704-588-2606
Ghost Town in the Sky 704-926-1140
North Carolina Zoological Park 910-879-7000
Tweetsie Railroad 704-264-9061

OHIO

American Funland 216-476-8300
Americana Amusement Park 513-539-7339
Cedar Point/Valley Fair 419-626-0830
Columbus Zoo 614-645-3400
Coney Island 513-232-8230
Geauga Lake 216-562-7131
Kings Island 513-398-5600
Sea World of Ohio 216-562-8101
Wyandot Lake Park 614-889-9283

Weight of Liberace's King Neptune costume, now at The Liberace Museum, Las Vegas: over 200 pounds.

OKLAHOMA

Arbuckle Wilderness 405-369-2397
Cowboy Hall of Fame (Ok. C.) 405-478-2250
Frontier City (Ok. C.) 405-478-2412

PENNSYLVANIA

Conneaut Lake Park 814-382-5115
Dutch Wonderland 717-291-1888
Hershey Park .800-437-7439
Idlewild Park .412-238-3666
Kennywood Park Corp. 412-461-0500
Knoebel's Amusement Resort 717-672-2572
Sesame Place 215-752-7070

PUERTO RICO

Plaza Acuatica 809-754-9800

RHODE ISLAND

Enchanted Forest 401-539-7711

SOUTH CAROLINA

Family Kingdom 803-626-3447
Fun Spot Inc. .803-448-5716
Gay Dolphin Park 803-448-6550
Gilligan's Island 803-651-4220
Jungle Lagoon 803-626-7894
Myrtle Beach Pavillion 803-448-6456

TENNESSEE

Dollywood 423-428-9488
Graceland 901-332-3322
Libertyland 901-274-8800
Opryland 615-889-6611

TEXAS

Astroworld (Houston) 713-799-1234
Fiesta Texas (San Antonio) 800-473-4378
Sandy Lake Amusement Park 214-242-7449
Schlitterbahn (New Braunfels) 210-625-2351
Sea World (San Antonio) 210-523-3611
Six Flags (Arlington) 817-640-8900
State Fair of Texas (Dallas) 214-565-9931
Wet 'N Wild (Arlington) 817-265-3356

UTAH

Lagoon Amusement Park 801-451-8000

VIRGINIA

Busch Gardens (Williamsburg) 703-522-1389
Kings Dominion 804-876-5000
Mount Vernon 703-780-2000
Pentagon 703-695-1776
Water Country USA 804-229-9300

WASHINGTON

Riverfront Park 509-456-4386

WASHINGTON, D. C.

White House Visitors Center 202-456-2322
Bureau of Engraving & Printing 202-874-3019
National Geographic Explorers 202-857-7588
Smithsonian Institution 202-357-2700
U.S. Capitol 202-225-6827

WISCONSIN

Circus World (Baraboo) 608-356-8341
Rainbow Falls 715-345-1950
Tommy Bartlett's Robot World 608-254-2525
Wisconsin Ducks, Inc. 608-254-8751

WYOMING

Wyoming Territorial Park 307-745-6161

FALL FOLIAGE HOTLINES

Alabama 800-252-2262
Connecticut 800-282-6863
Delaware 800-441-8846
Indiana 317-232-4002
Kentucky 800-225-8747
Maine 800-533-9595
Maryland 800-532-8371
Massachusetts 800-227-6277
Michigan 800-644-3255
Minnesota 800-657-3700
New Hampshire 800-258-3608
New Jersey 609-292-2470
New York 800-225-5697
North Carolina 800-847-4862
Ohio 800-282-5393
Rhode Island .800-556-2484
South Carolina 800-849-4766
Tennessee 800-697-4200
Vermont 802-828-3239
Virginia (Blue Ridge) 800-434-5323
Virginia (Shenandoah) 540-999-3483
West Virginia .800-225-5982
Wisconsin 800-432-8747
National Forest Service 800-354-4595

MOBILITY IMPAIRED TOURS

Able To Travel 800-986-0053
Access Tours .307-733-6664
Accessible Journeys 215-521-0339
Directions Unlimited 800-533-5343
Flying Wheels Escorted Tours 800-535-6790
Turtle Tours 800-453-9195

State with 70 cheese factories and 16 breweries, most offering tours and free samples: Wisconsin.

SKI RESORTS & AREAS RESERVATIONS & INFORMATION

Alpine Meadows-Tahoe City 800-441-4423
Angel Fire Ski Area-(NM) 800-633-7463
Aspen Central (CO) 800-262-7736
Beaver Creek (CO) 800-525-2257
Big Mountain Resort (MT) 800-858-5439
Big Sky Resort (MT) 800-548-4486
Breckenridge Ski Area (CO) 800-800-2732
Breeze Ski Rental Network 800-525-0314
Brian Head (Utah) 800-272-7426
Copper Mntn Ski Area (CO) 800-458-8386
Crested Butte Mntn Resort (CO) 800-544-8448
Keystone Resort (CO) 800-222-0188
King Pine Ski Area (NH) 800-367-8897
Pico Hotel (VT) 800-225-7426
Purgatory-Durango (CO) 800-525-0892
SilverCreek Granby CO 800-448-9458
Ski Cranmore (NH) 800-786-6754
Sugar Loaf Resort-Cedar (MI) 800-968-0576
Sugarloaf USA Ski Resort (ME) 800-843-5623
Timberline Ski Area (OR) 800-452-1335
Vail & Beaver Creek (CO) 800-525-2257

SPECIALTY DINING

Medieval Times Restaurants
    Buena Park, CA 800-899-6600
    Dallas, TX 800-229-9900
    Kissimmee, FL 800-229-8300
    Lyndhurst, NJ 800-828-2945
    Myrtle Beach, SC 800-436-4386
    Schaumburg, IL 800-544-2001
    Toronto, Ontario 800-563-1190

THEATRE

London Theatre and More 800-683-0799
Theatre Direct -New York/London 800-334-8457

TOURISM OFFICES

NORTH AMERICA

ALABAMA

Alabama statewide 800-252-2262
Alabama Mountain Lakes 205-350-3500
Auburn/Opelika 800-321-8880
Bessemer 205-425-3253
Birmingham .800-962-6453
Calhoun County 800-489-1087
Colbert County 205-383-0783
Decatur 205-350-2028
Dolthan/Houston Counties 334-794-6622
Huntsville 800-772-2348
Mobile 800-666-6282
Montgomery 334-240-9437
Road conditions statewide 334-242-4378

ALASKA

Alaska statewide 907-465-2010
Anchorage 800-446-5352
Fairbanks 800-327-5774
Juneau 907-586-2201
Sitka 907-747-5940
Road conditions statewide 907-273-6037

ARIZONA

Arizona statewide 800-842-8257
Flagstaff 800-842-7293
Mesa 602-827-4700
Northern AZ 602-779-2711
Phoenix 602-254-6500
Scottsdale .800-877-1117
Tucson 602-624-1817
Road conditions statewide 602-252-1010
Road construction (weekdays) 602-255-6588

ARKANSAS

Arkansas statewide 800-828-8974
Eureka Springs 800-638-7352
Hot Springs 800-772-2489
Little Rock .800-844-4781
North Little Rock 800-643-4690
Road conditions statewide 501-569-2374

CALIFORNIA

California statewide 800-862-2543
Anaheim Visitors 714-999-8999
Beverly Hills 800-345-2210
Carlsbad 800-227-5722
Lake Tahoe North 800-468-2463
Lake Tahoe South 800-288-2463
Los Angeles 800-228-2452
Newport Beach 800-942-6278

Average purchase price for cross-country skiing equipment: $245; for downhill equipment: $671.

CALIFORNIA (CONTINUED)

Oakland	800-262-5526
Palm Springs	800-967-3767
Sacramento	916-264-7777
San Diego	619-232-3101
San Francisco	415-391-2000
Sonoma Valley	707-996-1090
South Lake Tahoe	916-544-5050
Tahoe North	800-824-6348
Truckee-Donner	800-548-8388
Tuolumne County	800-446-1333
Road conditions statewide	916-445-7623

COLORADO

Boulder	303-442-1044
Colorado statewide	800-265-6723
Colorado Springs	800-368-4748
Denver Airport	800-247-2336
Denver	800-645-3446/303-892-1112
Durango	800-525-8855
Greeley	970-352-3566
Southwest Colorado	800-933-4340
Road conditions statewide	303-639-1234

CONNECTICUT

Connecticut statewide	800-282-6863
Hartford	800-446-7811
Housatonic Valley	800-841-4488
New Haven	800-332-7829
Winston American Coach	800-424-7767
Road conditions statewide (weekdays)	203-594-2650

DELAWARE

Delaware statewide	800-441-8846
Rehoboth-Dewey Beaches	800-441-1329
Wilmington	800-422-1181
Road conditions statewide	302-739-6677

FLORIDA

Florida statewide	904-487-1462
Central Florida	800-828-7655
Daytona	800-854-1234
Everglades	800-388-9669
Florida's Space Coast	800-872-1969
Florida Keys & Key West	800-352-5397
Ft. Lauderdale Area	800-227-8669
Jacksonville	904-535-9736
Lakeland	941-688-8551
Lee County	800-237-6444
Lee County/Ft. Myers/Sanibel	800-533-4753
Miami	800-283-2707
Naples	941-262-6141
Orlando	407-363-5862
Palm Beach	800-242-1774
Panama City	800-722-3224

FLORIDA (CONTINUED)

Pensacola	800-874-1234
St. Augustine	904-829-5681
Surfside	800-327-4557
Tallahassee	904-413-9200
Tampa-Hillsborough	800-448-2672
Road conditions statewide	904-488-8676

GEORGIA

Georgia statewide	800-847-4842
Amicalola Falls State Park	706-265-8888
Andersonville	912-928-2303
Atlanta	800-285-2682
Augusta	800-726-0243
Brunswick	912-265-0620
Cobb County	770-933-7228
Dekalb County	404-378-2525
Georgia Mountains	770-536-5209
Jekyll Island	800-841-6586
Lake Lanier Islands	800-768-5253
Macon-Bibb County	800-768-3401
Savannah	800-444-2427
Road conditions statewide (weekdays)	404-624-7890

HAWAII

Hawaii statewide	808-923-1811
Maui	800-525-6284
Molokai	800-800-6367
Wailea	800-782-5642
Road conditions statewide	808-536-6566

IDAHO

Idaho statewide	800-635-7820
Boise	800-635-5240
Sun Valley-Ketchum	800-634-3347
Road conditions statewide	208-336-6600
Highway Help-line	208-334-8888

ILLINOIS

Illinois statewide	800-487-2446
Bloomington	309-829-1641
Carbondale	800-526-1500
Champaign-Urbana	217-351-4133
Chicago	312-567-8500
Chicago Southland	800-873-9111
Decatur Area	217-423-7000
Galena/Jo Daviess	800-747-9377
Jacksonville	217-243-5678
Kankakee River Valley	800-747-4837
Mt. Vernon	618-242-3151
Peoria	309-676-0303
Rockford Area	800-521-0849
Springfield	800-545-7300
Road conditions statewide	312-368-4636
May-Oct	800-452-4368

Location of The Gallery of Also-Rans: Norton, KS, honoring U.S. presidential candidates who lost.

INDIANA

Indiana statewide	800-289-6646
Evansville	618-826-5000 ext 221
Indianapolis	800-323-4639
Laporte County	219-872-5055
Muncie	317-284-2700
Nashville/Brown County	812-988-7303
Terre Haute	800-366-3043
Richmond/Wayne County	317-935-8687
Road conditions statewide	317-232-5533

IOWA

Iowa statewide	800-345-4692
Burlington Area	319-752-7004
Cedar Rapids	800-735-5557
Debuque	319-557-9200
Des Moines	800-451-2625
Iowa City/Coraville	319-337-6592
Waterloo	319-233-8350
Road conditions statewide (weekdays)	515-288-1047

KANSAS

Kansas statewide	800-252-6727
Emporia/Lyon County	316-342-1600
	800-279-3730
Finney County	316-276-3264
Hutchinson/Reno County	316-662-3391
Lawrence	913-843-4411
Overland Park	800-262-7275
Salina	913-827-9301
Topeka	800-235-1030
Wichita	316-265-2800
Road conditions statewide	913-296-3102

KENTUCKY

Kentucky statewide	800-225-8747
Ashland	606-329-1007
Bardstown/Nelson County	502-348-4877
Bowling Green	502-782-0800
Cave City	502-773-3131
Elizabethtown	502-765-2175
Frankfort	502-875-8687
Harrodsburg/Mercer County	606-734-2364
Henderson	502-826-3128
Kentucky State Parks	800-255-7275
Lexington	800-845-3959
London/Laurel County	606-878-6900
Louisville	800-626-5646
Northern Kentucky	800-354-9718
Paducah	502-443-8783
Richmond	606-623-1000
Road conditions statewide (weekdays)	502-564-4780

LOUISIANA

Louisiana statewide	800-334-8626
Baton Rouge	800-527-6843
Houma-Terrebonne	504-868-2732
Iberia Parish	318-365-1540
Lafayette	800-346-1958
Lake Charles	800-456-7952
New Orleans	504-566-5085
Shreveport - Bossier	800-551-8682
St. Mary Parish	800-256-2931
St. Tammany Parish	800-634-9443
Tangipahoa	504-542-7520

MAINE

Maine statewide	800-533-9595
Road conditions statewide	207-287-3427
Road conditions statewide	207-287-2672
May-Oct weekdays	

MARYLAND

Maryland statewide	800-543-1036
Allegany County	301-777-5905
Annapolis	410-280-0445
Baltimore Area	800-282-6632
Frederick County	301-663-8687
Montgomery County	301-588-8687

MASSACHUSETTS

Massachusetts statewide	800-447-6277
Berkshire	800-237-5747
Boston	617-536-4100
Cape Cod	508-362-3225
Nantucket Island	508-228-1700
New England USA	800-847-4863
Pioneer Valley	413-787-1548
Plymouth County	617-826-3136

MICHIGAN

Michigan statewide	800-543-2937
Ann Arbor	313-995-7281
Bay County	517-893-1222
Detroit	800-338-7648
Frankenmuth	517-652-6106
Grand Rapids	616-459-8287
Grand Traverse	616-947-1120
Greater Battle Creek	616-962-2240
Kalamazoo	616-381-4003
Lansing	517-487-6800
Muskegon County	616-722-3751
Plymouth	313-453-1540
Saginaw County	800-444-9979
Upper Peninsula	800-562-7134
West Michigan	616-456-8557

Largest cave system on earth—Mammoth Cave National Park, Kentucky.

MINNESOTA

Minnesota statewide	800-657-3700
Bloomington	800-346-4289
Duluth	800-892-4997
Grand Rapids	800-472-6366
Minneapolis	800-445-7412
Saint Paul	800-627-6101
Road conditions statewide	800-542-0220

MISSISSIPPI

Mississippi statewide	800-927-6378
Gulf Coast	800-237-9493
Metro Jackson	800-354-7695
Vicksburg	800-221-3536
Road conditions statewide	601-987-1212

MISSOURI

Missouri statewide	800-877-1234
Branson/Lakes	417-334-4136
Cape Girardeau	800-777-0068
Columbia	314-875-1231
Hannibal	314-221-2477
Kansas City	800-767-7700
Springfield	800-678-8766
St. Charles	314-946-7776
St. Joseph	800-785-0360
St. Louis	800-325-7962

MONTANA

Montana statewide	800-541-1447
Road conditions statewide	800-332-6171

NEBRASKA

Nebraska statewide	800-228-4307
Buffalo County	308-237-3101
Lincoln	800-423-8212
Lincoln County	308-532-4729
Ogallala/Keith County	308-284-4066
Omaha	800-332-1819
Otoe County	402-873-6654
Road conditions statewide (weekdays)	402-479-4512
Road conditions statewide (winter)	402-471-4533

NEVADA

Nevada statewide	800-638-2328
Carson City	800-638-2321
Incline Village & Crystal Bay	800-468-2463
Pioneer Territory	702-482-3859
Pony Express Territory	702-423-4556
Reno-Tahoe	800-367-7366
Reno Weather Information	800-752-1177
Road conditions/construction for:	
South - Las Vegas	702-486-3116
Northwest - Reno	702-793-1313
Northeast - Elko	702-738-8888

NEW HAMPSHIRE

New Hampshire statewide	603-271-2343
Mt. Washington Valley	603-356-3171
Seacoast	603-436-9800
Road conditions statewide	603-271-6900

NEW JERSEY

New Jersey statewide	800-537-7397
Road conditions statewide	
Garden State Parkway	908-727-5929
Atlantic City	609-348-7130
Cape May County	800-227-2297
Monmouth County	800-523-2587
Ocean City	800-232-2465
Princeton	609-683-1760
Shore Region	800-365-6933
Trenton	609-777-1770

NEW MEXICO

New Mexico statewide	800-545-2040
Alamgordo-Intl Space Hall of Fame	800-545-4021
Albuquerque	800-284-2282
Farmington	800-448-1240
Gallup	800-242-4282
Grants	800-748-2142
Las Cruces	800-343-7827
Raton	800-638-6161
Red River	800-348-6444
Ruidoso	800-253-2255
Santa Fe	800-777-2489
Silver City	800-548-9378
Taos County	800-732-8267
Road conditions statewide	505-827-5118

NEW YORK

New York statewide	800-692-8474
1000 Islands Information	800-847-5263
Albany County	518-434-1217
Broome County	800-836-6740
Buffalo	800-283-3256
Catskills	800-882-2287
Chautauqua/Allegheny Region	800-242-4569
Dutchess County	800-445-3131
Finger Lakes Association	800-548-4386
Hudson Valley	800-232-4782
Long Island	800-441-4601
New York City	212-397-8222
New York State Visitors Info	800-225-5697
Niagara Falls	800-338-7890
Oneida County	800-426-3132
Ontario County	800-654-9798
Rochester	716-546-3070
Saratoga	518-584-3255
Syracuse	800-234-4797
Wayne County	800-527-6510

NEW YORK (CONTINUED)

Westchester .800-833-9282

NORTH CAROLINA

North Carolina statewide 800-847-4862
Asheville 800-257-1300
Cape Fear Coast 800-222-4757
From Canada .800-457-8912
Catawba County 704-328-6111
Charlotte 800-231-4636
Cherokee 704-497-9195
Fayetteville Area 800-255-8217
Greensboro Area 800-344-2282
Henderson County 800-828-4244
High Point 910-884-5255
Pinehurst Area 800-346-5362
Raleigh Area .800-849-8499
Wilmington 800-222-4757
Winston-Salem 800-331-7018
Road conditions statewide 919-549-5100

NORTH DAKOTA

North Dakota statewide 800-435-5663
Bismark/Mandan 701-222-4308
Fargo-Moorhead 800-235-7654
Grand Forks .701-746-0444
Jamestown 701-252-4835
Minot 800-264-2626
Road conditions statewide 800-472-2686

OHIO

Ohio statewide 800-282-5393
Akron/Summit 800-245-4254
Ashtabula County 216-576-4707
Athens County 800-878-9767
Auglaize/Mercer Counties 800-860-4726
Bellevue 800-562-6978
Cambridge/Guernsey County 614-432-2022
Canton/Stark County 800-533-4302
Cincinnati 800-246-2987
Cleveland Area 800-321-1001
Columbus 800-345-4386
Dayton Area .800-221-8235
Geneva-On-The-Lake 216-466-8600
Geuga County 800-775-8687
Green County 513-376-7482
Hamilton 513-844-1500
Hancock County 419-422-3315
Lima/Allen County 419-222-6045
Lorain County 216-245-5282
Mansfield/Richland County 800-642-8282
Marietta 800-288-2577
Marion 800-371-6688
Medina County 216-722-5502

OHIO (CONTINUED)

Meigs County 614-992-2239
Miami County 800-348-8993
Middletown 513-422-3030
New Philadelphia 800-527-3387
North Ridgeville 216-327-3737
Ohio Valley 800-765-6482
Ottawa County 800-441-1271
Oxford 513-523-8687
Pickaway County 614-474-4923
Portage County 800-648-6342
Portsmouth 614-353-7647
Ross County/Chillecothe 614-775-0900
Sandusky/Erie County 800-255-3743
Toledo 800-243-4667
Trumbull County 800-672-9555
Tuscarawas County 216-364-5453
Warren County 800-433-1072
Zanesville 800-743-2303

OKLAHOMA

Cherokee Heritage 918-456-6007
Oklahoma City 800-225-5652
Oklahoma statewide 800-652-6552
Tulsa 918-585-1201
Road conditions statewide 405-425-2385

OREGON

Oregon statewide 800-547-7842
Coos Bay/Bend/Charleston 800-824-8486
Eugene-Springfield 800-547-5445
Medford/Jackson County 503-772-5194
Newport 800-262-7844
Oregon Coast 800-858-8598
Pendleton 800-547-8911
Portland 800-345-3214
Salem 800-874-7012
Road conditions statewide 503-889-3999

PENNSYLVANIA

Pennsylvania statewide 800-847-4872
Armstrong County 412-548-3226
Beaver County 800-342-8192
Bedford County 800-765-3331
Berks County 800-443-6610
Blair County/Allegheny Mts. 800-842-5866
Brandywine Valley 800-228-9933
Cameron County 814-546-2665
Centre County 800-358-5466
Clinton County 717-893-4037
Crawford County 800-332-2338
Cumberland Valley 717-261-1200
Delaware County 610-565-3679
Elk County 814-834-3711
Endless Mountain 717-836-5431

Location of The Bull Hall of Fame: Plain City, OH, featuring graves of past studs and 1,000 live bulls.

PENNSYLVANIA (CONTINUED)

Erie	.814-454-7191
Fulton County	.717-485-4064
Gettysburg	.717-334-6274
Greater Scranton	.800-245-7711
Huntingdon County	.814-643-3577
Laurel Highlands	.412-238-5661
Lawrence County	.412-654-5593
Lebanon Valley	.717-272-8555
Lehigh Valley	.800-747-0561
Lycoming County	.800-358-9900
Mercer County	.800-637-2370
Northeast Territory	.800-245-7711
Pennsylvania Dutch	.800-735-2629
Philadelphia	.800-537-7676
Pittsburgh	.800-366-0093
Pocono Mountains	.800-762-6667
Valley Forge	.610-834-1550
Verango County	.800-776-4526
Washington County	.412-746-2333
York County	.800-673-2429
Road conditions statewide	.717-939-9551
PA Turnpike	.800-331-3414
Interstate Highways Conditions	.814-355-7545

RHODE ISLAND

Rhode Island statewide	.800-556-2484
Newport	.401-849-8048
Providence	.800-233-1636
South County	.800-548-4662
Road conditions statewide	.401-738-1211
Road construction statewide	.401-277-2468

SOUTH CAROLINA

South Carolina statewide	.803-734-0122
Charleston	.800-868-8118
Columbia	.800-264-4884
Greenville	.803-233-0461
Myrtle Beach	.800-356-3016
Seabrook Island	.800-845-2475
York County	.803-329-5200
Road conditions statewide	.803-737-1030

SOUTH DAKOTA

South Dakota statewide	.800-732-5682
Aberdeen	.605-225-2414
Black Hills/Bad Lands & Lakes	.605-341-1462
Pierre	.605-224-7361
Rapid City	.800-487-3223
Sioux Falls	.605-336-1620
Road conditions statewide	.605-773-3536

TENNESSEE

Chattanooga	.800-322-3344
Clarksville/Montgomery	.615-648-0001
Gatlinburg	.800-568-4748
Kingsport	.800-743-5282
Knoxville	.800-727-8045
Nashville	.615-259-4755
Memphis	.800-447-8278
Pigeon Forge	.800-251-9100
Smokey Mountains	.423-983-2241
Tennessee	.615-741-2158
Upper Tennessee	.615-753-5961
Williamson County	.615-794-1225

TEXAS

Texas statewide	.800-452-9292
Texas (out of state)	.800-888-8839
Abilene	.800-727-7704
Alamo	.210-225-1391
Alamo Village	.210-563-2580
Amarillo	.800-692-1338
Arlington	.800-342-4305
Astroworld	.713-799-1234
Austin	.800-888-8287
Bandara	.800-364-3833
Beaumont	.800-392-4401
Big Bend National Park	.915-477-2251
Big Thicket National Preserve	.409-839-2689
Brownsville	.800-626-2639
Corpus Christi Area	.800-678-6232
Del Rio	.210-775-3551
East Texas	.903-757-4444
El Paso	.800-351-6024
Fiesta Texas	.210-697-3980
Fort Davis	.800-524-3015
Ft. Worth	.800-433-5747
Fredicksburg	.210-997-6523
Galveston	.800-351-4237
Glen Rose	.817-897-2286
Granbury	.800-950-2212
Grand Prairie	.800-288-8386
Grapevine	.800-457-6338
Greater Houston	.800-365-7575
Guadalupe Mts. National Park	.915-828-3251
Henderson	.903-657-5528
Historic Accommodations	.210-997-3980
Houston	.800-231-7799
Irving	.800-247-8464
Jefferson	.903-665-2672
Kerrville	.800-221-7958
Kilgore	.903-984-5022
King Ranch	.512-592-8055
Laredo	.800-292-2122
Lubbock	.800-692-4035
Lufkin	.409-634-6305

TEXAS (CONTINUED)

Marshall 903-935-7868
McAllen.........................210-682-2871
Midland 800-624-6435
Nacogdoches 409-564-7351
New Braunfels 800-572-2626
Odessa 800-780-4678
Port Aransas 800-452-6278
Port Arthur 800-235-7822
Rockport-Fulton 800-242-0071
San Angelo 800-375-1206
San Antonio 800-447-3372
San Marcos 800-782-7653
Sea World of Texas 800-722-2762
Six Flags Over Texas 817-640-8900
South Padre Island 800-343-2368
Texarkana 903-792-7191
Tigua Indian Reservation 915-859-7913
Tyler 800-235-5712
Waco 800-922-6386
Waxahachie 214-937-2390
Weatherford 817-594-3801
Wimberley 512-847-2201
Wichita Falls 817-723-2741
YO Ranch 210-640-3222
Road conditions (weekdays) 800-452-9292

UTAH

Utah statewide 801-538-1030
Mountainland 801-377-2262
Moab-Green River 800-635-6622
Park City Area 800-453-1360
Salt Lake City 801-521-2868
Road conditions statewide 801-964-6000

VERMONT

Vermont statewide 802-828-3236
Kellington/Pico Area 802-773-4181
Stowe Area 800-247-8693
Sugarbush 800-828-4748
Road conditions statewide (weekdays) .802-828-2468

VIRGINIA

Virginia statewide 800-847-4882
Alexandria 703-838-4200
Arlington 800-677-6267
Charlottsville 804-293-6789
Colonial Williamsburg 800-447-8679
Eastern Shore 804-787-2460
Fairfax County 800-732-4732
Fredericksburg 540-373-1776
Hampton 800-800-2202
Lexington 540-463-3777
Lynchburg 804-847-1811
Newport News 800-333-7787

VIRGINIA (CONTINUED)

Norfolk 800-368-3097
Petersburg/Lee's Retreat 804-733-2400
Prince William/Manassas 800-334-9876
Richmond 800-365-7272
Shenandoah Valley 540-740-3132
Virginia Beach 800-446-8038
Virginia Golf Line 800-932-2259
Williamsburg Area 800-368-6511
Road conditions statewide 800-367-7623

WASHINGTON

Washington statewide 800-544-1800
Seattle 206-461-5840
Road conditions/Mountain Pass report
    Nov-Apr 206-434-7277
Road construction statewide(weekdays) 360-705-7075

WASHINGTON, D.C.

Road conditions (weekdays) 202-936-1111
DC Committee to Promote Washington .202-789-7000

WEST VIRGINIA

West Virginia statewide 800-225-5982
Charleston 800-733-5469
Jefferson County/Harpers Ferry .800-848-8687
Northern West Virginia 800-458-7373
Parkersburg 304-428-1130
Road conditions statewide 304-558-2889

WISCONSIN

Wisconsin statewide 800-432-8747
Eau Claire Area 800-344-3866
Fond Du Lac 414-923-3010
Green Bay 414-494-9507
Hayward & Sawyer County 800-724-2992
La Crosse 608-782-2366
Madison 608-255-2537
Milwaukee 800-231-0903
Oshkosh 414-236-5250
Racine 414-634-3293
Wisconsin Dells 800-223-3557
Wisconsin Indian Head Country ..800-826-6966
Road conditions statewide 800-372-2737

WYOMING

Wyoming statewide 800-225-5996
Buffalo Bill's Yellowstone 307-587-2297
Cheyenne/Laramie County 800-426-5009
Jackson Hole 307-733-3316
   800-782-0011
Riverton Area 307-856-4801
Road conditions statewide 307-635-9966
Road construction (weekdays) ...307-777-4437

Where to find a five-story Muskie: The National Freshwater Fishing Hall of Fame, Hayward, WI.

CANADA

Canada Consulate (USA) 214-922-9806

ALBERTA

Alberta 800-661-8888
Calgary 403-263-8510
Chinook 800-661-1222
Road conditions 403-246-5853

BRITISH COLUMBIA

British Columbia 800-663-6000
Vancouver 604-683-2000
Victoria 800-663-3883

MANITOBA

Manitoba 800-665-0040
Winnipeg 204-943-1970
Road conditions 204-945-3704

NEW BRUNSWICK

New Brunswick 800-561-0123
Saint John 506-658-2990

NEWFOUNDLAND

Clarenville 709-466-7953
Deer Lake 709-635-4100
Grand Falls .709-292-4300
St. John 709-729-2391
Newfoundland & Labrador 800-563-6353

NORTHWEST TERRITORIES

Northwest Territories 800-661-0788
Road conditions Hwy 1-7 403-874-2208
Road conditions Hwy 8 403-979-2678

NOVA SCOTIA

Dartmouth 902-466-2875
Halifax 902-421-8736
Nova Scotia .800-341-6096
Road conditions 902-424-3933

ONTARIO

Hamilton 905-546-4111
Keewatin/Kenora 807-468-8233
Kingston 613-548-4415
Kitchener 800-265-6959
London 519-661-5000
Niagara/Mid Western Ontario 519-756-3230
Ontario 800-668-2746
Ottawa 613-237-5158
Toronto 800-363-1990
Road conditions 800-668-2746

PRINCE EDWARD ISLAND

Prince Edward Island 800-565-0267
Road conditions (weekdays) 902-368-4770

QUEBEC

Montreal 518-844-5400
Quebec 800-363-7777
Quebec City .418-692-2471
Road conditions 514-873-4121

SASKATCHEWAN

Regina 306-789-5099
Saskatchewan 800-667-7191
Saskatoon 800-567-2444
. 306-242-1206
Road conditions 306-787-7623

THUNDER BAY

Thunder Bay .800-667-8386

YUKON

Yukon 403-667-5340
Road conditions 403-667-8215

MEXICO / LATIN AMERICA

Argentina 212-603-0443
Belize 800-624-0686
Bolivia 202-483-4410
Brazil 800-544-5503
Chile 800-244-5366
Costa Rica 800-327-7033
Guatemala 305-442-0651
Mexico 800-446-3942
Nicaragua 202-939-6570
Paraguay 202-483-6960
Peru 202-833-9860
Suriname 305-262-9922
Uruguay 305-443-7431

CARIBBEAN

Anguilla, British West Indies 800-553-4939
Aruba 800-862-7822
Bahama Islands 800-422-4262
Barbados (outside New York) 800-221-9831
Bermuda 800-237-6832
Bonaire 800-826-6247
British Virgin Islands 800-835-8530
Caribbean 212-682-0435
Cayman Islands 800-346-3313
Curacao 800-332-8266
Grenada 800-927-9554
Haiti 305-859-2003
Jamaica 800-233-4582

The four presidents honored on Mt. Rushmore: Washington, Jefferson, Lincoln and Theodore Roosevelt.

CARIBBEAN (CONTINUED)

Montserrat 800-646-2002
Puerto Rico 800-223-6530
St. Kitts-Nevis 800-582-6208
St. Lucia 800-456-3984
St. Maarten 800-786-2278
St. Vincent & the Granadines 800-729-1726
Trinidad & Tobago 212-682-7272
Turks & Caicos Islands 800-241-0824
US Virgin Islands 800-878-4463

EUROPE

Austria 212-944-6880
Belgium 212-758-8130
Cyprus 212-683-5280
Denmark 212-949-2333
Finland 212-949-2333
France 212-838-7800
Germany 212-661-7200
Great Britain 800-462-2748
Greece 212-421-5777
Hungary 212-355-0240
Iceland 212-949-2333
Ireland 800-223-6470
Italy 312-644-3019
Latvia 800-451-9511
Lithuania 202-234-5860
Luxembourg 212-935-3589
Malta 212-695-9520
Monaco 800-753-9696
Netherlands 312-819-0300
Norway 212-949-2333
Poland 212-338-9412
Portugal 800-767-8842
Romania 212-697-6971
Russia 212-758-1162
Scotland 800-462-2748
Spain 305-358-1992
Sweden 212-949-2333
Switzerland 212-757-5944
Turkey 212-687-2194
Wales 800-462-2748

ASIA / SOUTH PACIFIC

Australia 800-333-0199
Fiji 800-932-3454
Guam 800-873-4826
Hong Kong 708-575-2828
India 213-380-8855
Indonesia .213-387-2078
Japan 212-757-5640
Korea 312-819-2560
Macau 800-331-7150
Malaysia 212-754-1113

ASIA / SOUTH PACIFIC (CONTINUED)

Nepal 202-667-4550
New Zealand 800-388-5494
Papua New Guinea 202-745-3680
People's Republic of China 212-760-9700
Phillipines .212-575-7915
Singapore .800-283-9595
Sri Lanka 202-483-4025
Tahiti 310-414-8484
Thailand 213-382-2353

AFRICA/MIDDLE EAST

Egypt 312-280-4666
Israel 800-596-1199
Jordan 202-265-1606
Kenya 310-274-6635
Morocco 212-557-2520
South Africa 800-822-5368
Tunisia 202-862-1850
Turkey 212-687-2194

AUTOMATED TELLER NETWORKS

ATM Locators 800-248-4286
Cirrus 800-424-7787
Plus System 800-843-7587

CABLEGRAMS/TELEGRAMS

Moneygrams 800-926-9400
Western Union (US & Canada) 800-325-6000

LOST OR STOLEN CREDIT CARDS

American Express 800-992-3404
    (International) 910-333-3211
AT&T Universal Card 800-423-4343
    (International) 904-448-8661
Carte Blanche 800-234-6377
Diners Club/Carte Blanche 800-234-6377
Discover Card 800-347-2683
    (International) 801-568-0205
Master Card 800-826-2181
    (International) 314-275-6690
Visa 800-336-8472
    (International) 410-581-9994

Country with a golf course made entirely out of sand: Naura, between the Marshall and Solomon Islands.

LOST OR STOLEN TRAVELERS CHECKS

American Express 800-221-7282
    (International) 801-964-6665
Citicorp (US) 800-645-6556
    (International) 813-623-1709
Thomas Cook/Master Card 800-223-7373
    ...//www.mastercard.com
   609-987-7300
Visa 800-227-6811
    (International) 410-581-7931

REGIONAL PASSPORT OFFICES

Boston 617-565-6990
Chicago 312-353-7155
Honolulu 808-522-8283
Houston 713-653-3153
Los Angeles 310-235-7070
Miami 305-536-4681
New Orleans 504-589-6728
New York 212-399-5290
Philadelphia 215-597-7480
San Francisco 415-744-4444
Seattle 206-220-7777
Stamford 203-325-3530
Washington 202-647-0518

SHIPPING/AIR FREIGHT

Airborne Express 800-247-2676
American Airlines Cargo 800-227-4622
America West Air Cargo 800-228-7862
British Air 214-574-4842
Continental Airlines 800-421-2456
Delta Dash .800-638-7333
DHL Worldwide Express 800-225-5345
Federal Express 800-238-5355
    ...//www.fedex.com/
Northwest Airlines Cargo 800-692-2746
United Airlines 800-621-5647
US Air 214-574-5577
TWA 800-892-2746
Southwest Airlines Cargo 800-533-1222
UPS 800-742-5877
    ...//www.ups.com/

TRAVEL INSURANCE & ASSISTANCE

Access America 800-284-8300
International SOS Assistance 800-523-8930
Medic Alert .800-344-3226
Mutual of Omaha 800-228-9792
Travel Assistance International 800-821-2828
Travel Guard International 800-782-5151
TravMed Travel Insurance 800-732-5309
Wallach & Company, Inc. 800-237-6615

WEATHER

National Weather Service 301-763-8155
    ...//www.nws.noaa.gov/
The New York Times Weather Watch
    (TOLL CALL) 900-884-2278
Weather Channel Connection 900-932-8437
    ...//www.infi.net/weather/
USA Today's Weather & Travel Hotline
    (TOLL CALL) 900-555-5555
    ...//www.usatoday.com/ads.htm

MISCELLANEOUS

American Institute for Foreign Study
   800-727-2437
Association of Corporate Travel Executives
   800-228-3669
Consumer Information Center 719-948-3334
    ...//www.gsa.gov/staff/pa/cic/cic.htm

BEST FARES

DISCOUNT TRAVEL
M A G A Z I N E

A Monthly Publication of Insider Travel Secrets
Listing the Latest Discounts for
The Cost-Conscious Traveler

If You Think This Book Is Great...

Wait Until You See Our Magazine!

Special Offer for Insider Travel Secrets Readers!

Subscribe to *BEST FARES Discount Travel Magazine* and get over 250 of the hottest money saving deals in every issue–plus Tom Parsons' monthly insider secrets update. Our last Readers Survey showed that subscribers saved, on average, ten times the annual subscription cost and more.

Use the coupon below to order a year's subscription (12 issues) for only $49.95–$10 off the standard subscription rate. If you prefer, order by calling **800-880-1234** and be sure to mention "*Code Insider.*"

**Fax credit card orders to 817-548-9531
or mail your order to BEST FARES,
1301 S. Bowen Road • Suite 490 • Arlington, TX 76013.**

- -

Please enter a year's subscription to *BEST FARES Discount Travel Magazine* at a total cost of $49.95:

Name:_____

Address:_____
(Must be the same as your credit card billing address)

City/State/Zip:_____

Phone Number:_____

Credit Card Type:_____

Credit Card Number: _____ Exp. Date:_____

Signature: _____
(As it appears on your card)

WORLD TRAVEL
Puts The World On Sale!

Make international business and leisure travel affordable with just one phone call. World Travel's discount airfare experts cut the cost of international travel by as much as 50%. Savings on each ticket will vary but you can be sure of getting a great deal on every ticket you buy.

- Bargain hunters can get the very best fare from the over 300 worldwide consolidators in the World Travel network.
- Leisure travelers can choose from a world of choices at prices equal to some domestic tickets.
- Business, First and Premium Class travelers from over 100 U.S. cities can have comfort and savings with World Travel's hard-to-believe discount rates.
- Special offers may include free or low cost upgrades, two-for-one tickets and other destination-specific deals you can only get from World Travel.

Take the World Travel challenge.
Call around for your best quote, then call us.

WORLD TRAVEL
800-926-4400
Monday through Friday 9 a.m. to 6 p.m. CST

Sea the World

SAVE
$600-$2000
Per Cabin & More . . .

The Cruise Line, Inc.,
America's Foremost Cruise Center,
brings you special customer savings
and the best cruise values in the world.

• Caribbean • Mexico • Alaska • Europe/Mediterranean •
• Bermuda • Panama Canal • South Pacific • Orient •
• South America • New England/Canada •

Representing All Major Cruise Lines

For Reservations, Information and Free Brochure Call

OPEN 7 DAYS **1-800-685-6518** **U.S. & CANADA**

YOU MUST MENTION CODE BFBK01
TO RECEIVE YOUR EXCLUSIVE SAVINGS

BONDED MEMBER OF CLIA & UTA and MEMBER ASTA & NACOA

SAVE UP TO 65% OFF!

PREFERRED HOTEL RATES
Why Pay Full Price?

Hotel Reservations Network now offers discount hotel rates up to 65% off at top hotels in major cities including New York, Boston, Chicago, Los Angeles, Washington, D.C., San Francisco, Anaheim, New Orleans, Orlando, Miami, San Diego, London and Paris. They also offer the time saving convenience of comparing many different hotel chains with one easy phone call. The company uses its volume purchasing power to negotiate the lowest rates.

The service has a wide selection of properties in major cities in every price category, and at the **lowest rates**. The company staff personally inspects each of its "preferred" hotels to insure that it only offers customers the best values. The reservation agents are trained, courteous & thoroughly familiar with the properties.

This service is **FREE**. There are no membership fees, no minimum number of nights and even the phone call is free. Choose from among the most popular hotel chains including Sheraton, Marriott, Holiday Inn, Hilton, Doubletree, Radisson and many more. The service offers rooms (not discounted) for special events such as Jazz Fest in New Orleans and shopping weekends in New York City.

SAMPLE HOTEL DISCOUNT RATES

City	Economy	First Class	Deluxe	Daily Savings!
NEW YORK	FROM $75	FROM $79	FROM $129	*$35 TO $200*
BOSTON	FROM $59	FROM $69	FROM $109	*$35 TO $106*
CHICAGO	FROM $65	FROM $79	FROM $99	*$55 TO $220*
S. FRANCISCO	FROM $59	FROM $69	FROM $109	*$45 TO $190*
LONDON	FROM $99	FROM $109	FROM $149	*$40 TO $200*
PARIS	FROM $99	FROM $109	FROM $149	*$50 TO $250*

FOR RESERVATIONS CALL:
HOTEL RESERVATIONS NETWORK
1-800-96-HOTEL

8:00 am to 6:00 pm CST, Monday through Friday. For fax requests, please call 214-361-7299